A Spotlight on ACTION

This exciting new text takes readers to the roots of the social work profession, framing its historical development, practice settings, and career paths through the lens of advocacy.

Chapter 3: GENERALIST SOCIAL WORK PRACTICE

Layla Intervenes at All Levels to Help Immigrant Children

Layla, a social worker in an elementary school, helps the children of immigrants develop their ability to read and write. She also assists all the schoolchildren's parents with referrals to health and dental clinics. Layla thinks the children she works with have great potential as long as some of their basic needs are met on a regular basis. For this to be accomplished, Layla realizes she needs not only to assess particular individual needs but also to consider issues that affect groups and entire communities. She begins to attend the school's Parent Teacher Association meetings with the hope of better understanding the ways parents support the academic activities of their children. Layla also gathers ideas from the parents on ways the broader community offers to support them and their children's educational experience.

Chapter-opening vignettes introduce the real-life practice situations social workers encounter

---

"This book takes a historical approach to understanding the social work profession and advocacy as a fundamental responsibility of every social worker. Every social worker should know what is in this book."

—Rhonda Wells-Wilbon, Morgan State University

SOCIAL WORK IN ACTION: ISSUES IN DOMESTIC VIOLENCE

Attention on Strengths

COLE is a social worker at a domestic violence center that services primarily residents from the suburbs of a Midwestern metropolitan area. George, a client, came to Cole about his inability to manage the anger he expressed toward his wife of 10 years and their two children, a girl of 8 and a boy 5. Up to that point in time, George had not engaged in any physical violence toward his family, but he did punch a wall, destroy property, and threaten harm. George's wife had threatened to divorce George unless he curbed his angry outbursts.

Through conversations and role plays, Cole encouraged George to consider his life stressors. Over several sessions George came to realize that his anger stemmed from increased work pressures coupled with a decrease in salary and prestige. In fact, people younger than George were

being promoted over him. Cole facilitated a process whereby George began to reflect on his strengths. Interesting enough, George concluded that his w[...] strength for him, as was his [...]

1. Why would assessing [...] attempting to manage [...]

2. How does age play in [...]

3. What strategies did Co[...] ment of his life situatio[...]

4. What do you suggest [...] control his anger?

Social Work in Action and **Current Trends boxes** highlight contemporary, applied examples of social workers as advocates and activists

---

CURRENT TRENDS

Social Change Through Boycotts

ONE way those without much individual power can effect change is to band together to refuse to buy a product, use a service, listen to a radio station, or watch a television program—in other words, to conduct a boycott. During the 1950s, civil rights leaders such as the Rev. T. J. Jemison and Dr. Martin Luther King organized bus boycotts and alternative car pools in the cause of abolishing rules forcing African American riders to the backs of buses. In 1977, a boycott began in the United States, and eventually expanded into Europe, protesting Nestlé's promotion of breast milk substitutes in less economically developed countries. A boycott of U.S. firms investing in South Africa, which included protests on American college campuses, contributed to the end of official apartheid in South

Africa in the 1990s. These are just a few of the historic examples of effective boycotts.

In today's electronic world, groups such as Ethical Consumer enlist people in social change. Ethical Consumer publishes lists of companies that it believes should be boycotted on the basis of political oppression, animal abuse, tax avoidance, environmental degradation, supply chain issues, abuse of human rights, and exploitation of workers. When organized and conducted successfully, boycotts such as these bring publicity to issues and serve as powerful forums for advocating change.

When was the last time you heard of boycotting a business or enterprise as a means of exerting power to create change? What kinds of boycotts have you participated in?

A Spotlight on
ADVOCACY AND THE FUTURE

A model for advocacy practice and policy applies the components of advocacy to key areas of practice at client, community, national, and international levels

---

"There are several examples of very important connections being made across issues—for example, the emphasis on intersectionality and the multiple, overlapping experiences (and oppressions) that shape people's life chances. This is something that many intro textbooks lack and I'm happy to see here."

—John Q. Hodges, University of North Alabama

Spotlight on Advocacy boxes illuminate the transformative possibilities and contributions of social work

Careers in Social Work sections encourage self-reflection as readers consider a future in the field

Economic and Social Justice

Supportive Environment

Advocacy Practice and Policy Model

Human Needs and Rights

Political Access

YOUR CAREER IN MILITARY SOCIAL WORK

A great need exists to increase the capacity of community, behavioral health providers, programs, and organizations to counsel and serve vets. In addition, the needs of active duty members, reservists, National Guard members, veterans, and those connected to the global war on terror will increasingly exceed the capacity of the VA and Veterans Centers. The need for military social work is so great that civilian social workers will increasingly be required to help veterans and their families. So if you are looking for a career with lots of growth, military social work may be for you.

SPOTLIGHT ON ADVOCACY

Immigrant Children and Border Crossing

An estimated 52,000 children have been caught crossing the U.S. border from Mexico and countries in Central and South America. The reasons for the increase in unaccompanied minors tend to depend on the child's country of origin, poverty, violence, and political unrest. Most of the children are boys between 15 and 17 years of age.

To address the situation, the Department of Health and Human Services operates about 100 permanent shelters located primarily on the U.S.–Mexico border. Additionally, President Obama has urged Congress to authorize $3.7 billion in emergency aid to support border protection, deportations, and humanitarian efforts in Central America.

1. Given what you know about social work, what advocacy position do you think the profession will take in response to the current crisis?

2. Examine the Homeland Security Act of 2002 and the Trafficking Victims Protection Reauthorization Act of 2008. What is the defined role of Border Patrol regarding children?

3. Advocates contend that Border Control's screening of children traumatizes them. What are your thoughts?

4. Explore the website of Kids in Need of Defense (www.supportkind.org/en/), an advocacy organization for unaccompanied immigrant children, and list at least three strategies the organization supports to address the crisis. Would you add any strategies to the list? If so, what are they?

A Spotlight on CRITICAL THINKING

Robust chapter pedagogy includes learning objectives, discussion questions, exercises, exhibits, and Time to Think questions to encourage reflective practice and a deeper understanding of the field

TIME TO THINK

Social workers are often thought of as people willing to do good for others, which often means that others expect them to be willing to do good 24/7/365. Professional social workers must learn to maintain boundaries for relationships with clients and use of personal time. Contemplate your use of time, especially in relationship to potentially labor-intensive activities such as advocacy. Are you able to effectively set boundaries between personal and work time? For example, do you currently text message or e-mail family and friends during class time or at work? During personal time, are you tethered to work, answering work-related text messages and e-mails at all hours? If you were passionate about a cause, as Nancy is about licensure for social workers, would you be texting and e-mailing people all the time? What are the possible consequences of these kinds of behaviors?

"I've never read such a thoughtful analysis of social welfare and social work history in an intro text!"
——Alice Gates, University of Portland

"Cox, Tice, and Long provide an innovative text that positions social justice and advocacy as central to generalist social work practice. Their text goes further to highlight the career opportunities that will allow students with a hunger to change the world to also understand the many prospects for feeding themselves."
——Bonnie Laing, California University of Pennsylvania

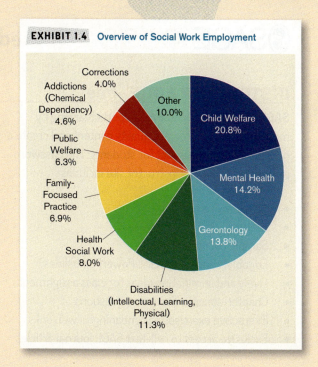

EXHIBIT 1.4 Overview of Social Work Employment

- Child Welfare 20.8%
- Mental Health 14.2%
- Gerontology 13.8%
- Disabilities (Intellectual, Learning, Physical) 11.3%
- Health Social Work 8.0%
- Family-Focused Practice 6.9%
- Public Welfare 6.3%
- Addictions (Chemical Dependency) 4.6%
- Corrections 4.0%
- Other 10.0%

DISCUSSION QUESTIONS

1. What do social workers believe and do?
2. Why is self-understanding so important to becoming a social worker?
3. Imagine that you meet a man who felt neglected as a child because his parents divorced and his father was an abusive alcoholic. As this man ages, he has choices. At one end of the spectrum, he may continue the cycle of addiction, drink heavily, and also become abusive. At the other end, he may choose never, ever to drink alcohol and become the most responsible person in all his relationships, always trying to please others. If you grew up in a family where alcohol was never around or was drunk only in moderation, how would you relate to and help this man?
4. What characteristics do you possess that make you behave ethically? Think of a time when perhaps you or someone you know did not act in an ethical manner. What was the rationale for the unethical behavior? Looking back, was that a good rationale? Why or why not?
5. What are the differences in where a BSW social worker and MSW social worker might work and in how they might practice?

EXERCISES

1. What is important to you in a career? Interview a social worker, and then interview a sociologist, a psychologist, or another human service professional. Compare and contrast their roles and responsibilities. Ask about their level of education and how quickly they got a job working with people upon graduation.
2. How would you respond to people (clients) who are poor, ill, or addicted—and oppressed? Find out more about these population groups: Read articles or stories; watch a movie, Fox News, or C-SPAN; listen to NPR; or interview social workers who work with addicted, mentally ill, impoverished, and oppressed people. Then record your thoughts and feelings about working with people who are vulnerable and in need of services. For example, here are some of the questions you might explore in a few relevant movies:
   a. *The Help*: What was your reaction to the oppression of lower-class African American women?
   b. *Losing Isaiah*: What was your reaction to this transracial adoption?
   c. *Maria Full of Grace*: What do you think about how drug/sex trafficking was portrayed?
3. What workplace features or career goals are most important to you? With which clients might you most like to work?
4. On the BLS website (www.bls.gov/home.htm), find the range of salaries for social workers in your local area or state. Compare salaries across practice settings, such as aging, child welfare, corrections, health, mental health, and school social work. Then compare the salaries for entry-level BSWs and advanced-practice MSWs.

A Spotlight on SUCCESS, FOR INSTRUCTORS AND STUDENTS

edge.sagepub.com/cox

INSTRUCTOR EDGE—free!

SAGE edge for Instructors supports teaching by making it easy to integrate quality content and create a rich learning environment for students. The password-protected SAGE edge instructor site includes

- An extensive test bank
- Lecture notes
- Sample course syllabi
- Editable, chapter-specific PowerPoint slides
- Lively and stimulating ideas for class assignments
- Chapter-specific discussion questions
- Interactive exercises and meaningful web links
- Exclusive access to full-text SAGE journal articles

STUDENT EDGE—free!

SAGE edge for Students provides a personalized, password-free approach to help students accomplish their coursework goals in an easy-to-use learning environment and features elements such as

- An online action plan that includes tips and feedback on course progress
- Learning objectives
- Case studies with follow-up activities
- Mobile-friendly e-flashcards and quizzes
- Multimedia content
- Exclusive access to full-text SAGE journal articles

PRICE EDGE

SAGE offers students a great value! *Introduction to Social Work: An Advocacy-Based Profession* is priced **30%+ less** than the average competing text price and is accompanied by FREE **SAGE edge** online resources!

INTRODUCTION TO
SOCIAL
WORK

INTRODUCTION TO
SOCIAL
WORK

AN ADVOCACY-BASED PROFESSION

LISA E. COX
The Richard Stockton College of New Jersey

CAROLYN J. TICE
University of Maryland

DENNIS D. LONG
Xavier University

Los Angeles | London | New Delhi
Singapore | Washington DC | Boston

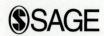

Los Angeles | London | New Delhi
Singapore | Washington DC | Boston

FOR INFORMATION:

SAGE Publications, Inc.
2455 Teller Road
Thousand Oaks, California 91320
E-mail: order@sagepub.com

SAGE Publications Ltd.
1 Oliver's Yard
55 City Road
London EC1Y 1SP
United Kingdom

SAGE Publications India Pvt. Ltd.
B 1/I 1 Mohan Cooperative Industrial Area
Mathura Road, New Delhi 110 044
India

SAGE Publications Asia-Pacific Pte. Ltd.
3 Church Street
#10-04 Samsung Hub
Singapore 049483

Acquisitions Editor: Kassie Graves
Associate Editor: Abbie Rickard
Editorial Assistant: Carrie Montoya
Production Editor: Libby Larson
Copy Editor: Megan Granger
Typesetter: C&M Digitals
Proofreader: Bonnie Moore
Indexer: Sheila Bodell
Cover Designer: Gail Buschman
Marketing Manager: Shari Countryman

Printed in Canada

Library of Congress Cataloging-in-Publication Data

Cox, Lisa E.

Introduction to social work : an advocacy-based profession / Lisa E. Cox, Richard Stockton College of New Jersey, USA, Carolyn J. Tice, University of Maryland, USA, Dennis D. Long, Xavier University, The University of North Carolina at Charlotte.

pages cm

Includes index.

ISBN 978-1-4522-4434-1 (hardcover : alk. paper) 1. Social service. I. Tice, Carolyn J. II. Long, Dennis D. III. Title.

HV40.C69 2015

361.3—dc23   2014047400

This book is printed on acid-free paper.

15 16 17 18 19 10 9 8 7 6 5 4 3 2 1

BRIEF CONTENTS

DETAILED CONTENTS

PART 1:   UNDERSTANDING SOCIAL WORK

1:   THE SOCIAL WORK PROFESSION   1

David Sacks/Digital Vision/Thinkstock.

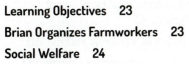

4:   ADVOCACY IN SOCIAL WORK   61

Tomas Abad/Alamy

PART 2:   RESPONDING TO NEED

5:   POVERTY AND INEQUALITY   85

©iStockphoto.com/tunart

6: FAMILY AND CHILD WELFARE 107

Jack Hollingsworth/Photodisc/Thinkstock

©iStockphoto.com/sshepard

©iStockphoto.com/nelsonarts

Hank Morgan/Science Source/Getty Images

iStockphoto.com/arekmalang

12: CRIMINAL JUSTICE 257

Medioimages/Photodisc/Thinkstock

13: COMMUNITIES AT RISK AND HOUSING 281

©iStockphoto.com/ginga71

15: VETERANS, THEIR FAMILIES, AND MILITARY SOCIAL WORK   327

©iStockphoto.com/DanielBendjy

©Infrogmation of New Orleans/CreativeCommons

Learning Objectives 353

Pam and Her Special Needs Students Volunteer in a Cleanup 353

Environmentalism and Social Work 354

Social Work Leadership in Environmentalism 354

Mary Richmond 354

Jane Addams 354

National Association of Social Workers 355

Council on Social Work Education 355

Ecological Social Welfare and Practice 356

Sustainability 356

Ecological Justice 356

Ecological Ethics 357

Environmental Issues 358

Overpopulation 358

Pollution 360

Climate Change 360

Environmental Disasters 361

Flooding 362

Drought 362

Hurricanes 362

Volcanoes 363

Famine 363

Diversity and Environmentalism 363

Age 363

Class 364

Gender 364

Sexual Orientation 364

Intersections of Diversity 365

Advocacy and Environmentalism 366

Economic and Social Justice 366

Supportive Environment 366

Human Needs and Rights 368

Political Access 368

Your Career in Environmentalism 368

Summary 369

Top 10 Key Concepts 369

Discussion Questions 369

Exercises 369

Online Resources 369

Boxes

16.1 Spotlight on Advocacy: Angus, the School Social Worker, and the Regional Trash Dump 355

16.2 Social Work in Action: Linda's Social Worker Encourages Her Environmentalism 359

16.3 Current Trends: Fracking 361

Exhibits

16.1 New Ecology in Practice 356

16.2 Sustainable Development and Social Work 357

16.3 Population by Race and Hispanic Origin: 2012 and 2060 358

16.4 Ten Key Questions to Be Addressed to Support Environmental and Cultural Diversity Policy 365

16.5 Seventeen Principles of Environmental Justice 367

©iStockphoto.com/Bartosz Hadyniak

FOREWORD

As the editor of Social Work for the New Century, I am very pleased to introduce the latest book in the series. The goal of this SAGE series is to provide students, faculty, and social work professionals with the theoretical foundation, conceptual tools, knowledge, and skills they will need to be effective practitioners in the rapidly changing global environment of the 21st century. Like other books in the series, this introductory text, targeted at undergraduate students who are considering social work as a career, includes an in-depth, multicultural perspective and integrates a social justice focus into each chapter. It also assesses the historical and contemporary role of the social work profession and discusses how such issues as the global economic crisis, climate change, demographic transformation, new technologies, war, and terrorism shape present and future social work practice.

The authors have been wise to emphasize the critical role that advocacy plays in social work practice. Advocacy is a core ethical obligation of social work; it distinguishes social work from other helping professions. Social workers advocate on behalf of individuals, groups, and families not only when they provide direct services but also when they administer programs, develop public policies, work to strengthen communities, and undertake research. This advocacy plays a critical role in enhancing the well-being of people in U.S. society and around the world—whether they are children or elderly, in urban or rural areas, in need of affordable housing or health care. As advocates, social workers help people gain access to existing services they are unable to obtain on their own and secure people's legal rights to a wide range of social benefits. All the skills social workers use in working with individuals, families, and groups are directly transferable to advocacy.

Since the emergence of the social work profession at the turn of the 20th century, social workers—as advocates—have responded to rapid demographic and cultural changes and been open to new concepts, ideas, and innovative approaches from other fields and other nations. They have forged collaborative relationships with clients, constituents, and colleagues from other professions and used new technologies to enhance the lives of people with whom they have worked. Through their advocacy, social workers have promoted individual and institutional change and a new, more inclusive vision of community. As advocates, social workers have taken personal and professional risks in their pursuit of social justice for all members of society and the satisfaction of common human needs.

Today, the challenges facing social workers, in the United States and abroad, are greater than ever. They include growing inequality and persistent poverty, fiscal austerity, and resistance to government intervention in the market economy; the increasing complexity of people's needs; persistent social tensions along racial, class, and religious lines; the unequal distribution of political power; the widening divide between the Global North and the Global South; the impact of new information and communication technologies; and the emergence of new problems such as climate change, terrorism, and epidemic disease.

Professors Cox, Tice, and Long have produced an exciting, informative, and inviting introduction to the field of social work—one that embraces the challenges of the new century and provides students with a solid foundation as they begin their professional education. Like the profession itself, their book is innovative and interdisciplinary, and reflects the dynamism that has characterized social work since its origins.

Michael Reisch, PhD, MSW
Daniel Thursz Distinguished
Professor of Social Justice
School of Social Work
University of Maryland

PREFACE

FOREWORD

When the idea of writing a book was first proposed, our thoughts turned to those people with whom we wanted to work over a long period of time. Said another way, we recognized that successful writing partnerships are built on trust, honesty, and commitment. We feel fortunate that those essential elements culminated not only in lasting friendships but in dedication to a profession that is very much part of our lives. Our collaborative work on *Introduction to Social Work: An Advocacy-Based Profession* over 3-plus years was often frustrating, confusing, and time-consuming, yet simultaneously exhilarating, stimulating, and rewarding. Undoubtedly, the positive emotions will be the ones we remember best.

OUR IMPETUS FOR WRITING THIS BOOK

We think *Introduction to Social Work* is a timely new text for adoption in introductory social work courses. Why? Because our book was crafted to align with the profession's historical roots of advocacy for economic and social justice. We know through our practice and community involvement with social service agencies that many social workers have been urging and taking a much more active approach in client and community-based advocacy. Throughout our book, advocacy is described at a clinical/client level and also at organizational, community, national, and international levels. We encourage readers to connect the needs of individuals with those of society by linking direct practice to policy development. Engaging in such analytical thinking integrates micro and macro practice into a holistic perspective of practice underpinned by human needs and rights.

A unique aspect of *Introduction to Social Work* is its advocacy framework for understanding the historical development of social work, important figures influencing social work history, multiple practice settings, and the types of practice performed. The advocacy practice and policy model comprising four interlocking components—economic and social justice, supportive environment, human needs and rights, and political access—provides a lens for viewing social issues of the day. Additionally, the model serves as a vehicle to place special emphasis on human diversity, cultural competence, and intersections of diversity.

Pertinent information is provided regarding professional use of self and contemporary applications to practice settings to adapt to a changing digital workplace and world. These applications view social workers as professional practitioners and client and community advocates, thereby offering a clear alternative to competing books. Features such as Time to Think boxes, Social Work in Action, Spotlight on Advocacy, and Current Trends provide examples of social work's dynamic force and contribution to confronting complicated life situations on individual, group, local, state, national, and international levels. Vignettes appear across all chapters and are modeled after real-life situations faced by professional social workers. Perhaps more important, the book's features prompt readers to pause in thought and consider their opinions, perspectives, reactions, and strategies related to events often far from their own reality. Our book encourages readers to stretch and think beyond, to connect the dots, and to critically analyze issues, concepts, and environments. These aspects of cognitive discourse set our book apart from other introductory textbooks.

STRUCTURE OF THE BOOK

Introduction to Social Work is organized into three parts. Part I introduces readers to a definition of social work, reviews the history of the profession, and describes advocacy as a major aspect of social work. In this section of the book, the advocacy practice and policy model is defined through examples and applications. Throughout the book, the elements of the model serve as themes for exploring practice and policy content areas and connecting them to vignettes that highlight critical features of each chapter.

In Part II, the chapters examine how social workers respond to human needs—poverty and inequality, family and child welfare, health care and health challenges, physical and mental challenges, mental health, substance use and addiction, challenges and rewards of aging, and criminal justice. The chapters in this section assess the strengths of people and communities in support of possible advocacy strategies. At every juncture, social workers are seen as leaders, experts, cofacilitators, and innovators who understand complexities, value diversity, appreciate the role of culture, and address ethical dilemmas.

We are pleased to write that Part III of *Introduction to Social Work* goes beyond the standard text coverage by including chapters on communities at risk and housing; the changing workplace; veterans, their families, and military social work; environmentalism; and global practice and international social work. Each of these chapters introduces material especially selected to stimulate intellectual curiosity about current topics of relevance, such as climate control and posttraumatic stress disorder. Additionally, the role of housing is examined in reference to quality of life and opportunity, the culture of the military is defined so as to better frame the needs of service personnel and their families, and environmental issues are described innovatively to encourage social work professionals to be more involved in all forms of life and service.

Each chapter ends with online resources that correspond to the chapter's content and offer readers the option to explore multiple topics in more detail. Discussion questions and key concepts are also provided to support class discussions and possible in-class and out-of-class assignments. A high-interest end-of-chapter feature titled "Your Career . . ." introduces possible career paths in social work related to the chapter content, along with thought-provoking questions and/or applications.

MAKING COURSE CONTENT COME ALIVE

Although we now primarily identify as educators, we have been molded by our social work practice experiences, current service endeavors, and the evolving world around us. No matter our work responsibilities, the classroom remains our playing field where we hope to convey the important role social workers play in society and people's lives. We contend that advocacy is critical to teaching, research, and service. Consequently, *Introduction to Social Work* is designed to generate discussion, encourage interactive learning and reflective thinking, and expand horizons. The text will be in e-book format, and ancillaries are also available. In other words, we took a multisensory approach to teaching and learning that extends the walls of the classroom to the community and well beyond.

To facilitate teaching, *Introduction to Social Work* is closely aligned with the Council on Social Work Education's new Educational Policy and Accreditation Standards and incorporates reflective practice, encouraging students to engage in critical thought and reflection and to contemplate a professional social work career. As suggested by the butterfly on the cover, life is precious, colorful, fragile, and ever changing. We hope this book will contribute to each reader's transformation as a person and aspiring professional.

SAGE EDGE

SAGE edge offers a robust online environment featuring an impressive array of tools and resources for review, study, and further exploration, keeping both instructors and students on the cutting edge of teaching and learning. SAGE edge content is open access and available on demand. Learning and teaching has never been easier!

SAGE edge for Students provides a personalized approach to help students accomplish their coursework goals in an easy-to-use learning environment. Here is a list of features:

- Mobile-friendly eFlashcards strengthen understanding of key terms and concepts
- Mobile-friendly practice quizzes allow for independent assessment by students of their mastery of course material
- Carefully selected chapter-by-chapter **video links** and **multimedia content** which enhanced classroom-based explorations of key topics
- A customized online action plan includes tips and feedback on progress through the course and materials, which allows students to individualize their learning experience
- Chapter summaries with learning objectives reinforce the most important material
- Interactive exercises and meaningful web links facilitate student use of internet resources, further exploration of topics, and responses to critical thinking questions
- EXCLUSIVE! Access to full-text SAGE journal articles that have been carefully selected to support and expand on the concepts presented in each chapter

SAGE edge for Instructors, supports teaching by making it easy to integrate quality content and create a rich learning environment for students. These features are:

- Test banks provide a diverse range of pre-written options as well as the opportunity to edit any question and/or insert personalized questions to effectively assess students' progress and understanding
- Sample course syllabi for semester and quarter courses provide suggested models for structuring one's course

- Editable, chapter-specific PowerPoint® slides offer complete flexibility for creating a multimedia presentation for the course
- EXCLUSIVE! Access to full-text SAGE journal articles have been carefully selected to support and expand on the concepts presented in each chapter to encourage students to think critically
- Multimedia content includes original SAGE videos that appeal to students with different learning styles
- Lecture notes summarize key concepts by chapter to ease preparation for lectures and class discussions
- A course cartridge provides easy LMS integration

ACKNOWLEDGMENTS

Despite our being experienced social workers, educators, and writers, publishing an introductory textbook has been a unique and demanding endeavor! The transition in writing style from journal articles and higher-level textbooks to an introductory book required patience and assistance from the SAGE team. Kassie Graves deserves much of the credit for her direct contributions to our writing and for surrounding us with highly talented and dedicated professionals, beginning with Michael Reisch, the series editor, and later Becky Smith, Abbie Rickard, Libby Larson, Carrie Montoya, and Mary Ann Vail. Each of our SAGE colleagues extended professionalism, tenacity, fortitude, and faith in our abilities. Our sincere gratitude and appreciation go to everyone at SAGE!

Life passes quickly, and we are ever cognizant of the influence and importance of the positive attitudes and demeanor of colleagues, family members, and friends who have been in our midst and part of our lives. Many of our thoughts and ideas were stimulated by people close to us. This was especially true of Joan H. Long, whose excellence in everyday practice as a social worker often served as an inspiration and valuable point of reflection. Karyn, Ellen, Judy, Joey, and Mary were consummate cheerleaders. Dr. David Burdick shared ideas and student interns, such as Gina Maguire, who provided insight about gerontological and military social work issues. Brittany LaRocca enthusiastically shared her love for social work practice and research as she located research articles and compiled references.

Dennis has appreciated having support from his university and colleagues, who have been understanding, supportive, and tolerant throughout his writing endeavors. He was encouraged by the words of interest extended to him by faculty, staff members, and professional friends. He is also grateful for mentorship from noteworthy role models and guides—Fr. Joseph Bracken, S.J.; Roger Fortin; Neil Heighberger; Tom Meenaghan; and P. Neal Ritchey. Their modeling of respect, a strong work ethic, time management, humility, and grace represent values that educators try to "pass forward."

For all of us, as professors, our students play a primary role in our lives. We learn from and with them, and our thinking and abilities are influenced and shaped by their mere presence. Professionally, there is little more rewarding than having former students return to campus, call, or send a message to provide an update and share their life experiences. Students in introductory classes are especially interesting and formidable. Our deep gratitude goes to our many students and alumni, who have provided us with inspiration and encouragement throughout our days in higher education.

Finally, a number of experienced educators and seasoned reviewers provided valuable and detailed feedback for our book. From the very beginning of the review process, they seemed to recognize and appreciate the advocacy direction we had taken, and diligently sought ways to enhance and improve our work.

D. Scott Batey, *University of Alabama at Birmingham*

Deborah G. Conway, *Community College of Allegheny County*

Bronwyn Cross-Denny, *Sacred Heart University*

Warren B. Galbreath, *Ohio University–Eastern Campus*

Alice B. Gates, *University of Portland*

John Q. Hodges, *University of North Alabama*

Carol Jabs, *Concordia University Chicago*

Bonnie Young Laing, *California University of Pennsylvania*

Ameda A. Manetta, *Winthrop University*

Donna Marie McElroy, *Atlantic Cape Community College*

John P. McTighe, *Sacred Heart University*

Marcia A. Shobe, *University of Arkansas*

Halaevalu F. O. Vakalahi, *Morgan State University*

Rhonda Wells-Wilbon, *Morgan State University*

ABOUT THE AUTHORS

Lisa E. Cox, PhD, LCSW, MSW, is associate professor of social work and gerontology and a former social work program coordinator at The Richard Stockton College of New Jersey. Prior to 1999, Dr. Cox held a joint faculty appointment at Virginia Commonwealth University's (VCU) School of Medicine (Richmond AIDS Consortium) and School of Social Work, where she taught MSW students and served as a pioneering AIDS clinical trial social worker with the National Institute of Allergy and Infectious Disease–funded Terry Beirn Community Programs for Clinical Research on AIDS. Dr. Cox received BA degrees in history/political science and Spanish from Bridgewater College, and her MSW and PhD degrees from VCU. Since 2007 she has served as research chair for The Stockton Center on Successful Aging. Dr. Cox teaches undergraduate- and graduate-level classes in social work practice, gerontology, HIV/AIDS, research, psychopathology, and cultural neuroscience, and she has co-led study tours to Costa Rica. She is a 2014 faculty scholar with the Geriatric Education Center Initiative and a 2014 governor appointee to the New Jersey Board of Social Work Examiners. As a long-standing member of the National Association of Social Workers (NASW), Dr. Cox has shared her vast practice experience by holding numerous leadership roles within NASW: National Advisory Board member to the Spectrum HIV/AIDS Project, chair of the Health Specialty Practice Section, Standards for Social Work Practice in Health Care Settings Task Force expert, long-term care liaison to The Joint Commission on Health Care, and unit chairperson. Dr. Cox has presented her scholarship nationally and internationally. She has authored several book chapters and numerous journal articles focused on health social work, gerontology, international social work, and social support. For relaxation, Dr. Cox plays the piano. E-mail: lisa.cox@stockton.edu.

Carolyn J. Tice, DSW, ACSW, has been professor and associate dean of the Baccalaureate Social Work Program, School of Social Work, University of Maryland since July 2002. Her prior appointment was chair of the Department of Social Work, Ohio University, a position she held for 9 years. At Ohio University, she was the first recipient of the Presidential Teacher Award for outstanding teaching, advising, and mentoring. Currently, Dr. Tice teaches a first-year seminar and social welfare policy. She received her BSW from West Virginia University, her MSW from Temple University, and her DSW from the University of Pennsylvania, where she worked with Hmong refugees. The coauthor of four books, Dr. Tice focuses her scholarship primarily on the development of critical thinking skills and social work practice and policy from a strengths perspective. She is a site visitor for the Council on Social Work Education and is on the editorial board of the *Journal of Teaching in Social Work*. She serves as a book prospectus reviewer for Wadsworth Publishers and John Wiley & Sons, Inc. Dr. Tice is a nominee for the 2015 McGraw-Hill Excellence in Teaching First-Year Seminars Award. In 2008 she was named a Fulbright specialist and traveled to Mongolia to assist in the development of social work programs. Her other international social work experiences include program development in Portugal, Taiwan, Vietnam, and China. Dr. Tice is a member of the Council of Social Work Education, the Association of Baccalaureate Social Work Program Directors, the National Association of Social Workers, and the Social Welfare Action Alliance.

For leisure, Dr. Tice operates Olde Friends, a booth in an antique store located on the southern New Jersey coastline, where she has a family home. E-mail: tice@umbc.edu.

Dennis D. Long, PhD, ACSW, is professor and associate dean of the College of Social Sciences, Health, and Education, Xavier University (Cincinnati, Ohio). Dr. Long previously served as professor and chair of the Department of Social Work at Xavier University, and from 2006 to 2012 was a professor and chair of the Department of Social Work at the University of North Carolina at Charlotte. He received his BA in sociology and psychology from Ohio Northern University, his MSW from The Ohio State University, and his PhD in sociology from the University of Cincinnati. The coauthor of four other books and numerous articles, Dr. Long has focused his scholarship and teaching in the area of macro social work, with special interests in community-based and international practice. He serves on the editorial board of the *Journal of Teaching in Social Work* and is a long-standing member of the National Association of Social Workers and Council on Social Work Education. Over the years, Dr. Long has provided leadership on numerous community and national boards, including the Butler County Mental Health Board, Oesterlen Services for Youth, Charlotte Family Housing, and the National Board of Examiners in Optometry. E-mail: longd3@xavier.edu.

With gratitude and love to my mother, Joyce,
who models how to help people and live life with faith, fortitude, and integrity; and to Jacques,
mon meilleur ami, for his unwavering loyalty, understanding, and pearls of wisdom.

LEC

In honor of my mother, Jeanne C. Tice, who is 86 years old and still has her own teeth.
In memory of Betty J. Laferty, who gave my brother and me a lifetime of love,
kindness, and opportunities.

CJT

With love to Hunter, Joanna, Griffin, and Kennedy—you are the sparkle in Papa's eyes.

DDL

UNDERSTANDING SOCIAL WORK

PART I

Chapter 1: THE SOCIAL WORK PROFESSION

Learning Objectives

After reading this chapter, you should be able to

1. Describe the work, goals, and values of social workers.
2. Explain the importance of diversity and advocacy in social work.
3. Appreciate the dynamic nature and roles of the social work profession.
4. Understand educational and practice options for social workers.
5. Compare a social work career to other human services occupations.

Mary Considers Social Work

While in high school, Mary volunteered at a vibrant day care center and a state-of-the-art long-term care facility. She loved working with the diverse people in both facilities and realized that she was a good listener, doer, and advocate for them. Mary's school counselor told her that she might make use of her newly discovered skills by becoming a social worker, a versatile "helping" career.

Mary has begun surfing the Internet and checking other resources, and has learned that with a bachelor's degree in social work (BSW) she could work as a generalist practitioner or apply to an advanced-standing Master of Social Work (MSW) program and quickly become either an advanced generalist or a specialist. MSW-prepared social workers can work in a wide range of specialty fields of practice, such as hospice, veterans services, and behavioral health. They can work in community-based settings; various types of institutions; state, federal, or local agencies; international disaster relief organizations; or political action campaigns.

Mary feels confident that she would enjoy social work, a field where she could advocate for people and causes, help develop policies, and provide services and resources to people who really need them. As a student, you may be wondering which career might best suit your personal values and the life you envision for yourself. Social work is a versatile and worthy profession to consider. Integrity, decency, honesty, and justice are values held in high regard by social work professionals. If you decide to become a social worker, you will also join a field that provides considerable career mobility and opportunity.

Social work is a helping profession, similar to counseling, psychology, and other human services. Social work is different, though, and will likely interest you if you care especially about economic and social justice and wish to advocate for individuals, groups, families, organizations, and communities that face disadvantages. To help these groups, social workers require an understanding of politics and power, and the ability to assess human needs and the environment.

This chapter introduces the goals, competencies, and responsibilities of the 21st century social worker. It describes social work's core values, roles, fields of practice, career paths, and employment opportunities to help you decide if the profession of social work is right for you.

THE PROFESSIONAL SOCIAL WORKER

Social work is categorized as a **profession** because it requires specialized, formal training and certification. Some of the other professions include law, medicine, accounting, teaching, and counseling. However, social work's unique purpose is to infuse change into the lives of individuals and into the community to reduce or eradicate the ill effects of personal distress and social inequality (Soydan, 2008).

Professional **social workers** generally graduate from a department, program, or school of social work with either a bachelor's or master's degree (or perhaps a doctorate) in social work. Although some social work jobs do not require certification, a professional social worker is generally considered to be someone who has received a social work degree and become certified or licensed by the state in which he or she practices.

Many social workers have achieved historical prominence, such as social work pioneer Jane Addams (who won a Nobel Peace Prize in 1931), civil rights activist Dr. Dorothy I. Height, and Frances Perkins (the first woman to serve as a Cabinet member, as secretary of labor in 1933). Social work pioneer Del Anderson transformed veterans services, Bernice Harper led hospice social work, Joan O. Weiss helped establish the field of genetic counseling, and Dale Masi developed the employee-assistance field (Clark, 2012).

Social work professor and researcher Dr. Brené Brown has become quite successful as a "public" social worker, offering the profession's perspective through books, television interviews, and online talks about shame, vulnerability, and courage. Others with social work degrees who have brought the profession's perspective to diverse careers include actor Samuel L. Jackson, writer Alice Walker, and personal finance guru Suze Orman. Their liberal arts–based social work education was a liberating experience that has served as the foundation for their life's work.

SOCIAL WORK'S UNIQUE PURPOSE AND GOALS

Throughout history, what human beings have seemed to need most are resources for survival as well as a sense that they matter. Beyond feeling secure and accepted for who they are, people also hope to live a meaningful, healthy, and successful life. These are the central concerns of social workers. Their professional role is to help people secure the basic **human needs and values**: food, water, shelter, and such intangible resources as emotional, economic, and social support.

The purpose of professional social work has been articulated formally by the **National Association of Social Workers (NASW),** the voice for the profession (NASW, 1973, pp. 4–5; 2012):

> Social work is the professional activity of helping individuals, groups, or communities enhance or restore their capacity for social functioning and creating societal conditions favorable to this goal. Social work practice consists of the professional application of social work values, principles, and techniques to one or more of the following ends:

- Helping people obtain tangible services (e.g., income, housing, food)
- Providing counseling and psychotherapy with individuals, families, and groups
- Helping communities or groups provide or improve social and health services
- Participating in relevant legislative processes

The NASW considers social work an applied science and art that helps people who are struggling to function better in their world and that effects societal changes to enhance everyone's well-being.

NASW describes four major goals for social work practitioners. The **Council on Social Work Education**

SOCIAL WORK IN ACTION

Dr. Brené Brown Speaks Out

DR. BRENÉ BROWN has a BSW, MSW, and doctorate in social work and serves as a professor and researcher at the University of Houston's Graduate College of Social Work. She is also a storyteller. Dr. Brown has authored a #1 *New York Times* best seller titled *Daring Greatly: How the Courage to Be Vulnerable Transforms the Way We Live, Love, Parent, and Lead* (2012), another *NYT* best seller titled *The Gifts of Imperfection* (2010), and *I Thought It Was Just Me* (2007). For the past decade she has also delivered national presentations on the concepts of courage, vulnerability, worthiness, and shame. Her work has been featured on *Oprah*, PBS, CNN, and NPR. In 2012, Dr. Brown gave a TEDx talk in Houston, Texas, on the power of vulnerability; more than 12 million people have watched this talk. (TED stands for Technology, Entertainment, Design; TEDx talks are modeled on TED talks, which feature engaging presentations by experts on a wide variety of topics, but are organized independently.) She is also the founder of *The Daring Way,* a training program for helping professionals who wish to implement her findings on courage, shame, vulnerability, and worthiness in their own work.

Source: Dell Inc./Flickr/CreativeCommons

In her YouTube clips on the "Power of Vulnerability" and "Listening to Shame," Dr. Brown discusses how social workers are called to "lean into the discomfort" and establish meaningful connections with people.

Brown concludes from her qualitative research that "vulnerability is not weakness"; vulnerability requires "emotional risk, exposure, uncertainty, and fuels our lives." Essentially, vulnerability is our most accurate measure of courage: "Innovation, creativity, and change is the birthplace of vulnerability."

In her clip about shame, she concludes that, although shame is not guilt, it is highly correlated with such behaviors as addiction, depression, suicide, and eating disorders.

Shame also reveals itself differently in women and men. For example, women experience shame due to unobtainable or conflicting expectations. By contrast, men experience shame when they believe that they are perceived as weak.

Dr. Brown exemplifies how a social work education can propel you into a many-faceted future. She is teaching social work students and the wider world about social work theory and methods. Dr. Brown's stories about courage, shame, worthiness, forgiveness, and vulnerability resonate with many. Now they are also adding richness to a social worker's tool kit.

1. How do Dr. Brown's ideas and stories help professional social workers eradicate personal distress and social inequality?

2. Consider how vulnerability makes you feel. What role might empathy play for social workers who counsel people who feel vulnerable?

(CSWE), the arbiter of social work education, adds another goal that relates to social work education. These goals are presented in Exhibit 1.1.

The general public often confuses social workers with other human service providers, among them school counselors, mental health counselors, psychiatrists, psychotherapists, public health workers and administrators, nurses, chaplains, and police or others involved in criminal justice and corrections. While the roles and settings for some of these occupations overlap, each has distinctive features,

EXHIBIT 1.1 Professional Social Workers' Goals

	PROFESSIONAL GOAL	SOCIAL WORKERS' ROLES
Goal 1 (Practice)	To enhance people's coping, problem-solving, and developmental capacities	*Facilitators* who "meet people where they are" and assess clients' environments Coaches, counselors, educators, trainers, and culturally competent solution-focused guides
Goal 2 (Practice)	To link people with systems that provide opportunities, resources, and services	*Brokers* who help build relationships between clients and service systems *Social media collaborators* who help clients connect with their environment
Goal 3 (Practice)	To promote the effectiveness and humane operation of systems that provide people with resources and services	*Advocates* of cases and causes who consider socioeconomic, political, and other contexts, and focus on the available resources for serving people *Administrative supervisors* who oversee staff and ensure that services are delivered efficiently and effectively *Consultants* who guide community organizations and agencies by identifying strategies to expand and enhance services *Coordinators and liaisons* who enhance communication and coordination among social and human service resources to improve service delivery, and who link an agency or program to other agencies and organizations *Program developers and evaluators* who design and evaluate programs or technologies to meet social needs
Goal 4 (Practice)	To develop and improve social policy	*Activists or advocates* who concentrate on the statutes, laws, and broader social policies that underlie the funding and provision of resources Policy practice analysts, developers, and planners
Goal 5 (Education)	To promote human and community well-being	*Activists* who use education, research, and service delivery to alleviate oppression, poverty, and other social and economic injustices

Source: Adapted from Zastrow (2014, pp. 50–51) from primary sites. Goals 1–4 from NASW (1982, p. 17); Goal 5 from CSWE (2008).

perspectives, methods, and areas of expertise. (See Exhibit 1.2 for more detail on the similarities and differences between social work and some of these other occupations.) But social workers incorporate the knowledge and skills of these other occupations as needed to serve clients and communities. They are not limited to a single perspective or set of methodologies. Thus, social workers are called **generalist practitioners**.

SOCIAL WORK AND HUMAN DIVERSITY

In helping and advocating for people in need, social workers inevitably learn about and interact with people from a variety of backgrounds. Many social workers would argue that one of the most interesting and rewarding aspects of their career

is the ability to expand their knowledge and appreciation of human diversity. They have an opportunity to learn about the strengths, needs, uniqueness, values, causes, and traditions associated with various forms of human difference. Consider how much you like hearing people's life stories. When you hear people's life stories, you get clues as to what they need, value, and dream about.

Clients and collaborators are often quite different from social workers in some significant ways. A person's life experiences and circumstances can influence how other people and situations are perceived. What social workers believe is true depends on their personal values and belief systems. Like everyone else, they are influenced by family, spiritual beliefs, **culture**, **norms**, race and ethnicity, gender and sexual orientation, as well as **life stage**, **socioeconomic status**, ability, and disability.

EXHIBIT 1.2   Comparison of Social Work and Similar Occupations

DISCIPLINE AND SIMILAR OCCUPATIONS	SIMILARITIES TO SOCIAL WORK	DIFFERENCES FROM SOCIAL WORK
Psychology: Study of behavior and mental processes; application of that knowledge to the evaluation and treatment of mental disorder Psychotherapists Psychologists (PsyD or PhD doctoral preparation) Psychiatrists (MD; physicians with an advanced specialty)	Is a practice profession Requires accreditation and postdegree supervision Requires graduate-level training for counseling clients (as psychotherapists) Can conduct psychotherapy Works in some of the same settings, with many of the same clients	Requires PhD or PsyD degree for practice Requires 2 years of supervised work experience before independent practice Focuses on client's psychological issues Administers psychological tests In some states, is allowed to prescribe medications MD training/degree is required for psychiatrists
Counseling: Practice of meeting with, listening to, and guiding individuals and groups with mental health, social adjustment, and relationship problems Therapists Marriage counselors Family therapists	Is a practice profession Requires a graduate degree Requires licenses and certifications Engages in psychotherapy Is not allowed to prescribe medications Works in some of the same settings, with many of the same clients	Focuses mostly on the individual as a problem requiring assessment and intervention Is not typically trained in community practice (advocacy, organizing) Requires a graduate degree for practice
Sociology: Study of characteristics and interactions of populations Sociologists	Studies patterns of human behavior, especially origins of that behavior and societal development Shares interests in human diversity and oppression	Is a social science, not a profession or practice Examines people's patterns and community's contexts
Nursing: Practice of caring for the physical and mental health of individuals, families, and communities to optimize quality of life Nurses (BSN, MSN, DNP)	Is a practice profession Has a caring/helping focus Is practiced in hospitals, clinics, and so forth	Offers RN and LPN designations denoting responsibilities and authority Focuses on health and well-being
Criminal justice: Practice of facilitating law enforcement, operating the court system, and investigating and preventing criminal behavior Police social workers Forensic social workers	Has a practice orientation Works in some of the same settings, with many of the same clients Shares concerns about individuals and families	Requires a BS in criminal justice or human services Focuses on the law and social order Supports authority structures Limited focus on the individual's environment
Public health: Practice of researching epidemiological and environmental health trends and protecting the health of populations Public health clinicians Human service workers	Has a practice orientation Focuses on groups and communities Practices in health clinics and community-based settings	Requires a BS in public health Requires training in epidemiology, biostatistics, and health policy and administration Focuses on health and the physical environment

However, social workers go to considerable lengths to broaden their perspectives. They increase their self-understanding by reading and taking classes (in the arts and humanities as well as on subjects such as psychology, sociology, sexuality, biology, neuroscience, and gerontology), learning foreign languages, engaging in personal therapy, participating in self-reflection, and receiving professional supervision and feedback (Green, Kiernan-Stern, & Baskind, 2005). Through seeking this type of self-knowledge, trained social workers are likely to become sensitized to the differences among people. They become better at appreciating other viewpoints and at developing and evaluating more creative policies and intervention strategies (Stoesz & Karger, 2009).

If you are contemplating social work as a career, you must look within and evaluate your readiness to **advocate** for the typical social work client, who is vulnerable and possibly affected by social injustice. You will also be required to respond to human needs very creatively, because resource availability and funding usually fall short of the need, although they vary across communities, regions, and states.

TIME TO THINK

How well do you think you know yourself? Do you believe you have empathy for others who do not have your privileges? What elements of your background might give you empathy for those whose human needs are not being met? Are you aware of how others perceive you and how you come across to others?

Diversity and Social Justice

As rewarding as the experience of human diversity can be, it can be troubling as well. Those who are different from the types of people with whom we are most familiar are often stereotyped as being inferior in some way. That prejudiced attitude may lead to actual discrimination in the way those who are "different" are treated. They may have a deprived and constrained childhood, struggle to meet their needs as they age, and feel a reduced sense of self-worth. Professional social workers are aware of this discrepancy and work toward economic and social justice, the fair distribution of rights and resources among all members of society.

The bases for prejudice and discrimination, which are discussed throughout the book, include the following categories of difference:

- *Class:* An appreciable number of social work clients are marginally employable because of low educational attainment and spotty work records. As a result, they are often stuck in poverty. The jobs that are available to them generally pay poorly, and so these clients may still struggle with transportation issues, affordable day care, mental health issues, physical challenges, and affordable health insurance. Since the beginning of the profession, social workers have advocated for services and programs for members of the lower classes who need support for a rewarding family life, stable housing, adequate nutrition, educational opportunity, and employability. Social workers recognize that use of public assistance is not simply a matter of personal shortcomings. Large-scale issues within the community or society as a whole (e.g., a shortage of good jobs, inadequate transportation systems, substandard schools, minimal child-support enforcement, or lack of quality, affordable day care) also undermine a person's efforts to advance in life (Seccombe, 2011, p. 74).

- *Gender:* Although women have made important strides in our society, they still face lingering and highly ingrained **gender stereotypes**, which are overgeneralizations about behaviors and characteristics based on whether a person is masculine/male or feminine/female. Social workers partner with women's rights groups, educators, and other helping professionals to advocate for and develop positive and meaningful services and programs for females, especially in education, employment, reproductive services, child care, and civil rights.

- *Race:* Race is still an issue in the United States, despite decades of social action and legislative and judicial remedies. Thus, opportunities to promote diversity and social justice for Americans with African, Latino, Asian, Pacific Islander, Middle Eastern, or Native American heritage are an important part of social work practice. Social workers who have gained cultural competence effectively help Bosnian refugees find employment and enroll in ESL (English as a second language) classes, and advocate for Latino clients who have a mental illness such as schizophrenia to help them avoid repeated hospitalizations because of language barriers and cultural misunderstandings. By 2050, the U.S. population is expected to increase by 50%, and minority groups will make up nearly half that population. One quarter of Americans will be Latino, and 1 in 10 Americans will be of Asian or Pacific Islander descent. The African American population is projected to increase from 41.1 million to 65.7 million by 2050, going from 14% of the U.S. population to 15% ("Minorities Expected to Be Majority in 2050," 2008).

- *Ethnicity:* Many people adhere to at least some of the traditions and beliefs of their ancestors. In a "nation of immigrants," many ethnic subcultures can be found. However, **ethnocentrism,** believing that one's own ethnic group and way of life are superior to others, can create intolerance and prejudice. In contrast, social workers promote respect for and understanding of all ethnic groups and cultures. For example, social workers frequently support ethnic centers, immigrant enterprises, language diversity, and cultural events that showcase ethnic pride and provide a forum for the public to learn about specific ethnic values and traditions. And well they should: By 2050, immigration will account for almost two thirds of the nation's population growth.

- *Sexual orientation:* In recent years, members of the LGBQT (lesbian, gay, bisexual, questioning, and transgender) community have become far more visible in the process of winning some degree of social justice for themselves. They have won the right in most parts of the United States to marry members of the same sex. It is becoming more acceptable in most quarters for LGBQT persons to be themselves, although discriminatory behavior and interpersonal slights have not disappeared. Social workers counsel LGBQT individuals facing prejudice and convene groups with them to discuss ways to cope with both subtle and aggressive discrimination. Social workers may also advocate for the LGBQT population on a community, state, or national level.

- *Age:* Older adults, who are ostensibly covered for many of their basic needs through Medicare and Social Security, often struggle with fixed incomes, health problems, and loneliness. Services such as home-delivered meals, transportation, and medical coverage for problems of aging may be underfunded or unavailable for practical reasons. Being acquainted with older adults and attentive to their specific needs enables professional social workers to improve older adults' situation. As the population of older adults grows in the 21st century—by 2050, the population of older Americans is expected to more than double—social workers will find themselves more and more challenged to help ensure "good aging" (Cire, 2014; Lieberman, 2011, p. 137).

Historically, social workers have advocated for justice and human rights for all people, despite their age, ability, class, race or ethnicity, religion, or sexual orientation. Social workers must challenge "isms"—such as ageism, ableism, classism, ethnocentrism, heterosexism, and sexism—as they advocate for vulnerable individuals and groups. However, because social workers are mere humans, mainstream culture influences their views of people and issues. Social workers are not immune to discriminatory language or "isms," so if you choose social work as your career, you must catch yourself and others when you hear language or see behavior that is ageist, classist, racist, sexist, or prejudicial or discriminatory in any way.

Intersections of Diversity

Social workers typically encounter multiple forms of diversity in a single individual. For instance, a woman experiencing a physical or mental challenge may also be old and poor. Holes in medical coverage (gaps among private insurance, Medicare, and Medicaid) may leave her without needed treatment and medications. The ever-changing complexity of medical protocols and health insurance coverage further complicate matters. In turn, the medical issues are an impediment to older, poorer people's ability to make doctors' appointments, keep themselves and their homes clean and in good repair, and buy medicine or even healthy food. On a regular basis, social workers find themselves creatively seeking to identify and fill gaps in services for clients with needs that span categories of difference.

Intersectionality refers to the entirety of a person's dimensions of difference and social identities. Most diversity includes a complex range or intersection of issues, not simply one. A person may be a poor, old, white, gay, Jewish man who was born with polio and lives in an urban environment. Or a person may be a single, middle-aged, Christian woman who emigrated from India and works as a nurse in a rural setting.

Some of those areas of difference may create problems in meeting one's human needs, but others may create advantages. For example, a man who is a retired middle manager has undoubtedly enjoyed some of the privileges of gender and class, but if he is also gay or lives with a disability, he may have faced difficulties in his life that require access to social services. His multiple social locations have sometimes placed him in the role of being the oppressed and sometimes the oppressor (Jani, Pierce, Ortiz, & Sowbel, 2011).

As a social worker you must understand the complex interrelationships that exist across all social identities so you can devise strategies that will make a difference and create social change (Adams & Joshi, 2010; Collins, 2010). Keep in mind that people are more than "labels" or any of their categories of difference.

THEORY AND PRACTICE

You may be starting to realize how complex the practice of social work can be. It requires knowledge of human development and behavior; of social, economic, and cultural institutions; and of the interaction of all these factors. The social work profession not only provides this knowledge but also educates its members to be proactive advocates for client systems. The essential lessons for aspiring social workers involve both theory and practice skills.

Social workers draw on ideas and theories to guide their assessments and intervention decisions. These perspectives emphasize the importance of resilience, strengths, solutions, social justice, and safe, sustainable communities. Professional social workers tend to adopt a primary practice theory that fits their views about human nature, particularly for the purpose of assessing a client, a situation, and the results of efforts to make changes. Chapter 3 describes these theoretical foundations in more detail.

In addition, many social workers are committed to **evidence-based practice,** which is, simply stated, using a particular intervention for an issue, problem, or disorder based on the results of research. They base their methods on the results of previous studies because they need to be accountable to clients and third-party payers (such as insurance companies). In addition, they want to use best practices as documented in their profession's knowledge base. Social workers are obligated to ask themselves, "What evidence do I have that my proposed idea or intervention will help my client?" Your reasoning skills will be enhanced by taking classes in research methods, policy, and statistics.

The knowledge base for social work is constantly evolving to match developments in other disciplines. Contemporary social workers embrace technology and neuroscience (Farmer, 2009). Environmental social work (Gray, Coates, & Hetherington, 2012) and models for social work in a sustainable world (Mary, 2008) now provide additional ideas and paradigms for social work professionals.

SOCIAL WORK VALUES

The mission of the social work profession is rooted in a set of core values that undergird social work's unique purpose and perspective (Barker, 2014, p. 190; Reisch, 2002):

- *Competence:* Having the needed abilities and skills to effectively help and work with clients

- *Dignity and worth of the person:* Esteeming and appreciating each individual's uniqueness and value
- *Importance of human relationships:* Interacting and communicating with clients and collaborators with a dynamic and reciprocal appreciation of one another's behaviors, thoughts, and feelings
- *Integrity:* Maintaining trustworthiness and adhering to moral ideals
- *Service:* Providing help, benefits, and resources to people so they can maximize their potential and thrive
- *Social justice:* Granting all citizens the same "rights, protections, opportunities, obligations, and social benefits," no matter their backgrounds or memberships in diverse groups (Barker, 2014, pp. 398–399)

The NASW Code of Ethics

Social work values are reflected in the NASW *Code of Ethics,* which serves as a social and moral compass for social work professionals. This code has four sections—Preamble, Purpose, Ethical Principles, and Ethical Standards—which are summarized in Appendix A of this book. The *Code of Ethics* serves six purposes (NASW, 2008):

- Identifies core social work values
- Summarizes broad ethical standards
- Identifies professional obligations when conflicts arise
- Holds the social work profession accountable
- Socializes new practitioners to social work's mission, values, ethical standards, and principles
- Defines unethical conduct

Ethical decision making is a process. Oftentimes, social workers struggle with complex scenarios, and the guidelines help direct their actions. In addition, although the *Code of Ethics* cannot guarantee ethical behaviors and a violation of standards in this code does not automatically imply violation of the law, these principles stipulate ideals to which all social workers should aspire.

TIME TO THINK

Are you ethical? How do your ethics stand up against social workers' professional ethics? In the workplace, what might make it difficult to adhere to a professional code of ethics?

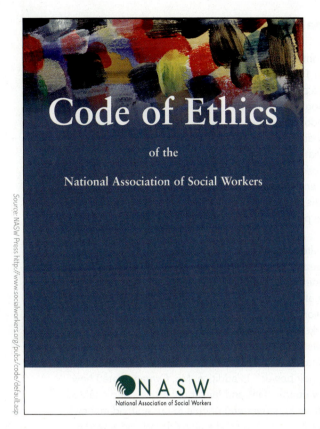

Source: NASW Press http://www.socialworkers.org/pubs/code/default.asp

Professionalism

In addition to valuing these ethics, social workers identify as professionals. With that status comes a set of characteristics that help ensure the highest standards of practice: a culture of professionalism, a professional authority setting standards, recognition of that authority by the community, a systematic body of theory, and a code of ethics.

Professional identity is currently a hot topic in the counseling profession. A strong predictor of professional identity is membership in a professional organization, such as the NASW, and pursuing leadership opportunities in professional organizations. It takes time for professional identity to develop, and it requires strong mentors who care about investing their time and energy in teaching, leadership, and advocacy. Professional identity results from a developmental process that facilitates a growing understanding of self in one's selected career. When a social worker is able to articulate her or his role to others, within and outside of the discipline, the process has begun. Next, developing social workers must learn how to merge the personal and professional by knowing themselves well. Social

workers must be in tune with their own personal beliefs and understand how their life experiences and gender role expectations have shaped them. As a social worker's professional identity develops, every area of her or his life will be reflected on.

Likewise, **self-awareness**—the ability to clearly understand one's own strengths, weaknesses, thoughts, and beliefs—is a process that is worthwhile yet not always easy to achieve. Much of the journey to becoming an effective social worker involves developing your own self-awareness—with classmates, professors, and clients who continuously challenge your thinking. Getting in touch with your feelings is extremely important. As you deepen self-understanding, both professionally and personally, you can develop a greater capacity to attend objectively to your clients' needs. Being aware and secure in thoughts and feelings leads to good health, moments of joy, and contentment, which is something every social worker should be mindful of.

Advocacy

A key element of social work values that is stressed in this introduction to the profession is **advocacy,** simply defined as activities that secure services for and promote the rights of individuals, groups, and communities. Advocacy covers everything from ensuring special educational services for a child with learning disabilities to presenting facts about poverty and needy Americans before the U.S. Congress. Social workers intercede in not only cases but causes.

One of the key differences between social workers and other service professionals is that social workers are expected to know and care about clients' environments. That is what undergirds and gives force to their advocacy.

On a broad level, clients' environments include issues of economic and social justice. As a professional matter, then, social workers embrace a political vision based on democratic values. They are also guided by the NASW *Code of Ethics,* which is influenced by the beliefs and tenets of the three great monotheistic religions (Judaism, Christianity, and Islam). Social workers envision solutions and engage in problem solving designed to protect legal and personal rights and to ensure a dignified existence for everyone. Social work professionals must also understand social and economic conditions. They must understand how economic

Suze Orman and National Social Work Month

▲ Suze Orman

March is National Social Work Month, first recognized by the U.S. Congress in 1984. It came about because the NASW had launched a public image campaign several years earlier to advertise what social workers do. President Ronald Reagan signed the resolution recognizing the many thousands of social workers who dedicate their lives to helping those in need. The resolution acknowledged that professional social workers are in the vanguard of the forces working to protect children and the aged, reduce racism and sexism, and prevent the social and emotional disintegration of individuals and families. Every March the NASW continues to celebrate the profession and raise awareness about what social workers do.

During the March 2012 celebration, NASW invited financial whiz, best-selling author, and television celebrity Suze Orman to help celebrate social workers. Ms. Orman had earned a bachelor's degree in social work from the University of Illinois at Urbana–Champaign but never formally worked in a social work agency. Although she took flak from a handful of social workers for lacking actual social work experience, Ms. Orman enthusiastically promoted the profession: "Social workers are vital to the fabric of the United States of America. . . . Those who enter the social work profession know about the low pay, so they need to 'stand in their power.'" In addition, Ms. Orman related how her social work studies helped her understand how people think and feel about money, and enabled her to talk about money on a personal level: "You have to understand people to understand money." Decent salaries can be earned in the social work profession, and so she also offered social workers some financial advice. While not all people who complete social work education will become "Suze Ormans," graduates who possess degrees in social work will locate meaningful work and be able to move from setting to setting quite easily. In some respects social work is a business and your degree is your ticket to success.

1. What role can social workers play in helping clients be financially literate and good stewards of their money?

2. What do you think about Ms. Orman's crediting her social work training for her success?

3. What might agencies do to celebrate National Social Work Month?

downturns, the changing balance between conservatism and liberalism, capitalism, and globalization affect their clients and their practice.

To become a more effective professional advocate, you should seek to expand your worldview. Social workers who have studied sociology, economics, political science, public health, and other social sciences can better help clients navigate social service systems and approach decision makers about changes in social policies.

SOCIAL WORK EDUCATION

Nearly every state in the United States requires a social work degree from an accredited school. The CSWE is the professional entity that accredits social work programs, by monitoring social work educators and ensuring high educational standards. CSWE is the authority that officially articulates the goals, values, and training objectives within the profession and oversees curricula development. Its mission is to ensure that social workers are trained to work at a professional level in many different dimensions of practice.

In 2008, CSWE delineated 10 social work competencies that students in the discipline must acquire and demonstrate before they graduate. These competencies reflect common practice behaviors and social work ethics and are measurable. They are intended to ensure that every social work graduate has "sufficient knowledge, skills, and values" to practice effectively. These competencies, known as the **Educational Policy and Accreditation Standards (EPAS)**, are summarized in Exhibit 1.3.

SOCIAL WORK DEGREES

Social work education is provided at both undergraduate and graduate levels. The CSWE has accredited undergraduate departments, programs, and schools in colleges and universities that offer social work training. If you complete an undergraduate degree in social work, you may proceed to graduate social work programs or immediately take social work positions in agencies.

Since 1971 the CSWE has authorized "advanced standing" for students who have finished approved undergraduate social work programs, and some schools of social work have made it possible for such students to obtain their master's degrees in less than 2 years, some requiring only 1 year of graduate work. Graduate training programs for the master's degree in social work in the United States usually take 2 years

and combine instructional classes with fieldwork practice in agencies.

The social work profession, like the psychology and nursing professions, is legally regulated by state licensing boards and offers specialized credentials and practice certifications. Unfortunately, in some states, no licensure certification exists for social workers who hold undergraduate degrees in social work. This means that people who possess other academic degrees can occupy social work positions and sometimes incorrectly call themselves "social workers," thereby confusing the general public. Too often the media blame social work for an act carried out by someone who never received a social work degree but still works in a human service agency.

Bachelor of Social Work

The **Bachelor of Social Work (BSW)** degree readies graduates for generalist social work practice, which will be described in more detail in Chapter 3. The BSW, or BS in social work, is the entry level for the profession. The academic credential is precisely defined: a bachelor's degree from a college or university social work program or department that is accredited by the CSWE.

An important goal of social work education is not only to cover social welfare content and practice skills but also to provide a liberal arts education so students can become good citizens. The liberal arts–oriented BSW curriculum

---

EXHIBIT 1.3   Ten Major Social Work Competencies From the EPAS

1. Identify as a professional social worker and conduct oneself accordingly.

2. Apply social work ethical principles to guide professional practice.

3. Apply critical thinking to inform and communicate professional judgments.

4. Engage diversity and difference in practice.

5. Advance human rights and economic and social justice.

6. Engage in research-informed practice and practice-informed research.

7. Apply knowledge of human behavior and the social environment.

8. Engage in policy practice to advance social and economic well-being and to deliver effective social work services.

9. Respond to contexts that shape practice.

10. Engage, assess, intervene, and evaluate with individuals, families, groups, organizations, and communities.

Source: CSWE (2008).

introduces student learners to social welfare history, communication skills, human behavior theories, and critical thinking about diversity and the human condition. Courses with an emphasis on human biology, economics, statistics, and political science enhance knowledge about human behavior and social policy development. Increasingly, BSW students also choose to learn American Sign Language or a foreign language.

Master of Social Work

A **Master of Social Work (MSW)** degree readies graduates for advanced, specialized professional practice. It must be obtained from a program or department accredited by the CSWE. The MSW degree is viewed as a terminal degree, meaning that select social work programs may hire MSW social workers as faculty to teach clinical courses or as non-tenure-track faculty—especially in fieldwork instructor roles.

The curriculum of master's degree programs builds on generalist, BSW content. MSW students develop a concentration in a practice method or social problem area; alternatively, some master's degrees focus on advanced generalist practice. Thus, the MSW social worker should be able to engage in generalist social work practice and also function as a specialist in more complex tasks.

The basic program for the MSW degree includes four core areas:

- Human behavior and the social environment
- Social work practice
- Social policy
- Research methods

Decades ago, social work education at the master's level placed considerable emphasis on specialization in fields such as psychiatric (mental health) social work, medical (health) social work, and school social work. Since the 1960s the training has centered on a generalist curriculum. Students complete a 2-year training program that qualifies them to work in some agencies. Additionally, at some schools, the research methods course requires students to complete an individual or group thesis, a research project, or multiple research classes. MSW programs also offer elective courses to provide a well-rounded program for graduate social work students. Dual-degree programs and certificates are offered at the master's level.

Doctor of Philosophy in Social Work or Doctor of Social Work

For most social workers, an MSW degree is sufficient for a rewarding career. Although the number of doctoral programs has been growing, only a small percentage of NASW members hold one of the two doctorate degrees:

- Doctorate of Philosophy in Social Work (PhD): Readies graduates to teach or conduct research or to specialize in clinical practice
- Doctorate of Social Work (DSW): Prepares graduates for advanced practice and administrative positions or other leadership in social work

Some MSW degree holders who are satisfied with this terminal degree or are working on their doctorates get jobs teaching at community colleges or in universities as part-time instructors or sometimes in nontenure-track "clinical faculty" positions. Other doctorate-level social workers assume administrative positions at agencies or enter **private practice** in psychotherapy.

These degrees involve advanced and specialized study, a focus on research, completion of a dissertation, and continuing education credits—especially in the areas of clinical work, **cultural competence,** and ethics.

FIELD EDUCATION

Whichever level of social work education you pursue, you can anticipate spending time in the "real-world classroom." Referred to as social work's signature pedagogy, **field education** is the part of the social work curriculum that students most eagerly anticipate. In the field you finally get a chance to apply what you have learned, under the supervision of a credentialed social worker who is approved by the college or university's social work program.

The placement settings for field education range widely. Students might be placed in hospitals, courts, domestic violence shelters, prisons, schools, mental health facilities, nursing homes, and community planning sites, or with political candidates or NASW chapter offices. In these placements, students engage in practice, conscientiously applying theoretical concepts and intervention skills learned in the classroom. When students have completed field education, they are expected to be able to demonstrate all the competencies required of the generalist social work accredited curriculum.

TIME TO THINK

How many hybrid or fully online (distance learning) classes are you currently taking? How many of these are social work courses? What are the advantages and disadvantages of learning about the profession of social work through an internship experience that is online rather than in person?

CERTIFICATES AND CERTIFICATIONS

In pursuit of their social work degrees, BSW students may complete minors or certificates that verify specialized knowledge and skills; for example, certificates in child welfare and gerontology are very popular. After graduation, social work professionals may also wish to obtain special certificates or certifications. Social work programs, departments, and schools collaborate with continuing-education partners to offer the following:

• Credentials such as Licensed Social Worker (LSW), Certified Social Worker (CSW), Academy of Certified Social Workers (ACSW), Licensed Master Social Worker (LMSW), and Licensed Clinical Social Worker (LCSW)

Beyond the social work degree and professional license, credentials (professional certifications) are often voluntarily sought by social workers to demonstrate professional commitment, achievement, and excellence in social work at the national level. The NASW Credentialing Center supplies information about credentials as they vary by state. NASW Specialty Credentials are open to all qualified LSWs. For example, certified social work case managers may receive this credential with only a BSW degree. The majority of other professional credentials (e.g., CSW, ACSW, LMSW, LCSW) require an MSW degree. The ACSW credential, established in 1960, is available to members and social work leaders in all practice areas and is a widely recognized and respected social work credential. CSWs and LSWs require an MSW degree. If a social worker is beyond 2 or 3 years of receiving her or his MSW degree and has accumulated a significant number of supervision hours and taken a standardized examination, she or he may qualify for the LCSW credential. LCSWs must have either an MSW, DSW, or PhD degree. Many LCSWs pursue a clinical or mental health counseling path because they can bill insurance companies for services—whether in private practice or with an agency (NASW, 2014).

• Special certifications such as a Graduate Certificate in Aging Studies or in Addictions and Substance Abuse

• Certifications such as in case management

In all 50 states, social workers have options for becoming certified or licensed at various levels of social work practice. In fact, it may be illegal to practice social work without a license, depending on the state and practice setting.

Social workers must be cognizant of four distinct sets of requirements and guidelines: constitutional law, common law, executive orders, and statutory law. And social workers' decisions should be morally defensible and aligned with the ethical standards of the social work profession (Reamer, 2005). For example, in New Jersey, hospital-based and MSW-degreed social worker Jessica may assist in-patient clients with discharge planning, information, and referral; however, without her LCSW credential, Jessica is not legally able to bill patients additionally for the time she spends assessing and counseling. In Florida, mental health social worker Ameda finds that the LMSW credential she received in New York will not suffice; by virtue of Florida law, practicing social workers must possess an LCSW credential and complete and document a specific number of continuing education credits in HIV and domestic violence before they can practice and bill insurance companies in the state.

SOCIAL WORK PRACTICE

The social work profession's dual purpose and responsibility is to influence social and individual change. Knowledge from a variety of disciplines, absorbed from formal classes and personal learning, helps social workers assess complex situations and determine effective interventions. Many people benefit from and appreciate these interventions, and our society is better for them. However, social work professionals often work with individuals and organizations that are not ready for or capable of change. So social workers also have to use such practice skills as assessing, strategizing, brokering, collaborating, intervening, linking, listening, motivating, and responding in their professional lives. In addition, they must be ready to pose alternative solutions, seek consensus, negotiate, and mediate (Theriot, 2013). It is no wonder that social work is considered a "doing" profession and that it is taught through experiential approaches such as service learning, internships, and fieldwork.

The multidimensional approach to social work education gives graduates at all levels the knowledge and skills they need to work in a variety of settings at various levels of practice. It also helps them prepare for a professional career that offers much personal satisfaction and a promising future, with many opportunities to grow and blaze new paths.

SOCIAL WORK ROLES AND SETTINGS

Traditionally, social workers have provided charity, created agencies and resources, developed or advocated for policy changes, and delivered services to people and communities in need. Historically, as Chapter 2 describes, they have been key to the development of social welfare policies, such as child labor laws, fair pay for minorities and other oppressed people, and relief for the aging and infirm.

Today, the main purpose of social work remains much the same: to empower people to grow and live healthy, productive, and meaningful lives. Social workers accomplish this purpose by working directly with people, organizations, and communities, and by acting to change society. Most people who consider social work as their career choice do so because they want to help people and make a difference.

But social workers' activities within their practice are more diverse than ever. They help people increase their capacities for problem solving and coping. They help people obtain needed resources, facilitate interactions between people and their environments, and make organizations responsive to people. Social workers are also professional social activists, working to influence social policies affecting their clients and their communities (Swank, 2012). Here are some examples of the broad array of practice activities they might undertake:

- Teaching people how to bring up and nurture children through training and small-group meetings
- Caring for older adults through case management and visits to senior centers and hospice facilities

- Privately counseling couples with marriage troubles
- Modeling how to preserve constructive, safe, and caring households through in-home visits and courses for family members
- Fighting for policy changes within institutions and local and state governments, and for the rights of persons who cannot fight for themselves, by organizing and leading meetings or writing letters and articles
- Advocating with the national government for veterans who have put their lives on the line for the sake of others, by writing position papers, speaking in public forums, and testifying before committees

Social workers undertake these activities in a wide variety of settings: medical facilities, government and nonprofit agencies, corrections facilities, home health and long-term care settings, state and federal government, schools, community-based mental health agencies, **faith-based organizations,** the military, veterans programs, corporations, and private practice. Social workers may also find employment in banks, theater groups, elder law firms, community gardens, police stations, and international agencies (Gambrill, 1997; Gibelman, 1995; Singer, 2009).

Exhibit 1.4 presents an overview of the primary fields of practice, industries, and employers for social workers.

LEVELS OF PRACTICE

No matter the precise setting, social workers also categorize their work on the basis of the **level of practice,** or the size of the client system with which they intervene: micro, mezzo/meso, or macro. Exhibit 1.5 delineates these three levels, with examples of each. The particular issues that enter into practice at each level are discussed in Chapter 3.

Professional social workers often operate on multiple intervention levels. Certainly, across a career, a professional social worker is likely to experience all three levels of practice. In addition, rarely does a case involve only one level at a time. For instance, a woman who has been raped on campus and feels traumatized may need individual counseling, and the social worker may also set up a meeting with her and her parents to ensure that they are sensitive to the woman's concerns; the social worker may also intervene with campus authorities to alert them to a problem that may affect other female students.

EXHIBIT 1.4   Overview of Social Work Employment

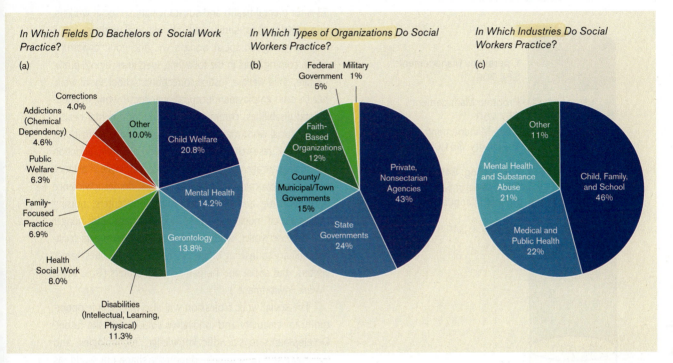

In Which Fields Do Bachelors of Social Work Practice?

(a)

- Corrections 4.0%
- Addictions (Chemical Dependency) 4.6%
- Public Welfare 6.3%
- Family-Focused Practice 6.9%
- Health Social Work 8.0%
- Disabilities (Intellectual, Learning, Physical) 11.3%
- Other 10.0%
- Child Welfare 20.8%
- Mental Health 14.2%
- Gerontology 13.8%

In Which Types of Organizations Do Social Workers Practice?

(b)

- Federal Government 5%
- Military 1%
- Faith-Based Organizations 12%
- County/Municipal/Town Governments 15%
- Private, Nonsectarian Agencies 43%
- State Governments 24%

In Which Industries Do Social Workers Practice?

(c)

- Other 11%
- Mental Health and Substance Abuse 21%
- Child, Family, and School 46%
- Medical and Public Health 22%

Source: Data from Bureau of Labor Statistics (2014, "Work Environment").

SOCIAL WORK AS A CAREER OPPORTUNITY

According to the U.S. Department of Labor's Bureau of Labor Statistics (Bureau of Labor Statistics [BLS]. 2014, "Pay"), the median salary for social workers was $44,200 in 2012. However, in social work the pay varies depending on where you work. For example, salaries for BSW-degreed social workers may start lower at nonprofit agencies than at government-funded child welfare agencies. Below, in order of annual median wages from high to low, are the industries that employ the most social workers:

1. Federal executive branch

2. General, medical, and surgical hospitals

3. Local government

EXHIBIT 1.5   Levels of Practice

LEVEL	SUBJECT OF INTERVENTION	EXAMPLES
Micro	Individual or couple	Counseling a traumatized woman who has been raped or a couple who are debating divorce
Mezzo/meso	Family, group, or organization	Facilitating a cancer support group or delivering a presentation on the needs of military families
Macro	Community or society	Working for a political campaign or advocating for legislative changes

EXHIBIT 1.6   Median Salaries for MSWs With Specialized Skills (2011)

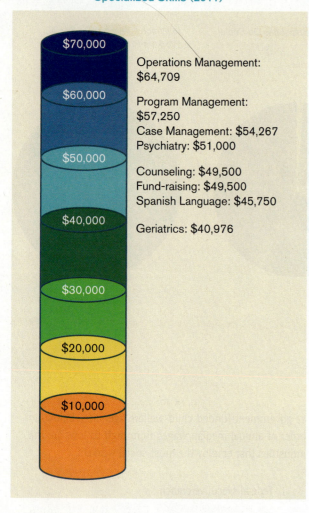

Operations Management:
$64,709

Program Management:
$57,250
Case Management: $54,267
Psychiatry: $51,000

Counseling: $49,500
Fund-raising: $49,500
Spanish Language: $45,750

Geriatrics: $40,976

Source: Data from "The 25 Best Master of Social Work Degree Programs" (2012).

4. State government

5. Individual and family services

Exhibit 1.6 shows the median salaries by skill or specialty of employees with an MSW degree. Keep in mind, however, that lower salaries may be offset by more opportunities to learn quickly about community resources, as is often the case when working for a nonprofit agency.

A 25% growth rate is expected for social work employment, which is faster than the average for all occupations. This expected job growth is a result of an increased demand for social services and health care. However, job growth will vary by industry. The BLS (2014, "Job Outlook") predicts a 27% employment increase for health care social workers, 23% for mental health and substance abuse social workers, and 15% for child, family, and school social workers.

MSW-degreed social workers will find good opportunities in coming years in the following specialties: aging, public welfare, child welfare, justice corrections, school social work, health care, employment/occupational social work, developmental disabilities, community organization, mental health/clinical social work, management/administration, international social work, research, politics, policy and planning, adoption and foster care agencies, private practice, employee assistance programs, advocacy and coalition groups, domestic violence agencies, drug and alcohol rehabilitation centers, nursing homes/skilled nursing homes, homelessness and hunger advocacy networks, women's shelters, long-term care facilities, military counseling offices, assisted-living facilities, senior centers, and social and human services centers (BLS, 2014, "Work Environment").

The social work profession will also offer ample opportunity for creativity and innovative solutions in the future. Developments in scientific knowledge, technologies, and the political economy will continually shape our world, as will globalization, the changing natural environment, and the aging population. Social workers' broad education and versatile skills will help ensure that all of us can keep up.

One appealing aspect of professional social work is that it reflects social and technological trends. Among the areas that promise to provide interesting challenges and opportunities for social workers in the next few years are the following:

- *Teaching and learning:* Outstanding communication skills are more essential than ever. Access to, and instruction in the use of, digital technologies is essential for social work clients. Streaming videos can teach client viewers about anger management, substance use interventions, or assistive devices to use at home. Online webinars can help social work professionals acquire new knowledge about mental health or health care reform.

- *Research:* Genetic counseling and neuroscience are burgeoning sciences that social workers are embracing. **Cultural neuroscience** elucidates how early childhood experiences affect our physical and mental health across the life span. Research that studies the meaning and nature of work is also vitally needed to inform social work practice. For example, one social

CURRENT TRENDS

Lifestyle and Technological Change

OVER the past three decades, some significant technological changes have occurred. For example, the following (Lindsell-Roberts, 2011, p. ix):

- Electric typewriters → High-speed computers
- Radio → MP3
- Encyclopedias → Wikipedia
- Wired → Wireless
- Letters → E-mail, instant messaging, and texting
- Rotary phones → Smartphones
- Kilobytes → Terabytes
- Local data storage → Cloud storage

These changes have been occurring simultaneously with a number of significant lifestyle changes:

- 9 to 5 → 24/7
- Jet-setters → Cybersurfers

- Office workers → Virtual workers
- Single skill set → Lifelong learning
- Shopping malls → Amazon.com, Craigslist, and eBay
- Brick and mortar → Virtual workplaces
- Security → Risk taking
- Status quo → Constant change
- National → Global
- Homogeneous → Heterogeneous
- Lifers → Job-hoppers

1. How will ever-changing technology likely influence the development of the social work profession?

2. What social work–related apps or e-therapy resources do you or your professors know about? How helpful are these resources to social workers or people in need?

work study comparing younger (19–34-year-olds) and older workers found that each group attached diverse meanings to the concept of "work" (Singh, 2013). In direct practice, social workers should ask which activities qualify as work and which sociocultural and situational factors influence the general public's interpretations of work.

- *Services:* Social work hails from a tradition of charity and service. In the future, social workers will need to become expert navigators and literate interpreters of services that are becoming digitized and being offered as part of a virtual marketplace so they can help clients receive what they need. Just as previous generations of social workers needed to adopt cultural competency, social workers now and in the future will need to embrace technical literacy (Belluomini, 2013). In addition, some social work practitioners are offering e-therapy interventions.
- *Social work education:* Social media and technology are radically changing social work pedagogy. Some graduate programs are now offered completely online. Social work education has also become part of the

global marketplace (Askeland & Payne, 2006; Garrett, 2009). Those who have the resources to produce and distribute social work literature digitally and through social media are able to disseminate their theoretical views and skills throughout the world. Social workers may have to adapt by researching and communicating about more universal topics, or on the learning end of the educational enterprise, taking into account the different local contexts in which information is produced and the different perspectives from which it should be read.

TIME TO THINK

If your friends or parents said to you, "Social work doesn't pay well. Why don't you major in nursing, psychology, or criminal justice?" how would you respond? How will social work prepare you to work with people and social problems differently than other professions would?

SUMMARY

Social workers are professionals who help individuals, families, groups, agencies and organizations, and communities. They work with people across the life span and across socioeconomic levels. They usually work with oppressed, vulnerable, and disenfranchised people. People who are suffering because they are ill, addicted, disabled, homeless, poor, immigrants, or discriminated against might very well be clients of social workers. On the other hand, social workers may also work with social and political elites, as when they serve as policy planners and program evaluators—although the plight of those at the fringes of society is always at the core of social work. Unique among other types of professionals, social workers are champions of economic and social justice.

Social workers can obtain employment in multiple settings, including traditional social service agencies, as well as courts and correctional settings, schools, the military, offices and factories, hospitals, mental health agencies, child and family welfare agencies, long-term care settings, addiction treatment centers, homeless shelters, nonprofit advocacy programs, local/state/federal government agencies, and legislative bodies. Social workers are found wherever people need help to alleviate personal or social problems.

No matter where social workers are employed, common skills and responsibilities exist across the profession:

- Providing services to support change not only in the individual but also in his or her environment
- Having a knowledge and understanding of human relationships
- Improving the problem-solving, coping, and development capacities of all people
- Serving as a broker by connecting individuals with resources
- Engaging and communicating with diverse populations and groups of all sizes
- Creating and maintaining professional helping relationships
- Advocating for individual clients or the community to solve identified problems

Job prospects for graduates with BSW or MSW degrees, who learn these skills through classroom learning and field practice, are very good for the future.

TOP 10 KEY CONCEPTS

Bachelor of Social Work (BSW)
Council on Social Work Education (CSWE)
field education
intersectionality
level of practice

Master of Social Work (MSW)
National Association of Social Workers (NASW)
profession
social work
social workers

DISCUSSION QUESTIONS

1. What do social workers believe and do?
2. Why is self-understanding so important to becoming a social worker?
3. Imagine that you meet a man who felt neglected as a child because his parents divorced and his father was an abusive alcoholic. As this man ages, he has choices. At one end of the spectrum, he may continue the cycle of addiction, drink heavily, and also become abusive. At the other end, he may choose never, ever to drink alcohol and become the most responsible person in all his relationships, always trying to please others. If you grew up in a family where alcohol was

never around or was drunk only in moderation, how would you relate to and help this man?
4. What characteristics do you possess that make you behave ethically? Think of a time when perhaps you or someone you know did not act in an ethical manner. What was the rationale for the unethical behavior? Looking back, was that a good rationale? Why or why not?
5. What are the differences in where a BSW social worker and MSW social worker might work and in how they might practice?

EXERCISES

1. What is important to you in a career? Interview a social worker, and then interview a sociologist, a psychologist, or another human service professional. Compare and contrast their roles and responsibilities. Ask about their level of education and how quickly they got a job working with people upon graduation.

2. How would you respond to people (clients) who are poor, ill, or addicted and oppressed? Find out more about these population groups: Read articles or stories; watch a movie, Fox News, or C-SPAN; listen to NPR; or interview social workers who work with addicted, mentally ill, impoverished, and oppressed people. Then record your thoughts and feelings about working with people who are vulnerable and in need of services. For example, here are some of the questions you might explore in a few relevant movies:

    a. *The Help:* What was your reaction to the oppression of lower-class African American women?

    b. *Losing Isaiah:* What was your reaction to this transracial adoption?

    c. *Maria Full of Grace:* What do you think about how drug/sex trafficking was portrayed?

3. What workplace features or career goals are most important to you? With which clients might you most like to work?

4. On the BLS website (www.bls.gov/home.htm), find the range of salaries for social workers in your local area or state. Compare salaries across practice settings, such as aging, child welfare, corrections, health, mental health, and school social work. Then compare the salaries for entry-level BSWs and advanced-practice MSWs.

ONLINE RESOURCES

- American Academy of Social Work and Social Welfare (aaswsw.org): Gathers ideas relevant to the future of the social work profession through its new initiative, called Grand Challenges for Social Work
- Bureau of Labor Statistics (www.bls.gov/ooh/Community-and-Social-Service/Social-workers.htm#tab-2): Categorizes jobs in social work by sponsorship (where the salary comes from to operate the agency and pay employees), by the kinds of clients or populations the social worker deals with, and by the kinds of services rendered
- Council on Social Work Education (cswe.org): The sole accrediting agency for social work education in the United States that advocates for social work research and education
- International Federation of Social Workers (www.ifsw.org): Contributes to achieving a socially just world through professional social work; comprises 90 professional social work organizations that care about setting and reviewing international standards for social work
- NASW chapters (www.naswdc.org/chapters/default.asp): All chapters, listed state by state
- NASW Occupational Profile Series (workforce.socialworkers.org/whatsnew.asp#profiles)
- National Association of Black Social Workers (nabsw.org): Composed of people from African ancestry and guided by the Principles of the Nguzo Saba to empower and advocate for people of African ancestry and work to create a world without racial discrimination and oppression
- National Association of Social Workers (www.socialworkers.org): The largest membership organization of professional social workers in the world
- *The New Social Worker* (www.socialworker.com/career.htm)
- Social Workers' Salary Guide (socialworklicensemap.com/wp-content/uploads/2013/05/The-Social-Workers-Salary-Guide.jpg)
- Suze Orman (www.socialworkersspeak.org/hollywood-connection/money-guru-suze-orman-offers-social-workers-financial-advice.html): Offers financial advice for social workers
- U.S. Center for Faith-Based and Community Initiatives (www.usaid.gov/faith-based-and-community-initiatives)

STUDENT STUDY SITE

Sharpen your skills with SAGE edge at **edge.sagepub.com/cox**

SAGE edge for Students provides a personalized approach to help you accomplish your coursework goals in an easy-to-use learning environment.

Chapter 2: THE HISTORY OF SOCIAL WORK

Learning Objectives

After reading this chapter, you should be able to

1. Recognize the forces shaping the American social welfare system and social policy.
2. Identify the historical relevance of major social welfare programs that assist people in need.
3. Describe the relationship between social welfare policy and the social work profession.
4. Explain why social welfare policies that address people's immediate needs are inadequate for promoting social justice.

Brian Organizes Farmworkers

Brian is a community organizer for an organization that supports farmworkers who travel throughout the northwestern United States. His job involves educating the public about farmworkers' significant contribution to the American economy and the food supply. With the farmworkers, Brian focuses primarily on the health needs associated with the pesticides and herbicides found in the agriculture industry. Since he is bilingual, Brian is often called on by health care providers to translate critical information and medication dosages to farmworkers and their families. Of late, Brian's focus has turned to immigration and health care policies. After researching the nation's history of farm labor relations, he has helped organize local and regional forums on citizenship and social welfare benefits and services for farmworkers. Also, Brian has connected farmworkers to other advocacy organizations.

The purpose of this chapter is to convince you that history matters. Specifically, the characters, landmark decisions, and political environments that encompass the history of social welfare and the development of the social work profession support a variety of educational purposes that extend beyond the memorization of facts, dates, and events. You will discover that the profession's history introduces you not only to social welfare policy and the practice of social work but also to American politics, diverse and marginalized groups, social reform movements, leadership strengths and weaknesses, and critical thinking. Perhaps most important, you will begin to consider how history can guide your development as an advocate for clients and causes, someone who challenges social injustices.

The historical context of American social welfare policy is a progression of dynamic events, leading incrementally to an expanded role for government in the human pursuit of the things needed to survive and even thrive. Examining the history of social work will help you consider two key points: the influence of political, social, and economic forces on policy development, and the parallel development of social welfare policy and the social work profession.

SOCIAL WELFARE

A critical concept in the history of social work is **social welfare**, or the array of governmental programs, services, and institutions designed to maintain the stability and well-being of society (Axinn & Stern, 2005). Social welfare requires both a common understanding and a formal arrangement between a government and its people. From this relationship, people have a sense of what they should receive for and contribute to their well-being. Social welfare reflects the beliefs and values of a nation. It involves the allocation of resources such as money, personnel, and expertise.

Source: ©iStockphoto.com/CaptLensCap

▲ American citizens can benefit from social welfare programs that maintain the well-being and stability of our society.

Take a moment to consider the services that citizens of the United States receive from the government. The list you generate might include education, transportation systems, national defense, and health care. All these services support people's well-being, and all could be considered social welfare. Despite this broad perspective, social welfare issues are hotly debated and central to local, state, and national politics. They are tied up with social trends, political ideologies, and notions of social control and social justice.

SOCIAL WELFARE POLICY

The services and programs made available to certain people for a specified period of time, based on established criteria, are the product of **social welfare policy**. Ever-changing social, economic, and political environments influence policy development and implementation, and so the services associated with policy are constantly changing. Depending on events, the role of government in improving people's lives also expands and contracts. For example, during the 1960s, when the United States experienced considerable public unrest associated with urban migration, urban violence, persistent poverty, discrimination, and an increasingly unpopular war, there was a significant expansion of support to poor people and an increase in the civil rights of a large spectrum of the nation's population.

Decisions regarding the direction of social welfare policy in the United States and around the world are always being made. Your conclusions on any given issue depend on your vision of society and sense of fairness in the redistribution of resources. How you think about policy issues reflects your political, social, religious, and economic ideologies. It is also likely to reflect your biases and values. Here are some current examples of policy-related questions for you to consider:

- Should we assist persons in poverty through direct cash transfers or services, through a combination of the two, or through a new approach that guarantees a universal standard of living?
- Which programs should be funded through local, state, and federal revenues?
- What is the role of the faith-based community in providing social services?

CURRENT TRENDS

Legalization of Marijuana

IN 2012 voters went to the polls in Colorado and Washington and legalized marijuana use for adults. The legal retail sales of marijuana started in Colorado in January 2014. Legalizing and regulating marijuana brings the nation's largest cash crop under the rule of law. Some people argue that legalizing marijuana will open new sources of tax revenue and create jobs and economic opportunities in the formal economy. Others say it is a gateway drug to the use of more harmful substances.

1. What does this law tell you about the citizens of Colorado and Washington, and possible political and voter trends across the nation?

2. What are your thoughts on the wisdom of this legislation?

3. What are the possible unintended consequences?

- How do social welfare policies in the United States affect or influence the policies of other nations? How can the social welfare policies of other nations guide the United States?

Your conclusions on policy questions and social welfare concerns necessitate a vision of society and a sense of fairness in the redistribution of resources. How you think about policy issues reflects your political, social, religious, and economic ideologies. Your ideas on social welfare policy are likely to include biases and value conflicts as you move forward in an effort to orchestrate reform or even a restructuring of the American welfare system.

In the United States, social welfare policies are generally intended to provide a **safety net** for citizens, services that protect people from spiraling downward economically or socially and hitting bottom. Eligibility for "safety net" services depends on meeting specific criteria, or **means testing**. Means testing is assessing whether the individual or family possesses the means to do without a particular kind of help. If not, the government will provide assistance for a designated period of time. Unfortunately, this assistance often produces only a temporary bounce upward and does little to improve the person's or family's overall status in life.

For social workers, social welfare policy is extremely important. It defines the profession's clients, specifies what services will be made available to designated populations,

Source: ©iStockphoto.com/helenecanada

▲ Social welfare policies provide a safety net for citizens in need.

describes how services will be delivered, outlines the duration of services, and indicates how intervention outcomes will be evaluated and measured.

CONSERVATIVE AND LIBERAL IDEOLOGIES

In the United States today, political ideology has a great deal of influence on how people feel about the social safety net. People with **conservative** political leanings tend to favor personal responsibility for one's own well-being over any form of government support or federally sponsored relief. The underlying premise is that people in the top echelon of

Nelson Mandela

In what became known as the Rivonia Trial, on October 9, 1963, Nelson Mandela joined 10 others on trial for sabotage in South Africa. Facing the death penalty, he addressed the court on April 20, 1964. His closing words in this "Speech from the Dock" have since been immortalized:

Source: South Africa The Good News/Flickr/CreativeCommons

> I have fought against white domination, and I have fought against black domination. I have cherished the ideal of a democratic and free society in which all persons live together in harmony and with equal opportunities. It is an ideal which I hope to live for and to achieve. But if needs be, it is an ideal for which I am prepared to die. (Nelson Mandela Foundation, 2014)

On June 11, 1964, Mandela and seven other accused men were convicted and the next day sentenced to life imprisonment on Robben Island. He was released on Sunday, February 11, 1990. During his imprisonment he rejected at least three conditional offers of release.

On May 10, 1994, he was inaugurated South Africa's first democratically elected president.

1. What does Mandela's life tell you about the consequences of advocacy?

2. Is there a cause you feel strongly about? If so, what time, energy, and other resources are you willing to dedicate to see the outcome you desire?

3. What other advocates stand out in your mind and why?

4. Mandela's autobiography is called *Long Walk to Freedom.* What would you expect to learn from this book and why?

society have worked hard, made smart choices, and earned their lot in life; similarly, people in distress have caused their own problems and should "pull themselves up by their own bootstraps."

Conservative political platforms often take firm stances against taxation (federal income tax, Social Security taxes, inheritance taxes, state income taxes, and local levies), which is the revenue source for many social welfare programs. More specifically, many conservative politicians and their constituents are of the opinion that the nation's income tax system is counterproductive and undermines a free enterprise, market-oriented economic system. Usually, conservatives oppose any form of graduated tax rates, which raise the percentage of taxes paid, or the tax rate, as a person's income increases. They think this so-called progressive program of taxation and the government intervention that goes with it place an unfair burden on businesspeople and entrepreneurs, who create economic expansion, employment opportunities, and the promise of subsequent wealth.

Liberal politicians also support a capitalist, free-market form of government, but they have a different view of the role of the federal government in social welfare. Liberals typically support a more robust safety net for poor people, one that attempts to address social issues through moderate or incremental forms of social intervention and change. Generally, liberals support various types of checks and balances within government, as well as regulatory and protective policies to help ensure fair competition in the marketplace.

As for taxes, liberals usually want a tax structure that rewards the work of people rather than the profits to be made through financial investment and manipulation. Liberal leaders also argue that the nation's tax code favors the wealthy through unique tax breaks and loopholes benefiting the rich. As a result, middle-class workers and families are seen as often paying proportionately higher taxes than do those from the upper class. Liberals generally want to help distribute more wealth and resources to people toward the lower end of the nation's socioeconomic structure.

TIME TO THINK

Read through the definitions of the conservative and liberal political perspectives one more time. Where do you consider your political leanings to be and why? What were the influences that pointed you in that particular political direction? Are you registered to vote? If so, do you vote? Consider why you do or do not vote.

SOCIAL CONTROL

The nation's social welfare system raises issues of **social control**, those policies and practices designed to regulate people and increase conformity and compliance in their behavior. Some people see social control as a motive embedded in social welfare policy (Trattner, 1999). They point out that many of the social welfare policies of the 1960s provided people in poverty with government housing, food stamps, and other kinds of relief in place of training and employment opportunities. Thus, reliance on the government increased while inequities in education and unemployment went unchecked (Trattner, 1999). Some would argue that these policies kept people socially controlled and regulated and separated from the rest of society, locked into unemployment, underemployment, and substandard living conditions (Harrington, 1962).

Social workers are in a position to build on individual and structural strengths while connecting to larger-scale change. The involvement of social workers in the policy arena helps our society address individual needs and confront social control—and perhaps shift or redistribute economic and political power so the poor and vulnerable can better help themselves.

SOCIAL JUSTICE

Social workers share the common goal of **social justice:** the endless effort to protect human rights and provide for everyone's human needs, such as housing, food, education, and health care, particularly for those in greatest need. The goal of social justice is what motivates social workers to be advocates. As you will learn, there are many forms of advocacy; however, here we are concerned with the advocacy that social workers undertake to challenge the "what is" in society with the "what should be" (Cohen, de la Vega, & Watson, 2001). Although this form of advocacy reflects the political, economic, and social environment in which it is conducted, some goals are consistent among social advocates across time and circumstance:

- *Fairness:* All citizens have the right to access resources and opportunities.
- *Equality:* All people are entitled to human rights without regard to race, gender, economic, or educational status, or other distinguishing features.
- *Freedom:* People share the need for independent thought and a sense of security.
- *Service:* The most needy of any society require the most commitment.
- *Nonviolence:* A peaceful approach to collaboration, mediation, or negotiation is more respectful of others' rights than is any form of violence.

If you take on a career as a social worker, you will recontextualize many of these goals of social advocacy in light of your personal and professional experiences.

THE INTERTWINED HISTORY OF SOCIAL WELFARE POLICY AND SOCIAL WORK

As the history of social welfare in the United States has unfolded, so has the history of the profession of social work. Social and environmental issues confronting various population groups in America (poverty, unemployment, discrimination, war, oppression, and the like) have helped shape human services and social programs as well as the nature of social work as a profession.

At times, the United States has developed positive strategies to address specific social problems; consequently, some groups within the population have made tenuous social and economic gains. However, lasting change for the larger society has been limited when measured against complex problems of human need and social justice.

The history of social work and social welfare can be divided into a series of policy eras, designated by landmark policy decisions and initiatives. Considering history in this way integrates the development of social work with a series of political issues and environmental factors that have affected what the nation has been willing and able to do for its citizens' welfare. The advocacy of social workers has helped ensure a degree of social justice when the government has addressed social concerns.

COLONIAL AMERICA: 1607 TO 1783

The early settlers who came to the United States carried with them the traditions, customs, and values of their countries of origin. Because the majority of the colonists were from England, they conceptualized and sought to address social problems such as poverty as they would have in England.

In colonial America, welfare assistance took the form of **mutual aid**; colonists relied on one another in times of need. It was the community's responsibility to provide assistance when an individual experienced a hardship such as a disease or home fire. Relatives and neighbors responded with the necessary assistance until the crisis situation passed or was somehow resolved. As churches took root in the colonies, they, too, would offer assistance to needy people. Overall the public attitude toward poor and needy people was respectful and benevolent, particularly since the harsh living conditions of the colonies placed all the colonists potentially in harm's way.

Although the initial systems of colonial assistance were informal, the severe economic and environmental conditions experienced by the American settlers prompted a more complex system of welfare assistance. The colonists turned to the principles outlined in the **Elizabethan Poor Laws,** which were instituted in England in 1601 (Axinn & Stern, 2005). These laws were a response to social and economic forces associated with the breakdown of England's feudal system, the reduction of the labor force, and industrialization, which increased the need for healthy workers. Further, the laws stipulated that taxes would be levied to finance welfare assistance (Axinn & Stern, 2005).

A concept underpinning the Elizabethan Poor Laws, and the poor laws of colonial America, was the distinction between the **deserving poor** and the **nondeserving poor** (Tice & Perkins, 2002). The deserving poor included orphan children, elderly individuals, and people with debilitating physical conditions, who could not provide for themselves through no fault of their own. In contrast, the nondeserving poor were able-bodied vagrants or drunkards, judged as lazy and unwilling to work for a living. Consequently, work and a person's capability or willingness to be self-sustaining through work became an integral part of America's social welfare system.

Settlement laws were another feature of the Elizabethan Poor Laws. Designed to control the distribution of public assistance, the settlement laws were the domain of small units of government and specified a period of residence for the receipt of assistance. They were implemented throughout the 13 colonies as a standard requirement for receiving welfare assistance and as a method for localities to monitor the cost of such assistance.

The colonists adapted other forms of relief from Elizabethan Poor Laws. **Outdoor relief** provided assistance to the deserving poor in their own homes and communities; **indoor relief** provided assistance in institutions where the nondeserving poor were sent to work (Rothman, 1971). Other approaches to poverty involved auctioning poor people to wealthy families who were willing to care for them in return for labor and services, and placing poor and sick individuals under the supervision of couples who were willing to assume responsibility for their care (Axinn & Stern, 2005).

TIME TO THINK

After reading the definitions of outdoor and indoor relief, please consider examples of those service perspectives today. For example, what perspective does the meals-on-wheels program represent? What about a mental health or long-term care facility? Are you able to recognize the influence of the Elizabethan Poor Laws on current social policies and services?

During the 1800s, the U.S. population expanded westward. In the new settlements, mutual aid remained the main source of help to those in need. An example of this expansion is the orphan trains that ran from about 1853 to the early 1900s, transporting more than 120,000 children, who were often abandoned and alone, from urban centers to 45 states across the country, as well as to Canada and Mexico. This controversial and unusual social experiment marked the beginning of the foster care concept in the United States.

However, the 1800s also saw the rise of advocacy on behalf of people who were poor, who had recently immigrated to the United States, or who were challenged on the basis of physical or mental ability. These people often faced unjust, inhumane, and harsh treatment. The early advocates were often trying to change conditions that had been created by local and governmental policies, ordinances, and rules. Dorothea Dix, for example, was a social activist who lobbied state and federal governments in the mid-1800s to create asylums for those who were mentally ill, especially those who had no other homes (Ezell, 2001, p. xx).

Advocacy also occurred as social workers became politically active and promoted legislation to protect children from oppressive labor practices and adolescents from severely punitive juvenile court systems. Activism by social workers eventually extended to the advancement of the rights of children, workers, women, the elderly, and racial and sexual minorities.

THE PROGRESSIVE ERA: 1890 TO 1920

By the end of the 1800s, the nation was rapidly urbanizing. There was an enormous influx of immigrants, and the economy had begun shifting from agriculture and resource based to industry based. These massive social disruptions led to the economic crisis of the 1890s. There was growing awareness in the United States of the value of social reform.

Some of the reformers of this era astutely recognized that documentation of human need through written records was a vital component of advocacy for new policies, practices, and laws. They realized that the general public and government decision makers could be influenced by numbers, categorizations, and qualitative accounts and descriptions of social phenomena. Importantly, they laid the foundation in social work practice for modern data collection systems, comprehensive community needs assessments, and precise descriptions of human conditions.

At the same time, two new social welfare movements—the Charity Organization Society and the settlement movement—emerged for dealing with dependency (Reisch, 1998). Each offered a significant contribution to the development of the social work profession.

Charity Organization Society

The **Charity Organization Society** (COS) was imported from England to the United States in 1877. The COS focused on the individual factors related to poverty, such as alcoholism, poor work habits, and inadequate money management. In general, the COS asked a family in need of relief to fill out an application, which was investigated to ensure a level of need. Then a **friendly visitor,** a volunteer committed to helping COS clients, was assigned to the family and asked to conduct regular home visits. Friendly visitors would attempt to address individual character flaws and encourage clients to gain independence and live moral lives (Chamber, 1986). The direct exchange of cash was strictly avoided.

In light of the growing need for a trained staff, charity organizations developed the paid position of "agent" to visit indigent persons and families and to investigate applications for charity. These agents were the forerunners of professional social workers (Chamber, 1986). Mary Richmond of the Baltimore and Philadelphia COS, and Edward T. Devine of the New York COS were early leaders in training agents. In 1898, Devine established and directed the New York School of Philanthropy, which eventually became the Columbia School of Social Work, America's first school of social work.

The **settlement movement** turned attention on the environmental factors associated with poverty. In 1889, Jane Addams, along with Ellen Gates Starr, founded Hull House in a poor Chicago neighborhood where immigrants lived in overcrowded conditions. Hull House was not the first settlement house in America; however, it pioneered advocacy roles in social welfare. Its staff collected information about Hull House's clients and the residents of the surrounding area and then used this information to influence legislation and social policy (Dolgoff, Feldstein, & Skolnik, 1993, p. 278). In response to the poverty that surrounded Hull House, the settlement house also offered day care for children, a club for working women, lectures and cultural programs, and a meeting place for neighborhood political groups (Axinn & Stern, 2005).

▲ Edward T. Devine, founder of the New York School of Philanthropy.

As a result of these efforts, settlement houses and their staff contributed community organization, social action, and social group work to the nascent social work profession. However, although Addams and many others in the settlement movement recognized the existence of class conflict as a reality in the U.S. economic system, they did not build a mass political organization. Consequently, they did not effectively confront social class differences on a national level and failed to challenge the overall distribution of the nation's resources (Galper, 1975). Instead, settlement house workers supported labor unions, lobbied city officials for sanitation and housing reforms, and fought discrimination in employment practices.

With the rare exception of Addams and a few other settlement house leaders, those involved in the social movements of the Progressive Era were not attuned to the needs of racially diverse populations, especially African Americans (Blau & Abramovitz, 2004). Most reformers took the second-class citizenship of African Americans for granted and did little to challenge racial barriers and assumptions. It was not until 1909 that W.E.B. Du Bois, the first African American to earn a PhD from Harvard University, formed the National Association for the Advancement of Colored People (NAACP). That organization gave African Americans a movement for fighting segregation in a mobilized and organized fashion (Blau & Abramovitz, 2004).

With social movements of the Progressive Era came the notion of a helping profession oriented toward social action—in other words, social work. In 1917 Mary Richmond wrote the first social work book, *Social Diagnosis*, which introduced a methodology and common body of knowledge for the practice of social work. Importantly, Richmond embraced assessment and understanding of human relations, social situations and surroundings, neighborhood conditions, and economic realities. Richmond's second book, *What Is Social Case Work* (1922), used six cases from industrialized urban areas to illustrate her definition of social case work. Thus, the case method of working with individuals and families provided an orderly process of practice with individuals, with an emphasis on documenting both need and social conditions to advocate for social change and reform.

WORLD WAR I: 1914 TO 1918

The political environment of the United States in the years before and following World War I supported the development of social work as a profession but marked a drastic change in its focus. The 1917 Russian Revolution caused a heightened fear of communism, "radicals" were under attack in the United States, and social workers retreated from reform to avoid the political arena and persecution. This turn was recognized at the 1928 Milford Conference, an annual meeting of social work leaders. It was here that Porter Lee, the director of the New York School of Social Work, reported that social workers had shifted their professional attention from **"cause to function"**—from a concern with politics to a concern with the efficient day-to-day administration of a social welfare bureaucracy (Blau & Abramovitz, 2004, p. 249).

The turn toward the "function" of social work gave rise to an expansion of practice settings for the profession, to include private family welfare agencies (as most charity organizations were then called), hospitals, schools, mental health facilities, guidance centers, and children's aid societies. The American National Red Cross employed social workers to provide case work services to families of servicemen and disaster victims in cities, small towns, and rural areas.

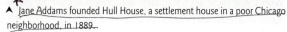

▲ Jane Addams founded Hull House, a settlement house in a poor Chicago neighborhood, in 1889.

▲ W.E.B. Du Bois established the National Association for the Advancement of Colored People (NAACP) in 1909.

It is important to note that throughout this time period, segregation within the profession continued. The National Urban League was developed by African Americans in response to their exclusion from much of mainstream social work services and settings.

The changes in the development of social work were also seen in the number of schools joining the American Association of Schools of Social Work, which was founded in 1919. The association standardized curricula and promoted a master's degree in social work. Both undergraduate and graduate programs became members of the association (Ginsberg, 2001).

THE GREAT DEPRESSION: 1929 TO EARLY 1940S

The stock market crash of 1929, followed by a far-reaching economic depression, brought the United States to the brink of economic disaster. Social service agencies were unprepared to address the mounting needs of not only the indigent but also members of the working class. In time, after listening to the narratives of their clients, social workers began to focus on individual deficits with a growing appreciation for the social and economic factors associated with dependency and need (Axinn & Stern, 1988). Social workers rekindled the "cause" orientation that had been abandoned in the 1920s and lobbied the government to provide an adequate standard of living for all Americans in this time of extraordinary need (Trattner, 1999).

In 1932, the governor of New York, Franklin D. Roosevelt, was elected the nation's 32nd president. He called for bold government action and instituted a large federal relief program for the needy. The vast majority of social workers endorsed President Roosevelt's New Deal, which included unemployment insurance and a social security system to deal with the financial insecurity experienced by older persons, dependent

Source: Http://www.loc.gov/pictures/item/00649036/

▲ President Franklin D. Roosevelt signed the Social Security Act on August 14, 1935.

children, and individuals with physical challenges. Harry Hopkins, a social worker, was appointed head of the Federal Emergency Relief Administration. This was the first federal program to provide relief to the nation's citizens on a major scale since the years following the Civil War (Trattner, 1999).

The New Deal provided additional employment opportunities for social workers, who were responsible for state and local public relief. The funds came from a combination of local and federal agencies. Unfortunately, the relief measures neglected to address racial discrimination; minority groups experienced more economic hardship than other Americans.

RANK AND FILE MOVEMENT

In the 1930s, progressive social workers organized the "rank and file movement" and began analyzing and criticizing aspects of the New Deal. More specifically, as new social service programs appeared, social workers were hired to administer the programs and service people in need. The social workers themselves realized they suffered as workers; they earned very low wages, faced massive case loads, and lived barely above their own clients. Consequently, large numbers of progressive social workers joined the rank and file movement to build labor unions at relief agencies. Additionally, they organized study groups on capitalism and socialism, established a newspaper called *Social Work Today*, and formed labor unions at relief agencies all over the country (see www.rankandfiler.net/about-the-contributors/). Some core leaders of the movement joined socialists and communist groups, and connected their efforts as social workers to a broader movement of the poor people and workers to fight for a more just economic system.

After World War II, the rank and file movement was disbanded with the nation's mounting anticommunist sentiments. In fact, the leaders and spokespeople for the movement were fired from welfare agencies and from their jobs at social work schools. The labor unions in welfare departments built by the rank and file movement were outlawed and broken.

The Great Depression and the New Deal had a lasting effect on the nation's social welfare system—most notably, enactment of the Social Security Act of 1935. Exhibit 2.1 details the major programs that were part of the act, which was the result of noisy political compromise. Whatever faults may be found in the legislation, the Social Security Act widely expanded welfare activities and advanced services and programs for poor persons. It helped prevent destitution and dependency. The fact that it provided cash benefits to recipients was a major step toward enhancing human dignity and personal freedom (Axinn & Stern, 1988; Trattner, 1999).

WORLD WAR II: 1939 TO 1945

World War II placed the United States squarely on the global scene and provided near full employment for most Americans. So during this time, issues of poverty were not on the national agenda or in the forefront of the social work. Still, throughout the war, social workers were involved in services to the armed forces and their families. In addition, the gains in jobs and income did not apply evenly across races, although Roosevelt did issue Executive Order 8802 prohibiting discrimination in the defense industries, a significant advancement toward civil rights in the workplace (Skocpol, 1995; Trattner, 1999).

WWII, and the prosperity that followed victory, changed the nation's political climate. But the Great Depression and the New Deal had lasting effects on the social work profession. There were new jobs for social workers, a deeper understanding of human needs in urban and rural areas, and a renewed interest in reform efforts. Private and public welfare agencies acknowledged the social work profession as both a "cause" and a "function" within various fields of practice. The National Association of Social Workers formed in 1955, helping unite the profession through guidelines and a code of ethics that defined roles and responsibilities associated with social work practice.

EXHIBIT 2.1   Programs Instituted With the Social Security Act

1935: President Franklin Roosevelt signs the Social Security Act, the foundation of the nation's social welfare system, in response to widespread economic insecurity during the Great Depression.

1936: U.S. Postal Service distributes applications for Social Security. More than 35 million people apply for the benefit, and distribution of the Social Security card begins.

1939: Social Security expands to include children, survivors of workers, and retirees.

1940: First monthly retirement check is issued for $22.54. About 222,400 people receive Social Security benefits.

1950: President Harry Truman signs an amendment to the Social Security Act to provide a cost-of-living adjustment to offset inflation.

1950s: Social Security benefits expand to include farmworkers, domestic workers, and self-employed people. Cash benefits are added for disabled workers. Early retirement, with reduced benefits, is approved for women at 62 years old.

1961: President John F. Kennedy approves amendments that allow male workers to select early retirement benefits at 62 years old, with reduced benefits.

1965: Medicare program is enacted, partially funded through Social Security payroll taxes.

1980s: To address signs of future insolvency in the Social Security Trust Fund, from which benefits are paid, Congress enacts an increase in the self-employment tax, partial taxation of benefits to early retirees, and a gradual increase in the retirement age.

2000s: Amendments to the Social Security Act are discussed, but all reform efforts fail. By 2010 the system is paying out more than it receives in payroll taxes, putting its future at risk.

Source: Adapted from "Social Security Timeline" (n.d.).

AMERICA'S WAR ON POVERTY: 1960 TO 1967

The 1960s was a time of social unrest and political change in the United States. With the Vietnam War escalating, students and like-minded individuals protested the war across the country. Other movements formed to protest rights for women, people with physical and mental challenges, gay people, and people of color. It was the civil rights movement that educated Americans on the extent of prejudice and discrimination in our society and its costs. Books such as Michael Harrington's (1962) *The Other America* made the issue of poverty a public concern and a rallying point for citizen protests.

President John F. Kennedy's New Frontier and President Lyndon B. Johnson's Great Society programs were federal responses to issues such as these. Both administrations spoke of poverty and instituted a variety of new social welfare initiatives, including Head Start, a program providing preschool education for disadvantaged children; Medicaid, health care for the poor; Medicare, health care for older persons; and the Food Stamp Program, a food purchasing program for needy people. Exhibit 2.2 lists some of the programs from this era that have had a lasting effect on social welfare.

Source: AP Photo/Anonymous

▲ A World War II soldier is greeted by his family upon his return.

CURRENT TRENDS

Social Movements

AS stated by President Lyndon B. Johnson, the goal for the nation's involvement in Vietnam was not to win the war but for U.S. troops to support defenses until South Vietnam could take over. By entering the Vietnam War without a clearly stated goal to win, Johnson set the stage for future public and troop disappointment when the United States found itself in a stalemate with the North Vietnamese and the Viet Cong (Rosenberg, n.d.).

1. Several movies depict the Vietnam War. Watch one of them and consider why social movements emerged from the Vietnam War that changed the way many people think about military service and issues of society.

2. What similarities does the nation's current involvement in Iraq and Afghanistan share with the Vietnam War?

3. What, if any, is the impact of voluntary military service on social movements about war?

EXHIBIT 2.2   New Frontier and Great Society Programs

NEW FRONTIER, PRESIDENT JOHN F. KENNEDY, 1961 TO 1963

- *1961:* Peace Corps is established by Executive Order 10924 to promote world peace and friendship.
- *1961:* The Area Redevelopment Act provides $394 million in benefits to "distressed areas" to combat chronic unemployment in impoverished cities and rural areas by increasing their levels of economic growth.
- *1962:* Rural Renewal Program provides technical and financial assistance for locally initiated and sponsored programs aimed at ending chronic underemployment and fostering a sound rural economy.
- *1962:* Aid to Families with Dependent Children replaces the Aid to Dependent Children program, as coverage is extended to adults caring for dependent children.
- *1963:* Community Mental Health Act provides assistance in improving mental health through grants for construction of community mental health centers and for other purposes.

GREAT SOCIETY, PRESIDENT LYNDON B. JOHNSON, 1963 TO 1969

- *1964:* Community Action Programs founded by Economic Opportunity Act to fight poverty by promoting self-sufficiency and depending on volunteer work.
- *1964:* Job Corp formed to provide free vocational training and education to young adults.
- *1964:* Office of Economic Opportunity created by Economic Opportunity Act to oversee a variety of community-based antipoverty programs.
- *1964:* Food Stamps Act designed to alleviate hunger and malnutrition of low-income families and individuals by providing the ability to purchase food.
- *1965:* Medicare part of Social Security Act enacted to provide federal funding for many of the medical costs of older Americans.
- *1965:* Medicaid part of Social Security Act enacted to provide medical care for families and individuals with low income and resources.
- *1965:* Volunteers in service to America founded as the domestic version of Peace Corps designed to fight poverty (incorporated into AmeriCorps in 1993).
- *1965:* Teachers Corp established by Higher Education Act to improve teaching in predominantly low-income areas.
- *1965:* Head Start established to provide early childhood education, health, nutrition, and parent-involvement services to low-income children and their families.
- *1966:* Model Cities Program established to develop antipoverty programs and alternative forms of local government.

A greater number of baccalaureate-level social workers were needed to fill the increasing demand for trained staff as these programs were established. The National Association of Social Workers and the Council on Social Work Education began accepting the Bachelor of Social Work as the entry-level professional degree in the field.

Tired of civil turmoil and the Vietnam War, Americans turned politically conservative and embraced the conservative ideals and concern with civil order promised by Republican President Richard Nixon (1969–1974). President Nixon left the presidency after his participation in the coverup of the Watergate scandal, a breaking-and-entering scheme at democratic headquarters in the Watergate Hotel in Washington, D.C. Vice President Gerald Ford became president (1974–1976) and eventually lost his election bid to one-term Democratic President Jimmy Carter.

Although President Carter (1977–1981) promoted social programs and showed compassion for disenfranchised Americans, his administration was marred by high inflation rates, spiraling gas prices, and an international crisis involving the taking of American hostages in Iran. These events contributed to President Carter's political demise and failure to gain reelection, while setting the stage for the election of President Ronald Reagan.

REAGANOMICS: 1981 TO 1989

The Republican presidential candidate, Ronald Reagan, beat the incumbent President Carter with a conservative platform that emphasized individual responsibility for one's own problems rather than the reform of existing systems for social welfare. Reagan called for a smaller federal government, a safety net for only the truly needy, and a lifetime limit on social services. He also embraced **trickle-down economics** (a version of classical economic theory also known as supply-side economics). The underlying idea was that reducing the tax obligations of the rich would stimulate them to spend more on the consumption of goods and services. In theory, the prosperity of the rich would "trickle down" to middle-class and poorer Americans via the creation of new industries and jobs. There was, however, nothing to prevent the rich from simply holding onto their profits, purchasing existing enterprises, or investing in enterprises overseas.

President Reagan's administration was largely successful in implementing his vision. It shrank government and social welfare programs and services at the federal level through budget cuts and the implementation of means-tested programs and services. It also curtailed programs sanctioned and funded by the Social Security Act, such as Medicaid, food stamps, loans for higher education, and legal assistance for poor people. To offset these federal reductions and maintain some programs and services, many states and communities increased taxation.

After President Reagan's two terms in office, the 1988 election of his vice president, George W. H. Bush, to the presidency continued Reagan's conservative approach. President Bush focused his energy on international affairs, showing little inclination to address social issues or domestic policy. Responsibility for social programs shifted from the public to the private sector. President Bush promoted a "thousand points of light" campaign, where communities would develop and often privately fund services and programs to address local needs. Impoverished communities had few resources to dedicate to such points of light, however.

Pushback against the nation's conservative era came by way of the election of William Clinton. President Clinton (1993–2001) was the first Democratic president since Franklin D. Roosevelt to win a second term of office. In revamping the welfare system, Clinton engaged in political compromise. One result was the 1996 Personal Responsibility and Work Opportunity Reconciliation Act, which reversed six decades of federal policy guaranteeing at least a minimum level of financial assistance, or a safety net, for indigent people.

PARTISAN GRIDLOCK

After a two-term Clinton presidency, Republican George W. Bush won the 2000 election. It was one of the closest and most controversial presidential elections in history, and was ultimately decided in the Supreme Court. A prior governor of Texas, President Bush described his political philosophy as "compassionate conservatism," a view that combined traditional Republican economic policies with concern for the underprivileged. His administration targeted education and volunteerism within faith-based and community organizations as a way of providing social services to the needy.

Source: AP Photo/J. Scott Applewhite

▲ All living U.S. presidents (L–R): President George H. W. Bush, President Barack Obama, President George W. Bush, President Bill Clinton, and President Jimmy Carter.

However, it was not domestic issues that marked the Bush administration. On September 11, 2001, terrorists attacked the World Trade Center towers in New York and the Pentagon in Washington, D.C., by flying passenger jets into them. A fourth suicide flight, en route to the White House or the Capitol Building, was thwarted by its passengers. All in all, some 3,000 people died. The event, now referred to as 9/11, defined Bush's tenure (see www.history.com/topics/9-11-attacks). He declared a "war on terror" and launched two wars in the Middle East. He also established the Department of Homeland Security, a vast bureaucracy charged with preventing any attack on the United States in the future. At the same time, he maintained his pledge to reduce taxes. The result was a huge national debt, a faltering economy, and a national and worldwide credit crisis.

The effect of many of his social initiatives was dwarfed by the wars in Iraq and Afghanistan, the fight against terrorism, and the global war on terror. By the end of his term, President Bush had a public approval rating of 20%, the lowest recorded for any sitting president (Pew Research Center, 2008).

The 2008 election was remarkable for the victory of Democrat Barack Obama, the first African American president. During the campaign, Obama had proposed a platform of change and reform in Washington, with domestic policy and the economy as central themes. In the midst of a downward spiral in the national economy, which became known as the "Great Recession," he had several serious domestic and international issues to address: the

transgressions of Wall Street, America's financial district, and the damage to the world economy; burgeoning, and suspect, foreclosures on American homeowners; a dysfunctional and unfair health care system; costly wars in Iraq and Afghanistan; increasing dissatisfaction with immigration policy; and increasing signs of global climate change. The Obama administration experienced intransigent pushback on nearly every issue from the Republican members of the House of Representatives and the Senate, who were committed to a smaller federal government and a reduction in the national debt.

The Obama administration's signature social welfare policy is the Affordable Care Act (ACA), signed into law on March 23, 2010. A controversial piece of social welfare policy because it expands the role of the federal government, the policy enacted comprehensive reforms to improve access to affordable health coverage and to alter insurance company practices. Exhibit 2.3 summarizes the ways the ACA protects the rights of patients and those who may become patients. Ideally, the ACA will decrease the nation's health care costs and make insurance companies more accountable for how premiums are spent.

The ACA primarily affects health care coverage in three ways: through health exchanges, which went into effect in 2014; by expanding Medicaid coverage; and when states decide to create their own basic health programs. In each case, social workers will help people "navigate" the new systems of health care to ensure they receive proper coverage and benefits. Further, the expanded health care provisions address mental or behavioral health, which represents another significant service area where social workers play a vital role.

TIME TO THINK

What stands out in your mind as you consider the development of social work and social welfare policy over time? What seems to drive the development of social welfare policy?

Is there a point in this history that you find particularly interesting? Why? What are the significant events in the development of the social work profession that draw you to consider social work as a career option?

EXHIBIT 2.3   Contents of the Affordable Care Act "New Patient's Bill of Rights"

BANS DISCRIMINATING AGAINST KIDS WITH PREEXISTING CONDITIONS

Insurance plans cannot discriminate against children because of a preexisting condition. Before reform, tens of thousands of families each year were denied insurance for their children because of an illness or condition.

BANS DROPPING COVERAGE

Insurance companies are banned from cutting off your coverage due to an unintentional mistake on your application. Before reform, insurance companies could cancel your coverage when you were sick and needed it most, because of a simple mistake on your application.

BANS LIMITING COVERAGE

Insurance companies can no longer put a lifetime limit on the amount of coverage; so families can live with the security of knowing that their coverage will be there when they need it most. Before reform, cancer patients and individuals suffering from other serious and chronic diseases were often forced to limit or go without treatment because of an insurer's lifetime limit on their coverage.

BANS LIMITING THE CHOICE OF DOCTORS

If you purchase or join a new plan, you have the right to choose your own doctor in your insurer network. Before reform, insurance companies could decide which doctor you saw.

BANS RESTRICTING EMERGENCY ROOM CARE

If you purchase or join a new plan, the insurance company is banned from charging more for emergency services obtained outside its network of health care providers. Before reform, insurance companies could limit which emergency room you could go to or charge you more if you went out of network.

GUARANTEES A RIGHT TO APPEAL

If you purchase or join a new policy, you will be guaranteed the right to appeal insurance company decisions to an independent third party. Before reform, when insurers denied you coverage or restricted your treatment, you were left with few options to appeal the decision.

GUARANTEES COVERAGE OF YOUNG ADULTS ON PARENT'S PLAN

Young adults can remain on their parent's plan until their 26th birthday, unless they are offered coverage at work. Up to 2.4 million young adults could gain affordable coverage through this provision of the new law.

GUARANTEES PREVENTIVE CARE WITH NO COST TO PATIENTS

If you join or purchase a new plan, you will receive recommended preventive care with no out-of-pocket cost. Services such as mammograms, colonoscopies, immunizations, and prenatal and new baby care will be covered, and insurance companies will be prohibited from charging deductibles, copayments, or coinsurance.

Source: Adapted from White House (n.d.).

THE LIMITATIONS OF SOCIAL WELFARE

Although social reforms have enriched the lives of millions of Americans (Jansson, 1999), they sometimes fail to meet stated or ideal goals. Consider how the notion of the "deserving poor" has affected the provision of social welfare. Our belief in supporting children and older people has characterized American society since colonial times. This fact sends a strong social signal to families that they should be responsible for their own.

Most of the social services that target young and old age categories are crisis interventions rather than preventions.

For instance, policies such as the Social Security Act and Temporary Assistance for Needy Families provide a safety net for children and older adults. However, the basic needs of food and clothing are met in a modest fashion under the guise of cost containment. In such an environment, clients live with uncertainty and the practice of social work is restricted.

Although the United States is a rich country, many people are working hard every day but living from paycheck to paycheck. Far too many Americans live in poverty, relying on social programs for their most basic needs. Ideally, changes in social policy would give these underprivileged groups greater access to jobs that pay a **living wage** and equip them with the tools, such as a good education, to raise their status in society. However, the nation's social welfare system does little to move working-class and poor people from their current socioeconomic class.

Tellingly, some communities experience persistent poverty and social inequality. In America, these groups are often the victims of racism. There are no policy examples and few social service programs that draw from and honor the cultural backgrounds and personal experiences of people of color. How can the effects of racism be challenged by the profession of social work? The history of social welfare policy suggests the need to address the root causes of social, economic, and political inequality. The 1963 March on Washington, followed by the 1964 Civil Rights Act, demonstrated that organizing people and taking united action can change the course of a nation.

For a more recent example of how movements for social justice can change society, consider the evolution of sexuality-based issues. History illustrates a long, hard struggle among women, lesbians, and gays for equality in all spheres of American life. Individually and collectively, they have been actively involved in civil rights. Through resilience and resourcefulness, this broad-based population has tackled barriers to its

own growth and participation in society. Subsequently, political institutions, American corporations, families, faith organizations, and other major American entities have changed power arrangements to ensure a greater degree of equality.

TIME TO THINK

What social issues concern you? Do you have student loans or pay taxes? Are you concerned about the environment, affordable health care, voting rights, military engagement, immigration, net neutrality, or legalization of marijuana?

What action could you take to influence a policy or concern? Do you see the federal government as a vehicle to address your concerns? What is your role in bringing a particular issue to the public attention? For example, do you vote, volunteer for campaigns, post to blogs, call in to radio shows?

Are organizations on your campus or in your neighborhood working on social issues? Have you participated or will you participate in such an organization? Why or why not?

SUMMARY

Approaches to social welfare have changed over the past few centuries of American life, and the social work profession has evolved alongside those changes. However, despite improvements in many realms of life, the problems to which social welfare responds have remained.

There is a rhythm of social responses to social welfare problems and social issues. As this chapter indicates, economic ups-and downs, wars, political shifts from conservative to liberal perspectives, and attitudes toward individual responsibilities are all factors that influence development of the social welfare system. The result is a fragmented approach to addressing human needs.

Currently many issues are facing the social welfare system. Debates over the nation's health care system and immigration policies, for instance, continue as cutbacks are made in programs to assist those in need. Determining how to intervene in issues such as these has always been a problem for our nation. This is particularly true in relation to providing assistance for those who are poor and appear to be able to work. Much depends on our willingness to commit to helping those in need.

TOP 10 KEY CONCEPTS

conservative
deserving poor
liberal
means testing
nondeserving poor

safety net
social control
social justice
social welfare
social welfare policy

DISCUSSION QUESTIONS

1. Think about your political ideologies and where they came from throughout your lifetime. Do they align with your parents' ideologies? Is this an issue? Why or why not? What experiences formed your opinions on social welfare services and social work?

2. As you read through the history of the development of social work, what period of time most captured your attention? What is it about this time that piques your interest?

3. Define the current political scene, environmental conditions, human needs, and social justice issues in the United States or your country of origin. How have these factors contributed to debate on a policy issue and a specific social welfare policy?

4. Take time to review Exhibit 2.1, the Social Security Act timeline. Discuss the issues and actions you think have been the most effective in helping the needy.

EXERCISES

1. Learn more about various political parties and their stances on social welfare by going to their websites. In addition to the Democratic and Republican parties, seek information about the Libertarian Party, the Green Party, the Progressive Party, the Constitution Party, or others that run candidates in your locale. Focusing on the issue of social welfare, locate the parties on a spectrum from most liberal to most conservative.

2. Read an editorial from one of the nation's leading newspapers or news websites. What political perspective does the editorial reflect, and how did you reach this conclusion?

3. Role-play a situation in which you must ask for public assistance. How did you feel about being in need and asking for help?

4. Review Exhibit 2.1, the social work and social welfare policy timeline, and select one landmark event. Read about the time period and list the relevant political situation, environmental factors, human needs, and social justice issues of the time.

5. Choose a social welfare service available in your community. Gather the history of this agency. In what ways does its history compare to what you read in this chapter?

ONLINE RESOURCES

- Affordable Care Act (www.hhs.gov/healthcare/rights): Lays out the health care rights of Americans under the act
- Great Depression (www.history.com/topics/great-depression): Defines the Great Depression and how it impacted the lives of people. Provides text, images, and video about the era that launched many new social programs
- Nelson Mandela (www.nelsonmandela.org/content/page/biography): Read about the remarkable life of South Africa's first democratically elected president
- Settlement movement (www.cfsettlements.org): Examine how the movement changed public health and working conditions for many workers
- Social Security Act (www.ssa.gov/history/pdf/histdev.pdf): Consider the significance of the Social Security Act from a historical perspective and as a safety network for Americans
- Social Welfare History Project (www.socialwelfarehistory.com): Provides more information about the Charity Organization Societies and other relevant topics
- War in Vietnam (www.history.com/topics/vietnam-war): Covers the relevance of the war in terms of public unrest

STUDENT STUDY SITE

Sharpen your skills with SAGE edge at **edge.sagepub.com/cox**

SAGE edge for Students provides a personalized approach to help you accomplish your coursework goals in an easy-to-use learning environment.

Chapter 3: GENERALIST SOCIAL WORK PRACTICE

Learning Objectives

After reading this chapter, you should be able to

1. Describe the knowledge base for generalist social work and direct practice.
2. Describe the five theoretical bases of generalist practice.
3. Define roles available for generalist social workers.
4. Identify the five steps in the client change process.
5. Explain how the advocacy program and policy model applies to the change process.
6. Explain how generalist social workers can advocate for change across client systems.

Layla Intervenes at All Levels to Help Immigrant Children

Layla, a social worker in an elementary school, helps the children of immigrants develop their ability to read and write. She also assists all the schoolchildren's parents with referrals to health and dental clinics. Layla thinks the children she works with have great potential as long as some of their basic needs are met on a regular basis. For this to be accomplished, Layla realizes she needs not only to assess particular individual needs but also to consider issues that affect groups and entire communities. She begins to attend the school's Parent Teacher Association meetings with the hope of better understanding the ways parents support the academic activities of their children. Layla also gathers ideas from the parents on ways the broader community offers to support them and their children's educational experience.

This chapter highlights **generalist social work practice.** The goal of generalist practice is to address problematic interactions between persons and their environments or surroundings. Most helping relationships and change situations within social work involve generalist skills. A generalist social worker may work in schools with children who have learning challenges, as Layla does, with people living in an institution who need help adjusting to life outside, on the street with destitute families who need immediate assistance with housing and food, with older people who can take care of most of their daily activities but need assistance with health care insurance and prescribed medications—or with any number of other types of clients. Community members who are organizing for change in their living environment, such as people fighting to reduce air pollution in their neighborhood, may also rely on a generalist social worker to help facilitate their efforts in the political arena.

Source: ©iStockphoto.com/vuk8691

▲ Generalist social workers work with individuals and families to assess their needs.

The knowledge, theoretical perspectives, roles, and skills of generalist practice are described in this chapter. You will see that generalist social workers, including those with a bachelor's degree in social work, have an array of employment opportunities. Social workers confront problems ranging from individual issues, such as domestic violence, to community issues, such as lead paint poisoning in federal housing projects, to national issues, such as gun violence and voting rights. Not all problems can be solved by generalist social workers, but they do possess the skills to assess many types of situations, plan a course of action, and evaluate outcomes.

This chapter emphasizes **direct practice,** or one-on-one interactions with clients. The social work profession has an important role to play in helping clients attain more social power, resources, and services. A generalist social worker needs problem-solving skills and the ability to determine a client's strengths or potential to participate in a change effort. Generalist social workers must also be able to think beyond current situations and to devise change strategies that build on strengths and capitalize on existing and potential resources. These skills are central to social work practice at the generalist level.

KNOWLEDGE BASE FOR GENERALIST SOCIAL WORKERS

The Bachelor of Social Work (BSW) degree, as Chapter 1 explains, is the entry-level credential for the social work profession. (In many states across the nation, baccalaureate social workers must also pass a state-administered examination to become licensed to practice.) The BSW degree provides the knowledge base for generalist social work practice. Although not required, membership in the National Association of Social Workers, the largest professional organization for social workers, helps generalist practitioners continue to learn and add to their knowledge bases throughout their careers.

The education for generalist practice is based on the liberal arts, a curriculum that provides a general fund of knowledge and academic skills. Courses within the **liberal arts foundation** that apply to a social work degree vary from university to university, but typically courses from sociology, psychology, biology, economics, political science, and statistics are included. The liberal arts foundation introduces students to the idea that a thorough understanding of a society, its people, and the challenges they face depends on knowledge, attitudes, ways of thinking, and means of communication. In addition to the required liberal arts courses, generalist social workers also take courses in the following subject areas:

• *Human behavior in the social environment:* Course material examines theory, research, and practice issues related to human development. Emphasis is placed on understanding the relevance and use of theory in practice, and the way diversity, such as in gender, race, ethnicity, sexual orientation, and economic circumstances, contributes to and influences personality development.

• *Social work research:* This course covers the formulation of research questions, data collection, and data analysis. Students are taught both to consume and generate research findings that support conclusions about life conditions. Most research courses introduce classic and contemporary studies, and point out how their findings apply to social work knowledge and practice.

• *Social policy:* Courses in this content area examine the nation's social welfare system and the development, implementation, and evaluation of policy. The social welfare policy course informs social work students of available services and programs, as well as which people are eligible for services and how long services can be provided.

• *Social work methods or practice:* These courses present a conceptual framework for social work intervention and cover common elements of social work practice, such as the social work process and the interaction of various kinds of diversity. Students are introduced to concepts and skills relevant for practice with individuals and groups, and in a variety of community settings.

• *Field education:* A requirement of all social work students, field education involves a placement in a social service agency, where students are required to complete at least 480 hours under the supervision of a master's-level social worker. Field education connects knowledge from the classroom with the opportunity to apply practice skills and knowledge in an agency setting with an array of clients.

• *Electives:* Social work students usually have the opportunity to select courses that complement their social work curriculum and expand on social welfare or social work issues that interest them. Electives may focus on addictions, domestic violence, international social work, aging, child welfare, or anything else that relates to today's social needs.

Exhibit 3.1 diagrams the interplay of these elements of the baccalaureate social work degree. Given the complexity of the problems they address, social workers need a broad knowledge base to develop a toolbox of interventions that can be used to undertake a change process.

Throughout the social work curriculum, students are repeatedly exposed to the profession's core values, which highlight individual rights and social justice. Social work's commitment to **self-determination**—the right of people, groups, and communities to make choices, design a course of action, and live as independently as possible—is stressed repeatedly.

EXHIBIT 3.1   Knowledge Base for Baccalaureate Social Work

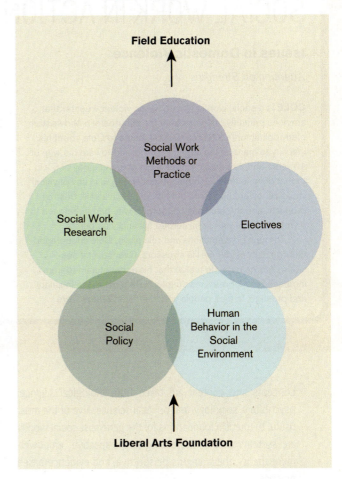

The baccalaureate social work curriculum also acts to expand students' skills in **critical thinking**—the ability to reflect on and integrate information from an array of sources to form a position, opinion, or conclusion. This is a critical skill for generalist social workers, who need to be able to express their views confidently and support them when questioned.

THEORETICAL FOUNDATIONS OF GENERALIST PRACTICE

Generalist practice is a comprehensive, multidimensional approach to social work that draws from a variety of intervention models and theoretical perspectives. Some of their

---

TIME TO THINK

Self-determination is a critical concept in generalist social work practice. As a college student, to what degree have you practiced self-determination in your career planning, course selection, and student activities?

Consider how exercising self-determination has caused you to think through options, evaluate alternatives, and solicit ideas from others. What did you learn from exercising your right to make decisions for yourself?

SOCIAL WORK IN ACTION

Issues in Domestic Violence

Attention on Strengths

COLE is a social worker at a domestic violence center that services primarily residents from the suburbs of a Midwestern metropolitan area. George, a client, came to Cole about his inability to manage the anger he expressed toward his wife of 10 years and their two children, a girl of 8 and a boy of 5. Up to that point in time, George had not engaged in any physical violence toward his family, but he did punch a wall, destroy property, and threaten harm. George's wife had threatened to divorce George unless he curbed his angry outbursts.

Through conversations and role plays, Cole encouraged George to consider his life stressors. Over several sessions George came to realize that his anger stemmed from increased work pressures coupled with a decrease in salary and prestige. In fact, people younger than George were being promoted over him. Cole facilitated a process whereby George began to reflect on his strengths. Interesting enough, George concluded that his wife and children were sources of strength for him, as was his educational status.

1. Why would assessing personal strengths be helpful when attempting to manage anger?

2. How does age play into George's circumstances?

3. What strategies did Cole use to facilitate George's assessment of his life situation?

4. What do you suggest Cole should do next to help George control his anger?

---

concepts and content are taken from biological science, psychology, sociology, and political science. Five of the most useful theoretical foundations for the generalist social worker are systems theory, the ecological perspective, empowerment theory, the strengths perspective, and evidence-based practice.

Source: ©iStockphoto.com/digitalskillet

▲ Parents and children are a part of a client system, which social workers using systems theory may use to help their clients.

SYSTEMS THEORY

Social workers engage in practice with individuals, groups, communities, and organizations. The multifaceted interactions that social workers encounter demand a comprehensive view of the world in all its complexity. The knowledge of **systems theory** facilitates a dynamic understanding of client interactions from various perspectives and in several settings.

To understand systems theory, begin by thinking of a system as a collection of elements, members, or parts of a larger whole. For example, a **client system** might consist of an individual; important family members and friends; relationships with work, church, and other organizations; and elements of large-scale institutions such as the economy. These elements are like pieces in a puzzle. For the puzzle to be complete or whole, the pieces must fit together in relation with one another. The interrelationship of puzzle parts is essential because they come together to make the entire picture. For the client system in the example, the individual's problems and the solutions to those problems are seated in all the elements of the system. In a similar fashion, the elements that shape your life—your family, friends, college and home community—reflect who you are and how you function as a whole person. These various elements are essential to your being and your ability to succeed in numerous circumstances. Exhibit 3.2 is an **ecological map,** a type of diagram that social workers use to represent a client system.

Social workers use systems theory to conceptualize all the elements of complex human problems and to introduce a change process. It allows for a multidimensional analysis of function, cause, and interrelations when considering avenues of change. For example, Pam is a single mother of three school-age children. Recently unemployed, Pam needs to find work to support her family in their small rental home. Although Pam has multiple challenges, she is optimistic and hardworking, with good parenting skills. A social worker would visualize Pam's interrelated system by considering her problematic life elements and unique resources as a network of patterns, purposes, and attributes. Thus, systems theory provides social workers with a backdrop for practice that recognizes complexities, strengths, and avenues for change.

EXHIBIT 3.2   Client System Represented in an Ecological Map

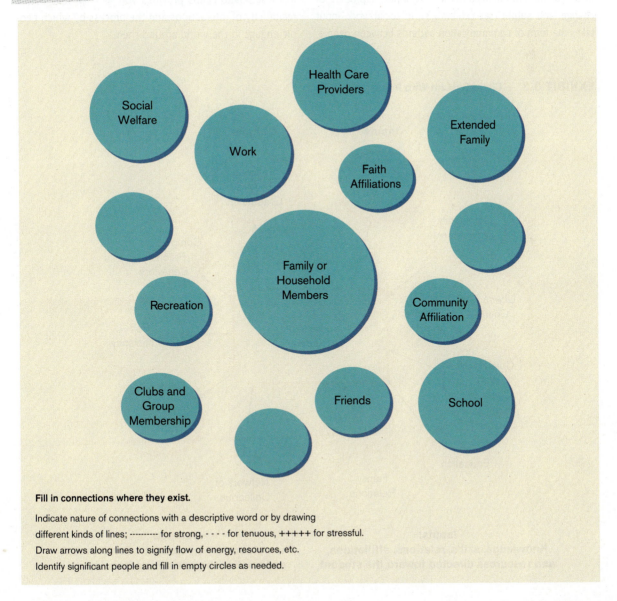

Fill in connections where they exist.

Indicate nature of connections with a descriptive word or by drawing different kinds of lines; ---------- for strong, - - - - for tenuous, +++++ for stressful.

Draw arrows along lines to signify flow of energy, resources, etc.

Identify significant people and fill in empty circles as needed.

The systems approach, which has been applied to disciplines from engineering to psychology, as well as social work, takes into account not only the complexity but also the dynamic nature of the interactions among the elements in a system. The interactions involve input, a process of change, and output (see Exhibit 3.3). In social work, input takes the form of communication patterns between people,

information transfer, and knowledge acquisition. Output takes the form of attitudes, behaviors, and role performance. The change process reflects the impact of the input on elements of the system and results in output that is noticeably different from the input and the elements at the beginning of the process.

It's important to keep in mind that human systems are always interacting with other systems, and inputs and outputs are continually changing those interactions. Consider the impact of the exchanges between a parent and a child, a student and a school, a family and a community, an employee and a workplace. The give and take in these relationships provides you with an idea of the reciprocity of interactions and the process by which people engage in the world around them.

EXHIBIT 3.3   Client System With Inputs and Outputs

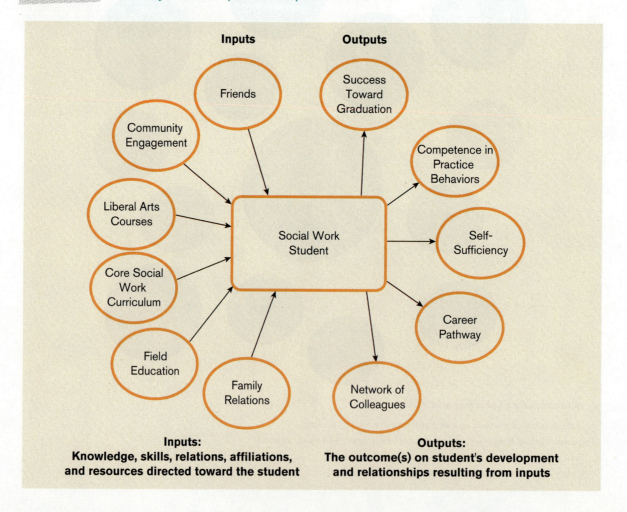

ECOLOGICAL PERSPECTIVE

Concepts from systems theory provide a foundation for the **ecological perspective,** which focuses on people and their environments. Those environments comprise the physical and social settings where a person resides or experiences life situations, including families and neighborhoods, communities and workplaces, and culture and institutions, such as places of worship and the education system. They are all part of a person's environment.

Generalist social workers learn to think of people as constantly interacting with their environment, a habit of mind called the **person-in-environment perspective**. It highlights how people are affected in positive and negative ways by their surroundings. Consider what it was like when you graduated from high school and entered college. You were faced with new circumstances, conditions, and expectations; however, you adapted to the change and soon found yourself comfortable in your new surroundings. This process of adaptation is critical to ecological or person-in-environment concepts. Adaptation requires the input from new ideas and experiences and the output of energy in the form of effort and flexibility. Fortunately you were successful in your adaptation to a new educational environment.

Exhibit 3.4 illustrates the elements of the environment that usually impinge on a person or a problem. Generalist practice with a person-in-environment perspective involves assessing all these elements of the environment:

- Political–economic system: Laws, political atmosphere, ideological trends, economic health
- Faith-based organizations, the marketplace, and human service systems: Providers of the resources (goods and services) that can be tapped to sustain a good life
- Education and employment systems: Developers and users of human skills, which promote well-being by giving people a place in society
- Family, **fictive kin,** and social support systems: The "home base" of friends and family (however *family* is defined by the individual) that provides a sense of safety and security and shapes the person's emotional life

The ecological and person-in-environment perspectives emphasize dynamic and complex relationships within an environment. Social workers understand that some people

▲ Social workers assess their clients' various day-to-day interactions.

struggle with adaptation to changes in the environment and need help in the process. Social workers also recognize that sometimes the environment needs to be changed to better suit the needs of a person. Sometimes improvements in social functioning correspond to change in social structures.

TIME TO THINK

The ecological and person-in-environment perspectives might be unfamiliar to you; people often blame personal qualities for their difficulties. Take a moment to think about how the concepts and terminology of the ecological perspective apply to your world. How has your community supported you throughout your development? Were you a member of a neighborhood sports team or club, such as a scout troop, or of some other supportive group while you were growing up? Was a place of worship significant to you as a child? What was missing from your community that you would like to add to the surroundings of other young people? Why?

EMPOWERMENT THEORY

A key term in both systems theory and the ecological perspective is *change*—change in individuals, families, groups, communities, organizations, institutions, and societies. **Empowerment theory** is a set of ideas that generalist social workers use to increase change possibilities. Social

EXHIBIT 3.4   Person-in-Environment Perspective

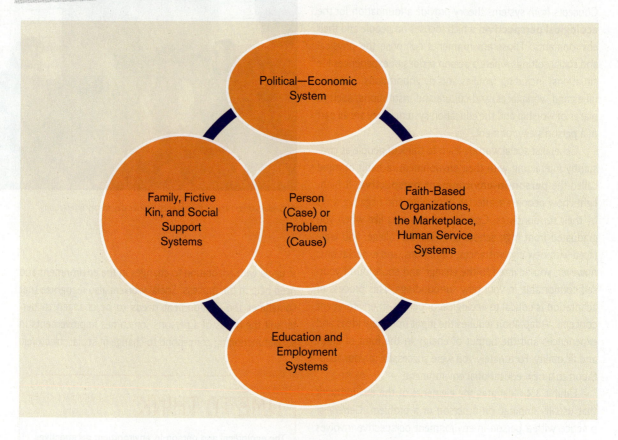

workers do not just provide the resources that people need; rather, they help people access resources on their own. **Empowerment** provides people with the means to attain their goals either directly or indirectly, through the help of others, such as social workers. Empowerment links the strengths and potential of individuals, systems, and behaviors to social action and societal change (Rappaport, 1981). For example, an empowered individual might challenge workplace promotion policies. A community can be empowered because citizens unite to improve conditions and the overall quality of life in their neighborhood.

A transformation occurs through the empowerment process. As individuals, families, and communities enhance their capacity, they begin to feel a sense of control over their lives as well as their environment. Thus, empowerment involves not only outward changes but also inward changes in self-esteem and the sense of personal value.

As a strategy for social work practice, empowerment necessitates collaboration with informal groups, such as

family and neighbors, and formal networks, such as agencies and organizations. The result is collective power that maximizes existing strengths and resources while tapping potential sources of renewal and change.

Closely connected to empowerment is advocacy, which in generalist practice encompasses all the activities that influence the allocation of resources and the decision making that occurs within social systems, institutions, and the political and economic arena. Influenced by a vision of a just society, social workers often find themselves questioning "why things are the way they are" and considering "what should be." That is the point where advocacy begins.

The empowerment aspect of advocacy links personal and political power to promote systematic societal change. Consider the dramatic societal change in support of marriage equality. It began when gay and lesbian individuals, seeking the rights and benefits of marriage, made their wishes known through the media and in public demonstrations. In moving from hopes and dreams to action, they accepted

▲ Changing one's environment, or the way they interact with the environment, can have positive results.

▲ LGBT Pride events create a space for individuals in a community to advocate for change and show support.

and embraced their sexuality, became empowered personally, and were able to organize a network of people and organizations that supported their position. The empowered gay and lesbian community successfully advocated at the local, state, national, and international levels for structural change to societal practices.

Using advocacy as a vehicle for empowerment supports social justice, which is a key concern of social workers. Social justice exists when everyone in a society shares in civil liberties, has a voice in political affairs, and has equal access to resources and opportunities.

STRENGTHS PERSPECTIVE

The cornerstone of generalist social work practice is the ability to assess and address problems related to people, groups, communities, and organizations. Although social workers recognize that problems do challenge clients,

sometimes grievously, they also recognize that clients in their environments have strengths, assets, resources, and knowledge that may be useful in solving those problems. The **strengths perspective** gives credence to the idea that every person has strengths to call on in solving their problems (Saleebey, 2009).

TIME TO THINK

Take a moment to consider the unique strengths you have. How have you used your strengths to address a personal problem or issue you've experienced?

Central to the strengths perspective is the role of assessment. Of course, in direct practice social workers assess their clients' situations. In addition, the clients themselves are also

Source: ©iStockphoto.com/temizyurek

▲ Though social workers acknowledge clients' challenges, they also understand the strengths, assets, and resources available to them.

called on to define or assess their conditions and state what they would like to change. In this way clients are empowered to act on their own behalf in conjunction with social workers. The resulting shift in power places clients in a prominent position in the helping relationship.

How does the strengths perspective manifest in generalist practice?

- Listening to the ideas of clients and communities to identify resources and opportunities
- Collaborating with clients as an equal partner in the assessment and change process
- Recognizing the unique potential and resilience of clients to challenge barriers
- Understanding that communities offer untapped resources that can be used individually and collectively

The strengths perspective complements systems theory, the ecological perspective, and empowerment theory by making people the primary experts in their own change processes (Saleebey, 2009). It ensures that the outcomes of change will reflect the needs and concerns of clients. The usefulness of the strengths perspective is in the values implicit in its approach and the direction it offers to social workers tackling a case or cause.

EVIDENCE-BASED PRACTICE

The goal of evidence-based practice (EBP) comprises four features: (1) the client's situation; (2) the client's goals,

values, and wishes; (3) clinical expertise/expert opinion; and (4) external scientific evidence. As is apparent, the client is an active participant throughout the intervention planning, implementation, and evaluation.

The use of EBP is thought to correlate with positive results in a selected intervention and the overall change process. Some social workers place emphasis on the findings derived from large-scale experimental comparisons to document the effectiveness of intervention against a control group that did not experience the intervention. In this way, the notion of cause and effect is approached. Other social workers honor the evidence generated from nonexperimental research, suggesting that some experimental research is too narrow and limited by conceptualizations, measures, participant samples, and specified interventions.

Generalist social work often describes EBP in the context of the decision-making process. The use of EBP is one way to help ensure that clients receive the best services possible. It also embraces a professional commitment by social workers to understand and critically appraise data from a variety of sources. Overall, adoption of EBP and current research findings upholds professional practice standards and serves as a means for practitioners to inform the course of social work research.

TIME TO THINK

Generalist social workers use all five of the theoretical foundations outlined here—systems theory, the ecological perspective, empowerment theory, the strengths perspective, and evidence-based practice—to help clients address the issues in their lives. Think of a time when you felt locked into a difficult set of circumstances. How would each of these foundations have helped you overcome those circumstances?

ROLES FOR GENERALIST SOCIAL WORKERS

People enter the social work profession for numerous reasons. Some want to make a difference in people's lives; others received services or care at some point in their own lives and want to give back as a form of reciprocity. The overriding reason is that people who enter social work care deeply about people, the conditions they live in, and the opportunities available to them.

CURRENT TRENDS

International Expansion of Generalist Practice

COUNTRIES such as China, Mongolia, Taiwan, and Vietnam are seeking social workers to develop educational programs in social work and design social service networks and programs. Often the programs are associated with national problems such as child abuse, substance abuse, and health care issues, including HIV/AIDS, tuberculosis, and malaria. Most of these countries are in the development stage of their economic base and welfare system.

1. Take a moment to read about the International Federation of Social Workers, at ifsw.org. Then review some of the

international employment opportunities and list at least three possible trends you see developing for generalist social workers on the international scene.

2. Why would developing nations seek support from U.S. social workers?

3. Do you think these international opportunities for generalist social workers are an option for you? Why or why not?

As Chapter 1 explains, baccalaureate-level social workers are prepared to practice with individuals, families, groups, organizations, and communities in entry-level positions in social service agencies, child welfare bureaus, shelters, community organizations, faith-based programs, schools, health clinics and hospitals, mental health and treatment centers, and criminal justice facilities. The types of clients encountered in these settings vary, as do their immediate issues, but in all cases the social workers' primary role is to be of assistance and service to people in need.

The specific roles of generalist social workers reflect how they see themselves and are viewed by others. Although it is difficult to comprehensively define all the roles of social workers, the following list is a good sampling:

- **Advocate:** Champions the rights of others with the goal of empowering the client system served
- **Broker:** Assists clients in identifying, locating, and linking to needed resources; establishes a network of services and providers in collaboration with clients
- **Case manager:** Oversees the services provided to clients to ensure that their needs are met through quality interventions and in a timely fashion
- **Counselor:** Provides direct services that help clients articulate their needs, problems, and goals; explores options and strategies for change in light of the clients' strengths and resources

- **Mediator:** Intervenes and resolves disputes in a fair and equitable fashion; finds common ground, compromises while reconciling differences, and assumes a neutral role
- **Navigator:** Assists clients in maneuvering through complex bureaucracies, such as the health care system, to gain needed services
- **Researcher:** Conducts research projects and program evaluations to gain evidence that informs practice and policy

LEVELS OF GENERALIST PRACTICE

Chapter 1 also introduced the levels of practice at which a generalist social worker might intervene. Here we can take a closer look at them and at how they may be expressed in generalist practice.

SOCIAL WORK WITH INDIVIDUALS (MICRO LEVEL)

This level of practice is often also referred to as direct practice. Social work with individuals one-on-one requires skills in communication, cultural sensitivity, empathy, genuineness, and solution-focused decision making. Refined assessment and interviewing skills (discussed later in the chapter) are also necessary to get people to trust you and open up about their deepest concerns and needs.

To be an effective social worker at this level of practice, you must strive to know yourself well. Social workers consciously use their selves as a tool to engage clients, by seeking areas of commonality and offering insights into differences. Social workers also rely on their sense of themselves to demonstrate healthy professional boundaries—that is, to show clients how the social worker can help and which activities the social worker cannot perform with clients.

SOCIAL WORK WITH FAMILIES AND GROUPS (MEZZO OR MESO LEVEL)

Social work with a family is very rewarding. It actually combines micro with mezzo practice because it includes the family (a small group) in addition to the individuals that compose that family. Note that social workers in the 21st century must be prepared to accept an array of different "family types."

Sources and dynamics of social support must be fully explored when working with families. How well family members provide emotional, economic, and day-to-day, practical support to one another matters. Social workers need to look at those forms of support as immediate and highly effective resources that buffer stress and facilitate clients' adaptation to changing conditions.

Group work is another mode of intervention at the mezzo level. In generalist practice with groups, a social worker may serve as a consultant, evaluator, facilitator, initiator, resource person, therapist, or a combination of these. It can be a challenging task to wear so many hats at once; however, it is important to keep in mind that group interaction, support, and interdependence have great potential to foster change, as group members experience and lend mutual aid to one another. Support groups, family education groups, resident councils, social or life skills groups, and anger management groups are all possible forums where social workers can use group process or facilitation skills. But although social work educators teach group process skills to all students, not all social workers identify group work as their primary practice area (Whitaker & Arrington, 2008).

SOCIAL WORK WITH ORGANIZATIONS, COMMUNITIES, AND SOCIETY (MACRO LEVEL)

Macro-level intervention has always been a part of social work. It can be considered synonymous with advocacy. The term *macro* has both general and specific connotations:

- In a general sense, within social work, macro-level intervention means engaging with large systems in the socioeconomic environment. Macro practice in this sense may include collaboration with individual clients to strengthen and maximize their opportunities at the organizational, community, societal, and global levels—what we have called case advocacy.
- In the specific sense, macro social work practice suggests that the strengthening of higher-order social systems (organizations, communities, societies) is the focus. This sort of macro practice is synonymous with cause advocacy and community organizing (Rothman, 2007). It is this sort of macro-level work that distinguishes social work from other helping professions (Glisson, 1994).

Indirect social work is another historical term that is synonymous with macro social work. This terminology is outdated but was used to connote social work's commitment to environmental change and the alleviation of widespread suffering and social problems. In contrast, *direct* social work practice referenced face-to-face contact with clients to support or strengthen them as people.

THE CHANGE PROCESS

As social work became more professional, its practitioners and theorists developed a framework of steps that would remind social workers about how they might best intervene in people's lives and help them meet their needs. The process begins when a social worker is assigned a client and does not end until the client–social worker relationship, which often includes aftercare activities, ends. The following are typical steps or phases identified in the change process:

1. Engagement
2. Assessment
3. Planning

4. Implementation

5. Evaluation

Although such frameworks are straightforward and work well to outline a general way activities occur in practice, it is important to realize that actual interventions do not always occur in a step-by-step, linear fashion. For example, implementation and evaluation may reveal that another round of assessment and planning needs to occur.

Many social workers acknowledge that the client–worker relationship is critical to the change process. As workers respond empathically to clients, warmth, genuineness, and trust are likely to develop over a period of time. As a result, the client will feel comfortable to explore issues, provide comments, and map a source of action that leads to change in his or her life. Arguably, perhaps the most important component of the change process is the client–worker relationship, which is based on a mutual bond of trust and confidence. Common steps in the change process are further examined and described below.

ENGAGEMENT

As the first step of the model, **engagement** sets the tone for the change process. The social worker interviews the client (or clients) to learn as much as possible about the person in the context of his or her environment. Skills in verbal and nonverbal communication are crucial for understanding the client and putting him or her at ease. Engagement is a key time for people to get to know each other and begin developing rapport.

To interview well, you must know how to listen actively, guide a conversation, and be open to clients' initial and perceived needs. Flexibility is a key attitude to respond to different contexts and individual preferences (Sidell & Smiley, 2008). There are many excellent books describing the relevance and importance of interviewing skills (e.g., Benjamin, 1981; Hepworth, Rooney, Rooney, Strom-Gottfried, & Larsen, 2010; Ivey, Ivey, & Zalaquett, 2010).

Effective interviews that promote revealing conversation about fundamental issues possess several characteristics (Evans, Hearn, Uhlemann, & Ivey, 2004; Sidell & Smiley, 2008). The interviewer must use visual means of communication that are sensitive to the culture, gender, and personality of the interviewee, such as appropriate eye contact, vocal qualities, and body language. Good interviewers are very skillful in knowing how and when to use closed- and open-ended questions.

During interviews, decoding clients' nonverbal behaviors is essential for successful communication. Some interviewers like using the PERCEIVE framework (Beall, 2004; Sidell & Smiley, 2008, pp. 74–76). PERCEIVE is an acronym for the types of communication behaviors the client may exhibit; see Exhibit 3.5 for the details.

EXHIBIT 3.5 PERCEIVE Framework for Decoding Nonverbal Behaviors

- **Proximity** is the distance between the interviewer and interviewee. Comfort zones must be assessed individually and culturally.
- **Expressions** are seen on faces. The six universal expressions are anger, fear, disgust, happiness, sadness, and surprise. Facial expressions may reveal what your client is thinking or feeling.
- **Relative orientation** is the degree to which people face each other. Attitudes and intentions may be decoded through your client's body positioning.
- **Contact** refers to physical contact. Familiarity, closeness, and degree of liking are conveyed by the amount and frequency of touch.
- **Eye contact** is a powerful way to communicate. Eyes reveal emotions, sensitivity, and understanding. Anxiety, intimidation, disinclination to communicate, and dishonesty are conveyed via lack of eye contact. The amount of eye contact, however, will vary by culture.
- **Individual gestures** are movements of the body when talking. Gestures indicate strong feelings.
- **Voice** reveals feelings. Listen to tones, volume, and level of control.
- **Existence of adapters** is the presence of small behaviors signifying when people are bored or stressed. Playing with one's rings, touching one's hair, and twirling a pen are the most common adapters.

Source: Adapted from Sidell and Smiley (2008, pp. 74–76).

Source: ©iStockphoto.com/vuk8691

▲ It is important for generalist social workers to engage with their clients through empathy and recognition of their strengths.

For an example of how the engagement process might take place in an intervention, consider Angus, a generalist social worker at a homeless shelter, and his client Hank. Angus begins by establishing a relationship with Hank through communication that displays empathy for Hank's current situation and concern as to what Hank will do on the city streets when the weather grows cold. Angus passes no judgment on Hank's spotty work history or sketchy friendships. Rather, Angus spends time listening to Hank's story of a recent apartment eviction and sense of failure as a retail clerk. Angus's formal and informal questions and willingness to discuss topics of interest to Hank place Hank in the position of expert (Tice & Perkins, 1996). Angus also fosters Hank's self-confidence by complimenting Hank on his strengths: his resilience and ability to think ahead about the approaching winter.

What slowly occurs between Hank and Angus is a collaboration or partnership. The engagement component of the change process initiates productive patterns of communication and a mutual sense of confidence about working together. In actual practice, forging client–social worker relationships often needs to be given priority over the completion of agency forms and paperwork. Indeed, without a relationship, it is often difficult even to collect client information.

ASSESSMENT

Assessment, the second step in the change process, is bidirectional in nature—a two-way street. The social worker is assessing the problems and strengths of the client, while the client is assessing the personality, professional skills, and demeanor of the social worker. These parallel assessments begin to intersect if they build on positive engagement and remain nonthreatening. For example, Hank was pleased when Angus endorsed his future plans and recognized his "can-do" attitude toward life. Sensing Angus's acceptance made it easier for Hank to discuss some of the problems that extended beyond his homelessness and included a description of sensitive and fragile relationships with his family. Some of Hank's other unique strengths were quickly apparent to Angus. Hank was resourceful, creative, and articulate. He was willing to accept feedback in a positive manner and reflected on options related to his situation.

During assessment, the generalist social worker also begins connecting individual or micro problems with macro or broader aspects of the situation. In Hank's case, Angus knew the city had a shortage of affordable housing. Many residents lived with the fear of homelessness, especially if an unexpected financial crisis resulted in—an inability to pay the monthly rent or mortgage installment. Working with Hank on his individual need for permanent housing connected both Hank and Angus to the larger issue of an affordable housing shortage throughout the city.

Another broader aspect of the situation was Hank's age. Approaching 60, he was older than most homeless people at the shelter. Angus realized that Hank was facing medical issues as well as great difficulty in finding a job because of employers' tendency to discount older individuals' ability to contribute. Challenges and discrimination on the basis of age take many forms and were clearly elements in Hank's life.

PLANNING

A third component of the change process is **planning,** or figuring out what to do—purposeful action—given the situation. In many instances, a written **case plan**, a contract designed collaboratively by the social worker and the client, is developed. Case plans comprise short- and long-term goals and corresponding strategies for achieving them. When appropriate, family members, friends, and the neighborhood can be included in the planning process and be part of the plan.

Planning documents often include a table delineating each strategy and assigning the name of the person responsible for that strategy, along with an estimated date for its completion. The signatures of both the client and the social worker formalize their collaboration and establish accountability for the agreed-on actions.

Contained within the plan are strategies and goals that directly impact the client—in other words, micro-level goals. One of Hank's individual goals was to secure a permanent residence close to public transportation. Hank also knew from his shelter experience that the city had a well-documented need for low-income housing in safe neighborhoods. He planned to attend city council meetings, along with others interested in housing issues, to better understand the bureaucracy associated with public housing and network with those involved in the city's housing development, with a focus on housing options for older people.

When Angus and Hank worked on this plan of action, Angus reinforced Hank's decision making and supported his right to select strategies that directed his life toward his personal goals. In the planning process, Hank was seen as the expert and Angus as the facilitator.

TIME TO THINK

Consider a time when you had to make a major decision, such as where to attend college. Did you ask anyone to help you with the decision-making process? If so, who did you ask and why did you select that person? Is it hard for you to ask for help? Why might some people have a problem seeking help?

IMPLEMENTATION

A typical next step in the change process is **implementation,** the actual performance of the activities outlined in the plan for reaching stated goals. The social worker and client monitor the plan during implementation to make sure their strategies are being followed and to make adjustments as deemed necessary. This is yet another meaningful way to connect the social worker and the client. Keep in mind that the actions called for in the plan reflect the client's situation and view of reality in the context of his or her strengths and specified problems.

For example, during this phase, Angus highlighted Hank's success and considered ways to improve any strategies that seemed inadequate. Hank found a place to live, which both Angus and Hank celebrated. Hank also attended a city council meeting. However, when Hank realized that attending one meeting would not likely improve the city's overall housing situation, he became discouraged. Angus suggested that Hank go to another meeting and introduce himself to attendees who might share his concerns. Angus's words of support and emphasis on Hank's success were critical to Hank at this stage. Maintaining motivation was crucial for implementing Hank's plan, as was affirmation of success in progress toward his goals.

EVALUATION

Evaluation, an often identified final step in the change process, is in reality integral throughout. The purpose of evaluation is to monitor implementation of the plan and ensure that designated activities are effectively accomplishing intended goals. Evaluation marks progress, provides insight into the success of initiatives, and informs future plans—including aftercare activities.

Evaluation gives meaning to the collaboration between the social worker and the client . It allows for an examination of what was accomplished and how change occurred for the client and the environment. It is an element that accentuates accountability between the social worker and the client, ensuring that both are working to accomplish the agreed-on goals in accordance with the negotiated timelines. In the end, evaluation reflects the quality of the plan and highlights what has and has not been accomplished.

TIME TO THINK

Given your strengths and interests, which components of the change process would you be most comfortable initiating? What would it take for you to become more comfortable with the other components?

ADVOCATES FOR CHANGE

Advocacy is integral to all social work practice, including generalist practice. It is rooted in an ethical obligation to address and diminish human suffering, discrimination, and oppression. The professional responsibility for advocacy provides social workers with a foundation and mandate to support political, reform, and action agendas to address issues of economic and social justice and rights. The professional commitment to large-scale change addressing social problems encourages advocacy as a means of improving an organization, community, and society through cause advocacy.

CURRENT TRENDS

Social Workers in Politics

SOCIAL workers often work directly with elected officials, but some have been elected to office, such as Senator Barbara Mikulski, a Democrat from Maryland. Senator Mikulski was raised in East Baltimore, where her father owned and operated a small grocery store. At an early age she saw the needs and struggles of working-class families. Senator Mikulski decided to become a social worker and graduated from the University of Maryland, School of Social Work. She went on to work with at-risk children and older adults.

At the community level, Senator Mikulski organized a successful protest that stopped the construction of a 16-lane highway that would have negatively impacted small communities and Baltimore's famous Inner Harbor. Eventually Senator Mikulski ran for the Baltimore City Council and for

Congress. In 1996 Senator Mikulski ran for the U.S. Senate and won, becoming the first Democratic woman to win a Senate seat in her own right. On March 17, 2012, she became the longest-serving woman in the history of the U.S. Congress (see www.Mikulski.senate.gov).

1. How do you think Senator Mikulski's childhood and education prepared her for the role of a U.S. senator?

2. Explain the overlap between the political arena and the social work profession.

3. What difference does it likely make if a woman is elected to the Senate, House of Representatives, or presidency?

At the same time, generalist social workers perform micro-oriented practice with individuals and families; much of their time is spent in case advocacy. By being cognizant of and envisioning a preferred state of affairs for clients— whether a permanent address for a homeless person, health care for a person with diabetes, or child care for a working mother—generalist social workers use their knowledge to develop helping strategies both for addressing immediate needs of clients and for creating larger-scale change.

The helping relationship between Hank and Angus exemplifies how the generalist social worker needs to be attentive to micro, mezzo, and macro levels of change. Social workers advocate not only to assist a particular client with obtaining specific services but also to create opportunities for others facing similar problems and issues.

The underlying process of advocacy does not depend on issue or client system level (e.g., individual, family, group, organization, community, or society) but, rather, is guided by the idea that social work is an empowering profession. In this context, advocacy is the active support of client involvement and impact concerning decisions related to an idea, need, or cause. Both case and cause advocacy are expressed through strategies and methods that influence the opinions and decisions of people and

organizations. Influence can be brought to bear through the following activities (UNICEF, 2010):

- *Defining the problem*: Examining the situation in detail to understand the underlying causes of the problem
- *Recognizing the strengths*: Assessing potential assets and resources within individuals, groups, and organizations
- *Raising awareness*: Educating the individual or the public by presenting evidence-based and solution-oriented messages
- *Developing partnerships*: Generating organizational support and momentum behind the issue being addressed
- *Lobbying and negotiating*: Discussing the issues and desired changes with decision makers and people of power in the situation
- *Generating and consuming research*: Examining the underlying causes of and solutions to a problem
- *Facilitating social mobilization*: Engaging allies and partners at multiple levels
- *Planning events*: Bringing together a variety of people to highlight the issue or concern and work toward solutions

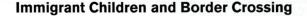

Immigrant Children and Border Crossing

An estimated 52,000 children have been caught crossing the U.S. border from Mexico and countries in Central and South America. The reasons for the increase in unaccompanied minors tend to depend on the child's country of origin, poverty, violence, and political unrest. Most of the children are boys between 15 and 17 years of age.

To address the situation, the Department of Health and Human Services operates about 100 permanent shelters located primarily on the U.S.–Mexico border. Additionally, President Obama has urged Congress to authorize $3.7 billion in emergency aid to support border protection, deportations, and humanitarian efforts in Central America.

1. Given what you know about social work, what advocacy position do you think the profession will take in response to the current crisis?

2. Examine the Homeland Security Act of 2002 and the Trafficking Victims Protection Reauthorization Act of 2008. What is the defined role of Border Patrol regarding children?

3. Advocates contend that Border Control's screening of children traumatizes them. What are your thoughts?

4. Explore the website of Kids in Need of Defense (www.supportkind.org/en/), an advocacy organization for unaccompanied immigrant children, and list at least three strategies the organization supports to address the crisis. Would you add any strategies to the list? If so, what are they?

SUMMARY

Social workers address problems and issues in a variety of settings and client levels—individuals, families, groups, organizations, and communities. Hence, generalist social workers need to possess a breadth of information and a broad array of skills. Their practice is based on a large body of knowledge, competencies, and practice behaviors, which are merely touched on in this chapter.

The change process used by the generalist practitioner is predicated on problem solving as well as a strengths-based perspective that requires social workers to assume a wide range of practice roles. Each component of the change process is based on collaboration and a sound working relationship between client and social worker. Critical thinking, the careful examination of facts and opinions (especially prior to formulating conclusions), is another key element of the change process. Similarly, reflective thought, acquired through interaction with clients and other knowledgeable parties, is a critical component for effective practice.

TOP 10 KEY CONCEPTS

client system
direct practice
ecological perspective
empowerment theory
evidence-based practice

generalist social work practice
person-in-environment perspective
self-determination
strengths perspective
systems theory

DISCUSSION QUESTIONS

1. Review the possible roles of generalist social workers, and discuss the role(s) that best match your interests and skills.
2. Consider the change process and discuss how you would engage a client. What does the term *rapport* mean to you? Provide an example of a person with whom you have established rapport.
3. Which component of the change process—engagement, assessment, planning, implementation, or evaluation—is most significant to the process, in your opinion? Why?
4. A case involving a social worker named Angus and a client named Hank was used as an example in the section on the change process. What were some of the strengths Angus displayed when working with Hank? What additional skills do you think would help Angus facilitate the change process for his clients?

EXERCISES

1. Investigate the baccalaureate social worker licensing procedures for your state. What do the licensure requirements tell you about the roles of generalist social workers?
2. Interview a generalist social worker to better understand how he or she applies generic skills to individual problems. Write a brief description of your findings.
3. Volunteer at a community agency such as a homeless shelter, food pantry, or used clothing store. Analyze your experience as a volunteer in terms of the information you read in this chapter. What information from this chapter was most relevant to your volunteer experience?
4. Research a national or international advocacy group, such as Amnesty International or Green Peace. Describe how the organization links individual concerns to national and global causes.

ONLINE RESOURCES

- Association of Baccalaureate Program Directors (www .bpdonline.org): Lists baccalaureate program guidelines
- Evidence-based practice (www.socialworkpolicy .org): The Social Work Policy Institute describes evidence-based practice and provides information on resources.
- National Welfare Rights Network (www.welfarerights .org.au): Describes a grassroots organization in relation

to advocacy by poor people on behalf of themselves and others
- Phi Alpha National Honor Society (www.phialpha .org): Provides details on membership and activities in this society for baccalaureate social work students
- Women's Empowerment Principles (www .weprinciples.org): Guidelines from the United Nations define the roles of women in the context of redistributing power and privilege.

STUDENT STUDY SITE

Sharpen your skills with SAGE edge at **edge.sagepub.com/cox**

SAGE edge for Students provides a personalized approach to help you accomplish your coursework goals in an easy-to-use learning environment.

Chapter 4: ADVOCACY IN SOCIAL WORK

Learning Objectives

After reading this chapter, you should be able to

1. Differentiate case advocacy and cause advocacy.
2. Summarize the ethical issues involved in advocacy.
3. Explain how advocacy is a signature aspect of social work practice.
4. Identify costs and benefits associated with advocacy.
5. Describe a cycle of advocacy.
6. List and describe four tenets of the dynamic advocacy model.

Nancy Advocates to Professionalize Social Work in Her State

Nancy is a BSW-level social worker residing in a state that recognizes and provides licensure only for MSW-level clinical social workers who have passed a national examination and completed at least 2 years of supervised clinical experience. The license is what allows clinical social workers to enter private practice with individuals and families, obtain reimbursement through insurance companies and other third parties, and tap into public funding sources. In contrast, BSW and nonclinical MSW social workers have been limited to obtaining state certifications in social work. These certifications lack credibility with potential clients and funding sources.

In Nancy's state, human service organizations rarely require proof of certification or of a degree in social work for employment as a social worker in nonclinical settings. So by law, just about anyone with at least a bachelor's degree can choose to be called a social worker. People who have majored in psychology, sociology, criminal justice, history, and English routinely obtain employment in human service and mental health agencies in her state. They often refer to themselves as social workers, care managers, caseworkers, and intervention specialists. As a result, the general public believes that the term social worker can be applied to nearly anyone doing good for others.

Nancy worked hard for her BSW degree and wonders how nonprofessionals can effectively do the work without the training she has received. It seems to her that the potential for doing harm is high.

The important point here is that Nancy is thinking and acting as an advocate. To ensure that clients receive quality services from competent social workers, Nancy works with her National Association of Social Workers state chapter and local social work educators to promote state legislation that will establish licensure and title protection for all social workers. As their recommended changes in state laws are considered, social workers and some client groups have also been talking with administrators of social work agencies about how important it is to require that every "social worker" in a human service position have a social work degree and be appropriately educated.

Source: ©istockphoto.com/PamelaMoore

▲ Social workers can act as advocates for their clients by promoting legislation that has a positive effect on the community.

The element of social work that greatly distinguishes it from other helping professions is advocacy. Social workers are unique in being oriented to and knowledgeable about **advocacy**—engaging in purposeful actions that will help people advance their rights, opportunities, causes, and human dignity—a hallmark of social work. Social workers believe in empowerment through advocacy to help improve people's lives, family dynamics, group processes, organizational functioning, community-based ventures and services, and policy-oriented decisions and guidelines.

Advocacy can involve one case (many times an individual or family) requiring some kind of change, which is known as **case advocacy.** It may also take the form of a larger structural or systematic effort to change policies, common practices, procedures, and laws to advance social justice for a larger segment of society, which is known as **cause advocacy.** Cause advocacy necessitates social workers to be knowledgeable about **social action** and ways to create social change. Social workers engage in many types of cause advocacy, such as legal advocacy, legislative advocacy, self-advocacy, and system advocacy.

The goals of case advocacy are often to meet individuals' **absolute needs,** or the basic goods and services that support human survival in the short term (water, food, shelter, sanitation, medical care). The goals of cause advocacy involve causes that impact a group of people and, like case advocacy, can encompass **relative needs**, which are the goods and services that promote human dignity and well-being over the long term: meaningful employment, equal status before the law, social justice, quality education, and equal opportunity.

THE NEED FOR PROFESSIONAL ADVOCATES

Many people are unable to provide adequately for themselves at one point or another; some people experience a lifetime of challenges from which they struggle to escape. The personal reasons vary, from physical or mental barriers to lack of proper socialization and education to lower social status through birth, custom, or misfortune. In addition, societal factors such as a lack of public resources and service, unsupportive political will, and entrenched systems of privilege and oppression impact and constrain the ability of people to move forward. Many people often struggle with the basics—food, water, shelter, health care—and human dignity.

Societies across the world have developed systems to create opportunities for people to rise above unfortunate

CURRENT TRENDS

Social Change Through Boycotts

ONE way those without much individual power can effect change is to band together to refuse to buy a product, use a service, listen to a radio station, or watch a television program—in other words, to conduct a boycott. During the 1950s, civil rights leaders such as the Rev. T. J. Jemison and Dr. Martin Luther King organized bus boycotts and alternative car pools in the cause of abolishing rules forcing African American riders to the backs of buses. In 1977, a boycott began in the United States, and eventually expanded into Europe, protesting Nestlé's promotion of breast milk substitutes in less economically developed countries. A boycott of U.S. firms investing in South Africa, which included protests on American college campuses, contributed to the end of official apartheid in South

Africa in the 1990s. These are just a few of the historic examples of effective boycotts.

In today's electronic world, groups such as Ethical Consumer enlist people in social change. Ethical Consumer publishes lists of companies that it believes should be boycotted on the basis of political oppression, animal abuse, tax avoidance, environmental degradation, supply chain issues, abuse of human rights, and exploitation of workers. When organized and conducted successfully, boycotts such as these bring publicity to issues and serve as powerful forums for advocating change.

When was the last time you heard of boycotting a business or enterprise as a means of exerting power to create change? What kinds of boycotts have you participated in?

circumstances. In Chapter 2, you read about the historical response to need, the development of social work as a profession, and the emergence of a unique system of social services in the United States. Social programs and services have helped millions of people live more fulfilling, healthier, and productive lives.

Often, however, social services are unknown or unavailable to those in need. It is difficult for people without resources to learn about sources of help and ways to challenge barriers suppressing human growth and development. Social workers have long worked to connect individuals, families, and communities with the available services in an effort to provide people with an opportunity to participate fully in society. In the process, they have become advocates, championing individuals, groups, and communities in their search for needed services. But social workers soon realized that when services were unavailable to meet serious needs within communities, they would also need to be advocates for policy and program changes with larger systems—organizations, communities, and society.

Both case and cause advocacy require knowledge, determination, and effort, many times with people consumed with just trying to survive. Social workers, on the other hand, have committed themselves to helping the needy as their life work. They have acquired education and training to develop knowledge and skills to use client strengths to challenge barriers. Social workers think in terms of a responsibility both to improve conditions for clients and to advance opportunities for other people facing similar struggles and problems.

POWER AND SOCIAL INEQUALITY

Implicit in this discussion of why professional advocates—that is, social workers—are needed is the idea of **social inequality.** Some people have more—access to society's benefits and resources, status, wealth, power—and some have less. Some inequality is part of the human condition. However, those at the top may use their advantages to organize society to suit their needs. Often they do so to the clear detriment of those below them on the social scale. Social workers are educated to understand these inequities and their effect on clients and social systems. They are also educated to combat social inequality at all levels and in various areas of practice, as you will learn in later chapters.

During the past several decades, social workers have embraced the concept of empowerment as a key feature of practice. In the context of advocacy, empowerment refers to clients' ability to exert influence over decision making and the process of determining the best outcomes for themselves and making life-changing decisions, both in service interventions and in the development of policies, programs, and legislation. Social workers are key players and leaders, but their role is to facilitate, work with, and support clients in their efforts to advance their own well-being and promote change.

Power is a factor in human services in another way. When social workers defend or represent others to secure social justice, they are challenging the people and special interest groups in power to exert their authority to assist and benefit those who are less powerful. When this type of advocacy is successful, the will and energy of clients and social workers, as well as the other advocates for change, yield desirable, measurable outcomes that produce additional opportunities, rights, and freedoms for clients.

Consider how Nancy, the social worker in our opening vignette, decides to approach those in power over licensing requirements for social workers. She realizes that her campaign may be an affront to certain groups. The likely opponents are individuals working in the field who do not have social work degrees, and budget-minded legislators and administrators. Antilicensure elements will question whether licensed social workers can do a better job than those who are already doing it without licensure. They will ask for evidence but may still dispute findings indicating that the quality of services is enhanced through the employment of professionally educated and degreed social workers.

So Nancy devises a strategy for challenging the status quo that involves empowering clients and enlisting the support of service groups. She has heard many disturbing stories of clients' receiving inappropriate or inferior services from non-professionals, and she believes those stories will sway decision makers. In addition, Nancy believes that clients' voices will resonate because each client brings unique passions and strengths for influencing change. Some clients are poised to step forward in the licensure debate and want to educate others to the ill effects of nonprofessional intervention. They, and the groups they form, will play a significant role in reaching out to administrators, leaders, and legislators in the state.

THE ETHICS OF ADVOCACY

Underlying their involvement in advocacy (and all forms of social work intervention) is the professional call for social workers to engage in ethical behavior in practice. The *Code of*

Source: ©istockphoto.com/Galvia

▲ Empowering clients to become involved in advocacy can help to effect change.

Ethics of the National Association of Social Workers (NASW) states that each social worker has an obligation to "advocate for living conditions conducive to the fulfillment of basic human needs" (NASW, 2008, Sec. 6.01). Social workers are also instructed in the *Code of Ethics* to approach, initiate, assist, educate, and organize clients for participation in advocacy. The responsibility for advocacy is also spelled out in the International Federation of Social Workers' (2004) statement of principles for ethical social work practice.

Advocacy is thus often viewed by social workers as a professional mandate and mark of competency. Nancy's call to license social workers in her state is a function of her ethical obligation to promote the well-being of her clients via competent practice. However, social workers exert care in advocacy not to impose their own values and interests. Social workers hold positions of power in helping relationships, which can influence client perceptions and actions. Ethical advocacy, whether efforts to advance competent practice or any number of issues or causes (e.g., safe and affordable housing, child welfare, affordable health care), is foremost centered on client needs and desires.

Client Self-Determination

Advocacy in social work practice is predicated on the principle of **client self-determination,** which dictates that consumers of services make decisions and choices based on their will and value orientations. Because there is a power differential between social workers and clients, it is important for advocacy to occur in a fashion that encourages and does not distract from or violate the client's right to self-determination.

With advocacy, the social worker is by definition taking up the cause of others. To promote client self-determination, social workers are attentive to setting aside their personal values and attempt to examine an issue or cause from the perspective(s) and voice(s) of the client. Placing oneself in the position of the client is difficult, as it necessitates learning from the client and the ability to successfully work through unequal power dynamics in the social worker and client relationship.

Self-Interest and Advocacy

It is important for social workers to know the differences between self-interest (defined as a focus on one's own benefit), case advocacy, and cause advocacy. Social workers should enter the profession to help other people, especially members of vulnerable population groups (e.g., people who experience prejudice based on gender, sexual orientation, economic status, race, or ethnicity), and not themselves. Social workers are client centered.

To understand the difference between self-interest, case advocacy, and cause advocacy, think about what college students might do when they are unhappy about a grade they received on a group assignment. One student might argue that the instructor should have graded his or her contribution higher because the other members of the group did not do as much work to complete an assignment. Another student might tell the instructor that the group deserves a higher grade. A third student might point out some weaknesses in the assignment or the grading rubric and that all students in the course should be given a higher grade. Which of these challenges constitute advocacy? Are any of them an example of case advocacy or cause advocacy? Which are based primarily on self-interest and personal gain?

As you may already sense, the concept of advocacy in social work is multidimensional and differs from the idea of advocating for one's own personal and private needs and rights. Case advocacy is important for helping specific individuals, families, groups, organizations, and communities address needs and concerns. Cause advocacy focuses on social change and enabling larger groups of people to improve their social and economic situation.

TIME TO THINK

What motivates you to consider social work as a profession? Have you experienced a loss, difficult living circumstances, a traumatic event, or a violation of personal rights? If so, are you motivated to consider social work out of self-interest or out of a concern that others benefit from your experience?

Social workers strive for objectivity in assisting clients. Could you be objective if your advocacy involved a significant event or factor in your life?

Individual Benefit Versus Community Benefit

In the United States, people often conceptualize needs in individualistic ways—what can be done for me or this person—as opposed to contextualizing them in group or community welfare and large-scale change. Although individual-level advocacy can produce needed benefits for the person, it frequently does not prompt community or institutional reform. One way to think about the difference between advocacy and self-gain is to determine whether the individual or a group of people is the primary beneficiary of the change process. The **individual reigns supreme perspective** equates individual gain and interest with the common good and is useful for seeing how case advocacy has limitations (McNutt, 1997). For example, advocating with a client to receive food assistance from an organization can be critical for addressing a person's immediate needs but may have little impact for subsequent people experiencing similar circumstances.

It is important to question whether promoting solely one's own rights in a single case constitutes effective advocacy and use of time. Many social workers argue that advocacy efforts should move beyond individualism and focus on efforts to promote social justice or improve social conditions or circumstances affecting other individuals or a group, community, or society. The attitude of placing self-interest in a context of promoting policies and practices for the common good aligns with the **community reigns supreme perspective** (McNutt, 1997). For example, taking the broader view of advocating with clients to promote just policies for receiving food assistance from organizations in a community can yield immediate assistance to a person in need and holds promise for benefiting other people as well.

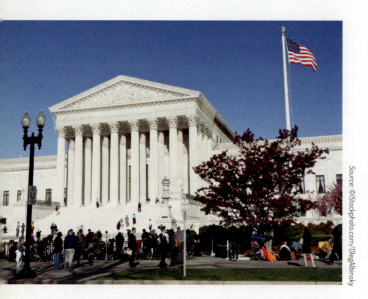

Source: ©iStockphoto.com/OlegAlbinsky

▲ Rallies and protests are one way clients can be empowered to participate in their community.

Although social workers are encouraged to focus on others, the motivation and ability to stand up for one's own rights can be a desirable personal attribute for social workers. How can people who are unable to muster the energy and passion to help themselves effectively promote fairness and social or economic justice for others? There is something to be said for people being willing to participate actively in a case or a cause rather than just look on passively. If you are seriously considering entry into the social profession, contemplate your abilities and potential to "stand up" and actively work with others to address clients' needs and address important issues and causes.

Pathways to Community Benefit

To promote social change, social workers advocate for pathways that will give groups of people access to resources, rights, and opportunities, and allow them to improve their life circumstances. The role of the social worker, therefore, involves "building avenues for clients to access power resources within themselves, their families, and their contexts . . . creating opportunities for significant participation in community and thereby freeing clients to experience themselves differently and act in new ways" (O'Melia, 2002, p. 3).

Using the example of requesting a grade change, consider the possibility that a number of students were adversely affected as a result of an unfair grading practice. The correction of a single grade would not facilitate grade changes for others also affected by that unfair or unjust grading practice. Possibly, if the course had large enrollments, the grading of essays was relegated to teaching assistants (TAs). If so, did the TAs receive proper training and clear instructions and grading rubrics to facilitate reliable and valid grading practices? One might question if scoring of essay answers varied appreciably between TAs. Or was there any political pressure from the professor, department, or university administration to keep grades low to combat grade inflation? Were environmental factors or conditions, such as assigning the group work during local fires and power outages, involved?

Identifying and asking important questions opens up pathways for possible resolution of the grading problem. For example, when prompted, the professor might review the grading practices of the TAs for consistency and fairness, and consider any necessary grade changes. The professor could also examine best practices of other professors and incorporate their perspectives concerning grading into a training program for TAs, to minimize bias and error. Or the professor might have been unaware of the impact of local fires on the group assignment. In the process of examining grading policies, the professor might have identified discriminatory grading differences from the TAs based on gender, race, or age of the students. Once again, advocacy involves a broad and dynamic assessment and understanding of political, economic, social, and environmental factors that can influence decision making affecting a number of people.

HUMAN ASPECTS OF HELPING

Social workers often work with clients and constituents who are under stress and feel desperate and powerless. When considering advocacy as a means of creating change, it is essential to keep the human aspect of helping in mind. People are susceptible to pain and permanent damage and can perish when critical needs go unmet. All people should be treated as human beings with dignity, not as problems, objects, or cases (Reynolds, 1951).

The human nature of advocacy involves both emotional and rational aspects. Passion to confront issues can be a powerful asset in promoting change, but it can also blur many of the realities associated with a situation or issue. Hence, objectivity is an important aspect of advocacy and a quality that social workers can contribute to the process. Social workers need to be able to put clients' values and interests first while providing professional insight concerning the realities, good and bad, associated with proposed change.

TIME TO THINK

As a social worker, you would want to see, appreciate, and respect the unique qualities of each person and group you encounter. You might think of social interaction as one big museum for discovering the commonalities and differences among people. In the context of advocacy, are you or could you be capable of viewing and appreciating the strengths and vulnerabilities of a variety of people—including those who think and behave quite differently than you do?

SOCIAL WORKERS AND SOCIAL CHANGE

Social work pioneers became aware of the need for cause advocacy when they recognized that addressing clients' immediate needs from a charitable perspective held little promise for creating substantial and sustainable change in people's lives. Temporary and survival-oriented efforts were analogous to using adhesive bandages for large, contagious sores. Although it was important to address individuals' needs for shelter, food, water, and sanitation, and to alleviate other forms of human suffering, it became apparent that collective and political action was also necessary. Confronting mechanisms of social control (such as policies, practices, and laws) and people in positions of power was necessary to promote human well-being and social justice.

Dorothy Height, Florence Kelley, and Whitney Young are important historical civil rights leaders who dedicated their lives to social reform and the expansion of social welfare and policies in the United States. For example, Dorothy Height was an African American woman admitted to Barnard College in 1929 but denied entrance to the school as a result of a racial quota—a practice Barnard College later discontinued and officially denounced. She earned her undergraduate degree (1932) and master's degree in educational psychology (1933) from New York University, later completing postgraduate education at Columbia University and the New York School of Social Work (now known as the Columbia University School of Social Work). Dorothy began her career as a caseworker with the New York City Welfare

Department and was a prominent leader during the civil rights movement of the 1960s. In addition to serving in a considerable number of national leadership positions, Dorothy served for four decades (1957–1997) as the president of the National Council of Negro Women. She is remembered nationally for promoting understanding of and rights for African American women, and she was honored with the Presidential Medal of Freedom in 1994 and Congressional Gold Medal in 2004.

CAUSE AND FUNCTION

The idea that cause advocacy is a key component of social work got a significant boost from a 1937 book, *Social Work as Cause and Function*, by social work educator Porter R. Lee. This was a question he addressed in the book:

> Are social workers merely part of a function, helping people adapt to the environment into which they are thrust, or do social workers intend to act in promotion of a cause, altering the social context to allow for higher-level changes in social problems? (Stotzer & Alvarez, 2009, p. 324)

Lee viewed social workers as professionals with responsibilities involving community practice, social action, and leadership. His vision of social work expertise went beyond

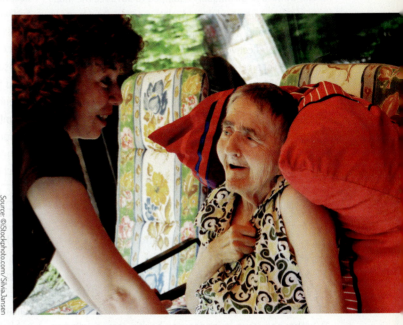

Source: ©iStockphoto.com/Silvia Jansen

▲ It is important to treat all clients with respect and dignity to best serve their needs.

Source: © Adrian Hood/CreativeCommons

▲ Dorothy Height was a prominent advocate for the rights of African Americans.

helping skills and focused specifically on the ability to create social change and lead social movements. He considered social workers to be uniquely equipped to advance the interests of those with absolute and relative needs. As experts in social action and as professionals, they could make social action more effective than could those taking the "emotional role" of a person not trained in social work (Stotzer & Alvarez, 2009, p. 325).

Lee's writings shaped the social work profession in a number of ways:

- Advancing the value of professional education and training in social work
- Moving the identity of social workers away from simple helper toward agent for systemic change
- Emphasizing objectivity (as opposed to emotion) in providing services and promoting social change

Lee's thoughts from the 1930s concerning the role of social workers in social action carry weight today. Whether the issue is inadequate health care; a faltering economy; oppression of women; challenges for older adults; oppression of racial/ethnic groups and people from the lesbian, gay, bisexual, and transgender community; or the plight of veterans, social workers are challenged to be resolute in their commitment to partner with vulnerable and disenfranchised groups.

RESPONSES TO HARD TIMES

A notable turning point for social welfare and cause advocacy in U.S. history occurred during the Great Depression of the 1930s, when social and economic conditions challenged prevailing assumptions about public assistance and the belief in individual responsibility. For the first time in their lives, many Americans were confronted with the reality that social and economic forces beyond one's control can have harsh consequences for individuals and families. Threats to average Americans' absolute needs produced a pervasive sense of desperation and helplessness. Many Americans began to see the wisdom of collective action to inform leaders about their common plight and to argue for social and economic relief programs.

Social and economic turmoil often serve as the stimulus for change in communities or societies. Change was also in the air from the mid-1960s to the late 1970s. Many people protested the nation's involvement in the Vietnam War, riots occurred in urban ghettos, civil rights protests abounded, and women sought relief from oppressive policies, practices, and laws.

Many social workers supported President Lyndon B. Johnson's 1964 declaration of a War on Poverty and advocated for the creation of programs and services to improve Americans' general welfare. "These initiatives included Volunteers in Service to American (VISTA), a domestic version of the Peace Corps; the Job Corps, an employment training program for school dropouts; and Head Start, a preschool educational program" (Long, Tice, & Morrison, 2006, p. 12).

During the politically conservative 1980s, social workers exposed the consequences of President Ronald Reagan's attack on social welfare programs for the poor and the windfall benefits for the rich of Reaganomics' tax reforms (Piven & Cloward, 1982). Social workers also brought new issues—problems of drug abuse, homelessness, and sexually transmitted diseases, among others—to the attention of the public and decision makers.

Source: © Leffler, Warren K./Library of Congress/CreativeCommons.

▲ Many Americans participated in the Civil Rights March on Washington in 1963.

educationally prepared for political participation and civic engagement (Rome, 2010, pp. 116–117).

CAUSE ADVOCACY TODAY

As a result of the election of President Barack Obama in 2008, on a platform of social change, many social workers experienced a renewed inspiration for advocacy. Social workers have actively partnered with client groups to advocate for federal funding to support those suffering from a failing economy and to research and advance the rights of a variety of vulnerable populations. These are some of the issues for which social workers have actively advocated:

- Health care reform (including national health insurance and parity laws to cover mental health services)
- Lesbian, gay, bisexual, and transgender rights
- Services for veterans returning from the wars in Iraq and Afghanistan
- Fair and just treatment of all immigrants in the United States, including those who are undocumented
- Affordable housing
- Independence and dignity for older adults
- Fair treatment of those infected with HIV/AIDS
- Quality delivery of social services based on practice-informed research and research-informed practice
- Substance abuse and mental health programs
- Environmental and climate change

The majority of social workers see cause advocacy as part of their professional identity. For example, in one survey of social workers, "more than half" agreed that political action is relevant to their jobs and that they are obliged to "stay informed, educate others, and advocate for constructive policies" (Rome, 2010, p. 115). Additionally, 78% reported being

TIME TO THINK

Have you participated in an advocacy event or movement? How comfortable were you, on a social–emotional level, with that involvement?

Social workers network and align themselves with diverse types of people to advocate for social change. Would you be able and willing to advocate for rights and opportunities for people of diverse gender, social class, race or ethnicity, age, physical or mental ability, or sexual orientation? If not, why? Do you think you might change your attitude to become a social worker?

THE COST OF ADVOCACY

Although advocacy is a core function in social work practice, it should not be undertaken without an understanding of the **cost of advocacy**—all the real, intangible, and unintended ways that undertaking advocacy can deplete resources and potentially work against the cause. For instance, bad publicity, adverse effects, and false hope can be just as detrimental as the expenditure of funds and other resources. Often the costs of advocacy are considerable (McNutt, 2011). However, comprehensive cost–benefit analyses of advocacy efforts take into account the costs, the prospects of attaining the goal, and the extent of the good to be derived from advocacy.

Assessment of the costs associated with any advocacy initiative, whether case or cause oriented, is likely to be multidimensional and can be time-consuming. Each agency or organization involved may incur expenses. In addition, the cost of advocacy includes determining the value of each person's time to engage in research, analyze and draft policies, attend meetings, develop media strategies, lobby, organize communities, and campaign. Communication itself—with constituent groups, leaders, politicians, and decision makers—requires a great deal of time, as well as expertise in various modes of communication, from the telephone and print media to text messages, websites, e-mails, blogs, wikis, and social networking sites.

Potential financial cost is not always an argument for abandoning or retreating from advocacy. A long-standing

In-Home Services for Older Adults

Joan is a social worker employed by her county's Council on Aging in a special extended stay program (ESP). Her primary responsibilities are to identify services and programs to allow seniors to reside in their homes. Several years ago, county officials and local social service leaders listened to the voices of older adults and decided to find ways for them to maintain their independence. A new county property tax levy allows Joan and her colleagues to fund in-home services for low-income clients, services such as "life lines" (medical alert systems), personal care, housekeeping, medical transportation, adult day care, home-delivered meals, and assistance with bill paying. Through an effective educational campaign, taxpayers have learned that it is more economical to provide services for low-income older adults in their homes than to rely on residential care (assisted living, nursing homes) and emergency hospital services.

Source: ©iStockphoto.com/Silvia Jansen

Joan advocates for seniors to address their needs and rights for care. She visits senior centers and forums to promote and explain the importance and virtues of the ESP. She works with provider agencies to ensure quality of care. At election time, Joan has used her personal time to hang posters in the community and at polling sites to promote funding for the ESP.

The vast majority of Joan's professional career has been dedicated to working with older adults. Providing support to older adults for independent living is her passion. Ask yourself, do you have a passion for a population group or problem area? Would you be willing to devote time, even if it involved your personal time, to political advocacy and action to promote your passion?

adage in business is, "You need to spend money to make money." For advocacy, this adage can be altered to, "You need to commit resources to effectively create change." The key in social work is to be mindful, intentional, and informed about the types of costs associated with planned changed.

Of course, on the other side of the ledger, advocacy has benefits. To evaluate the benefits of advocacy, those involved need to clearly define the criteria for success and ongoing means for evaluating whether advocacy outcomes are being reached. Once again, professional social workers can lend their expertise to the evaluation of the effectiveness of interventions and programs.

For example, Nancy has begun to consider benchmarks for success in reforming social work licensure requirements in her state. From the outset, she and the client groups and

advocacy partners with whom she is working will need to identify the goals and benefits, consider the costs associated with licensure reform, and develop mechanisms to monitor their progress.

A MODEL FOR DYNAMIC ADVOCACY

Chapter 3 introduces a model for generalist social work practice, along with the theoretical foundations for that practice. This chapter introduces a similar model for advocacy, the **advocacy practice and policy model (APPM)**. Exhibit 4.1 on page 72 depicts the theoretical foundations of the APPM:

- *Systems theory:* Although much of social work involves practice with individuals and families,

SOCIAL WORK IN ACTION

Competing Values and Goals in Advocacy

THOMAS is a social worker with an adoption agency. Today's court appearance is to advocate for the adoption of Jimmy, a 2-year-old boy, by Jill, a 30-year-old lesbian foster care mother. Jill has raised and cared for Jimmy for more than a year and lives in a discrete, committed relationship with her female partner.

Jimmy's birth mother is a crack addict, and her whereabouts have not been known for well over a year. In the past, this adoption judge has shown reluctance to approve adoptions without a biological parent's written consent and for gay or lesbian parents. Thomas's assessment and adoption study clearly indicate that Jill will be an excellent mother and that it is in the best interest of Jimmy (the client) for his adoption by Jill to be approved.

Although Thomas believes in the rights and merits of gays and lesbians' adopting children, in this example of case advocacy, his focus is on Jimmy's best interests, not on promoting or advocating for gay and lesbian adoption. Thomas is prepared to present the judge with all relevant information that will support Jill as an adoptive parent and, if necessary, debunk myths associated with gay and lesbian adoption. However, for Jimmy's interest and welfare, Thomas does not see this court appearance as an opportunity for larger-scale advocacy to advance (beyond Jimmy's adoption decision) the judge's views about gay and lesbian adoption. Indeed, Thomas has determined that dwelling on the sexual orientation of the adoptive mother in this instance would be inappropriate and potentially jeopardize Jimmy's adoption.

advocacy takes place with systems of all sizes—including groups, organizations, communities, and societies—as both clients and targets for change. A community could be the client for case advocacy, where a social worker advocates for a particular community seeking funding for a new social work agency. An example of cause advocacy is when a social worker partners with organizations to change a county or state policy or law restricting their ability to provide needed services (e.g., family planning and contraception education).

- *Empowerment theory:* Both case and cause advocacy involve social workers' building relationships with clients of various system sizes to participate in and impact decision-making processes. Empowerment-based case advocacy promotes the voice, perception, and ability of clients to influence a particular issue of importance to the client. Similarly, empowerment-based cause advocacy emphasizes the perspectives and abilities of clients to advance issues affecting them as well as others.

- *Strengths perspective:* In advocacy, it is important that social workers give appropriate attention to both the problems confronting client issues and the various strengths available to create needed change. Whether case or cause advocacy, clients of all sizes (e.g., individuals, families, groups, organizations, communities, and societies) bring to the advocacy process a variety of strengths, including resources, abilities, important relationships, knowledge, skills, insight, perspective, energy, and passion. For example, you may think that economically poor clients have limited strengths to advocate for change; yet their voices, knowledge, and perspectives are unique, and the very emotion and passion they bring to any situation can be especially convincing, powerful, and impactful in advocacy.

- *Ecological perspective:* When advocating for change, assessment of the total environment, not just people and social systems, is vital. Physical and natural resources such as technology, buildings, transportation, water, soil, air, plants, and animals

EXHIBIT 4.1   Theoretical Framework for the Advocacy Practice and Policy Model

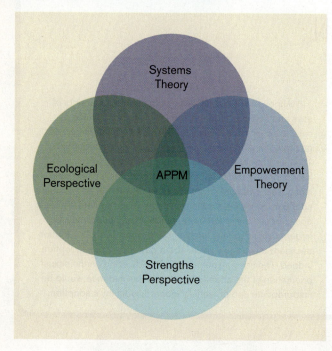

can be assets as well as challenges for case and cause advocacy. For example, consider the value of phone and Internet access for both case and cause advocacy. The poor are especially challenged in advocating for themselves and others without technological means (e.g., public access to the Internet and e-mail and to low-cost public transportation) to network and communicate with others to create change.

Several other features of generalist social work education and practice also are key to the APPM. The model assumes that advocacy activities, whether for client access to services or promotion of policies and programs, are conducted in an ethical manner. The APPM supports ethical behavior in assessing problems and strengths, planning strategies for change, and addressing dilemmas.

Social workers are also assumed to be critical thinkers with the ability to communicate effectively through oral and written means. In other words, social workers engaged in advocacy must be able to integrate multiple sources of information into a clear and coherent action plan. Furthermore, that action plan must reflect the interest of clients and connect individual needs to systematic change.

Recognizing the effect of diversity and culture in shaping life conditions is a particularly critical element in the APPM. Specifically, social workers engaged in advocacy must recognize their own values and biases and not let them influence their work. The APPM advances human rights by underscoring the need for social workers to understand various forms of oppression and discrimination, including their own prejudices.

As in generalist practice, the APPM uses concepts and insights from the person-in-environment approach to design research methodologies and program evaluations. The findings from the research inform practice and policy initiatives. This research also ensures that clients and the broader society will be exposed to scientifically tested intervention strategies throughout the change process.

THE CYCLE OF ADVOCACY

The change process for generalist practice, introduced in Chapter 3, can readily be adapted to guide social work advocacy and link practice goals and outcomes. Exhibit 4.2 illustrates the five steps in the intervention process in terms of the APPM. As in generalist practice, intervention is a dynamic process. The exhibit highlights the importance of considering both problems and strengths, and the encompassing nature of people and systems involved in advocacy—individuals and families (the micro level), groups and organizations (the mezzo level), and communities and societies (the macro level).

The feedback loop (in Exhibit 4.2, the dotted line that links evaluation and assessment) is very important in advocacy as in generalist practice. The greater the number of people collaborating in the change process, the more likely that adjustment and compromise will be necessary (Brydon, 2010).

In many ways, the cycle of advocacy describes a framework for guiding behaviors conducted by clients or collaborators in conjunction with a social worker. The success of the planned action is judged by the answers to such questions as, "Did the strategies work?" "Have life conditions improved?" and "Did systematic changes occur?"

One social work researcher and educator (Brydon, 2010, p. 129) suggests that practitioners follow these guidelines for increasing the effectiveness of the advocacy cycle:

- Begin collaboration. Think about the *big picture* and what might be different.
- Use your management and program planning skills to implement change. Ensure that there are review and evaluation criteria.

EXHIBIT 4.2   The Intervention Process and the Advocacy Practice and Policy Model

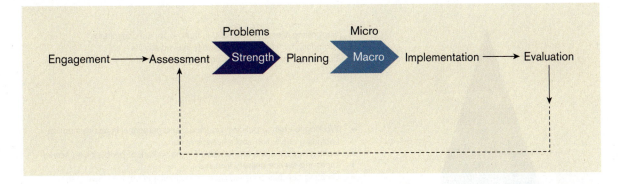

- Reflect on theory and practice. Apply critical and reflective approaches to review your practice experience.
- Collect and analyze evidence. Use your micro skills and research skills to gather evidence.
- Begin advocacy. Use your engagement skills to begin to persuade decision makers.

Nancy, in her advocacy regarding the licensure of social workers, followed most of Brydon's suggestions. She began by collecting relevant information and collaborating with key stakeholders. Both activities are labor-intensive. She became especially aware that building relationships with key stakeholders can be a challenge. In Nancy's state, politicians and decision makers are aware of their power and often guarded about forming new relationships or being courted by people aligned with special interest groups. Indeed, many legislators employ a chief of staff who serves as an official gatekeeper and controls contact with them. Nancy was aware of these challenges, however, and spent extra time figuring out how to link her cause to the legislators' interests.

TIME TO THINK

Although many social workers enter the profession to help others, producing and consuming research are integral functions in contemporary social work practice and advocacy efforts. Do you possess an interest and aptitude for research and statistics, or the willingness to produce and adopt research in practice?

THE ADVOCACY MODEL IN ACTION

Ask your family members, friends, and acquaintances about their perceptions of social workers and social work activities. They are likely to affirm that social workers are problem solvers, helpers for people trying to address daily needs, therapists, caseworkers, group workers, community organizers, and advocates for change to better people's lives and promote and advance human rights. Even relatively uninformed members of the general public will acknowledge that social workers are professionals willing to stand up and advocate with and for oppressed and disadvantaged groups.

It is far less clear to most people, including many helping professionals, how advocacy is integrated into social work practice. In this book, advocacy is broadly defined as actions taken to defend or represent others to advance a cause that will promote social justice (Hoefer, 2012, p. 3). More specifically, social workers promote fairness, secure needed resources, and empower people (especially members of disadvantaged groups) to take an active role in decision making. Some of the specific advocacy activities that social workers pursue in everyday practice, as well as efforts to advance policy development, are captured in Exhibit 4.3.

Although this list of advocacy activities looks straightforward, it is important to realize that conflicting goals and values often complicate advocacy. Social workers live and work in their own social worlds, which are frequently distinct from the social and economic realities of their clients. To support client self-determination, social workers must often ignore their own interpretations of the environment and commit to advocating for change based on the hopes, ambitions, desires, and interests of their clients. The social worker (or the agency) and the client may have "competing

EXHIBIT 4.3   Advocacy Activities in Social Work

- Supporting clients in court and in front of appeal committees
- Promoting human rights and dignity in everyday life
- Educating clients to advocate on their own behalf

Micro

- Working to change policies, practices, and personnel in an organization (including one's own social service agency)
- Making organizations accountable for the welfare of people being served
- Improving service delivery systems
- Creating new functions within organizations and communities so they can better address human needs

Mezzo

- Educating people about important social issues
- Conducting research to document the needs and the plight of disadvantaged population groups
- Campaigning for a new law or for politicians who support socially beneficial legislative initiatives
- Advancing projects and programs in communities and nationally
- Combating discrimination and oppression
- Educating communities to advocate on their own behalf

Macro

and sometimes contradictory values" (Boylan & Dalrymple, 2011, p. 20). When the values of clients conflict with professional values and ethics, social workers typically seek guidance from supervisors, professional ethics panels, and legal staff.

Keep in mind that advocacy typically occurs *with* clients and not simply *for* them. Although there are exceptions to this premise (e.g., mentally challenged clients and very young children), social workers make a special effort to ensure that client self-determination and the will of the client remain at the forefront of all forms of intervention, including advocacy. A social worker whose activities to advance the interests and rights of a client or population group have become misaligned with the desire and will of clients often ends up in a lonely place.

TENETS OF ADVOCACY PRACTICE AND POLICY MODEL

One of the signature themes of this book is the special place advocacy holds within social work practice. In each of the chapters that follow, you will find a section that examines

a particular practice population, need, or setting in terms of four basic philosophical principles, or tenets, that many social workers embrace. The diagram in Exhibit 4.4 depicts the **dynamic advocacy model,** a way of conceptualizing advocacy, and its four interlocking tenets—economic and social justice, a supportive environment, human needs and rights, and political access—to ensure ethical and effective practice. We say that these tenets are dynamic because they tend to shift constantly; we say that they are interlocking because it is hard to draw clear boundaries between, for instance, political access and economic and social justice.

We have identified tenets of advocacy that social workers often routinely use as a score sheet for their endeavors on behalf of a case or a cause. For instance, "Does my work promote economic and social justice? Does it promote a supportive environment, human rights and basic needs, political access?" There are other tenets that can motivate and guide advocacy, but this model helps aspiring social workers understand some of the most important elements associated with advocacy and policy practice.

It is important to point out that the four tenets identified in our dynamic advocacy model are not purely distinctive or independent. Instead, in social work practice with real people and situations, these tenets have considerable overlap with and influence on one another. For example, one's political perspective and involvement influence the definition of and thinking about economic and social justice. And environmental factors and context impact the conceptualization of economic and social justice in a specific time and place. The intent of the dynamic advocacy model presented throughout this book is to prompt critical and multidimensional thought and discussion about advocacy in social work practice.

ECONOMIC AND SOCIAL JUSTICE

Social justice is a core value of social work, as expressed in the *Code of Ethics* of the NASW (2008):

> These activities seek to promote sensitivity to and knowledge about oppression and cultural and ethnic diversity. Social workers strive to ensure access to needed information, services, and resources; equality of opportunity; and meaningful participation in decision making for all people. ("Ethical Principles")

In the APPM, the tenet of **economic and social justice** is closely related to the NASW definition of social justice. It involves "promoting and establishing equal liberties, rights, duties, and opportunities in the social institutions (economy, polity, family religion, education, etc.) of a society for all [people]" (Long et al., 2006, p. 208). Justice includes **relational justice,** which is people's ability to exert influence over decision-making processes and in relationships with dominant groups. Economic justice is captured in the concept of **distributive justice,** which is the ability to allocate or spread resources, income, and wealth in a manner that ensures people's basic material needs are met.

When social workers advocate for social change with clients, these activities should be justice centered. However, what does "justice centered" really mean for advocacy practice? Because there are a multitude of issues associated with economic and social justice, this is often a challenging question for practitioners. We can say that **just practice** involves equality, tolerance, and the promotion of human rights, as well as an active attempt to overcome social and economic inequalities (Finn & Jacobson, 2008).

Social work scholars have proposed a number of schemes for determining the degree to which advocacy is justice

EXHIBIT 4.4   Dynamic, Interlocking Tenets of Advocacy Practice and Policy Model

oriented. One of them (Hoefer, 2012, p. 80) emphasizes these four key aspects of social justice: respect for basic human rights, promotion of social responsibility, commitment to individual freedom, and support for self-determination. Scoring systems have also been devised for monitoring advocacy practice based on the type of justice being pursued (economic justice, distributive justice, relational justice, and so on), the strategy employed, or the underlying principles (Reisch, 2002, p. 350). Whichever scoring system is used, the point is that professional social workers need a way to determine whether advocacy has lived up to the tenets they espouse. The social and economic checklist might include the following:

- Am I sensitive to my client's right to think and act independently?
- Am I supporting equality of opportunity for my client?
- Am I encouraging my client's meaningful participation in decision making?
- Am I helping my client unearth opportunities for economic and social justice?
- Am I helping my client secure needed resources?

CURRENT TRENDS

Natural Disasters

SEVERE natural and weather-related circumstances—floods, tornados, earthquakes, wildfires, hurricanes, typhoons, blizzards—are often catastrophic environmental phenomena. People who are affected need immediate emergency services, water, food, shelter, clothing, medical assistance, and mental health services. Organizations such as the American Red Cross and World Food Program provide aid to communities devastated by these crises. Many social workers receive advanced training for responding to crises and implementing crisis intervention services.

Identify a recent natural or weather-related catastrophe that concerned you, and identify the organizations, professionals, and other people who responded to the needs of the people affected by this natural disaster. As an example, with Hurricane Sandy—a powerful storm that hit the northeast coast and New Jersey and New York shorelines in 2012—social workers partnered with the Red Cross and numerous crisis relief agencies to address the basic needs of people affected and to provide counseling. Social workers also advocated for the immediate availability and implementation of state and federal relief services and funds.

Note, advocating for resources to assist victims of natural and weather-related trauma is a year-round activity. Is this an area of interest for you in social work practice?

- Am I ensuring that all parties' rights are being respected?
- Am I advancing thought about the need for social responsibility?

Let's return to Nancy's advocacy for improving the licensure law in her state. Her motivation is firmly rooted in the tenet of economic and social justice and her desire to promote just practice. Many of her clients have received inferior services and experienced limited opportunities. She is dedicated to people's receiving effective, high-quality services from professional social workers who have earned appropriate degrees and credentials. Nancy also believes the meaningful participation of clients in decision making about the implementation of programs and services can best be accomplished by properly educated and trained social workers. Clients deserve and have a right to receive as high a quality of service as possible.

SUPPORTIVE ENVIRONMENT

The term *environment* is abstract, expansive, and loosely defined; yet the concept pervades social work theory and practice. Dominant theoretical approaches for intervention include the ecological perspective and the person-in-environment perspective (see Chapter 3). The underlying idea is that social work involves not just a client but a client system—all the people and social systems surrounding that client (e.g., significant others, friends, families, groups, churches, companies, associations, organizations, communities, societies), as well as natural and tangible resources (e.g., funds, land, buildings, time, computers, goods, water, food, housing, clothing). A thorough assessment and holistic awareness of the environment is essential for contemplating and enacting change.

For social workers engaged in advocacy and policy practice, an environmental perspective leads to the premise that clients need a supportive environment. Any key part of a client's environment that is not supportive needs to be considered. Social workers must be in tune with the social and physical conditions, human relationships, and interaction patterns involved in any aspect of social work practice, including advocacy. Ask yourself:

- Has a determination been made in collaboration with the client about which elements of the environment are currently supportive and which are detrimental or not as supportive as possible?

- Are existing resources available to advocate successfully?
- Is collaboration occurring to generate ideas for solutions and to make reasonable and effective choices about courses of action?
- Am I examining with the client ways to work with people and organizations to create a more supportive environment?

Nancy is encouraged that her social work colleagues, the state NASW chapter, a handful of elected state officials, and a couple of consumer groups want to pursue licensure reform for social workers in her state. However, she is cautious about and sensitive to the timing of a legislative initiative. She is undertaking this advocacy effort during a period of restricted funding for social services. Nancy sees social workers and clients who are overwhelmed by day-to-day operations and struggling to provide effective services in their agencies. Additionally, fiscally and socially conservative politicians are reluctant to advance legislation that would contribute to additional spending, or the expansion of regulatory bodies and the state bureaucracy. She and her colleagues must formulate a strategy for not only strengthening ties with allies but also approaching the skeptics and persuading them to change their minds. She knows how important creating a supportive environment will be for the success of her initiative.

TIME TO THINK

Social workers are often thought of as people willing to do good for others, which often means that others expect them to be willing to do good 24/7/365. Professional social workers must learn to maintain boundaries for relationships with clients and use of personal time. Contemplate your use of time, especially in relationship to potentially labor-intensive activities such as advocacy. Are you able to effectively set boundaries between personal and work time? For example, do you currently text message or e-mail family and friends during class time or at work? During personal time, are you tethered to work, answering work-related text messages and e-mails at all hours? If you were passionate about a cause, as Nancy is about licensure for social workers, would you be texting and e-mailing people all the time? What are the possible consequences of these kinds of behaviors?

HUMAN NEEDS AND RIGHTS

Human history is full of instances in which well-intentioned people (often white men) from dominant classes established programs and services for people they determined to be in need. People in positions of power and policymakers often decide who has needs, what is needed, and how programs and services should be implemented and evaluated. These top-down decision-making processes yield disconnects between how clients view their own needs and what others believe they deserve.

In contrast, the perception and reality of human need from the client's point of view is the primary concern of social workers. Need is to be framed in the spirit of what the person in need requires, not what others believe that person deserves or should receive. Social workers contemplating human need would ask:

- Who is defining the need and for whose benefit?
- What are the consequences for the client of such a definition of need?
- Are consumers of services being included or consulted when defining what is needed?

As important as it is to address the immediate human needs of clients in social work practice, doing so can often overshadow the relevance and importance of human rights and liberties (Murdach, 2011). It may appear that social work's dual obligations to address human needs and advance human rights are consistent and complementary, but in practice advancing human rights can too easily become secondary to the quest to address the immediate needs of clients.

Basic human rights can be thought of in a number of realms, such as personal, civil, and political rights. Generally, however, humans should be able to live free of persecution, discrimination, and oppression, and have access to important societal resources, which often include work, education, health care, and equality before the law. For many people and professions around the globe, an important source for defining and advancing human rights is the United Nations and the UN Human Rights Council, which disseminates up-to-date information and news about basic human rights. From a social work practice perspective, a key to promoting basic human rights is the ability for people to have meaningful participation in decision-making processes, which typically includes freedom of thought and expression.

The integration of human rights into the activities of social work practice has not been easy, especially in the United States (Witkin, 1998). In an individualistic and capitalistic society such as the United States, the general public and social workers tend to conceptualize human pain and suffering as the result of the individual's psychological makeup and choices in life rather than as the result of an unjust society (Witkin, 1998). Nancy, this chapter's featured social worker, believes that clients are people deserving of dignity. Clients have the right to receive high-quality services from competent and effective helping professionals. Advocating for the licensure of social workers in her state is one way of promoting professional services that recognize and support client respect, understanding, self-determination, and rights.

POLITICAL ACCESS

The crass reality of macrolevel decision making in much of the contemporary United States is that relatively few people have sufficient power to dictate policies, laws, and administrative orders. This situation exists in city, county, state, and federal governments as well as many private organizations and entities. Unfortunately, the primary interest of politicians (and CEOs and board members, in the case of private organizations) may not be what is best for the general welfare or for your clients. Instead, self-preservation, public perception and opinion, and reelectability (especially for politicians) or profitability (for CEOs) are often powerful concerns.

Politicians are elected because of their ability to acquire support and funding from others; CEOs are typically chosen because of their ability to focus on profits. Especially in the case of politics, being a candidate generally requires a considerable amount of funding and support from "heavy hitters" willing to donate appreciable money and time to the campaign. Of course, politicians are inclined to lend their ear and afford influence to major contributors. Politicians often feel beholden to longtime friends, loyal allies, dedicated supporters, and leaders of special interest groups and political action committees who have worked on their behalf. Often, key decision makers and policymakers meet with their allies and contributors to discuss "what ought to be" prior to asking for general input and taking a formal vote or action during a public forum or meeting—a practice sometimes referred to as "the meeting before the meeting." In such circumstances, newcomers and people outside of a politician's inner circle find it difficult to exert influence and sometimes even to provide information.

As a student considering the profession of social work, you might be asking yourself, "So what can I do to effect political change? Wouldn't it be a better use of my time to focus just on helping clients access existing services?" But consider that not becoming politically involved or active—through apathy, ignorance, or cynicism—can also be viewed as a political act. Effective social workers identify ways to become politically involved and develop political access for their clients as a means for "creating a dialogue and solution that view societal and structural inequities as the fault needing the fixing, not the people" (Haynes & Mickelson, 2006, p. 4).

Mary Richmond, one of the founders of social work, was impatient with "do-gooders" who gave little thought to the causes of their clients' troubles (Haynes & Mickelson, 2006, p. 5). Today, social workers are enjoined to care for their clients while advocating for clients' access to, and influence within, the political process. A scorecard for this kind of intervention might ask the following:

- Am I assisting clients to understand the bigger, fuller context of their problems?
- Am I facilitating the collaboration of others who have similar challenges or who work to overcome these kinds of challenges?
- Am I assisting clients with communicating their predicaments to politicians and policymakers?
- Am I enabling politicians and policymakers to look beyond these clients' situation to assess the structural and systemic issues contributing to the creation of private troubles?

To accomplish their goal of instituting a licensure requirement for social workers in their state, Nancy and her colleagues need to influence key political decision makers. Nancy has already completed a considerable amount of research to identify state legislators aligned with policies that are consistent with a new and improved licensure law for social workers. The voting patterns for state legislators are very clear and consistent. Proponents and supporters of social legislation aimed at protecting and advancing rights and opportunities for consumers of social services and programs come from progressive urban areas. Opponents of social legislation are elected in affluent, conservative, suburban and rural areas and frequently vote against government intervention.

Personally, Nancy has been considering the actions she is willing to take to achieve her goals. She is prepared to give expert testimony before legislative bodies or committees interested in examining the licensure issue. She is brushing up on the skills she needs to lobby legislators, being especially attentive to innovative forms of communication involving new technology and media. To learn more about the use of technology for lobbying, she plans to enroll in two new continuing education workshops examining the effectiveness of social media. Nancy has begun to assess the political action groups and special interest committees that might be good allies in the licensure cause. She has also considered running for the state legislature herself, or encouraging or supporting someone with similar views to do so. She knows that her willingness to participate in the political process is necessary.

SUMMARY

The next time you hear someone suggest that social work sounds like an "easy major," explain that the actions of social workers significantly impact lives and that the professional accreditation requirements by the Council on Social Work Education are high. Social work students are required to demonstrate their ability to perform specific practice behaviors, among them advocating for their clients and for communities. Social workers do not just match their clients with available resources; they actively attempt to change "the way things are" to improve their clients' lives and communities.

Advocacy requires value orientation, ethics, knowledge, skill, and passion. This chapter provides only a sprinkling of what is expected of social work students in terms of advocacy. As a beginning, however, the advocacy practice and policy model and the dynamic advocacy model derived from it provide conceptual orientations for entertaining the value and effectiveness of a social worker's advocacy efforts on a client's behalf. In the following chapters, these models are adapted to guide social workers through advocacy activities in relationship to particular social welfare issues. Regardless of the issue, advocacy should be collaborative, client centered, and ethical, and should act to help people in need.

TOP 10 KEY CONCEPTS

absolute needs	cost of advocacy
advocacy	dynamic advocacy model
basic human rights	economic and social justice
case advocacy	relative needs
cause advocacy	social action

DISCUSSION QUESTIONS

1. Identify the causes for which you feel particular passion (e.g., feminism, gay rights, gun rights, benefits for veterans, racial discrimination). Why do these causes seem particularly relevant to you? Consider your geographical location, current social conditions, and aspects of your own identity.

2. Is it possible to separate personal from professional values in practice, especially when engaged in advocacy? Identify a couple of personal values that would challenge your ability to advocate for a client population.

3. Can you hold conservative political views and be an effective social worker? How about an extreme or radical perspective?

4. Does the current "safety net" of services in the United States address the absolute needs of people in our society? If not, which groups of people are falling through

the safety net? To what degree are people's relative needs being met?

5. Should everyone holding the title of social worker be professionally educated in a program accredited by the Council on Social Work Education? Should government agencies and social welfare organizations reimburse only licensed professionals (e.g., social workers, counselors, psychologists, nurses) for services?

6. Would you ever consider running for a political office or becoming a volunteer for a political party? How might your sentiment affect your ability to be an effective social worker and advocate for causes?

7. On the website for your school, closely examine the research requirements for a BSW or MSW degree. Is this coursework congruent with your passion for helping others?

EXERCISES

1. Consider attending a rally or some form of public advocacy event. Can you identify the objectives and desired outcomes of the gathering? Are social workers involved in the demonstration? How do you explain their presence or absence?

2. Contemplate attending a political fund-raiser or rally for a candidate. Be attentive to the seating arrangements and interaction patterns of participants. Is there an "inner circle" of confidants surrounding the politician? How are those in attendance given opportunities to ask questions or enter meaningful dialogue with the candidate?

3. Many schools offer a legislative day in the state capitol. Sessions allow students to listen to legislators and their legislative aides describe how the business of state government and the legislative branch takes place. Attend and ask questions about effective ways to become involved in political processes. How challenging do you think it would be to get involved? What seems to be the secret to accessing decision makers and policymakers?

4. Select a human service organization in which to serve as a volunteer. Observe social workers at the agency and inquire about their typical workday and workweek. What kinds of activities do they perform? Use the chart in Exhibit 4.5 to record information about their time spent in activities such as advocacy and policy practice. Ask them directly, if necessary. In summary, how much of their work is related to advocacy?

EXHIBIT 4.5   Time and Advocacy Activities of a Social Worker

ASK A SOCIAL WORKER THE FOLLOWING QUESTIONS	COLLECT THIS DATA
In a typical workweek, how many hours on average do you spend engaged in advocating for clients and causes?	Average number of hours per week _____
What are some of the more common advocacy activities included in your job?	List the advocacy activities.
Do your advocacy activities take place during your paid or personal time?	Check the appropriate response: _____ Paid _____ Personal _____ Both
What is your employer's level of commitment to advocacy?	Check the appropriate response: _____ Just right _____ Not enough _____ Too much
On a scale from 1 to 10 (1 being lowest and 10 being highest), rank how important it is to you and your satisfaction as a social worker to be able to engage in advocacy activities during work time?	Provide a score of 1 to 10.

5. Attend a service learning immersion class, such as an "urban plunge" or trip abroad, that will expose you to people who have serious unmet absolute needs. As an alternative, talk with someone who has already had this type of experience. How does it challenge your thinking about the need to advocate for human needs and rights?

ONLINE RESOURCES

- *The Advocate*, a national gay and lesbian magazine (www.advocate.com): Exemplifies the use of technology to promote awareness and advocate for rights
- Council on Social Work Education (www.cswe.org/File.aspx?id=13780): Describes the criteria and expectations for the accreditation of educational programs in its Educational Policy and Accreditation Standards, including the competencies and practice behaviors required in social work curricula
- Evangelical Lutheran Church in America (www.elca.org/Our-Work/Publicly-Engaged-Church/Advocacy): Promotes social justice and advocates for ideals and values aligned with faith
- National Association of Social Workers (www.naswdc.org/advocacy/default.asp): Recommends ways to become involved in advocacy as a social worker
- Political Action for Candidate Election (www.naswdc.org/pace/default.asp): Provides information about social work participation in political processes and recommends action to elect candidates

STUDENT STUDY SITE

Sharpen your skills with SAGE edge at **edge.sagepub.com/cox**

SAGE edge for Students provides a personalized approach to help you accomplish your coursework goals in an easy-to-use learning environment.

RESPONDING TO NEED

PART 2

Chapter 5: POVERTY AND INEQUALITY

Learning Objectives

After reading this chapter, you should be able to

1. Define the term *poverty*.
2. Describe who is considered poor and why.
3. List various factors associated with poverty.
4. Define at least five programs or services designed to address poverty.
5. Apply the dynamic advocacy model to poverty and inequality.
6. Describe the role of social workers in addressing issues of poverty.

Steve Sees the Face of Poverty

Steve was not a likely candidate to begin his social work career in Appalachia, the region around the mountain range in the United States that stretches from the southern tip of New York to northern Alabama, Mississippi, and Georgia. Raised in an affluent community just north of Manhattan in New York, Steve wanted to work in the coal fields of Appalachia because he was intrigued with the resilience that seemed to come from living in isolated communities, as he imagined the coal camps to be.

Steve discovered that generalist social work positions were available in the rural towns he visited. In part, this was because there were few graduate social work programs in the region and people who earned a master's degree in social work did not necessarily want employment in rural communities such as the coal towns or coal camps. Eventually, Steve accepted a position with an outreach program operated by a community mental health center located in a county seat nestled in the Appalachian foothills. He was supervised about 1 hour each week by a psychologist. The majority of people served by the agency were long-standing residents of the area with large and often complex family systems. Steve's social work position required that he conduct home visits to people with persistent mental illness, many of whom had been institutionalized for a significant period of time in one of the state's large mental health facilities. Steve had to be quick thinking, flexible, agile, and resourceful on the job if he was to succeed, since the demand for services was high, the needs of people were multidimensional and often generational, and supervision was limited at best.

As a generalist social worker in the Appalachian region, Steve quickly learned that although America is one of the wealthiest nations in the world, it is also a country plagued by poverty. By visiting people in their homes and assessing their strengths and weaknesses within communities, Steve saw that prosperity and wealth are enjoyed by only a small portion of Americans.

Social work has a long-standing commitment to address the common needs of people who are poor and underrepresented. You will discover in this chapter that issues of poverty and inequality raise many concerns with regard to human rights and social justice. In this way you will begin to consider that poverty involves much more than money. Ideally, you will look beyond the symptoms to understand the root of poverty and how social work attempts to reduce poverty and inequality by applying knowledge through skills in practice.

As you read this chapter and consider the relationship between poverty and inequality, take time to think about the role of government in regulating fairness of opportunity and income. Generalist social work practice provides you with a lens through which to glimpse poverty. Ideally, the content of this chapter will stimulate new ideas and beliefs about the realities of poverty and alternative ways to frame the nation's response to common needs.

POVERTY

Discussions of poverty evoke strong responses from those concerned with society's welfare, such as social workers, because of its crippling effect on life conditions. The debate surrounding what to do about poverty reflects opinions on the role of government, government's contract with its citizens, and the distribution of wealth in the United States and other countries.

Poverty is not a new phenomenon, in our country or around the world. Yet the term *poverty* is difficult to define in a concise manner. Usually we consider **poverty** in the context of being without basic needs or resources such as money and all that it buys—food, clothing, housing, transportation, medical care. However, defining exactly what are basic needs within those categories and how much should be spent on them fuels the debate on poverty. As you probably see with your friends and family members, what is considered enough depends on the person or group of people discussing the need and allocating the resources.

For example, a worker may think basic needs include high enough wages to maintain a family with a few comforts, a house in a safe area, and a brief, thrifty vacation every year, but an employer may argue that a worker can survive on less and that raising wages to support the worker's aspirations will prevent the business from making a profit.

Most Americans do not know any poor people even though the number of people in poverty is increasing. Insulation from poverty is not all that uncommon in America. The nation's economic structure tends to restrict the interaction of poor people with those who are middle and upper class. In fact, just mentioning poverty, poor people, and issues of inequality will cause many people to change the subject abruptly. For this reason, we think it is critical for you to have an understanding of poverty in America and of the social welfare programs and services designed to address poverty.

MEASURES OF POVERTY

Economists and the governments of the United States and most nations of the world generally define poverty in terms of a quantitative measure referred to as **absolute poverty.** A fixed dollar amount, generally representing a person's wages, is used to designate poverty. The key factor in this absolute measure is agreement on the exact number that determines who is impoverished and who is not.

In contrast to an absolute measure of poverty is the concept of a relative measure. **Relative poverty** compares a person's wages with the norm or an average to determine if that person is experiencing poverty. Defining a relative level of poverty is extremely difficult, if not impossible. This is especially the case when you begin to compare what would constitute poverty in one place with the living conditions in other places—especially when comparing countries worldwide.

In 1963 the United States adopted the notion of a **poverty line**, sometimes referred to as the **poverty threshold** or **poverty index,** under the direction of Mollie Orshansky, director of the Social Security Administration (Orshansky, 1964). Each year the poverty line is adjusted to account for inflation. It is used by social welfare agencies and programs to determine a person's eligibility for benefits and services. Those whose income is above the poverty line do not receive services, or they receive lesser benefits than do those who are below the poverty line. The process of determining who qualifies for services and who does not is referred to as **means testing**. Means testing attempts to reduce some income inequality through the provision of services and benefits, but in no way does it attempt any major redistribution of wealth. For many social workers, documenting need through means testing is a hindrance to establishing rapport, because they must ask people personal and often intrusive questions about their income levels, expenditures, and insurance benefits.

The **poverty guidelines** are another federal poverty measure. They are issued each year in the *Federal Register* by the **Department of Health and Human Services**. The guidelines, a simplification of the poverty thresholds, are used to determine financial eligibility for certain federal programs and for other administrative purposes. Oddly enough, because the poverty guidelines vary from state to state, some people are poor enough according to federal guidelines to fall below the poverty line and receive services but not poor enough by state standards to receive other services.

Definitions of poverty and the way society responds to social need are based on assumptions and subjective values that constantly change over time. However, the poverty line remains useful. The measure helps in gathering data on the number of people experiencing poverty and the services people have requested and received or were denied. Reviewing the data provides a picture of poverty trends over time. The data also underscore poverty's relationship with quality of life and life choices, and the link between poverty and inequality.

TIME TO THINK

Take a moment to consider your definition of poverty and how you would describe poverty to someone. Is your definition based on personal experiences, readings, observations, or things people have told you?

Measuring poverty and determining who is poor reflects values and beliefs. How are your values reflected in your definition of poverty?

Do you think addressing poverty issues such as homelessness should be a priority of government? Why or why not?

POVERTY AND INEQUALITY

The distribution of income and wealth in the United States covers a wide spectrum. In this context, **wealth** refers to the accumulation of valuable resources and possessions, whereas **income** is a wage for work provided. Income is the money that flows into a household in a year, while wealth pertains to assets accumulated over time, such as stocks, houses, savings, and cars.

The U.S. Census Bureau aggregates the data on income and wealth and divides the nation's population into **quintiles,** or fifths. The "top quintile" is the top fifth of the population based on income and wealth; the "bottom quintile," which is the lowest fifth, is generally the target of programs for the poor. What analysis of the data has shown for decades is considerable, and growing, **inequality** in the distribution of wealth and income in the United States. The distribution of wealth is more unequal than the distribution of income, with the majority of wealth owned by about one tenth of the nation's population. Exhibit 5.1 depicts this inequality. What is important for you to remember is that while some people are very wealthy, others have accumulated essentially zero wealth.

This increasing inequality in income and wealth translates to a decline in opportunity for poor people. Consider these economic facts (Stiglitz, 2012):

- Income growth is occurring primarily within the top 1% of the income distribution.
- The unequal distribution of income results in growing social inequality.
- Inequalities are apparent not just in income but in other factors that reflect standards of living, such as housing and health.
- There is little income mobility.

As a result, the United States has more inequality than any advanced industrialized country, and it does less than other countries to correct these inequalities (Stiglitz, 2012, p. 25).

THE FACE OF POVERTY

No matter what your political leaning is, you probably recognize that equality is basic to American beliefs. However, poverty is real in the United States, and it is not evenly distributed across the population. The questions you, as a

EXHIBIT 5.1 Distribution of Income and Wealth in the United States

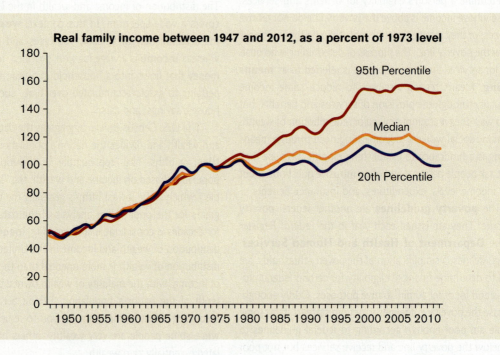

Real family income between 1947 and 2012, as a percent of 1973 level

Source: CBPP calculations from U.S. Census Bureau Data. Center on Budget and Policy Priorities, www.cbpp.org © 2008–2014 Center on Budget and Policy Priorities.

potential social worker, should be asking are, "Who are the nation's poor people?" and "Why are they poor?" To answer these basic questions, we look at the groups who are likely to experience poverty.

TIME TO THINK

Describe what the face of poverty looks like to you. Is it a woman, man, or child? What age is the person, and how does he or she appear?

Now consider where you got the ideas for your face of poverty. How did your life experiences, social media, films, books, and other representations influence your thinking?

Women

Throughout history and across the nations of the world, women are more likely to experience poverty than are men. This tendency is described as the **feminization of poverty** (Pearce, 1978).

A primary reason for this state of affairs is the difference in average earnings or income for women versus men. Women in the United States still earn only 77 cents on the male dollar. This figure drops to 68 cents for African American women and 58 cents for Latinas. Some of the discrepancy is due to discrimination against women in some higher-paying occupations. Women who can find work only in low-paying jobs experience a ripple effect of disadvantage: in lifetime wages, savings and investments, retirement benefits, and other types of wealth. The result can be a state of persistent poverty. If they cannot afford the many expenses associated with car ownership, they find that public transportation is extremely limited and incredibly time-consuming. The barriers to gainful employment are even more complicated when combined with race, leaving a distinct pattern of poverty for women of color (see Exhibit 5.2).

In addition, women tend to be at a disadvantage in the workforce due to societal changes in family structure—namely, high rates of divorce and separation and out-of-marriage births. Single and divorced mothers are more likely to be responsible for children than fathers are, and this extra

EXHIBIT 5.2   Women's Poverty Rates by Race and Ethnicity, 2010

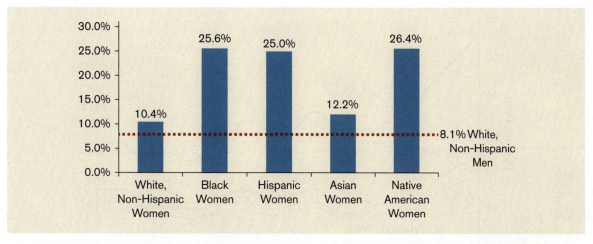

Source: Current Population Survey, Annual Social and Economic Supplement–www.nwlc.org © 2014 National Women's Law Center.

responsibility places an additional economic burden on them. Working mothers who are on their own often struggle to find and pay for quality child care. And when a family experiences a crisis that requires home-based caregiving, as when a child or parent suffers a chronic illness—women are usually the ones to leave the workplace.

People of Color

A history of prejudice and discrimination in the United States has largely disconnected people of color, such as Hispanics and African Americans, from economic opportunity and upward mobility. The concentration of poor minorities in certain neighborhoods has worked to enhance the disadvantages. Social services, public transportation, and quality health care may not be available close by. Often the schools in impoverished minority neighborhoods are substandard because the property taxes generated from the local residents cannot support high-quality schooling. A substandard education, in turn, chokes off the opportunity to succeed in occupational training programs and other advanced educational opportunities. Financial barriers to college are also a problem.

Without a good education, it is difficult to secure a well-compensated job. Decent employment, with benefits such as health care and retirement funds, is necessary for people to move beyond financial insecurity. The crippling of unions in some occupations has had a disproportionate effect on people of color in low-paying jobs, who usually lack the individual clout to advocate for better wages.

Although the media often depict the poor as people of color, the majority of the poor are white. However, people of color are disproportionately poor. In the case of Native

▲ Many women supporting themselves or their families with low-income jobs must take public transportation.

Source: Jupiterimages/Creatas/Thinkstock

EXHIBIT 5.3   Race, Ethnicity, and Poverty

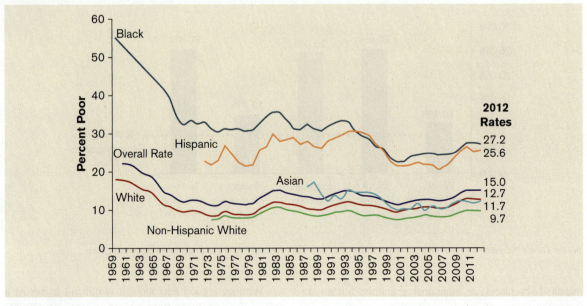

Source: U.S. Census Bureau, Historical Poverty Table 2; 2012 Census Report.

Note: Black poverty rate data from 1960 to 1965 is not available. The line shown connects the 1959 rate of 55.1 percent to the 1966 rate of 41.8 percent and is included to represent the trend but not to imply specific numerical data.

Americans, about 30% of all families are living below the poverty level. Exhibit 5.3 compares poverty rates for people of color in the United States.

Children

Poverty among children reflects the feminization of poverty. As can be imagined, caring for children is often costly, especially for working single mothers, and children's demands on parents' time can negatively impact parents' earning abilities.

In the past 20-some years, economic trends have hit families hard—particularly those families with young children, where the parents are usually young as well. The United States has experienced significant increases in unemployment and a general decline in the economy. Even when parents are employed, more of them have to work a second job to help make ends meet. Consequently, it has been increasingly difficult to support a family.

Unfortunately, children represent a disproportionate share of the poor in the United States; they are 24% of the total population but 36% of the poor population. In 2010, 16.4 million children (22%) were poor. As shown in Exhibit 5.4, the poverty rate for children varies substantially by race and Hispanic/Latino origin, as it does for adults.

Although their group is not included as a separate category in Exhibit 5.4,

Source: ©Alison Wright/Corbis

⌃ Approximately 30% of Native American families live below the poverty line.

American Indian children experience a very high level of poverty. In 2010, 29% of all American Indian children lived in poor families. In the states of Arizona, Minnesota, Montana, Nebraska, New Mexico, and North and South Dakota, more than 50% of American Indian children fell below the poverty line.

Homeless People

It is logical to think that poverty is a major contributor to homelessness. According to the U.S. Census Bureau, homelessness has worsened in the past decade because of increased housing costs, unemployment, and foreclosures, which were a result of the Great Recession and real-estate meltdown starting in 2008. A number of factors continue to influence the homeless rate on a national level:

Children make up a disproportionate percentage of the poor population, at 36%.

- Unemployment persists, particularly among those with little education or training and those who are older and have been unemployed for a long time.
- Average real incomes for the working poor have increased by less than 1%.
- Poor households are spending more of their income on rent.
- Foreclosure activity continues.
- Stocks of affordable, suitable housing units for families have decreased.

EXHIBIT 5.4 Children Under 18 Living in Poverty by Race and Ethnicity, 2010

CATEGORY	NUMBER (IN THOUSANDS)	PERCENTAGE
All children under 18	16,401	22.0
White only, non-Hispanic	5,002	12.4
Black	4,817	38.2
Hispanic	6,110	35.0
Asian	547	13.6

Source: U.S. Census Bureau (2010, Report P60, n. 238, Table B-2, pp. 68–73).

There is no easy answer to the question of how many Americans face homelessness. According to the National Coalition for the Homeless (2009), homelessness tends to be a temporary, rather than permanent, circumstance. The appropriate measure of homelessness is, therefore, not a static number but, rather, the number of people who experience homelessness or substandard housing conditions at any given time.

While homelessness affects people of all ages, races, ethnicities, and geographies, inequality is part of the homelessness equation. The people at increased risk are those living in "doubled-up" situations (living with friends, family, or other nonrelatives for economic reasons), people discharged from prison, young adults leaving foster care, and people without health insurance.

TIME TO THINK

Given the picture you now have of poverty, what approaches would you support to address it? Consider why you selected these approaches.

SOCIAL SERVICE PROGRAMS FOR THE POOR

As mentioned in Chapter 2, Americans began to broadly address poverty in the colonial period, through the Elizabethan Poor Laws. Today's social welfare programs originated with the New

SOCIAL WORK IN ACTION

Jacob Researches Poverty So He Can Help the Poor

Jacob works in a county human services department in California. His clients include many single mothers and their children, many people of color, some people who are disabled, some parolees and veterans who cannot find jobs, and some people who are homeless. Uniformly, they are poor.

Jacob has become disillusioned about his ability to help his clients. There are programs in place that could relieve their suffering, but due to budget cutbacks in federal and state programs, he simply cannot find all the needed help for his clients in a timely manner. He decides that he needs to push his concerns into the spotlight. But first he needs more facts and figures to bolster his campaign.

There are several social work institutes dedicated to understanding the dynamics of poverty, including the following:

- The Gerald R. Ford School of Public Policy Programs on Poverty and Social Welfare Policy
- National Center for Children in Poverty
- Institute for Research on Poverty

Jacob carefully notes data on poverty in his state, as well as details about the various populations that face difficulties in finding jobs, housing, health care, food, and other necessities. (The information in this chapter about the face of poverty is similar to what he finds; you might also wish to check these websites for additional information.)

Jacob realizes that he needs to narrow his focus to be effective. If he attacked poverty in general, he would likely never make a dent. So he resolves to pick an impoverished population or a cause of poverty or an aspect of need created by poverty.

1. If you were Jacob, how would you narrow your focus? Which group or groups would you concentrate on? Why do you choose that group?

2. Make a list of the aspects of life that contribute to poverty for that group. For example, how do age, education, residency, and gender impact the financial security of an individual?

3. What aspects of poverty would you like social workers to research? Why?

Deal of the 1930s. Programs to prevent poverty, usually referred to as **social insurance,** such as Social Security and workers' compensation, were designed to reward work and were funded through payroll deductions. People who could not work outside of the home, such as women with young children, people with disabilities, and older people, were thought to be the deserving poor and were provided for through **public assistance**, or means-tested programs.

The primary goal of programs designed to aid the poor, particularly when women and children are involved, has been to support the American economic and social systems, rather than to redistribute resources or change the value structure. People are always encouraged to work and participate fully in the economic system. Assistance programs by and large are designed to tide people over in times of downturn, not to redistribute wealth from the rich to the poor.

However, the American social welfare system was built on the fear of dependency on the government, government reluctance to provide social services, the work ethic, and rugged individualism. It is no surprise, then, that the system lacks coordination, cohesiveness, and a common sense of purpose. Today, federal public assistance efforts comprise as many as 75 different programs. They include the distribution of cash payments, direct services such as health care or training, and vouchers that can be converted into commodities such as heat, food, and clothing. Public assistance is also not so much a system as a network that operates across the federal, state, and local levels, and sometimes involves all three in a single program.

Before discussing each specific program, it is important to clarify some common values and perceptions of antipoverty programs. The American public has been reluctant to provide assistance to people who are poor. The distinctions between the worthy and unworthy helped ensure that only people deemed "truly deserving" of assistance received it.

The past 10 years have witnessed increasing levels of public frustration and resentment directed toward antipoverty programs and the poor themselves. Today the term most often used to describe efforts to assist the poor is *welfare*. **Welfare** has now become a vague, overarching term that stigmatizes people and conjures up images of handouts given to people who are marginally deserving or not deserving at all.

TEMPORARY ASSISTANCE FOR NEEDY FAMILIES

The largest, and perhaps most controversial public assistance program, is commonly known as **Temporary Assistance for Needy Families (TANF).** It was established through the Personal Responsibility and Work Opportunity Reconciliation Act, which was part of the welfare reform legislation of 1996, passed during the Clinton administration. The TANF program replaced Aid to Families with Dependent Children, the Job Opportunities and Basic Skills Training program, and the Emergency Assistance program.

Designed to help poor families achieve self-sufficiency, the TANF program provides states with **block grants,** which are large sums of money to be used for social services but without specific directions for how to spend the money. TANF funds are to be used to design and operate state programs with these goals:

- Assist needy families so children can be cared for in their own homes
- Reduce the dependency of needy parents by promoting job preparation, work, and marriage
- Prevent out-of-wedlock pregnancies
- Encourage the formation and maintenance of two-parent families

There is no guarantee that eligible individuals will receive assistance under TANF. The state-by-state system of determining need allows states to provide monthly payments only to the poorest of the poor who are thought to be the truly needy. In fact, according to federal law, families who have received five cumulative years of assistance will no longer be eligible to receive cash aid, federal funding for TANF block grants is capped at a set amount, and states must require adult recipients of TANF benefits to work after 2 years on assistance. Penalties for failure to work are set by each state.

Individual recipients who are unable to engage in work activities can elect to participate in community service or 12 months of vocational training, or they can provide child-care services to individuals who are participating in community services. As odd as it sounds, TANF does not provide child care, although single parents with children less than 6 years of age who cannot find child care will not be penalized for failure to engage in work activities.

MEDICAID

The **Medicaid** program was an addition to the Social Security Act of 1965. It provides federal matching funds to states to cover the costs of medical care and services for low-income people (Centers for Medicare and Medicaid Services, 2014), including the following:

- *Children:* Medicaid and the **Children's Health Insurance Program** provide health coverage to more than 31 million children, including half of all low-income children. An outreach program is in place to enroll eligible children in coverage.
- *Nondisabled adults:* Medicaid provides health coverage to 11 million nonelderly low-income parents, other caretaker relatives, pregnant women, and other nondisabled adults.
- *Pregnant women:* Medicaid plays a key role in child and maternal health, financing 40% of all births in the United States. Medicaid coverage for pregnant women includes prenatal care through the pregnancy, labor, and delivery, and for 60 days postpartum, as well as other pregnancy-related care.
- *Individuals with disabilities:* Medicaid provides health coverage to more than 8.8 million nonelderly individuals with disabilities, including people who are working or want to work.
- *Older adults and Medicare and Medicaid enrollees:* Medicaid provides health coverage to more than 4.6 million low-income older adults, nearly all of whom are also enrolled in Medicare. Medicaid also provides coverage to 3.7 million people with disabilities who are enrolled in Medicare, the federal health insurance program for people 65 years and older.

Each state designs and administers its own Medicaid program, following federal guidelines. All state Medicaid

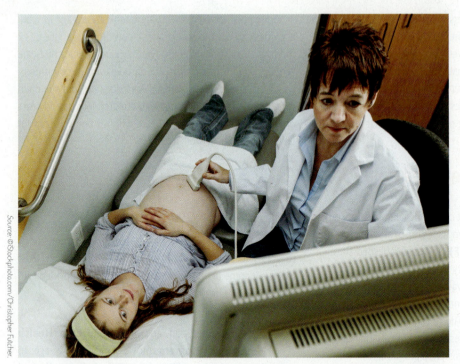

Source: ©iStockphoto.com/Christopher Futcher.

▲ Medicaid provides coverage for essential care for pregnant women.

programs must offer physician services, inpatient and outpatient hospital care, home health services, nursing home care, and some preventive services. States may elect to receive federal matching dollars to provide additional services such as dental care, eyeglasses, or medications.

SUPPLEMENTAL SECURITY INCOME

The **Supplemental Security Income (SSI)** program provides cash assistance to any person whose income falls below the poverty line and is 65 years or older or is blind or has a disability. A low-income person qualifies for SSI benefits if he or she is unable to participate in paid employment due to a medically determined physical or mental impairment or is over the age of 65. SSI also covers children with disabilities.

The various components of SSI were originally outlined by the 1935 Social Security Act. In 1972, the consolidation of two different programs—Aid to the Aged and Aid to the Blind and Disabled—coordinated eligibility and benefits under the federal government. Unlike many programs for poor people, funding for SSI comes entirely from federal revenues and is administrated through the Social Security Administration, resulting in uniform eligibility standards and benefits across all states.

HEALTHY MEALS FOR HEALTHY AMERICANS

Healthy Meals for Healthy Americans, funded by the federal government and operated by the states, provides food, nutrition counseling, and access to health care to eligible women, infants, and children. This type of program was first introduced in the social welfare system as the Special Supplemental Nutrition Program for Women, Infants, and Children (known as WIC). Initially a pilot program, WIC was made a permanent social welfare program in 1974. It is administered by the Food and Nutrition Service of the U.S. Department of Agriculture. WIC's name was changed under the Healthy Meals for Healthy Americans Act of 1994, to emphasize its role as a nutrition program (U.S. Department of Agriculture, Food and Nutrition Service, 2013).

To be eligible, women and their children must be at nutritional risk and have income below state standards for measuring need. The majority of Healthy Meals for Healthy Americans programs provide vouchers that women use at authorized food stores. A wide variety of state and local organizations cooperate in providing the additional food and health care benefits.

Healthy Meals for Healthy Americans has proven effective in improving the health of pregnant women, new mothers, and infants. Studies show that women who participated in the program during their pregnancies incurred lower Medicaid costs for themselves and their babies than did women who did not participate (California WIC, 2012). Participation in the nutrition program was also linked with fewer premature births, higher birth weights, and lower infant mortality rates.

TIME TO THINK

The United States is fortunate in that the country provides enough food to feed its entire population. Why do you think women and their children, as well as other sectors of society, such as older people, are still at nutritional risk? What are some of your ideas to improve the availability and accessibility of food across the nation?

▲ Social service programs for mothers and children, such as Healthy Meals for Healthy Americans, have proven to improve the health of pregnant women, new mothers, and infants.

Source: ©Jupiterimages/Stockbyte/Thinkstock

SUPPLEMENTAL NUTRITION ASSISTANCE PROGRAM

The **Supplemental Nutrition Assistance Program (SNAP),** formerly known as the Food Stamp program, helps low-income people buy food. SNAP—the nation's first line of defense against hunger—is a vital supplement to the monthly food budget for more than 46 million low-income individuals. Nearly half of SNAP participants are children, and more than 40% of recipients live in households with earnings below the poverty line.

Developed as part of the New Deal, the program was originally designed to distribute surplus agricultural goods according to federal standards and under the direction of state or local agencies. Support for government involvement in the purchase of food came from agricultural groups as a way to guarantee prices for farmers during periods of overproduction. Agricultural support for the food program resulted in its administration by the U.S. Department of Agriculture.

To participate in SNAP, a person must be determined eligible by income and be either a U.S. citizen with a Social Security number or a U.S. national or qualified alien. The SNAP application process includes an interview and documentation, including personal identification, such as a driver's license; proof of income for each member of the household; proof of child-care costs; rent receipts or mortgage payments; records of utility costs; and medical bills for household members 60 years or older and for those who receive government health care.

EARNED-INCOME TAX CREDIT

The **Earned-Income Tax Credit (EITC)** helps families who experience poverty in spite of having working family members. The general goal of the federal EITC program is to allow low-wage workers to keep more of their annual earnings. Thus, the program acts as a wage supplement for people in low-wage jobs and can decrease poverty for working families. The tax credit legislation was passed to offset the burden of Social Security taxes for low-income workers and provide an incentive to work. Congress originally approved it in 1975 and has expanded it several times since.

The EITC is administered by the Internal Revenue Service (2014). Participation requires the filing of a federal tax return and involves the same procedures as paying federal taxes. When the EITC exceeds the amount of taxes owed, the filer qualifies for a credit. The tax credit is based on family income and the number of children.

PUBLIC HOUSING

With the U.S. Housing Act of 1937, the federal government began financing low-income **public housing.** The Department of Housing and Urban Development (HUD) Act of 1965 expanded the program by creating HUD as a Cabinet-level agency (U.S. Department of Housing and Urban Development, n.d.-b).

People who qualify can rent a home (known as **Section 8 housing**) through HUD, with rental charges set by the federal government at about 30% of a person's monthly after-tax income. The federal government provides rental certificates and vouchers that can be used to subsidize the lease of a privately owned rental unit.

The Stewart B. McKinney Homeless Assistance Act, enacted by Congress in 1987, established distinct assistance programs for the growing numbers of homeless persons (U.S. Department of Housing and Urban Development, n.d.-b). It was the first comprehensive federal effort to aid people who are homeless. Included in the McKinney Act are 20 programs, including emergency food and shelter, transitional and permanent housing, education, job training, mental health care, primary health care services, substance abuse treatment, and veterans assistance services.

DIVERSITY AND POVERTY

In this chapter we have already learned about how diversity intersects with poverty. Women, people of color, children, and homeless people are all more likely to be poor than are other population groups. We have also seen the pernicious effects of intersections of diversity, such as the greater poverty experienced by women of color.

For social workers, being able to apply the concept of intersections of diversity to social work practice and to issues of poverty is not simply a benefit to poor people but a benefit to society as well. For example, when considering the wages of women, it becomes necessary to examine wages for all people across a spectrum of ages, working conditions, skills, and educational levels. A female client could be experiencing unemployment or underemployment based on several seemingly unrelated factors, including not only her gender but also disadvantages accrued from childhood poverty, such as a deficient education. Intervening by offering literacy services might be a good supplement to job counseling and training for jobs that are not traditionally held by women. Ideally, by thinking about intersections of diversity and women as workers we gain a better understanding of economic inequalities and their implications for social status.

ADVOCACY ON BEHALF OF THE POOR

We hope you begin to recognize that lack of earnings is by far the major reason why people are poor. When

Source: ©iStockphoto.com/jrling

▲ The federal government offers programs where individuals may rent housing at rates based on their after-tax income.

considering employment status, wage inequality is a key factor, and wage inequality is associated with age, race, gender, and family structure. Thus, it stands to reason that poverty disproportionately affects children, minority groups, families headed by single women, and young families. These population groups are more likely to encounter barriers to adequate employment in spite of wanting to work. So an increase in earnings is the most expedient way to confront poverty and challenge inequality. (Exhibit 5.5 provides information on federal poverty levels.)

The persistence of poverty suggests that economic uncertainty extending beyond individuals and toward the nation's social and economic structure is a factor. Social workers, and the nation as a whole, must not be concerned simply with poverty but with the risk of increasing economic insecurity for the entire society.

Why don't political and economic systems address poverty and inequality? The explanations span the ideological spectrum. Conservative ideology is likely to argue that poor people are uninterested in working because the public assistance system provides enough income for an adequate living, thus limiting incentives for securing employment. This perspective focuses on individual motivations. A more liberal ideology would suggest that structural barriers, such as the inability of the market to generate enough jobs and

an inadequate minimum wage, are a large part of the issue (Stiglitz, 2012).

CURRENT TRENDS IN ADVOCACY FOR THE POOR

Social workers have come to understand the importance of not just learning about the services available to needy individuals and families but also studying poverty. The best way is to learn from those who know best about poverty and injustice: the poor. Living among poor people is referred to as the accumulation of **life knowledge** (Krumer-Nevo, 2005). Integral to life knowledge are the interpretations, meanings, hypotheses, analyses, and theories provided by the people experiencing the life conditions that come from economic insecurity (Beresford, 2000). Understanding such life elements sheds light on the power structure and the resources of people living in poverty, and challenges preconceived notions of poor people as the "other"(Krumer-Nevo & Barak, 2007; Lister, 2004).

The ideas and perceptions gathered from life knowledge help form the **social constructs**, or perceived social reality, that social workers have about poverty and inequality (Hacking, 1999; Searle, 1995). Social constructs are important because they reflect beliefs. If the commonly

EXHIBIT 5.5   Federal Poverty Levels

What is the 2012 federal poverty threshold?

- $23,283 for a family of four with two children
- $18,480 for a family of three with one child
- $15,825 for a family of two with one child

Is a poverty-level income enough to support a family?

Research suggests that, on average, families need an income equal to about 2 times the federal poverty level to meet their most basic needs. Families with incomes below this level are referred to as low income:

- $46,566 for a family of four with two children
- $36,960 for a family of three with one child
- $31,650 for a family of two with one child

These dollar amounts approximate the average minimum income families need to make ends meet, but actual expenses vary greatly by locality. In 2010–2011, the cost of meeting basic needs for a family of four was about $64,000 per year in Los Angeles, California; $57,000 in Newark, New Jersey; $46,000 in Indianapolis, Indiana; and $42,000 in Jackson, Mississippi.

Source: United States Census Bureau, Poverty Thresholds, Thresholds by Size of Family and Number of Children (2012).

held belief is that people are poor because they are lazy, social welfare policies will be punitive and less inclined toward fairness in the distribution of resources. If the public belief is that poverty is the result of failures in the marketplace, economy, or political arena, social welfare policies will emphasize the value of equality. It is in the interest of social workers and the social work profession to link life experience to social constructs to better shape government attempts to create a fair society (Bullock, 1995; Groskind, 1994; Stiglitz, 2012).

Another point to consider is how life knowledge nurtures the development of skills needed for social work practice at all levels—from direct services with people to policy development. For example, a social worker with life knowledge who was involved with a program for homeless people would become mindful of how micro-level work to change an individual situation is connected to advocacy for macro-level policy change. The skills developed through life knowledge also help social workers develop partnerships with people in service communities and with programs across multiple levels of government, allowing them to share power and privilege to achieve effective interventions and social change (Krumer-Nevo, Weiss-Gal, & Monnickendam, 2009).

TIME TO THINK

Life knowledge is gathered from our first memory and throughout our lifelong development. Consider some of the skills you attribute to life learning. Where did you gather these skills and from whom?

DYNAMIC ADVOCACY AND POVERTY

Considering all the policies and programs the United States has in place to address issues of poverty, you might be wondering why so many Americans still live in poverty. Answers to that important question are found by examining the point where poverty intersects inequality: people working at low-paying jobs, single-headed households, and the fraying social welfare safety net. All three of these broad categories disproportionately impact women, children, and minority groups in both rural and urban areas.

The advocacy and policy practice model, described in detail in Chapter 4, is designed to assist social workers in analyzing and advocating for policies and services that help alleviate poverty. Ideally, applying the model to social constructs or beliefs about poverty enhances the integration of micro and macro social work practice to effect change in individual lives and in social, economic, and governmental arrangements.

Two broadly opposing values, personal responsibility and social responsibility, have prominently influenced public policies regarding poverty:

- **Personal responsibility** refers to the role people have in caring for their own needs, no matter the circumstances that have left them in need. Americans believe strongly in **individualism,** which is the belief that hard work is rewarded with success, virtue will also bring success, failure demonstrates a lack of virtue, and lazy and incompetent people attain success only through luck (Wilensky & Lebeaux, 1958). In essence, according to individualism, success or failure depends on the individual. Thinking about poverty in this context, we would see individuals, families, and possibly neighborhoods as being in charge of not only their employment status but also their health care, mental health, and housing.
- **Social responsibility,** in contrast, contends that society should assist those experiencing unfortunate or challenging circumstances (Segal & Brzuzy, 1998). It supports a collective approach to addressing need. It is important to realize, however, that social responsibility extends only to people considered to be worthy and by definition unable to support themselves because of age, disabilities, or child care responsibilities.

Social welfare advocacy reflects the struggle between individual and social responsibility. Those with conservative beliefs oppose broad-based policies and programs that expand the role of the federal government, believing that they nurture dependency rather than self-reliance in those who receive services. In contrast, a more liberal perspective supports an expansive role for government and for policies and programs with more universal coverage, such as Social Security. The tension between conservative and liberal policy positions plays out differently in different eras, depending on the political and economic environments.

CURRENT TRENDS

Life Knowledge

Increasingly, students are taking a "gap year" in between high school graduation and college. Also, some college students decide to spend a year or more engaging in volunteer work as a life experience and a way to enhance their résumés. In either case, programs such as the Peace Corps, Volunteers in Service to America (VISTA), and Teach for America offer life knowledge experiences. They provide potential social workers, as well as anyone who wants to make a difference for the poor, with opportunities to learn firsthand about the struggles that some people face just to meet their basic needs:

Peace Corps—International volunteer service primarily in developing nations. Requires a college degree and a 2-year commitment.

Volunteers in Service to America (VISTA)—Volunteer service in the United States. Requires at least a high school diploma.

Teach for America—Teaching commitment in often poor or vulnerable communities. Requires a college degree.

1. You may wish to review these programs online and consider if their mission and goals correspond to your career plans. What do you find?

2. Some universities have programs for returning Peace Corps volunteers that provide credits for participation as part of graduate coursework. Does your university have such a program?

3. What other experiences have given you or could give you life knowledge that applies to work with impoverished people and communities?

TIME TO THINK

If you think of the conservative and liberal stances on individual and social responsibility as being two ends of a spectrum, where do your beliefs fall? Which social programs do you think are good for society, and which are destructive?

Economic and Social Justice

Of the four tenets of the dynamic advocacy model, economic and social justice is perhaps the most basic. It underpins social work's professional commitment to helping people enhance their quality of life by addressing problems and matching resources with needs. Economic and social justice is based on a sense of fairness and the belief that people, no matter what their gender, race, age, or abilities, deserve equal economic and social rights and opportunities.

Social workers advocating for economic and social justice at the macro level address these particular questions (Kahn, 1994):

- How the power structure responds to the needs of poor people
- How the power structure has changed to address issues of inequality
- How well social welfare agencies are addressing the needs of poor people
- How the power structure recognizes and responds to the voices of poor people and their organizations
- How well the power structure recognizes and involves the leaders of poor people, such as clergy and union leaders
- How well poor people are represented in positions of power within the community

Advocacy for clients involves referrals to other social welfare agencies to ensure that poor people have the services they need, such as access to food stamps and health care. It can also mean protection from financial abuse by credit card companies, banks, check cashing establishments, student loan companies, and mortgage lenders. Finally, social workers are called on to ensure that clients receive the financial benefits owed to them from insurance policies and union membership.

Social workers also apply social justice principles to structural problems in the social service agencies in which they work, focusing on the long-term goal of empowering their clients. Social workers readily use their knowledge of legal principles and organizational structure to suggest changes that will protect their clients, who are often powerless and underserved. For example, a generalist social worker at a mental health clinic might help ensure that clients are treated respectfully by staff by negotiating with the clinic's director to appoint a client to the community governing board.

Supportive Environment

Social workers learn that their role is often to work with networks of people, in families, communities, and regions. Whether a problem is an individual issue or relevant to a group of people, the challenge is to help the community, when at all possible, define the situation in communal terms and take action that will support individuals in need (Ginsberg, 2001).

One of the advantages of working in communities is that many social work clients know one another. This sense of interconnectedness is generally positive. When the community is not supportive, the social worker has a point for assessment and possible change.

To form a social construct of how the area's overall environment addresses poverty and helps poor people, social workers can compose a list of questions that identify strengths and problems. The goal is to compile an objective profile of the area and its citizens to show the ways economics and politics are interrelated. The following questions illustrate how social workers might ask clients, colleagues, and community leaders about support for employment in a certain area (Kahn, 1994):

- Describe the jobs available for people who want to work.
- Do these jobs pay minimum wage or above?
- What are the working conditions for the available jobs?
- What are the opportunities for employment for women, minority and ethnic groups, teenagers and older people, and people with mental health challenges?
- Describe the benefits—for instance, health and mental health insurance—offered by the employers.
- What types of transportation to these workplaces are available?
- What are the day-care options in the community?
- What are the skills associated with these employment opportunities?
- What sorts of training programs currently exist in the community, and what programs are needed?

Source: © iStockphoto.com/peplow.

▲ Environmental factors may influence the types of jobs available in a community.

Social workers recognize that fostering jobs within the community is essential to reducing persistent and tenacious poverty. The connection of environmental factors to policy responses on employment requires broad community participation, greater opportunities, and more empowerment of poor people in their own development process. True to social work's principles on equality, the goal is to enhance economic development within a community.

Human Needs and Rights

Americans embrace the idea that all people are entitled to certain human rights regardless of nationality, sex, national or ethnic origin, race, religion, language, or other status. Those rights include civil and political rights, such as the right to life, liberty, and freedom of expression, and social, cultural, and economic rights, including the right to express one's culture, the right to food, and the right to work and receive an education. International and national laws and treaties uphold and protect human rights in most other parts of the world.

Social workers understand the concept of the indivisibility of rights. In their practice they see that civil rights without the security of food, shelter, and health care do little to enhance well-being. An advocacy orientation is perhaps the greatest social work strength and one that can make important contributions to human rights. Social workers take action; they engage in securing human rights for individuals and communities. What is missing is the ongoing link to build on individual case solutions to influence policy change.

The universality of human rights was first emphasized in the Universal Declaration on Human Rights in 1948, and has since been reiterated in numerous human rights conventions, declarations, and resolutions. Social workers often apply three key principles to their work, which are taken from the 1948 declaration and supported by the U.S. Department of State (2012) in its dealings with other countries:

- Learn the truth and state the facts in all human rights investigations.
- Take consistent positions concerning past, present, and future abuses.
- Maintain partnerships with organizations, governments, and multilateral institutions committed to human rights.

These principles provide social workers with a moral foundation for human rights practice, both at the level of day-to-day work with clients and in community development, policy advocacy, and activism (Ife, 2001).

Despite the array of programs that have been developed to alleviate poverty, social workers inevitably find that some services cannot meet common needs of the poor, such as food, housing, and medical care, in a timely manner. The service system is driven by bureaucracy and thus inflexible. In addition, the service system tends to minimize client needs, stigmatize those served, and intimidate clients with mounds of paperwork.

Further, to address human needs and rights on a broader level, social workers will sometimes turn to the lobbying arm of the National Association of Social Workers. The NASW lobbyist might help organize public forums that nurture public trust and promote the idea that change is possible through collective action.

Political Access

The practice of social work generally heightens the consciousness of social workers about economic instability and the alarming level of inequality in the nation. Looking at programs and how well they meet the needs of their clients, social workers often question the nation's essential fairness.

Many social workers find it increasingly difficult to ignore national and international poverty and inequality. It often appears as though political structures and established agencies are not truly responsive to all members of society. In fact, many of the funds that provide necessary services come through the federal government, and funding allocations are far below the need and in most cases shrinking.

Social workers sometimes work on voter registration campaigns in the hopes that getting their clients and people like them to vote will help change the equation in Washington, D.C., and in state legislatures. Clients and sympathetic community members are recruited by asking three broad questions (Kahn, 1994):

- What is your voter registration status?
- If you want to vote, what is your name, address, and other contact information?
- What is the contact information of any family member in the military, a nursing home, hospital, school, or other institution who might want to register to vote?

Involving clients in voter registration campaigns also helps inform them of the positions of various candidates.

Candidates who have expressed support for the needs of poor people in their community are likely to attract clients' interest. Whatever the ultimate success of the candidate, social workers see people's leadership skills, self-esteem, self-confidence, and self-reliance evolve as they make their needs known and exercise their rights through the ballot box.

THE CYCLE OF ADVOCACY

Seen in its totality, the dynamic advocacy model shines light on the skills, values, client knowledge, problem-solving orientation, and strengths assessments that define generalist social work practice. Social workers and their clients, working together, have the ability to research and analyze poverty and inequality and to advocate for change in people, communities, and agencies, and across all levels of government.

A first step in advocacy is envisioning improved conditions or a more ideal state of affairs (Jannson, 1999). For example, when thinking about social justice and poverty, social workers can use their analytical skills to assess structural problems in the agencies that serve their poor clients. The interactional skills of social workers often lead to a network of colleagues in human services, as well as new referrals for clients.

Realistically viewing the political structures that shape the lives of people living in surrounding communities is often a matter of integrating theory with practice. Social workers who apply different theoretical perspectives, such as the strengths perspective and empowerment concepts, often discover that economic and political systems are dysfunctional, exploitive, and unfair to many poor people.

Social work clients usually have limited experience with professionals and politicians; so they are reticent and even fearful about expressing their wants and needs. However, with knowledge of human behavior, social workers can identify strengths and leadership skills in their clients and mobilize them to vote and participate in political campaigns. Engaging poor people in the political process helps demonstrate their potential voting power.

Another important element of the dynamic advocacy model involves ethics. The impact of poverty and inequality violates social workers' belief in a moral or just world (Rawls, 1971). Thus, social workers aim to help relatively powerless groups, such as women, children, people of color, people with special needs, and poor people improve their resources and opportunities.

> ## TIME TO THINK
>
> **Do you think social workers contribute to the understanding of poverty and inequality through their practice? Please consider why or why not. What would you do differently to change attitudes toward poverty and inequality if you were in a social work position?**

YOUR CAREER AND POVERTY

As you think ahead to graduating from college and entering the workforce, consider how your selected career might help alleviate poverty and inequality. For social workers, poverty and inequality are at the core of their professional lives. In counseling, social workers typically address financial matters and employment status in relation to depression, anxiety, or life experiences such as domestic violence, substance use, and homelessness. On the policy level, social workers advocate and lobby for regulations and programs that enhance the well-being of people with limited resources.

You do not have to become a social worker to enter the Peace Corps or serve as a Volunteer in Service to America. In either of these organizations, a good portion of your time will be spent examining international or domestic distributions of resources. In most of the locales they serve, those resources are basics of life such as food, water, and shelter.

No matter where your career takes you, you can help alleviate the pain of poverty and inequality by keeping the needs and wants of others in your thoughts and displaying concern in your actions. Volunteering at a shelter, fostering a child, feeding and socializing with older people, and taking a stand on behalf of a policy or program are all components of the effort to change society for the better. And they can all make life a little better for those who have been forgotten.

SUMMARY

If a society cannot help the many who are poor, it cannot save the few who are rich.

John F. Kennedy

Poverty and inequality are not new phenomena in our country. The historical debate over what to do about these interrelated issues reflects the dilemma of reconciling unequal levels of power and privilege in the United States. Further complicating the task are contending forces whose political values and personal beliefs about the causes of life conditions influence the actions we take as a society.

If you conclude that the structure of the nation's economic system results in poverty and inequality, your macro-level advocacy will focus on far-reaching changes in policies relevant to the market and labor systems. If you think that individuals are responsible for their own poverty, your advocacy will emphasize changing people's behavior. Unfortunately, neither approach has been implemented effectively, and a large number of people are still experiencing poverty.

TOP 10 KEY CONCEPTS

absolute poverty
feminization of poverty
income
inequality
means testing

poverty
poverty line (poverty threshold or poverty index)
public assistance
relative poverty
wealth

DISCUSSION QUESTIONS

1. Much of the issue of poverty and inequality has to do with the role of government. Should the government ensure an adequate standard of living for all citizens? In responding to this question, first define the term *standard of living* and then consider how expansive you think the government's role should be.
2. As an advocate for poor people, toward which level of government (local, state, or national) would you direct your activities? Why?
3. Federalism is a form of government that combines individual states and an overarching national government. What role does federalism play in a democratic society such as ours? How does this relationship play out in U.S. programs and services to people who are poor?
4. In 2009, the nation's federal minimum wage was set at $7.25 per hour. Would you advocate for an increase in the minimum wage? Explain why or why not, with reference to poverty.

EXERCISES

1. Keep a log of your daily expenditures over a week. Given your cash outlays, do you have a sense of financial security or insecurity? If you had to trim your personal budget, what expenses would you reduce and how? How would you describe your socioeconomic level and why?
2. Take time to reflect on how your family's economic status impacts your life options. List the advantages you've experienced and also the challenges.
3. Read an editorial from one of the nation's leading newspapers that applies to the content of this chapter. Write and share with the class a letter of support or rebuttal to the editorial that expresses your thoughts in a clear, concise fashion.
4. Spend time examining the community you are most familiar with, such as the one you were raised in or the community where you currently live. Consider your selected community in light of the dynamic advocacy model's four interlocking tenets. Based on your analysis, list at least four possible advocacy actions related to poverty and inequality that you could organize in your community. What social work skills would you use in these advocacy actions? What results would you hope to achieve?
5. Consider attending a service-learning immersion class, such as an "urban plunge" or trip abroad, that will expose you to dire absolute needs. How do you think this type of experience might challenge your thinking concerning human needs and rights?

ONLINE RESOURCES

- Children and poverty (www.globalissues.org/issue/2/causes-of-poverty): Focuses on the reasons children experience poverty, from a family systems perspective
- Factors associated with poverty (www.stanford.edu/group/scspi/): Conducts regular surveys and aggregates data on poverty and factors associated with poverty
- Gender and poverty (www.legalmomentum.org/women-and-poverty-america): Examines poverty as it relates to issues of gender

- Global poverty (www.globalissues.org/issue/2/causes-of-poverty): Describes the leading factors related to worldwide poverty
- Worldwide data on poverty (databank.worldbank.org/data/): Provides comprehensive data on poverty experienced throughout the world

STUDENT STUDY SITE

Sharpen your skills with SAGE edge at **edge.sagepub.com/cox**

SAGE edge for Students provides a personalized approach to help you accomplish your coursework goals in an easy-to-use learning environment.

Chapter 6: FAMILY AND CHILD WELFARE

Learning Objectives

After reading this chapter, you should be able to

1. Define family in light of contemporary family structure.
2. Describe the tension between the rights of children and the rights of parents.
3. Describe services and programs designed to help children and families.
4. Describe the belief systems that underpin opinions about child and family services.
5. Identify how the education system could be improved to help families and children.
6. Explain how diversity affects family and child welfare.
7. Apply the dynamic advocacy model to family and child welfare.

Rosa Works to Strengthen Families for the Sake of Children

As a child protective services social worker, Rosa advances child safety and identifies ways to strengthen the ability of families to protect children. People have often told Rosa that they don't understand how anyone could possess the temperament to work all the time with cases of child neglect and abuse.

For Rosa, one of the most difficult hurdles has been working with young children living in dire poverty. Most of the children assigned to Rosa are under the age of 6 and live with a single teenage mother who has less than a 10th-grade education and little or no employment history. Many of these children do not eat properly, live in substandard housing, struggle with basic medical care, and receive little support or attention from their biological fathers.

Rosa is keenly aware of the effects of childhood exposure to traumatic events, such as verbal altercations, acts of violence in the home and outside of it, and substance abuse. She knows how hard it is for children to live with caregivers struggling with mental health and chemical addiction issues.

Although Rosa's caseload of 23 children and families is very challenging, she is dedicated to her area of practice. She actively advocates for meeting the unique social–emotional needs of young children in challenged families, as well as providing family aid and support in the form of employment assistance, adult education, self-help, health care insurance, mental health services, housing, and child care.

Interpersonal violence, poverty, and child maltreatment are just a few of the many issues social workers encounter when working with children and families. This chapter examines how the definition of family has changed over time and the diverse family types. Common problems facing the U.S. family, such as child abuse and violence, are also explored, along with the services available to children and families. A central theme in this chapter involves how social workers can advocate for children and families to create positive, lasting change.

Historically, child welfare has been a common and popular field of practice for social workers in the United States. Beginning in the early 20th century, protection of children from various forms of maltreatment and exploitation became a major concern. The early 1900s were characterized by industrialization, urbanization, and the rapid migration of people from various lands to an economically blossoming country. Economic growth, social disruption, and family stress went hand in hand. As economic growth and expansion took place, children were exploited for their labor in the workplace and very young children often faced harsh and neglectful living circumstances at home. These rapid and dramatic social and economic changes formed the backdrop for child and family services in the United States.

TODAY'S FAMILIES

The definition of what constitutes a family has changed in recent years and is often a source of debate in the United States. Most people would agree that a family is a social unit containing two or more members. However, families can vary significantly in composition, complexity, and size. For example, families can consist of a husband and a wife without children, cohabiting unmarried couples, single parents and their children, couples with children and extended family members, parents with children from previous marriages, and multigenerational family members. Although state laws differ concerning legal definitions, families also include same-sex marriages and partnerships.

Generally, regardless of its composition, the **family** constitutes a social unit where people form relationships and make a commitment to live together as a defined family group and provide for the group's social, emotional, and economic needs, including care of children.

Given such a broad definition of family, it is important to note that family structure may or may not be based on **kinship**, which is common ancestry, marriage, or adoption. No matter how families are constituted, they are a critical reference group for their members (Lamanna & Riedmann, 2012).

Traditionally, families have been classified as a **nuclear family**, in which one or more parents live with their dependent children apart from other relatives, or an **extended family**, in which, in addition to parents and children, other relatives live in the same household or in close proximity. Today, who can define what constitutes a family and a marriage is a topic of considerable debate among politicians, religious leaders, special interest groups, and people from various cultural backgrounds. Differing views on the issue are aligned with personal or group values, belief systems, and experiences. People with a conservative ideology often define families in more traditional ways, and people with a liberal ideology tend to define families in the broader, more contemporary ways.

DIVERSE FAMILY FORMS

The traditional image of family is a young husband and wife, each married for the first time, with one or two birth children of their own and living in a single dwelling. That image is now undergoing change. Because of advancements in communication and transportation, family units are not confined to single dwellings such as houses or apartments. Some families have been affected by **transnational migration** for economic and other reasons, a situation that separates family members into two or more countries (Furman & Negi, 2007). Also, diverse forms of family abound in the contemporary United States (and perhaps always have). Separation, divorce, blended families, single parenting, and gay and lesbian marriages are common occurrences. These diverse forms of family composition also influence living circumstances.

Social workers practice with a variety of family types and need to be knowledgeable, nonjudgmental, and competent in serving their needs. Each family form also possesses unique strengths. The social worker strives to understand the challenges and abilities associated with each family type to promote and support healthy child and family development.

Source: ©iStockphoto.com/inhauscreative

▲ Divorce may offer an opportunity for introspection for the parties involved.

TIME TO THINK

What were your family circumstances growing up? Did you consider your family to be typical or atypical? Can you see strengths in your type of family?

How did your family influence your values and outlook on life, including thoughts about career, marriage, and children?

Divorce

Once stigmatized as a sign of a failed marriage, divorce today is more commonly viewed as a legal process of ending a marriage that allows spouses to become single and, if they choose, to remarry. Spouses seek divorces for a variety of reasons, including unhappiness, infidelity, employment, unemployment, mental health, substance abuse, interpersonal violence, disapproval of the relationship by relatives and friends, and newfound romantic relationships. Another cause of divorce is **irreconcilable differences**, where the couple have disagreements that cannot be resolved and neither spouse is blamed for the breakdown of the relationship.

Divorce need not necessarily be a negative occurrence or experience. Spouses can end relationships in amicable ways that benefit them and other family members. In addition, divorce can represent an opportunity for introspection and personal realization, especially with the help of professionals. This type of growth is useful as a foundation for new committed relationships.

In the United States, the probability of a marriage ending in divorce is between 40% and 50%. Divorce rates are traditionally lower for spouses with college degrees (Cherlin, 2010, p. 404).

Separation

Spouses may also seek a legal separation from each other, often as a precursor to divorce. Separation can be temporary or permanent. Some states encourage or mandate a time-specific separation as a type of "cooling-off period" for spouses to reflect on and examine their relationship and begin to define parameters for it. Topics typically addressed include housing, living circumstances and child visitation, financial commitments (including financial support of children), distribution of possessions (e.g., furniture, electronics, cars, animals), and banking accounts and loans.

Although physically separated, separated spouses maintain the legal status of being married. This is an important attribute with regard to medical insurance, taxes, financial matters, and so on. As an example, spouses may decide to separate rather than divorce to maintain satisfactory medical insurance coverage for family members. Disruption in health and medical benefits and coverage could have a detrimental impact for treatment and use of medicine, with powerful and potentially life-threatening results.

Blended Families

The term **blended family** typically refers to a family unit with two adults in a committed relationship, children from previous marriages or relationships, and children (if any) from the newly formed committed relationship. Blended families work hard to define the relationships of the children with their biological parents and stepparents, as well as the relationships among the various siblings. Many children in blended families have to share time between two families and two sets of parents, which necessitates planning and decision making about activities, celebrations, holidays, and vacations. Social workers often work with blended family members to help define reasonable and functional parental and childhood roles.

Single-Parent Households

When a family unit is headed by only one parent, it is referred to as a single-parent household. Typically, that single parent is the mother. Without the help and assistance of a second parent, single parents face challenges in caring for and financially supporting their children. In two-parent households,

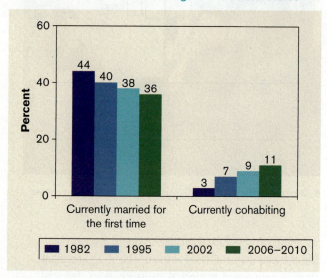

EXHIBIT 6.1　Marriage and Cohabitation Among Women 15–44 Years of Age in the United States

Source: Copen, Daniels, Vespa, and Mosher (2012, Fig. 1, p. 5).

children have two caregivers and parents can rely on each other for social and emotional support.

However, an advantage of single parenting is that single parents have no everyday obligations and commitments to a spouse. Advantages for children growing up in a single-parent household include the potential to develop a sense of responsibility and independence at an earlier age.

Gay Marriage and Parenting

Gay marriage is a relatively new phenomenon and an emotional and highly polarizing political issue. In 2004, Massachusetts became the first state to legalize gay marriage. Since then, California and a number of other states have passed legislation legalizing same-sex marriages. Other states legally recognize civil unions for gay and lesbian couples; civil union is a legal status that can be helpful with regard to child custody, family leave rights, and similar matters. However, other states have passed laws banning legal gay relationships and marriage.

Social workers need to maintain an open mind about gay marriage and parenting. Gay parents are often unduly placed under special scrutiny regarding their parenting practices. It is important to realize, however, that same-sex parents, like heterosexual parents, can offer children a loving and caring

environment for growth and development. The creation and maintenance of a stable, nurturing, and loving family unit is the key factor and does not depend on the sexual orientation of one's parents.

Cohabitation

When two adults decide to live together in a dwelling without legally formalizing their relationship through marriage, they are cohabiting. Cohabitation continues to be very popular in the United States (see Exhibit 6.1) and is employed by many couples as a step between being single and being married. Other adults, for a variety of reasons (e.g., lack of commitment, finances, legal issues, conflicting responsibilities) decide to forgo marriage altogether and live together as a couple. Gay and lesbian couples residing in states that do not allow same-sex marriage may have little other option than to cohabit.

FAMILY PROBLEMS

The family as a social structure is not necessarily declining in the United States, but it is most definitely undergoing change. With all the contemporary variations in family structure, children and parents need a range of programs and services that will help them adapt and adjust to new and evolving family roles and responsibilities.

The family unit and its members also face many of the social and personal problems of the day. Unemployment, poverty, mental health, substance abuse, interpersonal violence, natural disasters, and death of a loved one have powerful effects on families. Daily, family members struggle with these kinds of tribulations in the context of their unique family constellation and home. Social workers are employed to intervene with various family-based problems and advocate for programs and policies that strengthen and enrich family functioning and promote the rights and safety of children.

Domestic Violence

Domestic violence is a general term that references a broad range of acts of violence (including assault, injury, and rape) against family members. Predominantly, acts of violence are perpetrated by men and against women and children.

Wives and children can be especially vulnerable to men in family constellations because of their economic and social dependence as well as men's physical dominance.

CURRENT TRENDS

Child Trafficking

CHILD trafficking occurs when child victims are recruited, transported, harbored, and exploited. Child trafficking is often cited as a contemporary form of slavery. Children are exploited for their labor, deployed as soldiers, and put to work in the commercial sex industry as, for example, prostitutes, escorts, strippers, and nude models. The United States is both a source and a destination for trafficked children, and it is also a transit country. It is estimated that more than 12 million people are the victims of human trafficking worldwide, with more than a million being children, constituting a $32 billion worldwide trafficking industry (Catholic Relief Services, 2014).

Many of the victimized children do not have families or caring adults to advocate for their protection and rights. Perpetrators of child trafficking often take advantage of being the only adult figures active in the lives of these children, who are very vulnerable to adult influence.

UNICEF has been a leading force in working to protect the lives of exploited children across the globe. Social workers partner with organizations such as UNICEF to educate people concerning child exploitation and protection and to develop programs and services to help these vulnerable and severely abused children. In the United States, UNICEF and helping professionals, concerned citizens, and members of faith-based organizations have advocated for specific pieces of legislation. One success was the Trafficking Victims Protection Reauthorization Act, signed into law by President Obama in 2013. This act supports the President's Interagency Task Force to Monitor and Combat Trafficking in Persons and serves as a major entity for coordinating antitrafficking programs and initiatives.

Are you familiar with human and child trafficking issues and programs in your area or state? Is this a personal area of interest for social work practice—why or why not? Discuss with classmates and friends how human and child trafficking is an affront to the dignity and worth of people. Even if inadvertent, how do people in the United States directly or indirectly support human and child trafficking?

Domestic violence is typically an issue of power and control. Perpetrators take advantage of vulnerable people in the household as a demonstration of dominance and the perpetrators' desire to control family members' behavior.

Child Maltreatment

Child maltreatment is a broad term used to encompass the abuse and victimization of children. Children are vulnerable to several types of maltreatment because they are typically incapable of caring and advocating for themselves, and instead rely on the adults in their lives. For much of history, the treatment of children was considered a private matter. Children had no political power and no rights as independent human beings. Most societies considered children to be the property of their parents (Miller-Perrin & Perrin, 2013). But now their treatment has become a public matter as well as a private one.

The child-saving movement in the United States took place in conjunction with two noteworthy social changes (Finkelhor, 2008). First, social workers, nurses, schoolteachers, counselors, and legal advocates emerged as professionals and developed professional organizations devoted to seeking protection for children. Second, women entered the labor force in greater numbers and acquired newfound power to advocate for children's rights. As helping professionals, child advocates, and child advocacy groups became more plentiful and politically active, child maltreatment was criminalized, primarily through the passage of state-level child protective statutes. The child-saving movement is viewed today as a mark of societal development and modernization.

The practices, policies, and services put in place to promote child well-being and safety are generally referred to as **child welfare**. Child welfare includes a complex array of services provided by publicly funded child welfare agencies. **Child protective services,** programs through which social workers, law enforcement personnel, and health care workers respond to reports of child maltreatment, are a key component in publicly funded child welfare agencies.

Contemporary child welfare in the United States focuses on both children and families. The modern-day family is conceptualized as an adaptable social system that can be both functional and dysfunctional for children. For example, the family is the primary social unit for providing nurturance, sustenance, socialization, and care for children. Yet the family is also the social unit where most child maltreatment occurs, and parents are the primary perpetrators of violence against children 81% of the time (U.S. Department of Health and Human Services, Administration for Children and Families, Children's Bureau, 2011).

To understand child welfare, it is important to become familiar with several varieties of child maltreatment:

- **Child physical abuse:** Deliberately using physical force that injures or could potentially injure a child (Miller-Perrin & Perrin, 2009, p. 58). Examples of child physical abuse include forcefully hitting or punching, kicking, shaking, throwing, burning, choking, and stabbing.
- **Child sexual abuse:** Attempting (or succeeding in the attempt) to engage sexually with a child or to exploit a child for sexual purposes (Leeb, Paulozzi, Melanson, Simon, & Arias, 2008, p. 11). Examples of sexual acts include touching the genitals, engaging in sexual intercourse, penetrating the child, sexually exposing oneself to a child, and engaging in voyeurism if a child becomes exposed or is engaged in sexual acts.
- **Child neglect**: Failing to meet a child's basic needs (Miller-Perrin & Perrin, 2009, p. 152). Child neglect can include but is not limited to physical, emotional, educational, and medical needs.
- **Child psychological maltreatment:** Intentionally conveying that the child is "worthless, flawed, unloved, unwanted, endangered, or valued only in meeting another's needs" (Leeb et al., 2008, p. 11). Child psychological maltreatment can include public embarrassment, verbal cruelty, intimidation, threats, and deprivation of love.

Social workers practicing in child protective services receive special training for detecting and documenting various forms of child maltreatment. They learn to be suspicious of bruises and injuries that simply do not make sense or are illogical. For example, imagine that a parent claims that a small round burn on the child's arm was a result of play and skidding on the floor. The size, shape, and texture of the burn does not support that claim and instead is consistent with a cigarette burn. Additionally, social workers look for behavioral indicators of maltreatment, such as a child's extreme passivity and withdrawal to avoid the attention and provocation of a caretaker. Child protective social workers have a very demanding area of practice, and their abilities and decisions directly influence the quality of life and safety of children.

TIME TO THINK

Think about the factors that might motivate you to be a social worker. Do you think that working to make a difference in the lives of children would match your motivations? Would a practice focused on abused and neglected children be problematic for you? If so, why?

CHILD WELFARE SERVICES

In the United States, publicly funded child and family services are often the result of state or federal mandates to protect and support the well-being and development of children. **Public child welfare agencies** typically serve large numbers of people, offer a variety of programs, and are less costly to clients. Public child welfare programs are often located in county-based departments of social or human services and include adoption, family life education, foster care, child protective services, in-home family-centered intervention, and residential services.

Conversely, **private child welfare agencies** usually focus on specific problems and subpopulations, rely on pay for service, see fewer clients, and are less bureaucratic in nature. It is not unusual for a social worker to develop professional expertise in practice with children and families in public child welfare agencies and then be lured away to a private, more specialized child welfare agency. Although salary and benefits for social workers in the public sector in departments of social services are often very competitive, private agencies attract people through smaller caseloads, greater professional autonomy in decision making, focused

The Famous Mary Ellen McCormack Case

Although difficult to imagine, the United States has not always had policies to protect children from physical, sexual, and mental abuse. The case of Mary Ellen McCormack in the late 1800s is frequently cited as a landmark case that brought attention to the horrors of child abuse. Mary Ellen, a 10-year-old girl from the Hell's Kitchen section of Manhattan, reported being the victim of almost daily whippings and beatings by her adoptive mother.

Since child protection laws were nonexistent at the time, Mary Ellen's case was brought to the attention of the American Society for the Prevention of Cruelty to Animals, one of the only protective agencies in existence at the time. Eventually, Mary Ellen's heart-wrenching story made its way to a courtroom. Her case is credited as the impetus for the creation of the New York Society for the Prevention of Cruelty to Children in 1874, which is believed to be the first child protective agency in the world (Markel, 2009). The story was featured in an article in *The New York Times* on April 10, 1874.

Consider for a moment why the American Society for the Prevention of Cruelty to Animals was established in New York City before the New York Society for the Prevention of Cruelty to Children. At that time, were parental rights for children's upbringing and care more prominent and powerful than today? For example, were whippings and beatings seen as acceptable? Are such abuse practices condoned anywhere today?

services, and less bureaucracy. However, many social workers are also dedicated to providing clients reliant on public child welfare services with "top-notch," quality intervention and services.

TIME TO THINK

Would you feel more comfortable working in a public or private agency? Why? Consider the importance of factors such as professional autonomy, mission, population served, salary, benefits, geographical location, and the degree of specialization in service delivery.

HISTORY OF CHILD AND FAMILY SERVICES

In the United States, the development of child and family services can be traced to the early 1800s. Young children were often left alone to care and fend for themselves while their parents worked or sought work, sometimes traveling to the growing cities to do so. Older, more able-bodied children were exploited as a source of labor in emerging industry. Powerless and vulnerable, many children found themselves without basics such as food and shelter and in unsafe living conditions. The situation was so unacceptable that by the mid-1800s government-run institutions were being established to house abandoned and needy children.

During the 1900s, abuse against children was defined as criminal. Considerable progress was made at the state level to pass laws to protect children from abuse and neglect. Recognition by the states of their societal obligations to protect those who were unable to protect themselves was an important step in the development of child and family services. The stage was set for establishing procedures, funding sources, and policies to intervene with children and thwart their exploitation and abuse.

In the 1960s, a more robust recognition of child abuse as a social issue occurred when Dr. C. Henry Kempe identified the **battered child syndrome** as a clinical condition and advocated that physicians report cases of child abuse to authorities (Kempe, Silverman, Steele, Droegemueller, & Silver, 1962). Battered child syndrome can be a physical or psychological condition and typically involves persistent injuries (e.g., cuts, burns, bruises, broken bones, and emotional abuse) inflicted on a child by a caregiver. In recent years, child welfare researchers and neuroscientists have given considerable attention to **shaken baby syndrome**, where infants and toddlers sustain serious brain injury as a result of being physically shaken.

With support from the powerful medical community, child abuse and protection became further recognized, and by the end of the 1960s, professionals (e.g., social workers, physicians, teachers) were required to report suspected cases of child abuse in every U.S. state (Miller-Perrin & Perrin, 2009, p. 16). Today, state statutes also mandate that professionals report suspected elder abuse. Furthermore, there is emerging interest in cross-sector reporting of various forms of interpersonal violence and animal cruelty. Veterinarians and animal care professionals with reasonable suspicion of child abuse or neglect would be required to report to departments of social services, and helping professionals with suspicion of animal cruelty would report findings to animal care and cruelty organizations (Long, Long, & Kulkarni, 2007).

PARENTAL VERSUS CHILD RIGHTS

Attempts to protect children are complicated by the ongoing controversy over parents' rights versus their children's rights. In the United States, parents are granted considerable latitude in disciplining and maintaining control over the behaviors and development of their children. In some instances, parental rights to exert discipline can supersede children's rights to protection. Parents often assert the right to raise and discipline their children as they see fit, and they can question oversight by social workers and other child protection professionals. Some parents also attempt to justify child maltreatment as a parental right.

The overlapping needs and rights of parents and children are mirrored in the subtle (but important) distinction between child welfare agencies and family service agencies. The mission of **child welfare agencies** is to promote the safety, well-being, and best interests of children. Meanwhile, the mission of **family service agencies** is to provide programs and services to support and strengthen families during challenges and transitions. Although strengthening families and improving family functioning

are important for promoting the welfare and well-being of children, social workers are careful in practice to identify whether their client system is the child or the whole family. The interests of families and other family members (particularly parents) are sometimes at odds with the safety and best interests of children. For example, the rights of parents to discipline children who are disrupting family life can conflict with the goal of child protection.

A GLOBAL CONTEXT FOR CHILD PROTECTION

In the United States, **childhood** is often defined as the period from birth to age 18. The **UN Convention on the Rights of the Child (UNCRC)** defines a **child** as a human being under the age of 18. However, the notion of childhood can be conceptualized and defined in a number of ways. In some societies and cultures, the dividing line between childhood and adulthood is less a matter of one's age and more a rite of passage. For example, children may become adults when they exhibit certain forms of physical maturation (such as the emergence of secondary sex characteristics and ability to procreate) or have attained specific abilities (such as educational attainment or work skills). Or a child may become an adult when called on, often out of necessity, to fulfill vital roles as a caretaker of younger children or a provider for the family.

Around the world, there has also been considerable debate about what kinds of actions and behaviors constitute child abuse and neglect, especially since cultures vary considerably in child-rearing practices. However, the UNCRC has determined that all members of the United Nations must eliminate any customs that are abusive to children and has created guiding principles to protect the safety and rights of children across national borders (Miller-Perrin & Perrin, 2013, p. 10). Unfortunately, establishing widely shared definitions of what constitutes "abuse of children" is an ongoing challenge.

You might be surprised to learn that the United States has been one of two countries (Somalia being the other) to resist the ratification of the UNCRC treaty and policy statements promoting the protection of children and nonviolent discipline. The United States has been reluctant to restrict the individual rights of parents with regard to practices such as spanking of children (Miller-Perrin & Perrin, 2013, p. 11). For example, fundamentalist Judeo-Christian religious

SOCIAL WORK IN ACTION

Julian Supports HIV-Positive Children in Malawi

ESPECIALLY in developing countries, HIV-positive children with HIV-positive parents are often left to cope on their own. They face a double burden: the disease itself and its stigma, as well as life with chronically ill parents who often cannot adequately provide for them (Rowan, 2013, p. 241). HIV-positive children living under such circumstances are helpless and shunned. Being a survivor overshadows being a child.

As a social worker in Malawi, Julian has become very aware of these children and concerned about their bearing developmentally inappropriate responsibilities for taking care of not only themselves but also a dying parent. "Child" under these circumstances seems to Julian a misleading classification. This issue demonstrates how "childhood" varies and is relative to circumstances and context.

Much of Julian's time is spent finding guidance and support for these HIV-positive children, often from extended family members. As well as possible, Julian attends to the children's basic needs and safety, while advocating for additional goods, services, and any form of available social–emotional support.

Ask yourself, is it possible that in the United States, as in developing countries such as Malawi, some children could find themselves in situations where they must fend for themselves to meet their daily needs? What kinds of circumstances would put children in the position of assuming adult responsibilities over an extended period of time?

traditions condone spanking and other forms of corporal punishment as a means for creating discipline and making children more obedient.

KEY CHILD AND FAMILY SERVICES

A variety of child and family services are offered in many counties and municipalities across the United States. Social workers are employed both to provide these forms of services and to actively advocate for their enrichment, resourcing, and effective use. As is the case regardless of one's area of practice, social workers helping provide these services to children and families typically begin their interventions with engagement and assessment.

As you consider and reflect on your interests in social work with children and families, consider each of these services as an opportunity for future professional development and employment. For example, can you envision yourself working in child protective services, intensive treatment, or adoption services?

- *Child protective services.* Social workers employed in public child protective (CP) services practice on the "front lines" of child welfare and are exposed to a variety of forms of child abuse and neglect. When child abuse or neglect is reported, CP social workers are the ones who help investigate the charges, take the child into custody if necessary, and ensure that the child receives preliminary medical and psychological services. CP social workers are typically required to complete special education programs before employment. These education programs are often made available to social work students willing to commit to public CP practice and are offered through training centers operated by the state department of human services or departments and schools of social work.

- *Family-based services.* This is a broad category of services that are designed to enhance and strengthen the family unit, not simply children. **Family-based services** include counseling, therapy, skill building, advocacy, educational, and other services for children, parents, and families. Family-based services can be preventive and treatment oriented. Social workers are employed in a variety of public and private family service agencies. Often the client's ability to pay, either through medical insurance or out-of-pocket, determines whether public or private services are used. Many counties and states also work with school systems to organize and coordinate family-based services.

- *Family preservation services.* Social workers practicing in the field of **family preservation** focus on the early identification of families at risk of removal of a child and the implementation of concrete services to help prevent that outcome. In reality, however, family preservation services and intervention are often reactive rather than preventive and do not occur until a crisis increases the possibility that a child will be removed. This work involves case management, counseling, and skill building to enrich and strengthen the family and keep the family structure intact.

- *Family foster care.* If removal of the child for safety and well-being becomes necessary, one out-of-home placement option is family foster care. Immediate and extended family members are typically assessed as a first option. The second option is frequently **family foster care**, where children are cared for in a family setting by a certified foster care family. Although designed as a temporary form of placement, family foster care becomes a permanent status for many children, for a variety of reasons. It is also not unusual for children to be moved from one foster care family to another. With advanced training, some family foster care providers earn a special designation as treatment or therapeutic foster care placements. Social workers often work directly with children in family foster care, families of children in foster care, and foster care providers.

- *Family reunification services.* When children are placed outside of the home, family reunification is the first consideration and is oftentimes viewed as the most desired outcome for children and youth. It is not an easy path, however. Although parents may articulate love for their children and want to be with them, parents with children in out-of-home placement struggle to become capable of caring for their children full time. Social workers employed in family reunification services work with children in placement and their families, with the goal of successfully reconnecting them. This process often

requires parents to make significant improvements in their personal growth, parenting skills, financial commitment, and interpersonal functioning. Family reunification must also deal with the trauma children experience before being removed from the home and while going through the reunification process. Advocating for the rights of children during reunification processes is another social worker responsibility.

- *Adoption services.* **Adoption** is the permanent rendering of legal and parental rights by a child's birth parents to adoptive parents. Social workers promote adoption, seek prospective adoptive parents, screen adoptive parents, make arrangements for adoption, help choose the adoptive parents, assist adoptive parents in developing a new family, and help birth parents create a better life for their children and themselves. Some social workers focus on special needs adoptions with children facing unique conditions, which could include physical, mental, and/or emotional challenges. Adoptions typically take place through stepparent adoptions, independent adoptions (through attorneys, independent of agencies), agency adoptions (overseen by an agency), and intercountry adoptions (of foreign-born children). In each of these types of adoption, the needs and rights of children are the foremost concern.

- *Residential care.* The history of **residential care** for children in the United States can be traced back to the establishment of orphanages, which were designed to provide for the basic needs of children who had lost parents through death, disability, or abandonment. Interestingly, some current therapeutic group care facilities for children provide residential services in dwellings originally built as orphanages. However, today's contemporary residential group care facilities for children are treatment based, meaning that they are made available to some children and youth who need structure and stabilization in a nonfamily group setting. In recent years and for a variety of reasons—including lower cost and better therapeutic outcomes—residential group treatment services have given way to family-centered outpatient and family foster care. Social workers in group residential centers engage in treatment planning and implementation as well as aftercare planning and activities.

- *Independent living services.* An appreciable number of adolescents, many of whom are teenagers "aging out" of family foster care services (i.e., reaching the age of 18), are in need of independent living services. Social workers help these teenagers become independent by providing a range of services and promoting skills and abilities needed in adulthood. Support is often provided through collaborative efforts among foster parents, biological parents, and various service providers. Independent living services include transitional supervised living, group housing, scholarships, employment counseling, relationship building (with family members and friends), and connecting with needed resources. A special interest consideration is helping these older children develop and maintain constructive relationships with biological and foster family members.

- *Intensive treatment.* Social workers perform a variety of intervention services (specific types of therapy and counseling) that are classified as **intensive treatment**. Intensive treatment usually requires an appreciable time commitment and many resources during a condensed time; so social workers who operate in this specialty generally have smaller caseloads. Investing in intensive treatment with clients during crucial times in their lives is often more economical and effective than residential treatment.

Social Policy and Legislation Supporting Child and Family Services

In the United States, services to children and families are typically mandated and shaped by myriad state and federal policies and laws. Funding for children and family services is equally complex and relies on a combination of federal, state, and county or city monies, as well as insurance reimbursements and privately paid fees. To complicate matters, legislators are known to pass laws requiring children and family services without providing the necessary resources. Under these circumstances, it is understandable that the availability of quality services and programs for children and families can differ appreciably across state, county, and municipal boundaries.

Historically, the federal government has passed a number of laws to promote child and family welfare (see Exhibit 6.2).

Source: ©iStockphoto.com/Steve Debenpo

⌃ Independent Living Services offer teens opportunities to learn how to support themselves.

For example, the National School Lunch Program, Farm Bill, Supplemental Social Insurance, and Personal Responsibility and Work Opportunity Reconciliation Act established sweeping programs providing needy children and families with food and financial and health care benefits.

Other legislation listed in Exhibit 6.2 has had a narrower focus, such as the Education of All Handicapped Children Act and the Runaway, Homeless, and Missing Children Protection Act. Without these specialized intervention programs, however, vulnerable youth and their caregivers would suffer considerable deprivation and struggle with everyday needs.

An appreciable amount of time and effort is required to advocate for the passage of federal and state laws promoting child and family welfare. Countless groups and organizations, and hours of persuasion, were required to bring these laws to fruition. Yet gaps in service delivery for effective intervention and treatment of children continue to exist in the United States—for example, affordable day care and early intervention services to help prevent removal of children from their families (Pecora, Whittaker, Maluccio, Barth, & DePanfilis, 2009). Children have suffered as a result of underfunding, and the federal funds that are provided tend to be allocated to placement services instead of being allowed to flow to the family support services preferred by many states (Pecora et al., 2009). The lack of coherent funding for early intervention and family support services seems counterproductive to many social workers who are attempting to preserve families and keep children living at home.

EXHIBIT 6.2   Noteworthy Legislation Concerning Child and Family Welfare

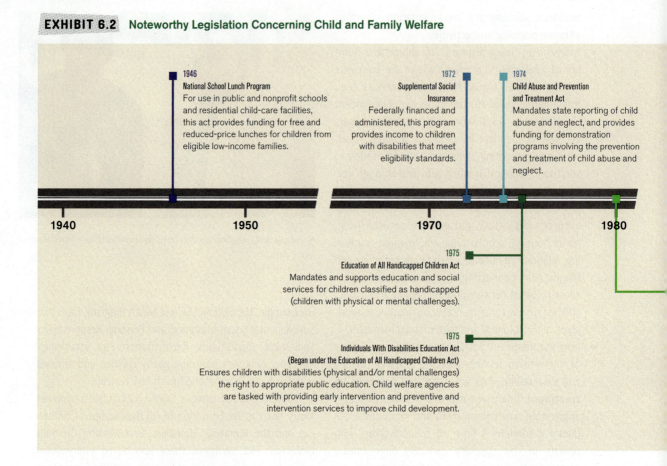

1946
National School Lunch Program
For use in public and nonprofit schools and residential child-care facilities, this act provides funding for free and reduced-price lunches for children from eligible low-income families.

1972
Supplemental Social Insurance
Federally financed and administered, this program provides income to children with disabilities that meet eligibility standards.

1974
Child Abuse and Prevention and Treatment Act
Mandates state reporting of child abuse and neglect, and provides funding for demonstration programs involving the prevention and treatment of child abuse and neglect.

1940   1950   1970   1980

1975
Education of All Handicapped Children Act
Mandates and supports education and social services for children classified as handicapped (children with physical or mental challenges).

1975
Individuals With Disabilities Education Act
(Began under the Education of All Handicapped Children Act)
Ensures children with disabilities (physical and/or mental challenges) the right to appropriate public education. Child welfare agencies are tasked with providing early intervention and preventive and intervention services to improve child development.

Public Attitudes Toward Services for Children and Families

Public support for child and family services is frequently mixed. It depends on people's belief systems and is frequently not informed by the perspective of social workers and their clients. For example, social workers often hear neighbors and friends complain about paying too much in taxes for services to children and families when they should be providing for themselves. Friends and family members can erroneously and naively suggest that problems with children do not exist with **traditional families**, when children are reared by two married, heterosexual parents. Others may acknowledge the need for social welfare but believe that recipients should be limited to only those experiencing the direst of circumstances, believing the priority should be encouraging older youth to get married before having children and for parents to work.

Two distinct viewpoints concerning social welfare programs and services can be articulated:

• **Institutional or primary view of social welfare:** Humans are inherently good but are confronted with challenging needs (e.g., employment, health care, housing) and circumstances (e.g., unemployment, illness, divorce, loss of a loved one). Social and economic conditions such as unemployment, recession, and prohibitive costs for health care may also contribute to human need. Communities and society as a whole have a responsibility to help people by providing economic and social support services.

• **Residual or secondary view of social welfare**: People, including the poor and downtrodden, should be responsible for their own lot in life and not expect government intervention. Social welfare programs should be limited to helping people only in the direst situations and should provide only a safety net—that is, those services that spare people from perishing. Social safety nets are not designed to assist people to overcome or move beyond their problems.

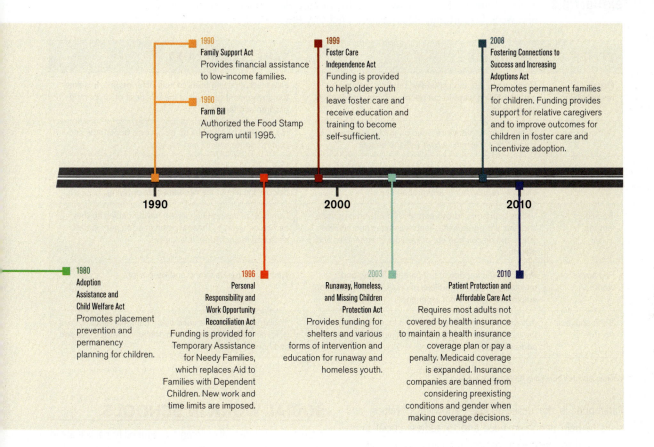

1980
Adoption
Assistance and
Child Welfare Act
Promotes placement
prevention and
permanency
planning for children.

1990
Family Support Act
Provides financial assistance
to low-income families.

1990
Farm Bill
Authorized the Food Stamp
Program until 1995.

1996
Personal
Responsibility and
Work Opportunity
Reconciliation Act
Funding is provided for
Temporary Assistance
for Needy Families,
which replaces Aid to
Families with Dependent
Children. New work and
time limits are imposed.

1999
Foster Care
Independence Act
Funding is provided
to help older youth
leave foster care and
receive education and
training to become
self-sufficient.

2003
Runaway, Homeless,
and Missing Children
Protection Act
Provides funding for
shelters and various
forms of intervention and
education for runaway and
homeless youth.

2008
Fostering Connections to
Success and Increasing
Adoptions Act
Promotes permanent families
for children. Funding provides
support for relative caregivers
and to improve outcomes for
children in foster care and
incentivize adoption.

2010
Patient Protection and
Affordable Care Act
Requires most adults not
covered by health insurance
to maintain a health insurance
coverage plan or pay a
penalty. Medicaid coverage
is expanded. Insurance
companies are banned from
considering preexisting
conditions and gender when
making coverage decisions.

As a prospective social work student, it may be hard for you to understand the residual view of social welfare. You may be interested, therefore, in the literature describing the belief systems behind some people's disapproval of the Personal Responsibility and Work Opportunity Reconciliation Act, federal legislation passed in 1996 (Long, 2000). Those beliefs are explained in Exhibit 6.3. Although belief systems for both individuals and groups change over time, many of these beliefs persist and continue to prevent improvements in programs and services for families and children.

TIME TO THINK

Do some of the beliefs and opinions recorded here reflect the sentiment of your friends and acquaintances, or perhaps your own sentiment? How do you imagine children and families struggling to meet basic needs would react to these opinions?

Social Workers' Attitudes Toward Child and Family Services

Social workers strive to be objective and use scientific inquiry and research to guide their views concerning child and family legislation and programs. Social workers are particularly interested in the effectiveness of child welfare laws and service delivery systems in the hope that the services and programs will permanently enhance and enrich the lives of children and families. Thus, when clients use school lunch programs, food stamps, Medicaid, and Temporary Assistance for Needy Families but are barely able to survive and unable to progress beyond their current living circumstances, social workers can share with the clients' frustrations. However, social workers realize that service provisions are limited and the ability of clients to move forward with their lives is influenced and limited by a number of factors, including upbringing, life experiences, personal motivations, social pressures, and the political environment (Kilty & Meenaghan, 1995).

Social workers use the National Association of Social Workers (NASW) *Code of Ethics* to ground their practice.

EXHIBIT 6.3   Beliefs Shaping Negative Attitudes Toward the Personal Responsibility
and Work Opportunity Reconciliation Act of 1996

BELIEF	DEFINITION	SAMPLE COMPLAINT
Fiscal responsibility	Emphasizes reducing spending on social programs and identifying ways to cut people off from government assistance	I am tired of paying taxes to help other people. It is time the government gets out of the business of supporting children and families.
Self-sufficiency	Seeks ways to reduce reliance on public assistance in favor of doing for one's own self and benefit	He needs to pull himself up by his own bootstraps and learn to do for himself and his kids.
Less eligible	Discourages individuals and families from participating in social welfare programs through the creation of complex eligibility requirements and procedures	Not everyone should be able to receive benefits and aid. We need to make it difficult to receive assistance and discourage all but the neediest from applying.
Traditional families	Values marriage and two-parent child-raising practices, and social programs that keep marriages and families intact and discourage out-of-wedlock pregnancies and parenting	I am tired of supporting women having babies so they can be on welfare. These women need to get married and raise their children in a family.
Primacy of work	Promotes the importance of parents' finding and maintaining work, regardless of one's health, education, employability, and work experience	That parent needs to find and keep a job.
State and local control	Advances the idea that states and local communities, not the federal government, should define and find ways to address needs	If children and families need help, then their state or local government is best situated to determine what is needed and how to respond.

Source: Adapted from Long (2000, pp. 63–64).

Paramount is the desire to use "knowledge, values, and skills to help people in need and to address social problems" and to "treat each person in a caring and respectful fashion, mindful of individual differences and cultural and ethnic diversity" (NASW, 2008, "Ethical Principles"). With the NASW *Code of Ethics* as a moral compass, social workers stay client centered and resist imposing or reinforcing counterproductive belief systems concerning children and families. A large part of the social work belief system is a commitment to client self-determination and the inherent dignity and worth of each person and each family.

TIME TO THINK

It is difficult for people, including helping professionals, to imagine themselves in a client's situation. Do you know any children who are at risk of removal from their homes? What kinds of services are available to them or have been implemented? Would it be difficult and stigmatizing for children and family members to partake of these services?

SOCIAL WORK IN SCHOOLS

In the United States, all children are required to participate in education. Thus, schools have been a long-standing venue for identifying and addressing the needs of impoverished, neglected, and abused children. **School social workers** emerged in U.S. schools in eastern cities (e.g., New York and Boston) toward the beginning of the 20th century, both to address student needs and to promote quality educational experiences. From the very beginning, school social workers were challenged with issues of racism, sexism, and social class (Joseph, Slovak, & Broussard, 2010), and many of those issues persist in contemporary school systems. Of particular note are the ways racial and ethnic discrimination has degraded educational opportunity for minority populations (Joseph et al., 2010).

The specific role of the school social worker varies in each school and organizational setting. School social workers practice in both primary and secondary school systems. They work with teachers, administrators, school counselors, community officials, agencies, and parents and children. A primary task is to promote and advocate for quality educational programs, outcomes, and experiences, and the well-being of students. Social workers assess the needs of children and participate in recommending and securing services for schoolchildren and their families (Constable, 2009).

It is understood that, for students to function effectively at school, it is important to address their needs at home (e.g., their physical and mental health, family stability, safety, nutrition, and sleep) and at school (including instruction, physical setting, curriculum, teacher–student relationships, and student relations). School social workers find themselves employed in an organizational environment advocating for interventions, programs, services, and organizational change that support the best interests of their primary client population—the students. In addition to counseling students, school social workers intervene with family members, school officials, lawmakers, and community leaders to identify ways to enrich social conditions and circumstances for student success.

With regard to professional qualifications, school social work has become an increasingly specialized area of practice in the United States. National and state policy has promoted the credentialing of professionals in school settings, which has led in turn to certification, licensure, and advanced training for school social workers (Constable & Alvarez, 2006).

CHALLENGES FACING SCHOOL SOCIAL WORKERS

School social workers become involved with students as a result of a variety of problems and behavioral manifestations, such as acting out in the classroom (verbally and physically), truancy, poor grades, interpersonal conflicts, a lack of personal hygiene, health issues (e.g., headaches, frequent illnesses), and inappropriate appearance (e.g., unkempt hair, dirty clothes).

Many factors are salient to problems with student performance and behavior. It is not unusual for school principals and teachers to point out student responsibility as well as the influence of family members and the home environment on school performance. Conversely, students and parents often allude to the importance of teachers, peers, and curricular matters in relation to student behavior. Frequently, students' problems are complex and involve many factors—not easily pinned on a single source.

Violence and Bullying

In the United States, children are exposed to multiple forms of violence. Modern media and entertainment expose children to guns, shootings, killing, interpersonal violence, verbal abuse,

aggressive behaviors, and bullying. Children witness violence at home, between adults and when adults inflict violence on children. In some communities, exposure to violence—punching, fighting, shootings, threat of physical harm, robbery, muggings, and use of weapons—is common and readily visible to children. Violent acts in schools include bullying, punching, fighting, homicides, and suicides.

Bullying is a form of aggression against others that is prevalent in elementary and middle schools. It involves physical, verbal, or psychological attacks, including harassment and intimidation, against weaker children or children who cannot defend themselves (Laursen, 2011, p. 4). Bullying can take the form of group bullying, racial bullying, cyberbullying, or gay bullying—among others.

In the United States up to 41% of students have been involved in bullying at school, either as a victim (23%), bully (8%), or both bully and victim (9%) (Bradshaw, Sawyer, & O'Brennan, 2007). However, much of bullying behavior goes unreported.

Psychologically, research indicates that

> bully/victims were most likely to display internalizing symptoms, problems in peer relationships, and have poorer perceptions of the school environment. Both frequent bullies and bully/victims displayed aggressive-impulsive behavior and endorsed retaliatory attitudes. High-school students frequently involved in bullying tended to display the greatest risk for internalizing problems, but less risk for aggressive impulsivity. (O'Brennan, Bradshaw, & Sawyer, 2009, p. 100)

Social workers need to remember that student bullying takes place in a social context. To effectively prevent and intervene with bullying, the individuals involved and the social context in which bullying occurs must both be addressed (Bradshaw & Johnson, 2011; Laursen, 2011). A healthy learning environment must include caring relationships and a safe and secure educational setting. Seven habits for professionals who are trying to construct caring relationships with young people when addressing bullying, are: be respectful, demonstrate empathy, be credible, actively listen, affirm positive behaviors, act as a positive role model concerning accountability, and take time to place youth as a priority (Laursen, 2011, p. 9).

Poor and Homeless Students

Poverty and homelessness constitute challenging barriers confronting school social workers. Whether poor and

Source: ©iStockphoto.com/Plougmann

▲ Teen girls often feel the consequences of pregnancy more than the father.

homeless as a result of unemployment, underemployment, or not being employable, poor and homeless families are highly transient, frequently changing home addresses and school systems. Although the homeless often find temporary housing in shelters, they are vulnerable and can easily find themselves out on the street at any time. Mental health and substance issues can also be contributing factors to instability. At a very basic level, poor and homeless children often arrive at school hungry and sleepy. These students are at considerable risk of poor school attendance and performance.

Parents and children also experience daily risk and considerable stress when everyday necessities and a dwelling become questionable. As a consequence, children adopt maladaptive behaviors, experience social and cognitive setbacks, and are prone to poor grades and high dropout rates (Groton, Teasley, & Canfield, 2013, p. 38). These are some of the reasons why school social workers and social work interventions focusing on the student's overall situation (family, teachers,

living circumstances, school policies, community safety) are vital to student success.

An important piece of national legislation focusing on the needs of homeless children and families is the **McKinney-Vento Homeless Assistance Act**. The act's mandates for homeless students include the following (Groton et al., 2013, p. 39):

- Streamlining enrollment procedures for homeless children so they can start school in a new place without all their previous school records, documentation of residency, and immunization records
- Employing homeless liaisons to advocate for the rights of homeless students
- Subsidizing homeless students' full participation in school events

Students With Physical and Mental Challenges

Knowing that language shapes social and personal realities and images, social workers are cautious and intentional with the use of words and language. In social work practice, care is taken not to label children with physical and mental challenges as being "disabled" or having a "handicap." Instead, social workers try to be positive and focus on strengths when referring to and working with children who have a physical or mental challenge.

Children with physical challenges face unique hurdles in schools, including limits on their participation in activities, being made to feel different through the use of accommodations, being stereotyped, and being bullied. School children with physical challenges have a right to be treated fairly, given their individual strengths and needs. Optimally, fairness is achieved when students and their parents participate in school decision-making processes that promote an appropriate and beneficial educational experience.

Children with mental challenges constitute a major public health issue. **Childhood mental disorder (CMD)** is a general term that includes all mental disorders that begin and can be diagnosed in childhood, such as Asperger's syndrome and developmental delays. CMDs are often identified during the school years and in conjunction with professionals in school systems. Estimates suggest that between 13% and 20% of children in the United States experience a CMD and that nearly $247 billion is spent each year on CMDs (National Research Council and Institute of Medicine, 2009).

CURRENT TRENDS

Best Buddies International

CHILDREN and adults benefit when they are surrounded by caring, loving, and supportive people, and provided with well-designed services. Best Buddies International is a global volunteer movement promoting opportunities and healthy relationships for people with intellectual and developmental challenges. Volunteers provide friendship, employment, and leadership opportunities for members of this population group. Best Buddies International programs foster one-to-one friendships between adults and between students. For additional information about Best Buddies International, visit the organization's website (www.bestbuddies.org).

To an extent, Best Buddies International is a worldwide adult program similar to local Big Brother and Big Sister programs—where boys are matched with positive male role models and girls are paired with positive female role models.

These types of programs offer people social–emotional support, constructive relationships, and opportunities for developing interpersonal skills with others. Social workers have traditionally been employed in these venues and often have served in leadership roles. When working with adults with challenges and child and adolescent populations, social workers often refer parents and clients to these types of organizations.

What is your initial reaction to organizations such as Best Buddies International that heavily rely on volunteers? Consider the importance of professional oversight and developing a sound application and background check system for volunteers. Would you ever become a Best Buddy—why or why not? Discuss with classmates and friends the level of commitment required to serve as a volunteer with such programs.

A major law advancing the interest of students with physical and mental challenges is the **Individuals with Disabilities Education Improvement Act**, reauthorized in 2004. This act promotes the rights of challenged students in a number of realms, including the following (Massat, Essex, Hare, & Rome, 2009, pp. 124–125):

- Using peer-reviewed research and scientifically based behavioral and instructional techniques for physically and mentally challenged students
- Expanding the definition of parent to include foster parents and nonparent caregivers
- Emphasizing a student's right to a free public education in the "least restrictive environment," in conjunction with a student's **Individualized Education Program**
- Bolstering the educational expectations and requirements of teachers and other educational staff

Teen Pregnancy

Teen pregnancy, sometimes referred to as "children having children," is frequently cited by politicians, social scientists,

and social service professionals as one of the nation's most serious social problems. Historically, people have objected to teen pregnancy on a values-oriented, moral basis involving a lack of responsibility and indulgence in premarital or casual sex. However, for many adolescent students, the everyday functional drawbacks of teen pregnancy and parenthood are as devastating as or more devastating than moral judgments.

Although teen pregnancy involves both a male and an adolescent female, the consequences of pregnancy for teenage girls are often far greater than for their male counterparts. Fathers may deny or contest paternity, or they may take responsibility for fathering and assist in caring and providing for their children. But if the father is also a teenager and a student, he may have very limited knowledge and resources for effective parenting. And it is often very difficult to legally mandate and enforce paternal responsibilities for fathers who have no employment or other resources.

For teen mothers, the pregnancy is a medical issue. Prenatal care also interrupts school attendance and extracurricular participation. Motherhood requires attention to child care, is a barrier to gaining experience and tenure in the labor force, and requires a reexamination of living circumstances. Reliance on parents, siblings, and extended family members for housing, food, clothing, and child care is common. But even with this help, teen mothers may not be able to continue in school.

School social workers and agency-based social workers assist teenagers and their families with transitions during this difficult time. They may explore with teen mothers enrolling in public assistance, such as Temporary Assistance for Needy Families and Medicaid, to provide minimal income and address medical needs. In addition to helping teen mothers with immediate needs for nutrition, clothing, furniture, shelter, and child care, social workers also focus mothers' attention on long-term issues involving continued education, father involvement, child support, transportation, affordable and safe housing, and employment.

IMPROVEMENTS IN EDUCATION TO HELP PARENTS AND CHILDREN

In the United States, public school systems are highly dependent on state and local funding for educational programming and services. This decentralized approach to supporting education lends itself to inequities, particularly on the basis of socioeconomic status. Students living in affluent areas are able to attend highly sought-after primary and secondary schools. Students living in economically disadvantaged areas, disproportionately from racial and ethnic minorities, are relegated to struggling school systems. Those school systems typically fall short in preparing students to work in a global economy (Heiner, 2013). Middle-class and rich kids, in contrast, attend better schools that help them prepare for better jobs. From this perspective, schools function to maintain class membership and distinctions.

Any real estate agent will tell you that one of the very first questions buyers will ask when looking for a desirable neighborhood is, "Where are the best public schools?" Even if the buyer does not have or expect to have children, purchasing in an area with an excellent school system protects property and resale values. Yet many Americans, especially the poor and disenfranchised, can't afford to live where they would like their children to attend school.

To improve education, social workers not only promote quality academic experiences inside schools but also advocate for laws, policies, funding, and programs to help ensure that students receive a quality education regardless of school location. The commitment people make when entering social work as a profession is both to help people in need and to address the social problems contributing to their difficulties. Advocating for quality educational systems and reducing inequities in education are excellent examples of how social workers can work toward larger-scale changes.

DIVERSITY AND FAMILY AND CHILD WELFARE

People often conceptualize diversity and associated types of oppression in terms of a form of diversity familiar to themselves. For example, teenagers often dream about what they would do if only they were old enough to vote, own property, drink alcohol, marry, and make legal decisions for themselves. They are focused on age discrimination. However, understanding how different forms of diversity impact individuals, groups, communities, and societies is vital in social work practice. Let's stretch our thinking beyond any personal form of diversity to examine how selected forms of diversity relate to child and family welfare and services.

- *Age.* Developmentally, young children are forming their personalities and learning about what is right and wrong. Children prosper through the presence of a stable family and positive adult and parental role models. Young children are especially vulnerable and dependent on family members for affection and basic needs, including food, shelter, clothes, medical attention, and nutrition. But they have limited rights and ability to advocate for themselves, especially when compared with parents and school officials.

- *Class.* Children living in economically challenged circumstances struggle with obtaining a safe living environment, quality child care or schooling, proper nutrition, suitable clothing, reliable transportation, and other basics. As for their families, unemployment, underemployment, and homelessness are common disruptive factors. Although many of the problems facing children and families transcend their socioeconomic status, having access to resources through social service agencies and the ability to secure needed help ameliorates the disadvantages of lower-class living.

- *Ethnicity.* Across the United States, many families identify themselves by ethnicity and enjoy strong bonds based on common ancestry, homeland, language, religion, and dialect. Members of a particular ethnic group also share values and expectations about individual behavior.

SOCIAL WORK IN ACTION

Pamela Facilitates Adoption for Gay and Lesbian Parents

PAMELA HOWARD is a BSW-level social worker employed at a large, urban children's advocacy center (CAC). She works in adoption services, especially for gay and lesbian parents. Primarily as a result of her practice experience, Pamela has an enriched sense of how members of lesbian and gay families can be stigmatized. She knows that adoptive gay and lesbian parents worry about their ability to gain legal custody and about their risk of losing it. There is a general lack of recognition of their parenting abilities, responsibilities, and rights.

In Pamela's state, gays and lesbians are allowed to form civil unions but not to marry. The legal ramifications for adoption by unmarried gay and lesbian couples are even greater than for married gay and lesbian couples. Many of Pamela's clients are concerned about their ability to adopt in the first place, as well as the limitations of their status in regard to custody, health care benefits, and educational rights and opportunities for their adopted children.

The CAC where Pamela works has an interdisciplinary and interprofessional orientation. Pamela has been able to work closely with a team of social workers, nurses, counselors, and other professionals to provide educational and supportive services related to the legal system, health care insurance, employers, and schools. One of Pamela's favorite colleagues at the CAC is an attorney, who has been a wealth of information for gay and lesbian adoptive parents. As a result of Pamela's interaction with this attorney, she is now entertaining the possibility of continuing her professional education in a program where she could simultaneously earn an MSW and a law degree.

Take some time to contemplate the host of professions (attorney, psychologist, public health official, nurse, counselor, and so on) that interface with social work and how each profession differs. Which professions focus on interpersonal, one-on-one intervention with children and families? Which professions focus on advocacy, policy development, and system-level change? Which types of helping appeal to you?

Some ethnic groups believe in individual responsibility and reliance on help from within the ethnic group; they tend to rebuff helping professionals and social service programs. Members of other ethnic groups recognize the value of child and welfare services but prefer to receive help from organizations and professionals aligned with their cultural heritage. As an example of how cultural values can shape attitudes about issues such as work and social welfare, many Latinos possess a strong work ethic but often lack education and job skills to secure nonmenial employment. As a consequence, Latino population groups can struggle with the idea that people with lower-wage employment can simply work their way out of poverty (Acevedo, 2005).

- *Race.* Despite decades of advocacy for desegregation, school systems in the United States remain segregated on the basis of race and social–economic status. Racial desegregation laws and U.S. Supreme Court decisions from the 1960s mandated the end of racially segregated schools, but the phenomenon of **white flight** has rendered those decisions moot in many U.S. cities. In the early years of desegregation, Caucasian families moved from the city to the suburbs to escape desegregated schools and enrolled their children in better-resourced public or private schools. Minority families, disproportionately poor, came to dominate urban neighborhoods. For example, many African American families live in poorer urban neighborhoods and consequently must send their children to less-desirable public schools. The inability for all students to attend schools characterized by quality instruction, extracurricular activities, and integrative support with family members is one form of structural discrimination and institutional racism that persists in the United States.

- *Gender.* In the United States, women continue to be commonly viewed as the primary caretakers of children.

Source: ©iStockphoto.com/elkor

▲ Families may represent several types of diversity.

When marital discord or family disruption takes place, mothers often assume custodial responsibilities for the children. Although state laws set standards for parental financial responsibilities and visitation with children, enforcement of legal obligations can be difficult. For example, it is not unusual for the noncustodial parent, often the father, to leave the state, be delinquent on child support, and seek undocumented forms of income. Also, women have been threatened by the fathers of their children not to pursue paternity or court-ordered child support. Women face unique and demanding situations, and they rely on child and family services for support in ways that often differ from those of their male counterparts.

- *Sexual orientation.* Marital and parental rights for gays and lesbians are currently grounded in state law and amidst change. In part, this is a social justice issue involving the ability of parents and children to be treated the same regardless of the parents' sexual orientation. However, this kind of legal limbo leaves many gay and lesbian parents with uncertainty and doubt. For example, what are the ramifications for parental and family rights if the family has to move from one state that protects their rights to another state that does not? If the parents divorce, separate, or split up, how do their parental rights differ from those of their heterosexual counterparts? With regard to everyday rules and practices, will school officials, employers, and health care providers treat gay and lesbian parents—and their children—with the same respect and dignity as they do heterosexual families?

- *Intersections of diversity.* It is not unusual for parents and family members to represent several types of diversity. For example, teenage mothers with little education, financial resources, or experience in the labor force are particularly vulnerable to poverty and a lack of economic opportunity. The cost of day care for a single, young mother is prohibitive, particularly when she may be qualified only for low-paying employment with irregular or unusual working hours. Young mothers from racial and ethnic minorities face the additional risk that prospective employers might discriminate on the basis of not only age but also race or ethnicity.

ADVOCACY ON BEHALF OF FAMILIES AND CHILDREN

Federal interest in children arrived on the heels of a variety of social reform initiatives of the late 1960s and can be traced to the presidency of Richard M. Nixon. In response to recommendations from the Joint Commission on Mental Health of Children and the 1970 White House Conference on Children, a National Center on Child Advocacy was established (McGowan, 1978). However, due to limited resources, shifting federal priorities, and mounting interest in the creation of a new National Center on Child Abuse, the National Center on Child Advocacy was never fully realized.

During the 1970s, recognition of the need for child advocacy led to strengthening of the services and programs serving children and families. The child welfare advocacy movement advanced the following major themes (McGowan, 1978, p. 277):

- Child development is influenced by interaction with families and transactions with other social systems (e.g., schools, child care providers, courts, medical providers, and court systems).
- Society has a responsibility for and obligation to children.
- Child and family services are a matter of right and entitlement.
- Children have rights in relationship to the social systems affecting them.

As with many social problems and issues, recognition of need and responsibility at the institutional, systemic level does not necessarily or immediately translate into social change or large-scale dedication of resources. The conceptual shift from rescuing and saving children from unfit parents to the development of comprehensive, integrated child and family services that support the healthy physical and emotional development of children and families has been decades in the making.

CURRENT TRENDS IN ADVOCACY FOR CHILD AND FAMILY SERVICES

The contemporary social worker is moving away from viewing advocacy for children and families as mainly a social work responsibility and toward viewing it in terms of interdisciplinary collaboration. In recent years, **children's advocacy centers (CACs)** have emerged. CACs typically provide a broad range of services for children and families and are known for their interdisciplinary and child-focused approaches. CACs often employ professionals from law enforcement, social services, and mental health, offering a unified, centralized agency for providing services and programming for children and their families (Wolfteich & Loggins, 2007, p. 334).

It appears that CACs can improve investigations of child abuse (Wolfteich & Loggins, 2007). However, the effectiveness of CACs for addressing other child and family needs and advocating for needed services remains unclear, especially in the realms of early intervention and child maltreatment. People who provide services to children and families are hoping that interagency collaboration and interdisciplinary teams, as employed in CACs, will broaden the reach and strength of a variety of advocacy initiatives.

DYNAMIC ADVOCACY AND FAMILY AND CHILD WELFARE

When advocacy involves children, who have limited rights, it continues to be relevant and important for social workers to advocate with in not simply for their clients. For social workers involved and child and family services, the concept of "best interest of the child" is a primary consideration. At the most basic level, children's needs for healthy development and maturation are the priority. But beyond that, the needs of children are often complex, multidimensional, and immersed in family problems and needs.

Determining the best interest of the child can be challenging for other reasons as well. Advocacy with children is centered on the question, "What do you want?" (Hoefer, 2012). However, children express their desires and needs through words, action, and inaction. Their cries for help can take a number of forms (e.g., acting out, bed-wetting, withdrawal, pleading or frightened facial expressions, clinginess, physical distance). Because the actions of children are open to interpretation, social workers must take care to ensure that they consider the individual before them and not make assumptions based on stereotypes about children (Boylan & Dalrymple, 2011, p. 24).

Economic and Social Justice

What constitutes just services and a just life for children? All children deserve the potential for health, well-being, and a good quality of life, as well as the ability to mature and develop in culturally appropriate ways. Children, especially young children, struggle intensely with their limited ability to exert power and impact decisions affecting their lives. Much of the history of child welfare has focused on saving children from maltreatment and abusive and neglectful circumstances, not empowering children to effect change. Children have been seen as dependents, without adult rights, and their perspectives have not typically been valued in policy and legislative development.

Social workers have challenged these premises and supported child advocacy initiatives in a number of realms. Organizationally, **guardian ad litem** programs appoint individuals to speak and advocate on behalf of children in court systems. Similarly, school social workers advocate for changes in policies, programs, and personnel in educational systems to benefit students.

Social workers can solicit the meaningful participation of children in decision making and educational processes in a number of ways:

- Conducting interviews and surveys designed to gain children's insight into issues, problems, and solutions
- Joining a child advisory or advocacy council
- Speaking at public forums and professional workshops about the needs and interests of children
- Organizing clubs to support children in need and at risk, and disseminating information
- Creating art, films, and music to express children's needs or working with the children themselves to produce such art, films, and music

Supportive Environment

The plight of many children and families is grounded in social–economic circumstances and conditions. In the United

States, the affordability of rent or the ability to make a house payment determines where you live. In turn, the location of your dwelling impacts your access to extended family members, employment, public transportation, health care, education, day care, social services, shopping, and recreation.

Exposure to crime and pollution are also based on place of residency. Social workers and clients partner with government and law enforcement officials and local businesses to advocate for community safety watches and groups, as well as entities dedicated to effective air, water, and waste-control systems. People living and working in impoverished neighborhoods share common interests and bonds to reduce crime and maintain a healthy and safe environment.

Human Needs and Rights

Through their education and training in the area of human behavior and the social environment, social workers acquire the theoretical foundations and knowledge they need to analyze human development from birth through childhood, adolescence, adulthood, and older age. This foundation is necessary for social workers to understand and facilitate both smaller, micro-oriented changes and large-scale, macro-oriented changes throughout various stages of human development.

When advocating for change with specific populations, social workers must be keenly abreast of the unique needs, limitations, and rights associated with various age groups. For example, in the case of early-childhood intensive treatment programs, it is unrealistic to believe that young children can verbalize and specifically ask for certain types of services. Children deserve the right to successful childhood development, and it is the social worker's professional and ethical responsibility to advocate for and pursue social change for one of society's most vulnerable population groups.

Political Access

Support for children and family services, as with many forms of social services, is a political issue based on dominant belief systems. For example, some politicians oppose social programs and services in an effort to demonstrate **fiscal responsibility**, reduce government intervention in the lives of people, and support traditional families and family self-sufficiency. Other politicians recognize the vulnerabilities and complexities associated with children and families in a complex and changing society. They often couch their

support for the funding of programs and services for children and families in terms of promoting compassion for and protection of children and strengthening the family unit, regardless of the family structure. It should be noted that support for children and family services cuts across party affiliation.

Provision of services for children and families is dependent on funding and resources. One way social workers may advocate for more funding and resources is by becoming more involved in the political process—whether campaigning for politicians, social service funding, levies, or legislation to protect children. In the process, social workers may align themselves with political figures, parties, and associations to educate people about and promote effective services and programs for children and families. Social workers have also been elected to political offices in local and state government as well as the U.S. Senate and House of Representatives, where they can become directly involved in crafting policies favorable to children and families.

YOUR CAREER IN FAMILY AND CHILD WELFARE

When working with children and families, social workers may be protective service workers, information and referral specialists, therapists, or program professionals. In each of these roles, social workers collect information and rely on data to inform best practices. Research skills are involved in a number of other social work roles as well:

- *Program evaluators* use their research abilities to provide information to help make decisions about the aspects of service programs that work best for children and families, and the ones that need to be adjusted.
- *Advocates* and *educators* collect and use data to educate the public, politicians, administrators, and other decision makers concerning the experiences and problems of children and families.
- *Community organizers* collect information and gather and rally consumers of services, professionals, and community members to promote changes in policies, practices, and laws to address the needs of children and families.

Each of these roles depends on the ability to use qualitative and quantitative research skills to collect and analyze information:

- **Qualitative research** highlights data that are descriptive in nature and not quantified into numbers. Data are gathered through methods such as case studies, focus groups, observation, interviews, and archival research. Generally, qualitative research focuses on small groups of people to understand a phenomenon or social unit in depth.
- **Quantitative research** involves collecting from a larger group of people data about social behaviors, phenomena, programs, and social units. Generally, it often relies on surveys and checklists, and it generates data that are converted into numbers and analyzed statistically.

TIME TO THINK

Think about a social work topic that is of particular interest to you. What kind of research, qualitative or quantitative, might be the most effective way of studying that issue?

How might you use qualitative and quantitative research in fields such as public administration, community relations, politics, management, or other social work–related careers?

SUMMARY

"There is no trust more sacred than the one the world holds with children. There is no duty more important than ensuring that their rights are respected, that their welfare is protected, that their lives are free from fear and want and that they can grow up in peace."

−Kofi Annan

The people of the United States are in the midst of a debate about what constitutes marriage and a family. Simply consider the debate about the rights of gays and lesbians to marry and assume legal responsibilities for each other and their children. Regardless of the outcome of these debates, the U.S. family has changed, and social workers practice with families in need, no matter their composition or circumstances. Child and family services should be viewed as a major element for helping maintain a social fabric that has always heavily relied on individuals committed to family and mutual support.

Social workers play an important role in assisting couples, parents, and children adapt to contemporary demands concerning work, child rearing, relationship building, and self-fulfillment. Social workers also advocate for social legislation, policies, and social welfare programs to address the rights and needs of children and family members. In practice, social workers both assist with the day-to-day trials and tribulations of family life and identify ways to protect and advance the rights of children and families.

TOP 10 KEY CONCEPTS

child maltreatment
child protective services
child welfare
domestic violence
extended family

family
kinship
nuclear family
qualitative research
quantitative research

DISCUSSION QUESTIONS

1. For social workers, what constitutes a family in the United States today? How does that definition align with your personal values and beliefs? How has the definition of family changed over the past four decades?

2. What attributes are needed to be a social worker in child protective services and to deal with instances of child abuse and neglect?

3. Why do parents have more rights than children do? Is this simply a matter of convention and tradition? Why or why not? Are there times when the rights of parents should supersede the rights of children? If so, when and how? Why are parents required to participate in intervention programs for the benefit of their children? To what degree is this requirement political? To what degree is it practical?

4. Why is advocacy such an important responsibility for social workers engaged in child and family services?

EXERCISES

1. Given the multiple definitions of family in contemporary society, determine whether gay and lesbian parents should have comparable rights to heterosexual parents. Base your conclusions on statistics from your state or locale describing the outcomes for children raised by same-sex parents, single parents, grandparents as parents, foster parents, and residential care for children.

2. On the Internet, identify a child welfare BSW or MSW program near you. How appealing is the program? Does the program sponsor an open house or any opportunities to talk with or contact the program coordinator, students, or recent graduates?

3. In a private setting with friends or family members, broach the topic of government spending for services and programs to protect children. Identify belief systems that support their opinions. Are their views surprising to you? What are the probable sources of their belief systems and thoughts?

4. Consider volunteering at a residential program for children. Research the type of commitment you would be making. Does it involve a criminal background check, references, and drug screening? Ascertain if and how services for families and parents are integrated with the residential program.

5. Research your local child protective services agency. Who provides and advocates for such services? For example, does your local child protective services agency hire licensed helping professionals (social workers and counselors), or are these positions filled by nonprofessionals? If the latter, in what areas of providing and advocating for services to children and families do you think the nonprofessionals would need to improve their skills?

6. Visit a family court and determine who appears to be looking out for the best interests of children. Is a guardian ad litem present? How are the views and interests of parents placed before the court?

ONLINE RESOURCES

- Child Advocates, Inc. (www.childadvocates .org/?gclid=CK-a07XGybECFUgDQAodWgsAsg): Describes how court-appointed volunteers advocate for children and child protection
- The Child Welfare League of America (www.cwla.org): Provides a description of this coalition of private and public agencies that serves vulnerable children and families through a variety of publications and services, including advocacy
- eHow money website (www.ehow.com/how_4685372_ becoming-child-protection-social-worker.html): Examines becoming a child protection social worker

- National Association of Social Workers (www .socialworkers.org/advocacy/updates/2003/081204a .asp): Provides a fact sheet on Title IV-E child welfare training program
- South Dakota Department of Social Services and Division of Child Protection Services (dss.sd.gov/cps): Describes state social and child protective services
- UNICEF (www.unicefusa.org/assets/pdf/Toolkit_End-Trafficking_Oct_2012.pdf): Informs and guides professionals on how to fight human trafficking

STUDENT STUDY SITE

Sharpen your skills with SAGE edge at **edge.sagepub.com/cox**

SAGE edge for Students provides a personalized approach to help you accomplish your coursework goals in an easy-to-use learning environment.

CDC
CENTERS FOR DISEASE
CONTROL AND PREVENTION
EDWARD R. ROYBAL
CAMPUS
DEPARTMENT OF HEALTH & HUMAN SERVICES · USA

Chapter 7: HEALTH CARE AND HEALTH CHALLENGES

Learning Objectives

After reading this chapter, you will be able to

1. Describe health challenges and the American health care system.
2. Recognize health disparities, stigma, and ethical dilemmas with health care.
3. Evaluate the current state of health care policy in the United States.
4. Articulate trends in health care.
5. Identify health care settings that employ social workers and the roles of social workers in those settings.

Gayle Practices Social Work in a Teaching Hospital

Gayle serves as a health social worker on the neurology floor of a fast-paced teaching hospital. She is an appreciated member of the multidisciplinary team because she efficiently assesses new patients' needs and their family dynamics. Gayle also quickly completes substantive chart documentation so appropriate and timely discharge planning can occur. Over the years, Gayle's community networking skills, policy knowledge, and resource savvy have given her the reputation of being the consummate professional and team player.

Gayle is a highly sought-after field instructor among students who wish to pursue health social work careers. This semester Gayle is supervising Becky, a student who is required to complete experiential service learning as part of her Introduction to Social Work class. Becky thinks she, too, may want to work in a health care setting.

During team meetings, Becky observes how Gayle—along with the dietician; speech, occupational, and physical therapists; medical students; and nurses—contributes important aspects about each patient as the attending physician, Dr. Iqbal, facilitates. The people discussed during today's rounds are recovering from strokes (cerebrovascular accidents), sickle cell anemia, accidents that have resulted in traumatic brain injury, myasthenia gravis, epilepsy, and Lou Gehrig's disease (also known as ALS—amyotrophic lateral sclerosis). Becky empathizes with how vulnerable and stressed each patient must feel. As well, she senses the strain and worry felt by family members and caregivers alike.

Becky admires Gayle's skill set, eclectic theoretical framework, policy knowledge, and life experience. As an MSW-prepared social worker, Gayle has worked in community and private hospitals, long-term care, home health, rehab, and hospice. Before her position on the neurology floor, she also worked as a clinical trials social worker with a National Institute of Health–funded community-based program that conducted clinical trials with people living with HIV/AIDS.

Twenty-first century health care issues and policies are so multidimensional and complex that innovative responses across professions and at all societal levels are required. Social workers and other health care providers see how the effects of negative social interactions and stigma affect health and well-being, and they keep updated on the latest medical practices and health-related resources. Whether working in hospitals, schools, government agencies, public health, or local community-based organizations, health social workers (especially the growing numbers of public health social work professionals) are actively making connections between prevention and intervention from one person to the entire population and advocating for people who are suffering from diseases.

In response to the politics and economics of America's dynamic health care system, social workers are required to have a broad range of knowledge that includes the leading causes of death, new health care concepts and practices, and federal, state, and local policies. The reality is that the health care one receives in the United States is tied to the insurance industry and government entitlements that may or may not be universally available. Because of disparities in health care access, service apportionment, and quality, populations such as the poor, illiterate, vulnerable, chronically ill and older adults need the skills and advocacy of social workers in the health care arena.

The multifold purpose of this chapter is to explore health challenges and diseases, identify health care system structures and realities, appreciate expanding roles for health social workers, and gain insight regarding how particular health care policies and programs affect Americans.

HEALTH CHALLENGES AND THE AMERICAN HEALTH CARE SYSTEM

The U.S. health care system, with all its strengths and shortfalls, is evolving rapidly. Social work advocates and practitioners, along with the general public and all those who work in the health care system, are in the process of grappling with the business and ethical realities of health care, political controversies, the practices of powerful pharmaceutical companies, and the implications of constantly emerging knowledge about the human body and its care.

Fundamental to these concerns are the definitions of health and illness. According to the World Health Organization, **health** is a state of complete physical, mental, and social well-being, and not merely the absence of disease or infirmity (cited in Barker, 2014, p. 190). In a sense, then, health is a metaphor for well-being. To be healthy means you are of sound mind and body, integrated and whole. By contrast, **illness** is a disease or period of sickness affecting the body or mind. Illness is costly, and health is a precious commodity.

Athletes, physicians, and nurses—and particularly social workers—all recognize that achieving good health is a matter of attending to a person's physical, mental, and social situation. Further, disease, disability, and death are the result of interconnections between human biology, lifestyle, environmental, and social factors (World Health Organization, 2003).

When good health is not sustained across a lifetime or accidents and genetic factors exist, illness and perhaps death result. The leading causes of death reported for people residing in the United States, illustrated in Exhibit 7.1, might surprise some.

EXHIBIT 7.1   Leading Causes of Death in the United States

RANK		PERCENTAGE OF TOTAL DEATHS
1.	Heart disease	28.5
2.	Cancer	22.8
3.	Stroke (CVA/cerebrovascular diseases)	6.7
4.	Chronic lower respiratory diseases	5.1
5.	Accidents (unintentional injuries)	4.4
6.	Diabetes	3.0
7.	Influenza and pneumonia	2.7
8.	Alzheimer's disease	2.4
9.	Kidney disease (nephritis/nephrosis)	1.7
10.	Septicemia (blood poisoning)	1.4
11.	Suicide	1.3
12.	Chronic liver disease and cirrhosis	1.1

Source: U.S. Census Bureau (2011).

TIME TO THINK

Think about your total well-being. Do you believe you are a healthy person overall? How much weekly exercise do you get, and what kind of food do you eat? Do you need to lose weight or stop addictive smoking or excessive or binge drinking? How well do you manage stress and your mental health? Do you have family members and a circle of friends who support you and spend time with you?

THREATS TO AMERICANS' HEALTH

Of 17 high-income countries studied by the National Institutes of Health (NIH) in 2013, the United States had almost the highest prevalence of infant mortality, heart and lung disease, sexually transmitted infections, adolescent pregnancies, injuries, homicides, and disabilities. Combined, these concerns put the United States at the bottom of the list for life expectancy. This means that, on average, a male American can be expected to live about 4 years less than a male in the top-ranked country.

On the other hand, in 1900, average life expectancy in the United States was 47 years. Today, average life expectancy is more than 77 years, which is an astounding increase of 30 years in the span of a century. Much of this improvement, especially during the first 50 years, has come from changes in lifestyle and living conditions. Advances in biomedical and sociobehavioral science have also increasingly contributed to life expectancy. In the past 30 years, almost 6 years of life expectancy gains have come from improvements in the management of cardiovascular diseases, spearheaded by research funded through the NIH (U.S. Department of Health and Human Services, National Institutes of Health, Office of Behavioral and Social Sciences Research, 2007).

At least 50 of the improvements in Americans' health have been attributed to sociobehavioral factors, such as malleable individual factors (e.g., smoking, poor diet, stress, inactivity, violence, substance abuse) and social and health care system factors (e.g., medical errors, gender bias, low health literacy, lack of insurance or access to health care). Many theories of health have been based on imbalances in the body, in the person, or in social relationships (Albrecht, 2006). Yet today lifestyle continues to threaten health and longevity in three key ways: chronic illness, heart disease, and stress.

Chronic Illness

Chronic illness is the personal experience of living with **chronic disease**, which is a persistent, long-lasting health condition. The term *chronic* is usually applied when the course of the disease lasts for more than 3 months and it can be controlled but not cured.

Chronic illnesses cause about 70% of deaths. Examples of chronic disease include asthma, chronic obstructive pulmonary disease, diabetes, depression, and heart disease. Chronic diseases are the leading cause of death and disability in the United States (Johnson & Johnson, n.d.). Exhibit 7.2 shows the proportion of various aspects of the U.S. health care system used by people with chronic illnesses.

People with chronic diseases often suffer from reduced quality of life. For example, progression of diabetes can result in amputation of lower limbs, and asthma can limit a person's ability to exercise and engage in pleasurable leisure activities.

Many chronic diseases are preventable and can be managed by mitigating risk factors, making lifestyle and dietary changes when necessary, and following prescribed treatment regimens. However, chronic illness and disease are greatly influenced by education, environment, employment, and socioeconomic status. Thus, people least advantaged will continue to experience more than their share of chronic illness. Social workers play vital roles in educating patients who are health illiterate, reinterpreting complicated medical jargon used by physicians, and connecting people to community resources so healing can continue at home. Social workers can also play a role in addressing underlying health determinants, a population's overall well-being, and the community context.

Heart Disease

Two thirds of Americans will die of heart disease, and it is the leading cause of death for both women and men. **Heart disease** comprises a range of conditions that affect the heart, including angina, congenital heart disease, congestive heart failure, and blood vessel diseases such as coronary heart

EXHIBIT 7.2   U.S. Health Care System Usage by Chronically Ill People

Hospital admissions	81%
Physician's visits	76%
$2 trillion spent on health care in U.S.	91%
Medicare spending	96%
Medicaid spending	83%

disease. More than half of all deaths from heart disease occur in men. Every year about 715,000 Americans have a heart attack, and 525,000 of these are people having their first heart attack.

Coronary heart disease is the most common type of heart disease, killing nearly 380,000 people annually. Alone it costs the United States $108.9 billion each year. This total includes the cost of health care services, lost productivity, and medications (Centers for Disease Control and Prevention, 2014b). Coronary heart disease results from coronary artery disease, where plaque buildup starts in childhood and worsens over time unless weight is controlled and prevention measures are taken.

Heart disease is the leading cause of death for people of most ethnicities in the United States, including African Americans, Latinos, and whites. For American Indians or Alaska Natives and Asians or Pacific Islanders, heart disease is second only to cancer as a cause of death. Deaths vary by geography, and death rates due to heart disease have typically been the highest in the South and the lowest in the West (Kulshreshtha, Goyal, Dabhadkar, Veledar, & Vaccarino, 2014).

Knowing the signs and symptoms of a heart attack and taking early action are key to preventing death. Many people are unaware of the signs, but social workers can help educate them.

Stress

Definitions of stress are highly subjective, and not all stress is bad. Basically, stress is our brain's response to any demand, including change. Changes can be negative or positive, real or perceived. They may be short-term, long-term, or recurring. Change can be mild and harmless or major and traumatic. Stress is a condition that has physiological impact. For example, stress affects a person's thoughts, feelings, mood, and body. If unchecked, stress affects sleep and leads to health problems such as heart disease, high blood pressure, obesity, and diabetes. Leading researchers at the NIH, including Dr. Anthony Fauci and his colleagues (2008), have described clinical manifestations of many stress-related disorders, including depression, ulcers, and hypertension (high blood pressure).

During the past 70 years, thousands of studies and technical articles have tried to explain stress theory and the stress response (e.g., Dohrenwend, Dohrenwend, Dodson, & Shrout, 1984; Frankenhaeuser, 1980; Lazarus, 1966; Selye, 1980). Stress responses have been studied in fields as diverse as anthropology, business, education, law, pharmacy, philosophy, physiology, psychology, and sociology (Rice, 2012). Most of the research has occurred in the scientific fields of medicine and nursing, because of the hypothesized relationship between stress and illness (Aldwin, 2007).

Social workers have not contributed much to this body of research, but they have incorporated many of the findings into their practice. For instance, social workers can assess and understand how clients get to their breaking point. They should realize that as stress levels increase, chemicals in the brain are released that affect the prefrontal cortex (decision-making area) and the amygdala (emotional system). People's ability to think logically and reasonably decreases as stress levels increase. Social workers can help clients develop stress management skills and strategies, and can point out the four types of stress: time stress, anticipatory stress, encounter stress, and situational stress. Through advocacy, when working with individuals, social workers help clients fully assess situations, learn how to relax, avoid self-medication, improve emotional intelligence, and practice time-management skills. When working with families, social workers help people keep a routine, encourage one another, listen and communicate better, and connect and relate well. Because social workers do not want to see people become sad, numb, or angry, or cry and cope poorly, much of their work and advocacy is about helping people manage stress.

Source: ©iStockphoto.com/huawadragon

▲ The health effects of stress have been widely studied in recent years.

Heartmates

After her own husband suffered a heart attack, author and clinical social worker Rhoda Levin (1994) founded the first hospital-affiliated program specifically designed to help the caregiver and the cardiac patient, a program called Heartmates. Her book details how coronary artery disease can be a catastrophic chronic illness that causes problems and stress for the entire family.

Levin notes these key risk factors for heart disease: high blood pressure, high LDL cholesterol, and smoking. Other medical conditions and lifestyle choices that put people at a higher risk for heart disease include diabetes, excessive alcohol use, physical inactivity, poor diet, and obesity. People who are described as high-strung, Type A, or extremely stressed are often implicated as prime targets for heart disease.

Levin tells caregivers and the public about these major warning signs and symptoms for heart attacks:

- Chest pain or discomfort
- Upper body pain or discomfort in the arms, back, jaw, neck, or upper stomach
- Shortness of breath
- Nausea, lightheadedness, or cold sweats

1. What kind of information needs to be conveyed to the family members of someone who has already had a heart attack?

2. Where can you find local, state, and national resources to help educate others about heart disease?

HEALTH DISPARITIES AND THE UNINSURED

Health science writers continuously reveal how the dynamics of health care, poverty, race/ethnicity, age, and gender intersect with disease. For example, not all Americans have access to the wondrous surgical procedures available to some, such as kidney transplants, technologically advanced rehabilitation processes, and psychopharmacology.

Socioeconomic status has been and remains persistently related to stressful and harmful living conditions, disease, and lack of access to adequate health care. For example, when waste plants are built near impoverished neighborhoods, health problems ensue in those neighborhoods. In addition, impoverished people often have less access to fruits and vegetables than to candy, cookies, snacks, and cheap foods containing large amounts of corn syrup, which leads to alarming rates of obesity and diabetes.

Unfortunately, impoverished and other oppressed people often do not have access to the health care that could help them treat their conditions. The term **health disparities** (also called health care inequality) refers to gaps between population groups in the availability and quality of health care, disease rates and severity, and overall health (U.S. Department of Health and Human Services, 2014). In the United States, health disparities are well documented in African Americans, Native Americans, Asian Americans, Pacific Islanders, and Latinos. Underprivileged groups distinguished by socioeconomic status or sexual orientation also experience health disparities.

One major contributor to health disparities has been a difference in access to health insurance. In the United States, health insurance is typically provided by employers but usually only to full-time workers who are not earning minimum wage. A 2013 report in *The New York Times*, using Census data, revealed that about 44 million Americans have no health insurance (Bloch, Ericson, & Giratikanon, 2013). People who are medically uninsured tend to postpone necessary care and forgo preventive care, such as childhood immunizations and routine checkups. Uninsured people usually have no regular physician and limited access to prescription medications. Therefore, they are more likely to be hospitalized for health problems that could have been avoided.

More than one third of uninsured adults state that they have problems paying their bills, which explains why many do not seek care until the last minute. When uninsured people cannot pay medical bills, the burden falls on those who do have insurance. Billions of dollars of "uncompensated care" drive up health insurance premiums for everyone.

HEALTH CARE POLICY IN THE UNITED STATES

Despite its continuing inadequacies, the U.S. health care system has traveled far. Long ago, a lone general practitioner would make house calls, offer folk or home remedies, and take livestock as payment. Today, the United States boasts a health care complex comprising general practitioners and specialists, clinics, hospitals, pharmaceutical companies, and health insurance providers.

Hospitals were first conceptualized during the Civil War, and new hygienic techniques were introduced. Much later, in 1846, the first surgery using anesthesia was performed at Massachusetts General Hospital, and diagnostic X-rays were first used in 1895. After the Great Depression in the 1930s, third-party payer (an organization other than the patient—first party—or the health

care provider—second party—involved in financing personal health services) insurance plans, such as those provided by the federation of separate health insurance organizations and companies referred to as the Blue Cross and Blue Shield Association, were devised to help pay doctors and not-for-profit hospitals for their ever-more-sophisticated services. Blue Cross and Blue Shield began as separate organizations in 1929 and 1939, respectively. In 1982, they merged to form the current association. For-profit hospitals arrived during the 1940s. These businesses required their customers (i.e., patients) to pay for services and eventually crushed the public health services sector. Once employers began providing insurance, people's access to health care became more complicated. Insurance needed to be portable so that when people went from one job to another, their health care would still be covered. Over time, health insurance has become a requirement to access good health care services (Green & Rowell, 2014).

Health Insurance

Health insurance is a service you pay for but hope you will never need. Most people want and value health insurance, but they cannot afford the coverage or have been shut out of the marketplace because they have a preexisting condition. If a person experiences a serious illness, accident, or traumatic event, staggering amounts of medical bills might build up and lead to bankruptcy or years of problems. Therefore, health insurance has become necessary for all Americans.

Fast-forward to 1996. During President Bill Clinton's administration, both Democrats and Republicans supported the **Health Insurance Portability and Accountability Act (HIPAA)**. The main goal of HIPAA was to ensure that people who already had been or were being treated for a health condition could not be discriminated against in receiving health insurance. Although HIPAA has expanded protections for people who belong to group plans, it has not helped people who have individual coverage (Pollitz & Sorian, 2000).

In 2007, as George W. Bush was winding down his two-term presidency, he put forward a comprehensive "Affordable Choices Initiative" to reform the private health insurance market. The goal was to harness market forces to make private health insurance cheaper for the people who needed it most. However, because the Democrats had just regained control of Congress, the plan was never passed. Today, Bush is best known for his 2003 Medicare prescription-drug benefit program, often referred to as **Medicare Part D**.

Today, American citizens under age 67 are mostly insured by their or a family member's employer. The U.S. government provides most of the insurance for public-sector employees. Medical care is paid for through private insurance, as well as by government programs and patients paying their own bills out of pocket. Yet others are uninsured. Medicaid, the State Children's Health Insurance Program, and Medicare are the federal resources that pay for health care. The U.S. government also provides medical programs for families of members of the armed forces and supports Veterans Affairs hospitals. A huge 65% of health care provision and spending derives from Medicare, Medicaid, TRICARE, the Children's Health Insurance Program, and the Veterans Health Administration.

Depending on their insurance status, ill or injured people can see generalist physician practitioners or get referrals to consult with specialists. People pay more to see "out-of-network" doctors, and some doctors are now offering "boutique-type services," where patients pay a yearly lump sum for present and future treatment.

TIME TO THINK

What has your experience been with the private insurance industry or with Medicare and Medicaid? What aspects of these types of health insurance worked well? What were their drawbacks? Consider carefully whether the difficulties you encountered were due to the insurance program itself or to your health issues or specific health care provider.

Affordable Care Act

Since the debate leading to passage of HIPAA during the Clinton administration, pressure only increased to reform the U.S. health care system more fundamentally so that more people would have insurance coverage (Odier, 2010). The United States toyed with multiple health care reforms and solutions, but there was contentious debate over how to balance government programs and the market-based insurance system, who deserved to be covered, and how to pay for expanding coverage. However, data from Switzerland showed that it was possible to provide market-based,

universal, private health insurance coverage at a far lower cost than that of health insurance in the United States, and that such an affordable health insurance system could work (Roy, 2012). Further, a state-supported health insurance system in Massachusetts showed how reforms might work in the American environment.

In 2010, the Patient Protection and Affordable Care Act, known simply as the **Affordable Care Act (ACA)** sometimes ObamaCare, became law. The ACA is a comprehensive health care reform law that includes provisions to expand health insurance coverage, improve health outcomes, control health costs, and improve the U.S. health care delivery system. The ACA also expanded public programs such as Medicaid as a "public option" to make more disadvantaged Americans eligible for health care.

The ACA bill was more than 2,000 pages long. Since 2010 insurance companies have not been allowed to deny coverage to children or adults for preexisting conditions such as asthma, HIV/AIDS, and so on. Also, children can now stay on their parent's policy up to age 26. Yearly limits on premiums are barred, which protects people with catastrophic illnesses. After the initial open enrollment period, every American citizen was required to have medical insurance by May 1, 2014, or face penalties from the Internal Revenue Service. By 2018, all insurance plans are supposed to offer preventive care with no copayments and no deductibles.

The ACA was a controversial law to begin with, with opponents believing that it would lead the United States toward socialized medicine. Some private insurance providers and health professionals opposed the law as well, because they believed that some of the reforms would decrease their profits. And then public enrollment in the plans in late 2013 was chaotic because of deficiencies in the computer technology undergirding the enrollment system. Many of ACA's opponents were quick to predict that the act would fail to achieve its goals.

By mid-2014, opinions varied as to the extent to which the ACA is making a difference. For example, doctor, bioethicist, University of Pennsylvania professor, and former advisor to the Obama administration Ezekiel Emanuel (2014a) passionately defends and lauds the ACA in his book *Reinventing American Health Care*, reminding readers that insurance companies and not doctors participate in the exchange. In contrast, Fox News host Bill O'Reilly provocatively countered that "ObamaCare is moving toward the direction of walk-in clinics, which are staffed by physician assistants and nurse practitioners" ("Debate: Are Doctors Fleeing the ObamaCare Exchange?" 2014).

HEALTH CARE TRENDS

Rapidly changing health care policy is accompanied by equally rapid changes in health care procedures and protocols. Overall, the health care system now places greater focus on "benchmark practice" or **continuous quality improvement,** which helps ensure that all medical personnel and administrators stay aware of developments in health care practice and choose those that have the best outcomes for patients (Spitzer & Davidson, 2013). Some of these systemic changes in U.S. health care are described here.

Integrative Medicine

Integrative medicine, or integrative health as it is called in the United Kingdom, is healing-oriented medicine that considers the whole person (body, mind, and spirit), including all aspects of his or her lifestyle. It emphasizes the therapeutic relationship and makes use of all appropriate therapies, both conventional and alternative or complementary.

These are some of the main principles of integrative medicine (Lemley, n.d.):

- A partnership between patient and practitioner in the healing process
- Appropriate use of conventional and alternative methods to facilitate the body's innate healing response

▲ Exercising is one way to promote wellness.

- Consideration of all factors that affect health, wellness, and disease
- Use of natural, effective, less-invasive interventions whenever possible
- Training to make health care practitioners models of health and healing, committed to the process of self-exploration and self-development

Social work majors can often choose to minor in holistic health, which enhances appreciation for medical interventions beyond Western medicine, such as acupuncture and herbal remedies.

Slow Medicine

Watch any of the multiple reality television shows about medical centers and you will observe that American medicine seems to excel at managing crises and supplying modern technological procedures such as joint replacements, organ transplants, eye surgeries, and cosmetic changes. For the more ordinary and common chronic problems of aging and slow-moving diseases, our medical care system has not done as well. All too often, patients are subjected to unnecessary, and unwelcome, stints in an intensive care unit. There is a rush to treat people aggressively.

Slow medicine, in contrast, is the avoidance of inappropriate or harmful care and a more deliberate approach to determining which medical procedures to follow. Family, friends, or neighbors team up with an older person who has health issues and with health care providers, including home health nurses and other providers, to improve the quality of life while the person is under medical care.

Slow medicine shares with hospice care the goal of comfort rather than cure. It is increasingly available in nursing homes. However, slow medicine is not a plan for getting ready to die; rather, it is a plan for caring, and for living well, in the time an older adult has left (McCullough, 2008).

Prevention and Wellness

Giving people the resources to maintain health is just as important as helping them when they are sick, ill, or injured. By encouraging healthy lifestyles, occurrence of preventable diseases can be reduced. Prevention and wellness include healthy behaviors such as eating a balanced diet, exercising regularly, scheduling regular physical examinations, and following a doctor's recommendations.

Recovery, Rehabilitation, and Resilience

When people become ill, injured, or disabled, time is often required to rehabilitate and recover. During the recovery and rehabilitation process, social workers educate people about how to reduce risk factors and increase protective factors.

Health care professionals may also assess resilience levels. **Resilience** is an interaction between risk and protective factors within a person's background that can interrupt and reverse a potentially damaging process. It is a trait, and a major strength, that allows a person to "bounce back" from difficulties. In the health care context, it may facilitate recovery from disease, injury, and medical procedures.

TIME TO THINK

How do you define resilience? How resilient do you think you are? How resilient do you perceive your parents to be? How has their resilience affected yours—or vice versa?

Inflammation

Inflammation—the body's attempt to protect itself from damaged cells, irritants, or pathogens so that a healing process can occur—is receiving an incredible amount of attention in medical journals these days. Inflammation, from the Latin *inflammo* (meaning "I set alight, I ignite") is part of our body's immune response and is initially beneficial; for example, when you hurt your knee, it swells and the tissues require time to heal. However, inflammation can be self-perpetuating and cause more inflammation.

There are two types of inflammation:

• **Acute inflammation** is the inflammation that occurs in the immediate or short-term aftermath of an injury or disease. The five hallmarks of acute inflammation can be remembered by the acronym PRISH, which refers to the signs of inflammation: pain, redness, immobility, swelling, and heat. **Pain** is when people have inflammation and it hurts; they feel stiff, uncomfortable, or distressed and in agony depending on its severity. Pain can be constant or steady, such as an ache, or it can be a throbbing type with pulsating pain or a stabbing, pinching pain. Pain is an individual experience, and the only person who can describe it properly is the one who is feeling it. Pain can be acute or chronic (www.medicalnewstoday.com).

• **Chronic inflammation** lasts for several months or years and can occur as a result of an autoimmune response, a chronic irritant, or failure to eliminate the cause of inflammation. Examples of diseases and conditions that produce chronic inflammation are asthma, chronic peptic ulcer, tuberculosis, rheumatoid arthritis, chronic periodontitis (infected gums), ulcerative colitis and Crohn's disease, chronic sinusitis, and chronic hepatitis, to name a few. The risk of chronic inflammation is much greater if the person is obese.

Inflammation may be treated with anti-inflammatory medications (naproxen, ibuprofen, aspirin), herbs (hyssop, ginger, turmeric), and other treatments (applying ice, taking fish oil or Omega-3, drinking green tea, eating tart cherries).

Managed Care

Managed care is a type of health care system created to manage, or contain, health care costs. Managed care is offered primarily through the private sector, although Medicaid and Medicare are also a form of managed care.

Managed care plans include the following variations:

• **Health maintenance organization (HMO).** An HMO is a coordinated delivery system that combines both the financing and delivery of health care for enrollees. In each plan a member is assigned a "gatekeeper" primary care physician who is responsible for the overall care of that member. In an HMO plan, patients pay less in insurance premiums and a nominal copayment at the time of service. The idea of a "health maintenance strategy" was first proposed by Dr. Paul Elwood in the 1960s, and the concept was promoted by the Nixon administration as a fix to rising health care costs. HMOs are licensed at the state level.

• **Preferred provider organization (PPO).** A PPO generally does not require copays and instead requires that patients cover a "deductible" (a preset sum for any service) before any benefits are provided. After the deductible is met, the insurance company and the patient split the costs of benefits. Because the patient is picking up a large portion of the "first dollars" of coverage, PPOs are the least expensive type of coverage.

CURRENT TRENDS

Medical Advice About Obesity

OBESITY has been linked to many diseases and types of illnesses, including inflammation, heart disease, diabetes, high cholesterol, and high blood pressure. In the past, doctors have not emphasized the risks of obesity to their patients. They would say, "You have a problem with your weight" (Perkes, 2013). The patient would agree and then go home and fall right back into old patterns. The weight would never come off, and the risks would remain.

Over the past couple of years, however, doctors have begun to try **motivational interviewing** as a way to get patients to change (Perkes, 2013). The technique centers on the patient and doctor deciding together what the patient wants to accomplish and how to go about doing it.

1. How can social workers respond on the micro, mezzo, and macro levels to lessen obesity?

2. How effective might motivational interviewing be in helping people change their eating habits?

A point-of-services plan combines features of PPOs and HMOs. What they all have in common is that patients must be preauthorized by an insurance carrier to qualify for specific services; patients with managed-care plans cannot simply make an appointment with any doctor. Exhibit 7.3 provides a breakdown of distinctions among managed-care organizations.

The growth of managed care in the United States was triggered by the enactment of the Health Maintenance Organization Act of 1973. Today managed care is almost ubiquitous in the United States but has been controversial because of its mixed results in trying to control medical costs. Proponents of managed care believe that it has increased efficiency, improved overall standards, and led to a better understanding of the relationship between costs and quality. It has promoted the practice of evidence-based medicine, which is now used to determine when lower-cost treatment may be more effective. Critics of managed care argue that "for-profit" managed care has been an unsuccessful health policy because it has contributed to higher health care costs, increased the number of uninsured citizens, driven away health care providers, and applied downward pressure on quality.

Electronic Medical Records

National policy changes have prompted the adoption of **electronic medical records (EMRs)**, which allow physicians to maintain electronic files of lab results, visit notes,

EXHIBIT 7.3   Managed-Care Organization Distinctions

	PHYSICIANS	INSURED
HMO staff model network	Employee network	Use HMO doctors in/out of network
HMO group model	Fixed, approved payment	Use HMO doctors
PPO	Payment for service (financial penalty for out-of-network doctor)	Use preferred providers
Point-of-service plan	Payment for service (high deductible for out-of-network doctor)	Must choose a doctor

Source: Odier (2010).

diagnostic test results, insurance information, demographics, health histories, and other medication information within their offices. The companion to EMRs are EHRs (electronic health records), which facilitate the electronic exchange of EMRs between providers, thereby allowing the medical record to "follow" patients when they see different providers (Spitzer & Davidson, 2013, p. 966).

EMR and EHR use is promoted by the ACA as essential to efficient health care delivery systems. Health care organizations are increasingly migrating toward a paperless environment. Exhibit 7.4 lists some pros and cons of electronic storage and transmission of individuals' medical records.

HEALTH CARE AND SOCIAL WORK

Health social workers have long provided people with **biopsychosocial-spiritual** support needed to cope with **acute illness,** chronic illness, or **terminal illness.** Services provided by professional health social workers include advocating for patients and family caregivers; assessing needs; providing care and case management; educating and counseling; intervening to promote health, prevent disease, and address disparities and barriers to health care; and providing information and referrals. Because health care is "big business," social workers can also take business and accounting classes to help prepare them to manage community-based agencies and social service organizations.

Health care social workers require interdisciplinary knowledge about acute and chronic illnesses, accidents and injuries, genetics and birth abnormalities, neuroscience, and death. Hospice workers in particular require a comfort level with end-of-life and palliative-care issues.

HISTORY OF HEALTH SOCIAL WORK

In 1905, at Boston's Massachusetts General Hospital, physician Dr. Richard Cabot hired a competent and dynamic medical social worker named Ida Cannon, who created the first hospital social work department. At this time, antibiotics, advanced X-ray technology, the human genome project, and managed-care organizations were nonexistent.

Health social work was one of the first three fields of practice established in the social work profession. Early medical or "health social workers" were the first social work specialty group to organize formally as professionals, and they shared a mutual concern for how poverty was affecting individual health outcomes and public health. Health social workers offered ill, injured, or suffering people and their loved ones social support and advocacy.

They endeavored to humanize people's hospital experiences and coordinate community resources. In 1918, the American Association of Hospital (Medical) Social Workers was founded and began publishing its own journal. In 1929, 10 college-level medical social work courses were created and offered. At this time, psychoanalytic thinking (or Freudian thought) was in vogue, and health social workers focused on diagnoses and mental health challenges. Community-based social workers focused on public health and social concerns such as tuberculosis, sexually transmitted infections, and sanitation.

EXHIBIT 7.4   Advantages and Disadvantages of Electronic Medical Records

ADVANTAGES	DISADVANTAGES
• *Reduced human errors:* No need to rely on illegible handwriting or inaccurate filing.	• *Perceived threat to privacy:* Some think that privacy via a digital system means confidentiality is lost and information can be accessed by unauthorized parties.
• *Safer and more secure:* While paper files can be lost, damaged, stolen, or subjected to natural disasters, computerized records circumvent these situations and provide greater safeguards.	• *Perceived loss of human oversight:* Some fear systems that are fully automated with no human management intervention.
• *Cost-efficient because of data consolidation:* A centralized location for digitized medical records can reduce duplication of efforts and documents, and increase the speed of exchanging information. This saves labor costs and enhances operational efficiencies that increase productivity through a greater volume of transactions.	• *Perceived lack of standardization:* Because electronic medical records are still a relatively new platform, many think that the standardization for quality, efficiency, and productivity has yet to be achieved.

Source: American Medical Association (2014).

When the Social Security Act of 1935 was passed and implemented, the social work presence in health settings grew. Social worker Grace Abbott helped write this legislation. Subsequently, the American Public Health Association and the American Hospital Association created standards for social workers.

Indirect social work practice in health settings began at the start of the 20th century, and sociologist Homer Folks, along with many others, worked hard to manage epidemics and debilitating diseases by focusing on prevention efforts and community systems change. In the hospital and in the community, Cannon, Abbott, and Folks advocated for good sanitation, adequate housing, and health improvements for individuals, families, and communities.

SOCIAL WORKERS' ROLES IN HEALTH CARE PRACTICE

The goals for health social workers are outlined in the revised *NASW Standards for Social Work Practice in Health Care Settings* (National Association of Social Workers, in press):

- Ensure that the highest quality of social work and client- and family-centered services are provided to clients and families in health care settings
- Advocate for clients' rights to self-determination, confidentiality, access to supportive services and resources, and appropriate inclusion in medical decision making that affects their well-being
- Encourage social work participation in the development, refinement, and integration of best practices in health care and health care social work
- Promote social work participation in systemwide quality improvement and research efforts within health care organizations
- Provide a basis for the development of continuing education materials and programs related to social work in health care settings
- Encourage social workers in health care settings to participate in the development and refinement of public policy at the local, state, and federal levels to support the well-being of clients, families, and communities served by the rapidly evolving U.S. health care system
- Inform policymakers, employers, and the public about the essential role of social workers across the health care continuum

Health care social workers provide services across the life span, from neonatal intensive care units to skilled-level long-term care settings. Their purpose is to help people and families cope with illness or injury, prevent emotional and social issues from negatively influencing health, and address service delivery shortcomings. They may be scheduled 24/7 or be on call in case an emergency or crisis arises.

As you might imagine, crisis intervention and grief counseling are common health social work roles, as are chart documentation and debriefing with colleagues. Some of the other roles are discharge planning; chemical dependency evaluation; mental health assessment; short-term decision-making counseling; ethical decision-making counseling; facilitating support groups (e.g., cancer support groups, rehab family groups); specialty evaluations and coordination, such as on a renal transplant team; and child abuse investigations and reporting.

Hospitals are a growing source of jobs for social workers, and those who work in hospitals expect to juggle hefty caseloads and remain on call. A typical day in a hospital may start with a review of new admissions, current referrals, walking rounds or sit-down multidisciplinary health care team meetings, family meetings, patient assessment, and discharge planning. Large teaching hospitals are found in cities and metropolitan areas; community hospitals are most often found in rural geographic areas. Social workers in teaching hospitals must have an MSW degree.

Regardless of workplace environment or client population, health social workers must be clinically and culturally competent. They must also be aware of factors driving health care practice, including the priorities, missions, capabilities, and limitations of the hospitals, clinics, and other organizations (Spitzer & Nash, 1996). Environmental and organizational awareness are essential to 21st century social workers who work in health and disability settings and fields of practice.

HEALTH CARE SETTINGS

Multiple types of health care organizations employ social workers. For example, health social workers work in acute care, hospitals, home health, long-term care, hospice and palliative care, clinics, and rehabilitation. All these health care settings are practice areas in which assessment, care, and treatment address the physical, mental, emotional, and social well-being of the person. Health settings address prevention, detection, and treatment of physical and mental disorders

SOCIAL WORK IN ACTION

Karyn Walsh Practices Health Care Social Work Across Multiple Settings

KARYN Walsh (LCSW, MSW) tells her own story: As an undergraduate, my degree was in social work. I felt a calling, of sorts, to help people. My first practicum experience was volunteering at a homeless shelter, where I learned much about community resources—food banks, congregate meals, and more.

As I pursued my MSW, I chose the health track over those in mental health, juvenile justice, and administration. In my first field experience, I felt fearful and uneasy helping hospice patients die with dignity. Eventually, I grew comfortable with end-of-life and palliative-care issues.

With my MSW degree, I landed a job at a community nonprofit hospital and was primarily assigned to orthopedics but also cross-covered neurology and oncology. I adored the fast pace of hospital-based health social work and became a whiz at efficient discharge planning. Sometimes after-hours oncology nurse Perry and I cofacilitated an "I Can Cope" support group for family members of patients who were living with and dying from multiple types of cancer. I participated in 7 A.M. walking rounds every Monday and Friday, and multidisciplinary team meetings.

After getting married and moving, I held a hospital social work position that served a wide range of populations and demographics, including military families. This position allowed me to accrue enough supervision hours to take the LCSW (licensed clinical social worker) exam, and I passed on my first try. My license allowed me to place my name on rosters with select insurance companies, and I began to provide per diem counseling to clients on the outside.

Following my family's second move, I became the program director for a grant-funded program that served people with hemophilia. In this capacity, I found myself working with clients who had hemophilia and HIV/AIDS. This job gave me an insider's view to the world of public health politics, stigma, and discrimination, as I watched several men with hemophilia die from the ravages of advanced AIDS (acquired immune deficiency syndrome).

Four years later when we moved to the suburbs of Washington, D.C., I accepted a job at the National Association of Social Workers headquarters. Great flexibility was afforded to me in this position. I worked some at home and took the metro or drove into the city a couple of times a week. Creativity, educational and technology skills, and macro social work skills were required for this position. I enjoyed designing curricula, organizing national webinars, revising policy brochures and practice standards, and interacting in a liaison capacity with other professional organizations. This position required that I keep up with the latest funding pots and policy changes being made by the Substance Abuse and Mental Health Services Administration, Center for Medicaid Services, Centers for Disease Control and Prevention, and more.

I next worked outside Washington, D.C., as a home health social worker. My child was in school, and I wanted the flexibility to accept work when I could and decline cases when I needed to attend to my child and her activities. The massive amounts of knowledge I acquired over the years in hospitals, outpatient clinics, clinical trials, and per diem hospice and mental health counseling work served me well. After a couple of initial orientations with other home health social workers and various therapists and nurses, I happily transitioned to the job I have today in home health social work.

Each day is an adventure. Some days I drive down dirt paths to small homes in impoverished areas. Then the next day I might park in a well-monitored parking lot and take the elevator up to a penthouse suite overlooking Washington, D.C. I help people who have illnesses, injuries, or disabilities and are in need of health care services, community resources, and/or counseling. As a frontline practitioner involved in direct social work, I increasingly see the immense influence of state and federal policies on my patients' ability to access services and get services paid for.

1. What benefits has Karyn derived from obtaining a social work degree?

2. How might Karyn's cumulative work experience benefit her clients?

with the goal of enhancing the person's biopsychosocial and spiritual well-being.

The health care setting includes personnel who provide the necessary services (e.g., physicians, nurses, social workers, hospitalists, care managers), appropriate service delivery facilities (e.g., hospitals, hospices, assisted-living facilities, nursing homes, medical centers, urgent care centers, and outpatient clinics), and educational and environmental facilities that work to help prevent disease.

In the United States, health care is provided by multiple distinct organizations mostly owned and operated by private businesses. For example, about 62% of U.S. hospitals are nonprofit, 20% are government owned, and 18% are for-profit.

Emergency Room Trauma and Urgent Care Centers

Emergency rooms (ERs) are equipped and staffed to deal with traumatic injuries and acute diseases. ER social workers require special training to work with patients experiencing chemical dependency and abuse concerns (Cesta, 2012; Fusenig, 2012). **Urgent care centers** or facilities are convenient walk-in options for people with non-life-threatening health situations, when their own doctor is unavailable. Some urgent care centers charge less than half the cost of an ER or hospital visit. Others offer self-pay discounts for the uninsured. Some of these centers use printable coupons that can be applied to the cost of self-pay pricing for urgent care on the patient's next visit.

Oftentimes medical residents moonlight at urgent care centers (also referred to as "doc in the boxes"—implying that any kind of doctor might be there when you walk in) for extra money and practice experience. But uninsured people often are unable to use community urgent care centers, unless they can financially manage the *posted pricing* fees; so they visit ERs instead. This has drastic effects on hospital budgets. ERs are expensive to operate, waits can be extremely long, and staff turnover is high.

Many of the ERs at public hospitals are especially impacted by heavy use by the uninsured and constant demands for budget cuts. As resource cuts continue, ER social workers may need to advocate on a macro level for continuation of services for poor and indigent patients. Social work's cost-effectiveness in hospital ER settings has been well documented (Auerbach & Mason, 2010). Emergency department (ED) social workers play a vital role in helping avoid unnecessary admissions and improving patients' quality of life. ED social workers possess good crisis intervention skills and can perform accurate and quick assessments. They quickly build rapport, help triage accident victims, manage people who have mental disorders, and counsel victims of violence and others. These same ED social workers can be tremendously supportive of other staff in the ER.

Hospitals and Acute Care

In-patient hospital care settings employ—in addition to social workers—nurses; occupational, physical, and speech therapists; dieticians; X-ray and operating room technicians; hospitalists; and more. Insurance reimbursement for in-patient hospitalizations varies depending on a person's age, diagnosis, and insurance coverage or work status.

Hospitals may be small or large, community-oriented nonprofit, private for-profit, or specialized to serve populations such as veterans and people with mental illness. Public, private, and Veterans Affairs hospitals all strive to equip themselves with specialized treatment equipment, laboratory facilities, and skilled technicians.

Hybrid hospital services also exist. Some ambulatory care entities integrate rehabilitative and mental health services for people capable of getting out of the hospital bed and beginning recovery. For extensive skilled or rehabilitative care, hospitals sometimes house transitional care units (or they may send patients to community long-term care settings).

Some health social workers are called to advocate for aging immigrants and refugees, who often present with anxiety, depression, and other mental health problems that may create physical health problems. It is not uncommon for immigrants and refugees to have been persecuted, to have lost loved ones, and also to be uninsured. When immigrants and refugees do not know where to go for illnesses or injuries, they may land in an ER or hospital bed feeling overwhelmed and alone. As the ACA hopes to provide health care coverage for the uninsured, social workers may likely be the people who help immigrants and refugees make sense of a "foreign system." Findings from some social work researchers reveal how the role of hospital-based social worker is changing, as a result of the ACA and immigration and deportation practices (Judd & Sheffield, 2010; Reisch, 2012; Sullivan & Zayas, 2013).

Direct patient care activities, such as discharge planning, consume the majority of hospital social workers' time. Direct practice includes counseling and crisis intervention, yet rarely includes bioethics, evidence-based practice, or income-producing projects (Judd & Sheffield, 2010).

Veterans Affairs Hospitals

Veterans Affairs (VA) hospitals and military social work emerged after World War II. Presently, VA hospitals are one of the largest employers of MSW social workers, as multiple members of the armed forces are returning home with trauma, physical injuries, and disabilities.

Critics have lambasted VA health care for excessively long wait times and bad practices (Olson, 2014). However, VA hospitals are leveraging technology to reduce the distance veterans have to travel, increase the flexibility of the system they use, and improve their overall quality of life. For example, in 2012, the Department of Veterans Affairs announced it would no longer charge a copayment when veterans receive care in their homes via video conferencing with VA health professionals. This clinic-based **telehealth** program involves more than 800 community-based VA outpatient clinics where many veterans receive primary care, and the program improves access to general and specialty services in geographically remote areas where it can be challenging to recruit mental health professionals. That same year, the VA added more than 1,600 mental health clinicians and more than 300 support staff to help address the increased demand for mental health services among veterans. The additional staff included nurses, psychiatrists, psychologists, and social workers. Pressing concerns for VA social workers revolve around compassion satisfaction, compassion fatigue, and burnout (Beder, Postiglione, & Strolin-Goltzman, 2012).

Home Health Care

Home health is both public and private. Agencies such as the Instructive Visiting Nurse Association, Anova Health Care System, and Jewish Family Service depend on the skills of nurses, occupational and physical therapists, and social workers to assess people and provide in-home health care services.

Because institutional structures are costly to maintain, the demand of home health care is expected to increase exponentially as the baby boomers continue to age and the population of people with chronic illnesses and disabilities continues to grow.

Long-Term Care

The term **long-term care**, often synonymous with nursing home care, implies that some people require supportive health care for a long time—maybe for the rest of their lives. Family or friends often cannot provide such intensive care themselves; the job is strenuous, laborious, and time-consuming (Meyer, 2000). By federal law (42 CFR 483.15) nursing homes with more than 120 beds are required to employ a full-time social worker with at least a bachelor's degree in social work or "similar professional qualifications." Facilities with fewer than 120 beds must still offer social services; however, they are not required to have a full-time social worker on staff. Preferably, a nursing home will hire a social worker from an accredited school of social work who is licensed, certified, or registered within his or her home state. Long-term care social workers make home visits, perform intake assessments, handle discharge planning, facilitate resident and family council meetings, provide educational training, and much more.

Hospice, End-of-Life, and Palliative Care

As the end of life approaches, health care can take a far different approach. Instead of aggressively treating a disease or injury—with surgeries, medications, and life-support devices such as breathing apparatus and feeding tubes—the patient is allowed to die peacefully and with dignity. Family and friends also get the support they need. Hospice and palliative care focus on caring, not curing.

Hospice care becomes available when a patient faces a terminal illness or painful injury and is believed to have 6 months or less to live. Hospice is not a place, per se; care often occurs in a person's home. Occasionally, hospice social workers visit residents in nursing homes and hospitals to conduct intakes. Hospice involves a team-oriented approach to expert health care, pain management, and emotional and spiritual support that is tailored to what individuals need and want. Support is also provided by and for a patient's loved ones. Hospice is considered the model for quality, compassionate care.

Palliative care focuses on relieving and preventing the suffering of patients, whether they are expected to die soon or not. It is provided by physicians, nurses, and social workers who specialize in the relief of pain, symptoms, and stress that accompany serious illness. However, like hospice, palliative care embraces the idea that at the end of life, comfort is

CURRENT TRENDS

Social Workers as Health Care Navigators

PRIMARY care used to be considered a client's first entry into the health system. Clients would call to make an appointment with a medical professional and put their health issues in that professional's hands. Increasingly, however, primary care in the United States and Canada is multidisciplinary and transdisciplinary, with nurses, social workers, and other community providers working in tandem and in teams with physicians, especially when the patient has a chronic illness. Health care has become, as a result, a complex process.

Vital Decisions is a U.S. company that represents a new trend in guiding those who are ill through the process (Gordon, 2014; Vital Decisions, 2014). It hires expert staff (who may be social workers) as navigators to help people make health care decisions. Via a series of phone calls, navigators review a person's medical situation and help develop a plan to address health care decisions that person is currently facing or may face in the future.

Social workers employed by Vital Decisions may also call terminally ill patients. The intent is to avoid futile medical care and thereby reduce health care costs by engaging in increased communication about palliative care.

1. With what ethical issues might a Vital Decisions social worker have to grapple?

2. What skills would be required to be a social worker for Vital Decisions?

---

more important than continued aggressive treatment. Social workers help people face terminal illness, find peace, and appreciate life (Faherty, 2008).

Rehabilitation Services

Rehabilitation in health care refers to bringing a person back to a normal, healthy condition after an illness, injury, drug problem, or the like. It can take many forms: vocational rehabilitation, rehabilitation after neurological or traumatic brain injury, addiction or substance abuse recovery, or physical and occupational therapy rehabilitation. It can take place in hospital-based transitional care units, or in community-based long-term care settings or other outpatient settings. Patients who reside in rural and suburban areas may have limited access to public transportation and depend on family to help them get the type and level of rehabilitation services they require.

Clinics

When doctors share offices, administrative personnel, and medical equipment for everyday health care needs, they are operating a **clinic.** Some clinics are privately owned by the doctors or by health care companies operating strings of clinics under a particular brand name. Public health clinics and ambulatory care clinics may be connected to large and small hospitals, and they often employ social workers to conduct assessments, link people with community resources and entitlement programs, and educate people about health diagnoses and prognoses.

Free-standing clinics for the homeless, indigent, or working poor also meet an important need for hundreds of uninsured Americans, especially in urban areas. Physicians may work **pro bono** to run these clinics. Social workers are also present to offer behavioral and cognitive interventions and care-management services to homeless veterans, the severely mentally ill, people with substance abuse problems as well as mental illness, and the uninsured working poor.

Public Health Services

A public health social worker focuses on the general well-being of small (villages or boroughs), medium (cities or towns), or large communities (nation) and their residents. Public health social workers may help implement communitywide programs or help alleviate individuals' suffering. Workers may make home visits and conduct community health fairs, or assist with seminars about vaccinations. Local, regional, state, national, and international entities may become involved in providing health services for a population. Public health care providers focus on prevention of disease, especially contagious diseases. Public health departments, which are usually local or state agencies, provide a broader array of services:

- Testing, counseling, and vaccinations
- Prenatal and postpartum care, nutrition, and medical care
- Physical rehabilitation to people who experience strokes and other debilitating health events
- School medical care to parochial and public institutions
- Codes, rules, and regulations to ensure that the air, water, and food are protected and that waste is properly disposed of (environmental sanitation)

In addition, state health divisions maintain records of area births, deaths, marriages, and current communicable diseases. At the state, national, and international level, public health agencies distribute health education and information to teach the general public about health and prevention of illness.

DIVERSITY AND HEALTH CARE

Health disparities that are experienced by disadvantaged populations result from multiple factors, including poverty, environmental threats, inadequate access to health care, individual and behavioral factors, and educational inequalities. Fortunately, health disparities are preventable differences in the burden of disease, injury, or violence, and in opportunities to achieve optimal health. However, it is important to recognize that health disparities are directly related to the unequal distribution of social, political, economic, and environmental resources (Centers for Disease Control and Prevention, 2013). Social workers have been staunch advocates for minimizing health disparities and lessening stigma toward people with health problems. In health care, the legacy of health social work is challenging, complex, and exciting.

- *Age.* Aging results in greater health care demands and increased costs. In America large numbers of people are aging and putting great pressure on the health care system. People over 80 are the fastest-growing segment of the population. When people age beyond 65, they

Source: © Luigi Novi / Wikimedia Commons.

ᐱ Free clinics allow individuals to access health care at little or no personal cost.

become eligible for Medicare. Both Medicare and Medicaid long-term care expenditures are doubling, thereby causing increased taxpayer-funded costs for younger working people. At the same time, efforts to put Medicare and Medicaid on a sounder footing have been victims of political debates about government budgets. The result is some so-far-mild resentment of retired workers who are assured of receiving health care in old age, whereas younger workers do not feel so secure.

- *Race and ethnicity.* By the year 2030, 1 in 4 Americans over age 65 will be from a racial or ethnic minority. Racial and ethnic minorities tend to receive lower-quality care than do nonminorities; therefore, patients of minority ethnicity experience greater morbidity and mortality from various chronic diseases than do nonminorities. For older adults of color, often their health issues are affected by their class, subculture, and sexual orientation. Consider how African American women over age 50 are contracting HIV disease at alarming rates, with little attention given to their prevention needs. Also think about why diabetes is the fifth leading cause of death in the Asian American and Pacific Islander population.

- *Class.* Health disparities are also related to class and inequities in education. Dropping out of school is associated with multiple social and health problems, and less-educated people are more likely to experience health risks, such as obesity, substance abuse, and intentional and unintentional injury. Higher levels of education are associated with a longer life and an increased likelihood of obtaining or understanding basic health information and services needed to make appropriate health decisions (Centers for Disease Control and Prevention, 2013).

• *Gender.* Ironically, women report more sickness than men, yet live an average of 7 years longer. While women are less likely to have a chronic health condition, they appear to be more at risk for acute illness and disability compared with men. There is concern that reductions in Americans' fertility, greater women's labor force participation, and increases in the divorce rate may reduce the ability of families to take care of older women who are ill, placing even greater demands on social and public programs.

• *Sexual orientation.* Sexual minorities are at increased risk for certain negative health outcomes. For example, young gay or bisexual men have disproportionately high rates of HIV, syphilis, and other sexually transmitted diseases. Adolescent lesbian and bisexual females are more likely to have been pregnant than their heterosexual peers (Centers for Disease Control and Prevention, 2012b). Gay men and women are also more likely to smoke cigarettes. Lesbian women and bisexuals are more likely to report having multiple risk factors for heart disease (Northeastern University Institute on Urban Health Research, 2010). Sexual minorities as a whole are more likely to report experiencing some form of sexual assault during their lifetime, compared with their heterosexual counterparts. Health care social workers will need to understand terms specific to gender expression, such as *cross-dresser*, *drag king* or *queen*, *passing*, and *transition*. Also, terms specific to sexual identity and sexual orientation require understanding, such as *bisexual*, *gay*, *lesbian*, *coming out*, *questioning*, and *MSM/ WSW* (men who have sex with men/women who have sex with women).

• *Intersections of diversity.* Multiple dimensions of diversity complicate and compound people's health care needs. We see how health care disparities translate into real health outcomes when we read how African American women with breast cancer are 67% more likely to die from cancer than are white women (Joslyn & West, 2000).

ADVOCACY ON BEHALF OF PEOPLE WITH HEALTH CARE CHALLENGES

When visiting or counseling patients or their families and friends in hospital rooms or hospice, social workers often witness physical and emotional pain. Those are the times that often galvanize social workers to become better advocates for people experiencing health care challenges. No matter the setting or client concern, human needs must be met so healing and acceptance can occur.

ECONOMIC AND SOCIAL JUSTICE

The complexity of the U.S. health care arena means that social work advocacy efforts are required in multiple places, spaces, and areas of health care. Health social workers, in particular, help people obtain insurance and translate or interpret complex and confusing insurance policy language. Older adults might need to better understand the intricacies of Medicare Part D, whereas parents of a young child with autism or epilepsy may benefit from understanding how such health concerns will change across the life course.

• *Insurance.* In the United States, accessing good health care services depends on one's insurance coverage. Marketplace values that are noted in policy language—for example, "levels of care," "market exchanges," and "medical homes"—are often incomprehensible to people seeking insurance. Government programs such as HIPAA, Children's Health Insurance Program, Medicare Part D, and the ACA also have complex rules and regulations. Social workers must often interpret the language of health insurance for clients.

• *Chronic disease.* The personal and economic burden of chronic disease and illness is a serious challenge for Americans and U.S. health care policy. Too often, health systems do not recognize chronic illness because it does not fit into biomedical or administrative classifications, and health care has become a business where bureaucratic systems reign supreme.

• *Hospitals.* Accessing hospital care is not simple. First you get a diagnosis, and then the expected medical activity of identifying and treating an unhealthy condition occurs. Additionally, much coordination of services and insurance tracking systems is required. Private for-profit organizations render health care services differently than do public government-supported entities. Administrative costs for insurance vary; hence, the implication is that the cost for premiums will vary and may be higher for those seeking care from private for-profit organizations rather than single-payer entities that accept Medicare or Medicaid insurance.

- *Outpatient services.* Some patients require services outside of a hospital. And now community-based physician group practices are charging fees for using their services, just like those patients would pay if they were being treated in a hospital.

- *Veterans health care system.* By law, the Department of Veterans Affairs is required to provide eligible veterans with hospital care and outpatient care services (treatment, procedures, supplies) that are defined as "needed" or that will restore health. Veterans may be eligible for health programs related to HIV/AIDS, Agent Orange exposure, or blindness rehabilitation. VA social workers may work with the Homeless Veterans Reintegration Program; counsel armed forces members living with posttraumatic stress disorder, a traumatic brain injury, or a substance abuse problem; or work with the Disabled American Veterans organization. Because of scandal and bad press related to health care at VA hospitals, veterans are now eligible for a portable and comprehensive health care package. However, to receive this health care, armed forces members and veterans must be enrolled. Military social workers can help educate people about the existence of such resources.

SUPPORTIVE ENVIRONMENT

There is no doubt that where you live, whether in a rural or suburban area or a city, dictates the type and variety of health care available to you. Accessing health care can be a problem when you reside in a remote area. You might not be able to get to a hospital quickly in an emergency. You also might not want to travel long distances to get routine checkups and screenings, and thus you may resort to telehealth services. Rural areas often have fewer doctors, dentists, and social workers, and certain specialists might not be available. People in rural areas of the United States have higher rates of chronic disease than do people in urban areas. They also have higher rates of certain types of cancer, from exposure to chemicals used in farming. Because it can be difficult to access care—especially for the poor and some people of color—health problems in rural residents may be more serious by the time they are diagnosed (Nelson & Gingerich, 2010).

The hallmarks of urban settings—size, diversity, density, and complexity—give rise to unique health problems having to do with sanitation and communicable diseases. However, suburban and urban residents also have greater access to advanced technology, screening services, and clinical trials, and they have greater proximity to dialysis facilities, VA hospitals, and long-term care or residential group homes. It is important to note, however, that taking advantage of these health care resources may require some sophistication, money or insurance, and transportation, and thus often requires social work advocacy.

TIME TO THINK

Do you think that space and place could have an effect on our immune system and stress response? Think about how different places affect your health. Does it seem as though you become more tired or stressed than usual or tend to get sick in any particular place? Are there environments that seem more supportive to your health?

HUMAN NEEDS AND RIGHTS

The adage, "If you have your health you have everything," speaks to the utmost value Americans place on good health. Living a disease- and illness-free life seems like a basic human need. However, too many youth, young adults, and poor people remain uninsured, and not everyone who has health insurance receives equivalent services. When serious illness strikes, only some people are able to access lifesaving treatments—for instance, not everyone is eligible for an organ transplant.

People at any level of society value health care characterized by personal choice, ethical decision making, resources to maximize health or well-being, and the chance to be understood and respected. When such values or needs are compromised because of health disparities or stigma and discrimination, we all suffer. Social workers get involved in health advocacy by helping someone with a substance abuse problem get into treatment, working in the foster care system, or helping families and children with mental illness. As consumer-driven health care plans and other cost-saving measures are shifting more responsibility to the employee, social workers render health advocacy via employee assistance programs to help people with complex health and life issues. Some health advocacy services are simply a call center staffed by health advocates and supported by social workers.

POLITICAL ACCESS

Health care–related policies are political. Perhaps the most glaring and recent example is the heated debate over the ACA, which continued for years after it was passed into law and began being implemented. Although it was popular among U.S. citizens, legislatures and courts continued to attack it.

Medicines have been a different matter. Because of a 1984 law, prompted in part by public outcry, America is blessed with the most efficient market for generic drug substitution in the developed world. About 80% of drugs prescribed in America are generics, compared with 12% in France and 7% in Italy—two countries with socialized systems and drug price controls (Organization for Economic Cooperation and Development, 2013). Prices

came down as well, because drug manufacturers were encouraged to compete with one another after a drug's patent expired.

Political factors affecting current health social work practice include both stressors and opportunities. Tremendous demographic, economic, social, political, and operational system issues are causing dynamic changes in the delivery of health care, and social workers need to respond with creativity and tolerance for ambiguity (Spitzer & Davidson, 2013). Consider the large aging population, the increased use of health care technologies, new integrated provider systems, models, anticipated changes in practice techniques, and skyrocketing costs and fees. Gerontology social workers can help create additional community health services that help older adults age in place, and help these same elders understand

EXHIBIT 7.5   U.S. Health Care Programs and Reforms

GOVERNMENT HEALTH PROGRAMS

Medicare

Medicaid/State Health Insurance Assistance Program

Federal Employees Health Benefits Program

Veterans Health Administration

Military Health System/TRICARE

Indian Health Administration

State Children's Health Insurance Program

Program of All-Inclusive Care for the Elderly

Prescription assistance (State Pharmacy Assistance Program)

PRIVATE HEALTH COVERAGE

Health insurance in the United States

Consumer-driven health care

Flexible spending account

Health reimbursement account

Health savings account

Private fee-for-service

Managed care

Health maintenance organization (HMO)

Preferred provider organization (PPO)

Medical underwriting

HEALTH CARE REFORM LAWS

Emergency Medical Treatment and Active Labor Act (1986)

Health Insurance Portability and Accountability Act (HIPAA, 1996)

Medicare Prescription Drug, Improvement, and Modernization Act (2003)

Patient Safety and Quality Improvement Act (2005)

Health Information Technology for Economic and Clinical Health Act (2009)

Patient Protection and Affordable Care Act (ACA, 2010) (aka ObamaCare)

STATE-LEVEL REFORMS

Massachusetts health care reform (aka RomneyCare)

Oregon Health Plan

Vermont Health Care Reform

SustiNet (Connecticut)

Dirigo Health (Maine)

MUNICIPAL HEALTH COVERAGE

Fair Share Health Care Act (Maryland)

Healthy Howard (Howard County, Maryland)

Healthy San Francisco

Source: http://en.wikipedia.org/wiki/Managed_care

how to use assistive devices and technology. Public health social workers can focus more on prevention and education and work collaboratively with other health care providers.

At the micro level, social workers can help clients access health services and obtain better health literacy—especially for people who speak different languages and do not understand complicated medical jargon, or do not have the capacity to comprehend policy language.

Another avenue for political advocacy is to learn more about the ways other societies address their health care issues and then share that information with clients, colleagues, and decision makers. Travel internationally and you will see how health care services in other countries are delivered quite differently than in the United States. Go to Norway and ask a citizen why they are required to pay more taxes that go directly to health services. Visit a hospital in Heredia, Costa Rica, and note how the corridors connecting hospital rooms are outdoors and greenery abounds. Both solutions create health benefits for the populations of those countries. For example, survey research has shown that when hospitalized patients saw water and trees, they were less anxious and required less pain medicine than those who looked at abstract art or no pictures at all (Franklin, 2012). Exhibit 7.5 lists the existing programs and reforms for health care in the United States.

YOUR CAREER IN HEALTH CARE

No matter the health care context, the health social work job market is exploding with opportunities as the ACA legislation rolls out, multiple veterans return injured from combat, and digital technology radically changes the fields of dentistry, surgery, and general medicine to help people live healthier and longer.

The Bureau of Labor Statistics (2014) *Occupational Outlook Handbook* reveals an expected 19% increase in job growth for health social workers over the next decade. The National Association of Social Workers (in press) assesses that 14% of social workers practice in health-related settings, and the number is expected to increase by 34%.

The Bureau of Labor Statistics (2014) *Occupational Outlook Handbook* for health care social work displays a plethora of interesting opportunities. For example, general medical and surgical hospitals, home health care services, individual and family services, skilled nursing facilities, outpatient care centers, psychiatric and substance abuse hospitals, grantmaking and giving services, health and personal care stores, specialty hospitals, employment services, insurance carriers, and agencies, brokerages, and other insurance-related activities represent but a few health care social work opportunities.

One area of growth is in clinical social work, whose practitioners collaborate with other health care professionals to diagnose and treat medical, mental, behavioral, and emotional issues. Because of relatively short lengths of hospitalization, more social workers are employed in outpatient rather than inpatient health care settings (Bureau of Labor Statistics, 2014).

To have a successful career in health social work, it is helpful to have

- knowledge of medical terminology,
- understanding of the roles of all health care team members,
- understanding of the biopsychosocial-cultural and spiritual aspects of illness and health,
- crisis intervention skills,
- short-term counseling skills, and
- knowledge about culturally competent planning and discharge planning processes and community resources.

When health social workers interview people, assess family situations, and document information, they use vernacular specific to the context within which they are employed. For example, clients are generally called *patients* in hospitals, *persons* in home health care, and *residents* in long-term care.

Prospective health social workers must also make sure they have dealt with their own fears of and issues surrounding illness and death with a strong family member, colleague, or friend beforehand. It is challenging to lose a young cancer patient or even an elderly patient with whom one has shared the emotional experience of dying. While health social work can be stressful, these professionals often serve as the "glue" for a health care team.

SUMMARY

Life is stress and stress is life.

—Hans Selye

Illness is a normal part of life; everyone gets sick at one time or another. Illness is usually felt somewhere in the body, but viruses such as tuberculosis and HIV may go undetected and be passed from person to person through the air or physical contact. Some illnesses come from bacteria in the environment—from food, drink, objects, people, or animals. Some illnesses result from genetic factors, and others have unknown causes. The diagnosis of a serious or chronic illness is a life-altering experience for a person and his or her loved ones.

When a person has no family, has trouble coping with a physical impairment, or has experienced undue pain, an injury, or suffering, social workers can help. Social workers are found in settings that range from community nonprofit hospitals and outpatient public or ambulatory care clinics to inpatient for-profit hospitals, transitional care rehabilitation units, assisted-living facilities, and long-term care settings, and they can also be found through home health agency referrals.

Health care is expansive, expensive, and complex. No matter their role or context, health social workers must understand the health care system and realize the prevalence of chronic illness in older adults, the concerns of veterans, and insurance and the implications of the Affordable Care Act.

TOP 10 KEY CONCEPTS

acute illness
chronic illness
electronic medical records (EMRs)
health disparities
hospice

integrative medicine
long-term care
pain
rehabilitation
resilience

DISCUSSION QUESTIONS

1. Do Americans take good care of themselves? Explain.
2. What does it mean to be chronically ill? Consider how your body functions as a sensory body, an emotional body, a spiritual body, an economic body, a productive body, a body of ideas and meanings, and a body in multiple garbs and spaces (wording inspired by DePoy & Gilson, 2007, p. 267).
3. What are the goals of the Affordable Care Act? Does the law itself seem likely to achieve those goals? Why or why not? What features are still missing?

4. How is technology and telehealth assisting people and diminishing health disparities?
5. What have you learned about illness and health disparities in this chapter? Why are people who are poor, less educated, and members of particular races and ethnicities more prone to certain illnesses? What can social workers do about these disparities?
6. How does health social work differ in rural versus urban parts of the United States?

EXERCISES

1. The opening vignette about health social worker Gayle identifies many practice settings where she has worked. Which of these settings might be places you would like to work? Why?
2. Locate some family or friends who have been hospitalized recently or have a serious health problem. Ask them what concerns they have about our current U.S. health care system, based on their own experiences or the experiences of other people they know.

3. Read about the life of Baseball Hall of Famer Lou Gehrig and the ALS that caused his early death. How did he face his illness? What lessons can we learn from the choices he made in life and while nearing death? What do you think about his famous final speech at Yankee Stadium?
4. How does the U.S. health care system compare with other countries? In what ways is it better? In what areas is there room for improvement?

5. Look at the list of U.S. health care programs in Exhibit 7.6. Research some of the programs. Which ones are your favorites? Why? What special health care programs exist in your state?

EXHIBIT 7.6   **Where Health Care Social Workers Practice**

Acute care hospitals	Hospice programs
Ambulatory care outpatient and public health clinics	Insurance companies
Children's and other specialized hospitals	Long-term care or nursing home settings
Clinical trials	Physician's offices
Community health centers	Private practice social work
Dialysis centers	Public health
Elder law attorney consultants	Rehabilitation services (including subacute centers and transitional care units)
Health maintenance organizations (HMOs)	Rural clinics
Health planning advisory boards	Veterans Affairs hospitals, clinics, and long-term care settings
Home health care agencies	Women's pavilions or health centers
Homeless shelter health clinics	

ONLINE RESOURCES

- Association of Oncology Social Work (www.aosw.org): Unifies and supports psychosocial oncology practitioners with the common mission of improving psychosocial support services for patients and families facing cancer
- Center for Medicare Advocacy (www.medicareadvocacy.org): Works to ensure that older adults and people with disabilities have fair access to health care and Medicare
- Centers for Disease Control and Prevention (www.cdc.gov): Works 24/7 to protect America from health, safety, and security threats in and outside the United States
- Centers for Medicare and Medicaid Services (cms.hhs.gov): An agency within the U.S. Department of Health and Human Services that administrates several key federal health programs (see also the official U.S. government site for Medicare information: www.medicare.gov)
- Council of Nephrology Social Workers of the National Kidney Foundation (www.kidney.org/professionals/ CNSW): Provides information about working with people who have chronic kidney disease
- National Association of Social Workers HIV/AIDS Spectrum Project (socialworkers.org/practice/hiv_aids/default.asp): Offers health and behavioral health care providers education and technical assistance related to the effects of HIV/AIDS on mental health and wellness
- National Patient Advocate Foundation (www.npaf.org): A national nonprofit organization providing patients a voice in improving access to, and reimbursement for, high-quality health care through regulatory and legislative reform at the state and federal levels
- World Health Organization (www.who.int/en): Within the UN system, responsible for providing leadership on global health matters, shaping the health research agenda, setting norms and standards, articulating evidence-based policy options, providing technical support to countries, and monitoring and assessing health trends

STUDENT STUDY SITE

Sharpen your skills with SAGE edge at **edge.sagepub.com/cox**

SAGE edge for Students provides a personalized approach to help you accomplish your coursework goals in an easy-to-use learning environment.

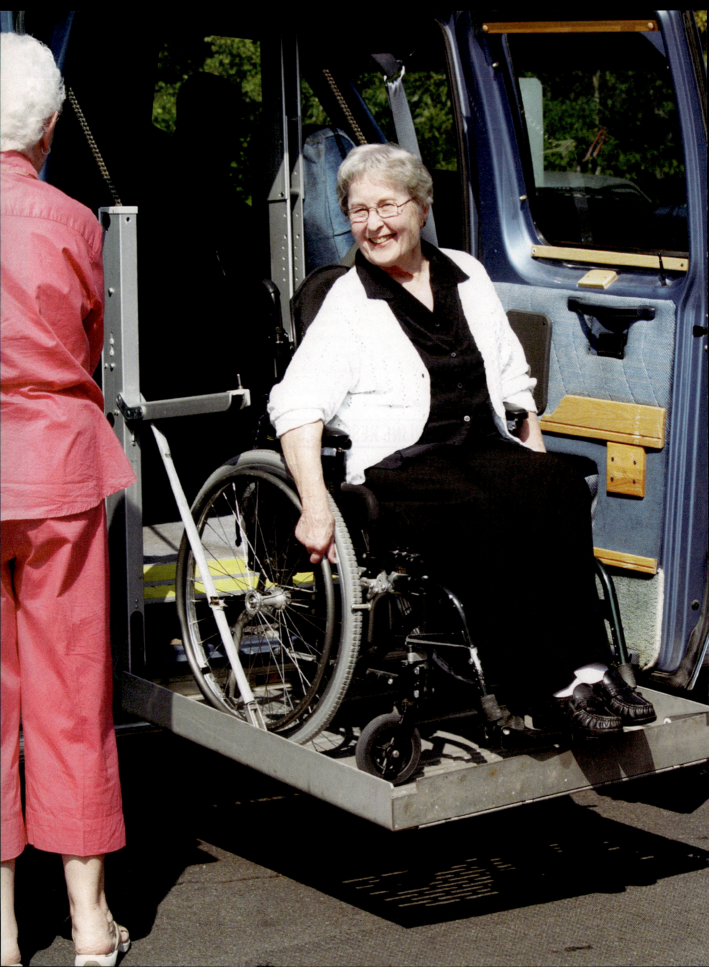

Chapter 8: PHYSICAL AND MENTAL CHALLENGES

Learning Objectives

After reading this chapter, you will be able to

1. Identify three main categories of physical and mental challenges, and types of disabilities within those categories.
2. Understand the importance of stigma in the lives of people with physical and mental challenges.
3. Distinguish between Americans' historical and current views of physical and mental challenges.
4. Identify federal policies relevant to people living with physical and mental challenges.
5. Understand why people with physical and mental challenges and developmental disabilities are more likely to experience disparities in health and health care.
6. Articulate social work roles and careers related to people with physical, mental and developmental challenges.

Joe Advocates for People With Intellectual Disabilities

As the administrator of The Arc (historically known as the Association for Retarded Citizens), an organization founded in 1950 by a small group of parents and others, Joe recognizes the invaluable social work services his staff renders to families and people with intellectual disabilities.

In addition to collecting community donations for The Arc's thrift stores, his staff promotes and protects human rights and supports the inclusion and participation of Arc clients in community life throughout their lifetimes. As Joe writes his reports, grants, and letters to legislators, he reflects on the strong grassroots network of the 140,000 members affiliated with more than 700 state and local chapters across the United States. When Joe drives to The Arc's national headquarters in Washington, D.C., he spends time continuing to educate policymakers and service providers on best practices and issues that affect people with intellectual disabilities and their families. Joe is proud that The Arc is a national force that creates the environment and opportunities for people with intellectual disabilities and their families to have choices as they live their lives.

When Joe supervises social work students, he makes sure to emphasize the crucial role of advocacy with the executive and legislative branches of government, administrative agencies, school districts, and other providers. Joe has students follow policies at the national level so they can learn how to influence federal agencies and policymakers, and obtain funding opportunities for disability programs and services (The Arc, 2014).

People with physical or mental challenges and developmental disabilities are people who have individual abilities, interests, and needs. They are mothers, fathers, daughters, sons, brothers, sisters, friends, neighbors, coworkers, teachers, and students. Their contributions enrich our communities and society as they live, work, and share their lives.

About 54 million Americans—1 out of every 5 individuals—have a disability. About 15% of the world's population has physical, mental, or developmental disabilities, and there are no available data for indigenous persons with disabilities (UN Enable, n.d.-a). Accidents, genetic diseases, viruses, and illnesses render many people disabled to a different degree. But the leading causes of disability are more mundane than you might imagine (see Exhibit 8.1).

Americans currently live in a rather inclusive society, yet people with physical or health-related psychosocial, sensory,

mental or psychiatric, cognitive or learning, neurological, or intellectual challenges and developmental disabilities still experience a reality that often includes limitations, stigma, discrimination, abuse, and poverty and loss of dignity. Historical mind-sets partly explain this behavior. For example, many colonial Americans shunned people who had mental or physical difficulties; family members hid disabled relatives. Early documentation also reveals, however, that renowned citizens such as Thomas Jefferson, Washington Irving, and Cotton Mather had speech difficulties, yet held formidable positions despite their physical impairment.

In corporate America today, much has changed. New laws for disability rights, disability activism, and expanded coverage of disability issues have changed public awareness and knowledge. Some stereotypes have been eliminated, but other misrepresentations persist. Consider how athletes and dancers with prosthetic legs compete on the world stage, and

EXHIBIT 8.1   Top Causes of Physical Disability Experienced in the United States

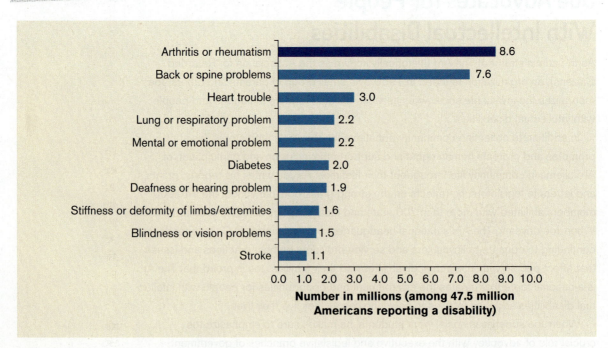

Source: Centers for Disease Control and Prevention (2012a).

how children with autism succeed in professions that require advanced degrees. Still, however, old attitudes, experiences, labeling language, and stereotypes exist in school settings, the workplace, health care settings, and within families.

People with physical and mental challenges and developmental disabilities crave accurate depictions that present a respectful, positive view of them as active participants in society, in regular social, home, and work environments. People with disabilities also focus attention on challenging issues that affect their quality of life, such as accessible transportation, affordable health care, discrimination, employment opportunities, and housing.

By virtue of the National Association of Social Workers (2008) *Code of Ethics*, social workers are called to support the worth and dignity of all people—including those with physical and mental challenges and developmental disabilities. Professional social workers also run groups, develop supportive services and programs, write grants, and advocate for the passage of legislation that benefits those living with any type of disability. Fundamental to advancing the science of disablement is the ability to communicate across disciplines and to speak a common language that is understood across related professional fields and disciplines (Bickenbach, Chatterji, Badley, & Üstün, 1999).

DEFINITIONS OF PHYSICAL, MENTAL, AND DEVELOPMENTAL CHALLENGES

There is no single, universally accepted definition of disability. More than 20 definitions of disability have been used for purposes of entitlement to government services, private or public income support programs, or statistical analysis (Centers for Disease Control and Prevention, 2014c; World Health Organization, 2013). For the purposes of this book, we can say that **disability** is a temporary or permanent reduction in function. Social workers really prefer to use the asset-promoting positive terms of *physical* and *mental challenges*, rather than *disability*, when working with client systems.

For some people, disability is the functional consequence of chronic mental or physical conditions; yet, for others, disability is the by-product of physical or social environments that do not accommodate people with different functional abilities. The health condition or impairment may be visible or invisible to others, and it may be present at birth or start at any age.

The body of law that protects people with a medical condition in the workplace also defines disability. To be protected, a person must be qualified for the job and show that she or he has a disability in one of three ways:

- A person may be labeled as disabled if she or he has a physical or mental condition that substantially limits a major life activity (such as hearing, learning, seeing, talking, or walking). For adults, this is reflected in whether they can engage in work, and for children, this is reflected in their ability to engage in age-appropriate activities.

- A person may be labeled as disabled if she or he has a history of a disability (such as cancer that is in remission).

- A person may be labeled as disabled if she or he is thought to have a physical or mental impairment that is not transitory (lasting or expected to last 6 months or less) and is severe and interferes with normal activities of living. The condition must have existed for at least 12 months.

TYPES OF PHYSICAL AND MENTAL CHALLENGES

People can have different types of challenges that most laws refer to as disabilities; in this book we classify them as developmental, physical, or mental. The severity of impairment varies as well. Also, people can experience more than one disability, or **co-occurring disabilities** (Gargiulo, 2006). An example of co-occurring disabilities is when a person with an intellectual disability also has vision and neurological impairments.

Disabilities can also be defined as "categorical" or "functional." In brief, people with **categorical disabilities** have a significant sensory impairment or mental illness and have developmental delays. They are likely to need long-term care and are eligible for special education. **Functional disabilities** limit a person's ability to perform physical activities, and they often can be ameliorated with assistive devices or technology.

DEVELOPMENTAL DISABILITIES

A **developmental disability** is a severe chronic disability that manifests before the age of 22 and is likely to continue indefinitely. It may occur because of a genetic predisposition or an issue before, during, or after the person is born (DeWeaver, 1983). Developmental disabilities are common and have increased, requiring more health and educational services.

Dr. Temple Grandin, Autism Advocate

Now a professor at Colorado State University, writer, and inventor, Temple Grandin (2011) was born August 2, 1947. Until she was almost 4 years old, she screamed instead of talked. Physicians diagnosed Temple as being autistic and told her parents to institutionalize her.

In response, Temple's supportive mother sought a second opinion, and that doctor suggested that Temple try speech therapy. Temple's very caring and creative mother proceeded to hire a nanny for her daughter. In 1966, Temple attended and graduated from a New Hampshire boarding school, where she was teased horribly and called a nerd. In 1970, she earned her bachelor's degree in psychology from Franklin Pierce College, and then she earned her master's degree in animal science from Arizona State University. Temple received her doctorate degree in animal science from the University of Illinois at Urbana-Champaign in 1989.

A beautiful and informative HBO documentary titled *Temple Grandin* (Jackson, 2010) reveals Temple's achievements as an animal welfare expert as well as a staunch leader in autism advocacy movements. Temple advocates for early interventions to help address autism and sensory issues. She also promotes having supportive teachers and mentors who can direct the fixations of children with autistic spectrum disorders in positive and productive directions. To this day, Temple remains hyper-sensitive to noise and sensory stimuli and she prefers being alone. She decided not to marry. Temple has published best-selling books on autism and humane treatment of animals. She has also designed several creative livestock handling facilities that keep cattle calm and prevent them from getting hurt.

Temple Grandin's story shows how someone with the label of autism, or any other physical or mental disability, should not be stigmatized or stereotyped as being "hopeless" or "helpless." Fortunately, Temple had loving family members, teachers, and mentors in her formative years that focused on her strengths and assets rather than her deficits. As a result, Temple has achieved a lot, including fame. Temple exemplifies how the disability label of autism spectrum disorder can be transformed into an asset. In 2010, she was listed among *Time* magazine's 100 most influential people in the world, in the "Heroes" category.

1. How does Temple's story reflect a focus on assets versus deficits for people with developmental disabilities?

2. What role(s) do family members, teachers, and health care providers play in relating to people with autism spectrum disorders?

A combination of causes can lead to a developmental disability being diagnosed, and genetic counselors are experts at understanding these connections. These are some of the most commonly encountered developmental disabilities:

• *Autism.* **Autism** is a neurobiological developmental disorder that generally appears before age 3 and affects the normal development of the brain in areas of social interaction, communication skills, and cognitive functions. People with autism have trouble in nonverbal and verbal communication, social interactions, and leisure or play activities. Asperger's syndrome is now considered a part of the autism spectrum. People with autism may be high functioning. Dr. Temple Grandin, for example, was diagnosed with autism but has earned a PhD and made a name for herself in the areas of animal welfare and autism advocacy.

- *Cerebral Palsy*. **Cerebral palsy** is a chronic condition affecting control of the body and/or limb movement, muscle tone, and coordination. It is caused by damage to one or more specific areas of the brain as the brain develops. Usually, there is no damage to sensory or motor nerves controlling the muscles. The brain change is not progressive, but the characteristics of disabilities resulting from brain damage often change over time.

- *Down syndrome*. **Trisomy 21**, commonly known as **Down syndrome,** is a chromosomal disorder caused by the presence of an extra 21st chromosome. It is associated with some impairment of cognitive ability and physical growth, as well as a distinctive facial appearance.

- *Epilepsy*. **Epilepsy** is a brain disorder that causes a person to have recurring seizures. Epilepsy is more prevalent than autism, cerebral palsy, multiple sclerosis, and Parkinson's disease combined. Globally, about 65 million people have epilepsy, and nearly 80% of cases occur in developing countries. The cause is usually unknown; however, brain trauma, brain cancer, stroke, and drug and alcohol misuse can result in epilepsy. Sustaining a concussion from a sports injury or having been dropped as a baby can also cause epilepsy. It becomes more common as people age and is controllable but not curable. Epilepsy kills thousands of people each year.

- *Fetal alcohol syndrome*. **Fetal alcohol syndrome** is a pattern of physical and mental defects that develop in some unborn babies when their mom drinks alcohol (or uses drugs) during pregnancy. It is one of the most common causes of intellectual disability and the only one that is 100% preventable. In addition, its lifelong effects could include growth deficiencies, central nervous system problems, poor motor skills, mortality, malformations of the skeletal system and major organ systems (heart and brain), and problems with learning, memory, social interaction, attention span, problem solving, speech, and/or hearing. Facial features may include small eyes, short or upturned nose, thin lips, and flat cheeks.

- *Fragile X syndrome*. **Fragile X syndrome** is the most common cause of inherited mental incapacities. It is one of the most prevalent intellectual disabilities inherited through generations. The clinical features are very subtle and difficult to diagnose. The impact can range from learning disabilities to more severe cognitive or intellectual

Source: Wikimedia Commons

∧ Temple Grandin gives a TED Talk called "The World Needs All Kinds of Minds."

disabilities. This syndrome is the most common cause of autism or "autism-like" behaviors. Symptoms can also include characteristic physical and behavioral features, and delays in speech and language.

- *Prader-Willi syndrome*. The most commonly known genetic cause of life-threatening obesity in children is **Prader-Willi syndrome**. This is an uncommon genetic disability. It causes low levels of sex hormones, poor muscle tone, and a constant feeling of hunger. The section of the brain that controls feelings of fullness or hunger does not work correctly in people with this syndrome. Their overeating leads to obesity. Babies with Prader-Willi syndrome are usually floppy, with poor muscle tone, and have trouble sucking. Later, other signs appear. These include short stature, poor motor skills, weight gain, underdeveloped sex organs, mild cognitive impairment, and learning disabilities.

PHYSICAL OR MOBILITY CHALLENGES

A physical challenge or disability is a highly individualized condition that substantially limits one or more basic physical activities in life (e.g., walking, climbing stairs, reaching, carrying, or lifting). A mobility impairment describes any difficulty that limits functions of moving, in any of the limbs or in fine motor abilities. It can stem from multiple causes and be permanent, intermittent, or temporary. The most common permanent physical challenges or disabilities are musculoskeletal impairments such as partial or total paralysis, amputation, spinal injury, arthritis, muscular dystrophy, multiple sclerosis, cerebral palsy, and traumatic brain injury. Rates of physical and mental challenges are growing due to population aging and increases in chronic health conditions, among other causes.

These are some common forms of physical or mobility disability:

- *Orthopedic problems.* **Orthopedic problems** are diseases or defects of the muscles and bones that cause people not to be able to move normally (Hallahan, Kauffman, & Pullen, 2012). Genetics or the results of injury, disease, accidents, or other developmental disorders may make it difficult or impossible for people to walk, stand, sit, or use their hands because they can't properly move their legs, arms, spine, or joints.

- *Hearing and vision problems.* Both these types of physical disability are challenges in perception. Visual impairment signifies a challenge in seeing. People can have a mild visual impairment and correct it with glasses, contact lenses, or laser surgery. The vision of others cannot be corrected, and they become functionally limited or visually impaired ("legally blind"). People's ability to hear also varies greatly. The term *hard of hearing* actually refers to people with mild to moderate hearing loss. By comparison, people who are deaf have moderate to severe hearing loss. Any of these people may or may not identify themselves as deaf. Two worldviews describe people with moderate to severe hearing loss: Deaf people may be considered to have a medical problem, or they may consider themselves part of the Deaf community, a unique cultural group whose members use sign language and emphasize strengths (National Association of the Deaf, 2011).

- *Epilepsy.* In addition to being known as a developmental disability, this seizure disorder is also considered a physical challenge. A seizure may involve a sudden change in a person's consciousness level or sensory distortions. Epilepsy can be caused by any type of injury to or condition in the brain, such as high fevers, infections, physical damage, or chemical imbalances. In about 70% of cases, the cause remains unknown.

MENTAL CHALLENGES

A **neurocognitive impairment** is an encompassing term to describe any **neurocognitive** characteristic that blocks the cognition process. The term may describe deficits in specific cognitive abilities, global intellectual performance, or drug-induced cognitive/memory impairment, such as from alcohol, glucocorticoids, or benzodiazepines. Neurocognitive impairments may be congenital or caused by environmental variables such as brain injuries, neurological disorders, or mental illness. Although a neurocognitive challenge is usually not visible, it is as legitimate an impairment to functioning as a physical disability is. Neurocognitive impairments include the following:

- *Intellectual disability.* **Intellectual disability** is a disorder characterized by significant limitations both in intellectual functioning and in the ability to adapt to circumstances, or **adaptive behavior**. The term *intellectual disability* is now used to describe the same population of individuals who were diagnosed previously with **mental retardation.** Every person who was eligible for a diagnosis of mental retardation is eligible for a diagnosis of intellectual disability. This disability varies in level, type, and duration, and degree of need for individualized services and supports. Intellectual disability ranges from mild (IQ 50–70) to moderate (IQ 35–49) to severe (IQ 20–34) to profound (IQ below 20), as measured by the Wechsler Intelligence Test.

- *Learning differences.* **Learning disabilities or differences** are neurological disorders that can make it difficult to acquire certain academic and social skills. They are not the result of poor intelligence or laziness. Well-known learning differences include dyslexia (hinders reading, writing, and spelling), dyscalculia (hinders math), dysgraphia (hinders writing, spelling, or putting thoughts to paper), dyspraxia (affects motor skill development), poor executive functioning (governs one's ability to plan, organize, and manage details), and attention-deficit hyperactivity disorder. Learning differences do not disappear with time.

- *Traumatic brain injury.* **Traumatic brain injury** usually results from a violent blow to the head or body, or when an object, such as a bullet, penetrates the skull. Such an injury can have wide-ranging physical and psychological effects due to damage to the brain. Some symptoms may appear immediately after the traumatic event, while others may appear days or weeks later (Mayo Clinic, 2014).

SOCIAL WORK IN ACTION

Iris Counsels a Family About Concussions in Sports

IRIS works on the rehab floor of the local teaching hospital. Tom, a high school athlete, now a junior, is one of her newly assigned clients whom she recently met and assessed. Later this afternoon Iris is scheduled to meet with Tom's parents, sister, and grandmother.

Tom told Iris that he lives for football. But he experienced his second moderate concussion during the Thanksgiving Day game. He feels nauseous and dizzy. Not to be deterred by his injury, Tom is motivated to recover and plans to continue playing football because he has always dreamed of obtaining a scholarship to play football in college.

Iris feels a bit anxious about talking with Tom's family, because she is aware of the serious consequences of sports injuries across the life course and doesn't want to dash Tom's dreams. She plans to share with Tom and his parents an article about concussions she read in a medical journal (DeKosky, Ikonomovic, & Gandy, 2010). It referred to the National Football League's creating a poster to be hung in league locker rooms, warning players of possible long-term health effects of concussions. It also cited how public awareness has been elevated due to the pathological consequences of traumatic brain injuries linked to high-contact sports and car crashes.

Iris is going to reinforce the article's recommendation that Tom and his family keep an accurate diary of his day-to-day progress in rehabilitation and his concerns with his physical and mental health over time. The diary will not only improve Tom's and his family's understanding of this chronic condition but also provide Tom's doctors with additional insights into traumatic brain injury.

1. What websites and community resources might Iris need to locate to best counsel Tom and his family?

2. How might Tom and his family be feeling?

TIME TO THINK

Neurocognitive impairments not only affect the person with the challenge/disability; they also have substantial influence on other family members. Imagine that one of your family members had a neurocognitive challenge/impairment. How might your family member's neurocognitive impairment affect you?

STIGMA AND DISCRIMINATION AGAINST PEOPLE WITH PHYSICAL AND MENTAL CHALLENGES

People with physical and mental challenges and developmental disabilities experience discrimination and injustices. Sometimes the discrimination is subtle and unconscious, as when people talk over the head of an individual in a wheelchair. Other times the prejudice and discrimination is blatant and intended. On a social level, people with physical and mental challenges are often overlooked. For example, they are seldom recognized as a group to be included in a national response to HIV/AIDS, and they are likely to be neglected or abandoned during evacuations in disasters and conflicts due to lack of preparation, planning, and transportation systems.

In the case of disability, discrimination is often due to **social stigma**, which is generally a "stain" on the way a person is perceived that leads him or her to be shunned by others. A famous 20th century sociologist, Erving Goffman (1963), noted that "stigma is a process by which the reaction of others spoils normal identity." Goffman identified three forms of social stigma:

- Visible or outer deformations such as scars, a cleft lip, or obesity—physical or social disabilities

- Deviations in personal traits, such as mental illness, alcoholism, drug addiction, or having a criminal background
- Imagined or real traits of an ethnic group, nationality, or religion that are thought to deviate from the prevailing norm, or "tribal stigmas"

Regardless of the form of social stigma, the stigmatized person is subjected to discrimination and loses status. Stigmatization can occur at work, in health care, in educational settings, in the criminal justice system, and in one's own family.

Disability specialist social workers have observed how stigma affects the behavior of people who are stigmatized. For example, by age 10, most children are aware of disability stereotypes, and children who are members of stigmatized groups are aware of the stereotypes at an even younger age. People who are stereotyped and stigmatized because of their disability begin to act the way that the people who are stigmatizing them expect them to act. Stigma can also shape people's beliefs and emotions, leading them to feel depressed or have low self-esteem.

TIME TO THINK

What are your thoughts about Americans' views of physical, mental, and developmental disability then and now?

Suppose you had either a visible or invisible disability. Would you disclose this information during a job interview?

SOCIAL WORK AND PHYSICAL AND MENTAL CHALLENGES

Most people will have a physical or mental challenge in their lifetime. Often that challenge or disability will last for a short time, but some people live with developmental, physical, or mental disabilities for a long time. Any of these people may require a social worker to help them navigate services, resources, and health care.

HISTORICAL BACKGROUND OF SERVICES FOR PEOPLE WITH MENTAL AND PHYSICAL CHALLENGES

Historically, people with disabilities have been regarded as people to be pitied, feared, or ignored. They have been portrayed as helpless victims, repulsive adversaries, heroic individuals overcoming tragedy, and charity cases who must depend on others for their well-being and care. Media coverage frequently focuses on heartwarming features and inspirational stories that reinforce stereotypes, patronize, and underestimate people's capabilities (Keller & Hallahan, 1990).

The historical roots of today's attitudes toward physical and mental challenges help explain why those attitudes are so complex today. Indigenous North Americans had no concept of disability (Nielsen, 2012). The Europeans who established the colonies, however, did have the concept that physical and mental differences required intervention. The Europeans also brought new diseases to the continent, which created more physical and mental infirmities that they defined as disabilities.

The colonists also introduced the notion that those who were disabled, along with children and newcomers, should not be punished for failing to observe some of the laws (Nielsen, 2012). Although people with intellectual disabilities were often abused and exploited, as they are today, disabled people were also cared for—mostly by families, although people with physical and mental challenges became a community responsibility if they were poor and could not be adequately controlled by their families. Of course, as is the case today, the treatment of people with physical and mental challenges depended a great deal on socioeconomic status, race, and gender.

During the 1840 census, people began debating society's role in taking care of disabled people, and race was a complicating factor (Nielsen, 2012). After the Revolutionary War, the approach to disability changed dramatically. Disability began to be explained as a biological matter. People considered those with epilepsy to be "idiotic" or insane, and heavy drinkers—along with people considered morally suspect, such as unmarried pregnant women—were often sent to almshouses, prisons, and asylums.

Treatments were sometimes gruesome, including "purging, bleeding, frights, hard labor, and immersion in cold water" (Nielsen, 2012, p. 38). After visiting some of the indigent and mentally ill people in Massachusetts, Dorothea Dix began advocating for reform. She found that people with intellectual disability and mental illness were sometimes penned up with criminals, sometimes chained and naked. The facilities were not always heated in winter, and the residents were abused, beaten, and not given adequate food.

CURRENT TRENDS

Confronting Stigma

MOST people with disabilities are well aware of the way other people perceive them. They understand stigma and discrimination. In the past few decades, however, people living with disabilities, as well as the people who love, support, and champion them, have developed some interesting—and even fun—ways to try to overcome stigma.

Sports for people with disabilities is one well-known activity that can help reduce stigma and discrimination. The Special Olympics, a movement founded in 1968, is now global. Its mission is to provide year-round sports training and athletic competition through "Olympic-type sports for children and adults with intellectual disabilities, giving them continuing opportunities to develop physical fitness, demonstrate courage, experience joy and participate in a sharing of gifts, skills and friendship with their families, other Special Olympics athletes and the community" (Special Olympics, 2014). Other examples include the Paralympics and wheelchair basketball for people with physical disabilities. Sports are an excellent platform for strategies of inclusion and adaptation because they have the unique ability to transcend linguistic, cultural, and social barriers. Sports and top athletes of all kinds are also universally popular. Concordia College's Social Work Club, for example, has participated in area Special Olympics (Taylor, 2012).

1. How might seeing people with intellectual disabilities participating in sports serve to put them in a new light for people who tend to stigmatize them?

2. Social workers are eligible to become members of the Special Olympics Global Scholars delegation, which allows them to travel internationally with people who have intellectual disabilities. What interest might you have in becoming involved with such a delegation?

Art created by people with physical or mental challenges also helps break down stigma. People with intellectual disabilities are often encouraged to create paintings, sculptures, and other *objets d'art,* some of them highly sophisticated interpretations of the world. Another interesting artistic effort was a documentary film on artists with disabilities, called *Shameless: The Art of Disability* (Klein, 2006).

The project was organized by an established director who experienced a debilitating stroke. She gathered a group of five artists with disabilities for a pajama party, where they identified some of the common stereotypes of people with disabilities in film and fiction (e.g., The Monster, The Saint, The Psycho, The Poor Little Crippled Girl). The artists made a pact to meet a year later at the KicksART Festival to present their own images of disability. The resulting film was praised as humorous, energetic, honest, and vulnerable. As the film tracks these artists, viewers come to recognize their passion for art and understand the everyday complexities and richness of life with a disability.

Once the industrial revolution got under way, in the 1890s and beyond, disabilities due to workplace accidents and exposure to harmful substances increased dramatically:

Textile mill operatives lost fingers, hands, and arms due to rapidly moving machinery. . . . Boilermakers, shipbuilders, and train engineers often lost hearing due to their noisy surroundings. Clock and watch painters, most of them female, experienced the paralysis and mental debility caused by lead poisoning as well as throat and mouth cancer. (Nielsen, 2012, p. 127)

In the late 1800s and early 1900s, the Progressive Era, new understandings of blindness and deafness led to reforms

of institutions that housed some of the disabled, and they experienced some measure of acceptance and empowerment (Nielsen, 2012). In contrast, people with intellectual disability and mental illness still were warehoused in bleak circumstances.

During World War I, adaptive technologies were developed for soldiers who became disabled (Nielsen, 2012). World War II brought new technologies, as well as a new cadre of rehabilitation experts.

People with physical and mental challenges began to be treated much more sensitively during and after the Great Depression (Nielsen, 2012). The League of the Physically Handicapped was formed and began promoting the idea that people with disabilities are entitled to the full rights of citizenship.

▲ Dorothea Dix advocated for the rights of the mentally ill.

principles of self-determination and deinstitutionalization. They are community agencies, usually staffed by people with disabilities, who use peer counseling and advocacy to help others live on their own. A distinct culture and philosophy resulted from this independent-living movement and now exists around independent-living centers.

However, in the 1970s and 1980s, professional care-givers, advocates, and decision makers were already beginning to realize that deinstitutionalization was leaving some disabled persons without enough support (Logsdon-Breakstone, 2012). Only the privileged or lucky few were able to be housed in independent-living centers, community-based mental health centers, or group homes. The rest were being left to fend for themselves on the streets or were incarcerated. Today, people who have intellectual disability and mental illness and who lack the resources for professional care most often end up in jail or prison.

However, in 2009 the Department of Health and Human Services created the **Community Living Initiative.** The initiative developed and implemented innovative strategies that increase opportunities for Americans with disabilities and older adults to enjoy meaningful community living. The Affordable Care Act, signed into law in 2010, expands the scope of the initiative and helps U.S. states promote and support community living for people with disabilities.

DEINSTITUTIONALIZATION

In the 20th century, as the horrors of some institutions for the disabled became better known, some reformers began advocating **deinstitutionalization,** or the removal of people with physical and mental challenges from institutions and better integration into the community. From 1965 to 1980, as the idea of deinstitutionalization took hold, public asylums lost about 60% of their inmates (Nielsen, 2012).

With the disability rights movement of the late 1960s, people with physical and mental challenges, along with their friends, family members, and professionals, endeavored to change the view that a person with a chronic illness or disability will always be unable to cope independently with life. The disability rights movement argued that just like other minorities, people with disabilities are disadvantaged as much or more by discrimination as by their physical limitations (Gliedman & Roth, 1980; Scotch, 1988). Many asylums and other institutions were closed, and their residents were sent home to enjoy life on their own. **Independent-living centers** began to appear in the late 1960s and espoused the

AMERICANS WITH DISABILITIES ACT

In 1990, the **Americans with Disabilities Act (ADA)** was passed. It was written to protect persons with disabilities from discrimination based on stigma. The ADA defines disability as any physical or mental impairment that substantially limits one or more major life activities such as caring for oneself, performing manual tasks, walking, seeing, hearing, speaking, breathing, learning, or working.

Enforcement of the ADA is handled on a case-by-case basis. People are not entitled to protection under the ADA simply because they have been diagnosed with a disability. The disability must substantially limit their ability to perform major life activities. The ADA uses a four-stage framework to categorize the level of difficulty experienced by an individual, ranging from least to most severe (Cornell University, 2013; Jette, 2006; Masala & Petretto, 2008):

1. Pathology

2. Impairment

3. Functional limitation

4. Disability

Multiple physical, mental, and developmental disabilities are covered by the ADA. Following is a partial list of these: (1) physical, sight, speech, or hearing impairments; (2) epilepsy; (3) muscular dystrophy; (4) multiple sclerosis; (5) cancer, heart diseases; (6) diabetes; (7) HIV or AIDS; (8) cognitive disabilities; (9) psychiatric disabilities; (10) specific learning disabilities; (11) developmental disabilities; and (12) recovered drug or alcohol addiction.

The law places strict limits on employers when it comes to asking job applicants to answer medical questions, take a medical exam, or identify a disability.

After a job is offered to an applicant, the law allows an employer to condition the job offer on the applicant answering certain medical questions or successfully passing a medical exam, but only if all new employees in the same type of job have to answer the questions or take the exam.

Once a person is hired and has started work, an employer generally can only ask medical questions or require a medical exam if the employer needs medical documentation to support an employee's request for an accommodation or if the employer believes that an employee is not able to perform a job successfully or safely because of a medical condition.

The law also requires that employers keep all medical records and information confidential and in separate medical files. (U.S. Equal Employment Opportunity Commission, 2014)

SOCIAL WORK PRACTICE WITH PHYSICAL AND MENTAL CHALLENGES AND DEVELOPMENTAL DISABILITIES

Social workers who specialize in knowledge about physical, mental, neurocognitive, or developmental disabilities may end up working in a hospital, mental health organization, supportive rehabilitative services, vocational rehabilitation, an employee assistance program, resettlement programs for refugees, sports clinics, HIV/AIDS clinics, disaster relief, the military, or residential treatment centers. Social workers observe how physical, emotional, or cognitive disabilities alter the lives or people they serve.

Source: Wikimedia/Healthcare bill.

∧ President Obama reacts to the passing of the Affordable Care Act in 2010.

Because social workers tend to learn about physical and mental challenges just at the time their clients are doing the same, they have come to view disability as rather stressful, where a sudden crisis turns into protracted, irremediable problems, strains, and disappointments. Social workers who help serve clients while under stress are encouraged to adopt the following practice behaviors (Mackelprang & Salsgiver, 2009; May & LaMont, 2014):

- Be person-centered and involve people with physical/mental challenges (disabilities) in decision-making processes that directly affect their lives
- Facilitate access and respect in a person's environment
- Focus on helping the person and his or her support system cope well with challenging situations
- Incorporate a strengths-based and resilience-oriented perspective to build on the person's inherent strengths and resources

Person-First Language

Another way social workers can better serve their clients is to be careful about the terminology they use. Because words are very powerful, the language we use to refer to people with physical, mental, and developmental disabilities shapes our beliefs and ideas about them. Old, inaccurate, and inappropriate descriptors perpetuate negative stereotypes and attitudinal barriers. When we describe people by their labels or medical diagnoses, we devalue and disrespect them as people. In contrast, if we use thoughtful terminology, we can foster positive attitudes about people with physical/mental challenges and developmental disabilities.

One of the major improvements in communicating with and about people with disabilities is **person-first language,** which emphasizes the person, not the disability. For example, we refer to a **person with a disability (PWD)** rather than "a disabled person." Saying our client is living with schizophrenia is more empowering than saying "our schizophrenic client." Instead of describing a person as "wheelchair-bound," we could say that he lives with a mobility disability or is a person that requires a wheelchair. By placing the person first, the physical or mental challenge is no longer the primary, defining characteristic of the individual but just one of several aspects of the whole person. Person-first language is an objective way of acknowledging, communicating, and reporting on disabilities. It eliminates generalizations and stereotypes.

The terminology used to refer to individuals with disabilities, as well as to the disabilities themselves, has also changed. Social workers avoid using the following words: *birth defect*, *deaf and dumb*, *fits* (epileptic seizures), *retarded*, *stupid*, *normal*, *cripple*, *handicapped*, *invalid*, *victim*, *insane*, *crazy*, *lunatic*, or *mental patient*.

TIME TO THINK

Do the words that others use to describe you have an influence on your life? To what extent do you think that language shapes attitudes and attitudes drive our actions?

What do you think about the concept of Person-first language? Why should we not use the term special needs?

Services for Persons With Physical and Mental Challenges

As direct service providers, social workers in disability settings are advocates, educators, clinicians, facilitators, group leaders, and program developers, and are employed in for-profit, non-profit, and public programs intended to serve people living with disabilities. Social workers assess severity levels of disability in clients who present with a chronic medical condition or a physical or cognitive impairment. Social workers engage in therapy groups; care management; assessment/information/referral services; individual or self-advocacy initiatives to address education, employment, health care, and other concerns; residential support; family support; employment programs; and leisure and recreational programs. Because people with physical and mental challenges or developmental disabilities also seek social services for situations not specific to issues presented by their impairments, a generalist social work approach to practice is very applicable.

Social workers can also help their clients with four specific issues relevant to their condition:

- *Civil rights.* Many clients with disabilities are protected by five particular acts that acknowledge the civil rights of people with disabilities. Exhibit 8.2 outlines these acts. Social workers who are familiar with the provisions of these acts will be more effective advocates for clients.

- *Income support.* Many people living with physical and mental challenges or developmental disabilities

EXHIBIT 8.2   Civil Rights Protections for People With Disabilities

ACT	YEAR	PROVISIONS
Architectural Barriers Act	1968	Requires buildings paid for by the federal government to be accessible and safe for PWDs; allows for public accommodation
Rehabilitation Act	1973	Prohibits job discrimination by federal contractors/grantees on the basis of disability; also funds independent-living centers
Education for All Handicapped Children Act	1975	Establishes that children with disabilities are entitled to an appropriate elementary and secondary education; reauthorized in 1990 and renamed the Individuals with Disabilities Education Act. As a result of this law, many children with disabilities are now educated in public schools and "mainstreamed" into regular classrooms as much as possible
Air Carrier Access Act	1986	Prohibits airlines from discriminating against air travelers on the basis of disability
Americans with Disabilities Act	1990	Prohibits discrimination in employment, public accommodation, public services, telecommunications, and transportation on the basis of disability by public- and private-sector employers, businesses, and service providers

Source: Adapted from Asch and Mudrick (1995, p. 758, Table 5).

cannot earn enough through a job to support themselves financially. They are often eligible for **income support**. Public assistance may also be available. Since 1950, when a fourth public assistance program titled Aid to the Disabled was added to the Social Security Act of 1935, federal and state governments have been able to provide assistance to the needy, blind, aged, and totally disabled through the Supplemental Security Income program. In addition, the Social Security Disability Insurance program provides long-term income support to workers whose disabilities prevent them from working, no matter the cause of their disabilities. Disability Insurance, workers' compensation, and Supplemental Security Income fall under the category of income support.

- *Education and rehabilitation.* A multitude of education and **rehabilitation** services are available to people with physical and mental challenges. Through the Rehabilitation and Services Administration, grants are distributed that help people with mental and physical challenges get work and live by themselves, as they are provided with supportive counseling services, medical and psychological assistance, job training, and individualized assistance. Also, clients who are older adults, have a disability, or are determined to be legally blind may receive Supplemental Security Income. The maximum monthly federal payments to these recipients in 2014 were $721.00 for an individual, $1,082.00 for a couple, and $361.00 for an essential person. Exhibit 8.3 indicates the types of services available to people with disabilities and their funding sources.

- *Genetic counseling.* Social workers can serve individuals or families as genetic counselors in hospital-based and other settings. **Genetic counseling** provides information and support to people who have, or may be at risk for, genetic disorders such as sickle cell anemia and Down syndrome. They may also counsel individuals whose illness or disability is based on lifestyle and environment, as with colon cancer. People may seek genetic counseling if they (1) have a personal or family history of a genetic condition or birth defect, (2) are pregnant or planning to be pregnant after age 35, (3) already have a child with a genetic disorder or birth defect, (4) have had two or more pregnancy losses or a baby who died, or (5) have had ultrasound or screening tests that suggest a possible problem. The National Society of Genetic Counselors (n.d.) advocates for improved access to quality genetic counseling and works to ensure that this profession is a recognized and integral part of the health care system. Genetic counseling is effectively accomplished by social workers who focus on psychological and social adjustment. Social workers need to know about the Human Genome Project, genetic testing, the biology of genetic inheritance, psychosocial counseling, values and ethics, and social policy in genetics (Mealer, Singh, & Murray, 1981; Schild & Black, 1984; Taylor-Brown & Johnson, 1998).

DIVERSITY AND PHYSICAL/MENTAL CHALLENGES

Disability is extremely diverse. More than a billion people, or about 15% of the world's population, have some form of

---

EXHIBIT 8.3   Federal, State, and Local Funding for Disability Services

FEDERAL AND STATE FUNDING

Vocational rehabilitation funding; Medicaid; Old-Age, Survivors, Disability, and Health Insurance; Supplemental Security Income; food stamps; workers' compensation program

STATE AND LOCAL FUNDING

Rehabilitation centers (vocational evaluation, sheltered employment, work adjustment training, counseling services, placement services, respite care, support groups for caregivers, recreational programs, educational programs)

Residential programs (group homes, halfway houses, long-term care/nursing homes, residential treatment centers)

Day care centers (child and adult)

Hospital services (public, private, Veterans Affairs)

Home services (meals-on-wheels, home health services, homemaker services)

SOCIAL WORK IN ACTION

Jade Develops a Transition Plan for a Young Adult With Developmental Disabilities

JADE'S social work position with people who are living with disabilities requires that she know how to develop treatment plans and individualized education plans. She must also be cognizant of the biopsychosocial features of multiple intellectual and developmental disabilities and co-occurring physical and mental disabilities. As skilled as she is, Jade is challenged to help Colin, and his family, given the limited amount of time she can spend with the client system.

One of Jade's clients is Colin, a 19-year-old male attending the local county special services school district. He is currently enrolled in a transition program designed to help students transition from the traditional high school program into the adult world at age 21. He also works in the cafeteria, preparing and serving food. The transition program helps instill a strong work ethic in students and encourages independence and social skills development. Colin also enjoys playing video games. At the center, he participates weekly in a group experience and receives one-on-one counseling with Jade.

However, Colin is diagnosed with autism, lacks good socialization skills, and trusts no one. He rarely makes eye contact and tends to avoid others. His family fears him because he is sometimes very aggressive. One goal in Colin's treatment plan is to reduce the amount of times he says, "I want to kill you," "I want to die," and "I don't want to go home." A second goal is to match Colin with a mentor so he can potentially learn to trust one person and receive cognitive behavioral interventions. A third goal for Colin is to graduate from high school. Jade has also prepared an individualized education plan for Colin to ensure that his educational needs are met. Because Colin is 19, he has been informed of his rights upon completion of the transitional program within the high school. Only if he still requires more behavioral skills to function adequately in the outside world will he be able to stay for an additional year.

The ADA relates to Colin's case. A variety of accommodations are required for Colin to adequately function at home and in groups. One accommodation at school is a scheduled break, because Colin is also diabetic and must eat properly to maintain his blood sugar and insulin levels.

How would you intervene if you were Jade?

---

physical or mental challenge or developmental disability. While some health conditions associated with disability result in poor health and extensive health care needs, others do not. Of course, some of the variation in independence among people with disabilities can be attributed to varieties of difference.

• *Age.* Some children with more severe disabilities are not enrolled in school. Also, adolescents with physical and mental challenges are more likely to be excluded from vital sexual and reproductive health education programs. Adults with disabilities have a 400% elevated risk of developing Type 2 diabetes. Diabetes is also highly correlated with vision loss (Yee, 2011). The aging process for some groups of people with disabilities begins earlier than usual. For example, some people with developmental disabilities show signs of premature aging in their 40s and 50s.

• *Class.* For people who can pay for assistive technology, such devices can help people with learning differences leverage their strengths and work around or compensate for learning problems, which is key to increasing independence in school and throughout life. All people with physical or mental challenges or developmental disabilities have the same general health care needs as everyone else, but they differ in socioeconomic status that dictates insurance resources.

• *Race and ethnicity.* Indigenous people with disabilities experience multiple forms of discriminations and face barriers to the full enjoyment of their rights, based on their indigenous status and also on disability. African American adults have higher morbidity and disability earlier in life compared with white adults; however, when socioeconomic resources, social integration, and other health indicators are adjusted for, the trajectories of disability by race are not significantly different over time (Kelley-Moore & Ferraro, 2004). See Exhibit 8.4 for a breakdown of how disability affects different racial and ethnic groups.

• *Gender.* Women with disabilities receive less screening for breast and cervical cancer than do women without disabilities. (For that matter, people with intellectual impairments and diabetes are less likely to have their weight checked.) Women with mobility difficulties are often unable to access breast and cervical cancer screening because examination tables are not height adjustable and mammography equipment accommodates only women who are able to stand. Women with disabilities face more public and private difficulties in attaining adequate housing, health, education, vocational training, and employment, and are more likely to be institutionalized. Women and girls with physical or mental challenges or developmental disabilities also experience higher risk of gender-based violence, sexual abuse, neglect, maltreatment, and exploitation. The global literacy rate is as low as 1% for women with disabilities (UN Enable, n.d.-b).

EXHIBIT 8.4   Disability Across Race and Ethnicity in the United States

Disability Among U.S. Adults*, by Race and Ethnicity	
RACE/ETHNICITY	**DISABILITY**
Non-Hispanic White	20.3%
Non-Hispanic Black or African American	21.2%
Hispanic	16.9%
Asian	11.6%
Native Hawaiian or other Pacific Islander	16.6%
American Indian or Alaska Native	29.9%

Source: Centers for Disease Control and Prevention (2008).

*Aged 18 years or older

• *Sexual orientation.* People who identify as lesbian, gay, bisexual, transgender, intersex, questioning, or asexual feel marginalized within two communities when they also have a disability. One factor links the two realms of difference: The sexual orientation of men and women is not always visible; similarly, oftentimes physical and mental challenges or developmental disabilities are not visible (e.g., learning difference, traumatic brain injury, multiple sclerosis).

• *Intersections of diversity.* As in other areas of need, multiple dimensions of difference further complicate the lives of those with physical and mental challenges and developmental disabilities. Consider gender and age. As Exhibit 8.5 shows, in all age groups women report more disabilities than men do. There are several reasons for the differences reported, but notice also that reported disability rises with age. As a result, women 65 and up are more than 5 times more likely to be disabled than are men 18 to 44. Women are more prone to disabling disorders such as arthritis, depression, and osteoporosis because they live longer than men and consequently survive to ages at which disability is more common. A woman who dies at 85 has a longer period of disability than a man who dies at 85. Typically, women with disabilities no longer have husbands to take care of them. Also, with aging come increased problems with mobility, and if people become overweight or obese they are at increased risk for developing potentially disabling chronic conditions such as heart disease, Type 2 diabetes, high blood pressure, stroke, osteoarthritis, respiratory problems, and some forms of cancer.

ADVOCACY ON BEHALF OF PEOPLE WITH PHYSICAL AND MENTAL CHALLENGES

In the United States, people living with physical and mental challenges or developmental disabilities who have been successful in their fields and careers are heralded as advocates, pioneers, and role models. Places such as Gallaudet University (for the deaf and hearing impaired), youth summer camps, and Special Olympics venues empower people to dream, achieve, and hope for a positive future.

Social workers who work with people who have physical and mental challenges and developmental disabilities must

EXHIBIT 8.5   Disability by Sex and Age Group in the United States

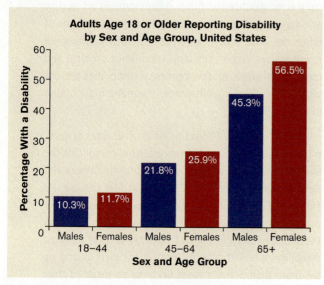

Adults Age 18 or Older Reporting Disability by Sex and Age Group, United States

(Y-axis: Percentage With a Disability; X-axis: Sex and Age Group)

- Males 18–44: 10.3%
- Females 18–44: 11.7%
- Males 45–64: 21.8%
- Females 45–64: 25.9%
- Males 65+: 45.3%
- Females 65+: 56.5%

Source: Centers for Disease Control and Prevention (2011b).

help them focus on their assets and advocate for cultural and policy changes that value people no matter their challenge or impairment. If people with a range of disabilities could figure out how not to isolate but instead unite as one, they would be a powerful lobbying force to be reckoned with on Capitol Hill and in the media.

Professional social workers who find themselves working in settings with people with a wide range of physical and mental challenges must be educated advocates who can teach others about how individuals, organizations, and government agencies define disability in so many different

Source: ©iStockphoto.com/Kevin Landwer-Johan.

⌃ Some countries do not provide accommodations for those with physical disabilities.

ways. Social work advocates require understanding of how disability can be an acute or chronic medical condition or a mental or physical impairment for some, and for others could manifest as a by-product of physical or social environments, or be a functional consequence of a chronic physical impairment or mental disorder.

Social workers can connect people living with physical and mental challenges or developmental disabilities to relevant services and resources, including rehabilitation services, employment services, public education, psychiatric care, disability insurance, income support, workers' compensation, and Supplemental Security Income. Competent social workers will understand the provisions of the ADA and connect people with health insurance, transportation, and more.

ECONOMIC AND SOCIAL JUSTICE

Since the deinstitutionalization movement and the technological advances in vision care, hearing devices, prosthetics, orthopedics, and more, people with any disability have more choices for recovery or adjustment than ever before. However, accessing such services is still limited by economic realities and injustices inherent in a marketplace-based system of care. When living with a disability of any type, people may need equipment, devices, respite care, acute care, or chronic caregiving assistance. These services are covered by the insurance industry and the law but with limits. The social work profession must serve as a "watchdog" as the private, for-profit sector commands an increasingly government-unsupervised role in delivering health care and disability services in both institutional and community-based settings (Reisch, 2000).

An important aspect of social and economic injustice toward people with disabilities is stigma and discrimination in the workplace. People who are disabled or live with physical and mental challenges are often unable to support themselves financially. To be successful advocates for clients with disabilities, social workers must be cognizant of disability policies. Stigma may keep a qualified individual with a disability from being hired or treated fairly.

However, the law requires an employer to provide reasonable accommodation to an employee or job applicant with a disability, unless doing so would cause significant difficulty or expense for the employer ("undue hardship"). The law also protects people from discrimination based on their relationship with a person with a disability (even if they do not themselves have a disability). For example, it is illegal to discriminate against an employee because her husband has a disability. The law forbids discrimination when it comes to any aspect of employment, including hiring, firing, pay, job assignments, promotions, layoff, training, fringe benefits and any other term or condition of employment (Waterstone, 2014).

SUPPORTIVE ENVIRONMENT

People with physical or mental challenges or developmental disabilities often face an uncaring environment with few **public accommodations** that would allow them to participate more fully in the community. Uneven access to buildings (hospitals, health centers), inaccessible medical equipment, poor signage, narrow doorways, internal steps, inadequate bathroom facilities, and inaccessible parking areas create barriers to health care facilities.

Private companies are becoming increasingly involved within the disability sector. Institutional living has largely been replaced by residential arrangements that accommodate the needs of PWDs, thereby increasing independence and freedom of choice. In ordinary residential areas, more special services areas are being provided.

Professional social workers may best maximize client self-determination and service provision for PWDs by being consumer centered, acquiring knowledge about resources and agency services, and advocating for PWDs across practice levels. Social workers empower PWDs best when they attune to what the client wants and refrain from making assumptions or labeling. Because policies that relate to people with physical and mental challenges often change, an effective social worker who works with PWDs will be aware of laws, statutes, and local, state, and federal regulations. The National Association of Social Workers regularly updates its published statement that highlights the promotion of self-determination in working with people who have physical or mental challenges. When clients with disabilities require more services than are available, social work advocates can work with the power players to have services for PWDs expanded.

HUMAN NEEDS AND RIGHTS

Institutionalization can be individually devastating, because residents not only lose most of their freedom but may be actively deprived of their civil rights and even abused (in the past especially). But institutionalization has been influenced more by economic factors than political ones. When families found it difficult to care for their family members, institutions became an option. Between 1880 and 1900 the intellectually/developmentally disabled population institutionalized rose from a little over 4,000 to 15,000.

When it comes to advocating for people's right to self-determination and ability to access appropriate health care or disabilities services, social workers would do well to attend equally to needs and rights. Giving clients and their families support and listening to their stories are essential components to understanding what services will be required and sharing the process of obtaining those services.

Members of stigmatized groups start to become aware that they are not being treated equally and know they are probably being discriminated against. That is the case with some members of the disabled community. For example, increasing numbers of people categorized with an intellectual disability, especially young adults, are indeed strengthening their resistance to being viewed as passive receivers of care.

POLITICAL ACCESS

Disability-related policies are political. The words and the meanings Americans use in everyday life create attitudes, influence feelings and decisions, drive social policies and laws, and ultimately affect people's daily lives. Words matter. Using a diagnosis as a defining characteristic reflects prejudice and also robs the person of the opportunity to define him or herself. Politically correct person-first language puts the person before the disability and describes what a person has, not who a person is.

Because politics is inextricably involved when helping people with physical and mental challenges, you may choose to become a disability policy social worker. These social workers may help update or craft brand new policies for corporations that cater to or employ PWDs. Disability policy social workers can also work to get laws pertaining to PWDs passed by lobbying to pass certain laws or by creating and writing the laws themselves. They can advocate for PWDs and investigate discrimination cases or help them file discrimination lawsuits.

SOCIAL WORK IN ACTION

Mike Learns His Responsibilities at a Residential Facility

MIKE has found employment at a community-based residential facility. Clients Mike works with have developmental and intellectual disabilities. During orientation week he got a sense of what his responsibilities would be:

- Outreach for PWDs in both residential facilities and private homes, where he would teach daily skills such as how to build self-esteem, how to budget and manage finances, and how to be assertive.
- Respite care for parents of children with disabilities, taking turns with other social workers to relieve the parents now and then and allow the parents to replenish themselves.

- Leadership of support groups for parents of kids of all ages and older adults who are living with a disability or disabilities. When he facilitates parent groups, attendees enjoy having special speakers from advocacy and service organizations come to share information and experiences.

1. What additional resources, websites, and reading materials might Mike consult to prepare himself for his work in residential facilities?
2. Which skills might Mike require to effectively facilitate parent groups?

YOUR CAREER WORKING WITH PEOPLE WHO HAVE PHYSICAL AND MENTAL CHALLENGES OR DEVELOPMENTAL DISABILITIES

Over the next decade, job availability for social workers in disability and rehabilitative services will increase. Often, social workers find work in a disability setting with a bachelor's degree. Social workers are found in all kinds of settings, from community nonprofit hospitals and outpatient public or ambulatory care clinics to inpatient for-profit hospitals, transitional care rehabilitation units, assisted-living and long-term care facilities, and through home health agency referrals. Social workers who practice with people who have disabilities may serve as residential counselors, consultants, group-home workers, or generalists. They provide information and referrals, serve on help lines, work in community-based residential facilities, advocate in supportive employment and vocational rehabilitation programs, and coordinate "day services" to maximize independent functional levels in self-care, physical and emotional growth, mobility, socialization, community transportation, leisure time and recreation, and educational and prevocational skills.

To have a successful career in disabilities social work, it is helpful to have the following:

- Understanding of the classification systems and diagnostic terminology for disabilities
- Understanding of the roles of all disability and vocational rehabilitation specialists
- Understanding of health disparities and stigma
- Understanding of the biopsychosocial-cultural and spiritual aspects of multiple types of disabilities
- Crisis intervention skills
- Short-term counseling skills
- Knowledge about culturally competent assessment, counseling, and community resources

They must also work to rid themselves of stereotypes and fear of people with physical and mental challenges and developmental disabilities.

Most people will have a disability in their lifetime, and people often live with disabilities for a long time. That means many people may at one point or another require a social worker to help them navigate services, resources, and health care. When a person has no family, has trouble coping with a physical or mental challenge or developmental disability, or has experienced undue pain, injury, or suffering, social workers can help.

SUMMARY

"Disability is not a brave struggle or 'courage in the face of adversity.' Disability is an art. It's an ingenious way to live."

–Neil Marcus

Because disability is equated with dependency and still stigmatized, it is positioned in direct contrast to American ideals of independence and autonomy. Social work must advocate for people not to be labeled as inferior citizens and for systems to be made equally accessible to all. Dependency is not bad–it is at the heart of both the human and the American experience. It is what makes a community and a democracy.

Over time, America has gone from relative homogeneity to increased levels of categorization for people who experience disabilities of any sort. It is important to remember, though, that disability is not the story of someone else; it is the story of someone we love and perhaps even the story of who we are or may become. That being the case, it is important to see the common humanity in all who have been diagnosed with a physical or mental challenge or developmental disability.

TOP 10 KEY CONCEPTS

Americans with Disabilities Act (ADA)
categorical disabilities
disability
functional disabilities
genetic counseling

independent-living centers
intellectual disability
person with a disability (PWD)
public accommodations
rehabilitation

DISCUSSION QUESTIONS

1. What does it mean to live with a physical or mental challenge or developmental disability?
2. How do social work values and the *Code of Ethics* guide social workers who practice with people who live with disabilities?
3. How do Americans still stigmatize people living with physical and mental challenges and developmental disabilities? Consider all the types of physical/mental

challenges and developmental disabilities, and name some specific actions, attitudes, and expressions.
4. What resources would you seek if you or a loved one had a chronic disability?
5. What roles do social workers assume if they work with people who have a physical or neurocognitive challenge or developmental disability?

EXERCISES

1. The opening vignette features Joe, an administrator who works with The Arc. Explore the history of The Arc and write a reflection on the importance of grassroots organizations for people with disabilities.
2. Locate a family member or friend who has a disability (physical or mental challenge). Ask this person what concerns she or he has about being disabled. Write a report on how this person has managed disclosure of the disability, issues at school and in the workplace, and activities of daily living.
3. What famous people (dead or alive) had or have a disability, yet still made valuable contributions to society? Start by investigating some of the following:

a. *Artists and musicians:* James Durbin (autism advocate, guitarist, and singer who finished fourth in Season 10 of *American Idol*); Ludwig van Beethoven (composer with a hearing disorder); Ray Charles (African American musician and singer who was blind); Francisco Goya (Spanish painter who became deaf at age 46)
b. *Actors:* Henry Winkler (played "The Fonz" on the TV show *Happy Days* and has dyslexia); Marlee Matlin (Oscar winner who is deaf and uses sign language); Michael J. Fox (lives with Parkinson's disease)
c. *Historical figures:* Julius Caesar (Roman Emperor who had epilepsy); General George Patton (WWII hero who had dyslexia); U.S. President George Washington

(had a learning disability that affected his spelling); U.S. President Franklin D. Roosevelt (childhood polio affected his mobility); Albert Einstein (physicist and mathematician who had a learning disability)

4. How can students become more aware of and engaged with people who live with physical, mobility, neurocognitive, developmental, or mental challenges?

5. How does your campus serve people who live with learning, developmental, or physical challenges?

ONLINE RESOURCES

- The Arc (www.thearc.org): Advocates for the rights and full participation of all children and adults with intellectual and developmental disabilities, such as autism, Down syndrome, fetal alcohol spectrum disorder, and a range of intellectual and developmental disabilities
- Disability Is Natural (www.disabilityisnatural.com)
- The International Network of Women with Disabilities (inwwd.wordpress.com): Comprises international, regional, national, and local organizations, groups, and networks of women with disabilities; seeks to enable women with disabilities to share knowledge and experience, enhance the capacity to speak up for rights, encourage empowerment, and promote relevant policies toward creating a more just and fair world that acknowledges disability and gender, justice, and human rights
- National Association of Social Workers' Help Starts Here (www.helpstartshere.org/health-and-wellness/disabilities/how-do-social-workers-help-the-families-of-children-with-

disabilities.html): Offers abundant resources for social workers who choose to specialize in disability services
- National Center for Learning Disabilities (www.ncld.org): Offers a plethora of resources for people struggling with learning disabilities, in school or work
- National Society of Genetic Counselors (nsgc.org): Involved in federal advocacy efforts aimed at improving access to quality genetic counseling services and ensuring that the genetic counseling profession is a recognized and integral part of the health care system
- Special Olympics (www.specialolympics.org): An international program, founded in 1968, that promotes fitness and athletic competition for children and adults who are living with an intellectual or physical disability
- UN Enable (www.un.org/disabilities): Works to promote the full and effective participation and inclusion in society of people with disabilities
- The World Association for People with Disabilities (www.wapd.org)

STUDENT STUDY SITE

Sharpen your skills with SAGE edge at **edge.sagepub.com/cox**

SAGE edge for Students provides a personalized approach to help you accomplish your coursework goals in an easy-to-use learning environment.

Chapter 9: MENTAL HEALTH

Learning Objectives

After reading this chapter, you will be able to

1. Explain the differences between mental health and mental illness, and between normal and abnormal mental health.
2. Identify at least five types of serious mental disorders.
3. Explain the medicalization of mental health and its effect on individuals as well as on mental health professionals and organizations.
4. Describe in broad terms how mental health has historically been defined and treated.
5. Understand the importance of mental health parity and its current status.
6. Identify mental health social work roles and settings.
7. Recognize how diversity affects mental health and mental health treatment.

Joyce Seeks Knowledge to Help With Her Broad Caseload at a Mental Health Center

Joyce's caseload at Henrico Mental Health fluctuates in size, yet steadily includes a wide range of ages and presenting issues. The agency has a respected, long-standing positive reputation in the community, and clinicians there use an array of intervention techniques and treatment modalities. They also accept multiple types of insurance. When insurance coverage ends, Joyce refers clients to other agencies—such as faith-based organizations or community support groups—for follow-up.

Joyce regularly attends local National Association of Social Workers chapter meetings and online webinars and workshops to keep current on mental health parity law, the *Diagnostic and Statistical Manual of Mental Disorders* classification system, and more. Such activities provide Joyce with important policy and practice information she requires to help her in her assessments, interventions, and advocacy efforts.

Social workers are the largest providers of mental health services in the United States (Masiriri, 2008; National Association of Social Workers, n.d.; Scheyett, 2005). Mental health social workers are known as **clinical social workers**, psychiatric social workers, psychotherapists, or behavioral health care specialists. These professionals help diverse individuals with mental or emotional disorders manage social problems and life's challenges.

Mental health social workers assess (evaluate) and work with people who have mental disorders and addiction problems that often occur alongside these disorders. (Substance use and addiction are discussed in more detail in Chapter 10.) Mental health social workers may specialize in child, adolescent, adult, or even older adult (geriatric) mental health; forensic social work; counseling for persons with developmental, physical, or neurocognitive disorders; or drug and alcohol rehabilitation. They regularly collaborate with a team of psychiatrists, psychologists, and nurses.

The purpose of this chapter is to describe the evolution and current state of mental health services in the United States and help you understand the roles social workers assume in mental health settings. You will find that ideas about the most effective treatment for people with mental illness have fluctuated over the years. The most recent policy trend—dehospitalization or deinstitutionalization—has served to increase the need for outpatient services, which is a key venue for social work with those who have a mental illness.

MENTAL HEALTH AND MENTAL ILLNESS

Failure to cope adequately with the demands of everyday life may be a sign of a mental health problem or disorder. When a person is suffering, **maladaptive** (a danger to self), unpredictable to the point of losing control and being irrational, causing an observer discomfort, and violating a moral or social standard, that person is failing to function adequately (Rosenhan & Seligman, 1989). Mental disorders are common in the United States and globally. Although mental disorders are widespread, the main burden of illness is concentrated in about 6% of the population. About 1 in 17 people suffer from a severe mental illness. Mental illness is caused by multiple factors, including accidents, poor choices, and genetic predisposition.

DEFINITIONS OF MENTAL HEALTH STATUS

Many people engage in behavior that is harmful, maladaptive, or threatening to self, but we don't necessarily classify them as abnormal. Consider participation in high-adrenaline sports, drinking alcohol, smoking, or skipping classes. Definitions have helped mental health professionals distinguish between good mental health and mental illness.

Mental health connotes a relative state of emotional well-being where one is free from incapacitating conflicts and is consistently able to make rational decisions and cope with environmental stresses and internal pressures. By contrast, **mental illness** is a disease that causes mild to severe disturbances in thinking, perception, and behavior. Mental illnesses are symptoms of **mental disorders,** which vary in duration and severity, and can affect persons of any age, class, race, and ethnicity. If these disturbances significantly impair a person's ability to cope with life's ordinary demands and routines, then they will likely require proper treatment from a mental health professional.

The terms *behavioral health* and *mental health* are often used interchangeably, and the term *perceptual health* has also been introduced because helping professionals' perceptions may often lead to harmful actions toward patients. **Behavioral health** includes prevention and well-being promotion and is a hopeful concept for people who feel that mental illness is a permanent part of their lives. Behavioral health is also a kinder term than *mental health* and may help reduce the **stigma.** Behavioral health can also place the onus on the individual to change rather than considering external environmental factors such as poverty, discrimination, or abuse, thus obliterating the underlying causes of suicidal behaviors and conveying a concept more reminiscent of an insurance company than of someone struggling with mental health issues (Sandler, 2009).

NORMAL VERSUS ABNORMAL MENTAL HEALTH

Undergraduate social work majors often take courses that debate what kind of behavior is normal versus abnormal. These courses may be called Personality or Abnormal Psychology, and they explore ways abnormality can be defined. The problem is that the multiple definitions of abnormality fail to distinguish between desirable and undesirable behavior. Statistically speaking, many very gifted people could be classified as "abnormal" by some definitions.

Also, social norms change over time and thereby complicate definitional matters. For example, homosexuality, until 1990, was considered a psychological disorder by the World Health Organization's International Classification of Diseases, and the American Psychiatric Association did not remove homosexuality from the *Diagnostic and Statistical Manual of Mental Disorders* (DSM) until 1973. Today, however, homosexuality is considered acceptable and not a mental disorder.

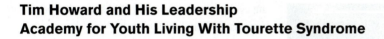

Tim Howard and His Leadership Academy for Youth Living With Tourette Syndrome

Tourette syndrome (TS) is a neurobiological condition characterized by tics. In the fifth edition of the DSM, it is referred to as Tourette disorder and listed among neurodevelopmental disorders usually first diagnosed in childhood and adolescence. People erroneously think that people living with TS curse sporadically or have intellectual challenges, because the media make fun of these people without understanding why they make noises, twitch, or move oddly or incessantly. The reality is that, although TS poses challenges, they can be overcome through various treatments, adjustments, advocacy, and education. Probably the biggest challenge for people living with TS is building the self-confidence to fulfill their potential (Benshoff, 2014).

Tim Howard, goalie for the USA World Cup soccer team who set a new world record of 16 saves in the 2014 game against Belgium, lives with TS. Given his success in sports, few have questioned his abilities. In conjunction with the New Jersey Center for Tourette Syndrome and Associated Disorders, Howard launched a leadership academy, envisioned as an annual event, to offer youth living with TS the skills they need to manage life's challenges.

Over 3 days, the leadership academy hosted three teams of teenagers, ages 14 to 17, and coaches, ages 21 to 29, who all have TS. Psychologists, educators, neurologists, and social workers offered workshops on the mind and coping psychologically and socially with life despite their TS. Building self-confidence, boosting self-esteem, and focusing on resilience were core goals of the academy. By engaging in workshops, team meetings, and experiential activities that involved creativity, advocacy, self-leadership, and teamwork, academy participants left thinking and acting more like Howard—a person who is a self-leader and advocate for TS. Because the youth attending the academy knew firsthand what it feels like to be bullied, isolated, scapegoated, and misunderstood, they absorbed knowledge about TS, acquired advocacy and social skills, and left the academy with a sense of empowerment, resilience, and realization that they can drive, attend a university, play sports on the world stage—and have TS (Fowler, 2014).

Most mental health care providers would agree that ideal mental health includes the following (McLeod, 2014):

- Accurate perception of reality
- Autonomy and independence
- Capability for growth and development
- Environmental mastery—ability to meet the varying demands of day-to-day situations
- Positive friendships and relationships
- Positive view of the self

The reality is that ideal mental health is not always obtainable, and the human brain affects human thoughts and actions. But because not all symptoms and problems in living are caused by mental disorders, mislabeling can be very harmful to people who are deemed "abnormal."

Similarly, when a person has been evaluated as having a mental illness or mental disorder, it is important to be sensitive about the language used to describe her or him. Person-first language, discussed in detail in Chapter 8 in relation to physical and mental challenges (disabilities), is meant to play up the individual's worth and downplay the disability. For example, instead of saying, "He's bipolar," it would be more appropriate to refer to "a man with bipolar disorder."

TIME TO THINK

What do you think the consequences might be of labeling any person "abnormal"? Similarly, what would be the consequences of referring to someone by mental illness—for example, as "a schizophrenic"? How might such a label affect a person who is managing life quite well? How might it affect someone who is struggling in one or more of the areas of mental activity listed as ideal?

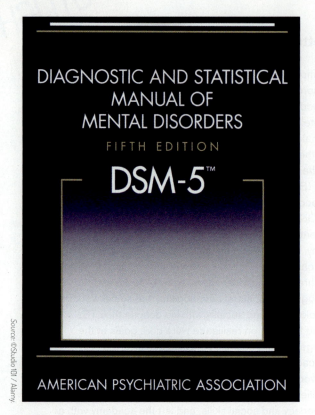

Source: ©Studio 101 / Alamy.

▲ The DSM-5 is a classification and diagnostic tool put out by the APA.

MENTAL HEALTH DISORDERS AND THE DSM

In America, mental disorders are classified and diagnosed based on the DSM. This manual, published by the American Psychiatric Association, serves as a universal authority for psychiatric diagnosis. Oftentimes, treatment recommendations and payment by insurance companies to health care providers are determined by DSM diagnostic codes. Mental health social workers routinely use the DSM to "label patients"—particularly at inpatient hospitals, mental health clinics, and outpatient health centers—so the client can be reimbursed through insurance.

The DSM is currently in its fifth edition (DSM-5; American Psychiatric Association, 2013), and every update has brought noteworthy changes. For example, the current edition dropped **Asperger's syndrome** as a mental disorder and changed the criteria for posttraumatic stress disorder (discussed in more detail below).

In its opening section, the DSM acknowledges that definitions of mental disorders are imprecise. The definitions actually describe patterns of behavior and severity levels that

are evident. Forthrightly, the DSM states that people are not diagnosed; their disorders are.

Although DSM classification occurs regularly in real-world social work practice, social work educators continue to debate the utility of teaching such classification schemas. The DSM has both proponents and critics. Critics find it necessary to remind mental health counselors that their relationship with a client should come first and that any diagnosis should be a team effort. In addition, a member of DSM task forces who is a clinician, educator, researcher, and leading authority on psychiatric diagnosis (Frances, 2013) has noted some specific problems with the DSM-5:

The DSM-5 suffers from the unfortunate combination of unrealistically lofty ambitions and sloppy methodology. . . . Unless diagnoses are used with restraint millions of essentially normal people will be mislabeled and subjected to potentially harmful treatment and unnecessary stigma. The DSM-5 has lowered the requirements for diagnosing existing disorders. For example, 2 weeks of normal grief have been turned into Major Depressive Disorder. The criteria for adult ADHD have been loosened, making it easily confused with normal distractibility and facilitating the illegal misuses of prescription stimulants for performance enhancement or recreational purposes. The DSM-5 has collapsed early Substance Abuse and end-stage Substance Dependence (addiction) into one category, confusing their very different courses and treatment needs and creating unnecessary stigma. (p. 5)

TIME TO THINK

Why do you suppose social workers perceive and use the DSM differently from the way it is perceived and used by psychiatrists, psychologists, and psychiatric nurses? As a prospective social worker, what are the advantages and disadvantages you see in using this type of a system to classify and code mental disorders?

Despite the controversy, social workers in the mental health field need to be familiar with these types of disorders and the way they are defined in the DSM-5:

• **Neurocognitive disorders:** The new descriptor for disorders that involve delirium or dementia. "Dementias" include diseases such as Alzheimer's, which leads to loss of mental functions, including memory loss and a decline in intellectual and physical skills.

- **Personality disorders:** The cause of vicious cycles of negative experiences where people cannot adapt to change and become distressed. **Personality** is an enduring pattern of behaving, feeling, interacting, and thinking that forms who we are. Ten personality disorders are classified in the DSM-5: borderline, antisocial, narcissistic, histrionic, obsessive-compulsive, avoidant, dependent, paranoid, schizoid, and schizotypal personality disorder.

- **Anxiety disorders**: Formerly lumped together with depressive disorder and bipolar disorder under the classification of "mood disorders," anxiety disorders, which include phobias and panic disorders, are common. People who suffer from **phobias** experience extreme fear or dread of particular objects or situations. **Panic disorders** involve sudden intense feelings of terror for no apparent reason and symptoms similar to a heart attack.

- **Depressive disorders:** Formerly categorized as mood disorders, along with anxiety and bipolar disorders, depressive disorders are also common. People lose their ability to concentrate, think clearly, or make simple decisions when they experience depression.

- **Bipolar disorder:** This was formerly listed among mood disorders such as anxiety and depressive disorders. Diagnoses of bipolar disorder abound. Between 1984 and 2014, diagnoses of childhood bipolar disorder have increased fortyfold, thereby becoming an epidemic and a "fad diagnosis." A bipolar diagnosis carries the connotation that it will last for a lifetime and require continuous treatment with medication (Frances, 2013, p. 53).

- **Schizophrenia** spectrum and other psychotic disorders: A serious disorder that affects how a person acts, feels, and thinks, schizophrenia is believed to be caused by chemical imbalances in the brain that produce multiple symptoms, including delusions, hallucinations, impaired reasoning, incoherent speech, and withdrawal.

- **Eating disorders:** This label includes **anorexia nervosa** and **bulimia**, which are serious, potentially life-threatening illnesses. People with these disorders have a preoccupation with food and an irrational fear of being fat. Anorexia is self-starvation, while bulimia involves cycles of bingeing (consuming huge amounts of food) and purging

Source: ©iStockphoto.com/kaylorg

▲ Austistic children can benefit from working with therapists.

(abusing laxatives or self-inducing vomiting). Behavior may also include excessive exercise.

- **Neurodevelopmental disorders**: This broad category includes three noteworthy disorders, usually first diagnosed in childhood and adolescence—**attention-deficit hyperactivity disorder (ADHD)**, autism spectrum disorder, and **oppositional defiant disorder**. Depending on its presentation, autism may be deemed a disability or simply a mental health issue. The fundamental truth about developmental disorders such as autism and dyslexia is that they are wrongly classified as childhood disorders. They are lifelong conditions that can be exacerbated by stress and unfamiliar situations, and can lead to mental collapse (Frith, 2014, p. 671). While autism has always been with us, it has been recognized only since the mid-20th century. Despite this slow start, the spectrum of autism is now incredibly broad.

- **Posttraumatic stress disorder (PTSD):** Applies when someone has suffered through an unusually dreadful trauma (e.g., combat, rape, torture, battery, or qualifying catastrophes such as fires, accidents, floods, earthquakes, hurricanes). However, the diagnostic criteria are more descriptive of the symptom-based outcome than of the precipitating event itself. One person may suffer PTSD due to a precipitating event that others might not consider "unusually dreadful." There are numerous variables that can influence whether and to what extent an event or experience is traumatic. Recovery from an accident, traumatic brain injury, or physical abnormality requires specialized treatment and an interdisciplinary team approach.

EVOLUTION OF THE MENTAL HEALTH SYSTEM

Chapter 8 includes a history of services for people living with disabilities—developmental, physical, and neurocognitive. In many ways, the history of perceptions of and treatment for mental illness tracks closely with that of disabilities; however, services and legislation for people with mental health disorders have traditionally been separated from those for people with physical disabilities.

TIME TO THINK

Does it make sense for disability and mental health services to be separate? Why or why not?

Do you think that people with physical and cognitive challenges (disabilities) and people with mental illness experience the same stigma and discrimination in employment, housing, and other areas? If not, how would you explain the differences?

INSTITUTIONALIZATION AND DEINSTITUTIONALIZATION

The institutionalization of people subject to bizarre outbursts dates back to the 13th century. European colonists brought their views of how best to care for people who were mentally ill to North America. They thought **institutionalization** of people who needed a safe, controlled environment was a good idea. However, in colonial America there was no institutionalization—if you were experiencing a mental disorder, you were left to your own devices or jailed as a criminal. It wasn't until 1773 that "hospitals" specializing in mental health opened in the United States.

Today, institutionalization is a core part of what many think about when talking about disability in the United States. However, in the United States, institutionalization has more often had the connotation of **criminalization** than of treatment. People in power often viewed people with mental health disabilities as a threat to social and political structures. Political thinkers supported a movement toward long-term hospitalization so the "insane" could not access the rights of citizenship and make societal decisions. Institutionalization can serve larger ideological purposes as well. The warehousing of those considered deviant, coupled with the threat of sterilization, literally controlled the reproduction of troublesome norms of behavior (Nielsen, 2012, p. 119). Consider

that suicide was not struck from all states' lists of felonies until the 1990s.

In the 1960s, U.S. policymakers and citizens began to embrace **deinstitutionalization**. It was in large part the philosophy behind the civil rights movement that put an end to long-term hospitalization for developmentally disabled people, mentally ill people, criminal offenders, and children and older adults (Segal, 1995). The rationale that helped make deinstitutionalization a reality, however, was preventing unnecessary admissions to institutions and thereby containing costs. As the United States closed down its large residential institutions, mental health care shifted to outpatient treatment in clinics, short-term hospitalization, and supervised group homes in the community.

After Medicaid was passed in 1965, community mental health centers tried to accommodate the patients who were being released from state medical hospitals. This strategy allowed Medicaid to extend coverage for psychiatric hospital care to poor people and created incentives for states to place in nursing homes older adults who manifested behavioral problems. As a result, during the 1960s the nursing home population doubled (Grob, 1991). Some who were released did not completely understand what was transpiring. Staffers in some of the facilities did not fully understand the mental health needs of their new charges.

Although the philosophy that undergirded deinstitutionalization was "laudable," it has been the "largest failed social experiment in twentieth century America" (Torrey, 1995, p. 1612, cited in Peternelj-Taylor, 2008, p. 185). In some jurisdictions, deinstitutionalization has dramatically increased homelessness and been blamed for the criminalization of the mentally ill.

MEDICALIZATION OF MENTAL ILLNESS

Another hotly debated policy of the era was the **medicalization** of mental illness. *Medicalization* is a 1970s term devised by sociologists to explain how medical knowledge is applied to behaviors that are not self-evidently biological or medical in nature, as a form of social control. One effect of medicalization is a conceptual shift from labeling disorders as "badness" to regarding people with mental disorders as "sick."

Medicalization is also referred to as "pathologization" and speaks to the role and power of professionals, patients, and corporations with ordinary people whose self-identity and life decisions evolve but amidst social control. In other words, medicalization is a social process whereby human experience is culturally defined as pathological and treatable as a medical condition. For example, alcoholism, childhood hyperactivity, obesity, and even sexual abuse have been defined as medical problems that are, as a result, increasingly referred to and treated by physicians.

Medicalization is a topic that generates mixed opinions and debate among social workers and others. Some of course see medicalization as taking control of a condition away from the person who has it and instead giving control to a medical professional. A potential advantage of this shift is the possible reduction of stigma associated with mental disorders (Payton & Thoits, 2011). In addition, medicalization can afford new opportunities for access to professional medical care and thus encourage optimism that a therapy can be developed to treat or cure the disorder.

TIME TO THINK

Do you think that by treating mental illnesses with medical interventions, individual responsibility, blame, and possibly stigma related to deviance can be reduced? Or do you think that medicalization of mental illness diffuses responsibility, increases dependence on medical interventions, and renders social interventions obsolete?

SOCIAL WORK PERSPECTIVES

In the mid-1800s, activist social worker Dorothea Dix heightened awareness of the inhumane treatment that was occurring inside institutions that housed people with mental health challenges, disabilities, and behavior problems (Caplan, 1969). In the early 20th century, Mary Richmond—the founder of social casework and author of the classic texts *Social Diagnosis* (1917) and *What Is Social Case Work?* (1922)—showed how poverty was closely linked to mental health, personality development, and effective coping skills in social work clients.

Richmond was a contemporary of Ida Cannon, the social worker employed by Massachusetts General Hospital to work with clients with mental health problems. In 1913, Mary Jarrett was hired by the Boston Psychopathic Hospital as its first director of social services. Jarrett is credited for coining the term *psychiatric social worker* (Grob, 1991).

Following World War I (1914–1918), social workers in hospitals and clinics helped soldiers with physical and psychological problems such as "shell shock" and trauma. Subsequently, hospital-based medical/health social work started to grow.

Freudian theory became popular in the United States during the 1920s, and people who could afford counseling services sought mental health assistance. Soon child guidance clinics and juvenile court systems opened to help children with emotional problems and mental health disorders. In 1922 in St. Louis, the first clinic staffed by a team that included a psychologist, a psychiatrist, and a social worker was opened, and this model evolved into what is now called a "mental health team."

During World War II (1939–1945), the Army created officer-level positions for psychiatric social workers, and they became members of neuropsychiatric teams. As World War II ended, Veterans Administration hospitals became the largest recruiter of professional social workers, a trend that continues today.

The National Mental Health Act of 1946 represented the first major piece of approved mental health legislation. This act federally supported demonstration projects, training, and research to examine effective prevention and treatment programs for mental illness. Subsequently, in 1949, the **National Institute of Mental Health (NIMH)** was created. Mental health social work continued to grow. In the 1950s, a social theorist named Helen Harris Perlman wrote *Social Casework: A Problem-Solving Process* (1957), and Florence Hollis wrote the classic social work text *Casework: A Psychosocial Therapy* (1964). From the 1960s until current times, social work mental health practice has also been influenced by other policies, court cases, and movements.

MENTAL DEFICITS VERSUS PERSONAL ASSETS

Prior to the major mental health movements, those who were experiencing mental illness were most often subjected to moral treatment. In the 1800s, moral treatment advocates, influenced by Enlightenment thinking, rejected using manacles, chains, and restraints. Instead, these advocates believed that people in asylums should be treated humanely, like children rather than animals. Yet asylum patients were still thought to have something wrong with them, deficits that needed to be overcome. As people learned more about the workings of the mind and body, the mental hygiene movement came into existence. Before it was called the mental hygiene movement, it strived to reform institutional

Source: iStockphoto.com/milenslavov

▲ Deinstitutionalization of the mentally ill has caused homelessness in many jurisdictions, and many believe it is to blame for the criminalization of the mentally ill.

care, establish child guidance clinics (1921), and educate the public about mental health. The movement promoted the idea that government was responsible for mental health and people with deficits, and played a significant role in organizing mental health care for the military in both World Wars. After the World Wars, mental health professionals garnered better publicity for mental health, and in return more funding was allocated to mental health care. After 1947, the mental hygiene movement supported community mental health centers' behavioral–scientific and collective approach. These centers were intended to treat people and change society.

Mental health care has evolved greatly since the days of the mental hygiene movement. As early as 1880, when the National Association for the Protection of the Insane and the Prevention of Insanity was formed, asylum physicians found it hard to defend their practices, which were mainly focused on a deficits approach. In the context of asylums, a deficits approach meant that more focus was placed on illness and disorders than on well-being. The goal was to prevent deviation rather than illness. The community mental health movement began to influence the treatment of mental illness after World War II. When hundreds of World War II veterans returned with psychological problems, trauma, and battle fatigue, beliefs about mental illness were questioned, but deficits in the soldiers' makeup were still the focus. Soldiers diagnosed with a mental health problem, such as depression, PTSD, or anxiety, felt stigmatized and were perceived as "weak." Therefore, many hesitated

to accept counseling services or pharmacologic treatment. Even later, in 1946, when Congress established a Mental Hygiene Division in the U.S. Public Health Service, and in 1949, when the NIMH research center began, deficits were the focus. Blame and responsibility for mental health challenges were attributed to the soldier rather than to the traumatic combat environment.

The legal advocacy movement and deinstitutionalization movement both continued to diminish the assets of people with mental illness. Following the civil rights movement, the 1960s marked the start of the legal advocacy movement in mental health. Essentially, the legal advocacy movement highlighted two landmark court cases: *Wyatt v. Stickney* (1971) and *O'Connor v. Donaldson* (1975). In these cases the Supreme Court ruled that mental illness and need for treatment were insufficient to justify involuntary confinement, thereby supporting deinstitutionalization but doing little to increase dignity and personal choice (Mu-Jung & Lin, 1995).

As medications were developed, in the 1960s and 1970s, the deinstitutionalization movement relocated people from state hospitals back into the community. Unfortunately, the deinstitutionalization movement's outcome illustrated how a piecemeal and nonintegrated approach to the social problem of helping the mentally ill results in spending more on determining eligibility than on providing food and shelter to people who live with mental illness. Following deinstitutionalization, America's mental health system was hideously expensive, wasteful, inefficient, and relatively devoid of dignified treatment and personal choice.

Today, the consumer movement has taken hold. Activists and established groups such as the **National Alliance on Mental Illness (NAMI)** are involved in advocacy efforts that dismiss deficits and stigma and strongly uphold a focus on assets. NAMI was founded in 1979 by people with mental illness who call themselves "consumers," along with their family members and concerned professionals. NAMI supports research, education, social policy, and political activities that help improve access to community-based services. Today, NAMI has affiliate offices in all 50 states. Mental health teams now collaborate to link clients with community-based day programs that teach skills to people diagnosed with mental health problems and urge physicians to prescribe a broad assortment of **psychotropic medications,** such as antidepressants and antimanic medications, that help people with mental illness function well in society.

The environment has changed significantly. In the early 1970s, when George McGovern was running for president, it came out that his vice presidential running mate, Thomas Eagleton, had suffered depression, been hospitalized for it, and received electroconvulsive therapy. The revelation was so shameful that Eagleton was dropped from the ticket without discussion, and McGovern lost the election in a landslide. Today, however, thanks to activists such as NAMI members, people with mental illness hold esteemed positions in the workplace and wider society. A few esteemed individuals who have overcome mental illness are actress Catherine Zeta Jones, who lives with bipolar disorder; Olympic swimmer Michael Phelps, who excels despite his ADHD; mathematician John Nash, who won a Nobel Prize despite living with schizophrenia; and guitarist Keith Urban, who successfully overcame alcoholism and continues to write songs and serves as a judge on the *American Idol* television show.

Exhibit 9.1 provides an overview of the important movements related to mental health care in the United States.

MENTAL HEALTH PARITY AND THE AFFORDABLE CARE ACT

Private practice or licensed clinical social workers may provide psychotherapy to treat mental disorders, which was the preferred treatment for mental illness for many decades. However, psychotherapeutic counseling has declined since the 1990s because of restrictions on the number and type of mental health services covered by insurance plans.

For decades, activists attempted to improve insurance coverage for the treatment of mental illness. They were interested in **mental health parity** with medical health policy. In other words, a person who has been diagnosed with a mental disorder should receive the same level of professional care as a person diagnosed with a physical disorder, and mental health professionals should be reimbursed for their services as are physicians and other medical personnel.

Initial reactions to the Mental Health Parity Act, which took effect in 1998, were positive. Under this act, employers who provided mental health benefits to their employees could not place stricter caps on those benefits than they placed on medical and surgical benefits. The National Association of Social Workers (NASW, 2001b) celebrated passage of the act and called it a "first step" toward mental health parity. However, it eventually became apparent that this act would not have the desired effect. It did not require employers to provide mental health benefits, and it did not keep insurance plans from imposing other restrictions on mental health benefits (Moniz & Gorin, 2014). In 2008, the earlier act was replaced by the Mental Health Parity and Addiction Equity Act, which fixed the gaps and added insurance coverage for addiction treatment as well. Up for debate is whether this act truly ensures parity now or still contains flaws.

Since passage of the Affordable Care Act (ACA) of 2010 (aka ObamaCare), Medicaid has become the major source of funding for mental health in the United States (Barry & Huskamp, 2011; Davis, 2008). The ACA emphasizes several

EXHIBIT 9.1   Mental Health Movements

MOVEMENT	TIME FRAME	BASIC STANCE ON MENTAL HEALTH AND ILLNESS
Moral treatment	Early 19th century	People treated in specialized psychiatric units/hospitals Deficits approach
Mental hygiene movement	Early 20th century	Government is responsible
Community mental health movement	Post–World War II	Community mental health centers established Stigma extended to veterans with mental illness
Legal advocacy movement	1960s	Involuntary confinement no longer supported
Deinstitutionalization movement	Post–civil rights movement	Care for mental health clients provided in the community instead of state hospitals
Consumer movement	1970s to present	Encourages independence and recovery Neuroscience appreciated

Source: Content modified from www.careerinfonet.org and www.mymajors.com

emerging models for mental health care (Isett, Ellis, Topping, & Morrissey, 2009; McConnell, 2013):

- **Integrated care:** Also referred to as collaborative care, this is care coordination for people with psychiatric disorders, including general medical illness and substance use disorders.
- **Medical home:** This is the medical care base (usually the primary care doctor) through which all patient care, for medical and mental health services alike, is tracked. This is a patient-centered rather than provider-centered approach. Ideally, the patient will have little sense of getting different kinds of services from different locations. The health care providers must always work collaboratively with the mental health team and the patient's family.
- **Accountable care organizations:** Groups of physicians, hospitals, and other health care providers who voluntarily join together to render coordinated high-quality care to their Medicare patients.

Reforms in the mental health care delivery system, embedded in the ACA, are meant to address long-standing system fragmentation. Typically, primary care doctors and specialty behavioral health care providers, such as therapists and counselors, have not coordinated their treatments for individual patients. Patients with coexisting mental health and addiction disorders are particularly in need of good coordination among all their care providers.

A series of government actions starting in the 1960s, summarized in Exhibit 9.2, has brought us to the current situation. People with mental health disorders are receiving more and better help than ever. Following the 2012 Newtown, Connecticut, tragedy where a man fatally shot 20 students and 6 staff members at Sandy Hook Elementary School, NAMI prepared a report that summarized trends, themes, and best practices in state mental health legislation, and circulated it to mental health advocates around the nation (Carolla, 2014; National Alliance on Mental Illness, 2013). Because Medicaid is the primary funding source for public mental health services, states guided by the ACA must now make decisions about expanding Medicaid for mental health services. NAMI's report outlines legislative goals for states to consider, such as mental health parity, civil rights protection and advocacy, integrated mental health/substance use/primary care, supported employment and housing; early identification and intervention, and more.

EXHIBIT 9.2   U.S. Legislation and Court Cases Related to Mental Health

POLICY/CASE	OUTCOME
Community Mental Health Centers Construction Act of 1963	President Kennedy supported this legislation that revolutionized the U.S. mental health system by providing grants to build community mental health facilities and led to the deinstitutionalization of patients.
O'Connor v. Donaldson Supreme Court case decided in the 1970s	Ruling released patients who were mentally ill or disabled if they had been committed to a hospital but were not receiving treatment. The language then stated that "care for mentally ill or retarded persons was to be provided in the least restrictive environment" (i.e., least confined and most homelike).
The Mental Health System Act of 1980	Continued funding for community mental health centers and endeavored to address deinstitutionalization.
The Omnibus Budget Reconciliation Act of 1981	President Reagan supported it, but the mental health field opposed it because it discontinued government leadership in developing mental health services and switched responsibility to individual states in the form of block grant programs.
President Clinton's 1992 health care plan and Mental Health Bill of Rights	Clinton's plan disappointed the mental health field, as it placed strict limitations on outpatient mental health care and required that patients pay 50% of the bills. Managed-care companies expanded during this time period. The Bill of Rights principles addressed eight areas and were implemented in the Federal Employee Health Benefit Plans in 1997. NASW was one of the supportive sponsors.
Mental Health Parity Act of 1996	Parity means efforts to equalize benefits for both physical and mental health care. This act prompted many states to pass their own parity acts.
The Affordable Care Act of 2010	Expands Medicaid, and emphasizes integrated care models, patient-centered medical homes, and accountable care organizations.

SOCIAL WORK IN ACTION

Asha Grapples With Ethical Issues

PSYCHIATRIC social worker Asha is well aware of how boundaries figure in the lives of social workers, especially those working one-on-one with people with mental illness. She lives in a remote rural area in Alaska, accessible only by plane or boat, and no other counselors are available in the region. Asha has to purchase her winter fuel supply from a man who is now one of her psychotherapy clients. John, of Pacific Islander descent, has been in therapeutic counseling with Asha for 2 months because of his divorce, depression, and co-occurring alcohol addiction.

Usually, the winter fuel purchase in this community is a major negotiating event because there are no other options for buying it. Asha grapples with how to haggle with her client and get a "fair market price" in light of the dual nature of their relationship. John's problems are far from being addressed, although he appears to be committed to treatment and recovery.

1. What would you do if you were Asha?

2. What options does John have, given the geographic context and availability of mental health professionals?

SOCIAL WORK PRACTICE IN MENTAL HEALTH

Mental health social workers often work across boundaries. Social workers see many clients who have combinations of health, mental health, disability, and substance use problems. At the same time, their work often requires collaboration among professionals in the medical, criminal justice, educational, and social services systems. A social worker often serves as the case manager—the one person, other than the client, who knows how everything interconnects.

SOCIAL WORK ROLES IN TREATMENT

Exhibit 9.3 outlines multiple tasks that are often the responsibility of either BSW- or MSW-prepared mental health workers. As you can see, the possibilities are expansive.

One of the most distinctive roles of social workers in the area of mental health is therapy, or clinical social work. **Licensed clinical social workers** are directly responsible for assessing, diagnosing, and treating all forms of mental disorders, including serious mental illnesses such as major depression, schizophrenia, and substance-related disorders (Theriot & Lodato, 2012). The job often requires great patience and ingenuity in breaking through the client's

disordered thinking and helping the client cope well with her or his social environment. Another reality is that people often "wait until their suffering is so desperate that it finally outweighs the fear, mistrust, or embarrassment that previously prevented them from seeking help" (Frances, 2013, p. 6). Other challenges confront the mental health social worker. For example, they often help families cope with trauma, loss, and addiction.

A good example of how complex a clinical social worker's role may become involves an increase in services for recovery from a combination of traumatic brain injury (a physical disability) and PTSD (a mental disorder often resulting from military service). These conditions are complex in and of themselves; together, they require integrated services from medical and mental health personnel. Sometimes the problem can be handled quite quickly, but other times it may require ongoing monitoring and care. PTSD can be addressed through individual or family counseling, or group therapy. Oftentimes, family members of patients with traumatic brain injury and PTSD require as much if not more counseling than do their family members, because while the patient looks the same as before, she or he now thinks and behaves differently and cannot necessarily control her or his thoughts and actions.

EXHIBIT 9.3   What Mental Health Social Workers Do

DIRECT SERVICES

- Interview clients to assess the presenting situation and client
- Counsel and aid family members to assist them in understanding, dealing with, and supporting the client or patient
- Counsel clients in individual and group sessions to help them manage their mental illness as well as physical illness, substance abuse, poverty, unemployment, or physical abuse

CASE ADVOCACY

- Refer patient, client, or family to community resources for housing or treatment to assist in recovery from mental or physical illness, and follow through to ensure service efficacy
- Review client records and confer with other professionals
- Collaborate with counselors, physicians, nurses to plan and coordinate treatment, drawing on social work experiences and patient needs
- Monitor, evaluate, and record client progress with regard to treatment goals
- Modify treatment plans according to changes in client status
- Advocate for needed change(s) with the client

CAUSE ADVOCACY

- Supervise and direct other workers who provide services to clients or patients
- Develop or advise on social policy and assist in community development
- Plan and conduct programs to combat social problems that typically affect people with mental disorders or to improve health and counseling services in the community
- Conduct social research to advance knowledge in the social work field
- Advocate with clients and stakeholders for larger-scale changes in policies, programs, and process

Source: CareerOneStop (www.careeronestop.org) and MyMajors (www.mymajors.com).

MENTAL HEALTH LITERACY

The term **mental health literacy,** first used by Australian researcher Anthony Jorm and his colleagues in the late 1990s as an extension of the term *health literacy*, refers to being able to recognize disorders and obtain mental health information (Mendenhall & Frauenholtz, 2013). Literacy facilitates understanding. The NASW (2009) has identified universal access to health and mental health care as one of social work's top priorities and includes health literacy in its initiative. However, largely excluded from the formal list of priorities is the need for mental health literacy.

Mental health literacy has value across multiple mental health settings. Social work clients and staff who have not had professional training need to understand the signs, symptoms, and treatments for various disorders. The most severely affected mental health consumers in community settings may not be able to achieve mental health literacy themselves and may be limited in their ability to share mental health information with others. Thus, social workers need to provide individualized psychoeducation for friends and family of people who live with mental health disorders. Social workers must also advocate for and prioritize mental health literacy as a goal of U.S. health care policy. Interventions could include public campaigns, agency- or school-based programs, online interventions, and information sharing through social media.

source: Linda Hosek/CreativeCommons

▲ Catrina Tomsich decided to close her business to care for her husband, Army Sgt. John Tomsich, after he was diagnosed with posttraumatic stress disorder.

MENTAL HEALTH SETTINGS

Current social workers provide mental health services in multiple settings, including the following:

- *Community mental health programs:* Overseeing assessments, interventions, and evaluations of people and programs related to mental health services
- *Disaster relief programs:* Planning and implementing international and humanitarian relief and response efforts for victims of natural and other disasters
- *Employee assistance programs:* Managing conflicts and providing information, referrals, and counseling to people with health, mental health, and other troubles
- *Hospitals and skilled nursing facilities:* Facilitating intakes, discharge planning, and monitoring of ongoing acute and chronic care needs
- *Military and veterans services*: Providing direct service, supervision, and administration, research, and policy formulation related to the Department of Defense
- *Rehabilitation programs:* Supporting clients to recover and rehabilitate from mental health and co-occurring disorders
- *Schools:* Helping teachers and educational professionals evaluate students' behavior at school to provide early intervention; sharing information with students, teachers, and administrators about mental health and mental illness; and guiding schools toward funding to expand mental health services
- *Private practice*
- *Employee assistance programs:* Counseling employees with personal problems and workplace issues
- *Inpatient and outpatient clinics:* Helping clients adapt to significant lifestyle changes related to a loved one's death, disability, divorce, or job loss; providing substance abuse treatment; and helping people who experience anxiety, depression, a crisis, or trauma

DIGITAL MENTAL HEALTH INFORMATION AND THERAPY

Young and old alike can experience mental health issues. When it comes to learning about mental illness and therapy

or treatment, however, adults respond best to brochures and self-help books, television or radio messages, paid advertisements, and face-to-face counseling. In contrast, the younger generation craves connection and information through social media and digital devices.

To provide effective mental health treatment to youth, 21st century health care providers must cross the "digital divide" and offer online and mobile options to support youth who wish to successfully manage their mental health problems. Young people respond to websites, Twitter, blogs, online questionnaires, and chat rooms. Therefore, providing mental health information via the Internet and social media platforms such as Facebook can enhance the self-help capacity of young people. Smartphone applications that can help improve some mental health habits also exist.

Computer-mediated activities such as e-counseling and e-therapy can also be used in treatment for people who are comfortable with digital technology and the Internet. Some treatment approaches can be applied even better in virtual environments, such as exposure-based therapies, which are efficacious for many phobia and PTSD issues. Other options involve using avatars or Comic Chat. Comic Chat, now called Microsoft Chat 2.5, allows players to take on the role of a character in a comic strip.

Many people find support and information through **peer support** sites, where people who share similar diagnoses can compare notes. However, it is important for mental health professionals, including social workers, to become comfortable with online media as well so their knowledge and experience can help inform people with mental health concerns (Rickwood, 2012, p. 25).

Whether counseling or resource information sharing occurs in person or through social media and the Internet, mental health social workers must remember that the client comes first and must be served with respect, worth, and dignity.

DIVERSITY AND MENTAL HEALTH

In and of itself, a mentally healthy population is paramount for enhancing unity, social integration, and inclusiveness in our society. Another consideration, however, is how the diversity of the American population plays out in the prevalence and treatment of serious mental illness. Exhibit 9.4 depicts the varying rates of mental illness among

CURRENT TRENDS

Peer Support

PEER support–based interventions are increasingly being deployed. One estimate suggests that groups, organizations, and programs run by and for people with serious mental illness and their families outnumber professionally run mental health organizations by a ratio of almost 2 to 1 (Lucksted, McNulty, Brayboy, & Forbes, 2009). Three forms of peer support include consumer-run services, naturally occurring mutual support groups, and the employment of consumers as providers within clinical or rehabilitative settings (Davidson, Chinman, et al., 1999).

Peer-based interventions have been developed based on the idea that people who experience mental illness can help others who experience similar mental health conditions. Although evidence exists to support the efficacy of structured self-management programs for chronic physical conditions such as diabetes and asthma, limited research has evaluated this approach for mental disorders. (Cook et al., 2009).

A review of peer specialist roles and activities demonstrated common activities, which include self-determination and personal responsibility; support health and wellness; address hopelessness; address stigma in the community; develop friendships and other social support; provide education, transportation, illness management, leisure and recreation; and assist with communication with health care providers. At a lesser level these roles support the development of psychiatric advance directives, and supports for dating, parenting, spirituality and religion, citizenship, employment, and family relationships (Salzer et al., 2010).

1. How can social workers encourage the creation and functioning of peer supports?

2. How can peer support be evaluated to assure they are encouraging self-determination, personal responsibility, and being supportive and health oriented?

Source: Allen S. Daniels, "Peer support services – What does the research reveal about peer support services?" Pillars of Peer Support-2 Summit. October, 2010. Atlanta, GA Carter Center. http://www.dbsalliance.org/pdfs/training/PillarsIIresearchPresentation10_10final-Daniels.pdfi

---

subgroups based on sex, age, and race or ethnicity. The paragraphs that follow elaborate on those differences.

- *Age.* Mental health problems can occur at any age; however, recognition of mental health problems and disabilities in children and adolescents is a relatively recent phenomenon that began in the late 19th century. That is not to say that mental illness does not exist in this age group: A large U.S. study found that "half of all mental disorders emerge by 14 and three quarters by 25 years of age. Translated this means that by the age of 21, 51% of young people will have experienced a diagnosable psychiatric disorder" (Rickwood, 2012, p. 18).

- *Class.* The relationship among health disparities, mental health disparities, and socioeconomic status is a complex and important one. The connection between the mind and the body is undeniable: Afflictions of the mind affect physiology, and afflictions of the body in turn affect psychology. The disproportionate rates of mental health problems in the lower social class show that mental health is associated with social inequality (Aneshensel, 2009). Additionally, the effects of negative social interactions and stigma are inversely associated with health and well-being (Chou & Chronister, 2011). Working-class people are more likely to be diagnosed with a mental illness than are those from nonmanual-labor backgrounds.

- *Race and ethnicity.* Although Exhibit 9.4 shows that African Americans have a lower rate of serious mental illness than the overall average for Americans, African Americans are more likely than their white counterparts to be diagnosed with schizophrenia (Bresnahan, Begg, Brown, Schaefer, & Sohler, 2007). On the other hand, non-Hispanic blacks are 40% less likely than non-Hispanic whites to experience depression during their lifetime. Exhibit 9.4 also shows that American Indians and Alaska Natives have a prevalence of mental illness far above that experienced by any other group shown in the chart. Historical traumas in the form of forced relocations, cultural assimilation, multiple broken treaties,

EXHIBIT 9.4   Prevalence of Serious Mental Illness Among U.S. Adults

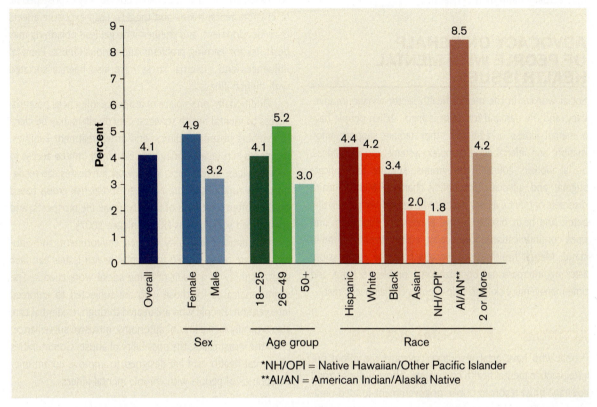

Source: National Institute of Mental Health (2013).

and other social and economic injustices have contributed to health and mental health disparities in this population. Mental health and disabilities also exert a disproportionately negative effect on racial and ethnic minority children. One reason for the disparity was cited in the final report of the President's New Freedom Commission on Mental Health (2003): "Specifically, the system has neglected to incorporate respect or understanding of the histories, traditions, beliefs, languages, and value systems of culturally diverse groups" (p. 49). Because some social work disability specialists and mental health service providers lack cultural competence, people of color frequently do not seek services in the formal system. Also, they are more likely to drop out of care, be misdiagnosed, or seek care only when their illness is at an advanced stage. "Fifteen percent of African Americans, 13 percent of Hispanics, and 11 percent of Asian Americans said there had been a time when they felt they would have received better care if they had been of a different race or ethnicity" (National Alliance on Mental Illness, 2012).

• *Gender.* In the United States, major depressive disorder is one of the most common mental disorders. Women are 70% more likely than men to experience depression during their lifetime. Comparatively, in the United Kingdom, depression is also more commonly identified in women.

• *Sexual orientation.* Lesbian, gay, and bisexual young people are at increased risk of mental health problems, particularly on measures of suicidal behavior and multiple disorders (Remafedi, French, Story, Reshnick, & Blum, 1998; Ryan & Futterman, 1998). Until recently, some gay men have also been pressured to "treat" their sexuality through mental health interventions. Most experts today agree that homosexuality cannot be "cured"—and in fact, should not even be considered a mental illness. The NASW (2000) position statement on this subject points out that research findings showing that **conversion therapies** work are confounded, and the organization does not stand by such therapies as a means of changing sexual orientation.

Indeed, the NASW has stated that conversion therapies may actually harm mental health.

ADVOCACY ON BEHALF OF PEOPLE WITH MENTAL HEALTH ISSUES

Social workers in the mental health sector engage in advocacy, and the demand for them is high. When people have a mental illness or addiction, they require support, information, and referral amid complex systems and insurances. Social workers counsel, run groups, educate to eradicate stigma, and advocate for policy changes. Mental health disorders or mental illness needs to be treated like cancer, diabetes, and heart disease, where prevention, education, and open communication occur in ways every citizen can understand. Mental health social workers have the compassion, listening, interpersonal, organizational, problem-solving, and time-management skills to help clients get their needs met.

ECONOMIC AND SOCIAL JUSTICE

People who have great insurance coverage can afford private practice mental health counseling. Those without good coverage must resort to public or government-funded organizations. Those in the middle often receive mental health services through managed-care organizations, which can limit the client's access to care and the ability for health providers to get paid. Mental health social work advocates need to keep up with ACA and mental health policy changes and subsequently counsel people about the best way to receive the best type of counseling services.

For clients who present with **co-occurring disorders**—for instance, depression and substance abuse or paranoia and aggressive tendencies—social work treatment is shifting to a holistic approach that involves combining rather than separating health care, substance abuse treatment, and mental health care. Increasingly, social workers in mental health will be required to have the skills and knowledge to provide treatment for co-occurring mental health disorders simultaneously.

SUPPORTIVE ENVIRONMENT

The physical place where people live affects health and mental health alike. For example, living on the street, under a bridge or boardwalk, in a rescue mission or Salvation Army shelter, near a railroad or shipyard, or in a home plagued with asbestos or an abandoned meth lab may expose people to environmental toxins and triggers. Lead exposure affects brain development, and children who get lead poisoning may be at risk for learning problems and serious illness. Prenatal influences and maternal stress have also been associated with mental illness.

Additionally, one's place of residence influences potential access to mental health services. City dwellers may be close to teaching hospitals, clinics, and other treatment facilities. Residents in rural areas may have extremely limited access to such services. In response, social work advocates can recognize how rural people are a diverse and at-risk group based on their often high rates of poverty, fewer life prospects, and stigmatized social status (Riebschleger, 2007).

No matter the quality of their environment, individuals who are being treated for mental health issues can face stigma simply as a result of being social work clients. The stigma increases for those who are subjected to enforced intervention. People who are treated through residential care also typically face a loss of autonomy, intrusive surveillance, or, in the worst cases, the possibility of abuse. Communities of mental health care are designed to improve community acceptance of people with chronic mental illness.

HUMAN NEEDS AND RIGHTS

People need and deserve respect and acceptance, regardless of their mental health. People with a mental disorder still require understanding, and people with substance abuse problems need to know that they have a disease and not a character defect. At the very least, social work professionals should support their feelings of self-worth by using person-first language.

Users of mental health services face risks from medication and other forms of treatment, and from services that fail to engage them effectively (Stalker, 2003, p. 225). Social workers can help clients living with mental illness better understand what types of medication they are taking, why they are taking them, and what side effects may occur. Also, some medications must be taken at particular times and with particular dietary restrictions, and doctors and nurses may not always fully explain these details to patients.

Another area of mental health services that requires advocacy related to human rights is the racial and ethnic disparity in treatment providers. Ten years ago a U.S. Surgeon General report recommended developing a more racially

SOCIAL WORK IN ACTION

John Beard Implements the Clubhouse Model

ONE example of an effective psychiatric rehabilitation model that focuses on providing people who are mentally ill with a supportive environment is the clubhouse model. Just about anywhere rehabilitation practitioners gather, they talk about this model. The term is often cited in professional literature and at conferences and seminars. Nearly synonymous with the clubhouse model is the Fountain House in New York City, which every year serves about 1,300 people who have severe mental disorders (Fountain House, 2014a). It has been praised widely and is the first of several other Fountain Houses worldwide. The man most responsible for this success is social worker John Beard.

An article in the *Psychosocial Rehabilitation Journal* describes the clubhouse model (Beard, Propst, & Malamud, 1982). The goal is to help severely disabled psychiatric patients improve their social skills through life in a community based on mutual support. The four core beliefs of the clubhouse model are productivity, work, social interchange, and autonomy. Each person in Fountain House is assigned to a work unit that is essential to operation of the facility, such as clerical, culinary, or maintenance work. A variety of living options are available, including shared onsite apartments offering support services and offsite apartments.

The ancillary components of Fountain House include a transitional employment program, an evening and weekend program, a thrift shop, and outreach programs. Every person in the community is expected to support every other community member. As one of the residents put it: "They helped me make it on my own, yet I was never alone" (Fountain House, 2014b).

Beard was executive director of New York's Fountain House for 28 years. Through his work, the clubhouse model was established and concepts that are seminal to the field of psychiatric rehabilitation were developed. Yearly, the John Beard Award is presented to someone who makes an outstanding contribution to the field of psychiatric rehabilitation.

1. What kind of knowledge and skills might mental health social workers require to work with the chronically mentally ill population in a setting that uses the clubhouse model?

2. How do the four core beliefs of the clubhouse model encourage personal empowerment for people living with mental health challenges?

diverse workforce to provide mental health services for racial and ethnic minorities (Lowry, 2014). Still today, however, more mental health social workers representing varied races and ethnicities are needed to meet the needs and numbers of consumers.

POLITICAL ACCESS

The mental health field of practice demands that social workers be involved in cause advocacy, such as these policy issues:

- Why so many nonspecialized providers are delivering mental health services and discussing psychotropic medications with clients

- Why both rural and urban areas experience a lack of available emergency care and residential treatment services
- What to do about cost containment and continuity of care issues
- How to increase the number of inpatient hospital beds to reduce the poor outcomes of shifting so many seriously mentally ill clients to outpatient care

These issues will not be easy to resolve. Presidents and Congressional leaders have claimed to want to stop ineffective policies and support funding for more inpatient beds and more community mental health centers; however, actual progress in the political arena has been slow.

Social workers and other mental health professionals have also been dismayed by the political factors, both blatant and hidden, that affect mental health disparities and mental health literacy. For example, patient preferences, cultural differences, medical mistrust, provider biases, stereotyping, and poor patient–provider communication can yield varying mental health outcomes. Most definitions of psychological abnormality have been devised by white, middle-class men, which has led to disproportionate numbers of people from certain races and ethnic groups being diagnosed as "abnormal" (Corcoran & Walsh, 2012).

YOUR CAREER IN MENTAL HEALTH SOCIAL WORK

As much as 35% of social workers list mental health as their primary practice (Whitaker & Arrington, 2008). As illustrated in Exhibit 9.5, the demand for social workers specializing in mental health is expected to increase, and future job opportunities are quite good. Government economists predict that job growth for mental health social workers will be much faster than the average for all careers through 2020. With the ACA, mental health parity is being rolled out, making more people eligible for mental health coverage under their insurance plans. Such policy changes will likely contribute to this increasing need for mental health social work professionals.

Mental health social work is also an attractive career because clinical social work tends to pay well. However, money is not normally the main factor that leads someone to become a mental health social worker. In fact, social workers throughout the mental health system have been willing to accept less pay than nurses, which has resulted in more social workers being hired (Beinecke & Huxley, 2009).

TIME TO THINK

What might be attractive about working as a clinical, psychiatric, or other mental health social worker, in a mental health setting or in private practice?

EXHIBIT 9.5   Expected Job Growth in Some Subfields of Mental Health

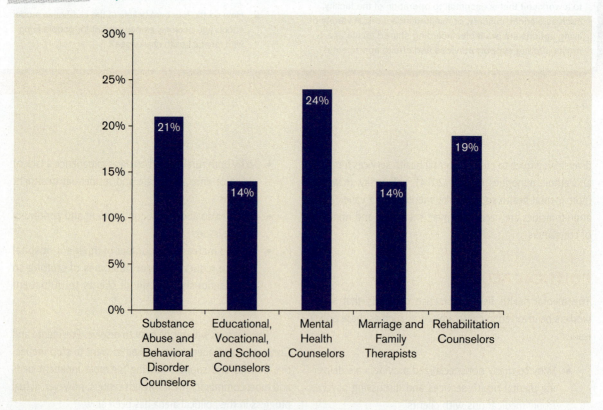

Source: Classes and Careers (2014).

CURRENT TRENDS

The Brain Initiative

THE Brain Initiative was conceived and funded by the federal government in 2014, with the goal of revolutionizing our understanding of the human brain. Researchers have craved this type of funding for a long time so they can seek new ways to cure, treat, and maybe even prevent brain disorders.

If we figured out how our brains work, maybe we could cure mental illnesses or create very smart robots. Scientists want to build a computer model of the brain, and the Department of Defense has invested about $40 billion to this project. The Brain Initiative differs from the Human Genome Project in that it plans to study individual neurons, focus on brain imaging, and do computer simulations of neuronal

networks. Essentially, the initiative will coordinate research on how the brain functions over an organism's life span. (For more information about this development that is funding neuroengineers and others, go to www.nih.gov/science/brain.)

1. How much more informative might brain images be than human behavior studies in teaching us about the human brain?

2. Why might social workers have a vested interest in the Brain Initiative?

BSW social workers often serve as behavioral assistants and care or case managers in mental health settings. They must be familiar with mental illnesses, be compassionate communicators, and know community resources and viable treatment strategies. By contrast, MSW social workers may be expected to provide psychotherapeutic counseling. In all states, social workers in clinical practice are required to be licensed, registered, or certified. Both BSW- and MSW-prepared social workers are required to know how to conduct thorough assessments, develop practical treatment plans, and evaluate progress. Both may serve as advocates for policy change and as activists to advance movements for the cause of people who are mentally ill. Burnout in the mental health social work field is a reality; so social workers must learn and use strategies to combat it (Acker, 2011). Meanwhile, advances in neuroscience, technology, and pharmaceuticals offer the potential for new treatments, prevention strategies, and policies.

SUMMARY

Out of suffering have emerged the strongest souls;
the most massive characters are seared with scars.

—Khalil Gibran

The mental health field grants multiple sources of identity, interest, status, and career opportunities for social workers at the BSW and MSW levels. Historically, a large number of social workers secured employment in private and public psychiatric hospitals, community mental health centers, general public or for-profit hospitals with psychiatric units, outpatient clinics and inpatient units in university settings, as well as private practice (Davis, 2008). Across these settings mental health social workers collaborated with multidisciplinary teams to offer therapy and other practical support, such as help with homelessness and unemployment, to people with mental health problems. Mental health social workers are involved in planning, policy, and administration of agencies.

Because treatment of mental disorders occurs frequently in general medicine, social workers may not be the first mental health professionals to identify a client's mental disorder or substance abuse treatment needs. As a result, some mental health patients are simply receiving medication from their physicians, without the counseling and other services that could help them overcome their symptoms as well as their problems with living. But times are changing in the field of mental health services, and with new policies favoring mental health parity, more people may receive effective treatment. Time will also tell how mental health services will evolve in the era of burgeoning technology, demographic changes, and a holistic, integrative focus among mental health practitioners.

TOP 10 KEY CONCEPTS

deinstitutionalization
Diagnostic and Statistical Manual of Mental Disorders (DSM)
medicalization
mental disorders
mental health parity

mental illness
posttraumatic stress disorder (PTSD)
psychopharmacology
psychotropic medications
stigma

DISCUSSION QUESTIONS

1. How come some social work professionals question the use of the DSM-5 classification system to understand mild, moderate, or severe mental disorders? What are the advantages and disadvantages of the DSM?
2. Would you be okay with a mental health facility's opening near your home? What stereotypes do you have regarding mental illness and those who are severely mentally ill?
3. What is your view on **psychopharmacology** (medication as treatment)?

4. What role does social support play in helping people cope with diseases or mental health conditions?
5. How do people, across cultures, use mental health care facilities and manage risk in their everyday lives?
6. How can the health beliefs and voices of people using mental health services be better understood and advocated for?

EXERCISES

1. Locate research articles or resources that examine how social workers are working to understand mental disorders, and write a report on your findings. These are some possible topics: What are social work researchers saying about the basis of mental illness? How can biomedical, behavioral, and social scientists work together to improve early detection, prevention, and treatment of mental disorders?
2. Choose a mental health disorder to report on. Then use Internet and library resources to gather articles and information about how this disorder is diagnosed and treated. Include both psychopharmacological and counseling interventions.
3. Research the types of mental health services available in your community. What types of settings and services are most common? Which seem to be in short supply? Draw a simple map that shows where those facilities are located. What are your conclusions about your community's ability

to treat all sorts of mental illnesses and disorders and all sorts of people who need mental health services?
4. Working in groups, research cultural diversity issues in mental health treatment. How do race and ethnicity affect access to treatment and its efficacy? What aspects of the treatment are insensitive to the needs of culturally diverse people? Explore the full array of available interventions for people with mental health problems:

- Behavioral approaches
- Psychopharmacology
- Community outreach
- Family therapy interventions
- Group counseling
- Program development
- Self-help groups
- Therapeutic communities
- Rehabilitation and support services

ONLINE RESOURCES

- American Association of Suicidology (www.suicidology .org): Seeks to understand and prevent suicide
- *The Contributions of Behavioral and Social Sciences Research to Improving the Health of the Nation* (obssr .od.nih.gov/pdf/OBSSR_Prospectus.pdf)
- "An Early History: African American Mental Health" (academic.udayton.edu/health/01status/mental01.htm)
- "Hammurabi's Managed Health Care–Circa 1700 B.C." (www.managedcaremag.com/archives/9705/9705 .hammurabi.html)
- "History of Social Work Research in Mental Health" (www .socialworkpolicy.org/research/history-of-social-work- research-in-mental-health.html)
- National Alliance on Mental Illness (www.nami.org): The nation's voice on mental illness and advocacy for people with mental disorders

- National Association for Rural Mental Health (narmh .org): Founded in 1977, develops and enhances rural mental health and substance abuse services, and supports mental health providers in rural areas
- National Institute of Mental Health (www.nimh.nih.gov): Seeks to transform the understanding and treatment of mental illnesses through basic and clinical research, paving the way for prevention, recovery, and cure
- PBS health care crisis timeline (www.pbs.org/ healthcarecrisis/history.htm)
- SAMHSA Center for Mental Health Services (beta .samhsa.gov/about-us/who-we-are/offices-centers/ cmhs): Leads federal efforts to promote the prevention and treatment of mental disorders; created by Congress to bring new hope to adults who have serious mental illness and to children with emotional disorders

STUDENT STUDY SITE

Sharpen your skills with SAGE edge at **edge.sagepub.com/cox**

SAGE edge for Students provides a personalized approach to help you accomplish your coursework goals in an easy-to-use learning environment.

Chapter 10: SUBSTANCE USE AND ADDICTION

Learning Objectives

After reading this chapter, you will be able to

1. Explain why substance abuse and addiction occur and why they are so hard to overcome.
2. Understand the role of codependency in substance abuse and addiction.
3. Explain why prevention of substance abuse and addiction is so important.
4. Understand social workers' roles in substance use and addiction.
5. Identify substance use and addiction treatment concepts and settings.
6. Explain why some forms of treatment present moral, personal, and social dilemmas.
7. Recognize how stigma and bias impede the drug-abuse recovery process.

Clayton Uses His Addiction Experience in Community Outreach

Before getting clean and becoming a street outreach worker, Clayton's walk on the wild side took him to crack houses and shooting galleries where he lost himself in the moment. He acquired hepatitis from sharing dirty needles and feared getting AIDS. Getting a hit, getting high was all that was important, until he landed in jail.

Several years later, Clayton got into a recovery rehab program and earned a BSW degree in social work. Now, Clayton possesses not only book learning but real-life experience about the world of mental health and substance abuse. Clayton attends 12-step meetings and knows the slang terms for drugs, and he's tuned into the excuses one can make when addicted to drugs. He strives to be committed to his work and relationships, and counsels clients with warmth, empathy, and natural genuineness. Clients adore Clayton—his genuineness and directness convey honesty, and they find it easy to trust him.

No longer is Clayton a hungry, angry, lonely, and tired person; instead, he works as an effective substance abuse counselor, sits on community consortiums and boards, and maintains a devoted relationship with his wife.

Sadly, one of Clayton's sons—a tall, handsome young man named Quincy—has followed in his dad's footsteps, seeking to escape from childhood pain through drug use. Quincy made some bad choices and is in jail. Clayton maintains a prayerful hopefulness for his son as he himself takes one day at a time. Clayton stays connected with his son, but he does not enable him.

Substance use problems are ubiquitous in the United States and globally. The substances could be alcohol, tobacco, or recreational or illicit drugs. Some use of these substances may not be a problem, such as limited use of alcohol; however, when a person goes overboard and uses substances to the point that relationships and the ability to cope with ordinary tasks and activities are affected, that person may be said to have a substance use problem. This definition of substance use and its related problems has opened helping professionals' eyes to other addictive behaviors that have little to do with substances, such as gambling and sex addictions.

The implication is that **addiction** is more than a behavioral disorder. Aspects of addiction include people's behaviors, thoughts, emotions, and interactions with others, including their relationships with family and community members, and their own psychological state.

Professionals who work in substance use may be case managers, clinicians, clinical social workers, counselors, community support workers, mental health therapists, psychotherapists, or probation agents. Social workers who specialize in substance use or addiction may be employed at addiction treatment or chemical dependency centers, community-based treatment programs, hospital-based treatment inpatient programs, education and prevention organizations, or private rehab centers established by people who have suffered from addiction themselves.

Some people believe that **substance use**—in this context the consumption of harmful, potentially addictive substances—should not be a matter for social concern. In reality, the use of some substances causes considerable health and social problems for users. The number one cause of preventable illness and death in the United States is **substance abuse**, which extends the idea of substance use to include maladaptive patterns of use despite adverse consequences. Each year, more than 500,000 deaths—or 1 in 4—in the United States are attributed to abuse of alcohol, tobacco, or other drugs (Schroeder, 2010). Those deaths include drug overdoses, teen suicides, traffic fatalities, murders, and manslaughter. As illustrated in Exhibit 10.1, substance abuse is also associated with rapes, assaults, burglaries, thefts, and child abuse. And the health care costs of substance abuse are immense when one considers cancer and cardiopulmonary disease from tobacco use, falls and oversedation from misuse of prescription drugs, or bacterial and viral infections (including HIV infection) from injecting illicit drugs.

EXHIBIT 10.1   Health Issues Related to Drug Use and Alcoholism

SUBSTANCE USE AS A MENTAL DISORDER

Substance use is also linked to mental illness. The fifth edition of the *Diagnostic and Statistical Manual of Mental Disorders* (DSM-5) defines **substance use disorder** as a mental disorder associated with the consumption of a harmful addictive substance. It is a general classification with a broad range of severity, from mild to severe (American Psychiatric Association, 2013, p. 484). Multiple definitions and criteria exist for the consumption of specific substances such as alcohol and tobacco.

The DSM-5 notes that the word *addiction* is not applied as a diagnostic term in this classification, even though it is commonly used in many countries to describe severe problems related to compulsive and habitual use of substances. The more neutral term *substance use disorder* is preferred in the United States. Gone is the diagnosis of substance dependence that caused so much confusion in previous editions of the DSM. **Substance dependence** refers to continued use or craving associated with greater tolerance to a substance, leading to ever-higher doses, and the risk of illness when a person stops using that substance (withdrawal symptoms). Previously, too many people linked the term *dependence*

SOCIAL WORK IN ACTION

Jessica Intervenes to Help Mason Recover

MASON, age 19, is a short, stocky young man with a ruddy complexion and shoulder-length hair. He is receiving counseling from Jessica, a clinical social worker at the college counseling center, for his depression and chronic episodes of binge drinking. He cannot seem to resist those beer pong events at frat parties and does not even think about the bacteria and viruses he might be picking up from this activity.

Mason does not adhere very well to the depression medication he has been prescribed. Sometimes he doesn't even remember when he last took it.

At his most recent appointment with Jessica, Mason confided that his father had a long-standing drinking problem.

As a child, Mason would also sometimes observe his father abusing his mother.

While in college and until he is 26, Mason is covered under his parent's workplace insurance policy. If after graduation Mason continues to experience depression and alcohol problems, he may be required to sign up for health coverage through the Affordable Care Act website.

What information does Jessica need to share with Mason to prevent his mental health and substance use behavior from worsening? To what extent might codependency issues be relevant to this client's situation?

with addiction, when in fact dependence can be a normal body response to a substance. However, some social workers in this field still use the word *addiction* to describe more extreme cases.

The DSM-5 still includes the term **addictive disorders,** but it is a new category based on behavioral, not substance, addictions. Gambling disorder is the only addictive disorder in the DSM-5 that is considered a diagnosable condition. This new term reflects recent research that links gambling disorder to substance-related disorders insofar as their brain origin, association with other disorders, physiology, and treatment.

Source: ©iStockphoto.com/vm

▲ Group counseling sessions are common in rehab.

CAUSES OF SUBSTANCE ABUSE

Similar to many psychological disorders, substance use disorder depends on two main factors: genes and environment. Genetic factors account for about half of the likelihood that a person will develop an addiction. An addicting drug causes physical changes to several areas of the brain, changes that exacerbate and are exacerbated by continuing use of the drug. In essence, addiction is a brain disorder with self-perpetuating tendencies. Although neurobiological researchers do not yet know exactly how genes influence a person's tendency to experience changes in the brain and become

addicted, they have found definitive signs that addictive tendencies run in families.

Environmental factors interact with a person's biology and affect the extent to which genetic factors exert their influence. The way a person is raised and later life experiences can affect the extent to which genetic predispositions lead to the behavioral and other manifestations of addiction. Culture also contributes to how addiction becomes actualized in people with biological vulnerabilities. Moreover, although addiction seems to be a matter of biology, the decision to start using a drug is influenced by your family's beliefs and attitudes and by exposure to a peer group that encourages drug use. People of any age, sex, or class can become addicted to a substance. However, addiction occurs faster or more readily for those who have a family history of addiction, have a neglectful family, are male, experience peer pressure to use a drug, experience anxiety and depression, or begin using a highly addictive drug such as heroin or cocaine.

TIME TO THINK

What features of American life do you think make American adolescents, adults, and older adults susceptible to addiction to alcohol and other drugs and harmful behaviors?

CODEPENDENCY

A substance use disorder may also progress because other people in the user's environment are enabling the substance abuse. The term for the relationship between the user and these other people is **codependency.** They rely on each other to meet reciprocal needs, especially unhealthy emotional needs. For example, a young woman puts up with controlling behavior and insults from her boyfriend because she wants to be with a man. Or a dad steps in to protect his son from the consequences of poor behavior instead of teaching his son the proper way to behave.

The person with a substance abuse problem needs treatment to break the grip of the substance or behavior. In addition, the people who have covered up or enabled the substance abuse (often referred to simply as codependents) need counseling to understand how their behavior is hurting everyone. Although they may accept that their "caretaking" behavior is making it more difficult for the person with the substance use problem to recover, they often have more difficulty understanding how codependency is hurting them in return. An example of this caretaking behavior is when a wife covers up for her alcoholic husband so he does not lose his job.

Researchers and clinicians have found that many codependents focus too much outside of themselves, do not express their feelings, and take too much personal meaning from their relationship with the person who has an addiction (Beattie, 2009, 2011; Knudson & Terrell, 2012, p. 245).

Codependency appears to originate primarily in the family of origin, particularly in families where the parents are perceived to have a turbulent relationship; interestingly, however, codependent behavior does not seem to be related to substance abuse in the family of origin (Knudson & Terrell, 2012). In any event, codependents may appear as people pleasers, denying themselves and their own needs because they are or have been so busy taking care of others.

ADDICTIVE SUBSTANCES AND BEHAVIORS

Many types of substances can be abused. Exhibit 10.2 is a chart from the National Institute on Drug Abuse that explains their effects and the dangers of abuse. Here we provide some additional information about the ways these substances (and a couple of behaviors) affect both those who abuse them and those who may suffer the consequences of others' abuse.

Alcohol

Alcohol is the most commonly used **psychoactive,** or brain-affecting, substance. About 1 in 4 people who drink heavily may have alcohol abuse problems (Larson, Wooten, Adams, & Merrick, 2012; Roman, 2014). **Alcoholism** is a chronic and often progressive disease that includes problems controlling your drinking, physical dependence on alcohol, or having withdrawal symptoms when you stop drinking.

Although it is not always associated with alcoholism, **binge drinking** is a common problem among young people. It means drinking so much within about 2 hours that **blood alcohol concentration (BAC)** levels reach 0.08%. For women this usually occurs after four drinks and for men after five. Drinking too much, whether as an alcoholic or a frequent binge drinker, can affect your brain, heart, liver, pancreas, cancer potential, and immune system.

Impaired driving related to alcohol, or drunk driving, is a significant public health problem. Generally, in the United States, a BAC of 0.08% is considered the legal limit for being charged with the criminal offense of driving while intoxicated (DWI).

The U.S. Department of Transportation found that in 2012, 10,322 people were killed in alcohol-impaired–driving crashes. Further, these fatalities accounted for 31% of the total motor vehicle traffic fatalities in the United States (Centers for Disease Control and Prevention, 2011a). According to the Centers for Disease Control and

EXHIBIT 10.2   Commonly Abused Drugs

SUBSTANCES: CATEGORY AND NAME	EXAMPLES OF *COMMERCIAL AND STREET NAMES*	DEA SCHEDULE*/ HOW ADMINISTERED**	*ACUTE EFFECTS/HEALTH RISKS*
Tobacco			
Nicotine	Found in cigarettes, cigars, bidis, and smokeless tobacco (snuff, spit tobacco, chew)	Not scheduled/smoked, snorted, chewed	*Increased blood pressure and heart rate/chronic lung disease; cardiovascular disease; stroke; cancers of the mouth, pharynx, larynx, esophagus, stomach, pancreas, cervix, kidney, bladder, and acute myeloid leukemia; adverse pregnancy outcomes; addiction*
Alcohol			
Alcohol (ethyl alcohol)	Found in liquor, beer, and wine	Not scheduled/swallowed	*In low doses, euphoria, mild stimulation, relaxation, lowered inhibitions; in higher doses, drowsiness, slurred speech, nausea, emotional volatility, loss of coordination, visual distortions, impaired memory, sexual dysfunction, loss of consciousness/increased risk of injuries, violence, fetal damage (in pregnant women); depression; neurologic deficits; hypertension; liver and heart disease; addiction; fatal overdose*
Cannabinoids			
Marijuana	Blunt, dope, ganja, grass, herb, joint, bud, Mary Jane, pot, reefer, green, trees, smoke, sinsemilla, skunk, weed	I/smoked, swallowed	*Euphoria; relaxation; slowed reaction time; distorted sensory perception; impaired balance and coordination; increased heart rate and appetite; impaired learning, memory; anxiety; panic attacks; psychosis/cough; frequent respiratory infections; possible mental health decline; addiction*
Hashish	Boom, gangster, hash, hash oil, hemp	I/smoked, swallowed	
Opioids			
Heroin	*Diacetylmorphine*: smack, horse, brown sugar, dope, H, junk, skag, skunk, white horse, China white; cheese (with OTC cold medicine and antihistamine)	I/injected, smoked, snorted	*Euphoria; drowsiness; impaired coordination; dizziness; confusion; nausea; sedation; feeling of heaviness in the body; slowed or arrested breathing/ constipation; endocarditis; hepatitis; HIV; addiction; fatal overdose*
Opium	*Laudanum, paregoric*: big O, black stuff, block, gum, hop	II, III, V/swallowed, smoked	
Stimulants			
Cocaine	*Cocaine hydrochloride*: blow, bump, C, candy, Charlie, coke, crack, flake, rock, snow, toot	II/snorted, smoked, injected	*Increased heart rate, blood pressure, body temperature, metabolism; feelings of exhilaration; increased energy, mental alertness; tremors; reduced appetite; irritability; anxiety; panic; paranoia; violent behavior; psychosis/weight loss; insomnia; cardiac or cardiovascular complications; stroke; seizures; addiction*
Amphetamine	*Biphetamine, Dexedrine*: bennies, black beauties, crosses, hearts, LA turnaround, speed, truck drivers, uppers	II/swallowed, snorted, smoked, injected	Also, for cocaine—nasal damage from snorting
Methamphetamine	*Desoxyn*: meth, ice, crank, chalk, crystal, fire, glass, go fast, speed	II/swallowed, snorted, smoked, injected	Also, for methamphetamine—severe dental problems
Club Drugs			
MDMA (methylenedioxymethamphetamine)	Ecstasy, Adam, clarity, Eve, lover's speed, peace, uppers	I/swallowed, snorted, injected	*MDMA—mild hallucinogenic effects; increased tactile sensitivity, empathic feelings; lowered inhibition; anxiety; chills; sweating; teeth clenching; muscle cramping/sleep disturbances; depression; impaired memory; hyperthermia; addiction*
Flunitrazepam***	*Rohypnol*: forget-me pill, Mexican Valium, R2, roach, Roche, roofies, roofinol, rope, rophies	IV/swallowed, snorted	*Flunitrazepam—sedation; muscle relaxation; confusion; memory loss; dizziness; impaired coordination/addiction*
GHB***	*Gamma-hydroxybutyrate*: G, Georgia home boy, grievous bodily harm, liquid ecstasy, soap, scoop, goop, liquid X	I/swallowed	*GHB—drowsiness; nausea; headache; disorientation; loss of coordination; memory loss/unconsciousness; seizures; coma*

(Continued)

SUBSTANCES: CATEGORY AND NAME	EXAMPLES OF COMMERCIAL AND STREET NAMES	DEA SCHEDULE*/ HOW ADMINISTERED**	ACUTE EFFECTS/HEALTH RISKS
Dissociative Drugs			
Ketamine	*Ketalar SV:* cat Valium, K, Special K, vitamin K	III/injected, snorted, smoked	*Feelings of being separate from one's body and environment; impaired motor function/anxiety; tremors; numbness; memory loss; nausea*
PCP and analogs	*Phencyclidine:* angel dust, boat, hog, love boat, peace pill	I, II/swallowed, smoked, injected	*Also, for ketamine—analgesia; impaired memory; delirium; respiratory depression and arrest; death*
Salvia divinorum	Salvia, Shepherdess's Herb, Maria Pastora, magic mint, Sally-D	Not scheduled/chewed, swallowed, smoked	*Also, for PCP and analogs—analgesia; psychosis; aggression; violence; slurred speech; loss of coordination; hallucinations*
Dextromethorphan (DXM)	Found in some cough and cold medications: Robotripping, Robo, Triple C	Not scheduled/swallowed	*Also, for DXM—euphoria; slurred speech; confusion; dizziness; distorted visual perceptions*
Hallucinogens			
LSD	*Lysergic acid diethylamide:* acid, blotter, cubes, microdot, yellow sunshine, blue heaven	I/swallowed, absorbed through mouth tissues	*Altered states of perception and feeling: hallucinations; nausea*
Mescaline	Buttons, cactus, mesc, peyote	I/swallowed, smoked	*Also, for LSD and mescaline—increased body temperature, heart rate, blood pressure; loss of appetite; sweating; sleeplessness; numbness; dizziness; weakness; tremors; impulsive behavior; rapid shifts in emotion*
Psilocybin	Magic mushrooms, purple passion, shrooms, little smoke	I/swallowed	*Also, for LSD—Flashbacks, Hallucinogen Persisting Perception Disorder*
			Also, for psilocybin—nervousness; paranoia; panic
Other Compounds			
Anabolic steroids	*Anadrol, Oxandrin, Durabolin, Depo-Testosterone, Equipoise:* roids, juice, gym candy, pumpers	III/injected, swallowed, applied to skin	*Steroids—no intoxication effects/hypertension; blood clotting and cholesterol changes; liver cysts; hostility and aggression; acne; in adolescents—premature stoppage of growth; in males—prostate cancer, reduced sperm production, shrunken testicles, breast enlargement; in females—menstrual irregularities, development of beard and other masculine characteristics*
Inhalants	Solvents *(paint thinners, gasoline, glues);* gases *(butane, propane, aerosol propellants, nitrous oxide);* nitrites *(isoamyl, isobutyl, cyclohexyl):* laughing gas, poppers, snappers, whippets	Not scheduled/inhaled through nose or mouth	*Inhalants (varies by chemical)—stimulation; loss of inhibition; headache; nausea or vomiting; slurred speech; loss of motor coordination; wheezing/cramps; muscle weakness; depression; memory impairment; damage to cardiovascular and nervous systems; unconsciousness; sudden death*
Prescription Medications			
CNS Depressants	For more information on prescription medications, please visit www.nida.nih.gov/DrugPages/PrescripDrugsChart.html		
Stimulants			
Opioid Pain Relievers			

*Schedule I and II drugs have a high potential for abuse. They require greater storage security and have a quota on manufacturing, among other restrictions. Schedule I drugs are available for research only and have no approved medical use; Schedule II drugs are available only by prescription (unrefillable) and require a form for ordering. Schedule III and IV drugs are available by prescription, may have five refills in 6 months, and may be ordered orally. Some Schedule V drugs are available over the counter.

** Some of the health risks are directly related to the route of drug administration. For example, injection drug use can increase the risk of infection through needle contamination with staphylococci, HIV, hepatitis, and other organisms.

*** Associated with sexual assaults.

Source: National Institute on Drug Abuse (2011a).

Prevention, young drivers (ages 16–20) are 17 times more likely to die in a crash when they have a BAC of 0.08% than when they have not been drinking. Also, 1 in 5 teen drivers involved in fatal crashes in 2010 had some alcohol in their system. Most of these drivers (81%) had BACs higher than the legal limit (Centers for Disease Control and Prevention, 2011a, 2012c).

Prescription Drugs

In 2010, about 16 million Americans reported using a prescription drug for nonmedical reasons in the past year (Wang, Fiellin, & Becker, 2014). Because older adults tend to be given more prescriptions, they represent a population with an increased incidence of prescription drug abuse and concomitant physical, mental, and social consequences. U.S. teenagers are increasingly using prescription drugs, and abusing prescription drugs, such as narcotic pain killers, tranquilizers, and sedatives, which can lead to addiction (National Institute on Drug Abuse, 2014). Exhibit 10.3 is a chart from the National Institute on Drug Abuse describing the effects of depressants, opioids and morphine derivatives, stimulants, and other substances that are meant for medical use but are frequently used in ways that are not intended or by people to whom they were not prescribed.

Illegal Drugs and Marijuana

Many psychoactive drugs have benign uses as medication or agents in brain research; however, they are frequently abused. The most commonly abused illegal drugs include cannabis (marijuana), organic solvents (e.g., toluene, which is used in dry cleaning and the aviation and chemical industries), amphetamines, and opioids such as morphine. "Designer drugs" are variants created by chemists specifically to avoid falling afoul of antidrug laws.

Many of these substances have been used for centuries; however, the recreational use of these drugs has been illegal since the federal law known as the Marijuana Tax Act was passed in 1937. Few may realize that newspaper mogul William Randolph Hearst used his newspaper to demonize marijuana and print stories that linked marijuana with violent crime (Deitch, 2003).

More recent stories report how these drugs can cause addiction and maladaptive behavior, as well as permanently impairing the brain and damaging other organs. For example, the effects of marijuana use include cognitive dysfunction, poor executive functions, and sedative effects. Heart problems and strokes have also been reported (Malick, 2014).

On a societal level, the global trade in these drugs has disrupted the lives of users and low-level functionaries working for dealers, often involving them in violence, the criminal justice system, and medical emergencies. The illegality of the drugs pushes the trade into the shadows and raises the stakes for people involved in the business. Weapons trading, money laundering, and cross-border disputes among drug cartels also threaten the security of numerous nations. And the problem is increasing. In the 2009 to 2012 reporting period, the U.S. Department of Homeland Security (2013) seized 39% more drugs, 71% more currency, and 189% more weapons along the southwest border than it had in the 2005 to 2008 period.

Anabolic Steroids

Anabolic steroids are similar to testosterone and have important medical uses. However, they are also abused by an unknown number of people, especially men, who want to "bulk up" for sports or look more imposing physically. Steroid users spend huge sums of money and a lot of time obtaining the drugs, which indicates a possible addiction. Another sign of addiction is a tendency for abusers to keep using steroids despite physical ailments such as feminization of the body (e.g., shrinking testicles and developing breasts) and negative repercussions in social relationships due to increased irritability and aggression. Withdrawal symptoms that steroid users may experience include depression, mood swings, fatigue, restlessness, loss of appetite, insomnia, reduced sex drive, and steroid cravings.

Tobacco and Nicotine

Tobacco is a relative latecomer to the list of addictive substances. The politics of the tobacco industry led to tobacco's classification as merely a "habit or habituation" in 1984 (Mars & Ling, 2008). However, the Philip Morris Tobacco Company publicly changed its position in 1997, and since then, nicotine, the psychoactive ingredient in tobacco, has been considered addictive. Multiple court cases also played a role in changing the classification of tobacco.

As an addictive substance, nicotine might be pleasurable during smoking, but the feeling does not last. Afterward, smokers feel anxious, moody, and depressed. In addition, nicotine can harm a person's heart, lungs, skin, and muscles,

EXHIBIT 10.3   Commonly Abused Prescription Drugs

SUBSTANCES: CATEGORY AND NAME	EXAMPLES OF *COMMERCIAL* AND STREET NAMES	DEA SCHEDULE*/ HOW ADMINISTERED	*INTOXICATION EFFECTS/* HEALTH RISKS
Depressants			
Barbiturates	*Amytal, Nembutal, Seconal, Phenobarbital:* barbs, reds, red birds, phennies, tooies, yellows, yellow jackets	II, III, IV/injected, swallowed	*Sedation/drowsiness, reduced anxiety, feelings of well-being, lowered inhibitions, slurred speech, poor concentration, confusion, dizziness, impaired coordination and memory/slowed pulse, lowered blood pressure, slowed breathing, tolerance, withdrawal, addiction; increased risk of respiratory distress and death when combined with alcohol for barbiturates—euphoria, unusual excitement, fever, irritability/life-threatening withdrawal in chronic users*
Benzodiazepines	*Ativan, Halcion, Librium, Valium, Xanax, Klonopin:* candy, downers, sleeping pills, tranks	IV/swallowed	
Sleep Medications	*Ambien (zolpidem), Sonata (zaleplon), Lunesta (eszopiclone)*	IV/swallowed	
Opioids and Morphine Derivatives**			
Codeine	*Empirin with Codeine, Fiorinal with Codeine, Robitussin A-C, Tylenol with Codeine:* Captain Cody, Cody, schoolboy (with glutethimide: doors & fours, loads, pancakes and syrup)	II, III, IV/injected, swallowed	*Pain relief, euphoria, drowsiness, sedation, weakness, dizziness, nausea, impaired coordination, confusion, dry mouth, itching, sweating, clammy skin, constipation/slowed or arrested breathing, lowered pulse and blood pressure, tolerance, addiction, unconsciousness, coma, death; risk of death increased when combined with alcohol or other CNS depressants*
Morphine	*Roxanol, Duramorph:* M, Miss Emma, monkey, white stuff	II, III/injected, swallowed, smoked	*For fentanyl—80–100 times more potent analgesic than morphine*
Methadone	*Methadose, Dolophine:* fizzies, amidone (with MDMA: chocolate chip cookies)	II/swallowed, injected	*For oxycodone—muscle relaxation/twice as potent analgesic as morphine; high abuse potential*
Fentanyl and analogs	*Actiq, Duragesic, Sublimaze:* Apache, China girl, dance fever, friend, goodfella, jackpot, murder 8, TNT, Tango and Cash	II/injected, smoked, snorted	*For codeine—less analgesia, sedation, and respiratory depression than morphine*
Other Opioid Pain Relievers: Oxycodone HCL Hydrocodone Bitartrate Hydromorphone Oxymorphone Meperidine Propoxyphene	*Tylox, Oxycontin, Percodan, Percocet:* Oxy, O.C., oxycotton, oxycet, hillbilly heroin, percs *Vicodin, Lortab, Lorcet:* vike, Watson-387 *Dilaudid:* juice, smack, D, footballs, dillies *Opana, Numorphan, Numorphone:* biscuits, blue heaven, blues, Mrs. O, octagons, stop signs, O Bomb *Demerol, meperidine hydrochloride:* demmies, pain killer *Darvon, Darvocet*	II, III, IV/chewed, swallowed, snorted, injected, suppositories	*For methadone—used to treat opioid addiction and pain; significant overdose risk when used improperly*
Stimulants			
Amphetamines	*Biphetamine, Dexedrine, Adderall:* bennies, black beauties, crosses, hearts, LA turnaround, speed, truck drivers, uppers	II/injected, swallowed, smoked, snorted	*Feelings of exhilaration, increased energy, mental alertness/increased heart rate, blood pressure, and metabolism, reduced appetite, weight loss, nervousness, insomnia, seizures, heart attack, stroke*
Methylphenidate	*Concerta, Ritalin:* JIF, MPH, R-ball, Skippy, the smart drug, vitamin R	II/injected, swallowed, snorted	*For amphetamines—rapid breathing, tremor, loss of coordination, irritability, anxiousness, restlessness/delirium, panic, paranoia, hallucinations, impulsive behavior, aggressiveness, tolerance, addiction* *For methylphenidate—increase or decrease in blood pressure, digestive problems, loss of appetite, weight loss*
Other Compounds			
Dextromethorphan (DXM)	*Found in some cough and cold medications:* Robotripping, Robo, Triple C	Not scheduled/ swallowed	*Euphoria, slurred speech/increased heart rate and blood pressure, dizziness, nausea, vomiting, confusion, paranoia, distorted visual perceptions, impaired motor function*

* Schedule I and II drugs have a high potential for abuse. They require greater storage security and have a quota on manufacturing, among other restrictions. Schedule I drugs are available for research only and have no approved medical use. Schedule II drugs are available only by prescription and require a new prescription for each refill. Schedule III and IV drugs are available by prescription, may have five refills in 6 months, and may be ordered orally. Most Schedule V drugs are available over the counter.

** Taking drugs by injection can increase the risk of infection through needle contamination with staphylococci, HIV, hepatitis, and other organisms. Injection is a more common practice for opioids, but risks apply to any medication taken by injection.

Source: National Institute on Drug Abuse (2011b).

and can lead to gum disease. **Nicotine addiction** is linked to serious health problems such as bronchitis, emphysema, heart disease, and various forms of cancer.

Nicotine addiction is difficult to overcome, in large part because of the social cues surrounding its use. Smokers come to value the ritual of lighting up and holding a cigarette. However, research shows that bupropion (aka Wellbutrin) is more effective than nicotine replacement gums or patches in reducing relapse in smokers, especially when co-occurring depression is present (Sinacola & Peters-Strickland, 2012, p. 99). The newer drug varenicline (Chantix) has been shown to be twice as effective as sustained-release bupropion because it blocks nicotine uptake in the brain.

Food and Caffeine

Recent research on the brain's mechanisms is revealing the psychoactive qualities of some common substances formerly considered benign. In fact, food is necessary for life; however, it can also be addictive in a way that shares a similar neurobiological and behavioral framework with substance addiction. Some people derive psychological pleasure from food.

The greatest potential harm from food addiction is obesity. However, researchers cannot agree on whether or to what degree food addiction contributes to obesity in the general population. A lone study on food addiction conducted by a research team in Newfoundland (Pedram et al., 2013) concluded that food addiction contributes to the severity of obesity. The finding is important, as obesity and overweight are the fifth leading cause of global death and the second most preventable cause of death in the United States.

Caffeine is not necessary to life, but it has long been incorporated into beverages that are consumed with pleasure—coffee, tea, carbonated sodas, and sports beverages. As with tobacco, there are social cues that popularize caffeine, and it is often consumed to improve performance. It is included here because it has some dangerous physiological and psychoactive effects. Data from college campuses reveal that students' caffeine consumption around exam time is excessive, causing anxiety and concomitant sleep deprivation (Hershner & Chervin, 2014).

According to the Mayo Clinic, there is no clear link between caffeine intake and depression. But caffeine can cause sleep problems that affect mood, and abruptly quitting caffeinated beverages can cause depression until your body adjusts (Hall-Flavin, 2011; Smith, 2002).

Gambling

As mentioned earlier, the DSM-5 reclassified pathological gambling with substance use disorders, under the heading of "Addiction and Related Disorders." Occasional, casual gambling may not be a problem, but compulsive gambling—the uncontrollable urge to keep gambling—can thoroughly disrupt a person's life (Mayo Clinic Staff, 2014). The gambling addict often keeps at it until all financial resources have been lost, which in turn destroys families and other relationships and increases the risk of the gambler's turning to crime as a way of either paying off debts or finding more money with which to gamble.

Compulsive gambling typically starts in the teen years and progresses over time. Causes are not fully understood, however a combination of biological, genetic, and environmental factors is implicated (Loecher & Harrar, 2001). Researchers have found that gambling addiction and substance use disorders are motivated by similar mechanisms in the brain (Thomas, Allen, Phillips, & Karantzas, 2011). In addition, as with substance use disorders, gambling can be controlled in part through social support.

Sex Addiction

Sex addicts are not just people who crave lots of sex. Underlying problems, including stress, anxiety, depression, and shame and guilt, drive their often risky sexual behavior.

Classifying certain types of sexual behavior as an addiction is controversial, and there are limited studies on the topic. Again, some of the brain mechanisms and psychological effects of so-called sex addiction mirror those of gambling and substance use disorders. The biggest impediment to accepting compulsive sex as an addictive disorder seems to be professional caution and misdiagnosis (P. Hall, 2011). Although the DSM-5 does not include sex addiction, some clinicians are alert to the problem that "hypersexual disorder" may pose to some people, especially because this behavior tends to put the individual at risk of contracting HIV/AIDS or other sexually transmitted infections.

Another aspect of sex addiction that has received attention recently is Internet sex addiction, from passive consumption to online pornography to the interactive exchange of sexual content in cybersex chat rooms. At this point, the data on the pathological use of Internet sex is inconclusive (Griffiths, 2012). Some therapists, however, have found that this sort of behavior can stress existing intimate relationships.

POLICIES RELATED TO SUBSTANCE USE

Legal drugs such as alcohol, tobacco, and prescription medications are loosely regulated and viewed as normal, and their users are not thought to have a disease. Colorado has even legalized the use of marijuana. By contrast, statutes and laws define illegal or "controlled" drugs and prohibit their use, possession, manufacture, and distribution. Legislative bodies have also passed laws associated with drug paraphernalia, money laundering, the sale of drugs to minors and on school property, and organized crime.

Over time, social policies related to substance use have influenced the development of practices and treatment programs. For example, in colonial America and the early 1800s, drinking alcohol was accepted, and opiates and cocaine were legal and widely used. In the 19th century, however, it became problematic to use alcohol and get drunk. Exhibit 10.4 illustrates a bit of policy history related to alcohol and drug problems in the United States.

Despite social work education's not focusing much on substance abuse, historically, social workers currently contribute greatly to the field of addictions. Because social workers are the largest group of U.S. mental health professionals, they must know how to assess, screen, intervene, use motivational interviewing, and make referrals to help people who have substance abuse problems. Social workers in addiction services must advocate for more innovative approaches and more inclusion of family members in treatment. At the policy level, social work advocacy is needed to ensure that state and federal policies are just and effective in addressing substance abuse issues. Social workers should realize that the field of addiction and substance abuse is constantly changing. Concepts and practice interventions that require understanding by substance use and addiction social workers include abstinence, recovery, stages of readiness for change, motivational interviewing, cognitive behavioral therapy, relapse prevention training, and harm reduction therapy, to name a few.

EXHIBIT 10.4   Historical Evolution of Policies Related to Substance Use

POLICY/ACT	EFFECT
1906 Pure Food and Drug Act *1914* Harrison Narcotic Act *1919* Volstead Act	Ushered in Prohibition in 1919; substance abuse viewed as bad and/or illegal. Prohibition repealed in 1933.
1937 Marijuana Tax Act	Criminalized substance users and limited access to medical treatment.
1970 Hughes Act	Established National Institute on Alcohol Abuse and Alcoholism and National Institute on Drug Abuse. Impetus to decriminalize public drunkenness; funded model treatment programs; allowed insurance coverage for alcohol and other drug treatment.
1971 Nixon declares "War on Drugs"	Special Office for Drug Abuse Prevention created; growing drug use among Vietnam veterans, armed forces, and general public.
1988 Reagan coordinates drug-related legislation, security, research, and health policy throughout U.S. government	Office of National Drug Control Policy created; director referred to as the "Drug Czar."
1997 Adoption and Safe Families Act	Child protection workers must identify the need for addiction treatment in parents and care providers.
2006 Substance Abuse and Mental Health Services Administration and Office of National Drug Control Policy have more responsibility in carrying out federal law and announce funding for Drug-Free Communities Support Program	Comprises a three-pronged approach: domestic and international law enforcement; focusing on "supply of drugs" to U.S. public; and addressing "demand" through (1) drug prevention and research and (2) drug treatment and research.

Source: Straussner and Isralowitz (2008); Department of Health and Human Services (HHS). SAMHSA and ONDCP: 2006 Drug Free Communities Support Program (2006).

CURRENT TRENDS

Colorado's Experiment With Legalized Marijuana

ON New Year's Day 2014, the state of Colorado began allowing licensed vendors to sell marijuana to anyone over the age of 21. Vendors expected marijuana sales to generate $30 million in revenues and taxes after 1 year. On that measure alone, the recreational marijuana industry seems to be improving Colorado's economy. In addition, the legal marijuana economy is expected to prompt new construction, new jobs, and new investments. Already, new categories of businesses have sprung up around legal marijuana (Yakowicz, 2014).

Although marijuana is legal in Colorado, it is still illegal according to federal law. This means that patients whose physicians recommend they use medical marijuana may be exempt from criminal prosecution in states that have passed medical marijuana laws; however, "federal laws make no such exception from the current drug prohibition policy" (FindLaw, 2014).

Not all Coloradans are happy with the new law. Although the law mandates that marijuana must be tracked until it is sold, some people are concerned about the effect legalization will have on children. In Denver, citizens and the city council expressed concern that they would soon see 12- and 13-year-olds selling marijuana on playgrounds or an increase in substance abuse problems.

1. What are the pros and cons of legalizing marijuana?

2. What is the advocacy role(s) of a social worker regarding passing laws on the use of marijuana?

TIME TO THINK

Do you believe substance abuse is a medical issue (physical illness), a moral issue, a law enforcement issue, or something else?

What policies do you think are needed to reduce substance use disorder and addiction in our country?

SOCIAL WORK PRACTICE IN SUBSTANCE USE AND ADDICTION

A substance use social worker might become involved in case management, crisis intervention, education, client advocacy, and group therapy. To carry out these tasks, social workers need to interview people, monitor progress, review records, conduct assessments, assess adherence with treatment plans, and consult other professionals. They must understand human behavior, personality, interests and hobbies, research methods, individual differences in ability, and learning and motivation. Also helpful is knowledge of relevant factors related to group dynamics, societal influences and trends, philosophical systems, religions, and ethnicity. It is also useful to know about relevant laws and court procedures. Substance use social workers very often need to read current literature, undertake research, and attend classes, seminars, and workshops. Quite possibly, drug testing will also be required. Above all, a substance use social worker must be emotionally mature, objective, sensitive to other people, independent, and responsible.

At least a bachelor's degree, preferably in social work, is required for work in substance use and addictions. BSW social workers often serve as behavioral assistants and generalist-prepared counselors in substance use and addiction treatment settings. Securing an entry-level position is sometimes possible with a degree in sociology or psychology. Many positions require an advanced degree such as a master's in social work.

Substance use social workers with MSW degrees often focus on counseling. Their clients tend to have issues that revolve around mental or physical illness, physical abuse, poverty, or unemployment. Social workers uncover hidden issues and intervene with solution-focused strategies. So along with all the other skills and knowledge required of social workers in this field, clinical social workers must understand the principles and methods of diagnosis and treatment of mental illness, and rehabilitation of those who have become addicted.

TIME TO THINK

Does clinical social work in a substance abuse treatment setting seem like a career that might interest you? Why or why not?

▲ Gambling addiction is a serious problem for many.

PREVENTION OF SUBSTANCE USE DISORDER

The best way to treat substance use disorders is prevention. Once a substance begins to affect the brain, the desire to use the substance increases and becomes difficult for the individual to control.

Many methods have been tried to prevent substance use. Schools and other community facilities may offer programs on understanding the ill effects of substance abuse and fighting peer pressure to use drugs, or require drug testing in certain circumstances. Some workplaces, especially those whose employees operate public transit and heavy machinery, also require periodic drug testing. Some require drug testing as a part of the hiring process. If companies do not drug-test employees, their business could be at risk for negligence lawsuits from employees and customers alike.

Many smaller businesses do not require drug testing, however. The National Drug-Free Workplace Alliance reports that small businesses employ the greatest number of substance abusers, because drug users tend to find work where there are fewer resources to perform drug tests (Konovsky & Cropanzano, 1991). The 2010 National Survey on Drug Use and Health found that 1 in 6 adults working full time in the restaurant industry had used illicit drugs (Substance Abuse and Mental Health Services Administration, 2011a). The phenomenon of substance abuse among restaurant industry employees has been attributed to a labor pool that averages in age from 16 to 25 years old, late hours, large availability of cash on hand, and low management surveillance (Kitterlin & Moreo, 2012).

TREATMENTS AND INTERVENTIONS FOR SUBSTANCE USE AND ADDICTION

Substance abuse and addiction services have been tailored to help diverse groups of people: people with co-occurring problems; people from different social classes and of different ethnicities and sexualities; people who belong to religious groups; athletes and intellectuals; people with physical and mental challenges; urban, suburban, and rural people; women and men; young people; unemployed people and people with jobs; old people; and so on.

Treatments and interventions have also been developed to deal with people having trouble with different sorts of addiction, from use of alcohol, opiates, and amphetamines to behavioral disorders. Moreover, their levels of addiction vary, although all tend to have gotten to the point where they are experiencing some type of problem with relationships or responsibilities.

No matter the specifics of the individual case, the substance abuse social worker should be concerned with assessing the following issues:

- Loss of control (inability to stop or limit drug use)
- Tolerance (the need to use more and more of the substance to avoid withdrawal or maintain a desired state)
- Impairment in functioning (e.g., failure to work or keep other life obligations)

Social workers may find employment in all the varied treatment settings outlined in Exhibit 10.5.

Detoxification and Recovery

The first step in overcoming either physiological or psychological addiction is **detoxification**. This short-term, medically supervised treatment program for alcohol or drug addiction is designed to purge the body of intoxicating or

EXHIBIT 10.5   Treatment Settings for People With Substance Use and Addiction Challenges

TREATMENT TYPE	SETTING	GOAL	TREATMENT APPROACH
Detoxification	Detoxification unit	To withdraw people safely from alcohol or drugs	Rapid detox may be dangerous and require medical supervision; detox phases in a drug rehab setting may take about 7 to 10 days or longer.
Inpatient rehabilitation	Hospital, residential rehabilitation facility, therapeutic community	To treat people via multiple methods, including family, individual, and group intervention	Treatment typically lasts 14 to 28 days in hospitals and rehab facilities but may last 1 to 2 years in therapeutic communities. Treatment may include individual, family, or group counseling, encounter groups, self-help meetings, and training in daily living skills.
Residential program	Community residence, halfway house, recovery home, self-run recovery home	To treat and counsel people and provide vocational training	Length of stay varies. Minimal programming is provided onsite; rather, residents are linked to outpatient treatment programs and self-help meetings.
Outpatient rehabilitation	Mental health clinic, methadone treatment center	To offer varied forms of "drug-free" programs and treatment, beginning with primary assessment and treatment for addiction and following up with aftercare	Intensive treatment lasts 4 to 8 weeks. Group treatment with individual counseling or group meetings often occurs 1 to 2 times a week for 3 to 24 months. Methadone maintenance programs for opiate addicts are sometimes offered but are controversial because they substitute a long-acting synthetic narcotic for the drug of abuse.
Screening and treatment	Host organization, such as business, court, prison, school, psychiatric facility, or welfare agency	To offer screening and treatment programs within or in conjunction with the host organization	Participants who exhibit signs of drug use are referred (or may self-refer) to employee or student assistance programs and prison drug treatment programs.

Source: Inspired by Smyth (1995).

addictive substances. Detoxing alone and at home is dangerous. If a person stops substances too suddenly, she or he can experience hallucinations, convulsions, or have a heart seizure that can turn deadly. Initial symptoms of detoxification include anxiety, nausea, insomnia, delirium tremens, shakiness, and seizures. People suffering multiple substance abuse issues need professional medical help to detox safely. Detoxification is only the beginning stage of addressing addiction.

Recovery follows detoxification and is the lifelong process of learning to live without the substance of abuse. The **Substance Abuse and Mental Health Services Administration (SAMHSA),** a federal entity that promotes prevention of and treatment for substance use disorders, announced a new working definition of recovery in 2011: "A process of change through which individuals improve their health and wellness, live a self-directed life, and strive to reach their full potential" (SAMHSA, 2011b).

SAMHSA has also delineated four major dimensions of life that support recovery:

- *Health:* Overcoming or managing one's disease(s), as well as living in a physically and emotionally healthy way
- *Home:* Maintaining a stable and safe place to live
- *Purpose:* Pursuing meaningful daily activities, such as a job, school, volunteerism, family caretaking, or creative endeavors, and the independence, income, and resources to participate in society
- *Community:* Forging relationships and social networks that provide support, friendship, love, and hope

SAMHSA has also developed some guiding principles for recovery, which are reproduced in Exhibit 10.6.

EXHIBIT 10.6   SAMHSA's Guiding Principles of Recovery

- *Recovery emerges from hope:* The belief that recovery is real provides the essential and motivating message of a better future—that people can and do overcome the internal and external challenges, barriers, and obstacles that confront them.

- *Recovery is person-driven:* Self-determination and self-direction are the foundations for recovery as individuals define their own life goals and design their unique path(s).

- *Recovery occurs via many pathways:* Individuals are unique, with distinct needs, strengths, preferences, goals, culture, and backgrounds, including trauma experiences that affect and determine their pathway(s) to recovery. Abstinence is the safest approach for those with substance use disorders.

- *Recovery is holistic:* Recovery encompasses an individual's whole life, including mind, body, spirit, and community. The array of services and supports available should be integrated and coordinated.

- *Recovery is supported by peers and allies:* Mutual support and mutual aid groups, including the sharing of experiential knowledge and skills, as well as social learning, play an invaluable role in recovery.

- *Recovery is supported through relationship and social networks:* An important factor in the recovery process is the presence and involvement of people who believe in the person's ability to recover; who offer hope, support, and encouragement; and who also suggest strategies and resources for change.

- *Recovery is culturally-based and influenced:* Culture and cultural background in all of its diverse representations, including values, traditions, and beliefs, are keys in determining a person's journey and unique pathway to recovery.

- *Recovery is supported by addressing trauma:* Services and supports should be trauma-informed to foster safety (physical and emotional) and trust, as well as promote choice, empowerment, and collaboration.

- *Recovery involves individual, family, and community strengths and responsibility:* Individuals, families, and communities have strengths and resources that serve as a foundation for recovery.

- *Recovery is based on respect:* Community, systems, and societal acceptance and appreciation for people affected by mental health and substance use problems—including protecting their rights and eliminating discrimination—are crucial in achieving recovery.

Source: Substance Abuse and Mental Health Services Administration (SAMHSA), 2011b.

Typically, a person in recovery is assisted by some kind of treatment center. The vast majority of treatment centers have a **zero tolerance** model that requires total abstinence from the substance that has led the client into treatment (Sinacola & Peters-Strickland, 2012). Beyond that, treatment centers may follow any of a number of models for promoting recovery (Sinacola & Peters-Strickland, 2012). Here are a few of the most common:

- **12-step approach**: Traditional treatment model based on a moral and spiritual understanding of addictive behavior.
- **Rational-recovery model**: Teaches addicts to recognize and dispute irrational thoughts that encourage substance abuse. Addictive thoughts are referred to as the BEAST—Boozing opportunity, Enemy voice recognition, Accuse the voice of malice, Self-control and self-worth reminders, Treasure your sobriety (Trimpey, 1994).

- **Harm reduction model**: A motivational approach to increase people's desire for better health and well-being. The model encompasses abstinence/harm elimination, recovery readiness, moderation management, substitution therapy, relapse prevention, and environmental prevention. The model is similar to moderation management and is often used with multiple substance use, because it views substance abuse behaviors on a continuum.

Motivational Interviewing

Clinical social workers who work with people in recovery have the full range of therapeutic techniques at their disposal. However, through research and practice experiences, it has become evident that a technique called motivational interviewing is especially effective in work with substance users/abusers.

Motivational interviewing grew out of the "stages of change" (or transtheoretical) model, which is based on

SOCIAL WORK IN ACTION

Judy Uses Motivational Interviewing to Assess Bob

DR. Judy Sames completed her social work dissertation on using groups in school settings. During her doctoral program, Judy noticed how particular mental health and substance use social work professionals tended to use motivational interviewing (MI) in groups and in counseling individuals. She bought books that described how and when to use MI, and recently attended a continuing education workshop on using MI with veterans. In her private practice, Judy is working with Army veteran Bob. Bob is 70 years old, recently retired, and challenged to take his medications as prescribed. Occasionally, flashbacks and nightmares trouble Bob; however, his main reason for seeing Judy is to learn how to adhere with his prescribed medication and stop imbibing whiskey nightcaps.

Judy has assessed Bob's readiness for change, and she believes the person-centered, directive method of MI will help Bob be adherent and alcohol free at bedtime. This week marks the third time Judy and Bob have met. Bob is aware of the five principles of MI that Judy anticipates incorporating into their therapy sessions: roll with resistance, express empathy, avoid argumentation, develop discrepancy, and support self-efficacy.

During their first session, Bob blamed his wife's nagging as the reason why he drank alcohol and forgot his medication. Judy did not argue with Bob; she simply involved him in a process of empathetic and respectful problem solving. In session two, with no coercion whatsoever, Judy asked Bob what was bad or not so good about his nonadherence and nightcaps. They explored his thoughts, and Judy acknowledged small positive steps that Bob appeared to be taking since they first met. This week Judy elicited more information from Bob about what strategies he thought would work, and she sensed that he understood what it would take to change his medication and drinking behaviors. Already, in 3 weeks' time, Judy sees progress. Last week, Bob asked his wife to assemble his weekly pill box and place it on his bedside table, along with a small glass of cranberry juice. MI seems to be working.

empirical research (Prochaska & DiClemente, 1982). These are the five stages of change through which the client moves with the assistance of the therapist:

1. Precontemplation (not yet acknowledging that there is a problem behavior requiring change)
2. Contemplation (acknowledging there is a problem but not yet ready or sure of wanting to make a change)
3. Preparation (determination: getting ready to change)
4. Action (willpower: changing behavior)
5. Maintenance (maintaining the behavior change) and/or relapse (returning to older behaviors and abandoning the new changes)

The concept of motivational interviewing evolved from experience using this five-stage model in the treatment of problem drinkers. Miller and Rollnick (2013) define **motivational interviewing** as a client-centered, focused, and goal-oriented counseling style for eliciting behavior change by helping clients explore and resolve their ambivalence about continuing to use the substance. On the one hand, they have come to enjoy using the substance, at least for a short time while the positive effects are strongest; on the other hand, they have come to recognize that habitual use of the substance is creating problems in their lives. The key to using motivational interviewing is to follow the client's lead and use the most natural skills possible to allow the client to open up. Those skills include warmth, empathy, and reflective listening.

Alcohol and Drug Treatment Programs

Groups are essential for the recovery of addicted individuals and their families, and that is part of the reason alcohol and drug treatment centers are successful. While at a treatment center, participants spend some time being counseled one on one and a lot of time attending group meetings. Group

CURRENT TRENDS

Celebrities in Rehab

EVERY month, it seems, we hear that a movie or TV star, a musician, an athlete, or a politician has gone into a rehabilitation facility because of problems with drugs or alcohol. Bicyclist Lance Armstrong disclosed in an August 2014 *Esquire* magazine interview how he is downsizing, dealing with lawsuits, and recovering from his doping scandal. After Armstrong confessed to Oprah Winfrey that he had used performance-enhancing drugs such as testosterone, human growth hormone, and erythropoietin, questions arose as to whether the blood doping was responsible for his 1996 testicular cancer diagnosis. At this point in Armstrong's life, his every move appears to be under scrutiny. His story illustrates the shame and pain that can occur when one begins abusing substances.

One celebrity who took his rehab experience a step further is rock star legend Eric Clapton, who established the Crossroads Center Antigua in 1998. It welcomes an international clientele to its drug and alcohol addiction treatment facility in Antigua and Barbuda in the Caribbean. It is a 32-bed residential facility with a 29-day treatment stay. Treatment is based on a 12-step, abstinence-based, modified Minnesota model. The Minnesota model is a 28-day inpatient/residential rehabilitation model based on 12-step AA (Alcoholics Anonymous) principles and a holistic approach that considers the whole person—body, mind, and spirit. After completing an inpatient program, people in recovery are referred to AA for continuing care (McKay & Hiller-Sturmhoefel, 2011).

The Crossroads Center Antigua facility was founded in 1997 as a for-profit venture and lifetime commitment built by Clapton. The 36-bed rehab center is not a nonprofit facility bankrolled by Clapton; the cost for 29-day residential detox is $27,500. Other fees are required for a 6-week extended stay and other adjunct therapies. In addition, the center on the island of Antigua boasts a family program to encourage the utmost in support. The center assiduously protects the privacy of its clientele, because addiction still carries with it a negative connotation in the eyes of the general public.

1. Why do you suppose treatment centers try to maintain their celebrity clients' privacy (beyond the obvious attempt to protect their celebrity status)?

2. How does reading about celebrities in rehab make you feel about those celebrities?

3. How does reading about celebrities in rehab make you feel about the rehab experience?

4. Locate literature about 12-step programs' principles. What do you think about the 12-step principles and utility of self-help groups ((Alcoholics Anonymous, 2001)?

therapy and addiction treatment are natural allies. Members of groups can reduce their own isolation, and support and help others who are recovering. Group participation helps people grow and be more healthy and creative as a result of the natural interpersonal process that occurs in groups. Research at Crossroads Centre Antigua, an international drug and alcohol treatment center, found that people who completed a 4-day program incorporating learning materials, workshops, group sessions, and individual counseling sessions, along with opportunities for interested family members to participate, experienced significantly improved recovery (Martin, Lewis, Josiah-Martin, & Sinnott, 2010). In other words, people who participate fully in group work at a treatment center tend to abstain from using their problematic substance longer than people who have participated in other kinds of treatment.

▲ Needle exchange programs are examples of harm reduction, hoping to prevent drug users from contracting diseases from sharing needles.

Source: ©Joe Mabel/CreativeCommons.

▲ Many individuals living in poverty also struggle with substance abuse.

Alcoholics and Narcotics Anonymous

One way of quitting addiction is attending Narcotics Anonymous (NA) or Alcoholics Anonymous (AA), which are both 12-step programs. No judging occurs in these programs. NA uses AA principles that focus on "working the 12 steps." Twelve-step programs involve admitting to having a serious problem, recognizing there is an outside (or higher) power that could help, consciously relying on that power, admitting and listing character defects, seeking deliverance from shortcomings, apologizing to people you have harmed, and helping others with the same problem.

Al-Anon Family Groups are related programs. The families of users share their experiences, strengths, and hopes in an effort to solve common problems. Like AA and NA, Al-Anon is not allied with any sect, denomination, political entity, organization, or institution. There are no membership dues, and the fellowship is self-supporting through members' voluntary contributions.

Needle-Exchange Programs

Needle exchange is a controversial intervention for reducing the transmission of HIV among those who inject drugs such as heroin. For one thing, needle exchange does nothing to treat the addiction itself. To some, it also seems to condone the use of injectable drugs. However, HIV prevention is relatively cheap. For the price of a condom or a sterile needle, lives and several thousand dollars in health systems costs from caring for an AIDS patient can be saved. However, politicians don't often do nice things for junkies (Bowen, 2012).

Methadone Treatment Programs

Methadone is a synthetic opioid mostly used to treat heroin and prescription opioid addiction. It can be used to detoxify opiate addicts or to maintain the addict on a stable dose so he or she can live a safer and more functional life. Its efficacy has always been hindered by negative stigma related to morality.

Since methadone's development in the 1960s, researchers have extensively scrutinized methadone maintenance treatment. Studies consistently find that it is more successful than other treatment models in the reduction of opiate/opioid misuse, transmission of HIV/AIDS and Hepatitis C, and criminal arrest and conviction rates. Nevertheless, methadone maintenance treatment is viewed negatively by the general public and vastly underused.

DIVERSITY AND SUBSTANCE USE AND TREATMENT

All kinds of people misuse or become addicted to drugs, alcohol, and other substances and behaviors; however, those who are more privileged members of society may find it easier to afford or hide their disorder. They are also likely to be treated more leniently by the criminal justice system. Here are some other ways diversity affects both substance use and addiction and its consequences.

- *Age.* When youth or adolescents experience substance abuse problems, family involvement is very important because parents have to finance and drive their children to care. The age at which adolescents begin using alcohol and drugs is a powerful predictor of later problems, especially if they begin using before age 15. Youth start with alcohol and cigarettes, then progress to marijuana and other drugs. Teens use mostly alcohol and tobacco (cigarettes). Those between ages 18 and 25 most likely use illicit drugs. Older adults misuse substances also, but they are underrepresented in treatment settings because health care providers tend to miss assessing substance abuse behaviors in this population. Treatment should be supportive and slower paced for older adults. Outpatient treatment programs work best for older adults when they are situated in settings they already frequent. Older adults often experience immense grief and loss surrounding their diagnosis of substance use disorder and can benefit from reminiscing or guided autobiography.

• *Class.* Despite what you may have heard, homeless substance abusers make up a small proportion of people with alcohol and drug problems. It is true, however, that those of lower socioeconomic status frequently face barriers to recovery that include unemployment, health disparities, and unsafe living conditions—all of which tend to create despair and make people in this socioeconomic stratum even more likely to relapse. Poor women might be able to afford only inexpensive crack, whereas affluent older adults with significant life savings have lots of disposable income to spend on expensive drugs and alcohol.

• *Race/ethnicity.* African Americans, Latinos, and Native Americans are frequently seen in drug treatment settings—and because of the higher rates of poverty among these groups, they are especially likely to be seen in public facilities. Although their treatment may be just as effective as that received in private settings, it also suffers because members of oppressed racial and ethnic groups may distrust agency professionals, especially if they are mostly white. Although substance abuse treatment should not center on race or ethnicity, it is important for the social worker to understand the role of culture, history, oppression, and ethnic pain. It is also important to realize that recent immigrants face a higher risk for drug and alcohol use and abuse than do other ethnic group members who have been settled in the United States. The stress of acculturation has been related to delinquency, drug abuse, and mental illness (Davis, 2008). Unfortunately, there is a tendency for minority groups to be punished more often for their substance use compared with the wider majority population.

• *Gender.* Female substance abusers typically have more frequent and serious health outcomes from addiction than males do and more psychiatric issues (such as depression), and except African American women, they are more likely to live with a partner or spouse who has a substance abuse problem (Blume, 1992; Mirick, 2014). On the positive side, women, along with older drivers, have fewer alcohol-related fatal crashes. Women make up 30% of the substance abuse recovery population in North America, but in the United States, 92% of women who need treatment for alcohol and drug problems do not enter a recovery program for multiple reasons (Young, 2010). A main reason for this lack of treatment seeking is that women need to have their situation considered in a broader context—family, extended family, support systems, economic and social environment, gender, and culture. Women have gender-specific treatment needs, yet few specific treatment models (Young, 2010).

• *Sexual orientation.* Historically, gay and bisexual men have used "club drugs" such as ecstasy, which lessens their inhibitions and increases their drug use. They are thus also at a higher risk of contracting HIV/AIDS than are other groups. Lesbian, gay, bisexual, transgender, and questioning (LGBTQ) clients may go unrecognized in addiction treatment centers, especially if they are assumed to be heterosexual. Recognizing LGBTQ clients is imperative to gain their trust and willingness to seek health care, mental health services, and addiction treatment. Historically, LGBTQ populations have lacked places to socialize, and women's particular issues have been unattended to. In the 21st century, however, gay bars exist out in the open and the media are more accepting of people who identify with the LGBTQ community.

ADVOCACY AND SUBSTANCE USE DISORDER

Social workers require an ecological perspective to work effectively in the substance use field. They will not only focus on a person's addiction or substance use problem but also help clients in relation to their family, the neighborhood, social support system(s), prevailing cultural attitudes and policies, and the cosmic or spiritual level. Social workers trained in substance use and addiction may find themselves advocating for clients directly in the process of case management, individual and group therapy, and family counseling. They will also engage in advocacy for jobs and housing, community development of resources, educating, policymaking, and sometimes a combination of these.

ECONOMIC AND SOCIAL JUSTICE

People who have great insurance coverage can afford nice, private, for-profit addiction treatment centers. Those without good coverage must resort to public or government-sponsored organizations. When clients do not have insurance, social workers advocate in such a way that the clients can better access services and thereby obtain improved treatment. Social work advocates also help clients understand insurance options and apply for insurance.

For clients who present with co-occurring disorders and misuse of multiple substances, the social work treatment field is shifting to a more holistic approach. Health care reform in the United States is encouraging integrated and integrative treatment by linking treatment for addiction and other behavioral health conditions into primary care practices and federally qualified health centers (Quanbeck et al., 2014). Consequently, social workers will be required to have the skills and knowledge to provide treatment for substance use disorders and additional co-occurring mental health disorders simultaneously.

SUPPORTIVE ENVIRONMENT

The physical place where people live, geographically, affects their initiation into drug use. To ameliorate the effects of environmental factors, social workers can serve on planning boards that make decisions about where drug rehabilitation centers will be located. They can also advocate for uninsured clients to gain access to integrated community health centers.

Additionally, one's place of residence influences potential access to substance abuse services. City dwellers may be close to teaching hospitals, clinics, and addiction treatment facilities. Residents in rural areas may have extremely limited access to such services.

HUMAN NEEDS AND RIGHTS

People need and deserve respect and acceptance, despite their substance use disorder. People with substance abuse problems need to know that drug abuse and addiction is a disease and not a character defect. Professional social workers play vital roles in helping family members understand what the detoxification and recovery processes are all about and what will likely happen to their relative who requires medical treatment by physicians and follow-up meetings with a school, the courts, or other personnel.

At the same time, people being treated for substance abuse and addiction have the right to know that over the long term, drug abuse and addiction will likely result in physical harm, behavioral problems, and association with other people who also abuse drugs. Along with human rights, personal risk requires consideration.

Nevertheless, social workers need to acknowledge that people have the right to go uninsured, abuse over-the-counter drugs, or refuse to take antidepressant medications, if they want to. However, when people's poor choices risk the endangerment of others, professionals must intervene. A professional social worker is responsible for reporting cases when he or she sees that children are at risk for maltreatment, due to a parent's addiction problem, or senses that adults might attempt or complete suicide.

TIME TO THINK

Imagine that someone in your family or a close friend has a substance use disorder or addiction. You are sensitive to this person's rights as a human being but also aware of the physiological, mental, and social consequences of his or her behavior. You have already tried hard to help. At what point would you decide not to try any longer?

POLITICAL ACCESS

Legalizing drugs in the United States is far from an innovative idea. Consider how long public debates have been addressing the legalization of performance enhancing drugs in sports. Lance Armstrong's case, for instance, forces us to consider a philosophical problem that torments those who love watching Tour de France bicyclists and MLB (Major League Baseball) and NFL (National Football League) players. Promoters, sponsors, leagues, and advertisers all dangle incentives for athletes who can reach record-breaking performances.

Debates also focus on how to handle border police responsible for catching drug dealers at the Mexican border. Politicians and scholars, including social workers, have for decades articulated arguments to legalize or decriminalize drugs; however, they have failed to address the issue of drug trafficking and the rise of international markets for illegal drugs (Jenner, 2011). The NASW (2013) Social Justice Brief titled "A Social Work Perspective on Drug Policy Reform: Public Health Approach" reminds social workers that they are integrally involved with the criminal justice service delivery continuum and should therefore serve as "stakeholders in the national movement to bring about reforms in how drug-related offenses are processed" (p. 1; see also Gorin, 2001). This brief also states that by virtue of social work's historical advocacy for people with limited resources and no political power, social workers must be involved in drug policy reform. In addition to advocacy, social work professionals are responsible for conducting objective research and studying the pros and cons of legalization, as well as noncoercive methods to prevent drug abuse.

YOUR CAREER IN TREATMENT FOR SUBSTANCE USE AND ADDICTION

Job growth for substance abuse social workers is expected to be much higher than the average for all careers through 2020. This increase is partly thanks to new laws that send drug users to treatment programs instead of jail (Peternelj-Taylor, 2008). Employment growth will also be driven by an increased overall need for health care. Returning veterans with mental disorders such as posttraumatic stress disorder (PTSD) are at risk of drinking more alcohol to cope with their stresses; Veterans Affairs may consequently increase job opportunities for mental health and substance use social workers.

Additionally, a surprising number of baby boomers are abusing not only alcohol but also illicit drugs such as cocaine, heroin, and marijuana (Reardon, 2012). Social workers have a role to play in counseling some baby boomers who have long "experimented" with drugs and are now experiencing the stresses of transitioning into older adulthood. Aging baby boomers may also need to be updated on recent research into the mechanisms and consequences of using these drugs.

Regardless of the population being served or the setting in which treatment takes place, social workers should become familiar with the programs of SAMHSA. SAMHSA disseminates national data on the characteristics of people admitted into treatment and their substance abuse problems. Substance use social workers also benefit clients greatly when they possess a working knowledge of psychopharmacology and keep up-to-date with the vocabulary that describes a plethora of mind-altering substances. Understanding this new terminology, as well as neuroscience and the dynamics of co-occurring substance use, abuse, addiction, and dependence, is essential to effective practice.

SUMMARY

Determination, patience, and courage are the only things needed to improve any situation.

–Peter Sinclair

Substance abuse disorder and addiction is a chronic disease of circuitry in the brain related to reward, motivation, and memory. Addiction affects neurotransmission and thus the ability of those who have the disorder to control their own substance use, especially when they are under the influence. Therefore, it is crucial that substance use social workers possess an understanding of the neurobiology of addiction.

Recovery from substance abuse is a lifelong journey. People in recovery require support lest relapse occur as a response to almost any kind of stressor. Social workers must be aware of how substance abuse affects and costs the person, the family, and the community in so many ways, including loss of work, impaired physical or mental health, increased crime and violence, reduced quality of life, and more.

Substance use social workers collaborate with multidisciplinary teams to offer people with substance abuse problems psychotherapy, access to treatment programs, and help with drug-related problems in relationships and life. Social work professionals have a unique role and skill set to offer the multidisciplinary team. They consider the person in their environment, advocate for timely access to rehab treatment and follow-up community services, and offer hope. Skills in motivational interviewing and an understanding of 12-step principles and change processes help social workers garner their clients' trust and encourage their growth.

TOP 10 KEY CONCEPTS

addiction
alcoholism
codependency
harm reduction model
motivational interviewing
recovery

substance abuse
Substance Abuse and Mental Health Services
    Administration (SAMHSA)
substance use
12-step approach

DISCUSSION QUESTIONS

1. In the vignette at the beginning of the chapter, Clayton is successful as a substance abuse and addiction counselor but has had less success in keeping his son from misusing substances. How would you explain this discrepancy?
2. Should marijuana be legalized or decriminalized on a federal level? Why or why not?
3. Why is prevention so important in the field of substance abuse treatment?
4. What role does social support play in helping people cope with addictive substances?
5. What is your opinion of needle exchange and methadone treatment programs? For you, do the moral issues they raise outweigh their effectiveness? Why or why not?
6. How can the health beliefs and voices of people using addiction services be better understood and advocated for, regardless of their cultural backgrounds?

EXERCISES

1. Locate research articles or resources that examine how social workers are working to understand a particular substance use disorder or addiction, such as alcoholism, drug use, or food addiction. What seem to be the most effective interventions to date?
2. Peruse the SAMHSA website and reflect on the array of information available there. What part of the website would be valuable to ordinary people? What part would be valuable to substance use disorder professionals? Does this entity seem to be a worthwhile expenditure of public funds? Why or why not?
3. Examine the community where you live or attend school, and assess what substance abuse and addiction programs exist. What are they called and where are they located?
4. Every now and then, the media run exposés on 12-step programs. Research the social work literature to discover how effective 12-step programs are.
5. Visit the website of singer Eric Clapton's Crossroads Center Antigua. What do you think about the addiction services offered there? Evaluate the programs and outcomes, as well as the way clients are selected.

ONLINE RESOURCES

- National Institute on Alcohol Abuse and Alcoholism (www.niaaa.nih.gov): Conducts research and promotes understanding about alcohol use and abuse
- National Institute on Drug Abuse (www.drugabuse .gov): Conducts research and promotes understanding about drug abuse
- SocialWorkLicensure.org (www.socialworklicensure .org/types-of-social-workers/mental-health-substance-abuse.html): Provides information about mental health and substance abuse social workers
- Substance Abuse and Mental Health Services Administration (www.samhsa.gov): Agency within the U.S. Department of Health and Human Services that aids programs and efforts to help people with substance abuse or mental illness problems and gives money to programs for research and demonstration projects

STUDENT STUDY SITE

Sharpen your skills with SAGE edge at **edge.sagepub.com/cox**

SAGE edge for Students provides a personalized approach to help you accomplish your coursework goals in an easy-to-use learning environment.

Chapter 11: CHALLENGES AND REWARDS OF AGING

Learning Objectives

After reading this chapter, you should be able to

1. Understand the variations in normal aging.
2. Appreciate the biopsychosocial-spiritual and family aspects of aging across the life span.
3. Describe gerontological social worker practice and policy roles.
4. Identify and understand available services and policies that relate to older adults.
5. List at least three ways the aging population is changing American society.

Emilee Adores Gerontological Social Work

Emilee warmly greeted the family members as they arrived to the caregiver support group at The Royal Suites, the assisted-living and long-term care nursing home where she works. Virtually all the attendees at these group meetings are experiencing stress because their spouses or parents are suffering from some type of dementia or neurocognitive disorder. To begin this week's session, Emilee wisely distributes handouts on elder abuse and resource lists for respite care while the caregivers take a little time for themselves. Emilee well realizes how quickly stress can escalate into mistreatment.

Since graduation as a BSW-trained social worker who also minored in gerontology, Emilee has had no problem finding work with older adults. In Sun City, Arizona, Emilee worked in sundry assisted-living facilities. Now in Vermont, she uses comparable skills. As the social work director, Emilee's main responsibility at The Royal Suites is to keep the facility full and meet the biopsychosocial-spiritual and safety needs of residents. Emilee's five major roles are as a decision-making and transition coordinator, resident advocate, mental health assessor and counselor, family social worker liaison, and care planner (Koenig, Lee, Fields, & Macmillan, 2011). She competently provides information and referral resources to family members who know little about all the care options for older adults with dementia and other neurocognitive impairments. In addition, she also coordinates support groups, supervises students, and collaborates in marketing efforts.

To provide the best possible information to family members, she stays updated on Medicare, Medicaid, and insurance changes by visiting the Centers for Medicare and Medicaid Services website, attending online webinars and statewide conferences, and reading news blasts from AARP and several aging-related online listservs to which she belongs.

Emilee fortifies the image and presence of her workplace by providing tours to the public and holding educational lectures for staff and community social workers that award them continuing education credits. Speakers from the nearby university's Center on Successful Aging spark lively discussions at breakfast meetings about the latest concepts in gerontology, such as culture change, assistive technology, guided autobiography, slow medicine, and palliative care.

Emilee feels blessed to have grown up with all four of her grandparents and her two great-grandmothers, who lived to be 99. Fortunately, Emilee enjoyed many positive images of active and successful aging as she observed her energetic and engaged grandmothers and her witty, intelligent, and fun-loving grandfathers.

Today's **cohort** of older adults has a variety of expectations about what the experience of aging will bring. In part, those expectations are generational (see Exhibit 11.1 for a breakdown of the generations in the United States). Generation X, who are in their mid-30s, 40s, and early 50s at this point, are typically just beginning to think about their lives in older adulthood. They feel considerable anxiety about their finances in retirement. The "boomers," the generation born between 1946 and 1964, are the ones now entering older adulthood. Their expectations are quite different from those of their predecessors, the "traditionalists." Traditionalists have often been surprised that they lived so long and so well, given their parents' problems with aging, relatively early demise, and financial struggles in old age. Boomers, on the other hand, expect to remain active and healthy well into their proverbial golden years, with good health care and social support. Consider the images of happy, engaged aging currently portrayed in the media.

There are some grimmer realities, however. A large number of very old single or widowed women who are childless live in nursing homes. Increasing numbers of older people are continuing to work out of necessity. Although older Americans tend to be among the wealthiest groups in our nation, some of them are among the poorest.

This chapter urges you to view aging realistically and positively. Content explores the realities of the biological aging process, defines aging and gerontology, explores psychosocial-spiritual issues surrounding older adulthood, and identifies policies and services important to older adults. Both specialized gerontological social workers and generalist social workers across multiple agencies, organizations, and fields of practice will be required in growing numbers to fulfill the care needs of older adults and their families and caregivers.

It is important to keep in mind that we are all aging and would like to maintain our independence as long as possible. To maximize older adults' independence, social workers must join other specially trained professionals to create innovative and responsive policies, programs, structures, and practice modalities.

> ## TIME TO THINK
>
> What does it mean to be "old" or an "older adult"? How come older people do not want to be labeled as "elderly" or "senior citizens"? Why do you suppose television shows mostly cast younger leading characters and magazine ads mostly feature young, sexy people on their covers?

AGING AND OLDER ADULTS

American society has not fully come to terms with the meaning of **aging,** the process of change that occurs in an organism during its life span. More precisely, we are concerned about **senescence,** which is the gradual decline of all organ systems, leading inevitably to death. Thus, aging at its core involves a confrontation with one's own mortality.

Because American culture fears aging and death, we often devalue older adults. Social forces such as age discrimination and **ageism,** even among professionals, make the process of biological aging sometimes seem more negative

EXHIBIT 11.1   American Generations and Their Expectations of Older Adulthood—Fiction or Reality?

GENERATION NAMES	BIRTH DATE	CHARACTERISTICS AND EXPECTATIONS OF OLDER ADULTHOOD
Mature/Silents Generation The Greatest Generation	Born into a world of crisis 1927–1945	Civic minded, loyal, vote, work till you die, avoid debt Compliant children, honored elder's sacrifice Growing sense of cultural decay
Baby boomers	"Graying of Disability" Born 1946–1964	Savvy, assertive, health conscious, engaged in care, workaholics, self-centered High expectations for wellness/independence
Generation X	Born 1965–1980	Entrepreneurial, flexible, creative, skeptical, cynical, slackers, question authority Expect multiple employers and careers
Generation Y/millennials	Also called "echo boomers" Born 1981–2000	Mostly children of baby boomers High rates of narcissism, materialism, inflated expectations, and lack of independence Lack basic literacy Tech savvy, tuned into diversity Detached from institutions and networked to friends
Generation Z/boomlets	Travel is cheap and communication is free Born after 2001	"Digital natives," innate multitaskers Globalized empathy, less parochial, teamwork oriented View boomers and their institutions as parasitic aliens
GI Generation	Young in the Great Depression Born 1901–1926	Community minded, assertive, energetic doers Strongly interested in personal morality and near-absolute standards of right and wrong

Source: Kruse (2005) and Novak (2014).

than it needs to be (Moody & Sasser, 2012). At the same time, optimists think that medical science will soon find a way to delay senescence. Marketers play on that hope, plying us with cosmetics, elixirs, and procedures that promise to postpone aging. And, indeed, senescence often does not stop individuals from enjoying life.

Social work with older people encompasses both the positive and the negative aspects of aging. It often involves making health, housing, and social security systems work for clients, and ensuring that systems respond appropriately to older people's needs. It may also mean helping older people and their families manage issues of chronic illness, financial and social stress, and death and dying.

Social workers who specialize in this field of practice may call themselves gerontologists. **Gerontology** is the comprehensive study of aging and the problems of older adults. Gerontologists are multidisciplinary, usually combining expertise in biology, psychology, and sociology. Gerontology

professionals work in health care, government, nonprofit agencies, the business community, and university settings.

MEANINGS OF "AGING" AND "OLD"

When people in the United States turn 50, they typically receive an invitation for membership in the AARP (formerly the American Association of Retired Persons). It is something of a rite of passage for adults, signifying they are entering the years when their perspective on life might begin to change and others might start to consider them old. AARP is one of the most powerful lobbying organizations in America, taking up such causes as the preservation of social security for future generations. Its magazine covers feature celebrities who just turned 50, providing visual proof that despite fame or fortune, all humans become chronologically older. But the stories of vibrant 50-plus individuals inside the magazine point out that aging is in part an attitude.

Source: ©iStockphoto.com/AlexRaths

▲ Aging is in part an attitude.

Source: iStockphoto.com/GeorgiosArt

▲ Otto Von Bismarck is often incorrectly attributed with establishing 65 as the age of retirement.

Another marker of entering old age was established by the Social Security Act of 1935, which set 65 as the official retirement age and the age of eligibility for Social Security retirement benefits. (Changes to the law are gradually increasing the age of full eligibility, however; some people will reach full eligibility at age 66 or 67.) Scholars have mistakenly credited German chancellor Otto Von Bismarck with spreading the idea that old age begins at 65, because in 1889 he introduced a pension schedule in Germany for those 65 and older (Hayflick, 1994). However, recent research reveals that it was well after Bismarck died, in 1916, when the retirement age in Germany was reduced to 65 years (von Herbay, 2014).

Being defined as "old" may be desirable or undesirable, depending on one's culture and values. Some people dread the approach of their 65th birthday (or their 50th or 70th or whichever birthday seems to them to mark the beginning of old age); others look forward to retirement, relief from many of the more burdensome family and work obligations, and all the "senior discounts" that will be available to them.

This range of responses is another hallmark of aging. Developmental scholars have found that there is more variation, in terms of health and human development, among older people than among any other age group. Two-year-olds predictably have similar developmental experiences; however, 65- or 75-year-old people widely vary in their employment situations, family responsibilities, and health experiences. Some retire, while others assume encore careers and embark on creative new journeys and adventures. Although many older people live alone or with only a spouse, others may become responsible for the care of their grandchildren or children who are permanently impaired physically or mentally, or struggling financially (preferably not permanently). Although about 80% of older adults will likely have at least one chronic condition at some point, many control their conditions with medication, and 20% age with older but still-healthy bodies and minds (Centers for Disease Control and Prevention, National Center for Chronic Disease Prevention and Health Promotion, 2011).

STAGES OF OLDER ADULTHOOD

Gerontologists use special terms to refer to age groups among older adults, in an attempt to categorize some of the variations they encounter. Exhibit 11.2 summarizes these categories. The **oldest-old** are usually frail and need the most assistance. But the **young-old** and **middle-old** tend to be able to live independently and function well, despite the possible need for health, mental health, and social services to maintain and maximize their independence and functioning.

Dan Buettner Publishes Lessons for Long Life

One way for gerontological social workers to advocate for lifestyle changes in clients is to refer them to Dan Buettner's research. Buettner is an explorer and educator who has authored *The Blue Zones: Lessons for Living Longer From the People Who've Lived the Longest* and *Thrive.* He also served as keynote speaker for the Gerontological Society of Aging annual meeting for professionals in 2014.

For *The Blue Zones,* Buettner received funding from the National Geographic Society to investigate where in the world people lived the longest and why. On the sleepy Greek island of Ikaria, one in three Ikarians reach age 90. This group showed virtually no Alzheimer's disease or other dementia. As he interviewed 90– and 100-year-old people, he found 13 likely contributors to Ikarian longevity. So here is one possible "fountain of youth formula":

- Graze on greens.
- Sip herbal teas.
- Throw out your watch.
- Nap daily.
- Walk wherever you're going.
- Phone a friend (maintain strong social connections).
- Drink goat's milk (rich in the blood-pressure–lowering hormone tryptophan).
- Maintain a Mediterranean diet.
- Enjoy some Greek honey.
- Open the olive oil.
- Grow your own garden (or find farmer's markets).
- Get religion.
- Bake bread (the island's sourdough bread is high in complex carbohydrates and may improve glucose metabolism and stave off diabetes).

1. What additional lessons do you know of that might contribute to a longer and healthier life?

2. How can social workers use this information to educate and help others?

Additional labels that have entered our vernacular, related to aging, are *centenarian* and *supercentenarian.* **Centenarians** are people who arrive at age 100. One in twenty-six baby boomers are expected to live to age 100, and legions more will likely reach their mid- to late 90s. **Supercentenarian** is a more recent descriptor for a person age 110 or over.

LONGEVITY

Gerontologists also distinguish between the terms *life expectancy, life span,* and *longevity:*

- **Life expectancy** is how long on average a person is expected to live at a given age.

EXHIBIT 11.2 Subcategories of Older Adults Recognized by Gerontologists

LABEL	AGE RANGE	FUNCTIONAL LEVEL
Young-old	65–74	May choose to work; enjoy good physical and mental health
Middle-old	75–84	Early mobility restrictions; self-identify as older adults; are no longer in the workforce
Oldest-old	85 or older	May require assistance with personal care (bathing, dressing, eating, using the bathroom, walking, etc.); often have serious health conditions

EXHIBIT 11.3   An Aging Populace

LIFE EXPECTANCY

YEAR	WHITE MEN			BLACK MEN		
	AT BIRTH	AT AGE 65	AT AGE 85	AT BIRTH	AT AGE 65	AT AGE 85
Additional Years	28	4	2	35	5	2
Percentage Change	60%	33%	50%	106%	50%	50%
1900	47	12	4	33	10	4
1910	49	–	4	34	–	5
1920	54	–	4	46	–	5
1930	60	–	4	47	–	4
1940	62	–	4	52	–	5
1950	67	13	4	59	13	5
1960	67	13	4	61	13	5
1970	68	13	5	60	13	6
1980	71	14	5	64	13	6
1990	73	15	5	65	13	5
2000	75	16	6	68	15	6

YEAR	WHITE WOMEN			BLACK WOMEN		
	AT BIRTH	AT AGE 65	AT AGE 85	AT BIRTH	AT AGE 65	AT AGE 85
Additional Years	31	7	3	41	7	2
Percentage Change	63%	58%	75%	121%	63%	40%
1900	49	12	4	34	11	5
1910	52	–	4	38	–	5
1920	66	–	4	45	–	5
1930	64	–	4	49	–	6
1940	67	–	4	55	–	6
1950	72	15	5	63	15	6
1960	74	16	5	66	15	5
1970	76	17	6	68	16	7
1980	78	18	6	73	17	7
1990	80	19	7	74	17	6
2000	80	19	7	75	18	7

Data Source: National Vital Statistics Reports, Vol. 50, No.6. *Life Expectancy at Birth, by Race and Sex, Selected Years 1929-98.;* National Vital Statistics Reports, Vol. 49, No.12. *Deaths, Preliminary Data for 2000.;* U.S. Census Bureau. P23-190 Current Population Reports: Special Studies. *65+ in the United States.*

- **Life span** is a person's lifetime, the number of years a person actually lives.
- **Longevity** refers to living an active life longer than the average person.

Most people wish to experience longevity—that is, to have a life span that is beyond their life expectancy. Insurance companies are expert tabulators of life expectancy, and they, among others, provide online calculators that can help estimate your likely life span.

Longevity is partly a matter of your genetic heritage (how long did your grandparents live?) and partly a choice you make by the way you live your life. The influence of your poor choices can actually be tabulated. According to the Population Health Institute, when calculating mortality rates, almost one third of the influencing factors are health behaviors, medical care, socioeconomics, and physical environment. So if you want to live a long, healthy life, you can choose to live in a low-stress, low-pollution environment; eat nuts, fruits, and vegetables; drink red wine; and work out—or you can choose to smoke, binge drink, eat unhealthy food, and engage in other risky behaviors.

TIME TO THINK

How long do you expect to live? What do you know about your family medical history or the geographic environment where you live? Do you have "good genes" and live in a place where people thrive and have a long life expectancy? Are your personal habits conducive to longevity?

AN AGING POPULACE

From the 19th to the 21st century, improvements in sanitation, diet, and medical care have led to a dramatic increase in life expectancy. At the same time, birth rates and death rates are declining. As a result, the population of older people as a percentage of the total population has been growing (see Exhibit 11.3).

The growing number of older people is very visible in the United States and worldwide. This "aging of the population" is concerning to political leaders, government planners, and average citizens. It is affecting all kinds of social institutions, including families, education, the workplace,

and health and mental health, as well as the leisure and hospitality industry.

For example, the rapidly growing population of adults aged 65 and older is outpacing the U.S. current health care system's capacity to care for them. Each day between now and 2030, an average of 10,000 people will turn 65. Without immediate action, the health care workforce will lack the capacity, both in size and ability, to meet the needs of this number of older Americans (Bragg & Hansen, 2011).

During the next three to four decades, there will also be a significant increase in certain vulnerable populations of older adults in the United States—particularly the oldest-old (people 85 and over), unmarried women, women who live alone with no children or siblings, and older racial minorities who live alone with no nearby kin. The number of older adults and the oldest-old who will require long-term care is projected to rise astronomically during the ensuing decades.

GERONTOLOGICAL SOCIAL WORK PRACTICE

Social work practice with older adults actually includes two specialties:

- *Gerontological social work* is based on biopsychosocial-spiritual knowledge of the aging process. Gerontological social workers enhance developmental, problem-solving, and coping abilities of older people and their family members; promote effective and humane operation of delivery systems that provide services and resources to older adults and their families; link older clients with systems that provide them with opportunities, resources, and services; and enhance the creation and improvement of social policies that better people's functioning across their life course (Berkman, Dobrof, Damron-Rodriguez, & Harry, 1997).

- *Geriatric social work* is grounded in interventions with older adults who have health concerns; **geriatrics** is thus focused on physiological changes in aging and on health care. Geriatric social work practice mostly centers on family caregiving, because about 80% of the care for older adults is rendered by informal support systems (Rizzo & Rowe, 2006). Geriatric social workers also provide community care via hospitals or facilities (e.g., long-term care, assisted living, **respite care**, dementia care), home environments, and communities.

EXHIBIT 11.4   Theories of Aging

THEORY OF AGING	MAIN TENETS
Activity theory	The more active people are, the more satisfied with life they will be; assumes we think of ourselves based on roles or activities in which we engage.
Cellular (DNA) theory	Human aging results from cellular aging whereby cells reach senescence, a terminal stage in which they stop dividing; when cells cease to divide, the body is limited in its ability to regenerate and respond to injury or stress.
Continuity theory	People who grow older are inclined to maintain as much as they can the same habits, personality, and style of life they developed in earlier years (Atchley, 2009; Costa & McCrae, 1980).
Disengagement theory	Old age is a natural time when both the older person and society engage in mutual separation, such as retirement from work.
Modernization theory	The status of older adults declines as societies become more modern.

Source: Moody and Sasser (2012, pp. 7–14).

EVOLUTION OF GERONTOLOGICAL PRACTICE

Gerontological (and geriatric) social work practice is a relatively new specialty. The social work profession formally recognized the need for specific gerontological or geriatric knowledge in the mid-20th century. In the late 1960s and early 1970s, the social work profession finally began to consider older adults a target population that required specialized knowledge and training (Damron-Rodriguez, 2006). Closer ties between social workers and medical professionals dealing with older people took a bit longer. In 1995, the Bureau of Health Professions held a National Forum for Geriatric Education that for the first time included social work. Soon thereafter, the John A. Hartford Foundation began to fund social work research projects to improve the medical care of older people (Berkman et al., 1997). The Hartford funding has positively influenced the fields of geriatrics and gerontology because social work research has yielded a great deal of new information about useful interventions, resources, and advocacy strategies (Greenfield, Morton, Birkenmaier, & Rowan, 2013; Hooyman, 2006; Robbins & Rieder, 2002).

Over time, biological, psychological, and social science theories about aging have also evolved. They focus on the social consequences of biological aging for older adults and for their families, communities, and society as a whole. Exhibit 11.4 lists some theories of aging that help social workers avoid assumptions about aging, and create better policies and practice interventions. Social work's focus on human values is reflected in these theories.

SOCIAL WORK ROLES IN GERONTOLOGY AND GERIATRICS

As Exhibit 11.5 shows, gerontological social workers assume multiple and complex roles involving all levels of practice: micro, mezzo, and macro. Social workers go to older adults' homes to do assessments and provide clinical counseling to individuals and families. They also work within institutions such as hospitals and rehabilitation or residential settings, and throughout communities. Their primary role is to provide education and training about aging and older adulthood, conduct support groups, make sense of medical diagnoses and prescriptions, deliver counseling and case-management services, and advocate for environmental and legislative changes. They might also design and facilitate intergenerational programs, such as an adopt-a-grandparent program.

These are some of the specific direct, client-focused services they provide:

- Help clients choose the best Medicare Part D plan
- Tell families about adult day-care services and refer them to agencies that provide those services
- Make referrals to **adult protective services** when they perceive that an older person is being abused or neglected
- Intervene in crisis situations and devise ways to navigate immediate solutions
- Counsel older individuals experiencing grief over terminal diagnoses and offer grief or bereavement

EXHIBIT 11.5   Settings and Roles for Gerontological Social Work

AGING SETTINGS	GERONTOLOGICAL SOCIAL WORKER ROLES
Nursing homes Assisted-living facilities Independent residential facilities for 55+	Administrator; admissions or intake coordinator; case manager; social service coordinator or director; activities department coordinator or director; counselor; building manager
Hospital	Case manager, inpatient or outpatient; geriatric psychiatric unit
Outpatient diagnostic or rehabilitation center	Counseling; crisis worker; educational specialist; research coordinator
Health-related nonprofit	Administrator or manager of program(s); education of public professionals and/or clients; advocacy-related work; research-related work; case management; counselor
Area agency on aging/senior center	Case manager; support group facilitator; activities director; abuse assessment
Mental health agency	Case manager; counselor; outreach advocate
Caregiving for-profit agency	Care manager; marketing coordinator; intake assessment

counseling to family, often by providing links to hospice or chaplain services

- Provide referrals to home health or respite care services and explain how to activate insurance coverage for them
- Provide (and help complete) applications for housing and transportation services and help coordinate them

Geriatric social workers, in contrast, have a more direct role with clients and their families overall. They help clients best when they participate as interprofessional and collaborative team members, with the client and family at the center (see Exhibit 11.6). Social workers often observe, oversee, and negotiate their older clients' relationships with family members, nurses, geriatricians (doctors), neuropsychologists, and pharmacists. Social workers reinterpret for clients the medical diagnoses and prescriptions they get from geriatricians and pharmacists. When dementia is suspected, social workers will link clients with a neuropsychologist or home health nurse for additional assessment and assistance with **activities of daily living (ADLs),** such as taking medicine, bathing, and preparing meals, as well as more instrumental activities such as managing money, shopping, and housekeeping.

EXHIBIT 11.6   Ecology of Geriatric Social Work

NATIONAL INSTITUTE ON AGING
AGEPAGE
ELDER ABUSE

Gerald, 73, had a stroke. Unable to care for himself, he moved in with his son's family. His son tried to help, but it was Frances, his daughter-in-law, who usually cooked special meals and helped him bathe and dress. Frances was already busy staying ahead of two teenage boys and teaching third grade. At first everyone was glad to have Gerald living with the family. But after a few months, Frances was yelling at him often and sometimes didn't help him get dressed until late afternoon. Gerald was upset, but he didn't know what to do.

Many Kinds of Mistreatment

Many older people are victims of elder abuse, sometimes called elder mistreatment. It can happen to anyone—no matter what their race, religion, or background. And, it can happen in many places including the older person's home, a family member's house, assisted living facility, or nursing home.

(Continued)

(Continued)

Caring for someone who is physically or mentally disabled can be demanding and exhausting. Some caregivers become frustrated, and some type of physical or emotional abuse may occur.

- *Physical abuse* happens when the caregiver causes bodily harm by hitting, pushing, or slapping.
- *Emotional abuse* can include a caregiver yelling, saying hurtful words, threatening, or repeatedly ignoring an older person. Keeping an older person from seeing close friends and relatives is another form of emotional abuse.
- *Sexual abuse* involves a caregiver forcing an older adult to watch or be part of sexual acts.
- *Neglect by caregiver* occurs when the caregiver is not responsive to the other person's needs.
- *Abandonment* is leaving an older person alone without planning for his or her care.

Money Matters and Abuse

After Victor's mother died, he started looking after his elderly grandparents. Victor insisted they add his name to their bank account so he could pay their bills. For the last 6 months, Victor has been taking money from their account for his own use. He feels guilty, but tells himself that the money will soon be his anyway.

Financial abuse happens when money or belongings are stolen. This can include forging checks, taking retirement and Social Security benefits, or using another person's credit cards and bank accounts. Financial abuse includes changing names on a will, bank accounts, life insurance policies, or the title to a house. Financial mistreatment is becoming widespread and is hard to detect.

Many older Americans are victims of financial abuse. It can be very upsetting. In addition to losing money, some older adults never regain their sense of trust and self-worth.

Healthcare fraud can be committed by doctors, hospital staff, and other healthcare workers. It includes overcharging, billing twice for the same service, falsifying Medicaid or Medicare claims, or charging for care that wasn't provided.

Who Is Being Abused?

Most victims of abuse are women, but some are men. Likely targets are older people who have no family or friends nearby, and those who suffer from physical handicaps or memory problems.

Abuse can happen to any older person, but often affects those who depend on others for help with activities of everyday life—including bathing, dressing, and taking medicine. The frailest people are often abused because they appear to be easy victims.

How Can You Tell If Someone Is Being Abused?

Two years ago, the doctor diagnosed Eduardo's mother with osteoporosis. When she needed more help, he moved her into a nearby nursing home. For the last few months she's been depressed and withdrawn. Eduardo doesn't like the way a nurse talks to his mother.

You may see signs of abuse or neglect when you visit an older person at home or in an eldercare facility. You may notice the person:

- Has trouble sleeping
- Seems depressed or confused
- Loses weight for no reason
- Displays signs of trauma like rocking back and forth
- Acts agitated or violent
- Becomes withdrawn
- Stops taking part in activities enjoyed in the past
- Has unexplained bruises, burns, or scars on the body
- Looks messy, with unwashed hair or dirty clothes
- Develops bed sores or other preventable conditions

What Causes Abuse?

Nancy reassured her siblings that she would take good care of their oldest sister, Agnes. And she has; but now Agnes has been diagnosed with Alzheimer's disease. At night she is so restless that Nancy can't get her to bed. Nancy feels tired, lonely, and angry that her brothers and sisters don't help. More and more she feels like shaking Agnes.

Caring for an older person can be a demanding and difficult job. It can be very stressful. The caregiver may need to be available 24-hours a day to fix meals, provide nursing care, take care of laundry and cleaning, drive to doctor's appointments, and pay bills. Caregivers may have additional worries. Many put their own financial future on hold when they give up paying jobs to care for an older friend or relative.

Are You Thinking About Caregiving?

If you are going to be a caregiver for someone in your family or for a friend, ask yourself these questions:

• Do I have a good relationship with this person?
• Is the person difficult?
• Am I being pressured into this job by other family members?
• Are other family members going to help me?
• Will I have time to rest and take care of my needs?
• Can I afford to care for this person?
• Are there community resources that can help me?
• What are the other options for caregiving?

Being a caregiver can be even harder when the older person has dementia or memory loss. It can be upsetting, even annoying, to be asked the same questions over and over again. You can lose sleep worrying about night wandering or being asked for help at any hour of the night or day.

Caregiving can also be rewarding, but it may be hard to keep a positive outlook when there's little hope of the older person's physical and mental condition improving. All of these may play a part in caregiver burnout, neglect, or abuse.

Who Can Help?

Elder mistreatment will not stop on its own. Someone else needs to step in and help. Many older people are too ashamed to report abuse. Or, they are afraid if they make a report it will get back to the caregiver, and the abuse will get worse. If you think someone you know is being abused—physically, emotionally, or financially—talk to him or her when the two of you are alone. You could say you think something is wrong and you're worried. Offer to take him or her to get help; for instance, a local adult protective service agency.

The Administration on Aging has a National Center on Elder Abuse where you can get listings of Government agencies and learn about State laws that deal with abuse and neglect. Go to *www.ncea.aoa.gov* for more information. Or, call the Eldercare Locator weekdays at 1-800-677-1116.

Many local, state, and national social service agencies can help with emotional, legal, and financial problems.

If you think the older person is in urgent danger, call 911 or your local police to get help right away. Most states require that doctors and lawyers report elder mistreatment. Family and friends can also report it. Do not wait. Help is available. If a crime has been committed, the police will be called.

What Is the Long-Term Effect of Abuse?

Most physical wounds heal in time. But, any type of mistreatment can leave the abused person feeling fearful and depressed. Sometimes, the victim thinks the abuse is his or her fault. Protective service agencies can suggest support groups and counseling that can help the abused person heal the emotional wounds.

For More Information

Here are some helpful resources:

Eldercare Locator
1-800-677-1116
www.eldercare.gov

Long-Term Care Ombudsman
Resource Center
Washington, DC 20036
1-202-332-2275
www.ltcombudsman.org

**National Adult Protective
Services Association**
920 South Spring Street
Suite 1200
Springfield, IL 62704
1-217-523-4431
www.apsnetwork.org

National Center for Elder Abuse
Center for Community Research and Services
University of Delaware
297 Graham Hall
Newark, DE 19716
1-302-831-3525
www.ncea.aoa.gov

(Continued)

(Continued)

National Domestic Violence Hotline
24-hour a day reporting 1-800-799-7233 (toll-free)
1-800-787-3224 (TTY/toll-free)
www.thehotline.org/get-help

National Family Caregiver Support Program
Administration on Aging
Washington, DC 20201
1-202-619-0724
www.aoa.gov/AoA_programs

National Library of Medicine MedlinePlus
www.medlineplus.gov

Office for Victims of Crime
U.S. Department of Justice
810 Seventh Street, NW, Eighth Floor
Washington, DC 20531
1-202-307-5983
http://ovc.ncjrs.org/findvictimservices

For information on nursing homes, nutrition, exercise, and other resources on health and aging, contact:

National Institute on Aging Information Center
P.O. Box 8057
Gaithersburg, MD 20898-8057
1-800-222-2225
1-800-222-4225 (TTY/toll-free)
www.nia.nih.gov www.nia.nih.gov/espanol

To sign up for regular email alerts about new publications and other information from the NIA, go to *www.nia.nih.gov/health*.

Visit *www.nihseniorhealth.gov*, a senior-friendly website from the National Institute on Aging and the National Library of Medicine. This website has health and wellness information for older adults. Special features make it simple to use. For example, you can click on a button to have the text read out loud or to make the type larger.

Source: National Institute on Aging (2011, May).

The provision of these services varies widely by client and client system. In their assessments, social workers must continuously evaluate such factors as access, desire, and capability, and the interrelations of complex phenomena in the lives of clients and their families:

- Marital status
- Living arrangements
- Education
- Labor force participation and economic dependency
- Numbers and capabilities of the client's children
- Client's home and its suitability
- Resources, including income and insurance

Important questions include, "How educated is my older adult client?" "Does my client have children who live nearby?" "Has my client been married?" "Does my client live in a clean and stable environment?" "Does my client have savings and retirement income?"

RESOURCES FOR SUCCESSFUL AGING

Active and successful aging are popular perspectives that resonate with gerontological and geriatric social workers who already lean toward interventions based on strengths and resilience (Greene, 2002; Greene & Galambos, 2002):

- **Active aging** is becoming older but continuing to grow and participate in family, community, and society.
- **Successful aging** is becoming older but avoiding disease and disability, and continuing active engagement in life.

Social workers in these fields thus try to promote older adults' self-direction and self-advocacy that colors their recommendations for community resources, programs, services, and policies for and related to older adults. Such services fall into the subcategories of living spaces and places; day programs and activities; and resource, discount, and benefit programs.

Living Options

Most older adults prefer to live at home as long as possible, perhaps until death. However, they may choose instead to reside in a homelike environment that ameliorates some of the problems of living at home:

- **Assisted living:** They are in their own unit but can gather with other residents for meals and recreation, and are monitored for health problems.
- **Continuing care retirement communities:** They can stay in one setting but move to more appropriate living units depending on the level of health care and attention they require.
- **Nursing homes** (intermediate or skilled level of care): They receive more intensive nursing care; some nursing homes specialize in caring for people with Alzheimer's disease.
- **Foster care homes**, **group homes,** and **Housing and Urban Development housing projects**: Older adults who have lifelong developmental or intellectual disabilities or are impoverished can live in an environment suited to their needs.

Social workers help family members and older adults understand the culture of the setting and sources of financial assistance to pay for the housing (especially for assisted-living and nursing homes).

Day Programs

For the majority of older adults who are able to stay in their homes, a multitude of daytime services and opportunities exist that can help relieve loneliness and depression, and maintain health:

- Clubs and volunteer programs
- Congregate meals
- Adult day-care centers
- Fitness centers with special classes for older adults (e.g., Zumba Gold, ActiveForever strength training, aqua aerobics)
- Senior centers, which offer games, crafts, speakers, and day trips
- Foster grandparent programs, which are intergenerational experiences that match elders with children for mutually beneficial relationships

Social workers assess, coordinate, develop, intervene, and provide information and referrals to all these community-type services.

One of the challenges of social work with older adults is honoring their strengths. One solution is to encourage older adults to participate in ordinary activities that take advantage of the knowledge and skills they have developed over a lifetime. Organizations such as SCORE, for instance, employ older people who have had a business career to advise small-business owners. Another solution is to encourage participation in art and creative work, which enhances social interaction and provides a sense of fulfillment. People of all ages receive a boost from seeing an enjoyable result from their work, and older adults once again have the time to pursue those kinds of activities. Creative work can also be a diversion from depression or difficulty (Payne, 2012, p. 128).

Benefit Programs

An assortment of community services exists for older adults. Social workers often help older people with disabilities and older adults who are very poor apply for services and entitlement programs to meet their living requirements, such as food stamps; home health services; meals-on-wheels; nutrition programs; old age, survivors, disability, and health insurance; ombudsman programs to investigate nursing home resident concerns; property tax relief; respite care and rehabilitation services; and special federal income tax deduction for those over age 65. Social workers may also be able to help older adults find and secure special discounts for things such as bus tickets, cultural events and movies, special shopping days, and telephone reassurance (lifeline) services.

Medicare and Medicaid and/or Supplemental Security Income are indispensable resources for older adults who require home health, in- or outpatient physical or occupational therapy, or nursing home services:

- **Medicare**, the U.S. national social insurance health care program for everyone older than 65, includes coverage for hospital stays (extended hospital care), home health services, hospice care, and voluntary medical insurance (e.g., doctor's fees, outpatient services). Medicare also covers people with end-stage renal disease. Medicare Part D, a relatively recent benefit, pays for part of prescription drug costs. Funding for Medicare comes from Social Security contributions, monthly premiums from participants, and general federal revenues (Barker, 2014, p. 264).

• Medicaid, a health care program created in 1965, pays for medical and hospital services for people who cannot afford them. Eligibility is based on income level and inability to pay for health care insurance. Funding comes from federal, state, and sometimes county governments. In most areas, Medicaid is administered via local public assistance offices.

• Supplemental Security Income (SSI) recipients may also receive other services in their local Social Security offices, such as help applying for Medicaid (Barker, 2014, pp. 263–264). SSI is designed to provide income to those who have little financial gain and are also blind, disabled, or aged. SSI provides cash to meet basic needs for food, clothing, and shelter.

Social workers often help clients understand how to apply for and use these programs properly and effectively. Clients in both rural and urban areas often require additional information about where to go and how to apply for SSI.

Culturally Competent Care of Older Adults

Gerontological social workers must consider the language, customs, history, and preferences of racial and ethnic groupings of older adults. Cultural values of respect for elders' wisdom and accomplishments, and obligations to care for extended family members require humble consideration, as do holidays, special celebrations, and level of Americanization.

The number of older adults who belong to ethnic and cultural minorities is growing faster than the average for the United States as a whole. People of color may have increased needs for social services because they are especially vulnerable to poverty and experience continued discrimination. Some of these older adults also experience abuse.

ISSUES OF AGING AND OLD AGE

Why are some older adults quite active and vital at age 90 while others are frail at age 60? What causes aging, and why is there so much variation in aging among human beings compared with other species? How come some older adults perform as well as younger people on cognitive tasks while others show significant deficits in cognitive functioning? Is "keeping active" the secret to avoiding memory loss? How come some social contexts and societies provide significant care for their elders while others leave it to the individual and

his or her resources? And why is there so much variation in public policy about aging? These are some of the issues that confront anyone working to help older adults cope with aging (Manfredi, 2009).

BIOLOGICAL AND PHYSIOLOGICAL ASPECTS OF AGING

All humans age, and after 30, there is a gradual decline in all organ systems (Hooyman & Kiyak, 2010). All perceptual and sensory systems, as well as coordination, speed, speed of response, and strength, also decline with aging. However, within individual people, biological change rates vary for different physiological systems, organs, tissues, and cells. Furthermore, practically every aspect of aging and development for adults is determined by the interplay among hereditary and age-related biological process and the environmental or cultural influences. A healthy lifestyle, good diet and exercise, good health care, and self-management of chronic stress are known to increase longevity and life span.

A great deal of anxiety surrounds the **four Ds** of aging—death, dementia, depression, and disability. Everyone will experience death, but the others are not inevitable. It is realistic to assume, however, that about 80% of older adults will likely have at least one chronic condition that may or may not interfere with their ADLs, such as arthritis or high blood pressure. Geriatric studies estimate that between 25% and 50% of older adults living in the community suffer from chronic pain that affects their daily functioning (Park & Hughes, 2012). Examples of pain-related disorders are osteoarthritis, osteoporosis, neuropathic conditions (nerve-related diseases), and degenerative spine conditions (Cavalieri, 2005; Park, Hirz, Manotas, & Hooyman, 2013). Other broad categories of physiological issues commonly found in the geriatric population include vision impairment, incontinence, depression, hearing loss, balance and mobility issues, and memory disorders. Today, many options exist to enhance fitness and maintain a person's ability to remain active and independent into old age. Exercises such as yoga, Pilates, and tai chi can be wonderful options to help older adults stay fit and strong.

Improvements in **assistive technology** also help. Some examples of the new technologies are voice-activated devices (e.g., wheelchairs), mobile applications, home telecare (a more sophisticated version of medical alert systems), and specially designed tools for performing tasks that have become difficult for older adults, such as picking up things from the floor.

SOCIAL WORK IN ACTION

Alysia and Rachel Educate Staff and Older Clients About Sitting Disease

TWO gerontological social workers at the Seashore Garden Living Center (SGLC), Alysia and Rachel, read a study published in the *Journal of Physical Activity and Health* that revealed how sitting too much may increase the risk of disability in people over age 60. Specifically, the research has linked too much sitting to increased risk of heart failure, Type 2 diabetes, and death from cancer, heart disease, or stroke. Sitting too much may also affect mood and creativity (Hellmich, 2012a, 2012b).

Health problems related to sitting disease are increasing universally, and the SGLC social workers have observed this phenomenon among the residents they serve. Alysia and Rachel have introduced this research at multidisciplinary team meetings. Through education and counseling, the staff members at SGLC intend to heighten their residents' awareness of the importance of remaining physically active.

1. How can the social workers collaborate with other SGLC staff to ensure that sitting disease is avoided in their facility?

2. What creative solutions, from community supports and connections, could be devised to encourage residents to remain active?

COGNITIVE AND PSYCHOLOGICAL ASPECTS OF AGING

Psychologically, aging people experience changing sensory and cognitive processes. For example, perception, motor skills, problem-solving ability, and drives and emotions often change as people age. Also, age-related slowing in processing speed greatly affects cognitive functions, such as the speed of encoding and retrieving information, selective attention, integrating information, and switching between multiple tasks. Cultural factors and personal factors such as age stereotypes and self-esteem exert huge effects on memory and the allocation of attention.

Fortunately, age-related differences in cognitive performance are minimal when older adults can draw on previous knowledge or experience. Memory performance can improve when older adults are taught ways to remember information, such as making word lists or shopping lists. Brain gyms, learning how to play an instrument, or doing word or Sudoku puzzles, as well as participation in therapeutic arts (e.g., music, sculpture, drawing) also facilitate brain health.

The **five-factor model (Big Five)**, a trait approach, has been extremely influential in describing personality across the adult's life span. The five traits are neuroticism, extraversion, openness to experience, agreeableness, and conscientiousness. This model is used because personality traits predict mortality; for example, people who score high on conscientiousness are at lower mortality risk across the entire life span. Conscientious people are more likely to manage their lifestyles for greater health and to maintain healthy relationships (Friedman & Martin, 2012). They end up in happier marriages, better friendships, and healthier work situations, which create healthy, lifelong pathways for them.

In addition, realistic pessimism may be better for one's health than unrealistic optimism (Friedman & Martin, 2012). Unrealistic optimism can lead to underestimation of risk—for example, health hazards. Negative emotions and unrealistic optimism are both associated with higher levels of stress and more intense reactions to stressors.

TIME TO THINK

Do you have habits and traits that will help maintain good cognitive and psychological functioning as you age? Do you stretch your mind from time to time? Are you conscientious? Are you a realistic pessimist?

Neurocognitive Disorders (Dementias)

There is a great deal of confusion, as well as anxiety, about dementia. Social workers help family members understand

CURRENT TRENDS

Assistive Technologies for Aging in Place

60 Minutes ran a segment in 2014 on the fascinating Lift Labs sensor spoon. It was created by an engineer who wanted to help improve the quality of life of older adults who experience hand tremors, such as from Parkinson's disease. The International Essential Tremor Foundation (n.d.) website features the spoon, which has sensors in the handle that detect a hand tremor and quickly respond to cancel the tremor and steady the spoon. The spoon helps a person focus less on how he or she is eating and more on the people he or she is eating with.

In addition, the site features technology such as the SpillNot mug for beverages; the Soap Safety Sack, which keeps soap from slipping out of people's hands and causing accidents; the MagnaReady clothing line, which features dress shirts with magnetically infused buttons that help people with limited motor skills dress independently; and multiple iPad apps to help with typing and so much more.

1. How helpful might assistive technology and novel devices be to maximize good nutrition and minimize the need for extra staff in a long-term care setting?

2. How might assistive technology and novel devices be used for older people who live at home or are alone?

Source: iStockphoto.com/arekmalang

▲ Active aging is becoming older but continuing to grow and participate in family, community, and society.

that dementia is not a specific disease. Essentially, **dementia** refers to a group of symptoms that affect social and thinking abilities so severely that everyday functioning is affected. Dementias are classified as mild, moderate, or severe neurocognitive disorders. Some causes of dementia are treatable and even reversible.

Families need to know that memory loss usually occurs in dementia, but this alone does not mean someone has dementia. According to the Mayo Clinic, dementia is diagnosed when the following two types of neurocognitive deficits both occur:

- Problems with at least two brain functions—for example, memory loss and impaired judgment or language
- Inability to perform some ADLs, such as paying bills or driving without getting lost

Alzheimer's disease is the most common cause of a progressively degenerative dementia, accounting for between 60% and 80% of all dementia cases (Burock & Naqvi, 2014). The second most common type of dementia, which is caused by stroke and not Alzheimer's disease, is **vascular dementia.**

In 2011, President Obama signed the National Alzheimer's Project Act into law, making Alzheimer's disease a medical

MoMA Alzheimer's Project

In 2009, the Department of Education in the New York Museum of Modern Art (MoMA) published *Meet Me: Making Art Accessible to People With Dementia,* a comprehensive resource for creating art programs for individuals with Alzheimer's disease and their caregivers. The museum decided to use the resource to create a project of its own, called Meet Me at MoMA, which is an outreach program encouraging this population to visit and helping them enjoy the museum's art.

It was such a success that the museum created the MoMA Alzheimer's Project, a nationwide expansion of Meet Me at MoMA and the museum's other art and dementia programs. It was funded by a major grant from the MetLife Foundation. For the project, museum staff, along with Alzheimer's specialists, have developed resources that can be used by museums, assisted-living facilities, and other community organizations serving people with dementia and their caregivers.

At the easy-to-use website (www.moma.org/meetme/index), you can read interviews with experts in the field of art, aging, and Alzheimer's disease; learn about the findings from an evidence-based research study conducted by New York University School of Medicine to evaluate the efficacy of the Meet Me at MoMA program; review guides for creating arts-related programs in various settings; and explore works from MoMA's collection through thematic art modules or by browsing the artwork section. In addition, this site includes special multimedia content pertaining to the museum's overall programming in art and dementia.

1. How can social workers draw more from the arts to help clients who experience various forms of dementia or neurocognitive disorders?

2. In what types of policy advocacy might social workers engage to reproduce projects such as this in other communities?

---

priority for the United States. This plan aims to encourage research that will improve prevention and treatment by enhancing quality and efficiency of Alzheimer's care, expanding supports for people with Alzheimer's disease and their families, and enhancing public awareness and engagement. Alzheimer's disease appears repeatedly in the news as a public health problem, because the disease is burdening a growing number of U.S. older adults and their families (Stix, 2012).

Depression, Mental Health, and Other Emotional Problems

Aging is not always accompanied by worsening mental health; however, it may occur. Depression and anxiety are especially problematic because they affect a person's ability to make good choices and participate in health-promoting behaviors. But when dealing with older adults, it is important to keep in mind that depression is not a normal part of aging.

Depression is widely underrecognized and undertreated. One reason for such underrecognition is that families rarely realize that people who are experiencing other major illnesses, such as cancer, diabetes, heart disease, Parkinson's disease, and stroke, are frequently depressed as well.

Clearly, depression and social relationships are intertwined. The experience of grief, interpersonal strife, or role transitions, which are common as people age, may indeed influence mood. The other side of the coin is that older adults who receive a diagnosis of depression then experience stigma because of reactions from other people and themselves.

Whether the older adult's problem is depression or something else, gerontological social workers work with family members as well as the older adult. Their client could be a middle-aged and overwhelmed caregiver of a 97-year-old widow or adult children feeling anxiety and guilt because they do not know how to help their 80-year-old dad who is a veteran diagnosed with diabetes and dementia.

▲ Alzheimer's disease is a growing public health problem in the United States.

Substance Abuse/Addictions

Unfortunately, when major depression hits, some older adults resort to abuse of alcohol or other substances. Detecting alcohol or drug problems in older adults is challenging. Because of ageism, family members and clinicians are reluctant to ask about it or do not think to assess for addiction. When a substance abuse problem is detected, doctors may fail to realize that even modest amounts of alcohol or drugs can be problematic. Older patients have a significantly reduced ability to metabolize these substances, as well as increased brain sensitivity to them. And the cognitive impairments common with advancing age make self-reporting—as well as self-monitoring—unreliable.

Even small amounts of drug and alcohol use can have serious consequences for older adults. For some who have never used substances or consumed alcohol, substance abuse may start when they begin to experience losses or unwanted transitions. Also, prescription medication use or misuse may be associated with falls in older populations, and substance-abusing older adults may be at higher risk for different cancers and organ damage (Schulte & Hser, 2014).

A particular problem is a growing epidemic of alcohol and drug abuse and mental illness among the 78 million retiring, aging boomers that have wealth, health, and education (Friedman, 2013). Boomers came of age in the 1960s and 1970s, when illicit drug experimentation with cocaine, opiates, and marijuana was pervasive. Therefore, younger social workers should consider the contextual realities in which baby boomers have grown older and maybe not always wiser.

Although alcohol is the most commonly abused drug among older adults, nonmedical use of prescription drugs is a rapidly growing problem. Some studies estimate that nearly 10% of older adults misuse prescription drugs, with serious abuse potential—most often antianxiety benzodiazepines such as Klonopin, sleeping pills such as Ambien, and opiate painkillers such as Oxycodone. When it comes to nonmedical use of prescription medication, women far outnumber men.

Sexual Activity

Many older adults still want and need to be intimate with others, and want to have an active and satisfying sex life. But physical or emotional problems may thwart their desires. Both men and women experience normal physical changes as they age that affect their ability to have and enjoy sex. For example, an older woman's vagina may become shorter, narrower, thinner, stiffer, and drier, all of which affect function and pleasure. As men age, impotence or erectile dysfunction becomes more common. With erectile dysfunction, a man loses his ability to get and keep an erection for sexual intercourse, or it may take longer for another erection to become possible.

Sexual problems may also be due to illnesses, disabilities, medicines, or surgeries. The main physical problems that affect sexual relations include arthritis, chronic pain, dementia, diabetes, heart disease, incontinence, stroke, depression, surgery (e.g., hysterectomy, mastectomy, prostatectomy), medications, and alcohol.

Older adults can also contract sexually transmitted disease (e.g., syphilis, gonorrhea, chlamydial infection, genital herpes, Hepatitis B, genital warts, and trichomoniasis). Almost anyone who is sexually active is also at risk of being infected with HIV, the virus that causes AIDS. The number of older adults with HIV/AIDS is growing (Stine, 2014).

Emotions also play a role in sexuality. How you feel affects what you can do. Many older couples find greater satisfaction in their sex life than they did when they were younger, because they have fewer distractions, more time and privacy, no concerns about pregnancy, and more intimacy with their lifelong partner. However, older women may be unhappy because their looks have changed and they feel less attractive. Older men may fear that erectile dysfunction will become even more common as they age, and stress can trigger it. Older couples face daily stresses like everybody else, in addition to having concerns about age, illness, retirement, and other lifestyle changes.

CURRENT TRENDS

Senior Sex–and the Disease That Comes With It

EZEKIEL Emanuel (2014b), an oncologist at the University of Pennsylvania and contributing opinion writer for *The New York Times,* wrote a titillating column headlined "Sex and the Single Senior." Emanuel's Sunday op-ed piece cited four factors contributing to an increase in sexually transmitted infections among older Americans:

- Retirement communities and assisted-living facilities have lots of similarly aged people living in close proximity to one another.
- Older people are living longer and healthier lives, and remaining sexually active much later into life (e.g., the National Survey of Sexual Health and Behavior has reported that among people over age 60, more than half of men and 40% of women are sexually active).
- Older adults grew up before the safe-sex era and don't tend to think they should use condoms.

- Older men who use Viagra and similar drugs are 6 times less likely to use condoms than are men in their 20s (according to a study published in the *Annals of Internal Medicine*).

Social workers must be aware of these trends and assess older adult clients for sexually transmitted diseases. Also, a public health campaign on safe sex aimed at older adults living independently is needed.

1. Should the AARP cajole its members to be sexually responsible? Should Social Security include some information on sexually transmitted diseases and proper condom use when it sends out checks?

2. What are some other ways to effectively prevent sexually transmitted diseases among older persons?

Relationship problems can affect a couple's ability to enjoy sex as well. Marriages differ substantially in their starting levels of marital quality, and multiple contextual factors can accelerate or delay the rates of change for certain marriages. For example, the presence and age of children in the home, work demands, and family support or interference affect the experience and quality of marriage over time. Intimacy—mutual sharing of personal feelings, honesty, and respect—becomes increasingly important as relationships develop and mature. Enjoying time with friends and relating to each other with acceptance and respect both enhance the intimacy between a couple (Blieszner, 2014; Qualls, 2014; Syme, 2014).

Social workers must adopt the attitude that sexuality in older adults should not be stigmatized or considered taboo. If partners are available, the potential for passion exists. Passion, caring, and intimacy are enduring socioemotional needs for adults of all ages. Sexuality is equally important to single, partnered, widowed, married, and LGBTQ (lesbian, gay, bisexual, transgender, and questioning) couples.

Loneliness

Some aspects of aging, such as blindness and loss of hearing, place people at special risk for becoming isolated and lonely. People also become lonely as mobility decreases and friends pass away.

According to leading experts, feeling extremely lonely can increase an older adult's chances of premature death by 14% (Harms, 2014). Compare this statistic with the finding that disadvantaged socioeconomic status increases by 19% the chances of dying early. Loneliness is a risk factor for such physiological responses as high blood pressure, insulin resistance, obesity, inflammation, and diminished immunity (Harms, 2014).

Two types of loneliness have been noted: emotional isolation (loose emotional attachment) and social isolation (loose social ties). Both kinds of loneliness affect well-being and physical health across time (Weiss, 1973). What is important for social workers to discern is that being alone differs from being lonely. There are many older adults who actually crave solitude, and for them aloneness can be a healing power. For others, however, loneliness can hurt. These variations in loneliness actually seem to have a genetic component (Boomsma, Cacioppo, Muthén, Asparouhov, & Clark, 2007). Thus, it is not solitude or physical isolation itself but, rather, the subjective sense of isolation that is profoundly disruptive (Harms, 2014). In other words, older people living alone are not necessarily lonely if they remain socially engaged and enjoy the company of those around them.

Suicide

Late-life suicide is concerning and requires more attention from health care providers, researchers, policymakers, and society at large (Joiner, 2005; Manetta & Cox, 2013). Of all age/gender/race groups, white men over the age of 85 are at the greatest risk of completing suicide. Comparatively, the rate of suicide for women tends to decline after age 60 (after peaking in middle adulthood, ages 45–49; American Association of Suicidology, 2012).

Although older adults attempt suicide less often than people of other age groups, they have a higher completion rate. Firearms are the most common means used for completing suicide among older adults, with men using firearms far more often than women (Callanan & Davis, 2012; Lester, Haines, & Williams, 2012).

A leading cause of suicide among older adults is untreated depression. Gerontological social workers need to ask relevant assessment questions to determine their clients' suicide risks. Common risk factors include the recent death of a loved one; physical illness, uncontrollable pain, or the fear of a prolonged illness; perceived poor health; major changes in social roles (e.g., retirement); and social isolation and loneliness.

SOCIAL ASPECTS OF AGING

The human need for connectedness is tangible, and social workers must be ready to assess the following key dimensions that sustain healthy relationships (Wilmoth, Adams-Price, Turner, Blaney, & Downey, 2014):

- Intimate connectedness (from someone who affirms you)
- Relational connectedness (from face-to-face contacts that are mutually rewarding)

- Collective connectedness (from feeling that you are part of a group or collective beyond individual existence)

All these forms of connectedness help older adults cope with the changing roles and definitions of self that society places on them. For example, the role expectations and status of grandparents differ from those of parents, and the roles of the retired are remarkably different from those of people who are employed.

Ageism

Negative stereotypes hurt older people and may shorten their life span. A longitudinal study of 600 people over age 50 found that those with more positive self-perceptions of aging lived 7.5 years longer than those with negative self-perceptions of aging (Levy, Slade, Kunkel, & Kasl, 2002). The study also found that older adults exposed to positive stereotypes have significantly better memory and balance, whereas negative self-perceptions contribute to worse memory and feelings of worthlessness. Negative perceptions of aging are difficult to combat, however. Age stereotypes are often internalized at a young age—long before they are even relevant to people. By age 4, children appear to be familiar with age stereotypes that are then reinforced over their lifetimes (Levy, 2003).

Most older adults are acutely aware of the negative stereotypes. Doris Roberts, the actress who played Raymond's mother on the hit television show *Everybody Loves Raymond*, testified in 2002 at a Senate hearing before the Special Committee on Aging about the effects of age stereotypes. This Emmy-award–winning actress in her 70s said that she and her peers are all too often portrayed as dependent, helpless, unproductive, and demanding rather than deserving. She further noted, "In reality, the majority of seniors are self-sufficient, middle-class consumers with more assets than most young people, and the time and talent to offer society" (Dittman, 2003, p. 50).

Social workers must dispel myths about aging, be aware of the extreme emphasis on youth and the discrimination of elders in the United States, and advocate for respect, equality, and visibility. The value that the media and society place on youth seems to explain why cosmetic products and surgeries have increased.

TIME TO THINK

Do you consider yourself to be ageist? What stereotypes about aging do you have? What have you learned in this chapter about older adults that might help dispel those stereotypes?

Think of an older adult you know. In what ways are the stereotypes invalid for this person?

Aging in Place

Aging in place is the ability to live in one's own home and community safely, independently, and comfortably, regardless of age, income, or ability level (Wiles, Leibing, Guberman, Reeve, & Allen, 2014). The idea is growing in popularity, although housing and health care programs and policies require alteration to support this level of independence, such as rethinking housing design, developing better assistive technology, and revising health care delivery practices.

Aging in place is also a movement that supports the notion that older people should be permitted to stay in their own homes rather than forced to go to an assisted-living facility or nursing home. The movement was created to help American communities prepare for the aging population. Multiple agencies and organizations, including the National Association of Area Agencies on Aging, support this movement. One concept the aging in place movement supports is **naturally occurring retirement communities**, which are buildings or neighborhoods that were not originally built to serve older adults but over time have attracted a large proportion of older residents who intend to age in place. Nine laboratory communities have also been established by the movement. Elders Village is a similar network. In addition, a wide variety of websites and organizations have sprung up across the United States to help people remain in their own homes for as long as possible.

The term *aging in place* is used widely in aging policy and research but is rather underexplored with older people themselves. Gerontological social workers realize how much older people desire choices about where and how they live as they age and are prepared to provide information about options. They know that aging in place supports independence, autonomy, and the maintenance of caring relationships and familiar roles for aging adults.

Caregiving

Caregiving is an act of love, a necessity, and priceless. American families provide 80% to 90% of all in-home long-term care services for their aging family members and other loved ones. These services often include help with ADLs, medical services coordination and supervision, administration of medications, and help with emotional, financial, legal, and spiritual concerns. One researcher defines caregiving as **care work** (Meyer, 2000) and notes the immense load carried by American women. If caregiving services were provided by America's national health care system, the estimated costs would be about $250 billion per year.

The **Sandwich Generation** is a buzz term coined to describe caregivers who find themselves squeezed in between caring for their children and their elder parents or other older adult family members. While the Sandwich Generation is not a new form of family caregiving, these caregivers are getting lots of research attention. Currently, the typical American Sandwich Generation caregiver is in her mid-40s, employed, married, and cares for her family and older parent(s) (Cravey & Mitra, 2011; Smith-Osborne & Felderhoff, 2014). Increasingly more men are finding themselves in a caregiving role, too.

An ever-growing portion of family and Sandwich Generation caregivers reside in rural communities where they find themselves with geographic barriers to resources and isolation from other caregivers, family members, or informal supports. Lack of service availability, lack of care networks, and isolation from other caregivers and family members add to rural caregiver stress, burnout, and depression.

Caregiving is not the same for all cultures, and social workers must understand this reality. Unique traditions, values, and rituals exist within cultures and populations, and the diversity among older adults and within subtypes of the population is often ignored. Increasing numbers of people of color are aging, and each population group may have its own set of family values, help-seeking behaviors, access to resources and services, and so on. Other special populations include people who live in rural areas and those who have developmental disabilities.

Long-Term Care

Wishing to avoid placing the burden of caregiving on others, or not having other family members to depend on in old age, some people secure long-term care insurance, a type of

CURRENT TRENDS

The Village Concept

ORIGINATING in Beacon Hill in Boston more than a decade ago, the village concept for aging in place has since spread rapidly throughout the United States. Each village is independent and diverse, and each works a little differently depending on the layout and makeup of the community or village it is serving. However, they all share the common goal of providing a way for older adults to age in place with dignity.

The basic structure works like this: Members of the village pay a monthly or annual fee into a fund that will help them obtain services when needed. Transportation and home maintenance are at the top of the list for most members. Providers, which include individuals and businesses, have been vetted and approved by the organization. These providers offer the same range of services found in assisted-living places in a cost-effective manner, but village members remain at home (Accius, 2010).

The financial benefits are great. For example, in New Hampshire the cost of assisted living is $3,000 or more per month. By contrast, the annual yearly membership fee to belong to one of the village networks in New Hampshire is between $300 and $600 (Doherty, 2013).

1. How might social workers be involved in the village movement in rural and urban areas?

2. What would be important considerations in implementing the village concept in your neighborhood?

---

policy that covers basic daily needs over an extended time and helps people cope with the cost of chronic illnesses, such as Alzheimer's disease or various disabilities.

The policies typically cover out-of-pocket expenses for assistance with everything from the basics—bathing and dressing—to skilled care from therapists and nurses for months or even years. Long-term care insurance typically covers home care, assisted living, and nursing homes. These are costly services. For example, 1 hour of care from a home-health aide can cost about $20, while the average private nursing home room for someone with dementia costs $87,000 a year or $7,500 a month (Geewax, 2012). Neither routine employer-based medical insurance nor Medicare will pay for extended periods of custodial care.

Most long-term care policies have a waiting period that works like a deductible. So if a home nursing aide is needed, you may have to wait 90 to 120 days before your benefits start to cover those costs. Only a fortunate few will have long-term care insurance; out of more than 313 million Americans, only about 8 million have any such protection (Zamora, Nodar, & Ogletree, 2013). The low participation rate largely reflects the high cost of long-term care insurance, which averages about $400 per month.

A fortunate few will have long-term care insurance, but even that option is looking sketchy as more companies exit the business. Insurance giants such as Prudential and MetLife have recently pulled back from offering long-term care policies. Companies such as John Hancock and Genworth Financial have turned to state regulators, seeking permission to hike premiums dramatically. Depending on the location, insurers have requested rate increases of 18% or 40%, or in a few cases even 90% (Geewax, 2012).

The 78 million baby boomers now entering retirement are likely to suffer from the lack of long-term care insurance. Many of them have been hurt deeply by the Great Recession, losing good jobs and being "too old" or too discouraged to find new ones, and losing nearly half the value of their retirement funds with little time to earn it back. Many in this generation do not have children to care for them in old age. Few have long-term care insurance; so they are expected to fall so far into poverty trying to provide themselves with paid care that they will qualify for Medicaid, the medical care program for the deeply impoverished.

Elder Abuse

Sometimes the stress and demands of caregiving are so overwhelming to family and other caregivers that **elder abuse**, or maltreatment of an older person, occurs. Physical or mental ailments may cause older adults to be more trying companions than usual for loved ones living with them.

Older adults may be victimized by noncaregivers as well. As older adults become more physically frail, they are less likely to stand up to bullying or fight back if attacked. They may not hear, see, or think as well as they used to, allowing space for unscrupulous people to take advantage of them. In addition, their retirement funds and benefit checks, unmortgaged homes, and belongings collected over a lifetime make them tempting targets.

Only recently have the nature and extent of victimization been recognized as a problem. Unfortunately, older adults across America are being abused and harmed in some major ways. More than half a million occurrences of abuse against older Americans are reported yearly, and millions more go unreported. Those who are most likely to be victimized are unemployed, traumatized by a prior event, getting by with a low household income (less than $35,000 per year), social services clients, in need of assistance with ADLs, or in poor health.

Elder abuse takes many forms:

- **Physical abuse:** Nonaccidental use of force against an older person that results in physical pain, injury, or impairment; includes hitting, shoving, and inappropriate use of drugs, restraints, and confinement. Serious violence in the form of murder, rape, robbery, aggravated assault, and kidnapping also occurs with older adults. Although most of those who physically maltreat older adults are family members, acquaintances account for 19% of physical maltreatment and strangers for 3%.

- **Emotional or psychological abuse:** Speaking to or treating older persons in ways that cause them emotional pain or distress. Verbal forms include intimidation through yelling or threat; humiliation and ridicule; and habitual blaming or scapegoating. Nonverbal abuse is ignoring the older person; isolating the person from friends or activities; or terrorizing or menacing the person. Emotional or psychological abuse is a challenge to detect, and what social workers observe may reflect a lifelong history of harsh-sounding communication. This may take the form of infantilizing or willfully isolating an older adult family member (McInnis-Dittrich, 2014).

- Sexual abuse: Intimate contact with an older person without the person's consent. Sexual abuse includes physical sex acts and also forcing the person to watch pornographic material or watch sex acts.

- **Neglect** (and abandonment): Caregivers' failure to fulfill a caretaking obligation. Neglect or abandonment constitutes more than half of all reported cases of elder abuse. It can be active (intentional) or passive (unintentional, based on factors such as ignorance or denial that an older person needs as much care as she or he does).

- **Financial abuse** (and exploitation): Unauthorized use of an older adult's funds or property, either by a caregiver or an outside scam artist. Financial exploitation is especially problematic. Noncaregivers may victimize older adults in the form of fraud through investments; charity contributions; car and home repairs; sweepstakes and prizes; home mortgages; health, funeral, or life insurance; health remedies; lottery scams; or telemarketing. Older adults are vulnerable because they often have medical needs, diminished capacity, and a pool of financial resources to exploit.

Exhibit 11.7 breaks down the perpetrators of physical and emotional abuse. The clear majority is family and friends, but acquaintances and strangers also account for a fair number of the perpetrators.

SPIRITUAL ASPECTS OF AGING

Much variability exists as to the definitions of spirituality and religion. **Spirituality** equates to a person's individually experienced connection to a higher being and a "felt" experience of connectedness and transcendence. **Religion** is organized spiritual practice that tends to focus on the link between a higher power and human existence, whereas spirituality is more about where and how one finds meaning in life.

Living in and for the moment, asserting oneself against loss and fate, and transcending the previous limits of self in society are spiritual dimensions and opportunities older adults face. "Meaning and spirituality are the drugs of age, the consolation prizes" (Thomas & Eisenhandler, 1999, p. 211). In other words, people generally seek meaning and a renewed spirit as they move deeper into old age.

Benefits of Spirituality and Religion in Old Age

Gerontologists now recognize that religion and spirituality are part of older people's physical and mental health (Carr & Sharp, 2014). They appear to be related to enhanced feelings of well-being, inner emotional peace, and satisfaction with life—which all help maintain health and overcome illness. In addition, the opportunity to help others in times of need has been noted as a part of the reason religious participation and spirituality have a positive influence on health.

EXHIBIT 11.7   Perpetrators of Elder Abuse

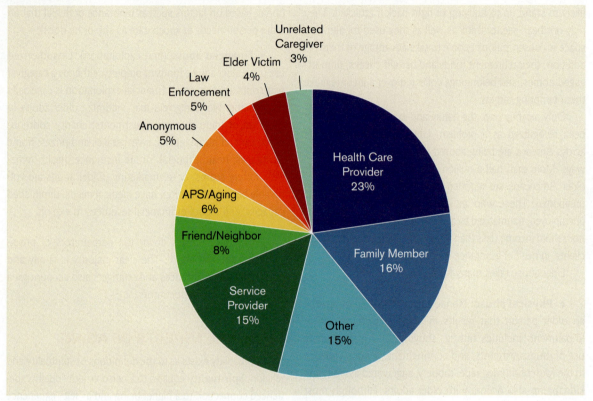

Source: UNC Center for Aging and Health (2005).

Affiliation with religious institutions also tends to promote connectedness and decrease isolation. Many centenarians identify regular participation in formal religious services as important. Older adults who regularly attend religious services show improved health status, reduced incidence of chronic disease, and more effective coping with stress (Hoeger & Hoeger, 1995).

Illness, Death, and Faith

Spirituality is the most frequently addressed topic of hospice visits with the terminally ill, with death anxiety a distant second (Reese & Brown, 1997). Hospice social workers often note that the greatest fear people express related to death is that they will lose control over the circumstances of their dying and be forced to endure pain, suffering, and indignities they did not choose. Many people fear this more than they fear death itself (Atchley, 2009, p. 140).

Americans' discomfort with aging and dying is often unveiled in debates about governmental policies. For example, New Jersey's assisted suicide bill underwent a contentious and controversial debate. Those in opposition to the bill were concerned about the spiritual dimensions but focused their talking points on the practicalities: It allowed poisonous drugs to be used without requiring an independent, disinterested witness to be present. Those who favored the bill believed it would allow people to die with dignity.

POLICIES AFFECTING OLDER ADULTS

Before government began to address older adults' needs, family members were responsible for their aging family members. Amid agrarian life, older adults helped their families by doing farm chores. People without family depended on faith-based organizations or the almshouse. Older adults living in the 21st century receive support from family in exchange for serving as babysitters to grandchildren and as housesitters. However, government-provided resources are still greatly needed for the aged poor to survive and thrive.

- *Pensions.* The U.S. government offers pension plans to older adults who exhibit a good work history. The best known of these is Social Security. The Social Security Act of 1935 served to enact a nearly universal pension plan for older Americans who paid into the Social Security system. Widows and their children were included in a 1939 expansion of this legislation. Subsequently, other categories were included, such as domestic and farmworkers, government workers, military veterans, religious personnel, and self-employed people (Huttman, 1985).

- *Health insurance and Medicare.* Older people had to pay for their own health care until the Medicare legislation was enacted as part of the Social Security Act of 1965. For a very low monthly fee, Medicare Part A covers hospitalization and some follow-up care. Medicare Part B pays for outpatient hospital care and some doctor's services (older adults must pay an additional premium to get Part B coverage). Medicare C only partly covers around 100 days for nursing home care and blood draws. The relatively new Medicare Part D provides for prescription drug coverage.

- *Area Agencies on Aging.* In 1965 the very important federal-level **Older Americans Act** was enacted. Its mission was to keep older adults living independently for as long as possible by providing information on services that are available to them. To do so, it authorized state units and local **Area Agencies on Aging.** Amendments to the Older Americans Act, approved in 1981, allowed for information and referral services for non-English-speaking older adults; provided legal services and transportation; and offered in-home assistance in the form of health aides, homemakers, and visiting and telephone reassurance activities.

TIME TO THINK

What if the Social Security program stopped and you had to invest individually for your own retirement? Do you think you would do so with adequate investments to make sure you had a secure retirement income?

DIVERSITY AND AGING

The experience of aging in America differs for people across different cohorts, social classes, races and ethnicities, abilities, religious and spiritual beliefs, and genders. Educational and economic factors also affect attitudes about health, health literacy, and exposure to health information.

Gerontological social workers realize that health and mental concerns increase with age as older adults cope with the loss of their spouses or partners and their friends, and manage verbal or physical abuse. No matter the social worker's or client's age or race/ethnicity, respect and trust are crucial wherever older clients are aging and wherever the social worker is working (Joo, Wittink, & Dahlberg, 2011).

AGE

Age is a multidimensional concept that comprises multiple meanings:

- **Chronological age** (the number of years that have elapsed since birth)
- **Biological age** (an estimate of one's potential life span—measures a person's vitality or neurobiological health level)
- **Psychological age** (one's adaptive capacities related to learning, memory, intelligence, emotional control, motivational strengths, coping styles)
- **Social age** (social roles and expectations people hold for themselves and others, such as "mother" and the behavior that accompanies that role)

Ageism and negative stereotypes are serious problems that affect older adults globally. People may have overly positive views of aging (idealizing old age), or they may have overly negative views of aging and older adults (viewing elders as useless and inadequate). Labels of age cohorts also stereotype people. For example, an older adult male may be from the "Greatest Generation" or a "baby boomer." One label makes the man seem noble and competent, while the other makes him seem whiny and arrogant.

TIME TO THINK

What stereotypes do you have about people from different generations? Which are most positive and which more negative?

Do you feel that the label for your generation is positive or negative? How accurately does it reflect your self-identity?

CLASS

During their lives, older adults are usually assigned to social classes on the basis of their occupations, which vary in pay structure, prestige, and the power to influence others. Once they retire, they are stereotyped on the basis of their economic resources and living conditions. Thus, a person who may have been considered solidly middle class during youth and middle adulthood may come to be seen as lower class if for some reason he or she is reduced to living in smaller, less-prestigious quarters in old age.

The U.S. Census Bureau reveals the percentage of elders who have incomes just above the poverty line. About 40% of Americans aged 60 to 90 have experienced at least 1 year of living near or below the poverty line. The percentage sharply increases for unmarried blacks with less than a high school education (Hoyer & Roodin, 2009, p. 44).

The inequities of class also extend to those who care for older adults. Lower-class and relatively uneducated certified nursing assistants provide hard labor and the lion's share of physical and direct care in nursing home settings; yet these workers get much less pay than does the social worker or nurse caring for the same residents.

ETHNICITY AND RACE

Older adults come from all ethnic and racial backgrounds. However, by 2050, the percentage of people of color over age 65 in the United States is projected to increase; their rate of growth is faster than that of the white population.

Ethnicity and race are a factor in longevity as well. The average life span of an African American man is less than that of a white man, and African American women are the most likely racial group to become widowed. Asian and Latino older adults appear to have longer life expectancies than do whites; however, predictions indicate that this rate

may change as the poor-nutrition and low-exercise American lifestyle takes hold among immigrants of these ethnicities.

There is a paucity of information about race and ethnicity in the area of caregiving. However, there is a discernible lack of diversity within caregiving programs, perhaps because many people from ethnic and racial minorities are reluctant to seek services, existing programs and supports erect cultural and language barriers, and services are not always designed to meet varied cultural needs.

It is worth noting the cultural beliefs of Native Americans regarding old age, which could be a model for the rest of the population. Tribal elders are respected for their knowledge and experience, and they bear the responsibility of passing down wisdom to the young. All members of a tribe care for the older adults. Death is an accepted fact of life, a "changing of worlds" that is not to be approached with fear, for the soul is thought to be immortal.

GENDER

Women represent the fastest-growing segment of the older population, especially among the oldest-old. Yet older adult women are at risk for higher levels of poverty and lower Social Security benefits compared with men. Several factors contribute to this disparity:

- Lower lifetime earnings due to job discrimination and interrupted work history due to child rearing and caregiving for a spouse or other family member (fewer work credits accumulated)
- Changes in marital status (divorced, widowed) that tend to leave women in worse shape financially because their husbands had a higher income than they did
- Preexisting economic status (career choice, educational level obtained)
- Length of time spent as a widow (women have a higher life expectancy than men)

Because of economic realities, many female heads of household are now supporting three or four generations within their homes. And the majority of grandparents who are raising grandchildren and serving as caregivers are women. One reason grandparents may be raising their grandchildren is that their own children are struggling with addiction.

Gender influences the experience of old age in another way. Women are more likely to experience the death of a spouse than men are. Widows and widowers experience loneliness and depression that may lead to unhealthy behaviors. In addition, women are lonelier living with their children without a spouse, while men are lonelier living alone (Cornwell & Waite, 2009).

SEXUAL ORIENTATION

Older LGBTQ individuals are a hidden population that is expected to increase. LGBTQ individuals have the same concerns as all older adults do, with regard to long-term care, housing, employment or encore careers, health care, and transportation. LGBTQ older adults also serve as caregivers for parents, siblings, spouses, or partners. But they are also doubly stigmatized, having experienced living in at least two different cultural networks simultaneously and having had to cope with multiple barriers.

Some older LGBTQ individuals hesitate to disclose their sexual orientation at this late stage because they fear that family members or friends will reject them when they most need support. Also, because the social stigma of homosexuality and bisexuality is still abundant (even virulent) in many settings, they fear making their sexual orientation known when seeking senior services and housing. In addition, assisted-living and long-term care facility policies are established for heterosexual or single residents, so older LGBTQ people may have limited options if they are seeking a gay-friendly long-term care environment. Exhibit 11.8 provides a model for social work practitioners to better serve the aging LGBTQ population.

ABILITY

The numbers of older adults across all levels of physical and mental challenges are growing rapidly, and the number of people who are severely or moderately disabled is expected to more than triple by 2040 (Choi et al., 2014; Hermans & Evenhuis, 2013). Serious health or disabling conditions usually lead to residence in a nursing home because of the grave hardships of caring for a disabled person at home. Increasing age is much the same. According to one survey, at ages 65 and over, only 5% of the population were in nursing homes, but for ages 85 and over, the figure was 22%. This wide gap is likely to persist indefinitely (Reardon, Nelson, Patel, Philpot, & Neidecker, 2012).

EXHIBIT 11.8   R-E-S-P-E-C-T Model for Helping Older LGBTQ Clients

- **R**—Review agency policies and practices. How are LGBTQ consumers treated?
- **E**—Educate residents, staff, and administration on taboo topics related to human sexuality and gender differences.
- **S**—Share experiences and ideas for overcoming homophobia and heterosexism.
- **P**—Promote diversity and prevention of homophobic practices. Uncover *isms*.
- **E**—Evaluate and explore areas for education and ongoing learning.
- **C**—Change belief systems and taboos that devalue (sexual) diversity.
- **T**—Transition to a diversity-friendly facility that supports and attends to older LGBTQ people.

Source: Metz (1997).

A huge number of people who reside in nursing homes and are in the severely disabled category are those with clinically diagnosed Alzheimer's disease. Alzheimer's disease affects both physical and mental functioning. At first, slight memory losses occur, followed by a shuffling gait, stooped posture, and loss of bowel and bladder control. The symptoms progress at different speeds for each person because, researchers think, various areas of the brain are affected by the disease process. Despite the sad long-term prognosis for people with Alzheimer's, social workers in long-term care settings can optimize the functioning of older adults by helping them actively exercise their bodies and minds.

INTERSECTIONS OF DIVERSITY

The majority (three fourths) of older men but only a minority of older women (one third) are currently married and living with their spouses—a pattern that is expected to continue over the next several decades. Solitary living increases with advancing age. In 1990, 47% (35,000) of those aged 85 and over lived alone; projections show that 83,000 will live alone in 2030. However, the proportion of Latinos living alone in 1990 (22%) was considerably lower than that of whites (31%).

In addition, about 8% of older adults live alone and have no children. The figure for blacks and Asians and Pacific Islanders is substantially higher (11%) than for whites (8%). There are serious implications for caregiving as these populations age.

ADVOCACY AND AGING

When people refuse assistance or caregiving responsibilities, social workers ethically must intervene to help family members act, make difficult decisions, let go, or legally prepare for changes in environment or care. Resources that many older adults require are in the form of nutrition (meals-on-wheels, congregate meals, or food stamps), long-term care, home health, housing, and respect.

ECONOMIC AND SOCIAL JUSTICE

As advocates for social and economic justice, social workers must be a voice for older people approaching or living in poverty. In the 1970s benefit increases helped boost standards of living for older adults, even though they also created subsequent concerns about the programs' sustainability. At the same time that the economic and political landscapes are causing doubt about how older adults will be able to afford to live, options for self-support are dwindling as well. The Great Recession hollowed out many retirement accounts, and long-term care insurance can be crushingly expensive. These are issues that must be addressed for both individuals and society as a whole, and gerontological social workers could help make a case for the needs of older adults.

Social workers can also advocate for older adults who no longer drive or who have ambulation difficulties (Berg-Weger, Meuser, & Stowe, 2013; Rusch, Schall, Lee, Dawson, & Rizzo, 2014). Services are available to help them obtain food, medical care, and other homemaking necessities. However, wait lists of 6 months or more exist for some older adults who reside in particular states and desire home-delivered meals. As well, older adults residing in rural areas may have difficulty accessing transportation to medical appointments or home shopping services to acquire groceries.

With their respect for diversity, social workers are also well trained and positioned to combat ageism. Society resists embracing the aging population. Battling "old geezer" stereotypes and trying to obtain equal standing in the workplace continue to be struggles for those age 60 (or even 50) and older. In one survey of 84 people age 60 and older, nearly 80% of respondents reported experiencing ageism—such as other people's assuming they had memory or physical impairments due to their age (Palmore, 2001). The most frequent type of ageism—reported by 58% of respondents—was being told a joke that pokes fun at older people. Thirty-one percent reported being ignored or not taken seriously because of their age.

Unfortunately, ageism has seeped into mental health care. Older patients are often viewed by health professionals as set in their ways and unable to change their behavior. As a result, mental health problems—such as cognitive impairment or psychological disorders caused at least in part by complex pharmacological treatments—often go unrecognized and untreated. This deficit in treatment needs to change, because people over the age of 85, who often depend on medication for an active lifestyle, are the fastest-growing segment of the U.S. population.

SUPPORTIVE ENVIRONMENT

Older adults who live in inner-city and suburban areas and those who are homeless, uninsured, or live alone present with varying risk factors in later life. Suburbanites tend to have nice homes and cars, while inner-city dwellers reside in cluttered and decrepit projects. Substance use and addiction may be part of the scenery. Community outreach in the form of distribution of condoms and bleach to clean needles may be required in some cities where drug dealing and use are rampant (Boeri, Sterk, & Elifson, 2008; Namkee & DiNitto, 2013).

Environmental factors related to caregiving affect both the physical and mental wellness of caregivers. It is predicted that caregiving will become more complex in part because of the need for long-distance caregiving. Children and their aging parents often live in different cities, and it may be difficult for the caregivers to take time from work or family to travel to their parents' homes. Mental health practitioners must continue to respond to the concerns of these caregivers and develop options that recognize the precious nature of time. These same counselors must create ways to use technology effectively to compensate for lacking resources in environments where the parents reside.

HUMAN NEEDS AND RIGHTS

Older adults, like everyone else, have the right to make bad decisions throughout their lives. However, many who have made bad decisions have reached a point where they have few means—mental, physical, or financial—of mitigating the consequences. Gerontological social workers cannot change the past, but they can help find the resources for a safe old age. For example, older adults who have not planned well economically will require special counseling to help them manage long-term care or aging-in-place needs.

Addiction is another bad choice that gerontological social workers can address. However, social workers must recognize that older adults rarely use alcohol or drugs to "get high." Drug or alcohol use that begins after age 60 appears fundamentally different. Typically, people who begin as teenagers or young adults are sensation seekers with significant rates of psychiatric disorders and antisocial traits. In contrast, older adults tend to turn to alcohol and drugs to alleviate the physical and psychological pain from the onslaught of medical and psychiatric illness, the loss of loved ones, or social isolation. The problem is that these psychoactive drugs are all addicting and can impair cognitive functioning, cause depression, increase the risk of falling, and interact dangerously with other medications. Moreover, drug and alcohol abuse in older patients occurs alongside other medical and psychiatric illnesses. You cannot treat either problem in isolation. There is little doubt that America faces a looming public substance use and mental health crisis in the aging population. The question is whether we can meet this daunting challenge with the investment in research and mental health that is currently allocated. Gerontological social workers can help keep the problem in the public eye (Wu & Blazer, 2011).

Regarding caregiver stress, ethnicity and race, emotional support, and the quality of the current and past relationship may help mediate caregiver burden. An effective gerontological social worker can help stressed caregivers improve their relationship with the older adults they care for and also receive the services they need. Social workers need to point out that caregiving may yield some positive outcomes as well. For example, through the act of caregiving, individuals can grow in mastery and personal efficacy, and enhance well-being or self-worth. Caregiving may increase feelings of personal achievement and pride, and enhance meaning and heighten the sense of closeness and warmth between caregiver and care recipient.

POLITICAL ACCESS

Ozawa and Yeo (2011) explore how older adults, across their life spans, make decisions for how to spend, save, or give away money. Depending on one's cohort, whether part of the Greatest Generation, a baby boomer, a Gen Xer, or a millennial, Social Security payouts and the eligibility age to receive Social Security benefits differ (Ozawa & Yeo, 2011). Thus, social workers have a role to play not only in helping older people maximize their resources and receive aid when needed but also in teaching middle-aged people how

to save money and invest in stocks, bonds, and IRAs (individual retirement accounts). At the same time, social workers should be advocating for legislation that helps fund resources and programs for older adults now and in the future.

The Affordable Care Act's emphasis on prevention and Medicaid expansion will surely have ramifications for older adults. Aging in place is an ideal for which social workers must advocate. Also, social workers can work to influence government policies related to public funds for nursing homes and services.

Social workers may expand their clout by partnering with sympathetic lobbyists and national organizations such as the American Association for Retired Persons and the Gray Panthers. Both organizations have long existed to provide support and services to all older adults. Currently, AARP has 97 million members and collaborates with more than 93 product companies. AARP is a powerful lobbying organization with a substantial mailing list of older adults. Social workers need to have a working knowledge of policies and potential political partners to ensure a mutually beneficial relationship with organizations such as these.

YOUR CAREER IN GERONTOLOGY

Well-respected and accredited colleges and universities across the United States have created degree and certificate programs for individuals who wish to embrace the challenging and compassionate field of gerontology. Bachelor's, master's, and doctoral degree programs are available that focus on gerontology's multidisciplinary approach. Courses can include topics such as theories of aging, ethics, housing, geriatric psychology, research methods, physiology of aging, social services, government policy, and interesting electives (e.g., aging and spirituality, aging and the family, women and aging, therapeutic arts, aging and the law, economics and aging—to name a few). Gerontology minors and graduate certificates in aging studies are also options for social workers pursuing an MSW degree.

Social workers with gerontology specialties can assess economic well-being, discern political and religious orientations and promote engagement, link older adults to work (i.e., encore careers), link them to leisure opportunities (e.g., senior centers, Road Scholar program), connect them to nutrition programs (e.g., congregate meals, meals-on-wheels), provide health care and home health social work services, develop programs and policies, and serve as consultants (e.g., acting as a thought leader for AARP to guide the organization on how to market products better or collaborate with new resource partners).

Lessons related to gerontology and geriatrics will serve social workers well across practice areas. For example, social workers in child welfare, family services, mental health agencies, schools, AIDS treatment clinics, homeless shelters, and Veterans Affairs and naval hospitals may at one time or another be required to assist older adults and understand the policy issues that affect them. Gerontological or geriatric social workers are called to help people age resiliently despite the numerous vulnerabilities, inequities, and ageism elders may experience.

To provide better care for older adults and better support for worn-out caregivers, social workers need to embrace new interdisciplinary, multidisciplinary, and transdisciplinary integrative models of care that traverse physical and mental health, long-term care, community-based settings, and social services. And given the expected increases in the numbers and challenges of older Americans, social workers must endeavor to educate and recruit more qualified BSW- and MSW-prepared gerontological social workers (Greenfield et al., 2013; Hooyman, 2006; Hooyman & Kiyak, 2010; Hooyman & Lubben, 2009). More gerontology scholars are also welcome.

The biggest barrier to attracting social work students to gerontology may be pervasive ageist attitudes. Many Americans still fear the processes of aging and dying. Younger and healthier people unfortunately tend to avoid thinking about the issues of mortality and loss of independence, and so they avoid older adults as well. A comprehensive literature review has noted multiple reasons why social work students hesitate to work with older adults (Wang & Chonody, 2013):

- Limited experience with and exposure to healthy older adults (Reed, Beall, & Baumhover, 1992)
- Anxiety related to personal aging (Anderson & Wiscott, 2003)
- Perception that older adults cannot change (Gellis, Sherman, & Lawrance, 2003)
- Perception that older adults are depressed and lonely and have poor hygiene (Mason & Sanders, 2004)
- Belief that geriatric social work provides a low salary (Hooyman & Lubben, 2009)
- Perception that working with older adults is not challenging or rewarding (John A. Hartford Foundation, 2009)
- Perception that they will have a higher status in the field if they work with children or adolescents (Reed et al., 1992)

Keep in mind, however, that the number of workers in gerontology and geriatrics is declining precisely when their services are needed the most. America has certified about half the number of geriatricians it needs, and few medical students are choosing geriatrics. By 2020 the geriatric nursing workforce is expected to drop by 20%, and geriatric psychiatrists have been decreasing in numbers since 2001. Eldercare is projected to be the fastest-growing employment sector within the health care industry. The demand for gerontological and geriatric social workers is growing as well. The U.S. Bureau of Labor Statistics classifies gerontological social workers as health care social workers and notes how nursing homes and home health care agencies are prime employers of social workers specializing in gerontology. Without a strong, well-trained cadre of gerontological social workers, greater demands will be placed on families and caregivers, and of course on older adults themselves.

SUMMARY

It's not how old you are, it's how you are old.

—Jules Renard

We all grow older and experience physical changes as we age. We also age in social places and within social relationships and contexts that have shaped our lives. Humans create their old age as part of life, and societies construct their own views of aging. Gerontological social workers assess clients by discerning differences between normal and abnormal aging processes within those contexts. The goal of social work with older adults is to help people live well with their aging process and empower societies to engage with aging along with other aspects of life.

Social workers who decide to work with older adults are and will continue to be in demand. From program and product development to counseling, and everything in between, diverse jobs are available for social workers who have a passion to serve older generations. Gerontology is a science and an art; it is the point where education and research meet advocacy and care for the older adult generation.

TOP 10 KEY CONCEPTS

activities of daily living (ADLs)   gerontology
ageism   nursing homes
aging in place   Older Americans Act of 1965
Alzheimer's disease   Sandwich Generation
assisted living   senescence

DISCUSSION QUESTIONS

1. What effect does an aging population have on the U.S. workforce, pension system, and health care services?
2. What biopsychosocial-spiritual challenges do aging Americans face?
3. How well will you manage the four Ds (death, depression, dementia, disability) of aging?
4. How can social workers help bust the myth that older adults are not sexually active?
5. How can ageism be combated?

EXERCISES

1. Why does the United States seem to emphasize youth and deem older adults as lower status?
2. What do gerontological social workers do, and how can they creatively address gaps in service that older adults experience when they quit working, remain single, become widowed, decide to move or marry late in life, or raise grandchildren?
3. Research workplace issues in social work and management resources: How do generations interact in the workplace? What are effective strategies for managing and supervising older and younger workers on the job?

How do organizations manage the unique and sometimes competing priorities of multiple generations in the workplace? What are the strengths that older workers and their younger counterparts bring to the workplace? What are your views on work and older adults? When should people retire?

4. Conduct research to determine how economic and political issues and the status of entitlement programs (e.g., Medicare, Medicaid, Social Security, long-term care insurance) are affecting the lives of older adults in all parts of our nation.

ONLINE RESOURCES

*   AARP (www.aarp.org): A nonprofit, nonpartisan membership organization for people age 50 and over, dedicated to enhancing quality of life for us all as we age; delivers value to members through information, advocacy, and service, and publishes a monthly bulletin
*   Alzheimer's Association (www.alz.org): Formed in 1980 to advance research to end Alzheimer's and dementia while enhancing care for those living with the disease
*   Association for Gerontology in Higher Education (www .aghe.org): Aims to advance gerontology and geriatrics education in academic institutions, and provide

leadership and support of gerontology and geriatrics education to faculty and students at educational institutions
*   Centers for Medicare and Medicaid Services (cms.hhs .gov): Administers the Medicare and Medicaid programs, and the State Children's Health Insurance Program, which provide coverage for close to 1 out of 4 Americans
*   Facts on Aging Quiz (cas.umkc.edu/gerontology/ agingfactsquiz.asp): Lists questions that can lead to a lively discussion on aging

- Gerontological Society of America (www.geron.org): The nation's oldest and largest interdisciplinary organization devoted to research, education, and practice in the field of aging, with the principal mission of advancing the study of aging and disseminating information among scientists, decision makers, and the general public
- "Human Values in Aging" e-newsletter (subscribe via valuesinaging@yahoo.com): Publishes items on positive aging, including spirituality, autobiography, lifelong learning, and late-life creativity

- National Center for Gerontological Social Work Education (www.cswe.org/CentersInitiatives/GeroEdCenter.aspx): Provides resources for social work faculty, students, and practitioners who are committed to enhancing gerontological competence
- National Institute on Aging (www.nih.gov/nia): One of the 27 institutes and centers of the National Institutes of Health; leads a broad scientific effort to understand the nature of aging and to extend the healthy, active years of life, and is the primary federal agency supporting and conducting Alzheimer's disease research

STUDENT STUDY SITE

Sharpen your skills with SAGE edge at **edge.sagepub.com/cox**

SAGE edge for Students provides a personalized approach to help you accomplish your coursework goals in an easy-to-use learning environment.

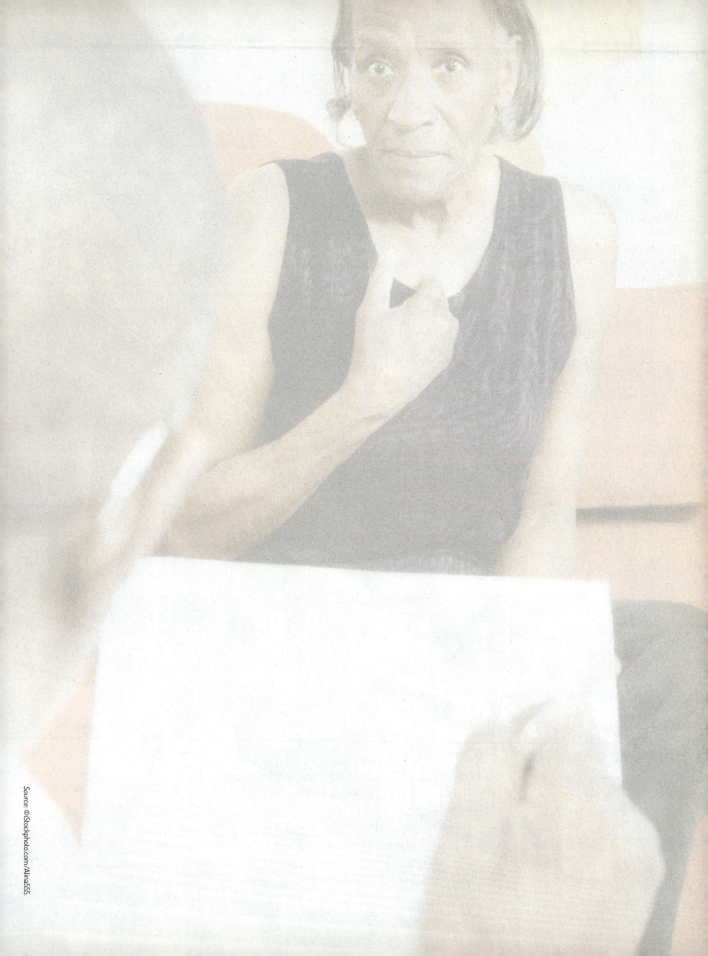

Chapter 12: CRIMINAL JUSTICE

Learning Objectives

After reading this chapter, you should be able to

1. Identify and describe important concepts and terms in the criminal justice system.
2. Analyze the contextual nature of criminal behavior, as politically defined and relative to time and place.
3. Identify and describe the intended functions of punishment and imprisonment in the United States.
4. Describe and explain the differences and tension between social work and criminal justice perspectives concerning criminal behavior.
5. List and explain areas to advocate for change and reform in the criminal justice system.
6. Describe and analyze how specific population groups are advantaged and disadvantaged in the criminal justice system.
7. Describe the importance of empowerment of victims and criminals in advocating for fair and just legal processes and systems.

Michelle Combats Racial and Ethnic Imbalances in the Juvenile Justice System

As a BSW-level social worker employed at an urban juvenile probation agency, Michelle interacts with a variety of teenagers and encounters a wide range of situations involving criminal acts. Michelle's clients have experienced numerous forms of trauma, such as physical and sexual abuse, and have been diagnosed with various mental health and substance problems. Michelle works mainly with juveniles and probation officers to conduct assessments and coordinate referrals to mental health, family, and substance services.

Michelle has learned a great deal about exposure to trauma, dysfunctional family dynamics, and legal systems from her day-to-day contact and discussions with her clients and their families. She has learned as well from attorneys, police officers, social workers, judges, and administrative staff at her agency.

As a social worker practicing in a criminal justice setting, Michelle is mindful of her responsibility to identify and address larger-scale, structural issues impacting her clients. Glaringly, 55% of her clients are members of a racial minority group, largely African American, even though only 30% of the juvenile population in her urban area comprises members of a racial minority group. The disproportionate involvement of minorities in the juvenile criminal justice system is a problem in Michelle's city as well as in many areas across the nation. She has heard that Washington State has been successful in documenting the racial and ethnic imbalance in its juvenile justice system and has passed laws to monitor and reduce this imbalance in its legal systems (Hsia, Bridges, & McHale, 2004). Helping professionals and leaders in Michelle's juvenile justice system would benefit from additional information and better data to understand why youth from ethnic and racial minorities appear to become disproportionately involved in the juvenile justice system and how they might help combat the imbalance.

The profession of social work has experienced a lengthy and at times tension-filled relationship with the field of criminal justice. Although the criminal justice system is an important arena for employment and includes therapeutic and rehabilitative services, the historical roots of criminal justice in the United States have focused on law enforcement, incarceration, and the punishment of criminal behavior. Traditionally, professionals in criminal justice have approached crime and delinquency as a matter of personal responsibility and thus have tended to work in law enforcement and judicial and correctional settings with a heavy emphasis on individual accountability. Although social workers share the view that people involved in the criminal justice system have responsibility for their actions, criminals are also seen as a product of their **biopsychosocial environment**.

TIME TO THINK

What are some distinct advantages that Caucasian and affluent people have in minimizing contact with the court system? How might parents and family members use their status to influence and intervene when their young people become involved with it?

Social workers respect criminals for their inherent worth as individuals and often represent people in need of help, especially with mental health and substance abuse issues. In practice, social workers have influenced criminal justice interventions by advocating for entities such as drug and mental health courts, where judges can explicitly consider, order, and support therapy and intervention plans for criminals as an alternative to punishment.

Differing perspectives about the nature of criminal behavior can create tension in the relationship between social workers and criminal justice professionals. It is too simplistic but also true to a degree to say that law enforcement professionals, correction officers, and court officials often view social workers as being too understanding, caring, and compassionate. Social workers struggle to accept what they often think of as rigid, dehumanizing, and punitive practices in legal and correction systems. Exhibit 12.1 highlights some of the tensions between social workers and juvenile justice personnel (e.g., probation officers, court officials, law enforcement officers) and the social work perspective on those tensions (Peters, 2011).

CENTRAL CONCEPTS IN CRIMINAL JUSTICE AND CRIME

Crime in the United States is a long-standing and significant social problem resulting in the creation of myriad federal, state, and local organizations, and a complex labor force charged to process and respond to criminal activity. The **criminal justice system** refers to a large network of organizations (e.g., courts, police departments, prisons, jails, probation agencies) dedicated to the enforcement of laws and the administration of justice.

Crime refers to acts or behaviors that are prohibited by criminal law and punishable by negative sanctions (e.g., probation, fine, jail term). **Laws** are legislative acts passed at the local, state, and federal levels by corresponding political entities (e.g., city councils, state legislators, the U.S. Congress) to define and regulate acceptable and unacceptable behavior. Although debatable, the presumption in the United States is that people, even after being charged with a violation of law, are innocent until proven guilty. But if they are found

EXHIBIT 12.1   Tensions Between Social Workers and Juvenile Justice Personnel

SOURCES OF TENSIONS	BRIEF INTERPRETATION USING A SOCIAL WORK PERSPECTIVE
Historically gendered nature of social work and law enforcement	Social work is a female-dominated profession, and the helping role of social worker has appealed largely to women. Law enforcement officers have been predominantly men who view their role in a less casework and more corrective, punitive fashion.
Social workers' embracing theoretical orientations for assessment and intervention, which is seen by correctional staff as irrelevant to their work	Social workers began by using psychodynamic theory and casework to assess and develop interventions for clients, and then adopted additional theories to guide practice. The view of law enforcement and corrections officers remained narrowly focused on correction.
Cynicism that rehabilitation-oriented services provided by social workers are ineffective in corrections work	Officials in criminal justice systems have traditionally expressed skepticism about the effectiveness of rehabilitation services. However, advancements with mental health and drug courts are a testimony to a contemporary convergence between court systems and a rehabilitation perspective.
Founding of the American Probation and Parole Association by probation officers in 1975, which required only a baccalaureate degree (any type) and deemphasized social work education in favor of a punitive approach	Probation officers became organized, and their role became formalized outside of the realm of social work. Social workers and social work theory did not provide a guide for probation interventions (Diana, 1960). Probation continues to focus on enforcing and policing functions.

Source: Peters (2011, pp. 357–363).

guilty of having committed a crime, they are classified as **criminals**.

TYPES OF CRIMES

Crimes are typically classified into two general categories:

- **Misdemeanor crimes** are relatively minor crimes (e.g., traffic violations, public drunkenness, shoplifting) and are punishable by a fine and a small amount of time (e.g., less than 1 year) in jail.
- **Felonies** are serious crimes (e.g., murder, rape, aggravated assault) and are punishable by extended imprisonment and sometimes death.

It is important to note that both types of crime are recorded and become part of a person's legal record. A criminal record is ordinarily a public document. It creates a stigma for the person. One's criminal record is frequently reviewed in relationship to applications for employment, apartment rental, and insurance, and in the event of any subsequent criminal behavior. If you enter a professional major, do not be surprised if your field agency, licensing board, or future employer requires a criminal background check prior to field placement, licensure, or employment.

Crime is classified in several other ways:

- **Violent crimes** are typically crimes against other people that involve the use of force or threatened force. Examples of violent crimes include **robbery** (stealing from another person), **aggravated assault** (attacking another person physically), **rape** (sexual penetration through the use of force), and **homicide** (illegally causing the death of another person).
- **Property crimes** involve the taking of money or property from others without force or destruction. Examples of property crimes include **arson** (malicious burning of property), motor vehicle theft, **larceny** (stealing of property), and **burglary** (breaking into a house or building to steal).
- **Victimless crimes** involve illegal acts that (arguably) do not have a readily identifiable victim. Examples include prostitution, illegal gambling, and the selling of drugs. Many social workers would suggest that family members and loved ones are victims of this type of crime.
- **Hate crimes** involve intimidation and the intent to hurt people based on race, ethnicity, national origin, religion, sexual orientation, disability, and other forms of diversity. Hate crimes include the use of

verbal threats, acts of violence, fear, physical attack, and explosives.

- **White-collar crime** involves acts (e.g., fraud, theft, falsification of records) that occur in the course of employment or normal work activities. **Corporate criminals** commit crimes on behalf of a corporation and with its support.

The primary source for crime information in the United States is the **Uniform Crime Report**, an annual publication of the Federal Bureau of Investigation (FBI). The accuracy of information from this report is always a concern, as data reflect the number of crimes reported, not the number actually committed.

Nevertheless, the preliminary 2011 report indicates that violent crimes and property crimes in the United States are down 4% and 0.8%, respectively, from 2010 figures (Federal Bureau of Investigation, 2012). These declines continue a yearly trend (since 2006–2007) in which U.S. crime rates have fallen in nearly every category. Despite a common misperception advanced by the sensationalizing of crime in modern media, television crime series, computer games, and movies, crime rates in the United States have been falling in recent years, as illustrated in Exhibit 12.2.

THE CONTEXTUAL NATURE OF CRIME

In the United States, laws that have been passed are modified or amended on a regular basis. In addition, although some laws apply across states, they are political acts passed by legislative bodies in a particular time and place. As a consequence, a behavior legislated as illegal at one point in time

▲ NASCAR cars often sport ads for alcoholic products.

Source: Night Gyr/CreativeCommons

and within a specific jurisdiction may in a different locale or during a different time be deemed legal.

To exemplify the contextual nature of laws and criminal behavior, consider Prohibition. During the Prohibition Era in the United States (1920–1933), it was illegal to sell, manufacture, and transport alcohol. Defying these laws, "bootleggers" manufactured alcohol in homemade stills and set out in "souped-up" cars that could outrun police to transport and distribute their contraband to alcohol users and distributors in nearby counties. When the prohibition laws were repealed, however, alcohol became legal in the United States, and it has since become a multibillion-dollar industry. The legacy of bootleggers lives on in the organized racing of "stock cars"—similar to the souped-up cars of the Prohibition Era—overseen by the National Association for Stock Car Auto Racing (NASCAR). In fact, some of the early NASCAR drivers had been bootleggers. Today, alcohol is readily sold at many sporting events, including the popular NASCAR races. Several alcohol manufacturers prominently advertise their products through car sponsorship in NASCAR. Despite this dramatic turnaround, people who were convicted of the sale, manufacture, and/or transportation of alcohol during the Prohibition Era would continue to be classified as criminals.

The contextual nature of crime is also demonstrated in the label of "criminal" or "juvenile delinquent." This label is formally bestowed after a person is caught, charged, and deemed guilty of committing a crime. However, decisions by police officers, prosecutors, magistrates, and juries impact whether a person is charged, prosecuted, and ultimately found guilty of violating a law. Some people charged with a crime avoid being found guilty of criminal acts, whether through legal counsel, persuasive argument, or other forms of influence. Those with power, resources, and clout may be able to avoid the label of criminal, but people unable of mounting meaningful defenses often cannot avoid it. Affluent community members possess resources and hire attorneys to enable maneuvering around and through the criminal justice system to have cases dropped or reduced to a lower charge. Additionally, at times, people who have been found guilty of crime can petition to seal their records from public view.

THE CORRECTIONAL SYSTEM

Once a person has been convicted of a crime, and if the crime is serious enough and the judge deems fitting, the person enters the **correctional system.** There are three particularly important aspects of corrections:

- **Probation** constitutes a sentence given to an offender by a judge, typically in lieu of prison, carrying specific requirements and conditions, such as regular reporting, counseling, drug testing, and substance treatment. A person on probation is monitored by a probation officer. If an offender violates the terms of probation, a warrant for arrest can be issued and the offender may serve time in prison.
- **Parole** is the early release of an inmate from prison, supervised by a parole officer. Much like probation, parole specifies conditions for offenders. If parole requirements are violated, the offender can be sent back to prison.
- **Prison** is frequently viewed by judges as the most expensive and last-resort correctional option for offenders. *Prison* is a broad term that encompasses being held in local and county jails as well as state and federal prisons. In many jurisdictions, prisons are full and the cost of **incarceration**, being placed in prison, is prohibitive. For 2011, it was estimated that the average cost of incarceration for federal inmates was $28,893.40 per year and $26,163 per year for an inmate in a community corrections center (Prisons Bureau, 2013).

JUVENILE JUSTICE AND CORRECTIONS

Juvenile justice and corrections deserves special recognition because **juveniles,** who are people under the age of 18, are typically viewed and treated differently from adults in the criminal justice system. The UN Convention on the Rights of the Child defines a child as any human being under the age of 18; however, in many states, youth can be tried as adults in an adult criminal court. Some states (e.g., Connecticut, New York, and North Carolina) automatically prosecute 16- and 17-year-olds as adults. Other states allow judges the discretion to have youth tried in adult criminal courts. An **emancipated adult** is a juvenile who has been granted the status of adulthood, usually by court order. These types of legal distinctions add to the confusion of who is considered a juvenile and an adult.

Juveniles are deemed to be under the supervision and control of parents or guardians, who bear oversight and some responsibility for the minor's behavior. However, especially with adolescents, parental control of children becomes a challenge and often problematic.

Crimes committed by juveniles typically involve sexual or antisocial "acting out" (impulsively and uncontrollably behaving in a forbidden way, usually to get attention), truancy, running away, illegal use of drugs (including alcohol), shoplifting, property damage, fighting, and gang behavior. Appropriately, a juvenile who becomes involved in the criminal justice system is often brought to helping professionals (including social workers), agencies, and programs for help. Many times, the criminal actions of the juvenile involve and reflect interpersonal and family conflicts and dysfunctions.

Juvenile corrections refers to intervention, services, and programs for minors as a result of their involvement in the criminal justice system and courts. Juvenile corrections can include the use of locked juvenile detention facilities.

TIME TO THINK

How does public opinion and policy differ for criminal behavior by juveniles versus adults? Does the age of the juvenile or child make a difference, or are the type of crime and circumstances surrounding the act more important? Throughout this chapter, ask yourself how juveniles and adults are viewed and treated differently by police, courts, judges, and other elements of the criminal justice system.

CONFLICTING ATTITUDES ABOUT THOSE WHO COMMIT CRIMES

In the United States there are two dominant underlying values with regard to dealing with criminals: the need for transgressors to take individual responsibility and the need for society to punish transgressions. These perspectives are so pervasive among voters that many politicians include "anti-crime" and "hard-on-criminals" messages in their election campaigns. Of course, it is difficult to imagine a politician being in favor of crime. Politicians seldom speak kindly of criminals either (except perhaps powerful white-collar or corporate criminals), but their disdain for criminals overlooks the fact that many people who become involved in the criminal justice system have experienced mental and emotional challenges and addictions. Additionally, many criminals have been victims of trauma, abuse, and exploitation.

EXHIBIT 12.2   Changes in Crime Rates by Type of Crime, 1992–2011

YEAR	POPULATION[1]	VIOLENT CRIME	VIOLENT CRIME RATE	MURDER AND NONNEGLIGENT MANSLAUGHTER	MURDER AND NONNEGLIGENT MANSLAUGHTER RATE	FORCIBLE RAPE	FORCIBLE RAPE RATE	ROBBERY	
1992	255,029,699	1,932,274	757.7	23,760	9.3	109,062	42.8	672,478	
1993	257,782,608	1,926,017	747.1	24,526	9.5	106,014	41.1	659,870	
1994	260,327,021	1,857,670	713.6	23,326	9.0	102,216	39.3	618,949	
1995	262,803,276	1,798,792	684.5	21,606	8.2	97,470	37.1	580,509	
1996	265,228,572	1,688,540	636.6	19,645	7.4	96,252	36.3	535,594	
1997	267,783,607	1,636,096	611.0	18,208	6.8	96,153	35.9	498,534	
1998	270,248,003	1,533,887	567.6	16,974	6.3	93,144	34.5	447,186	
1999	272,690,813	1,426,044	523.0	15,522	5.7	89,411	32.8	409,371	
2000	281,421,906	1,425,486	506.5	15,586	5.5	90,178	32.0	408,016	
2001[2]	285,317,559	1,439,480	504.5	16,037	5.6	90,863	31.8	423,557	
2002	287,973,924	1,423,677	494.4	16,229	5.6	95,235	33.1	420,806	
2003	290,788,976	1,383,676	475.8	16,528	5.7	93,883	32.3	414,235	
2004	293,656,842	1,360,088	463.2	16,148	5.5	95,089	32.4	401,470	
2005	296,507,061	1,390,745	469.0	16,740	5.6	94,347	31.8	417,438	
2006	299,398,484	1,435,123	479.3	17,309	5.8	94,472	31.6	449,246	
2007	301,621,157	1,422,970	471.8	17,128	5.7	92,160	30.6	447,324	
2008	304,059,724	1,394,461	458.6	16,465	5.4	90,750	29.8	443,563	
2009	307,006,550	1,325,896	431.9	15,399	5.0	89,241	29.1	408,742	
2010[3]	309,330,219	1,251,248	404.5	14,722	4.8	85,593	27.7	369,089	
2011	311,591,917	1,203,564	386.3	14,612	4.7	83,425	26.8	354,396	

[1] Populations are U.S. Census Bureau provisional estimates as of July 1 for each year except 2000 and 2010, which are decennial census counts.

[2] The murder and nonnegligent homicides that occurred as a result of the events of September 11, 2001, are not included in this table.

[3] The crime figures have been adjusted.

Note: Although arson data are included in the trend and clearance tables, sufficient data are not available to estimate totals for this offense. Therefore, no arson data are published in this table.

TABLE 1   Crime in the United States

Percent Change in Volume and Rate per 100,000 Inhabitants for 2 Years, 5 Years, and 10 Years

YEARS	VIOLENT CRIME	VIOLENT CRIME RATE	MURDER AND NONNEGLIGENT MANSLAUGHTER	MURDER AND NONNEGLIGENT MANSLAUGHTER RATE	FORCIBLE RAPE	FORCIBLE RAPE RATE	ROBBERY	ROBBERY RATE	
2011/2010	−3.8	−4.5	−0.7	−1.5	−2.5	−3.2	−4.0	−4.7	
2011/2007	−15.4	−18.1	−4.7	−17.4	−9.5	−12.4	−20.8	−23.3	
2011/2002	−15.5	−21.9	−10.0	−16.8	−12.4	−19.0	−15.8	−22.2	

Source: Federal Bureau of Investigation (2011).

ROBBERY RATE	AGGRAVATED ASSAULT	AGGRAVATED ASSAULT RATE	PROPERTY CRIME	PROPERTY CRIME RATE	BURGLARY	BURGLARY RATE	LARCENY-THEFT	LARCENY-THEFT RATE	MOTOR VEHICLE THEFT	MOTOR VEHICLE THEFT RATE
263.7	1,126,974	441.9	12,505,917	4,903.7	2,979,884	1,168.4	7,915,199	3,103.6	1,610,834	631.6
256.0	1,135,607	440.5	12,218,777	4,740.0	2,834,808	1,099.7	7,820,909	3,033.9	1,563,060	606.3
237.8	1,113,179	427.6	12,131,873	4,660.2	2,712,774	1,042.1	7,879,812	3,026.9	1,539,287	591.3
220.9	1,099,207	418.3	12,063,935	4,590.5	2,593,784	987.0	7,997,710	3,043.2	1,472,441	560.3
201.9	1,037,049	391.0	11,805,323	4,451.0	2,506,400	945.0	7,904,685	2,980.3	1,394,238	525.7
186.2	1,023,201	382.1	11,558,475	4,316.3	2,460,526	918.8	7,743,760	2,891.8	1,354,189	505.7
165.5	976,583	361.4	10,951,827	4,052.5	2,332,735	863.2	7,376,311	2,729.5	1,242,781	459.9
150.1	911,740	334.3	10,208,334	3,743.6	2,100,739	770.4	6,955,520	2,550.7	1,152,075	422.5
145.0	911,706	324.0	10,182,584	3,618.3	2,050,992	728.8	6,971,590	2,477.3	1,160,002	412.2
148.5	909,023	318.6	10,437,189	3,658.1	2,116,531	741.8	7,092,267	2,485.7	1,228,391	430.5
146.1	891,407	309.5	10,455,277	3,630.6	2,151,252	747.0	7,057,379	2,450.7	1,246,646	432.9
142.5	859,030	295.4	10,442,862	3,591.2	2,154,834	741.0	7,026,802	2,416.5	1,261,226	433.7
136.7	847,381	288.6	10,319,386	3,514.1	2,144,446	730.3	6,937,089	2,362.3	1,237,851	421.5
140.8	862,220	290.8	10,174,754	3,431.5	2,155,448	726.9	6,783,447	2,287.8	1,235,859	416.8
150.0	874,096	292.0	10,019,601	3,346.6	2,194,993	733.1	6,626,363	2,213.2	1,198,245	400.2
148.3	866,358	287.2	9,882,212	3,276.4	2,190,198	726.1	6,591,542	2,185.4	1,100,472	364.9
145.9	843,683	277.5	9,774,152	3,214.6	2,228,887	733.0	6,586,206	2,166.1	959,059	315.4
133.1	812,514	264.7	9,337,060	3,041.3	2,203,313	717.7	6,338,095	2,064.5	795,652	259.2
119.3	781,844	252.8	9,112,625	2,945.9	2,168,459	701.0	6,204,601	2,005.8	739,565	239.1
113.7	751,131	241.1	9,063,173	2,908.7	2,188,005	702.2	6,159,795	1,976.9	715,373	229.6

AGGRAVATED ASSAULT	AGGRAVATED ASSAULT RATE	PROPERTY CRIME	PROPERTY CRIME RATE	BURGLARY	BURGLARY RATE	LARCENY-THEFT	LARCENY-THEFT RATE	MOTOR VEHICLE THEFT	MOTOR VEHICLE THEFT RATE
−3.9	−4.6	−0.5	−1.3	+0.9	+0.2	−0.7	−1.4	−3.3	−4.0
−13.3	−16.1	−8.3	−11.2	−0.1	−3.3	−6.6	−9.5	−35.0	−37.1
−15.7	−22.1	−13.3	−19.9	+1.7	−6.0	−12.7	−19.3	−42.6	−47.0

SOCIAL WORK IN ACTION

Dr. Tina Maschi and Diverting Delinquent Youth

DR. Maschi is a social worker, researcher, and college professor. She has conducted research and published widely in the area of criminal justice and juvenile delinquency. In one of her many publications, Dr. Maschi points out "the need to create more opportunities to divert delinquent youths into community-based interventions to prevent or delay institutional placements" (Schwalbe, Hatcher, & Maschi, 2009, p. 31). The general premise is that when problems for youth arise, early use of counseling and intervention services holds promise for preventing or minimizing involvement with the juvenile justice system.

Social workers practicing in community-based youth treatment centers and child welfare agencies play an important professional role in intervening with youth who are exhibiting problems with school, drugs, inappropriate behavior, and their family. When counseling and interventions are effective, the quality of life for a juvenile becomes enhanced and her or his life course can move away from crime and exposure to juvenile and adult justice systems.

One of the more rewarding aspects in the life of a social worker is helping people change their lives. Practice with troubled youth can be both challenging and rewarding and often involves a family system. Do you have an interest and temperament for providing services to youth, many of whom are at a pivotal time in their biopsychosocial development and face challenging parental influences?

Working with youth and juveniles requires both compassion and the ability to hold youth and parents responsible for their actions. Are these types of professional expectations in your comfort zone?

This is not to say that criminals should not be held accountable for their actions. Instead, it behooves us all for criminals to be treated in a just fashion and, upon their release, to be able to move forward in their lives as productive members of society. Interestingly, many Americans seem to be single-minded about crime, tending to see the purpose of incarceration as either punishment or rehabilitation.

ATTITUDES TOWARD PUNISHMENT

The system for the punishment and imprisonment of criminals in the United States is designed to fulfill four functions (Kendall, 2013), although its success in fulfilling them is uneven:

- *Social protection.* It is true that criminals who are in jail will no longer be able to commit crimes; so the public is protected. However, many times society is protected only temporarily, until the criminal is released from jail.

- *Deterrence.* It is thought that fear of punishment will prevent future criminal activity. It is not clear, however, that punishment does have a deterrent effect. Criminologists have noted that many crimes are committed in the heat of the moment, with little consideration of the consequences, and 30% to 50% of those who are released from prison commit additional crimes. In addition, much of the criminal justice system is predicated on a reactive approach, taking action only after a crime has occurred.

- *Rehabilitation.* Providing services and programs to offenders while they are incarcerated is supposed to facilitate their successful, law-abiding reentry into the community. Unfortunately, rehabilitation programs are few in number, understaffed, and underfunded.

- *Retribution.* The belief that penalty or punishment should match the severity of the crime to provide "payback" is popular. For example, by this thinking, people who commit homicide should be punished more severely than people who commit fraud.

Currently, criminal punishment in the United States tends toward the retributive end of the spectrum. People joke about the indignities of being incarcerated and react negatively to appeals for funding for more humane conditions, believing that criminals are getting "what they deserve." Thus, jails and prisons in the United States are overcrowded, forcing prisoners into cells designed for far fewer inhabitants. Many states have turned to private prisons as a means to control costs. But this outsourcing approach tends to reduce appropriate oversight concerning the humane treatment of prisoners and the impact of prisoners' living in close quarters with one another.

Yet, at the same time, crime and criminals are often glamorized. Popular television shows such as *Breaking Bad, The Good Wife,* and *Blue Bloods* provide a misleading and glorified depiction of crime, law enforcement, and the legal system. National and local news programs exploit criminal activity as a mechanism to boost ratings and capture the attention of viewers. What the general public views has little relationship to the everyday workings and proceedings of law enforcement, criminal justice, and correctional systems.

ATTITUDES TOWARD REHABILITATION

Another place where American values conflict with reality is in the professed desire to have criminals "pay their dues," become rehabilitated while in the system, and then return to society as productive citizens. In fact, many helping professionals are concerned about the lasting negative effects of being found guilty of committing crimes. Being labeled as a criminal can present significant challenges for obtaining employment, housing, and credit, as well as damaging one's self-image and self-esteem. **Recidivism**, the tendency for former inmates to return to prison, is common because people who have been labeled as criminals find it so difficult to reintegrate into society. Exhibit 12.3 lists some facts about recidivism in the United States.

In fact, it is common for people who are incarcerated to become even more expert at crime at the same time as they are becoming less employable. People have a greater tendency to participate in criminal activities and deviance when they frequently associate with criminals and those deemed to be deviants (Sutherland, 1939). Thus, overcrowded prisons can be viewed as educational grounds for future criminal behavior.

Source: Peabody Awards/70th Annual Peabody Awards/CreativeCommons.

▲ Television shows, such as *The Good Wife,* can glorify crime.

SOCIAL WORKERS AND THE CRIMINAL JUSTICE SYSTEM

People working in the criminal justice system focus on the law's definitions of what is acceptable or unacceptable and enforce those laws through arrest of people accused of crime, through prosecution, and through sentencing. In contrast, social work intervention requires a thorough understanding of client behavior and contextual factors influencing criminal acts, such as upbringing, family, friends, subculture, and community. Social work is thus more than affirming and reinforcing social norms through the enforcement of laws. People do not live in isolation but are social beings. To be an effective social worker requires the ability to influence criminal behaviors and confront social conditions that give rise to and support criminal action.

FORENSIC SOCIAL WORK

Much of what social workers do within the criminal justice system can be called **forensic social work.** Forensic social work applies a social work outlook to legal issues and systems and litigation. These are some of the tasks forensic social workers perform:

evaluating criminal and civil competency, court-ordered psychotherapy, evaluation of suitability to parent, child and adult custody evaluation, mediation services, probation and parole services, consultant to attorneys, termination of parental rights

EXHIBIT 12.3   Recidivism of Prisoners in 30 States, 2005–2010

Selected Highlights

- 67% of released prisoners were arrested for a new crime within 3 years, and 76.6% were arrested within 5 years.

- More than 36.8% of all prisoners who were arrested within 5 years of release were arrested within the first 6 months of release, with 56.7% arrested by the end of the first year.

- 16.1% of released prisoners were responsible for 48.4% of the nearly 1.2 million arrests that occurred in the 5-year follow-up period.

- Within 5 years of release, 84.1% of inmates who were age 24 or younger at release were arrested, compared with 78.6% of inmates ages 25 to 39 and 69.2% of those age 40 and older.

Source: Durose, Cooper, and Snyder (2014, p. 1).

evaluations, bonding and attachment assessments, correctional services, domestic violence services, international child abduction, . . . protective shelters, [and] rebuttal witnesses. (Munson, 2011, pp. 39–40)

The **National Organization of Forensic Social Work** was established to advance education in the field of forensic social work. It supports annual conferences, political action, a professional literature newsletter and journal, and networking opportunities. Social workers and their clients benefit from specialized education and training opportunities provided by organizations such as this one.

As an area of practice, forensic social work requires social workers to learn and share specific ways to promote effective social work practice and human rights in areas such as racial and ethnic imbalances in the criminal justice system, dehumanizing aspects of and conditions in prisons, mental health and addiction services, and living conditions that place people at risk of committing crimes (Maschi & Killian, 2011, pp. 30–31).

SOCIAL WORK VALUES REGARDING CRIMINAL JUSTICE

If you are interested in social work and criminal justice, it is important to understand the need to hold people who have committed crimes responsible for their actions. But at the same time, it is also important to have compassion for those caught up in the system. The following values are key to contemporary social work practice:

- *Prevention*—This should be the first goal. Lawbreakers are often between the ages of 15 and 25. Social workers should be concerned with designing, implementing, and funding programs and services that will keep children and young adults away from antisocial activities and out of the criminal justice system. Prevention of crime reduces the number of victims and is more humane than letting crime occur and then punishing offenders.

- *Justice*—Members of certain population groups (especially those of diverse race, ethnicity, and social class) have distinct advantages and disadvantages in the criminal justice system. Advocating for fair and equitable access to information, services, and resources across population groups is crucial to promote social justice.

- *Dignity*—In addition to being treated fairly, people accused and found guilty of crimes, as well as their victims, deserve to be treated in a respectful and humane fashion. It is important to recognize and take into account their challenges, which may include mental health, addiction, and trauma of victimizations.

- *Best practices and quality services*—Offenders and victims of crime should have access to appropriate and effective legal representation, mental health programs, and addiction services. Social workers in the criminal justice system provide many of these services and must focus on the dignity and needs of each person, whether offender or victim. In addition, social workers should advocate at the local, state, and federal levels for access to competent professionals implementing best practices in their respective disciplines.

Source: ©iStockphoto.com/grahambedingfield

▲ Forensic social workers examine issues such as disproportionate minority contact in the criminal justice system, and work to affect change in these areas.

INTERACTIONS WITH THE CRIMINAL JUSTICE SYSTEM

The criminal justice system and its various components and players constitute a complex structure of officials and programs in the United States. At times, attorneys are needed and hired simply to help clients navigate the system. To be effective practitioners, social workers must also become familiar with the people, places, processes, and organizations within their local and relevant criminal justice systems.

Police

There are many different types of **police officers**, individuals sworn and authorized by local, state, county, or federal authorities to enforce and uphold laws. *Police* in its most general use includes city and township officers as well as county sheriffs, state highway patrol officers, and federal enforcement agents—FBI agents; agents of the Bureau of Alcohol, Tobacco, Firearms and Explosives; and so forth. Police officers are usually called on to be the first responders to criminal activities.

Social workers often work closely with police officers, especially in relationship to specific problems (e.g., child neglect and abuse investigation) and population groups (e.g., victims of domestic violence). In some jurisdictions, police officers and social workers share their expertise as members of uniquely designed and trained teams to investigate certain incidences of rape, child abuse, and domestic violence. Additionally, when social work intervention is mandated by court order, police officers may be called on to enforce the relevant aspects (e.g., placement of a child) of the court order.

Courts

Courts determine whether people accused of committing crimes are guilty or innocent. **Judges and magistrates** are attorneys elected or appointed to lead and rule over court and its processes. Judges hire court staff to assist in conducting court procedure. Courts are found at various jurisdictional levels (e.g., city, county, state, federal). People are tried in the court that is appropriate given the offenses and charges brought against them. Because courts are capable of hearing only a portion of cases, it is not unusual for the accused, typically through his or her attorney, to negotiate with the prosecution for a reduced charge or sentence, called **plea bargaining**.

Social workers are called or brought before courts to provide information and their expertise. They often investigate and describe the circumstances of a crime and offer psychosocial assessments of the accused and relevant others. These social workers may be considered "officers of the court" and sworn to uphold confidentiality and other rules.

Attorneys

The practice of law is regulated through state law. Attorneys graduate from law schools and then pass appropriate state bar examinations. Attorneys acquire expertise and specialize in specific areas of practice, such as real estate, estate planning, divorce, and of course criminal law and appeals. The **prosecutor** is an attorney representing a government entity (e.g., city, county, state, federal) and arguing that the accused is guilty. A defense attorney represents the accused and argues his or her innocence. If people cannot afford a defense attorney, some jurisdictions offer court-appointed public attorneys or defenders. Additionally, certain private attorneys will agree as a commitment to personal and/or civic duty to provide legal services on a pro bono basis (i.e., without payment or at a reduced rate) to people unable to pay. Defense attorneys often rely on the expertise of social workers to better understand their clients' situation. Attorneys also partner with social workers to advance legislation and

SOCIAL WORK IN ACTION

Betsy Biben Supervises Forensic Social Workers

BETSY Biben, chief of the Office of Rehabilitation and Development in the Public Defender Service for the District of Columbia, supervises forensic social workers. Although Betsy indicates that forensic social work can be a challenging field, she became "inspired to enter the field as a way to address the inequality of treatment and sentences for defendants lacking privilege and money" (Pace, 2012). Her group is dedicated to ensuring that attorneys, judges, and juries have an opportunity to review a comprehensive profile of a defendant, which includes information about the person's mental health, substance abuse, brain development, medical conditions, and other mitigating factors. The social workers in her group also advocate for rehabilitation services and appropriate reentry planning.

For people interested in pursuing a career in forensic social work, Betsy suggests entering an MSW program "that focuses on child and adolescent development, trauma, mental illness, psychopharmacology, intellectual disabilities, and criminal justice" (Pace, 2012). She also recommends that students consider internships in public defender offices.

Should courts consider background information when a crime has been committed, or should the focus be solely on the crime itself? If a county or state did not offer similar public defender services, which would be better: allowing no defendants to submit profiles or allowing those who are better off and able to pay for their own assessments to place their profiles before court officials?

Does your county or state offer similar public defender services? If not, is there a reason? Are there any student volunteer or internship opportunities in local public defender offices?

policies to promote justice and client rights. Attorneys may refer clients to social workers and social service agencies to promote the clients' stability and well-being.

Corrections Officers

Where people are imprisoned or in custody awaiting trial, corrections officers are hired to oversee inmates and maintain order. They enforce jail and prison rules with the inmate population and consequently have a stressful and dangerous job. Qualifications for becoming a corrections officer vary by state and correctional facility but typically require completion of a training program or graduation from an academy. Social workers' direct exposure to corrections officers is typically limited to visits with clients in jails and prisons.

Social workers frequently practice with offenders and the family members of people who have served prison terms or been placed on probation and/or parole. Collaboration with court officials and probation and parole officers to coordinate the best correctional strategy for moving forward in life and promoting well-being is an important interprofessional function. Social workers also work to ensure that the rights and perspective of the client are understood and considered in correctional decisions and processes. A common goal among all professionals is to reduce recidivism, the tendency for inmates to return to prison.

VICTIM ASSISTANCE PROGRAMS

In the criminal justice system, the clients of social workers can be both perpetrators and victims of violent crime. **Perpetrators** are people who inflict violence on others. **Victims** are people who have experienced a traumatic or violent act committed by a perpetrator. Because the term *victim* carries negative and helpless connotations, many professionals prefer the term *survivor*. Being a survivor suggests strength and resilience to move forward after experiencing a violent and/or traumatic event.

Social workers have been long-standing advocates for the creation and development of **victim assistance programs**, designed to support and help survivors and witnesses of acts of victimization. These unwilling participants in crime are counseled so they can better understand what has happened and seek appropriate crisis help and services. Survivors often struggle with investigative processes and testifying in court as to what happened. Social workers have advocated for victims to be interviewed and assessed by specially educated and trained police officers, prosecutors, medical staff, and helping professionals such as social workers, counselors, and psychologists. Volunteer programs have been developed to provide social support (e.g., a peer group, buddy systems, and accompaniment to court) to survivors. In the political realm, victim assistance services and programs may support the campaigns of sympathetic elected officials (e.g., sheriffs, prosecutors, and judges) or work to remove from office those who are deemed to favor the accused over the victims.

Social workers, especially those employed in victim assistance programs, seek to hold criminals socially accountable to the people they have wronged. A **restorative justice perspective** highlights the notion that many crimes are first and foremost an offense against human relations and offenders should be held accountable to the people they have violated (Finn & Jacobson, 2008, p. 341). Offenders are asked to acknowledge the harm they have done and apologize to the survivors, and the survivors are encouraged to forgive the offenders in return. The goals are "justice, healing, and reconciliation" (p. 341).

DEVIANT BEHAVIOR AND SOCIAL STATUS

In 2008, a banking crisis occurred in the United States. As a result of misleading and illegal business and lending practices in the banking and financial industry, many people suffered very real and painful losses. Real estate values plummeted, and home foreclosures and unemployment skyrocketed. Mortgage fraud was common, with lenders using inflated appraisals and false information for properties to justify unwarranted mortgages. Their reward was inflated bonuses based on a misleading volume of business.

The banking crisis damaged the national economy severely and forced the U.S. government to "bail out" a failing banking industry. Yet few banking officials in the United

States were held legally accountable for their actions. The entire episode added credence to the notion that in the legal system, different rules apply to different people, depending on their social–economic status and the nature of their crime.

The criminality of a deviant behavior is relative and based on societal or community values, norms, and standards, as well as social status and perception. Additionally, the wrongfulness of a criminal behavior is not necessarily related to the harm caused by the act. For example, faulty and ostensibly illegal loans by bank officials caused great personal pain and anguish, but these actions were often justified as overzealous business practices of people "caught up" in a quest to be successful. Corporate leaders often attempt to justify actions of corporate criminals as simply bad judgment by lower-level employees, even when the leaders actually encouraged a culture of fraudulent criminal activity in the name of personal gain and corporate profit.

Compare the possible perceptions of and reactions to white-collar crime and "welfare fraud," or fraudulent behavior by recipients of public assistance. People relying on benefits such as food stamps and Temporary Assistance for Needy Families have passed means tests (qualification requirements) documenting their dire economic circumstances. Presumably, people struggling to provide for children and families sometimes falsify information to qualify. Although their actions are illegal, their desperation to provide for family members is perhaps more justifiable than the greed of corporate criminals. Yet the general public often views "welfare cheats" as more reprehensible than corporate criminals. Although welfare fraud has an economic and political impact on government spending for social services, that impact usually pales in comparison with the extent and depth of the pain caused by greedy financiers and investment bankers.

TIME TO THINK

Think about your own attitudes regarding work, individual responsibility, and success. How might those values affect your ability to work with people who have been convicted of a crime?

CURRENT TRENDS

Prosecution of Fraud

FRAUD is endemic to our society, for the same reasons theft is endemic. However, fraud typically involves people in positions of trust and power, presenting unique challenges for detection and prosecution. Even following the financial shenanigans during the mid-2000s, few cases of fraud were brought to court. However, the ramifications of fraud, a crime perpetrated by the people we entrust with our financial resources, can be broad and long lasting. Some fraud victims become impoverished and never recover, and their trust in people with power and privilege is destroyed.

One notorious case of fraud that was prosecuted was perpetrated by Bernie Madoff, arguably the world's most famous white-collar criminal. Over a number of years, Madoff swindled thousands of investors out of an estimated $50 billion, falsely and fraudulently offering them high return rates for their money. He operated a Ponzi scheme, in which earlier investors received relatively little in returns but instead got some of the investment money coming from later investors.

Madoff's fraudulent work impacted the value of stocks and in many cases wiped out entire retirement accounts. The devastation was not limited to individual investors; investment accounts of charitable organizations (e.g., the Betty and Norman F. Levy Foundation and the Picower Foundation) also suffered losses, undermining their ability to operate their organizations and provide support and grants to various nonprofit and social service organizations.

Unlike many people of power and privilege who are convicted of fraud, Madoff was punished severely. Although he was an older adult when convicted, he is now serving a 150-year sentence in prison, sending a message that this type of behavior is highly unacceptable.

▲ Bernie Madoff was convicted in 2009 of operating one of the largest Ponzi schemes in American history.

How does white-collar crime impact social work practice? What kinds of services can social workers offer to victims of white-collar crime, who may struggle with both economic loss and trust issues?

MENTAL HEALTH AND CRIMINAL JUSTICE

One prevailing belief in the United States is that the criminal justice system is a haven for people with serious mental illness. As Chapter 9 explained, in the 1960s, mental health services were deinstitutionalized, and jails and prisons increasingly became the default residence for people with serious mental illness who caused too many problems in the community. Simply stated, in lieu of receiving the residential mental health services they needed, members of this population were arrested for manifesting symptoms of their mental illnesses.

Social workers have been long-standing advocates for programs to address the needs of people experiencing mental health challenges. People with mental illness who end up in jail for inappropriate and unlawful behavior particularly need assistance. The increasing number of mental health and drug courts is a sign of progress, but convincing public officials and decision makers to invest in mental health programs and decriminalizing mental health is a challenge.

EXHIBIT 12.4   Five Premises About Criminal Justice and People With Severe Mental Illness

PREMISE	SUPPORT AND CONSIDERATIONS FOR PREMISE
People with serious mental illness have been criminalized.	It has been determined that a disproportionate number of people in the criminal justice system are experiencing mental health challenges.
Deinstitutionalization is the cause of criminalization.	Deinstitutionalization of people with severe mental illness appears to be a valid consideration for the criminalization of that population.
The number of people with severe mental illness continues to grow.	This premise requires more research. The answer is important to advocate for appropriate services and programs, especially in relation to the criminal justice system.
Treating people with severe mental illness will lower recidivism.	This premise requires more research. However, as a human rights issue, it can be said that people with severe mental illness deserve humane treatment and appropriate intervention that could prevent future imprisonment.
The criminal justice system is ill equipped to handle people with severe mental illness.	This is a premise that few would argue against. Support within prisons for the population of people with severe mental illness is inadequate in terms of both availability and quality. Although costly, additional mental health services are a more appropriate and humane alternative to prison.

Source: Lurigio (2011, pp. 11–15).

Social workers can educate and challenge people in positions of power about people with mental health issues in the criminal justice system (Lurigio, 2011). Exhibit 12.4 lists five underlying premises about criminal justice and people with severe mental illness that social workers tend to accept; it also describes the degree to which those premises are supported by research and values.

ISSUES AFFECTING CHILDREN AND YOUTH

Children and youth are of particular interest to social workers practicing in the criminal justice system because it is possible, with early and appropriate interventions, to help them avoid becoming embroiled in the system themselves. Young people may benefit from help in coping with the traumatic and subversive effects of the crime around them. They may also need social workers' intervention to help them overcome the influence of their life experiences and keep them out of the criminal justice system.

Social workers in various practice areas become familiar with many of the available services and methods for helping children and youth. Beyond child protective services, social workers assist and partner with family support and training programs, early childhood intervention programs, programs for offenders and victims, and educational awareness campaigns. Two common issues impacting children and youth are examined here in greater depth.

Exposure and Desensitization to Violent Behavior

Many factors contribute to the development of criminal and violent behavior among children and youth. Exposure to violence via television, movies, social media, music, and video games is commonly cited. For example, violent video games appear to increase aggressive thoughts and behavior and physiological arousal; additionally, they negatively influence helping behavior (Anderson & Bushman, 2001). As a result of repeated exposure, youth can experience **desensitization**, decreased sensitivity to fear about certain acts, which increases their risk of engaging in violent behavior toward others.

One social work response to this issue is advocacy for violence rating systems for media and games, as well as parental education about overseeing children's exposure to violence in media. Social workers also partner with other professionals and parental groups to advocate for legislation, policies, and practices that promote technological capabilities to help parents monitor and block violent media and programming (Long & Holle, 2007, p. 52).

Parental Imprisonment

Social workers commonly work with families in which one or more parental figures have been or are presently imprisoned. The impact of parental imprisonment on children is complex. It includes loss, trauma, lack of understanding, anxiety, frustration, embarrassment, stigma, and instability in income and supervision. Social workers help children and families with these issues. For example, children are prone to bottling up their emotions. They may also need reassurance that they have not done anything wrong or do not bear responsibility for the ill fate of their parent. Social workers also serve as change agents advocating for policies and practices protecting the rights and developmental needs of children, regardless of their parents' criminal status.

DIVERSITY AND CRIMINAL JUSTICE

People from all social and economic backgrounds commit crimes. However, variables such as race, age, gender, and social class are related to crime and punishment in a variety of ways, influencing who is investigated, charged, and sentenced. The demographics of criminals are also associated with the types of crimes they commit. Social workers are also aware that members of various population groups have varying levels of trust in police officers, court officials, prosecutors, attorneys, and corrections officers. Trust or mistrust is developed as a result of cultural beliefs as well as previous experience, observation, and perception.

Law enforcement officials have their own issues with trust and mistrust. They are known for **profiling** criminals, using their stereotyped understanding about the types of people who commit crimes to identify and question suspects. For example, the phrase "driving while black" is a reference to racial profiling, indicating traffic police's tendency to stop African American drivers for presumed illegal activity more often than they stop people from other racial and ethnic groups (Carl, 2012).

Here are some other ways diversity affects a person's experience with the criminal justice system:

- *Age.* Crime has a long-known and distinct relationship with age, often referenced as the "age–crime curve." Crime rates peak during the teen years, followed by a rapid decline that continues through adulthood. The profound and complex developmental changes that occur during adolescence and young adulthood—related to maturity, impulse control, peer-group association, and identity formation—impact interpersonal functioning as well as the likelihood of involvement in crimes (Sweeten, Piquero, & Steinberg, 2013).

- *Class.* People from impoverished areas are more likely for many reasons to be identified and classified as criminals. One of these reasons is that, because of their limited resources, poor people are easier both to catch and to convict (Carl, 2012). Affluent people can afford to hire expensive attorneys and build formidable defenses that challenge prosecutors, who might back away from full prosecution of the crime if going forward would result in time-consuming and expensive trials. In contrast, poor people rely on court-appointed attorneys with large caseloads and less time to devote to their clients. Many social work clients cannot afford costly legal services and, as a result, are disproportionately at risk of being labeled as criminals and subjected to stiffer legal charges and penalties. The disadvantage of the poor in the legal system is why social workers advocate for quality legal services for all.

- *Ethnicity.* Crime statistics show strong variations in the links between ethnic groups and crime rates and types of crime. For instance, African Americans and Latin Americans are overrepresented in crime rates, and European Americans and Asian Americans are associated with the lowest crime rates. Asian Americans, frequently referenced as a "model minority" because of their high median levels of education and income, include Asian Indians, Chinese, Filipinos, Japanese, Koreans, Vietnamese, and people from other, smaller Asian countries. When Asian Americans are convicted of crimes, the severity of their punishment is similar to that of European American offenders, which is less severe than that of African American and Latin American offenders (Johnson & Betsinger, 2009).

- *Race.* The relationship between race and crime in the United States has been a long-standing topic of research and debate. Considerable data exist describing how African Americans disproportionately account for arrests and face discriminatory prison terms. It is also true that African Americans and Caucasians view the criminal justice system very differently. Blacks and Hispanics are wary of police

The Death Penalty and the Developing Brain

In 2009, 11-year-old Jordan Brown was accused of the murder of Kenzie Houk, a Pennsylvania woman who was 8 months pregnant, and her unborn child (Chen, 2010). Jordan is the son of the victim's fiancé. It is unusual for a child this young to be accused of murder and to be considered for trial as an adult. If convicted as an adult, Jordan faced the possibility of 14 years to life in prison without parole.

Many people and organizations, including Amnesty International, asserted that Jordan was too young to be sentenced as an adult, no matter how heinous the crime. Laurence Steinberg of Temple University drew the following analogy: "The teenage brain is like a car with a good accelerator but a weak brake. With powerful impulses under poor control, the likely result is a crash" (Chen, 2010). Indeed, at the age of 11, Jordan's impulse control would conceivably be even less mature than that of a teenager.

In fact, in 2005, the U.S. Supreme Court banned the death penalty for juveniles after considering the research literature on adolescent brain development (Chen, 2010). Jordan was sentenced in 2012 to a state juvenile facility, where he will remain until he turns 21.

What is your opinion about how Jordan should be punished? What kind of proof of rehabilitation would you require for him to be released from incarceration, as opposed to his simply turning 21 years old?

and the courts because of their historical and contemporary experience of prejudicial treatment; whites tend to believe that police and law enforcement are benign and necessary to people's safety (Weitzer & Tuch, 2004). It is important for social workers to understand that although racial minorities may exhibit a degree of skepticism and doubt about the criminal justice system, they may not be specifically antipolice.

- *Gender.* Women do commit crimes, but in the case of violent crime, a woman is more likely to be the victim than the offender. To identify problems, provide intervention, and advocate for services specific to female victims, social workers strive to understand the contextual factors. For example, women who are victims of violent crime (especially rape) vary in reporting those crimes based on whether they live in an urban, rural, or suburban area (Rennison, Dragiewicz, & DeKeseredy, 2013). In rural areas, women are less likely to report rape because of social pressure, especially from the "good ol' boy network." Social workers must be ready to work with women and others in the community to confront people and practices dedicated to maintaining a patriarchal status quo (Rennison et al., 2013).

- *Sexual orientation.* Victims of hate crimes based on sexual orientation often find it difficult to report offenses. Perpetrators include neighbors, coworkers, and relatives but can also be strangers in public places. Victims struggle over whether to report crimes to police, in fear of disclosure of their sexual orientation and concern about whether perpetrators will be charged and how they will be punished (Herek, Cogan, & Gillis, 2002). Insight concerning the impact of antigay crimes is vital when practicing with this population group. Often, LGBTQ (lesbian, gay, bisexual, transgender, and questioning) victims educate social workers as to various types of hate crimes and the associated behaviors. Through this knowledge, social workers not only better understand the intricacies associated with hate crimes, but they learn how to partner with and empower LGBTQ victims to improve reporting processes and develop effective policies and legislation governing disclosure of hate crimes.

- *Intersections of diversity.* Consider the challenges that might be associated with being a young Latino male living in an impoverished section of town. Profiling is nearly a certainty, whether by police, bystanders, prosecutors, teachers, medical personnel, or the general public. The tendency would often be to identify such a young man as a criminal or gang member. But is such an inclination based on ethnicity, age, gender, class, or a combination of these characteristics? Social workers are dedicated to seeing each person as a unique human being and debunking stereotypes and detrimental labels in everyday life. They realize that various forms of diversity are elements of one's sense of self and need not define a person's overall being.

ADVOCACY AND CRIMINAL JUSTICE

Social workers enter their profession because they not only want to help people but are dedicated to advocating for and with the disadvantaged (Whitaker, 2008, p. 4). Empowerment is a primary tenet in advocating for changes and reform in the criminal justice systems. The perspective of persons who have been involved with the system and who are oppressed by it is necessary for creating fair and just policies and practices regarding laws, courts, and corrections. Victims of crime know best what can be helpful for their recovery and well-being; criminals have firsthand experience with unjust treatment.

Community leaders, police officers, attorneys, judges, correctional staff, and other officials in the criminal justice system do not always agree with the premise that social work clients (victims and criminals) should be afforded an active voice to inform or impact change. This is especially true for criminals, as many people believe an incarcerated person should have few or minimum rights.

People in positions of power (such as politicians, elected officials, and community leaders) also have a vested interest in the status quo and may believe their ideas about what is right or wrong and legal or illegal should prevail. Their views extend into decisions about law enforcement, punishment, and correction. Typically, social workers are hired in agencies and programs supported by funding sources controlled by powerful people. In an organizational environment dedicated to conformity, control, and punishment, a social worker's advocacy for reform and the rights of criminals can be risky.

In such an environment, advocating for the rights and fair treatment of clients who are criminals and victims of crime depends on having accurate data. Social workers play an important role in identifying, acquiring, analyzing, and disseminating information, as well as educating the public and decision makers about the causes and impacts of crime.

ECONOMIC AND SOCIAL JUSTICE

Unfortunately, justice in the legal system depends in large part on the accused person's status and assets. People with influence and money who are accused of crime not only acquire some of the best legal representation available but also can mount a formidable challenge to a legal system and its resources. Their money and status buy them access to research, expert witnesses, and consultants. Prosecutors do in fact make decisions to pursue cases, settle for plea bargains, or dismiss charges based on the merits of the evidence as well as expected use of public resources to pursue a charge through trial. In contrast, people without money or status who are accused of a crime have to rely on legal aid services.

Social workers involved in the criminal justice system advocate for the protection and rights of the poor by

- identifying and promoting competent legal representation for all;
- working with attorneys and court and corrections officials to advance just policies, practices, and laws for victims and criminals;
- confronting and combatting discriminatory practices in the criminal justice system;
- ensuring that the accused are assessed properly and are competent to face charges and stand trial; and
- promoting safe, proper, and humane treatment of the poor in correctional facilities.

SUPPORTIVE ENVIRONMENT

In many respects, people are a result of their environment. Healthy living conditions and circumstances for children, adolescents, and young adults can be instrumental in discouraging and thwarting criminal behavior. Safe neighborhoods, a stable family unit, good schools, extracurricular activities, positive peer relations, quality mental health and addiction services, positive role models and support networks (e.g., friends and churches), comprehensive health services, and enriching recreational facilities are valuable environmental assets in human development. However, they are not available to everyone. Social workers involved with children, youth, and families can help forestall criminal behavior by advocating for all these kinds of environmental support.

CURRENT TRENDS

Privilege and Prosecution of Crimes

DR. Atiq Durrani was a prominent spine surgeon in the Cincinnati area. He is facing federal criminal charges for fraudulent charges to Medicare and dozens of lawsuits from former patients who accuse him of performing unnecessary surgeries.

Durrani pleaded not guilty to federal charges in August of 2013, but 4 months later the U.S. Attorney's Office reported that he had fled the country. This occurred even though Durrani had been forced to hand over his passport to federal officials and was forbidden to travel outside of the country (Bernard-Kuhn, 2014). An international warrant for his arrest was issued.

Speculatively, Durrani used his resources to flee to a country that refuses to extradite (return) people to the United States. Physicians are respected and well-compensated professionals, and they have the resources to flee punishment in ways that less-privileged individuals cannot. Durrani is believed to be residing in Pakistan.

How do crimes such as this affect the victims and society as a whole? What needs might Durrani's former patients have that could be met by social workers?

Conversely, consider life in crime- and gang-ridden neighborhoods. Gangs offer teenagers and young adults a social unit to meet their personal, economic, and social needs. Gangs also provide a source of identity and power to their members. To combat the influence of gangs, social workers partner with community officials to provide healthy alternatives, such as job training, employment, mentorship programs, and sporting activities. Environments characterized by economic deprivation are especially challenging. Without real economic and social opportunity, many youth are lured toward gang life and lucrative criminal behaviors such as selling drugs and theft, which offer quick but dangerous relief from their deprivation.

HUMAN NEEDS AND RIGHTS

Social workers are uniquely educated and trained to assess the complex, multifaceted needs of victims and criminals. Their holistic outlook and biopsychosocial-spiritual perspective, as compared with that of individualism, differentiates social workers from other helping professionals. In assessing a client's situation, social workers seek to respect the person's inherent worth and ability to define what she or he needs given a particular social situation and circumstances. Thus, advocacy is centered on what the client presents as

needs, not necessarily what the social worker believes the client needs.

Within criminal justice, however, social workers have a dual responsibility both to their clients and to the greater society. This is how the National Association of Social Workers (2008) *Code of Ethics* states it:

Social workers should promote the general welfare of society, from local to global levels, and the development of people, their communities, and their environments. (Sec. 6.01)

Social workers should engage in social and political action that seeks to ensure that all people have equal access to the resources, employment, services, and opportunities they require to meet their basic human needs and to develop fully. (Sec. 6.04)

Thus, while social workers respect and abide by laws, they also seek to change and advance laws that both benefit their clients and protect all people. Advocacy for needs and rights is not without boundaries. For example, it would be contrary to the *Code of Ethics* to advocate for policies and laws that exploit, dominate, oppress, or discriminate against people.

POLITICAL ACCESS

Laws and criminal behavior are by definition political. Legislative bodies make laws defining criminal behavior for implementation in a jurisdiction. Social workers advocate and support politicians and pieces of legislation to address the needs and rights of all people, including clients labeled as criminals. As earlier noted, this type of advocacy is often unpopular with politicians and the general public. Even when prisoners are mistreated and abused during incarceration, there is a tendency for people to blame the victims.

To complicate matters, in recent years, support for social programs, including services for victims and criminals, has faced stiff political opposition based on both ideology and concerns about funding, "as government coffers have been drained by increasing need, economic troubles, and anti-tax philosophy among the vocal public" (Hoefer, 2012, p. 21). Unfortunately, decisions made on these bases can have a serious effect on poor and oppressed people interacting with the criminal justice system. Ultimately, society as a whole may suffer an increase in crime and a decrease in security when programs to help these people are underfunded or eliminated.

social workers listing mental health as their primary practice (Whitaker & Arrington, 2008). Arguably, social work has a limited presence of employment within the criminal justice system. A number of factors conceivably contribute to this employment outlook, including a gender factor (e.g., the predominance of women in the profession of social work), the rehabilitative and treatment orientation of social work, restrictive work conditions, and the politicized nature of hiring in the criminal justice system.

Even if a social worker does not work in the area of forensic social work, she or he will likely practice at some point with victims of crime and offenders. This is true for social workers in schools, health care facilities, family service organizations, nonprofit agencies, and a variety of public and governmental entities. Social workers also serve as consultants, expert witnesses, parole and probation officers, as well as court officials and legislators. In many human service agencies, social workers partner with attorneys and judges to create and implement entities such as mental health and drug courts, where offenders are provided with opportunities to undergo treatment instead of imprisonment.

BSW social workers can find job opportunities in this field. However, a growing number of social workers are interested in acquiring advanced education and training in criminal justice social work via MSW and law programs. Some graduate programs in social work have already partnered with law schools to offer students the ability to acquire MSW and law degrees simultaneously. Graduate education in **criminology** (the scientific study of criminal behavior) is another option for enhancing a BSW degree.

TIME TO THINK

To what extent should the rights of criminals be limited? Criminals are expected to follow rules and regulations during their incarceration. However, should criminals have the right to quality health and mental services during imprisonment? What are the potential ramifications for prisoners and the general welfare of society if prisoners do not receive appropriate health and mental health services?

Who should bear the responsibility of funding services and programs for prisoners? Why?

YOUR CAREER IN CRIMINAL JUSTICE

Interestingly, only 1% of social workers report their primary practice area as criminal justice, compared with 35% of

TIME TO THINK

What is your history with victims of crime and criminals? When considering your experiences and value orientation, would you be able to effectively practice with members of these population groups? Is employment involving legal, court, and correctional systems appealing to you. If so, why? Is forensic social work a viable career option?

SUMMARY

Injustice anywhere is a threat to justice everywhere.

—Martin Luther King Jr.

In nearly every walk of life, people are confronted with crime and criminal behavior. Only a relatively small percentage of social workers will enter forensic social work and specialize in criminal justice–oriented practice. However, most social workers will interface with the criminal justice and legal system, primarily in the context of their practice with individuals and families.

Social work's comprehensive, biopsychosocial view of offenders and victims of crimes is especially noteworthy. People are unique and are all entitled to their dignity. They are influenced by and products of a social and cultural and familial environment over which they may not have had much control.

It is important to remember that many offenders have been victims themselves. For a variety of reasons, they are likely to view their criminal acts differently than helping professionals and officials of the criminal justice system do. We should listen to those views and have compassion for their predicament.

TOP 10 KEY CONCEPTS

correctional system
crime
criminal justice system
criminals
forensic social work

laws
plea bargaining
recidivism
restorative justice perspective
Uniform Crime Report

DISCUSSION QUESTIONS

1. Are any crimes victimless? Use drug addiction as an example. How does drug addiction impact other people and society as a whole? Should people with addictions be viewed as criminals or as people with a treatable disease or both?

2. When is a person labeled as a criminal? Who bestows the label and why? How does labeling constitute a challenge in social work practice?

3. As a result of incarceration, what (if any) rights should a prisoner have to relinquish? Does the answer to this

question have any relationship to the type and severity of crime—if so, why?

4. How can social workers advocate for rehabilitative services and programs in the criminal justice system?

5. Why aren't more social workers and helping professionals employed in the criminal justice system? If social work practice has lost a foothold in legal and criminal systems, how might it be regained?

EXERCISES

1. Visit a court proceeding. What are the characteristics (e.g., gender, race, ethnicity, age) of people being prosecuted in comparison with those of court officials? Is the culture of the courtroom control and punishment oriented? Are people simply being processed, or is there an effort to understand their background and rationales? How do the attorneys differ in how they show respect in the courtroom?

2. Consider joining a volunteer group that visits prisoners. After your visit, describe how it feels to be in a prison and behind bars. What are topics of interest among prisoners?

Do prisoners accept responsibility for their actions? Do they receive help during incarceration and articulate any sense of being able to move forward in their lives?

3. Investigate the duties and procedures of your university's student disciplinary board. Does it seem that student criminal activity is viewed differently than criminal behavior in the general population? If so, how? If you know someone involved in the student disciplinary board, ask that person about her or his perceptions of the system. You might also consider becoming a member of the disciplinary board.

4. Some community leadership academies offer "ride alongs" with police officers. People can accompany on-duty police offers in their patrol cars. Sign up to participate and then report on what you observed. How would you characterize the authority and discretion afforded police officers in the community?

5. Ask a criminal defense attorney about her or his practice and the types of criminals served. How does the attorney view helping professionals, particularly social workers? Would the attorney recommend law school as an option for social workers—if so, what kind of law?

6. Have you ever been charged with or convicted of a crime? Would your criminal record pose a problem for your entry

into a professional field such as social work? Depending on the charge(s), many state social work boards provide applicants with the chance to describe and explain the circumstances surrounding a crime and what the applicant has done since the criminal behavior. If you are interested in social work as a major and have a criminal record, examine your state's licensure board website and the content relating to criminal records and licensure. You might also want to discuss the ramifications of any criminal past with one of your social work professors, who could share or point you toward relevant information for your state.

ONLINE RESOURCES

- Corrections.com (www.corrections.com): Provides news, perspectives, and stories about prison and parole issues
- FBI's Uniform Crime Reports (www.fbi.gov/about-us/cjis/ucr/ucr): Serve as the primary source of information about crime in the United States
- Mental Health and Criminal Justice website (kristinarandle.com/blog/15-criminal-justice-career-options-for-social-

workers): Describes criminal justice career options for social workers
- National Organization of Forensic Social Work (nofsw.org): Promotes and is recognized as a leading national organization for forensic social work
- Social Work and Criminal Justice website (sw-cj.org): Promotes social work research and teaching with regard to criminal justice

STUDENT STUDY SITE

Sharpen your skills with SAGE edge at **edge.sagepub.com/cox**

SAGE edge for Students provides a personalized approach to help you accomplish your coursework goals in an easy-to-use learning environment.

WORKING IN CHANGING CONTEXTS

PART 3

Chapter 13: COMMUNITIES AT RISK AND HOUSING

Learning Objectives

After reading this chapter, you should be able to

1. Describe the relevance of community practice in social work.
2. Explain what puts communities at risk.
3. List the major forms of housing.
4. Define major considerations for a person buying a home or renting an apartment.
5. Explain the link between poverty and segregation and their effect on communities.
6. Describe social work advocacy with housing and communities at risk.

Tonya Supports Residents of Federally Subsidized Housing

Tonya is one of two social workers providing outreach, crisis, and preventive services to residents living in a 250-unit apartment building operated and managed by the City Housing Authority (CHA). In an attempt to "take social services to the clients," city and county officials have partnered with several private organizations to employ the two social workers at the CHA apartments.

Located in a densely populated and economically depressed borough of a large northeastern city, the CHA apartments provide federally subsidized housing to predominantly single-parent mothers receiving Temporary Assistance for Needy Families, Medicaid, and food stamps. Individual apartments are older one- and two-bedroom units, frequently in need of repair (e.g., carpets, plumbing, appliances). The surrounding neighborhood is characterized by a high crime rate, very few job opportunities, vacated buildings, a struggling public school system, ineffective public bus transportation, and an abundance of convenient food and alcohol marts.

Most of Tonya's career as a BSW-level social worker has been in the area of domestic violence. The CHA hired Tonya to work with residents to address basic needs, perform crisis intervention, enhance the stability of residents, assist residents with educational and employment opportunities through a public assistance to work program, and provide individual- and group-level support to women and their children who have experienced domestic violence.

Tonya has formed a resident council to advocate alongside residents for needed services as well as policy changes at the CHA apartments. The resident council has secured a meeting space and organized support groups, which meet at convenient times and provide organized child care. The leadership of CHA relies heavily on the resident council as an important voice and source of information for CHA program and policy development.

Client success outcomes have been impressive, with the average resident at CHA apartments exiting subsidized housing a full 9 months earlier than several years ago. One of Tonya's responsibilities is to track client success. Survey data indicate that since the implementation of social work services at the CHA apartments, residents have become increasingly hopeful and positive about their futures.

Housing constitutes a basic human need and is a key factor for defining one's social status and well-being (Rizvi, 2012, p. 14). Safe, affordable, and adequate shelter for living can be viewed as a fundamental right for human beings but in reality involves major expenses and considerable human effort. For many Americans, some of the priciest items on their budgets involve housing (e.g., rent, house payment, utilities, upkeep, etc.). The "upfront" costs (e.g., housing deposit, utility activation fees, home furniture/furnishings, and moving costs) can be especially prohibitive for first-time independent dwellers. Out of necessity, many people rely on family members and friends to help offset the expense and labor associated with moving into a new residence.

Housing in the United States not only provides people with places to live but is an important industry in the country's economy. Building and housing involve labor-intensive markets for employment and produce important commodities (e.g., houses, rental properties, condos, retirement communities, dormitories) for constructing, selling, buying, financing, maintaining, insuring, and renting. Consider the number of occupations, skilled and unskilled, associated with real estate and temporary and permanent forms of housing. One measure of the vibrancy of a nation's economy is the strength of its housing and building markets. When housing-oriented markets experience a downturn—as occurred in 2007 at the start of the recession—economic and labor markets falter.

The poor have traditionally experienced **residential instability**, moving frequently and often once a year. They rely on the availability and affordability of inferior housing options, located in less-desirable and economically depressed (slum) dwellings and communities. Add mental health and/or substance issues, and housing decisions for the poor often teeter among low-rental apartments, **doubling up** (temporarily living with relatives or friends), residential treatment sites (e.g., group homes, residential facilities,

sober-living houses), and homeless shelters with episodes of homelessness.

It is important to remember that housing is not available or accessible to all people in the United States. For a variety of economic, social, and health-related reasons, people routinely struggle with the ability to secure safe and adequate housing. In the United States, living circumstances are contingent on one's income, finances, and the availability of affordable housing. People are required to pass credit checks to rent an apartment, townhouse, or home and to qualify for loans in purchasing a home. People at the lower end of the socioeconomic spectrum often have trouble meeting the requirements for good housing.

Beyond its relation to quality of life, where and how a person lives routinely defines and labels that person. In everyday conversation, questions and comments about the community or part of town in which one lives frequently come up, demonstrating the importance of community and housing.

TIME TO THINK

Is homeownership still a part of the American Dream? Think about your reactions to learning where your acquaintances and friends live. Do you view acquaintances and friends differently depending on the community and place in which they dwell. If so, why?

CENTRAL CONCEPTS REGARDING COMMUNITIES AND HOUSING

In the United States, people commonly make reference to living or residing in a particular community, as in a specific geographical area. However, a **community** is a social unit that can be based either on shared geography or similar interests. Nongeographical communities are groupings of people who regularly associate and meet with others to share common interests and concerns (e.g., mutual aid groups, learning communities). **Geographical communities,** in contrast, create social connections through a defined physical territory (locality). Communities develop distinctive identities and subcultures. They are usually a link between individuals and the larger society (Long et al., 2006, p. 118).

With the exception of dwellings in country areas (e.g., farmland and mountains), housing typically exists in the context of a geographical community. If a housing or apartment complex is large enough, with a distinctive subculture, people (e.g., residents in the City Housing Authority apartment building, discussed in this chapter's opening vignette) may view their building and its immediate geographical surrounding as a community. In rural areas, small towns and villages are frequently identified as communities. In large urban areas, geographically defined sections of the city, such as boroughs and neighborhoods, constitute communities.

Communities can be described and classified by a number of characteristics, including the social–economic, racial, sexual orientation, and ethnic composition of their members. Communities also vary concerning the social and economic amenities available. Typically, communities with highly desirable characteristics (e.g., close proximity to water, aesthetically pleasing views, high-end stores, convenient transportation, good schools, quality parks/recreation, entertainment value, etc.) command higher housing costs. Location, convenience, amenities, and appeal are key ingredients for housing values. The name or nickname of a community may be symbolic of the image, charm, or socioeconomic status of that community.

COMMUNITY PRACTICE

Social work has a rich tradition of practice in communities. **Community organizing** is a term used to capture the process by which social workers bring interested people together through neighborhood associations, block parties, organizational affiliations, and religious entities to address social issues and seek solutions (e.g., policy changes, new laws, programs, and services) to community problems. Soliciting the voice and involvement of community members is a key to the success of community organizing. Meaningful

community change occurs when ordinary people partner with community leaders and government officials to identify the specifics of community need and how to take necessary action. Community organizing is a means by which social workers solicit the full and rich involvement of community members in community-level decision making.

Social workers are at an advantage for conducting **community practice** (Perlman & Gurin, 1972). For one thing, they are **analytical** in their ability to use theoretical and research knowledge to inform community practice and change efforts. Social workers also possess **interactional abilities** for relationship building and interpersonal interaction. Effective community practice involves both understanding key components of a community, including the relevance of important factors such as housing, and being able to bring various community actors and stakeholders together for change.

AT-RISK COMMUNITIES

For any number of social and economic reasons, certain communities are deemed as presenting their residents with a higher risk of uncertainty in several areas:

- Public services (e.g., law enforcement, garbage pickup, sewage, electricity, sanitation)
- Hazard (e.g., crime, accidents, unsafe housing, pollution)
- Social norms (e.g., school truancy, begging, prevalence of illicit drug use)

These geographical locations are categorized as **at-risk communities**. At-risk communities can also be thought of as disenfranchised communities. Care should be given to labeling a community as being at risk, however, because the uncertainties constitute only a partial reflection of a community. In addition, being labeled an at-risk community leads to lower property values and a narrower range of businesses and other services, which further degrades the community's reputation.

In social work practice, the relationship between communities at risk and housing is quite relevant, particularly with regard to poverty and inequality. Communities at risk often serve as an undesirable housing option (e.g., temporary refuge) for poverty-stricken people, while many times adding to their overall stress, economic woes, and instability. Poverty-stricken clients who take what they hope will be temporary refuge in a community at risk often describe being stuck and unable to get out. As their overall stress, economic woes, and instability increase, they lose hope of being able to improve the community and make little effort to enhance it. At the same time, the very presence of the poor can deter community investment and social and economic development.

Consider some of the dynamics associated with a crime-ridden urban community characterized by low rent and few, if any, legitimate businesses. Politicians and government officials would typically be reluctant to build or maintain public gathering areas (e.g., parks, theaters, and museums) for fear that they could not keep visitors to these facilities safe and that vandalism would ruin their investment. Police chiefs would question the wisdom and efficacy of deploying police officers into such areas. Business leaders would in turn hesitate to establish economic enterprises in communities with high crime and turn to more affluent and convenient suburban areas. A vicious cycle takes place, ultimately leading to a high concentration of poverty and public housing in specific residential neighborhoods.

HOUSING

In the United States, a major component of the American Dream has been homeownership. However, a great many Americans live in other types of housing. Some people who are capable of buying a home may prefer to rent—perhaps because they are in the midst of a transition or do not want the responsibilities of homeownership, or because the current economy in a locale makes renting more attractive financially. Exhibit 13.1 shows the percentages for renting and owning in the United States.

For the poor, finding housing is mainly an issue of matching available personal resources with very limited, if any, choices. A death or serious illness in the family, personal illness, loss of employment, divorce, or natural disaster can quickly render a person of limited means unable to maintain housing (Giffords & Garber, 2014, p. 147). A logical source of information about possible housing options is family members, friends, and acquaintances, and they can provide information about little-known opportunities, such as room rentals and multifamily space. But looking for new housing through "for rent" postings on the street, in the newspaper, or online often results in finding the smallest affordable spaces and dwellings that are in poor condition or in unsatisfactory neighborhoods (Skobba, Bruin, & Yust, 2013, p. 248). With little money and limited information about housing options, finding new housing often means accepting the "housing of last resort" (Cook, Crull, Fletcher, Hinnant-Bernard, & Peterson, 2002, p. 311).

Homeownership

Homeownership constitutes an important form of investment and savings for many Americans. By purchasing a home in a desirable community, the buyer hopes to maintain or improve the condition of the dwelling so the house experiences **appreciation**, an increase in value. For people able to secure housing loans, homeownership can improve quality of life, is a potential source of pride, and constitutes an important form of investment.

The jump from renting to homeownership is a financial threshold in the United States. People save money and seek the support of family members to secure a down payment for the house, which typically varies between 5% and 20% of the purchase price. In addition to a down payment, buyers

EXHIBIT 13.1   U.S. Households: Renters and Owners

TYPE OF HOUSEHOLD	HOUSEHOLDS (000s)	% OF U.S. TOTAL	RESIDENTS (000s)	% OF U.S. TOTAL
Renter-occupied	43,018	35%	104,194	33%
Owner-occupied	79,484	65%	206,923	67%
Total	122,502	100%	311,117	100%

Source: National Multifamily Housing Council (2013).

are often responsible for realtor fees, closing costs, inspection charges, prepaid insurance, and appraisal costs, which add to the upfront costs and factor into the feasibility of purchasing a home. The remainder of the purchase price is usually covered by taking out a **mortgage**—a long-term housing loan (e.g., for 10, 15, or 30 years) provided through a bank, savings and loan, home lender, or credit union. Getting a mortgage, and a low interest rate on it, requires a good credit history, a reliable source of income, and a prospective home that will hold or increase its value. The interest on a mortgage can be deducted from federal taxes and is a valuable means for further enhancing one's credit history. For poorer Americans, though, building a successful credit history, saving a down payment, and securing a housing loan are substantial barriers to homeownership.

In many ways, the term *homeownership* is a misnomer, as only a relatively small percentage of people in the United States fully own their homes. Instead, until the mortgage is paid off, the purchaser is only paying toward ownership of a home. Because a buyer's **home equity** (paid-off portion of the house value) can be borrowed against, people do not need to own it outright to realize some of its appreciation soon after purchase, assuming home prices are stable or rising. Thus, there are incentives to be in the process of buying a home rather than renting.

Financial planners often caution against investing a vast majority of one's financial resources into any single form of investment, including one's home. Many people learned this lesson the hard way: Faltering housing values from the 2008 recession confirmed the importance of diversified investment strategies.

Rental Housing

Renting a room, apartment, condo, or house typically requires a stable background as well. Renting often involves an application (and fee), background checks (such as criminal, employment, and credit checks), a rental deposit, a legally binding lease agreement, rental insurance, and arrangements to receive and pay for utilities, such as electricity, water, heating, and fuel. People without sound employment, good credit, and a clean criminal background struggle to have rental applications approved.

Out of necessity, people who cannot meet these requirements turn to undesirable and less selective rental properties. One way for people to secure better housing is to have a reputable cosigner share responsibility for rent and damages

⋏ Wells Fargo has been a dominant housing loan originator in the United States.

Source: ©iStockphoto.com/wdstock

to the dwelling. But potential cosigners may be reluctant to enter into a rental agreement, particularly if they are concerned about the inhabitant's ability to pay rent and cover damages. As an example, people with substance and chemical dependency issues may have alienated friends and family members to the degree that they will avoid any financial entanglements.

Subsidized Housing

Subsidized housing is a general term referencing government-supported housing, which is willing to accept low-income populations as renters as long as the renter or housing owner is receiving official financial assistance. Historically, in the United States there have been many forms of housing subsidies, including the following:

- Nonprofit housing
- Public housing
- Rent supplements
- Interest deductions (a federal tax break afforded to home buyers to subsidize housing costs)
- **Section 8 vouchers** (certificates provided through the U.S. Department of Housing and Urban Development [HUD] for use with both nonprofit and for-profit housing)

Federally assisted housing often also includes social services to help low-income residents transition and move to nonsubsidized housing (Cohen, Mulroy, Tull, White, & Crowley, 2004). In this chapter's opening vignette, the City

SOCIAL WORK IN ACTION

Joanna Finds Housing for Clients in a Rural Area

JOANNA is a social worker employed with the Department of Children and Family Services in a rural county in the Midwest. As one of three social workers at her agency, she has a wide range of responsibilities, including identifying and promoting community-based housing with her clients. Joanna works closely with the local Salvation Army, homeless shelter, and United Way office to maintain a current list of subsidized and unsubsidized rental units. Although Joanna avoids endorsing particular landlords or rental properties, she remains familiar with the strengths (e.g., affordability and access) and challenges (e.g., safety and transportation issues) associated with each rental option. Immediate occupancy is frequently a key issue for her clients. Joanna has developed relationships with landlords and rental property managers to advocate for the ability of her clients to sign a lease and transition quickly into a housing unit, often with a minimal security deposit. Within the past year, area churches have initiated a program for converting former parsonages, houses designated for

a minister's dwelling, into a network of affordable housing units for the poor. Joanna has been a partner and advocate for this effort. Many congregations have developed plans to transform parsonages into duplexes—separate, two-family dwellings.

Churches and many charitable organizations possess vacant space. Converting unused space into suitable housing must conform to zoning restrictions and can be expensive and labor intensive. However, initiatives such as Habitat for Humanity have demonstrated that volunteers, helping professionals, nonprofit organizations, and corporate partners can be very successful in working hand in hand to develop affordable housing for the poor.

Does this level of community involvement with organizations, programs, and professionals excite you? What are your beginning thoughts about working with religious organizations and churches that have beliefs and values different from your own?

Housing Authority is an example of both subsidized and federally assisted housing.

Shared Housing

During difficult times, low-income people may be able to live temporarily with family members or friends, an arrangement sometimes referred to as doubling up. This is a traditional form of informal housing assistance and support. At face value, the sharing of one's home with others appears both admirable and gracious, but it does have costs. Allowing others to stay in your home increases expenses for utilities and food, provides additional household wear and tear, and strains relationships.

Homes can be conceptualized as protective spaces that allow people to eat, sleep, relax, converse, express intimacy, exercise, play, and work in privacy and at times of their choosing. Guests, especially people living in another person's home, disrupt lifestyle and violate personal space. Doubling up also creates a risk that family members and friends will

step across relational boundaries and become intrusive and overly involved in the lives of others.

When household costs mount, tensions about contributing to rent, utilities, and food may become points of discussion and conflict. Thus, although doubling up typically does not involve a formal leasing agreement, it can be helpful to establish mutually agreeable social and financial expectations before people double up. This is a proactive task that can be facilitated by a social worker.

Halfway Houses

Another form of temporary housing, **halfway houses** are designed to facilitate transition from a restrictive inpatient residence or incarceration to independent, community-based housing. Staffing, supervision, and structure are provided to allow residents to gradually assume responsibility for the activities and responsibilities necessary for independent living.

Many halfway houses employ behavior modification and reinforcement techniques, where residents acquire points for

CURRENT TRENDS

More Beds for Heroin Addicts

BUTLER County (Ohio), located just north of Cincinnati, is creating additional residential beds for treating heroin addicts. Readily available and low cost, heroin has resurfaced in many communities as a highly addictive and destructive drug of choice. In Butler County, overall residential treatment space has increased to 82 beds, and for men space has doubled to 24 beds (McLaughlin, 2014). The need for additional residential services for men is of particular concern. Fortunately, "Medicaid expansion has made it possible to offer residential treatment for more men in Butler County, who weren't eligible for Medicaid before" (p. A12). Agencies in Butler County are planning to add two new residential facilities and expand intensive outpatient services to address the heroin epidemic.

Butler County is not alone in this, as many U.S. counties and states are overwhelmed by heroin addiction, often viewed as a cheaper alternative for people addicted to pain pills and medication. In nearby Kentucky, heroin addiction is such a hot topic that politicians have actively embraced support for preventive and rehabilitative services in their political campaigns

Who should bear the responsibility for paying for costly residential addiction services? When appropriate services are unavailable, are addicts simply prone to end up in jail or dead?

---

completion of mutually agreed-on activities needed for independent living—for example, cleaning one's room, seeking employment, attending school, maintaining personal hygiene, observing curfew, making meals, demonstrating appropriate interpersonal actions, completing house chores, and participating in group meetings. Residents accumulate points for completing these tasks, and with a certain number of points, they can obtain additional privileges, such as extended curfews, more groceries, visitations, and accelerated transition to independent living. Failure to obtain a specified number of points could lead to expulsion from the halfway house.

Shelters

Shelters are short-term havens for people to inhabit during a life transition. Emergency shelters are constructed to provide immediate accommodations for victims of natural catastrophes, such as hurricanes, floods, earthquakes, and tornadoes. Homeless individuals and families may also temporarily rely on homeless shelters for a place to stay. Female survivors of domestic violence may seek safe living conditions in undisclosed shelters for women and their children.

To use limited resources efficiently, shelters frequently involve **communal living**, where people eat and sleep in common, shared areas. Although shelters are designed to address the basic needs of shelter and food, they often lack privacy and impose restrictions governing the length of one's stay. They often also mandate participation in assessment for placement in an alternative form of housing. Shelters are designed to accommodate a disruption in life, with admirable intentions, but their temporary and communal nature can be a source of anxiety and stress for the people who use them.

Residential Treatment Centers and Hospitalization

Inpatient treatment refers to intervention taking place in an overnight residential treatment center or hospital. **Outpatient treatment**, sometimes called partial treatment, occurs when clients partake of intervention services at a treatment center without staying overnight. Residential treatment centers and hospitalization are appropriate options when people require intensive therapy and a high degree of professional supervision (e.g., for detoxification, drug treatment, or stabilization with mental health) and outpatient treatment has been deemed insufficient (e.g., the client could be harmful to self or others).

Residential treatment and hospitalization are costly; so people recommended for this type of treatment are carefully scrutinized by insurance companies and providers, who seek to reserve inpatient treatment for only the most difficult and needy clients. Inpatient treatment is often **capitated** by insurance companies, meaning that they place strict limitations on the number of nights or amount of service allowable, depending on diagnosis.

SOCIAL WORK PRACTICE IN HOUSING AND COMMUNITIES

Social workers are frequently called on as educators and sources of information for clients who need referrals to housing options managed by organizations, providers of services, and agencies. Many people in the United States struggle with basic knowledge concerning housing terminology and types of housing. To complicate matters, when in a crisis situation, people find it very difficult to think about crucial needs such as housing. In almost any area of practice (e.g., health, mental health, children and families, substance abuse), social workers develop expertise with regard to community housing resources and options for their clients. They also advocate for client rights with landlords and promote the availability of affordable, safe, healthy, and supportive community housing.

This aspect of social work can be more difficult than it sounds because of the discrepancy in social status between social workers and clients. Many professionals, including social workers, live in circumstances that are much less risky than those of their clients. Professionals have a college or graduate degree, relatively stable jobs and homes, and family incomes that are at the median or higher for this society. They can afford to ignore the riskiness of daily life. Their clients' lives typically exist on shakier ground (Meenaghan, Kilty, Long, & McNutt, 2013, p. 164).

CLIENTS' HOUSING ISSUES

Even once social work clients find housing, maintaining a stable place to live can be difficult. Their precarious finances leave them vulnerable to risks and losses of various kinds. Social workers can help clients mitigate these risks by encouraging financial and career planning, and wrapping around appropriate supportive services (e.g., outpatient mental health, family, and addiction services).

Foreclosure

Foreclosure occurs when a residential mortgage borrower ceases making loan payments or otherwise violates the terms of the mortgage. The lender then has the right to take legal action to terminate the loan and repossess or sell the property. By foreclosing on the loan, the lender hopes to protect and recoup its assets. The recession and housing meltdown of the 2000s resulted in a proliferation of foreclosures. Some lenders greatly profited from making unrealistic, "bad" loans to people incapable of assuming such debt. Meanwhile, sudden, widespread layoffs impacted the ability of many homeowners to keep up with their mortgage payments.

Because foreclosure involves a legal process, homeowners at risk of falling behind on their payments and failing to comply with the terms of their mortgage are often counseled to seek legal advice. For example, lenders may be willing to negotiate with an attorney and work with an individual or family to save the investment in the home if a good-faith plan to meet the terms of the mortgage can be put into action.

From a social work and social justice perspective, it is important to point out that with the 2008 mortgage and foreclosure crisis, many social work clients lost their homes and were penalized for their bad choices. Many of these poor mortgage decisions were a result of bad financial advice by lenders, who failed in their duty to vet potential buyers for creditworthiness; yet the affluent banking officials and others who did so much to precipitate the foreclosure crisis were insulated from the suffering experienced by people who lost their homes.

Social workers employed in a variety of social service agencies routinely work with homeowners experiencing setbacks to identify ways to save their homes and navigate challenging economic circumstances. Social workers also advocate for fair lending policies, programs, and processes that promote the abilities of clients to buy homes and maintain homeownership.

Landlords

The person or entity renting a housing unit to a renter or tenant is a **landlord**. Larger rental companies typically own a number of rental properties in a geographical area and employ property managers, leasing representatives, and maintenance people for management, upkeep, and repair responsibilities. Individual landlords owning a limited number of dwellings for rent often manage and maintain their own properties, contracting out for repairs only when needed.

Slum landlord is a negative term applied to landlords who specialize in the purchase and renting out of inferior, low-cost units in need of repair, often to desperate tenants. These rental properties may be in violation of housing codes and are often located in severely depressed neighborhoods, where the landlord has acquired the property at little cost and with minimal intention of providing upkeep or repair.

All landlords maintain specific rights concerning their properties, as specified in the lease agreement. For example, it is not unusual for landlords to retain the right to inspect and repair their property with advance notice to the renter. Landlords are not usually responsible for the loss of the renter's personal possessions, even in the event of a natural disaster or crime. A renter is well advised to purchase rental insurance if the loss of certain items is a concern. However, people on a tight budget often consider this type of insurance a luxury. In "high-risk" areas, it might also be expensive and difficult to obtain rental insurance.

Eviction

Another legal process, **eviction**, occurs when tenants or homeowners are removed from their housing, commonly for missing rent or mortgage payments. The procedures for evicting people from their homes vary by state, city, and county. Typically, however, eviction involves the landlord or lender filing a legal notice to be served to the renter or homeowner. Written notices specify the date by which a tenant must leave the premises. When an eviction is legally conducted, homeowners and renters can be forced to leave their homes and their personal possessions can be removed. Often those possessions are simply set out at the curb.

As with foreclosures, seeking legal counsel concerning evictions is advisable, especially when renters and homeowners are being treated unfairly. Being evicted from a home is often a traumatic experience and results in a housing crisis for the tenant or homeowner. With evictions, social workers often assist clients by identifying emergency or transitional housing and implementing crisis counseling.

Substandard Housing

Many people live in housing that fails to meet local health and/or building codes, labeled **substandard housing**. Living conditions in such housing are unsafe and a risk to health or occupants, representing a worst-case housing option. Many states and municipalities have established laws and zoning requirements prohibiting people from dwelling in

Source: ©iStockphoto.com/kalifcam

▲ Social workers whose clients live in substandard housing may have to consider scheduling visits at a different location.

housing characterized by infestation (e.g., by rodents, cockroaches, or bedbugs), flooding, structural decay, dangerous electrical systems, gas leaks, broken plumbing pipes, and other serious flaws.

Substandard housing poses a risk to both dwellers and visitors, including social workers. For clients living in substandard housing, social workers need to consider scheduling home visits at an alternate location. Social workers may also have an ethical obligation to report the condition of the housing to authorities, such as Child and Adult Protective Services or police. Social workers would help clients identify more suitable housing and secure resources, employment, and support to transition to a safer and more suitable form of housing.

SOCIAL WORK WITH AT-RISK COMMUNITIES

There are a number of routine considerations for social workers dedicated to the improvement of social and economic conditions in at-risk communities. **Community development** is a multifaceted endeavor, and advancing positive housing options and quality living circumstances for all people is a mainstay function for many social workers. In this section, a few examples of common housing factors associated with communities at risk are examined.

When practicing with people living in economically challenged areas, special consideration should be given to the perspectives and circumstances influencing residents (Kleinhans, van der Land, & Doff, 2010). Whether they remain in or leave poor neighborhoods depends on much more than the state of the housing, the poverty, or even the crime. Despite those undesirable conditions, residents may decide to stay because of their attachment to the neighborhood, their ability to cope with conditions there, constraints on their ability to leave, and the social networks that exist there. It is important to recognize that clients often differ with respect to their motivation, willingness, and ability to move. Generally, residents of poor neighborhoods can be conceptualized as falling into one of two categories (Kleinhans et al., 2010, p. 382):

- *Movers:* Poor residents who can be induced to move, with assistance, from their poverty-stricken neighborhoods to lower-poverty areas
- *Stayers:* People who cannot or are not willing to move out of poor neighborhoods

TIME TO THINK

In social work practice, clients often live in poor and crime-ridden neighborhoods. Their living conditions can include exposure to vandalism, poor sanitation, and various forms of infestation. Social workers adopt procedures for safely conducting home visits in these neighborhoods. When considering social work as a career option, would visiting these sorts of neighborhoods be a problem for you?

When considering social work's commitment to client self-determination, would you be able to work with "stayers"?

Segregated Communities

One factor that affects both movers and stayers is segregation, which occurs when groups of people are separated in social settings (e.g., workplaces, housing, communities) based on human characteristics. The term **segregated communities** refers to people living in communities separated on the basis of factors such as race and ethnicity. As an example, Chicago is a city with some of the most racially and ethnically segregated communities in the United States (Carl, 2012, p. 228). Segregated communities are often poor; some people want to get out and go to more diverse communities, and some want to stay where the culture is familiar to them.

Historically, for decades, distinct residential segregation patterns have been found across the nation in many

communities and in urban and rural areas. Segregation in the United States occurred as a result of migration patterns and social, economic, and political conditions. In the past, discriminatory practices were not only condoned but legal. Before the passage of fair housing laws, the real estate and housing industry openly participated in redlining and blockbusting policies, which were designed to restrict persons of color from obtaining housing in racially designated geographical and residential areas.

Although now prohibited by law, the discriminatory housing practices of the past contributed to the establishment of current residential segregation patterns, which have been crystallized by contemporary racial economic disparity. In other words, although people are no longer prohibited from buying and renting housing on the basis of race, many people from racial minorities continue to experience challenges in buying and renting in segregated neighborhoods because of their own income and wealth. Housing segregation is a major social issue and is explored in greater depth later in this chapter.

Equal Opportunities for Housing

Discrimination in the sale, leasing, rental, or disposition of housing properties on the basis of race, color, national origin, sex, disability, age, or religion is prohibited in the United States by a number of federal fair housing laws and presidential executive orders. The basic premise is that people should possess a fair and equal opportunity to obtain housing via both policy and practices. Landlords, property managers, and sellers are prohibited from using any methods to discourage individuals and families from seeking housing. Although seemingly a simple and straightforward position, ongoing oversight and monitoring of housing rental and purchasing processes for fair opportunity is necessary to protect housing rights.

The Office of Fair Housing and Equal Opportunity, a division of the HUD, is dedicated to promoting equal housing opportunities for all people and prohibiting discrimination in housing. Additionally, many cities and communities have created local organizations to promote equal and just housing opportunities. Social workers partner with these federal and local officials, as well as community-based organizations, to ensure that clients are afforded lawful and fair access to housing.

Housing discrimination affects people who are trying to leave at-risk communities and move to more desirable ones.

For reasons of self-interest, landlords have been known to illegally seek control of the types of people living in their property by discouraging some groups of people from renting and encouraging others. Similarly, people leaving at-risk communities can face landlords in more desirable locations seeking to manage the types of people residing in their property by dissuading renters from even completing applications so that the landlords can avoid any documentation or evidence of discriminatory practices.

An effective technique for identifying and disclosing discriminatory practices and techniques in housing is for two independent sets of professionally trained "secret shoppers" to visit the same rental or housing unit to ascertain if potential renters or buyers are treated differently on the basis of race or some other dimension of difference subject to discrimination. One set of secret shoppers represents the oppressed group and the other set represents the preferred group. If the oppressed group is treated differently from the other group—perhaps told that the unit is no longer available or shown a less desirable unit—the assumption is that illegal discrimination has occurred, is likely to have occurred in the past, and will likely continue in the future unless the authorities intervene.

Imagine that an African American family visits an apartment rental property and the rental agent shows the family small, subground-level units with little natural light. Later, the same agent shows a Caucasian family spacious apartments in prime locations, with lots of windows and plentiful natural light. Whether intentional or not, this practice constitutes discriminatory behavior. Progressive housing owners and landlords will hire outside "secret shoppers" themselves to ensure that their employees are behaving in a standardized and nondiscriminatory way.

Through relationships with clients, social workers hear about or may even witness discriminatory housing acts. Using case advocacy, social workers partner with clients to promote and defend their fair right to access and acquire housing from a landlord, leasing representative, or realtor. From a cause advocacy perspective, social workers seek ways (e.g., secret shoppers) to identify and advance policies, personnel, and practices to systematically protect and promote fair housing practices.

Transportation and Connectivity

Geographical location is one of the key reasons at-risk communities struggle to encourage the creation of new businesses and job opportunities. When a community lacks connectivity (easy access via transportation for large groups of people) with other communities and industry, it suffers from social and economic isolation. As a result, the tax base erodes and property values plummet. In turn, support for education and social services also becomes challenging.

Without affordable and well-organized transportation, social work clients, particularly those living in at-risk communities, struggle to secure and maintain employment and are cut off from support systems such as family members living in other communities, medical and social services, and jobs. Employers routinely sort applicants on the basis of where they live and their ability to commute to work on a timely and regular basis. Clients and residents in rural areas may need to rely on family members, friends, coworkers, car pools, churches, and van services when available. People with physical challenges and limitations often struggle with identifying accessible living conditions and forms of transportation. For example, consider the importance of housing ramps and transportation lifts and accommodations for people who use wheelchairs.

Community-based transportation is therefore an important asset for enriching communities at risk. Transportation includes efficient bus routes, rail systems, bike paths/lanes, walkways, and highways/streets. Economical, effective, and reliable modes of transportation facilitate many forms of social interaction and commerce, allowing groups of people to commute readily within as well as among communities. Social workers not only assist clients with identifying transportation but also advocate for public and private support to develop transportation systems and services.

Community Development and Resources

In addition to housing and transportation, a number of other key community assets and resources contribute to quality of life and are frequently in need of community development, particularly within at-risk communities. In terms of human biopsychosocial needs, the following are important elements of a thriving community:

- Health providers such as physicians, dentists, and optometrists
- Mental health services
- Grocery stores with economical and nutritious food
- Clean water, good sanitation, and unpolluted air
- Just law enforcement
- Quality educational systems

- Parks and other recreation facilities
- Support systems such as churches and friendship networks

Social workers partner with community residents, leaders, and stakeholders to secure funding to advocate for and sustain these kinds of community resources.

A valuable research method for social workers involved in community development is a **community needs assessment**, which specifies the magnitude and types of community problems and the availability of local resources for addressing them. Community leaders and government officials are often reluctant to enter discussions about allocating resources to address community needs without sound research documenting needs and existing services and programs. Community needs assessments often involve surveys and focus groups of the target community's residents. Exhibit 13.2 provides more information about the considerations addressed in community needs assessments.

POLICY ISSUES RELATED TO COMMUNITIES AND HOUSING

Stable housing and safe living conditions are key ingredients for human well-being and quality of life. Many people struggle with obtaining safe and nurturing housing because of its unaffordability, which is both a community and a national concern. The following sections highlight several contemporary issues in the realms of housing and communities at risk.

HOMELESSNESS

Dependent on the source, there are a number of official definitions of homelessness. Most definitions of **homelessness** focus on individuals or families lacking a fixed, regular, and adequate nighttime residence. Although homelessness has been declining nationally since 2010, the number of people experiencing homelessness in the United States remains staggering, with many national estimates depicting more than half a million people affected. The HUD is the primary source for collecting and disseminating this type of information in our nation. But because people experiencing homelessness do not have an address and frequently move, they are a difficult population to document and research.

EXHIBIT 13.2   Common Considerations With Community Needs Assessments

- *Purpose of community needs assessment:* Is it to determine what types of specific services are needed for clients? Or is the purpose centered on the development of community assets?
- *Definition of need:* What is it specifically? Is it something the community desires (such as a park or museum), or is it something necessary to the community's safety (such as sanitation, healthy food, or shelter)?
- *Stakeholders:* Who is asking that a community needs assessment take place? What is the purpose? Who is defining the need being assessed (clients, experts in community services, community leaders)? Who will be affected by the outcome?
- *Research methods:* What research methods will be used to document, describe, and quantify the needs? Will data be based on the perceptions of key stakeholders, obtained through focus groups and surveys? Or will data be more objective, based on counts of requests for services and demand from agencies?
- *Uses for results:* Will community leaders, funders, and helping professionals use the results to decide on the funding programs and services needed? Or will clients make these decisions?

Source: Powers, Meenaghan, and Toomey (1985, pp. 114–115).

Nevertheless, the HUD sponsors an annual homelessness assessment on a single night in January of every year. Local planning agencies and comprehensive service organizations conduct the survey. In 2013, the U.S. Department of Housing and Urban Development reported the following:

- The total number of people experiencing homelessness was 610,042—64% of them individuals and 36% families.
- Nearly two thirds of these people were living in emergency shelters or transitional housing programs, and 35% were living in unsheltered locations such as under bridges, in cars, or in abandoned buildings.
- The number of veterans experiencing homelessness was 57,849, a decrease of 24.2% since January 2010.
- Chronic homelessness among individuals and temporary homelessness among individuals and families had both declined since 2010. Statistics regarding the decline in homelessness among families between 2007 and 2013 are shown in Exhibit 13.3.
- Nearly 20% of people experiencing homelessness were in either Los Angeles or New York City. Los

EXHIBIT 13.3 Changes in Family Homelessness, 2007–2013

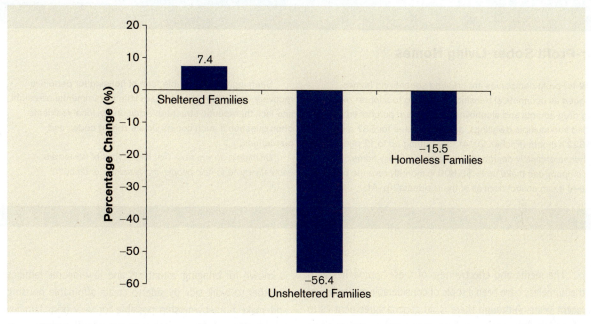

Source: U.S. Department of Housing and Urban Development (2013).

Angeles experienced the largest increase among major cities, reporting a 27% increase in homeless individuals in 2013 compared with 2012; New York City reported a 13% increase.

Many people conceptualize homelessness in stereotypical ways: homeless men, skid-row alcoholics, runaway kids, "crazy people," addicts, and bums. However, the homeless population also comprises entire families trying to make ends meet and return to a more stable existence. Homelessness can occur as a result of health/mental health problems, unemployment, substance abuse, and abandonment, but those problems alone do not define people experiencing homelessness. Many times, the conditions or circumstances that led to homelessness are outside of individual or family control.

Two distinct strategies for addressing homelessness in the United States offer hope for easing the problem:

- **Continuum of Care program**: A community-based approach where clients progress through a series of programs to become "housing ready,"

▲ Homelessness is prevalent in many large cities.

typically requiring sobriety and a commitment to mental health services (Groton, 2013, p. 51)

- **Housing First programs:** Emphasize the rapid provision of permanent housing for the homeless, with the subsequent offering of supportive services such as employment and vocational counseling, mental health services, and addiction programs

CURRENT TRENDS

For-Profit Sober-Living Homes

NEW for-profit companies are creating sober-living homes, designed as economical transitional housing to support recovering drug addicts and alcoholics. Houses are purchased and divided into multiple dwellings, and then rented for $87 a week or $322 a month (Pilcher, 2014). "By putting up to 12 people in a house originally designed to be a single-family home, the company can make up to $3,800 in monthly revenue per home—if it can collect from all of the residents" (p. A1).

Seemingly an affordable form of housing for people in recovery, sober-living homes have little governmental oversight and lack therapeutic structure. Additionally, local residents often question if such homes violate zoning codes and restrictions.

Ultimately, do you think that these types of homes are earnestly trying to help people, make money, or do both?

The merits and effectiveness of these approaches with the homeless have been a topic of considerable research over recent years. Although there is no general agreement as to which housing strategy is best, many social workers agree that the use of effective substance treatment and mental health services is a key factor when addressing the housing needs of the homeless population.

AFFORDABLE HOUSING

The concept of **affordable housing** is a topic of considerable debate among researchers and scholars. Federally, housing is deemed to be affordable when a household has to pay no more than 30% of its income on mortgage or rent, including taxes and utilities (U.S. Department of Housing and Urban Development, n.d.-a). Particularly for low- or no-income individuals and families, a 30% threshold limits housing options considerably. For example, a person working 40 hours each week at $8 per hour (calculated on 4.3 weeks to a month) would be seeking a rental with utilities at $412.80 per month. Dependent on state and locality of residence, the affordable housing guideline would likely relegate this renter to very specific low-income rental properties located in communities at risk.

Many communities work with development corporations and nonprofit housing groups to establish low-income residences. For example, **Habitat for Humanity International (HFHI)** is a highly recognized faith-based nonprofit organization dedicated to building and rehabilitating homes across the United States to provide affordable housing. HFHI is known for bringing volunteers and low-income families together to work side by side to create affordable housing and make homeownership possible for very poor families (Smith, 2013, p. 95). HFHI has partnered with communities to rehabilitate entire subdivisions in communities at risk. At times, groups opposing changes in their neighborhoods (generically called "Not in My Back Yard" or NIMBY groups) have organized against HFHI projects. The NIMBY groups are afraid that having new low-income neighbors will lower their property values (p. 103).

TIME TO THINK

Social workers attempt to place themselves in the role of the other, which professionally means seeing things from the perspective and view of the client. Imagine that you are a 22-year-old married mother with two young children. You have very little employment experience, no extended family members, and few friends. Your husband has abandoned the family and fled to parts unknown, leaving you in considerable debt and with unpaid rent. In the midst of crisis, where do you turn for housing and financial support for your children?

If you found suitable housing in a public affordable housing project, how would you feel about neighbors' hostility? How would you attempt to overcome it—or would you?

COMMUNITY ASSET BUILDING

All communities possess strengths. One way to accentuate and develop those strengths is through identifying, mapping, and developing community assets (Kretzmann & McKnight, 1993). The term **community assets** encompasses physical resources (e.g., buildings, housing, parks), businesses, schools, transportation, community participation, associations, leadership, civic groups, interorganizational networks, organizations, shared values, and the ability to exert power over decision makers.

Various community assets contribute to housing stability, such as homeowner associations, property management organizations, renter coalitions, housing rights organizations, nonprofit housing advocacy entities, and builder associations. Social workers can be members and leaders of these organizations to advocate for affordable housing and the rights of clients. Social workers can also help these organizations develop contacts with similar organizations and housing officials, and find locations for information and referral activities. Social workers help clients find rental assistance, acquire information, and develop relationships through neighborhood events, meetings, and celebrations.

SEGREGATION

A rich body of literature and research describes housing segregation on the basis of race, ethnicity, and income in the United States. Housing choice is dependent on what and where a person or family can afford to rent or buy, as well as preferences for living, influenced by the social and economic characteristics of community members. For example, white middle-class families are well-known for living in middle-class communities near people similar to themselves. There are three ways communities often segregate on the basis of race/ethnicity and income (Quillian, 2012):

- *Segregation due to simple racial discrimination*—for instance, whites in one neighborhood and blacks in another
- *Segregation within a race based on poverty status*—for instance, middle-income or wealthy black people in one neighborhood and poor black people in another, or middle-income or wealthy white people in one neighborhood and poor white people in another

- *Segregation due to simple income discrimination*—for instance, white and black people with mid- to high incomes in one neighborhood, and poor white and black people in another

Too often, when people of different races and ethnicities isolate themselves or segregation occurs, neighborhoods of poverty appear. As community racial and ethnic diversity increases, concentrated residential segregation in neighborhoods can occur, exacerbating poverty. For example, in an area that is becoming home to both white and black people, "poverty is concentrated in communities [or smaller neighborhoods] of high-poverty racial groups while low-poverty racial groups are shielded from poverty contact," resulting in even further segregation of high-poverty racial groups (Quillian, 2012, p. 356). In other words, poverty segregation is complex and can occur in both communities and smaller neighborhoods, across and within racial and ethnic groups (Quillian, 2012).

Power and control by the dominant group also seem to be issues leading to racial and ethnic discrimination. Historically, much of residential segregation in metropolitan areas in the United States has been attributed to the discriminatory reactions of the white population when the minority population in a community appears to be growing (DeFina & Hannon, 2009, p. 373). As minority groups begin to move into new areas, the dominant status of whites and their ways seemingly become threatened. The result is white resistance or flight. However, research findings suggest that people living in areas that are already ethnically diverse do not perceive the arrival of racial minorities to be nearly as big a threat as do people who live in ethnically homogeneous neighborhoods (p. 373).

TIME TO THINK

Are discriminatory practices and processes that contribute to segregation part of everyday, accepted culture in the United States? For example, landlords have a legal right to deny housing to people with criminal records. How might this practice disproportionately impact racial and ethnic minorities? How are people with criminal backgrounds disadvantaged in obtaining adequate housing?

DIVERSITY AND HOUSING

Safe, affordable, and healthy housing, especially in communities at risk, matters to people. For many social work clients, housing is also a topic that readily demonstrates inequities and the importance of such personal variables as age, class, ethnicity, race, gender, and sexual orientation. However, social workers view clients in the context of their overall living circumstances and conditions, not just their dimensions of difference, taking care not to generalize one client's living experience to other people and settings.

Because the United States is such a geographically, socially, economically, and culturally diverse country, housing factors differ tremendously across urban areas, between rural and urban areas, from state to state, and by region. Based on multiple factors (e.g., location, prestige, economy, cost of living), consider how housing challenges and communities differ depending on whether you live in New York City, San Francisco, Boston, Kansas City, a town of 600 people in North Dakota, a rural community in South Carolina, Anchorage, Honolulu, Las Vegas, farmland in Iowa, or a remote area in Arizona. As various dimensions of diversity are examined in relationship to community life and housing, consider regional and local differences as well as historical and cultural components.

- *Age*. Housing options for older adults at retirement age heavily depend on financial planning and assets, and personal health. Many people do not conceptualize older adults as a population that will become homeless or live in substandard housing; however, older adults often experience physical limitations restricting employment, may not qualify for a pension program or Social Security benefits, and may have little or no savings or possessions that can be readily sold for cash. Older adults without the assistance of family members and friends may be found by social workers (especially those working in Adult Protective Services) in unsafe and unsanitary conditions and exploitive relationships. The availability of subsidized housing for older adults varies appreciably depending on the person's health care needs and the particular locale in which the person lives. The stereotypical image of an older adult living in a retirement community in Florida assumes the availability of resources to support a desired lifestyle.

- *Class*. For most Americans, housing and community of residence are a direct reflection of economic status, income, and wealth. Wealthy people often own several homes in various locations for recreation or relaxation, convenience, extended family gatherings, or investment purposes. Homeowners in urban areas are known to move to suburban areas to avoid city taxes, and they may choose to dwell in self-contained, isolated communities or gated subdivisions. Although politicians and elected officials are often required to own a residence in their elected district, it is not unusual for them to spend limited time each year residing in that particular dwelling. Affluence and wealth carry many privileges, and being able to live where and how one likes is often at the top of the list of advantages.

- *Ethnicity*. The United States is often referenced as a "melting pot" nation, where people from multiple ethnic origins have come to reside, work, and enjoy the freedoms and opportunities of American life. The melting pot analogy suggests a certain degree of blending among people. However, people of the same ethnic background tend to reside in communities representing their ethnic culture and traditions. This is simply because they tend to move to the communities where they know people, and among recent immigrants in particular, that usually means people of the same ethnicity. In some urban areas, ethnic neighborhoods are distinct and identifiable and less integrated. In other cities, ethnic distinctions are less clear and are simply unique elements of a less segregated community. Ethnic identity and networking is typically viewed as a strength in social work practice, a source of support, power, and pride. Other residents and tourists may also find ethnically distinct neighborhoods to be charming.

- *Race*. Housing segregation based on racial oppression takes many forms, some of which have already been discussed in this chapter. In addition, oppressed minorities may be harmed by **gentrification**, in which poor people, often racial minorities, are displaced from their community when developers and investors purchase low-value dwellings for renovation, resale, and profit taking. When this occurs, residents are required to relocate. It is often difficult for these people to find comparable affordable homes. In addition, gentrification is disruptive for the people who are forced to move and can be a source of crisis and grief. Beyond the loss of physical space, housing provides a sense of security, and communities are often the basis for friendships, supportive relationships, and a sense of belonging. Although new housing sometimes creates new and better housing opportunities for the original residents, those affected by gentrification may also experience a loss of control, anxiety, and depression.

• *Gender.* In the United States, women tend to be the primary caretakers of children, and a significant number of women are single parents. Identifying safe, affordable, and appropriate housing is a particular challenge for mothers with dependent children. Limited or unreliable income, which may result from irregular child support or conflicts between employment and child care, is also problematic. The availability of subsidized housing for women with dependent children varies considerably by county, state, and region. Doubling up is a common but often temporary option. Some community shelters are designed for families, but often they place time restrictions on residency. When desperate, women have resorted to undesirable and potentially exploitive relationships as a means to secure financial support and housing. Such relationships can place the mother and children at risk of abuse.

• *Sexual orientation.* As with other population groups, when working with gay, lesbian, bisexual, and transgender clients concerning housing and community options and issues, social workers need to avoid being presumptuous. For example, some people prefer privacy in living, while others desire the ability to lead life in an open and transparent fashion. Acquiring housing in a community safe from discrimination and violence on the basis of sexual orientation will be a priority for some people and not for others. At the macro level, social workers advocate for policies and practices that advance fair and safe housing—as well as community standards, rights, and protections—for gay, lesbian, bisexual, and transgender people.

• *Intersections of diversity.* People with mental health challenges frequently struggle with securing appropriate housing. They may require inpatient and residential treatment. Add poverty and inadequate mental health insurance, and people with untreated mental health conditions have very limited options for securing appropriate residential care. Many residential mental health facilities will accept only specific insurance or out-of-pocket payment, once again separating the affluent from the poor. Although jails and correctional facilities often function as default housing for people with untreated mental health issues, they are overcrowded. In addition, administrators and mental health professionals in public and private hospitals face pressure from funding sources to reduce overnight stays unless the client is deemed a potential harm to self or others.

▲ Same-sex couples have to consider which communities they feel comfortable living in.

Source: ©iStockphoto.com/Juanmonino

ADVOCACY AND HOUSING

Social workers' commitment to promoting human rights and challenging social injustice extends to where and how people dwell. In the United States, quality of life is predicated on the ability to obtain and maintain a safe and secure residence, not simply a roof over one's head. In the United States, people living day to day and place to place experience great difficulty securing a government identity card, completing applications for employment and housing, getting a bank account without an established address, and receiving mail.

Advocacy in the area of housing and community enrichment primarily involves addressing individuals' basic needs. In other words, case advocacy often takes precedence over cause advocacy in this area. Clients are often in a crisis, and their immediate concern is for personal housing, not necessarily a macro-level change to advance housing and community opportunities for others. In addition, clients who are experiencing instability in housing and may be transient have limited time and energy to devote to issues of social justice and human rights. The same is often true of the social workers who work so hard to help them meet their immediate needs.

ECONOMIC AND SOCIAL JUSTICE

It is an oversimplification to suggest that the ability to obtain money, income, and wealth can overcome various forms of economic and social injustice. However, this chapter clearly illustrates the advantages when people in need of housing and communities at risk have access to financial resources. For poor individuals and families, educational and employment opportunities provide a means for improving quality of life and housing circumstances. For communities, the addition of business, industry, and public transportation can be a conduit for promoting affordable and safe housing as long as people of lower social–economic status are included in prosperity and not displaced or pushed to the side.

Companies and people in positions of affluence and power are potential partners for advancing housing and community assets. It should not be assumed that the wealthy have little interest in improving the quality of life for all people, including the poor. Each person, group, and company brings to the decision-making table a story and life experiences, and a religious or philosophical orientation that may include economic and social justice. Many astute business leaders strive to identify meaningful ways to contribute to the lives of people and communities—if for no other reason than because they believe that creating opportunities for upward mobility is a righteous and just action.

In promoting and advocating for economic and social justice, social workers are encouraged to view each and every person they interact with as a potential ally for improving access to housing and creating healthy communities. Although real estate and housing officials may not be in the typical social and occupational circles of social workers, they can be key players for promoting and advancing the well-being of client population groups and communities at risk.

SUPPORTIVE ENVIRONMENT

The natural environment is an element of individual and community health often overlooked. Residing in an area prone to floods, hurricanes, fires, earthquakes, pollution, or tornadoes carries inherent risks and may limit or preclude housing options and make insurance either prohibitively expensive or unavailable. Because of financial limitations, the poor are often relegated to substandard housing in areas prone to or having been impacted by natural disasters. Government officials and investors are often reluctant to assist with housing development and protection in such locations in anticipation of further natural problems.

The flood-prone neighborhoods of New Orleans and the catastrophic impact of Hurricane Katrina not only illustrate how natural environment can contribute to housing and community challenges but also provide insight as to how

social workers partner with landlords, community leaders, government officials (local, state, and federal), engineers, emergency relief organizations, law enforcement officials, and public utilities. Following Hurricane Katrina, large coalitions of concerned parties advocated for timely response to future disasters and preventive measures such as flood walls and hurricane-resistant dwellings for residents and communities at risk.

Advocacy concerning environmental issues in connection with housing and communities can take many forms (e.g., elimination of pollution, recycling, garbage removal, clean water, use of efficient and green energy, food production, historic preservation). Encouragingly, entire communities, subdivisions, and neighborhoods can be transformed when people unite with a common goal to overcome environmental issues and create safe and environmentally stable and sustainable places to live, work, and play.

HUMAN NEEDS AND RIGHTS

The United States is a plentiful country with large disparities between the rich and poor in many domains, including housing. People experiencing homelessness represent the very poorest of people in America, and advocacy for this population has resulted in a number of federal acts to address the housing needs and rights of the poor, including the following:

• The Housing and Community Development Act of 1974—Created the Housing Choice Voucher Program, also known as Section 8 housing. This program allows eligible participants to use federal vouchers to choose housing, including nonpublic dwellings, that meets program requirements.

• The McKinney-Vento Act of 1987—Established funds to maintain emergency shelters for temporary housing.

• The Veterans Affairs Supportive Housing Act of 2008—Provided funding for supportive housing, case management, and clinical services for veterans through the Department of Veterans Affairs.

• American Recovery and Reinvestment Act of 2009—Created the Homeless Prevention and Rapid Rehousing Program to provide resources to newly displaced families in an effort to help them immediately secure housing.

SOCIAL WORK IN ACTION

Tamara Collaborates With Private Companies to Build Community Assets

TAMARA is a social worker and a program coordinator for her city's "drop-in" shelter, which serves single homeless adults. Daily, free dinners are provided to men and women, and emergency shelter is also available for single men and women in large, overnight sleeping rooms segregated by gender.

Tamara has been active with local real estate and property management groups to advocate for additional affordable housing for the poor. As economic development has begun in the shelter's neighborhood, many community residents and professionals have grown concerned about gentrification and the displacement of low-income residents and shelters. A developer and property management group recently purchased a large apartment building and is making plans to rehab it. Tamara and other members of the local coalition for affordable housing successfully negotiated with the developer, property management group, and government officials to secure a commitment that 20% of apartments in the renovated apartment building will be dedicated to low-income residents at prescribed affordable rental fees. The developer and property management group have also pledged to find ways to support the "drop-in" shelter and various forms of community asset building.

Are the goals of businesses and social services agencies necessarily at odds with each other? What common concerns and interests might they share?

Although many helping professionals would argue that federal housing legislation does little to confront the root causes of homelessness and the lack of affordable housing (Giffords & Garber, 2014), federal intervention is valuable. Comprehensive action to address the housing needs of the poor requires more than private, local, community, and state intercession. Federal legislation and programs provide states and communities with much-needed funding to address very real and immediate housing needs. Additionally, federal support and oversight prompt discussion about optimal expectations for programs and services for addressing basic housing needs and rights. The HUD is an excellent example of a federal agency formed to create and sustain affordable and inclusive homes for all people.

POLITICAL ACCESS

Throughout this book, it has been argued that liberals often support governmental intervention to address human needs and rights, while conservatives favor **privatization**, transferring governmental duties, functions, and roles to businesses or private organizations. The key premises of privatization are described in Exhibit 13.4. Privatization is a common theme found in conservative circles and confronted by helping professionals and their clients when advocating for legislation and public programs to address housing and community needs. With privatization as a dominant value, "government becomes the problem whereas champions of social programs become the enemy" (Fisher & Harding, 2008, p. 16).

One way to overcome some of the resistance among conservatives may be for social workers to try to involve private businesses when advocating for government intervention and designing social programs related to housing. As you have seen, there are ways to do so, and when social workers find business allies, they will have more clout with politicians and political organizations.

YOUR CAREER IN HOUSING SERVICES AND COMMUNITY PRACTICE

Social workers participate in home visits and develop relationships with clients in at-risk communities to assist with immediate individual and family needs through case management services, by conducting community needs assessments to document and prompt community development, and via advocacy both to improve and enrich community conditions and the client's quality of life. Hence, social workers

EXHIBIT 13.4   Underlying Premises Regarding Privatization of Social Services

PREMISE	DESCRIPTION
Primacy of economy and business	Priority is given to business considerations and actors in most aspects of domestic activity, including housing.
Importance of private markets	Private markets are given preference and power over public policies and programs with regard to political and social decision making.
Devaluation of public intervention	Private market processes are preferred over public intervention. If public intervention occurs, then it is supplementary to the private market and private sector processes.
Private sector as model for public sector	When public programs occur, they should be modeled after the methods and processes found in the private business sector.

Source: Adapted from Fisher and Harding (2008, p. 16).

routinely act to produce change in a number of ways, including the creation of housing opportunities, on multiple system levels (e.g., with families, organizations, communities, and society). Although full-time employment in community practice is often limited, social workers are routinely expected to be involved in larger-scale change as part of their everyday practice.

BSW social workers possess knowledge and abilities well suited for occupations involving housing and communities at risk. For more specialized practice in these areas, social workers might want to consider advanced coursework in community practice and housing. As an alternative to traditional social work practice, social workers can explore employment as property managers, leasing representatives, and realtors, where their interpersonal skills, ability to work with diverse populations, and commitment to fairness and nondiscriminatory practices will serve them well. Social workers are also well prepared to appreciate and understand the housing difficulties in at-risk communities and to work with people and organizations under trying circumstances.

Employment and leadership within community development and housing rights organizations are also possibilities. Public service with the HUD, or its affiliate agencies and programs, couples social work's professional commitment to human rights and fairness with the social worker's ability to collaborate effectively with clients and various stakeholders (public and private). Social workers possess a background in policy analysis and implementation, community organizing, and advocacy for services and programs.

It is not unusual for social workers to change their employment with regard to client population groups served, problems addressed, employer, and area of practice. Social workers regularly evaluate their practice within and outside of traditional social work employment, sometimes inspired by personal circumstances, shifts in interests, professional passion, and agency environment and leadership. For example, a career in the housing industry may not be an apparent career choice for many social workers, but people-oriented employment involving basic needs such as housing, public utilities, transportation, or education is a worthy consideration.

SUMMARY

We cannot seek achievement for ourselves and forget about progress and prosperity for our community. . . . Our ambitions must be broad enough to include the aspirations and needs of others, for their sakes and for our own.

—Cesar Chavez

Inadequate, outdated, and poorly constructed and maintained housing is often a major contributing factor in making a community "at risk." It is also a contributing factor to segregated living. Out of economic necessity, the poor and homeless gravitate toward communities with low-cost housing. Conversely, business and industry generally avoid poverty-stricken areas, unless they are targeted for urban renewal or gentrification.

Social workers in this area of practice strive to help impoverished, poorly housed, and homeless clients find permanent, suitable housing and to convert at-risk communities to vibrant, cohesive neighborhoods. But when clients progress and are able to acquire credit, savings for a housing deposit, and steady employment, they typically consider upgrading their housing, which often means moving out of a community. As clients make strides in life, the social worker often loses them as clients. But the commitment to community development and activism remains.

TOP 10 KEY CONCEPTS

affordable housing
at-risk communities
community
community assets
community organizing

homelessness
Housing First programs
privatization
residential instability
segregated communities

DISCUSSION QUESTIONS

1. What are the major hurdles for moving from renting an apartment to buying a house? How problematic is a down payment? How can social work clients overcome this difficulty?

2. Do social workers need to live in the communities in which they practice? How about communities at risk? Explain your thinking and responses.

3. If you buy a home in an area experiencing gentrification, are you contributing to asset building and the rejuvenation of the community or in the displacement of low-income people?

4. Is the federal affordable housing guideline of paying no more than 30% of your income on mortgage and rent, including taxes and utilities, a realistic premise? Why or why not?

5. What are some of the flaws associated with privatization of services and programs for the poor, particularly in the realm of housing? Why are government offices such as the U.S. Department of Housing and Urban Development needed?

EXERCISES

1. Search the website of your nearest public bus or rail system. Identify routes, times, and commitment needed to travel from your home to work or school. Then consider taking a route between a nearby community at risk and your workplace or university. List your observations about the affordability and efficiency of transportation on both routes. As a bonus, add your observations about the characteristics, including apparent housing options, in various communities through which you would pass in your travels.

2. Run a credit report or credit rating for yourself. You are guaranteed one free credit report per year from each credit report bureau—Equifax, Experian, and Transunion—which you can access through www.annualcreditreport .com. The site provides information on the way to establish a good credit rating. Given this information, what do you consider doing differently with your credit? How would

low-income individuals struggle with establishing a good credit rating?

3. Consider volunteering time at a homeless or emergency shelter. Observe the food and overnight conditions and services. What are common characteristics of the people using this form of temporary shelter?

4. Search the Internet and identify a recent community needs assessment for a community of interest to you. What are some of the key needs identified? Are they a surprise? How might this information inform decision making in that community?

5. Interview a family member, friend, or acquaintance who has doubled up with someone in a housing unit. What were some of the issues or problems this person experienced? What would he or she recommend to other people prior to participating in doubling up?

ONLINE RESOURCES

- AnnualCreditReport.com (www.annualcreditreport .com/index.action): A source for requesting a credit report
- Housing Opportunities Made Equal (www.cincyfairhousing .com): An example of a community-based housing opportunity and rights agency
- The National Alliance to End Homelessness (www .endhomelessness.org): Works to end homelessness through education and policy development

- Realtor.com (www.realtor.com/home-finance/buyers- basics/?source=web): Provides tips for first-time homebuyers
- U.S. Department of Housing and Urban Development (www.hud.gov): Serves as the primary federal entity to coordinate housing and urban policies and programs in the United States

STUDENT STUDY SITE

Sharpen your skills with SAGE edge at **edge.sagepub.com/cox**

SAGE edge for Students provides a personalized approach to help you accomplish your coursework goals in an easy-to-use learning environment.

Chapter 14: THE CHANGING WORKPLACE

Learning Objectives

After reading this chapter, you should be able to

1. Describe how the organization of work reflects advances in the economy, production methods, and society.
2. Define the concept of the "changing workplace."
3. Explain five work-related issues of current concern.
4. Explain the difference between social insurance programs and social welfare policies.
5. Describe the role of social workers in workplace issues.
6. Apply the dynamic advocacy model to the changing workplace.

Deidre Experiences Firsthand the Realities of the Contemporary Workplace

Deidre is an adjunct instructor in an undergraduate social work program at a midsize university and a recently divorced mother of two young children. To support her family, Deidre cobbles together an adjunct teaching schedule dependent on the instructional needs of the social work program, picking up an assortment of courses that meet at different times each term. Thus, she needs to prepare constantly for new courses, and her schedule is unpredictable from term to term. But she agrees to teach almost any course that is offered to her, because she needs the money.

On the average, Deidre earns $26,000 annually. She receives no benefits from the university, such as health care insurance or a retirement fund. Deidre's university intentionally limits her instruction to avoid laws and policies requiring provision of benefits. Deidre has noted, with a little bitterness, that tuition at the university is more than $18,000 per academic year.

Although Deidre holds a PhD in social work, she has discovered that tenure-track positions as a social work professor are few and far between. Further, given her family responsibilities, Deidre has recognized that she could not allocate the time needed to launch the research agenda required for an assistant professor position.

She is both a social work instructor and a social work client. She has been visiting with a clinical social worker to discuss her recent divorce and to assist her children through the transition. During her most recent visit, Deidre also asked for assistance in forming strategies to advocate for better working conditions.

As you well know, work is an essential feature in American society. People's employment status defines their position in society and their **standard of living** or the level of wealth, material goods, housing, services, and education available to them. Being gainfully employed also brings self-esteem, respect from others, friendships, socialization, and a daily routine. Therefore, the social work profession considers both access to work and an adequate standard of living as human rights.

The world of work involves the intersection of workers, employers, the marketplace for goods and services, the economy, educational status, and the work environment. The workplace is constantly evolving because of ongoing changes in culture, politics, economics, and technology. All these changes present issues relevant to social work and social welfare. This chapter explores the changing workplace, on a national and international scale, and highlights many current concerns associated with work in the context of human rights and social justice. It is designed to highlight the features of a meaningful work environment and the contribution of social work to positive workplaces and social justice for workers.

THE HISTORY OF WORK

Whether in or out of the home, work is what sustains individuals, families, communities, and societies. Most of us have the privilege of thinking of work as a source of income and perhaps even as a pleasurable pastime; however, in less-developed societies, work is linked to survival. Work also has a societal function, serving to organize people in small groups (as embodied in an expression such as, "We're like a family here in the accounting department") and in large, complex systems with bureaucratic structures.

Our society places a great deal of value on the **work ethic:** the moral belief in the necessity and benefit of work. The work ethic is often associated with the character of an individual and the perceptions others have of that individual. All people who are capable are expected to work and if they do not, they are viewed as "unworthy" or "undeserving" of government support. Although the work ethic is not unique to the United States, the moral virtue of work permeates American society. Thus, the relationship a person has with the workplace is important. Work positions a person in a social system and structures a great deal of life, including the social welfare system. For example, those who have limited

skill sets may find themselves out of work when the economy shifts. They often find themselves unemployed, and then they might need to rely on social welfare. Said another way, poverty and poor people in the United States are defined by their ability to work and their employment status.

Work and the workplace change with changes in the economy, technological advancements, and fluctuating relations between employers and the employed. Here we examine broad time frames to better understand transitions in the workplace and the evolving relationship between the workplace and the social work profession.

TRADITIONAL SOCIETIES

From the beginning of history, the labor necessary for survival and well-being has been divided into tasks, and those tasks have been assigned to specific members of society. The organization of work by task and responsibility is referred to as the **division of labor**.

Initially, labor was divided according to gender and age, which is still the case in many developing nations of the world. Traditionally, the men engaged in physical labor requiring strength and endurance, while women were assigned tasks related to child care and household duties such as cooking and cleaning. Children and older people also worked to the capacity of their physical capabilities. Specifically, older people assisted with child care and food preparation and children who were old enough tended the garden and fed the animals. Race, ethnicity, and religious affiliations also factored into the division of labor.

This model of labor began to change to an agricultural model not too long before the colonists moved from their homelands in England and Europe to the Americas. The division of labor and the location and character of some tasks began to shift.

AGRICULTURAL ERA: 1630 TO 1760

For well over a century, the main occupations in the American colonies were based in subsistence agriculture in rural contexts. As the nation expanded, agricultural occupations associated with lumber, food, cotton, and dairy rose to meet the demands of a developing nation and a growing population.

Agricultural work was often divided according to gender. Men tended to plow, sow, till, and chop, while women gardened, sewed, and cooked. Over time, specialists emerged from this division of labor. For example, a woman who was especially gifted at sewing could earn a reputation as a seamstress and become established in a cottage business. Some men began to distinguish themselves as especially talented in making weapons or farm equipment such as wheeled plows. Others were recognized as craftsmen in leather, metal, or wood.

The cultivation of tobacco required heavy labor and gave birth to a plantation system that allowed workers to be close to both home and the sugar mill. The requirements of sugar planters brought the introduction of agricultural slavery. This practice began in 1518 and spread throughout the sugar-growing areas during the next two centuries. The institution of slavery was abolished between 1863 and 1865, a change set in motion by President Lincoln's Emancipation Proclamation. However, the discrimination against and oppression of the former slaves had a lasting impact on the education opportunities, trade and union membership, and occupations available to African Americans (SenGupta, 2009).

The social welfare system in place during this time reflected the centrality of the family in maintaining social and economic stability. When a family experienced difficulty, the typical colonial response was one of the following:

- **Farming out** members of the family to provide labor for others in return for food and shelter
- **Indenturing** workers from the family to another farm or business for a specified period of time
- **Apprenticing** selected family members to expert craftsmen so they could learn a trade such as shoemaking or blacksmithing

In all these cases, the goal was to make family members economically useful to their own families and worthy members of society.

INDUSTRIAL REVOLUTION: 1760 TO 1840

Marked by a transition to new manufacturing processes, the industrial revolution impacted almost every aspect of work and family life. Water and steam power, iron making, and machine tools elevated the living standards of ordinary people, while the United States gained a worldwide presence as an industrialized nation. Family life changed as people left their homes and searched for work. Men, women, and

Source: Wikimedia/NARA

▲ Several American families ran their own farms.

children were welcomed into the labor force and were needed to advance the industrial base of the nation.

A hallmark of the industrial revolution was the introduction of **wage laborers,** who sold their work hours to a factory, mining operation, or business owner in exchange for a salary. Wage laborers worked under strict workplace rules and all too often lived in deplorable conditions. For instance, factory-based families in Philadelphia "lived fifty-five to a tenement, usually in one room per family, with no garbage removal" (Zinn, 1980, p. 213). In New York, the poor lived in slums, "and filthy water drained into yards and alleys, into cellars where the poorest of the poor lived" (p. 213).

Integral to the rise of wage labor was Francis Cabot Lowell's power loom, which synchronized weaving with spinning and changed a labor-intensive method of textile production into an automated weaving system (Rosenberg, 2011). Even young girls could do the work of the mechanized mill system. They were called Lowell Mill Girls and lived in dormitories or boarding houses supervised by matrons. At the height of the textile industry, more than 8,000 women worked in the mills, forming about 75% of the mill labor force (Zinn, 1980).

The sense of community that arose from working in close quarters and living together in tenements and boarding houses nurtured the growth of friendships, alliances, and unified action among wage laborers. Many of the Lowell Mill Girls joined the American union movement to protest their living and working conditions, forming the Lowell Female Labor Association. One protest song describes their plight:

Oh! Isn't it a pity, such a pretty girl as I

Should be sent to the factory to pine away and die?

Oh! I cannot be a slave,

I will not be a slave,

For I'm so fond of liberty

That I cannot be a slave. (Robinson, 1898)

In response to working conditions and the inequality of incomes, workers united in action and demanded these reforms (Axinn & Levin, 1992, p. 41):

- Equal and universal free education
- Public lands for settlements
- No more abuse of child labor and apprentices
- Restrictions on competitive prison labor
- Better working conditions for women
- Establishment of a 10-hour workday without any decreases in wages
- Governmental control of currency
- The right to organize
- Jobs for the unemployed in public works programs

A new attitude toward social problems emerged during the industrial revolution. Public issues were identified, examined, analyzed, and publicized. Living and working conditions and labor regulations regarding children and women were addressed legislatively or voluntarily by factory owners (Hartwell, 1971). Equally important, women were earning money as part of the workforce in various occupations, including nursing and teaching.

URBANIZATION: 1860 TO 1950

One of the defining features of the industrial revolution was the development of cities—vast urban areas with roads, public transportation, railroads, and waterways. Prior to industrial growth, about 80% of people lived in rural areas. However, high rates of labor turnover caused people to move to where the jobs were located. Hiring unskilled workers on a daily basis, laying off workers during slow periods of production, and seasonal work contributed to unsteady employment and transience among the working class. In addition, from the mid-19th century to the start of the 20th century, the growth of American cities was supported by an influx of 1,285,349 immigrants looking for work (Ward, 1971). Immigrants and African Americans tended to work on the lowest rungs of urban employment, largely due to the lack of better alternatives.

The turmoil of labor force disruptions was a threat to the business community. Thus, business owners introduced policies and programs that became associated with the welfare movement. Their involvement was sometimes referred to as **welfare capitalism.** It had two basic goals: supporting a diverse workforce that would maintain the established values and goals of management, and discouraging workers from union membership. These goals were addressed through schools and training programs, nonprofit lunchrooms and company stores, company houses and apartments, and health clinics.

The growth of the welfare movement required staff—namely, **welfare secretaries.** Interestingly, although welfare secretaries had been hired to help laborers, laborers resented their paternalistic attitude and unconditional support of management. Welfare secretaries received little or no support from union leaders, who concluded that welfare capitalism could not accept any attempt to organize workers.

The **human relationship school of management** emerged with the decline of the welfare movement, originating from a set of studies conducted at the Western Electric Hawthorne Works in Chicago. Researchers were interested in the impact of physical factors such as light or temperature on production rates but found that the attention they paid to the workers during the studies was in itself motivating. The human relationship school of management focused on the changes in the labor force due to military service and the diversity of workers, who were increasingly inexperienced, female, older, and members of minorities. In essence the role of the human relationships school of management was to stabilize shifts in the labor force and the workplace to ensure a high level of productivity and profits.

Attention to the work environment was apparent throughout the 1940s. For example, in 1941 the National Community Service Committee was formed by the Congress of Industrial Organizations to train union counselors for manufacturing plants. Bertha Reynolds, a social worker and union organizer, worked with members of the National Maritime Union and their families (Carter, 1977). Also, the branches of the military for the first time employed professional, trained social workers as commissioned officers to deal with the many problems military personnel encountered in relation to their work.

SOCIAL WORK IN ACTION

Mark Serves Both Workers and Administrators in an Employee Assistance Program (EAP)

The world of work is complex and changing. Social workers interested in a career in EAPs quickly learn that problems impacting the workplace involve employers, workers, and family members. There is also a correlation between the work environment and the efficiency and effectiveness of an organization. It is no wonder that the number of EAPs is expanding nationwide.

After completing his master's degree in social work, Mark began his professional career as a social worker in a nursing home. He now works as a social worker in a hospital-based EAP. On a daily basis he learns from hospital workers of problems related to the misuse of prescribed medication, financial insecurity, domestic violence, and mental health conditions such as depression and anxiety, just to name a few of the complex issues facing workers. Mark is skilled at assessing environmental life stressors that cause hardship to individuals and their families. He takes satisfaction in facilitating the resolution of individual and family crises among his coworkers.

Interestingly, it's also up to Mark to address some of the dysfunctional aspects of the workplace. For instance, a couple of the licensed vocational nurses have talked with Mark about their difficulty finding child care on short notice, as they receive their weekly schedules, which vary, the day before the week starts. This is an area where Mark might be able to help at the organizational level. He meets regularly with hospital administrators and department heads to talk about the types of issues he uncovers and offers suggestions for changing policies and procedures to reduce hospital workers' stress in the future.

1. Why do you think EAP services are needed?

2. What skills, experiences, and personal qualities do you think would be essential to a social worker employed in an EAP?

Although the majority of occupational social service programs faded in importance after World War II, there was an increase in the number of occupational alcoholism programs (Googins & Godfrey, 1987). By the 1950s a large number of companies had established occupational alcoholism programs for workers and their families. The majority of the workplace programs were modeled on the 12-step Alcoholics Anonymous program.

INFORMATION AGE: 1960 TO PRESENT

From the 1960s onward, the increasing number of women in the workplace, the civil rights movements, the use of ever-more-sophisticated technology, and the growth of multinational corporations have increased issues facing workers and management alike. In response to the stresses of work associated with disrupted employment, competition, and changing markets, **Employee Assistance Programs (EAPs)** were developed.

An employer-paid benefit, EAPs are designed to provide services that address issues that negatively impact job performance, work attendance, and collegial relationships. Personal problems, such as domestic violence, parenting, and mental illness, also come under the purview of EAPs. Some of the services may be offered onsite. If appropriate, referrals can also be made to offsite providers with a particular area of expertise. Whether the services are provided on- or offsite, EAPs usually offer a limited number of annual sessions.

Social workers provide the majority of EAP services (Jacobson, 2006). Trained in an ecological perspective, EAP social workers view the person in the environment, which includes relevant individuals, groups, and communities. The goal is to assess environmental stressors that may be contributing to a problem and then intervening to bring balance into the employee's work and life.

Source: ©iStockphoto.com/Blend_Images.

▲ The gender pay gap is starting to close due to more educated women entering the workforce.

TIME TO THINK

After reading this history of work, what era was most interesting to you? Why?

During that era, what were the social and economic implications of work for men and women? Regardless of era, women have traditionally been paid less for their work than have men. Why do you suppose that is?

CURRENT SOCIAL TRENDS RELATED TO WORK

Political, social, and economic shifts have changed the way work is carried out. Digital advances and expectations from a new generation of workers have shifted the way we produce and collaborate, transforming the workplace and with it our lives. Further, the nonwork responsibilities of American workers have changed dramatically over the past 50 years, largely as a result of the entrance of women into the workforce in large numbers (Boushey, O'Leary, & Glynn, 2013). These are some of the other major changes related to work:

• *More people work at home.* One third of Americans (17 million people) are freelancers, contractors, and consultants, and most of them work at home instead of in a traditional office setting. By about 2020 there will be more of these nonpayroll workers than full-time employees (Boushey et al., 2013). A key factor in this change is the digitization of the workplace, which allows people to work at home and closer to family. Such a workplace environment may sound less stressful than the traditional setting, but it requires time management, home-office outlays, and well-defined work hours.

• *Workforce ages are decreasing.* The baby boomers, those individuals born between 1946 and 1964, are starting to retire, causing major shifts in workplace demographics. Next year, millennials—people born in the early 1980s to early 2000s—will account for 36% of the American workforce. New opportunities will be created for people from younger generations who are skilled, forward thinking, and flexible. One of the biggest problems workplaces will have is ensuring continuity as people with deep knowledge of the company's business leave and new ones come in.

• **Gender pay gap** *is starting to close.* Only 24% of women are happy with what they earn at work, compared with 32% of men (Parker & Wang, 2013). But those statistics may start to change. As indicated in Exhibit 14.1, the gap between women's and men's pay is smaller for younger workers than it is for workers overall. It is expected to shrink even more, because more women than men are becoming educated and more men are leaving the workforce.

• Anemic *economy is delaying career growth.* The decline in the nation's economy during the Great Recession, which began in 2008, negatively impacted the workforce. Long-term joblessness has become a fixture of our economy, which still has an unemployment rate of nearly 7% to 8%. Most American workers are now 30 years old before they start receiving the median wage of $42,000; back in 1980, they tended to be earning the median wage by the time they were 26 (White House, 2014). Recent college graduates who have not been able to find good jobs have sought internships to gain work experience, which sounds like a good strategy but may actually delay their ability to get a full-time job.

• Global *markets are becoming more integrated.* Global commerce will experience significant growth in the next decades as developing nations and emerging markets benefit from a new generation of businesses and

EXHIBIT 14.1   The Narrowing of the Gender Wage Gap, 1980–2012

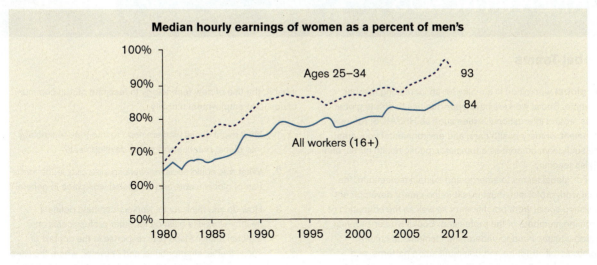

Median hourly earnings of women as a percent of men's

Note: Estimates are for civilian, non-institutionalized, full- or part-time employed workers with positive earnings. Self-employed workers are excluded.

Source: Pew Research Center. (2013, December 11.)

consumers. The likelihood of cultures, ideas, and commodities integrating around the world holds promise for international agreements, industrial combinations, and innovative connections. Globalization will highlight new ways of engaging people in the workplace and implementing new technologies. Embedded in global integration, however, is the issue of diversity. Differences in language and culture must be recognized and managed.

• Job *searches are continuous.* Research shows that people are always searching for new jobs and opportunities. Fifty years ago, Americans tended to find a good job and stay with that employer for most of their working life. But people are just not satisfied anymore with the work they do; so they are continuously searching, and the search sometimes begins promptly after getting a new job. Today people have, on average, about 11 jobs between the ages of 18 and 34 (Bureau of Labor Statistics, 2012).

WORK-RELATED ISSUES

Sometimes a person's participation in the workforce is interrupted for reasons unrelated to work performance. For example, the employer may go out of business, a new technology may make some workers expendable, or the

economy may be disrupted. Regardless of the cause, being without work leaves a person financially, emotionally, and socially vulnerable.

The following sections examine employment issues of concern not only to social workers but also to policymakers, because of their impact on broad swaths of workers. They are primarily related to financial security.

UNEMPLOYMENT

Unemployment is a fear of every worker. Discussing unemployment is difficult because the subject is complex, with multiple dimensions, most of which require an understanding of micro- and macroeconomics and business cycles. There are three basic types of unemployment:

• **Frictional unemployment:** Part of the normal labor cycle and considered unavoidable. Frictional unemployment is triggered when people leave their place of employment or are fired from their job. Unemployment occurs not because jobs are unavailable or the unemployed lack skills; rather, frictional employment reflects the amount of time it takes an employer to find another worker. Two critical factors contribute to frictional employment: Employers are unaware of available workers and their specific skill sets, and available

CURRENT TRENDS

Global Teams

The global workplace is a reality for an increasing number of people. Social workers have opportunities to create global teams around international issues such as HIV/AIDS, refugee settlement, primary health care, and environmental concerns. One such team comprises a translator, public health nurse, and English teacher.

For global teams to emerge and sustain momentum, the social work profession must invest in the career development of existing social work practitioners as well as the education of upcoming members of the profession. Social workers serving on global teams need to understand elements of culture, organizational structure and communication patterns, and individual and cultural values. These social workers must also be flexible in thinking about the physical workspaces they may

inhabit, the use of new technology to facilitate global communication, and employment mobility.

1. How might social workers need to integrate technology into global practice and policy development?

2. What role could social networking sites play in the formation of global teams and the global workplace in general?

3. How do you think social workers can help define a healthy work–life balance for other professionals on a global team? Place your response in the context of social media, smartphones, and telework, where the lines between personal and professional lives often blur.

---

workers are unaware of the open jobs. In essence, frictional employment is the result of an inadequate exchange of information, and so the solution is to make sure information about jobs and workers is freely available.

- **Structural unemployment:** Caused largely by conditions in the economy that mismatch available jobs and potential workers (Diamond, 2013). The skills of potential employees and those required for available jobs are different. Consequently, there are workers wanting jobs and employers needing workers, but because the available workers lack the necessary skills, the jobs go unfilled and the workers remain unemployed. The effective response to structural unemployment is training programs that help workers develop skills that match the work requirements of available jobs.

- **Cyclical unemployment:** When businesses downsize and lay off workers because of a decrease in demand for goods and services. For example, when banks increased the interest rates on home mortgages and lending funds were limited, the construction of new houses declined. As a result, construction workers were laid off, as were sales clerks

in home appliance and hardware stores and employees of companies such as cabinet and carpet manufacturers. The solution to cyclical unemployment is to improve economic conditions and thus increase the need for workers.

In frictional and structural unemployment, there are enough employment opportunities, but they remain unfilled because of the inadequate exchange of information or workers' lack of necessary job skills. However, cyclical unemployment involves an insufficient number of employment opportunities. Cyclical unemployment usually requires that the federal government expand its fiscal policies so that people and businesses have more money to spend on goods and services and on paying new employees.

UNDEREMPLOYMENT

People who are employed but frustrated in their ability to do a job commensurate with their skills and availability exemplify the concept of **underemployment.** Imagine a worker with a graduate degree working as a library assistant because there are no other employment openings. Or consider the worker who needs full-time employment to cover living costs but has a part-time job with no possibility of advancement or additional work hours. Another example is immigrants who have skills or education credentials that are not needed or recognized in the country where they currently live.

The end result in these situations is work dissatisfaction and an inadequate income. To address underemployment, the labor market has to expand to include and reward employment potential and income needs, which would mean a decrease in profits for businesses. Given the economic philosophy of the United States, such an action is unlikely.

TIME TO THINK

You've probably held jobs to help defray the cost of college or to support your family in some way. Have you ever changed from one place of employment to another? Why? Based on your experiences, what do you think is the main difference between unemployment and underemployment?

Describe your emotions during a time when you needed a job and didn't have one. How did the lack of work and income impact your attitude and activities?

MINIMUM WAGE

The following excerpt from President Obama's 2014 State of the Union address summarizes the major issues surrounding **minimum wage**, the lowest hourly-rate wage that employers may legally pay their workers.

After four years of economic growth, corporate profits and stock prices have rarely been higher, and those at the top have never done better. But average wages have barely budged. Inequality has deepened. Upward mobility has stalled. The cold, hard fact is that even in the midst of recovery, too many Americans are working more than ever just to get by—let alone get ahead. And too many still aren't working at all. (Obama, 2014)

In 2009, the federal government mandated a minimum wage of $7.25 per hour, which is the hourly rate paid to about 1.6 million workers (White House, 2014). Although some justify such a low wage by claiming that minimum-wage

workers are young people just entering the workforce, the reality is different, as Exhibit 14.2 shows. Nearly half of those earning the minimum wage are 25 and older; 17% are 45 and older, and likely to have serious financial obligations. Even when working 40 hours per week, workers paid the minimum wage are earning only $15,080, which is below the poverty line of $15,130 (Desilver, 2014).

Many who are concerned about the financial well-being of American workers argue that the minimum wage should be increased and indexed to inflation (i.e., increased at the same rate as inflation). Increasing the minimum wage would ensure that workers earn enough to live on, add to a family's financial stability, decrease turnovers and training costs when people leave to find better jobs, and stimulate the economy. Those in opposition to increasing minimum wage are also quite vocal. They contend that a higher minimum wage would result in businesses' passing higher costs on to consumers, cause teenagers and unskilled workers to lose their jobs, and lead to a spike in unemployment.

The overall effects of increasing the minimum wage are unknown at this point, given the wide range of existing estimates, and there is clearly a lack of consensus about the best steps to take. For example, recent research indicates that raising the minimum wage does not reduce employment, although some would argue that it does (Neumark & Wascher, 2006).

GENDER INEQUALITY

Globally, **gender inequality** is reflected in the fact that women primarily work in low-paying positions: hair stylists, house cleaners, cooks, child-care workers, nurses, and teachers. Although sex discrimination laws have been passed in the United States, gender-based job discrimination persists, and many women continue to be relegated to low-paying jobs. Women with full-time employment are paid about three fourths the salary of full-time working men.

In some places around the globe, the difference between men's and women's earnings for comparable full-time work, which is referred to as the **gender gap,** is nearly nonexistent. However, as Exhibit 14.3 shows, American women earned about 82% of men's median weekly earnings in 2011, even in the same jobs (Hegewisch, Williams, Hartmann, & Hudiburg, 2014). You will note that only women employed as "stock clerks, order fillers" and as "bookkeeping, accounting, auditing clerks" make slightly more than their male

EXHIBIT 14.2   Distribution of Minimum-Wage Workers by Age Group

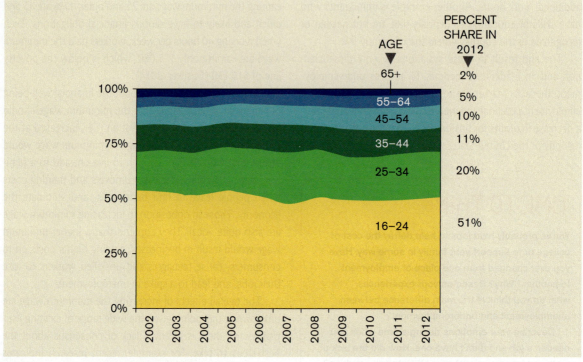

Source: Pew Research Center. (2013, December 4).

counterparts. The gender gap is most significant among CEOs and financial managers. Female chief executives earned only 69% as much as male bosses, resulting in $658 less in median weekly earnings (Hegewisch et al., 2014).

Gender inequality extends to the nation's political environment. Women represent less than 20% of federal and state elective offices. The vast majority of senators and representatives in Congress are men, as are the presidential-nominated members of the Supreme Court. Thus, as in the workplace, the higher the status of a position or office, the lower the percentage of women holding that position. The possible political influence of women should not go unnoticed, however, since women constitute a majority of the nation's voters.

OCCUPATIONAL HEALTH HAZARDS

The social and economic development of a nation is dependent on a healthy workforce. Illnesses, diseases, and disorders, whether physical or emotional, tend to affect a

person's earning ability, but those conditions often arise for reasons other than work. When they do arise from work, the causes are called **occupational health hazards**.

Since 1950, the International Labor Organization and the World Health Organization have shared a common definition of occupational health: "Occupational health should aim at: the promotion and maintenance of the highest degree of physical, mental and social well-being of workers in all occupations; the prevention amongst workers of departures from health caused by their working conditions."

To ensure health and safety in the workplace, legislation and inspection standards for workplaces have been enacted. Since the industrial revolution, this approach has been effective in controlling occupational health hazards.

One special concern in the contemporary era is the effect of stress on worker health. Layoffs and the increased workloads that result for those left on the job contribute significantly to stress. Exhibit 14.4 categorizes those stressors and others associated with the workplace. It is important for employers to realize how stress is likely to impact overall

EXHIBIT 14.3   U.S. Gender Wage Gap for Selected Occupations, 2011

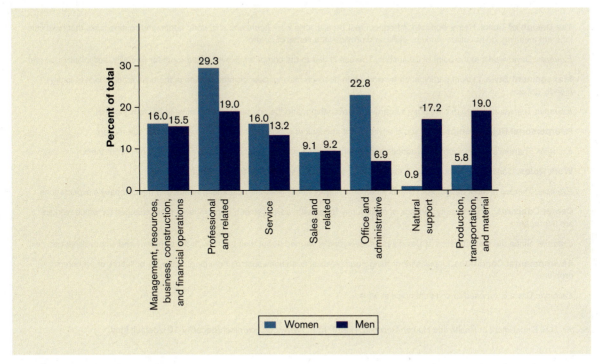

Source: U.S. Department of Labor (2011).

employment performance and for everyone to recognize the consequences of stress for quality of life.

SOCIAL WELFARE AND THE CHANGING WORKPLACE

One way to address changes in the workplace is to have social welfare programs and social welfare policies that protect workers against situations they have no control over, such as the loss of a job, employment-related injuries, old age, and discrimination. Think about the jobs you have held. Chances are your payroll deductions included Social Security taxes. Although you might think you do not need compulsory savings for future workplace events, the day will undoubtedly come when you are entitled to the program benefits and glad to have them.

SOCIAL INSURANCE PROGRAMS

Some of the work-related social welfare programs, such as unemployment insurance and workers' compensation,

are referred to as social insurance. Such programs involve employers and workers sharing the risks associated with employment by paying premiums through deductions from their earnings, which are recorded for workers under their Social Security numbers. There are other social insurance programs that may come into play earlier in one's career.

Unemployment Insurance

The Unemployment Insurance Program, a federal–state program, provides benefits to eligible workers who are unemployed through no fault of their own. Workers must also meet other eligibility requirements of specific state law. The payments or benefits of unemployment insurance are designed to provide temporary financial assistance to unemployed workers as a strategy to reduce the risk of poverty.

In the United States, there are 50 state unemployment insurance programs, plus one each in the District of Columbia, Puerto Rico, and the U.S. Virgin Islands (U.S. Department of Labor, Office of Unemployment Insurance, 2014). The federal government lends money to the states

EXHIBIT 14.4 Job Conditions That May Lead to Stress

The Design of Tasks. Heavy workload, infrequent rest breaks, long work hours and shiftwork; hectic and routine tasks that have little inherent meaning, do not utilize workers' skills, and provide little sense of control.

Example: David works to the point of exhaustion. Theresa is tied to the computer, allowing little room for flexibility, self-initiative, or rest.

Management Style. Lack of participation by workers in decision making, poor communication in the organization, lack of family-friendly policies.

Example: Theresa needs to get the boss's approval for everything, and the company is insensitive to her family needs.

Interpersonal Relationships. Poor social environment and lack of support or help from coworkers and supervisors.

Example: Theresa's physical isolation reduces her opportunities to interact with other workers or receive help from them.

Work Roles. Conflicting or uncertain job expectations, too much responsibility, too many "hats to wear."

Example: Theresa is often caught in a difficult situation trying to satisfy both the customer's needs and the company's expectations.

Career Concerns. Job insecurity and lack of opportunity for growth, advancement, or promotion; rapid changes for which workers are unprepared.

Example: Since the reorganization at David's plant, everyone is worried about their future with the company and what will happen next.

Environmental Conditions. Unpleasant or dangerous physical conditions such as crowding, noise, air pollution, or ergonomic problems.

Example: David is exposed to constant noise at work.

Source: U.S. Department of Health and Human Services. (1999) http://www.cdc.gov/niosh/docs/99-101/default.html.

for unemployment insurance when the states run short on funds. In general, this can happen when the unemployment rate is high. All loans must be repaid with interest. The need for loans can be exacerbated when a state cuts taxes and increases benefits.

Individual states and territories raise their own funds for unemployment insurance from workers. The federal government sets broad guidelines for coverage and eligibility, but states vary in how they determine benefits and eligibility. In general, eligibility is determined when a person has worked a certain amount of time in a covered program, is willing and able to work, files a claim for benefits and registers in a public employment office, and demonstrates that the unemployment status is due to a lack of local work opportunities (Bureau of Labor Statistics, 2014).

Benefit amounts and the length of time they are available are also determined by state law. Generally, eligible workers receive between 40% and 50% of their previous pay (Bureau of Labor Statistics, 2014). The standard length of unemployment compensation payment is 6 months, although extensions are possible for certain individuals. Once this 6-month time period elapses and payment ceases, an individual who

remains unemployed is at risk of falling into poverty, as he or she no longer has a safety net on which to rely.

Workers' Compensation

Workers' compensation is a social insurance program that provides most employees who are injured on the job the right to medical care for any injury and, in many cases, monetary payments to compensate for resulting temporary or permanent disabilities. Further, benefits are provided to the families of workers who are killed on the job, such as in a coal-mining disaster or other work-related accident.

The workers' compensation system is administered on a state-by-state basis, with a state governing board overseeing a system that includes some combination of public and private funding. The Office of Workers' Compensation Programs administers four major disability compensation programs: wage replacement benefits, medical treatment, vocational rehabilitation, and other benefits to certain workers or their dependents who experience a work-related injury or occupational disease.

Workers' compensation is financed by a tax on employers. With the goal of protecting the interests of workers who are injured or become ill on the job, the program is designed to (1) provide timely reviews of claims, (2) process and pay benefits, (3) assist workers to obtain timely treatment and rehabilitation, (4) maintain quality work environments, and (5) provide oversight to the workers' compensation program across states (U.S. Department of Labor, Office of Unemployment Insurance, 2014).

Social Security

The nation's **Social Security** system (formally Old-Age, Survivors, and Disability Insurance) supports retirement for workers who contribute to the federal social insurance program. About 94% of all workers participate in the program. Deductions for the program are taken directly from a worker's paycheck. The Social Security taxes are levied on a fixed amount of wages and do not take into account individual situations, such as the number of dependents (Social Security Administration, 2014).

Although people can begin receiving Social Security benefits at 62 years of age, the majority of Americans' expectations regarding retirement have changed in recent years. Gradually, workers have presumed they will need to work to an older age, and fewer are expecting to enjoy a financially secure retirement, particularly those nearer retirement age. Exhibit 14.5 indicates that the average nonretired American now expects to retire at age 67, up from age 63 a decade ago and age 60 in the mid-1990s.

The changes associated with anticipated retirement are understandable given the nation's economy and stock market volatility. However, these attitudes may indicate a more permanent change in Americans' outlook, rather than a temporary downswing. As the majority of the population enjoys a longer and more vibrant life, workers have extended their careers and think long and hard before leaving the workplace.

SOCIAL WELFARE POLICIES

In the past few decades, social policies have been enacted to help ensure equality in the workplace. Such policies are based on the idea that women, members of minority groups, and people with challenging conditions have civil rights that guarantee them opportunities in employment without prejudice or discrimination.

Affirmative Action

In the United States, **affirmative action** refers to equal opportunity employment measures that federal contractors and subcontractors are legally required to adopt. These measures are intended to prevent discrimination against employees or applicants for employment on the basis of "color, religion, sex, or national origin."

The rationale for affirmative action policies is to redress the disadvantages associated with overt historical

EXHIBIT 14.5   Expected Age of Retirement, 1996–2012

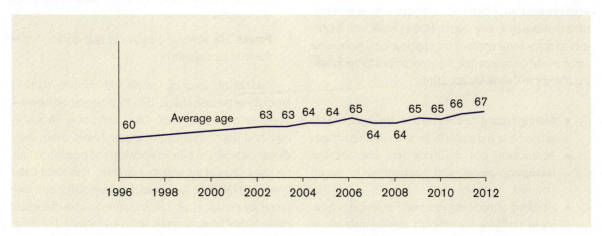

Source: Jones (2012).

discrimination. A further intention is to ensure that public institutions, such as universities, hospitals, and police forces, are more representative of the populations they serve. Thus, affirmative action programs require employers to (1) actively locate and recruit minority applicants and (2) in certain circumstances hire a specified number of minorities for vacant positions (American Civil Liberties Union, n.d.). Affirmative action programs offered by the U.S. Department of Labor include outreach campaigns, targeted recruitment, employee and management development, and employee support programs.

Americans With Disabilities Act

The Americans with Disabilities Act (ADA) supports people with disabilities in employment, transportation, public accommodation, communications, and governmental activities. It covers employers with 15 or more employees, including state and local governments. It also applies to employment agencies and labor organizations.

The ADA prohibits private employers, state and local governments, employment agencies, and labor unions from discriminating against qualified individuals with disabilities, whether in job application procedures, hiring, firing, advancement, compensation, job training, or other conditions and privileges of employment (U.S. Equal Employment Opportunity Commission, 2014). An individual with a disability is a person who has a physical or mental impairment that substantially limits one or more major life activities and who has a record of or is regarded as having such an impairment.

Significant to the ADA is the concept of **reasonable accommodation,** which refers to adjustments or modifications provided by an employer to enable people with disabilities to enjoy equal employment opportunities. Reasonable accommodation may include but is not limited to the following (American Cancer Society, 2014):

- Making existing facilities used by employees readily accessible to and usable by persons with impairments
- Restructuring jobs, modifying work schedules, and reassigning people with impairments to vacant positions
- Acquiring or modifying equipment or devices; adjusting or modifying examinations, training materials, or policies; and providing qualified readers or interpreters

An employer is required to make a reasonable accommodation to the known impairment of a qualified applicant or employee if it would not impose an "undue hardship" on the operation of the employer's business. As you might imagine, disputes do sometimes arise regarding what constitutes a reasonable accommodation or an undue hardship.

TIME TO THINK

Do you know someone who has a mobility, vision, or hearing impairment? Have you noticed the types of difficulties this person experiences when participating in work or campus life? Social events? Have you noticed accommodations that ease the way for this person?

How does reading about the ADA change the way you think about people, their work, and their community engagement?

DIVERSITY AND THE CHANGING WORKPLACE

The stratification of the workplace, which produces unequal opportunity and unequal rewards, was described by German sociologist Max Weber (1922/1964). He speculated that three factors in the stratification of society are also reflected in the workplace:

Class: A person's economic position in society

Status: A person's prestige, social recognition, honor, or popularity in society

Power: The ability of a person to gain control despite the resistance of others

Traditionally speaking, people with minority status—especially on the basis of race, ethnicity, or religious affiliation—have been deficient in class, status, and power. Thus, they have held labor positions that require harder, dirtier, more dangerous work and offer less privilege and prestige. In turn, the lowly nature of the work they do lowers their social status (Weber, 1922/1964). Because of their low social status, such people are excluded from specializations in labor that would enhance their financial status and overall standard of living. It is a vicious cycle.

This phenomenon, in which social status is based in part on labor, has been referred to as the **environment of work** (Wilson, 1996). The environment of work supports the social advancement of some workers, while others are marginalized. For example, the person at a fast-food restaurant who takes orders and prepares food does not have the same employment opportunities, social status, or financial incentives as the manager or owner of the restaurant does, although the work is likely to be demanding.

AGE

In effect, older adults are a recently discovered minority. The most striking example of age discrimination in the workplace was the practice of mandatory retirement, whereby people were forced to leave their jobs at a certain age. Even though employers can no longer force workers to retire, many exert subtle pressures on older workers.

Currently, older people are subject to many stereotypes. Older workers are thought to be less healthy, clumsier, more prone to absenteeism and accidents, and slower in task performance (U.S. Department of Labor, Office of Disability Employment Policy, 2014). Research has shown that these myths are erroneous. In fact, older workers tend to be highly productive, dependable, and cooperative.

In response, social workers are taking a leading role in identifying the problems of older adults in regard to work. To provide older adults with a productive, meaningful role in society, it is suggested that they be encouraged to work as long as they are productive and have an interest in working to maintain their standard of living.

CLASS

Ideally, the workplace should be a positive environment that enhances the growth and productivity of the people who work there. Workers should have the opportunity to develop their capabilities through their work. The outcome of work should better the lives of workers and contribute to society through cooperation that encourages people to become and remain interconnected. For such an ideal workplace to occur, groups must develop their potential and influence, and this can be realized through cooperative action.

Yet the structures of work create a variety of problems. More specifically, they are alienating for many people.

Alienation refers to the cognitive separation of people from one another and from the control of their work; it can lead to the exploitation of workers, resulting in inequality in the distribution of work and its rewards. Exploitation in a work context is seen when individuals gain little from their work but those who supervise them gain much.

Consequently, the organization of work creates a system of class in the nation's profit-based economy. Such a system creates incentives to keep wages down and invests little in working conditions. The class-based labor market affects older people, women, people of color, and the lesbian, gay, bisexual, transgender, and questioning (LGBTQ) community because traditionally these groups do not have the same power within the workplace as white men do. Social workers are urged to address the question of power in the workplace by recognizing the political character of work, highlighting the leadership roles displayed by disadvantaged groups, and favoring the expansion of worker rights through unionization.

GENDER

We discussed gender equality in the workplace earlier in this chapter, and it is certainly an issue in the context of pay, promotion, and power in the workplace. The experience of being segregated into low-paying jobs provides a set of grievances shared by all women. The historic conflict women have waged for a fair share of resources generates a powerful critique of denial of basic rights, withholding of economic opportunities, and exclusion from the center of power that have affected their ability to earn a living and more.

But other factors come into play when thinking about women in the workplace—for example, flexibility to care for a sick child or a child who has special needs, to attend school visits and parent–teacher interviews, or to support the special needs of older relatives. The position of women (and some men) in the workplace would be enhanced if access to affordable, convenient child-care or elder-care services was provided either onsite or through a consortium with other employers.

Social workers recognize that the development of consciousness, leadership, and organizational capacity are needed to change women's position in the workplace. By challenging the status quo, the goal is to provide something more to those with less in the workplace.

SEXUAL ORIENTATION

LGBTQ people and their heterosexual coworkers consistently report having experienced or witnessed discrimination based on sexual orientation. In response to such discrimination, courts and administration agencies have recognized the need for greater protections for LGBTQ workers under federal law.

In addition, there has been a surge in the number of LGBTQ-inclusive corporate policies. There are 21 states with laws protecting LGBTQ workers from discrimination (Human Rights Campaign, 2014). The majority of the largest employers (those with 5,000+ employees) now provide benefits to same-sex partners and spouses of employees. However, these private policies do not provide the protection of a state or federal law with an external enforcement agency and a clear right for individuals to seek redress in court.

Social workers have the opportunity to advocate for legislation to enact explicit protections for the LGBTQ community. Such bills have been introduced in every Congress since 1994. In 2014 the Employment Nondiscrimination Act (ENDA) was passed by the Senate. ENDA is a political compromise, however; the bill passed by the Senate does not require equal access to employee benefits (Pizer, Sears, Mallory, & Hunter, 2012). Nevertheless, ENDA introduces a federal statute that supports piecemeal state and local protections for LGBTQ people.

INTERSECTIONS OF DIVERSITY

Most women of color experience workplace discrimination somewhat differently than do women in general. Women of other racial and ethnic groups may be relegated to "female" jobs such as office work, nursing, and teaching. But women of color are disproportionately employed in low-income jobs in retail, child care, and janitorial services.

In addition, it can be argued that the lack of social, legal, and economic support available to families of color has intensified the need for women of color to work inside and outside of the home. Thus, the family life of minority women has not been shaped as much by the idea of the family as by that of an emotional haven separate and apart from the demands of the economic workplace.

ADVOCACY AND THE CHANGING WORKPLACE

A similar dynamic seems to affect older people, people of lower socioeconomic classes, women, and sexual minorities in the workplace. Long-standing discrimination and complexities involving equality and needs seem to be more obvious in that context. Is federal law prohibiting employment discrimination still needed? The answer is clearly yes. A developing body of research confirms that discrimination is persistent, widespread, and harmful. Likewise, social workers' advocacy is needed to help everyone who wants to work find employment that supports their well-being.

ECONOMIC AND SOCIAL JUSTICE

Social justice ensures that all members of society share in the benefits that society offers and have opportunities to reciprocate with their own contributions. A just order accords every societal member the same basic social rights and opportunities. However, the working conditions of women, older people, people of color, working-class people, and LGBTQ people contradict the notion of a just workplace, in which workers receive resources and benefits through equal distribution.

In the workplace, **redistributive justice** frames the political and economic agenda for policy initiatives and practice interventions. For example, the stratification in the workplace results from inequality related to power, privilege, wealth, and prestige. Workers' position in the workplace hierarchy determines their potential for either earning a livable wage or experiencing barriers to career advancement. Social workers can help by advocating for systematic change to shift this sort of inequity from being seen as a personal problem to being acknowledged as a societal one. Such advocacy can take the form of referring people to programs and benefits, developing social welfare policy, union organizing, and writing editorials and other documents for public education.

SUPPORTIVE ENVIRONMENT

The work environment can set the stage for discriminatory actions and prejudicial attitudes. Employers can do a great deal on their own to make the environment more supportive for employees. For one thing, executives can mandate that

Lilly Ledbetter and the Fair Pay Act

Social workers often advocate for changes to policies and laws that affect the workplace, in such areas as occupational safety and health, and worker rights and benefits. Their tools include public relations, conflict resolution, and coalitions, collaborations, and support groups.

An example of this type of advocacy is passage of the Lilly Ledbetter Fair Pay Act of 2009, an equal-pay lawsuit signed by President Obama. The act states that pay discrimination claims on the basis of sex, race, national origin, age, religion, and disability "accrue" whenever an employee receives a discriminatory paycheck (National Women's Law Center, 2013). Lilly Ledbetter was one of the few female supervisors at the Goodyear plant in Gadsden, Alabama, and worked there for close to two decades. Ledbetter did not know she was the subject of discrimination until she received an anonymous note revealing the salaries of three of the male managers (National Alliance for Partnerships in Equity, n.d.). After she filed a complaint, her case went to trial, and the jury awarded her back pay and about $3.3 million in compensatory and punitive damages for the extreme nature of the pay discrimination to which she had been subjected.

1. Do you think you would be able to pursue a cause like this to the point of passing a law? If not, what skills do you feel you would need to develop? What types of allies do you think you would need?

2. If you were counseling a woman who was not receiving fair pay, what would you tell her about the Lilly Ledbetter Fair Pay Act? Assuming that she would be discouraged and tired of fighting the injustices she was facing, and would have problems with financial security, how might you convince her to move forward?

employment policies apply consistently across their organization, and they can ensure that managers and supervisors follow through.

Often the line between employment protections from discrimination and protections from harassment is not clearly defined. Antidiscrimination policies typically emphasize the responsibility of the employer, and antiharassment policies emphasize the responsibility of employees. However, antiharassment and nondiscrimination statements are wrapped into the same policy language.

An employer's nondiscrimination policy, or equal employment opportunity policy, typically covers conditions of employment such as hiring, promotions, termination, and compensation. Employers should include "gender identity" and "sexual orientation" as protected classes in nondiscrimination policies, in addition to other federally protected classes. Specifically referencing "sexual orientation" and "gender identity" in antiharassment policies sends a clear message that all employees will be respected and able to work free of any kind of harassment, and that no form of harassment or offensive conduct directed at individuals on those bases will be tolerated.

Social workers often support nondiscrimination or equal employment opportunity policies in government agencies by conducting program evaluations that gather data or evidence that indicates the degree to which policies are effective and efficient. Such evaluations are rational and scientific but often threatening to political forces such as elected or agency officials, because they might reveal inadequacies or poor administrative practices. Consequently, a social worker's role as an evaluator involves complexities that extend to the political arena.

HUMAN NEEDS AND RIGHTS

According to the dynamic advocacy model, human rights can be divided into three categories: (1) civil and political rights, (2) social and economic rights, and (3) collective rights. All these rights provide or support fundamental entitlements that are necessary for personal development and human potential (DuBois & Miley, 2014).

This chapter has primarily focused on civil and political rights, which provide protection against discrimination and oppression in the workplace. In the world of work, it is civil rights that ensure fair treatment, as guaranteed by the nation's Constitution.

Throughout its history the social work profession has been concerned with civil rights in relationship to women, older people, workers, and LGBTQ people. Currently social workers are also concerned about the social and economic rights of workers—LGBTQ people and women in particular. They are also concerned about the widening salary gap between the most highly compensated workers, such as executives and financiers, and lower- and middle-class workers. Social workers will work in community agencies, large service organizations, and local, state, and federal offices to ensure programs and policies that move forward an agenda relevant to the needs of these groups.

POLITICAL ACCESS

The dynamic advocacy model's political component suggests that "educator" is a significant role for social workers. In the workplace and in agencies, social workers can educate people about their rights as employees and about the resources that should be available to them if they are not employed. Employee rights cover everything from salary levels to appropriate physical work environments and benefits, including child care, sick days, and mental health services. Social workers can also educate workers about the structural elements that support discriminatory practices, fuel prejudicial treatment, and ignore civil rights.

In the political arena, social workers can both educate policymakers and advocate for particular pieces of legislation. Social welfare policies are fundamental to social work practice in the occupational arena, and politicians are the people who make decisions about key workplace issues associated with procedures, standards, and resource distribution (Reisch, 1998). The need for social workers to engage in employment-related politics is made more pressing given the economic times and increasing globalization of the marketplace. The dynamic advocacy model urges social workers to understand the influence they can have by participating in the political and policymaking processes and becoming involved in the effort to enhance the workplace for workers and their families.

YOUR CAREER IN THE WORLD OF WORK

Since work is an essential part of most of our lives, you might be interested in a career in a hospital, corporation, social service agency, or government-related organization. Social workers are involved in the majority of workplaces, through direct practice with individuals, families, and groups; service systems, including housing, health, and education; policy development at the local, state, and federal level; advocacy in unions, associations, or membership affiliations; offices of human services; insurance offices; schools; correctional and mental facilities; and service agencies across all levels of government.

When thinking about a career in the world of work, consider what is important to you in a workplace. Is it the benefits (e.g., health care, continuing education), environment, location, coworkers, or salary that will draw you to and keep you at an employment site? It is likely to be a combination of factors that make for a healthy and rewarding workplace. For the most part, what you want to experience in the workplace is what others will also want; thus, a career in the world of work involves embracing people's individuality and needs as a matter of basic human dignity and civil rights.

SUMMARY

Success is liking yourself, liking what you do, and liking how you do it.

–Maya Angelou

For most people worldwide, the family and the workplace are the two major domains of everyday interaction. Often social workers focus on the family and overlook the importance of the work environment. Yet, because social work uses a systems–ecological approach to issues of human needs, social workers are positioned to advocate for better working conditions in the context of family life.

As suggested by the dynamic advocacy model, the future direction of social work advocacy should be broad based to include organizational and political change supportive of a diverse workforce and their families. Ideally, introducing policies, programs, and procedures that enhance the workplace will improve family life while simultaneously increasing productivity and profitability for the work organization.

TOP 10 KEY CONCEPTS

affirmative action
Employee Assistance Programs (EAPs)
gender gap
gender inequality
minimum wage

occupational health hazards
Social Security
standard of living
underemployment
work ethic

DISCUSSION QUESTIONS

1. Think about your employment history in terms of the work environments and your assigned duties and responsibilities. What were the strengths and areas to improve in those workplaces? How did your experience in the workplace influence your career plans?

2. What are the issues that concern you about the changing workplace? List the issues and brainstorm what advocacy strategies could be introduced to prevent or alleviate the issues. How does your list of issues relate to social justice?

3. What aspect of the history of work did you find most interesting or informative when assessing the current workplace environment?

4. Would you advocate for or against an increase in the minimum wage? Please explain the reasons behind your position.

EXERCISES

1. Make a "dream list" of the economic and social status and other benefits you hope to gain from your professional career. Do you think your goals are realistic? Why or why not?

2. Schedule an interview with a professional who's currently employed in a position that you might be interested in pursuing. Before conducting the interview, please be sure to construct a list of questions that will guide your discussion. What does the list tell you about your values and also about your career expectations?

3. The unemployment level is high worldwide and causes civil unrest in some countries. Read an article that describes an international work-related incident. How does the situation impact workers and their families? Is there a role for the United States in the issue? If not, why? If so, what is it?

4. Visit a large retail store and note the people working: what they do, what they wear, how they interact, and the general work environment. Based on your observations, describe how and why the components of the dynamic advocacy model apply to the workers in the store. What advocacy skills would you use to enhance this workplace?

5. Social work education builds on a liberal arts foundation. Use the Internet to examine how the following individuals contributed to social work's perceptions of the workplace. Please list the experiment, theory, or concept each individual offered to the understanding of the workplace.

   a. Adam Smith
   b. Karl Marx
   c. Emile Durkheim
   d. Elton Mayo
   e. Frederick Winslow Taylor

6. Take a walk across your campus or community and list the modifications that have been made to assist people with special needs. Consider mobility, vision, and hearing impairments in particular. Are there more than you realized? What others are needed?

ONLINE RESOURCES

- "Employee Rights" (www.dol.gov/olms/regs/compliance/EmployeeRightsPoster11x17_Final.pdf): Provides a broad overview of the national rights of workers across a spectrum of employment situations

- "Immigrant Workers' Rights and Remedies" (www.nelp.org/content/content_issues/category/immigrant_workers_rights_and_remedies): Outlines the needs of immigrants to gain access to legal residence in the United States and to find financially sustaining employment opportunities

- Institute for Women's Policy Research (www.iwpr.org): Provides research findings on international women's issues

- "Nine Trends Defining the Future World of Work" (www.newworldofwork.co.uk/2012/01/27/ten-trends-defining-the-future-world-of-work): Considers factors that will influence the workplace and employers in the next decade

- "Succeeding in the World of Work" quiz (quizlet
  .com/5520481/succeeding-in-the-world-of-work-unit-1-self-
  assessment-wy-flash-cards): Offers an interactive survey
  related to success in the workplace
- TEDBlog (blog.ted.com/2014/01/15/further-reading-on-
  women-and-the-workplace): Depicts the role of women in
  various workplaces

- "Types of Retirement Plans" (www.irs.gov/Retirement-
  Plans/Plan-Sponsor/Types-of-Retirement-Plans-1):
  Encourages workers to consider the financial needs of
  retirement and how to plan for it
- World-of-Work Map (www.act.org/wwm/): Summarizes
  similarities and differences among various occupations

STUDENT STUDY SITE

Sharpen your skills with SAGE edge at **edge.sagepub.com/cox**

SAGE edge for Students provides a personalized approach to help you accomplish your coursework
goals in an easy-to-use learning environment.

Chapter 15: VETERANS, THEIR FAMILIES, AND MILITARY SOCIAL WORK

Learning Objectives

After reading this chapter, you will be able to

1. Understand military culture, values, and beliefs.
2. Understand the history and practice of military social work with veterans, members of the armed services, and their families.
3. Identify contexts where soldiers and veterans may seek social services, health care, and mental health/addiction counseling.
4. Understand challenges and stressors in military families.
5. Identify policies, models, and interventions to assist veterans and their families.

Veteran Javier Experienced Military Life and Now Counsels Families

Javier Melendez joined the U.S. Army after high school, served as a service member for 6 years, and experienced the ground invasion of Baghdad in 2003. In combat, he sustained a mild traumatic brain injury. He was honorably discharged with the rank of staff sergeant and received outpatient clinical treatment for his symptoms of posttraumatic stress disorder (PTSD).

After receiving therapy, Javier decided to take advantage of his GI benefits, which are available to honorably discharged veterans, and enrolled in classes at a county college. While sitting in classes, Javier sometimes daydreamed about returning to familiar military duty. He longed for the purpose and meaning he had felt in combat, where he was called to protect his comrades.

One of Javier's classes was an introduction to social work course. The professor was himself a veteran. He noticed Javier's leadership and empathy skills and suggested that Javier major in social work. Javier successfully completed his BSW degree while working full-time in an electronics shop. After college Javier excitedly accepted a counselor position at the Covenant House, where he counseled runaway and at-risk youth.

Despite his absence from combat, Javier still gets startled whenever someone wakes him or touches him to get his attention. He additionally experiences flashbacks, insomnia, and hyperarousal. Javier is flirtatious but hesitates to get involved in a romantic relationship. As an unmarried, 27-year-old Latino who does not converse well in Spanish, Javier realizes he may continue to be at a greater risk than some of his fellow veterans of ongoing PTSD and readjustment issues, which are exacerbated by his ethnic issues. He understands that symptoms related to his traumatic brain injury may linger for a lifetime.

As a social work counselor Javier clearly sees how change is a process rather than a single event—for his clients and for himself. He still feels the need to reintegrate with his own family of origin here in the states. On the plus side, because of his military experience, Javier is punctual, adherent to a structured life, a creative problem solver, and natural leader, and he possesses excellent interpersonal skills and a strong work ethic. Next, Javier plans to acquire his MSW degree.

To work most effectively with service members, veterans, and military families, social workers must understand why people join the military, as well as military culture and service experiences predeployment, during deployment, and postdeployment. Surprisingly few civilians are aware of military demographics, events, culture, or stressors. In this chapter, you will learn about military history and a culture that esteems authority and expects conformity "in the workplace."

Following World War II, social workers provided increasing behavioral health care to military personnel, veterans, and military families across multiple branches and contexts. Today, licensed social workers may choose to work as full-time uniformed military officers or as civilians for the **Department of Veterans Affairs (VA)** and veterans' centers. Social workers can also work part- or full-time as civilians who are contracted by the armed forces or the VA. Social workers can also work with veterans and military families as private practitioners through the military's health insurance plan.

The attitudes and concerns of service members have changed a great deal between the Vietnam era, when many young men were forced to join the military through **conscription** (forced military service), to the present day, when men and women are in the military only because they have volunteered to join. Service members now define their military service more as a career than a difficult phase of life through which they must pass on the way to adulthood.

Enlistment in today's military is also characterized by special benefits designed to make a military career more attractive. For example, families left behind when their loved ones deploy receive much more care and concern than in previous eras. At the same time, developments in weaponry, wartime tactics, and trauma care have allowed more service members to survive serious physical and mental injury. They return from war with extensive needs. Even those who are not gravely injured may have trouble reintegrating into society. Commendably, the military is stepping up to take responsibility for the long-term care of these people.

THE ARMED SERVICES AND MILITARY CULTURE

No matter how much the military tries to treat its members like their peers in the work world, being in the military will always differ from being in other professions. In the military, failure or success in performing duties may affect the survival of a country. Military personnel realize they may be placed in danger. They are required to take an oath when they enlist to abide by the **Uniform Code of Military Justice** and the moral principles found in the Constitution and the Declaration of Independence.

The **Department of Defense (DoD),** otherwise known as the Pentagon and illustrated in Exhibit 15.1, is the headquarters of all five branches of the U.S. armed forces: Army, Navy, Marine Corps, Air Force, and Coast Guard. The U.S. president is the head of the armed forces; second in command is the secretary of defense, a civilian appointed by the president.

The military is extremely hierarchical and bureaucratic. Each branch of the armed forces is headed by a member of the military. Except for the head of the Coast Guard (who reports to the secretary of homeland security) and along with the head of the National Guard, the top leaders of the various branches are known as the Joint Chiefs of Staff. Below them is a hierarchy of smaller and smaller

EXHIBIT 15.1   Department of Defense Organizational Chart

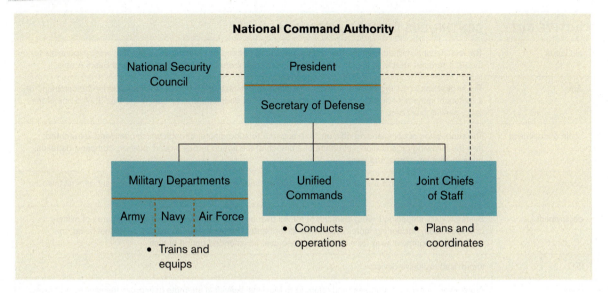

Source: http://en.wikipedia.org/wiki/File:US_National_Command.png

units, down to the squad, which usually consists of 8 to 14 people.

Such a distinctive institution has, of course, its own jargon. The special terms defined in Exhibit 15.2 will often come up in conversations with veterans and military family members, and are helpful for social workers to know.

TIME TO THINK

How does your current workplace environment (or college or university) differ from a military environment? How is it the same?

WHAT IT MEANS TO BE A SOLDIER

The American military subculture rests on four distinct pillars that set it apart from mainstream culture, as shown in Exhibit 15.3 (Kudler, 2010; cited in Pryce, Pryce, & Shackelford, 2012, p. 20):

- It requires strict discipline throughout the hierarchy.
- It relies on soldiers' values of loyalty and self-sacrifice to keep order in battle.

- It uses ceremonies and rituals to create common identities among its members.
- It emphasizes group cohesion and esprit de corps to keep soldiers interconnected.

The core values that guide service members are evidenced in creeds such as, "I will bear true faith and allegiance" and "I will obey my orders" (U.S. Marine Corps values; cited in Rubin, Weiss, & Coll, 2013, p. 23).

This subculture appeals to young Americans who decide to join the military, although there are also practical reasons for becoming a soldier. Soldiers most commonly cite the following reasons for enlisting: identification with the warrior mentality, family tradition of military service, benefits of being a member of the military, and escape from difficult life circumstances (L. K. Hall, 2011; Wertsch, 1991). As a matter of fact, since 1973, when the all-volunteer force replaced conscription, the economy and the job market, along with an individual's call to service, have tended to motivate people to join the ranks.

The strong identity of being a soldier continues after a person separates from the military. The following definition comes from a website for the 1886 Welcome Home Farm (www.1886welcomehomefarm.org), an organization that

EXHIBIT 15.2   Glossary of Military Terms

ACTIVE DUTY	CONTINUOUS DUTY ON A DAILY BASIS
al-Qaeda	The multinational militant Islamic organization, previously headed by Osama bin Laden, that was responsible for the 9/11 terrorist attacks in the United States. Current members are mainly from Egypt and Saudi Arabia.
Army	The largest unit in the organizational chain of command, comprising 50,000-plus soldiers under the command of a lieutenant general or higher officer. Army groups have not been employed since World War II. Also one of the major service branches.
chain of command	The succession of commanding officers, from superior to subordinate, through which command is executed; also the following organizational structure of a branch of the armed forces: squad, platoon, company, battalion, brigade, division, corps, and army.
corps	The Marine Corps; also a unit of 20,000 to 45,000 soldiers under the command of a lieutenant general (also Jar Heads)
deployment	Systematically stationing military persons or forces over an area, or moving forces within an area of military operation; also, positioning forces in a formation for battle. The term refers to military personnel being on temporary assignment away from their home base over an extended period of time.
IED	Improvised explosive device
jihad	Arabic word meaning "struggles" and referring to Muslims' individual attempts to improve themselves and grow closer to Allah
Shiite	Those who follow the Shia branch of Islam; Shiites believe that the only legitimate leaders of Islam must be blood relatives of the prophet Muhammad. Most Arabs are Sunni Muslims, and relations between Sunnis and Shiites are poor.
soldier	Technically and specifically a member of the Army (as opposed to a marine, airman, or sailor, for instance) but in general parlance a member of the armed forces
Sunni	The largest branch of Islam. Unlike the Shiites, this branch does not require that religious leaders be blood descendants of the prophet Muhammad.

EXHIBIT 15.3   Four Pillars of the American Military Subculture

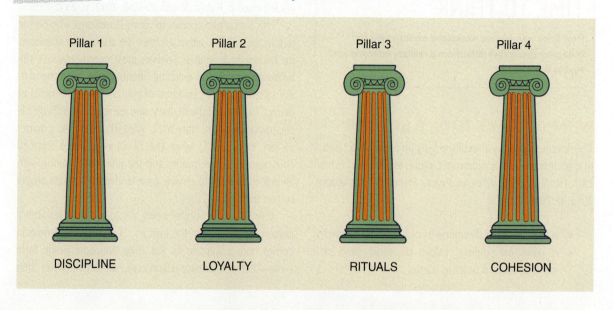

Pillar 1	Pillar 2	Pillar 3	Pillar 4
DISCIPLINE	LOYALTY	RITUALS	COHESION

CURRENT TRENDS

Reminiscences of World War II Veterans

THOSE who fought in World War II are becoming more and more scarce as they age and die. Historians and journalists are feeling a great deal of pressure to interview as many of them as possible before all personal witnesses to the war are gone. One of those interviewed in 2014 was Ewing Roddy, a 90-year-old World War II veteran from Egg Harbor Township, New Jersey. This is an excerpt from the article written on the basis of his interview:

> Roddy, 90, was an engineer and B-17 gunner in the U.S. Army Air Force 490th Bombardment Group in World War II, flying 22 missions over Germany and German-occupied Europe. . . .
>
> . . . Roddy now lives at an assisted-living facility in Egg Harbor Township, surrounded by photos and mementos of his flying days. A certificate designating him as a veteran of the Battle of the Bulge hangs near the door, a miniature B-17 bomber sits on one table—press the button at the base and the sounds of roaring engines and flak explosions fill the room—and on another table, the funeral card for his wife, Delores, who died earlier this year.
>
> "We would have been married 60 years in a couple of weeks," Roddy said. . . .
>
> Despite his encyclopedic memory of his flying days, Roddy was surprised to be reminded of one important anniversary: his very first mission was flown 70 years ago this Saturday.
>
> "My first mission?" he recalled. "I was completely scared to death. . . . But we never said so. Everybody was scared to death."
>
> Roddy was in his senior year in high school in Uniontown, Pa., outside Pittsburgh, when he and several other players volunteered in 1943. . . .
>
> It was the bitter cold at thousands of feet above ground that he remembered most—from one crewmember's nose injury freezing the blood as it poured out of his face, "like the Frosty you'd get in a store," to the time he took his gloves off and his fingers froze to a metal gun. . . .
>
> His worst injury came when a piece of flak hit one of the shells stored in the turret, which "went off just like being in a shotgun." A flash like something from a welder's torch damaged his eyes.
>
> "They just patched it up, put some salve in it and some cotton," Roddy recalled. He lost about 70 percent of the vision in his left eye—but since it was never determined whether the shell that hit his plane was enemy or friendly, he never received a Purple Heart.
>
> But he knows he was lucky. A ball turret gunner was transferred from his crew to another plane—which was shot down—and Roddy said he was executed by the Germans. . . .
>
> When the war in Europe ended, his crew had flown 22 missions—but they needed 25 before they could be grounded. So they trained to fly B-29s in the Pacific, until Japan's surrender ended that. His post-war life was interrupted, however, when he was almost called back up to fly in the Korean War.
>
> "I told them I had two babies and a house on the way up," he said. "They finally let me stay home." But he did get a promotion to master sergeant upon his discharge.
>
> Roddy received four Air Medals during the war—the last one for kicking the stuck bomb out of his plane—which made him eligible for the Distinguished Flying Cross, he said.
>
> "But anyway, I still haven't gotten it," he said with a shrug. "The medal doesn't mean a thing. Life is precious."

1. What is the purpose of collecting these reminiscences from older generations of soldiers? Why is it so important?

2. What would you say has been the long-term psychological effect on Roddy of having flown in World War II?

Source: Lemongello (2014).

takes in homeless veterans and puts them to work in charitable enterprises:

Who is a VETERAN?

A veteran, whether active duty, discharged, retired, or reserve, is someone who at one point in his life, wrote a blank check made payable to "The United States of America" for an amount of "up to and including his/her life."

HOW WAR AFFECTS SOLDIERS

Implicit in the quote above is the understanding that, despite all the other activities soldiers may undertake, ultimately they are obligated to engage in battle if their superiors call on them to do so. The risk, of course, is that soldiers will be killed or maimed. But war has not only physical consequences for the soldiers but also psychological ones.

The United States has been involved in multiple international conflicts that have resulted in multiple deployments for service members. Exhibit 15.4 provides a chronology of the most important wars fought by the United States, beginning with the Civil War.

Both the harsh environments and the extended duration of two recent conflicts, **Operation Enduring Freedom** in Afghanistan and **Operation Iraqi Freedom**, have led to unusual work demands for armed services members. Huge numbers of combat veterans have survived serious burns, amputation, and other physical injuries. The three traits of secrecy, stoicism, and denial that are crucial for a contemporary warrior's success on a mission may also cause psychological trauma. It is difficult to live in a strange environment with constant fear, continuous planning for disaster, and constant readiness for change (L. K. Hall, 2008, 2011). Psychological injuries include PTSD, helplessness, shame, and survivor's guilt (Larson, Wooten, Adams, & Merrick, 2012). Along with these injuries come high rates of co-occurring physical, psychological, and substance abuse problems.

EXHIBIT 15.4   Selected Wars Involving the United States

WAR	TIME PERIOD	NOTES
U.S. Civil War (War Between the States)	1861–1865	Union vs. Confederacy, fought to preserve the union of the USA.
World War I	1914–1918	Fought for complicated causes of imperialism, nationalism, militarism; European countries making mutual defense agreements and the assassination of Archduke Franz Ferdinand. In 1917 the United States joined on the side of The Triple Entente (Britain, France, Russia) against The Triple Alliance (Germany, Italy, and Austria-Hungary).
World War II	1939 or 1941–1945	Bloodiest war of the 20th century to defeat Germany/Japan. (September 16, 1940, FDR approved Military Draft.)
Korean War	1950–1953	Fought during Cold War to stop communism.
Vietnam War	1962–1975	Fought during Cold War to stop communism in Southeast Asia; very unpopular war. (Military Draft stopped after this war.)
Persian Gulf War (Desert Storm)	1990–1991	When Iraq invaded Kuwait, this was the first war fought by the new all-volunteer force.
Global War on Terror	2001–	Began with September 11, 2001, attacks on the World Trade Center and Pentagon; started as a fight against radical fundamentalist Islam.
Afghanistan War (Operation Enduring Freedom)	2001– December 2014	Purpose was to remove the radical Islamist Taliban from political dominance, destroy al-Qaeda, and kill Osama bin Laden. American forces are still involved in this first protracted war that uses an all-volunteer force that has required military personnel. (President Obama announced May 27, 2014, that the U.S. combat mission will end December 2014.)
Iraq War (Operation Iraqi Freedom, or OIF)	2003–August 2010	Guerilla-type war that captured Baghdad in a month and continued, with U.S. active and reserve component military personnel often being deployed for a year, coming home, and being redeployed; this protracted unpopular war resorted to enlisting felons for a brief period; the motives for U.S. invasion are debatable.
OIF renamed Operation New Dawn	September 2010	Reduced role of U.S. troops in Iraqi cities and towns. December 15, 2011, American troops lowered the flag over Baghdad, symbolizing the official end of America's presence in Iraq.

TIME TO THINK

In your opinion, what is the purpose of war?

Think about enlisted service members. From what you have learned so far, what do you think would be important needs for them?

HOW THE MILITARY TAKES CARE OF ITS OWN

After deployment, soldiers and veterans return from war with multiple needs and reintegration challenges that traverse issues of physical impairment, economic distress, employment, domestic violence, family services, housing, health, mental health, and substance abuse. As a direct result of their military service, veterans' personal relationships, careers, education, and physical independence often suffer. Consequently, the DoD has established a vast system of services for soldiers, veterans, and their families. VA hospitals and **TRICARE** military insurance benefits were created specifically to respond to predeployment, deployment, and postdeployment military needs.

Military families also experience considerable stress, periods of long separation, and changes to the family system when a family member enters or returns from a war zone (Simmons & Rycraft, 2010). In the military, the definition of family has evolved. Twenty to thirty years ago, the norm for a service member's family was usually the husband in uniform and the wife at home with the children. Now the military has extended families, blended families, single-parent families, dual-career families, multicultural and multiethnic families, and service members in committed relationships, as well as combinations of all these.

In 1864, William Tecumseh Sherman, a general in the Union Army during the Civil War, had this to say about how important it is to soldiers to be ensured of their families' well-being:

> Man has two supreme loyalties—to country and to family. . . . So long as their families are safe, they will defend their country, believing that by their sacrifice they are safeguarding their families also. But even the bonds of patriotism, discipline, and comradeship are loosened when the family itself is threatened.

SOCIAL WORK WITH THE MILITARY AND VETERANS

Members of our armed services who have returned from the Afghanistan and Iraq wars face similar challenges to those other soldiers have faced throughout history, such as physical injury, emotional anguish and grief, and combat stress and fatigue (Flynn, 2010). In addition, contemporary veterans and their families face the aftereffects of combat experience caused by extended and multiple deployments, traumatic brain injury (TBI), posttraumatic stress disorder (PTSD), and bodily injuries from explosive devices.

Since World War I, social workers have helped veterans cope with the aftermath of war (Yarvis, 2011). In response to increasing need, veterans hospitals have hired multiple social workers, in all parts of the United States and the world. These social workers must be prepared to help veterans deploy and reintegrate into society despite the multiple personal, community, and social obstacles they face.

Military social workers form a distinctive cadre of social work professionals who help combatants cope with the negative mental health effects of war and deal with stigma. Over the years, thousands of social workers have successfully balanced their personal and professional ethics with the military's ethics and codes, as they have observed the military model change from an institutional to an occupational one (Knox & Price, 1995).

Today, civilian and military social workers require knowledge about physical injuries, mental health, homelessness, criminal justice systems, **GI Bills,** and women and LGBTQ (lesbian, gay, bisexual, transgender, and questioning) veterans' experiences, and how to manage secondary traumatic stress. They must also be clinically astute and recognize how the multiple branches handle pre- and postdeployment, as well as recognize the importance of quickly engaging the trust of clients connected to military culture. To build a therapeutic alliance with vets and to be credible to military personnel, veterans, and their families, social workers are required to understand the military's power and authority structure, military culture, and its influence on people's lives. Effective military social work practice also requires a sensitivity to ethnic, gender, and sexual identity diversity within the military culture.

A HISTORY OF MILITARY SOCIAL WORK

Since Civil War times, social work professionals have been involved with helping service members, veterans, and military family members. In 1943, the Army designated psychiatric social work as a separate job category (Simmons & Rycraft, 2010). Today there are uniformed social workers in the Army, Navy, and Air Force. Then and now, social workers have had to know how to render clinical and other psychosocial interventions for the veteran, couples, and the family, because change, separation, and stress were and are apparent phenomena experienced by all military families (Laser & Stephens, 2011).

History reveals that three organizations, (1) the Wartime Committee on Personnel of the American Association of Social Workers, (2) the National Committee for Mental Hygiene, and (3) the War Service Office of the American Association of Psychiatric Social Workers, were instrumental in getting a social work branch established in the U.S. Army (Rubin et al., 2013, p. 6). Commissioned status for social workers in the U.S. Army was accomplished in 1945 when Major Daniel I. O'Keefe became the first chief of the Army's Psychiatric Social Work Branch.

After the demobilization after World War II, urgent recruitment of master's-prepared social workers, especially males, was enacted to help Army veterans. The Air Force's military department of social work was created in 1947 and expanded from the original 6 commissioned social work officers in 1952 to 225 social workers by 1988 (Jenkins, 2000; cited in Rubin et al., 2013, p. 7). The Navy Relief Society was one of the largest social services agencies to give social support to families. In the Vietnam War era, the number of military social workers in the Navy expanded greatly. During this time the Red Cross stopped providing psychosocial services despite the great need for mental health counseling, as many prisoners of war (POWs) were missing in action. In response naval treatment facilities began to employ numerous social workers to help coordinate community services and facilitate the transitioning of repatriated POWs and their families.

During the 1970s Navy drug rehabilitation centers, family advocacy programs, and family service centers were developed; yet only 29 civilian social workers were then employed in naval hospitals. Meanwhile, the other branches of the armed services had well-functioning social work programs. The paucity of social workers caused problems in treating sailors and marines, so the Navy got a boost in 1979 when the Bureau of Medicine and Surgery was approved to recruit and commission 13 social workers in the Medical Service Corps (Rubin et al., 2013, p. 11).

For the most part, however, the evolution of the professional role of social work has taken place within the VA, and social workers now have treatment responsibilities in all client care arenas. For example, social workers at VA hospitals and clinics promote psychosocial and vocational rehabilitation and help VA patients and families cope better with the new realities of their lives. As members of multidisciplinary teams, social workers both develop and implement treatment approaches for armed services members, veterans, and military families. Military social workers also assist with discharge planning and provide ongoing case-management services.

BEHAVIORAL HEALTH PROBLEMS OF SERVICE MEMBERS AND VETERANS

One in five veterans meet diagnostic criteria for PTSD, and many others experience anxiety, depression, or other mental health issues. Besides their invisible wounds of PTSD and TBI, veterans have a heightened risk of homelessness, substance abuse, suicide, and unemployment (Yarvis, 2011).

Today the DoD and VA have significantly increased their attention to the behavioral health of military personnel. Service members not only have to be physically fit for duty but also must meet behavioral standards that demonstrate self-discipline. Thus, services for prevention and resilience, assessment and outreach, and counseling have been expanded for service members and veterans. Four of the main health and interrelated behavioral health problems social workers see in the military are TBI, PTSD, substance use disorders, and increasing cases of suicide.

Traumatic Brain Injury

TBI caused by blast exposure is the signature wound of recent warfare. In the wake of Operation Iraqi Freedom, Operation Enduring Freedom, and Operation New Dawn alone, more than 195,000 service members have been screened for a suspected brain injury (Defense and Veterans Brain Injury Center, 2014). In the aftermath of TBI, adjustment to civilian life becomes more complicated than usual for returning soldiers.

TBI ranges in severity from mild to severe. Skull fractures, contusions, and ocular/eye injuries are commonly found in moderate to severe brain injuries. An array of acute symptoms can follow from moderate to severe TBI: severe worsening headache, dizziness, fatigue, sleep problems, vomiting, seizures, pupil dilation, problems speaking, limb weakness, loss of coordination, confusion, restlessness, and agitation.

Posttraumatic Stress Disorder

Defining PTSD is difficult and much debated. Research on proper and specific treatments for PTSD has also proven difficult, especially with regard to veterans of combat and peacekeeping missions. Combat PTSD is harder to treat than the civilian type because it is more chronic and complex (Rubin et al., 2013, p. xxiv).

The term PTSD was coined during the Vietnam War. Many veterans of that war had high scores on measures of depression, hostility, and psychoticism, as well as survivor's guilt, unreality, and suicidal tendencies. Also, Vietnam vets had a greater lifetime frequency of panic disorder and an earlier age of onset for alcoholism. Today the signs and symptoms of PTSD are described more in terms of an anxiety disorder (American Psychological Association, 2013; cited in Rubin, 2012, p. 87). It is unique among psychiatric diagnoses because of the great importance placed on the stressor that caused it. Events such as rape, torture, genocide, and severe war zone stress will be experienced as traumatic events by almost everyone; however, there are some unique features of PTSD in warrior populations. For example, combat veterans may relive experiences through flashbacks, nightmares, and trigger responses. Vets may also try to avoid crowds, driving, or war movies if such remind them of a combat situation. As well, veterans with PTSD may feel keyed up (hyperaroused) and experience negative changes in feelings and beliefs (e.g., not trusting people, thinking the world is a dangerous place).

Substance Use Disorders

Historically, substance use has been a problem in U.S. military settings. During the American Civil War, alcohol was used medically and daily consumption of rum was common to help soldiers cope with battle. Opiates were used for pain when limbs were amputated, and many soldiers became addicted to these substances as well.

During the Vietnam War, the pattern of substance abuse changed. While alcohol continued to be prominent, marijuana use increased. Later in the war heroin use surpassed marijuana use. In 1971, the Army began urine testing for opiates, barbiturates, and amphetamines.

Concern about substance use in the military is extremely elevated today. In response, substance use disorder prevention efforts have been developed based on a community-based model. One such model is the **community capacity model** used by the Air Force (Rubin et al., 2013, p. 193). This approach has two components: shared responsibility and collective competence. Shared responsibility implies that one is concerned, and collective competence conveys that one is motivated and will take action. An example of using the community capacity model to help treat postdeployment mental health problems in veterans is when local, nature-based efforts grounded in conservation psychology and horticultural therapy—for example, gardening, hunting, planting trees—are used to promote individual and community resilience in traumatized veterans who need to adapt and function more positively (Straits-Troster et al., 2011; Tidball & Krasny, 2014). Veterans in the process of healing may be less likely to abuse alcohol or drugs. The Army, however, is moving toward a public health model. Army installations employ prevention coordinators, risk-reduction specialists, and employee assistance professionals to help improve the health and wellness of the total force.

Suicide

Social workers need to be cognizant of military-specific and other factors that might increase a service member's risk for suicide. An increase in suicide among military personnel in the all-volunteer era seemed to be related to the number, length, or operational tempo of military deployments, until in 2014, findings from a large study were unveiled (Zoroya, 2014). The study found that many suicides also occur among service members who have never been deployed. However, the highest suicide rates are among soldiers who have been to war. Suicide data in the military point to three primary risk factors: relationship, legal, and financial troubles (DoD, 2010; cited in Rubin et al., 2013, p. 226).

Resilience is often required to prevent self-directed violence in the military. Evidence-based, cognitive-behavioral strategies are used by counselors to assess and intervene with clients who have experienced suicidal ideations or attempts. In addition, a mind–body framework (depicted in Exhibit 15.5), which draws on resources within the individual, family, and organization, has been used with some success to prevent suicide. The domains within the framework include medical fitness, environmental fitness, psychological fitness, nutritional fitness, behavioral fitness, social fitness, physical fitness, spiritual fitness, and family fitness. This framework helps prevent suicide, as social workers help military members identify stress and proactively enhance resilience by getting fit across all these domains. Essentially, Total Force Fitness is a new way of improving mental health by focusing on well-being (Jonas et al., 2010; Mullen, 2011).

ISSUES AFFECTING WOUNDED MILITARY VETERANS

Advances in both medical care and technology have resulted in new challenges for veterans of war. Because of better

medications, efficient medical care, and Kevlar body armor that protects the vital organs, 90% of soldiers who are wounded now survive injuries to their head and limbs (Jackson, 2013). They are coming back to the United States for medical care in droves. Unfortunately, injured soldiers have been returning to myriad economic woes and a U.S. society that incompletely comprehends the exact nature of their military service.

Social workers may be required to assist wounded soldiers in VA hospital settings, in their homes, or in the community. Veterans and their family members often require assistance in adjusting to physical impairments that end or greatly alter plans for the future. In addition, they require assistance in navigating systems of care. Therefore, social work professionals must have a working knowledge of eligibility and enrollment criteria, service-connected disabilities and compensation resources, Vet Centers, homeless veterans programs, suicide prevention, transition assistance resources,

EXHIBIT 15.5   Suicide Prevention Through Family, Organization, and Environment

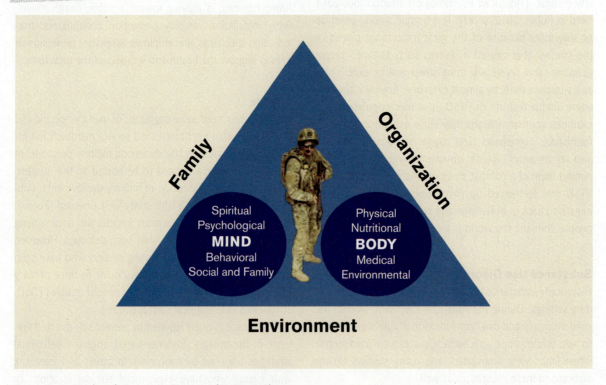

Source: Jonas et al. (2010); illustrated in Rubin et al. (2013, p. 230).

and the special needs of women veterans. Vet Center programs, established in 1979, help veterans and their family members have a successful postwar adjustment experience.

ISSUES AFFECTING MILITARY FAMILIES

Dependent family members outnumber military members in all services (Pryce et al., 2012, p. 25). Since the terrorist attacks in the United States on September 11, 2001, family separation as a result of deployment has become more frequent and unpredictable. The deployment puts strain on military families. Family members fear for their soldier's safety, living conditions, and health. Spouses become lonely and apprehensive about adapting to unfamiliar roles. Negative media reporting about war and conflicts exacerbates stress levels. Younger families, families with a pregnant spouse, families whose soldier is deployed alone to join an unfamiliar unit in-country, and families with multiple problems and special needs are especially vulnerable (Pryce et al., 2012, p. 26).

It is very important for social workers to understand how mobilization may adversely affect the families of people in the military reserves in particular. **Reservists** are service members who are civilians during peacetime but may be obligated to report for duty during conflicts. They serve in all branches of the military. They tend to be older and married longer than those actively serving in the military. During the war on terror, many reservists were "called up," requiring a sudden disruption in their lives. Monthly income for families of reservists often decreases by more than $1,000 once the reservist leaves his or her civilian job and enters active duty (Pryce et al., 2012, p. 27). To serve them, the DoD has put in place family assistance centers and community outreach partnerships with civilian, faith-based, and veterans organizations.

Whether the soldier is on active duty or a reservist, postdeployment household roles and routines require renegotiation, and soldiers must reconnect with their children. Because combat changes a soldier's mood and personality, both physical and invisible emotional wounds require healing. In addition, veterans with TBI may require extensive health care, and much of the burden falls on their spouses, partners, and parents. These civilians often feel emotionally and practically ill equipped. Because many veterans are married with children, the trauma of war causes collateral damage to children, parents, and of course spouses. As the

▲ A soldier who lost a limb in combat attends a rally.

veterans' problems mount, they may also fear being stigmatized and resist mental health care (Jackson, 2013).

Clinical social workers may work with armed service members and veterans who have experienced combat in the World Wars, Korea, Vietnam, the Persian Gulf, Iraq, or Afghanistan (Rubin, 2012). Regardless of the war fought in, they face similar mental health challenges. When they return to their families, they cannot debrief quickly or in isolation. Instead veterans may require counseling, treatment, and/or assistance to best manage medical issues (e.g., TBI, amputations, or surgeries), mental health problems or disorders, military sexual trauma, parenting and family communication, domestic violence, homelessness, substance abuse or addiction issues, stress, and attempted suicide.

Data show that about 37% of the spouses of returning soldiers have mental health issues to contend with (Makin-Byrd, Gifford, McCutcheon, & Glynn, 2011). In addition, military families may move a lot, and housing on bases tends to be located next to predatory lending companies, which are tempting resources when money runs short. Their home lives may be complicated by domestic violence or unemployment.

Children in military families, one third of whom are between the ages of 5 and 12 years old, are challenged to adjust to the relocations and prolonged periods of separation from one or both parents. In essence, their situation resembles that of children living with a single parent. These experiences require recognition and often individual or family counseling.

The high rate of unemployment among returning service members during an economic downturn increases the temptation to reenlist. Reenlistment bonuses may be as much as $60,000 (U.S. General Accounting Office, 2003; cited in Rubin et al., 2013, p. xxvi).

Social work professionals would do well to consider aspects of stress and traits of resilience in clients they counsel. Fortunately, because social workers view clients through a person-in-environment lens, they can help families see the big picture, the interconnectivity of problems, and the sources of support available to them.

TIME TO THINK

How can social workers help veterans and their families process the experience of war and adapt to biological, psychological, social, spiritual, and financial issues that result from exposure to war?

PROGRAMS AND POLICIES FOR MILITARY PERSONNEL, VETERANS, AND THEIR FAMILIES

Multiple military programs and policies are available to members of the military and their families (see Exhibit 15.6), and those programs and policies must be a part of military social work professionals' knowledge base, wherever they practice. For example, social workers employed by VA hospitals require knowledge about disabled transition assistance and military programs that help wounded service members. They also have to know about TRICARE military insurance benefits and how to uphold confidentiality and minimize stigma so service members get needed treatment. Civilian social workers in private practice will help veterans most when they possess knowledge and resources to assist reintegration in personal, social, and community situations related to civilian life.

The good news is that over the past 100 years, the presence of social workers and social work–initiated reform

programs has dramatically increased. Today social workers must have at least an MSW degree to work with veterans and to serve in the military. The DoD prefers that social work professionals have 2 years of postgraduate experience and/or a license to practice independent clinical social work before they serve in the armed services. However, each branch has developed internships for newly minted MSWs to help them get their clinical licensing while in the service. At a minimum, social work professionals who help military personnel and family members should be familiar with the programs and policies listed in Exhibit 15.6.

SOCIAL WORK ASSESSMENT AND INTERVENTION SKILLS

Knowledge about physical injuries is essential to a military social worker. For example, TBI is the most significant wound of recent warfare. Therefore, social workers must know about its prevalence, diagnosis, and treatment; its influence on psychosocial functioning and the family; and its implications regarding the treatment of and recovery from co-occurring disorders. Knowing about treatment phases is important to working with veterans who have TBI.

Social workers can increase their effectiveness in this field of practice through a **systems–ecological approach**. For instance, active duty personnel and veterans display a high prevalence of comorbidity of PTSD and TBI with substance use disorders. In fact, military clients often have the triple threat of PTSD, TBI, and substance use disorders. Clinical interventions should encompass both individual and systemic variables and cultural/worldview variables, and use a biopsychosocial approach.

Skills required by military social work personnel include case management, counseling, motivational interviewing and cognitive-behavioral therapy (among other therapies), advocacy, medical social work, and hospice care. Effective social workers will also understand at least basic content about neurobiology, because such relates to comprehension of PTSD symptoms. Because of the high incidence of substance use problems in military personnel, social workers also require knowledge about psychopharmacological interventions for PTSD and co-occurring disorders.

Social workers who help military personnel also need to know how to prevent homelessness, rehabilitate, and navigate systems. They must realize how the social work *Code of Ethics* may conflict with military codes. For example, the

EXHIBIT 15.6   Military Social Programs and Policies

PROGRAMS	POLICIES
Family programs	Family Advocacy Program
Air Force	Child Advocacy Program (1975)
Armed Services YMCA	Military Family Resource Center (1980)
Substance abuse prevention (EAP)	Public Law 92-129 (1971) [12-step model]
Vet Centers	Veterans Health Care Amendments Act of 1979
Comfort and Mercy/Fleet Hospital Five	First social workers deployed to combat zones on ships (1990s)
New Parents Support Program	Family Advocacy Budget designed (1995)
ADAPT program	Air Force Alcohol & Drug Abuse Prevention & Control (1998)
Services for Women Veterans	Veterans Health Care Act of 1992
First VA center for women only	DoD policy following the Tailhook scandal and military sexual trauma
Homosexuality support	Don't Ask, Don't Tell policy overturned (2009)
SAPRO	Sexual Assault Prevention & Response created (2000s)
Veterans Crisis Line	Suicide Prevention (2007)
VA affiliation with MSW programs	Department of Veterans Affairs

admonishment to preserve confidentiality may conflict with military mission preparedness and a commander's need to know about the service member's fitness for combat.

Social work practitioners who long practice with military veterans and their family members may experience **secondary trauma**. A social worker who counsels veterans who have been physically or emotionally handicapped from traumatic combat experiences may experience vicarious trauma similar to that of their clients. Social workers who help these veterans must learn how to assess, prevent, and treat secondary trauma in other service providers and in themselves.

Common Types of Therapy

Clinical social workers can draw from a wide variety of empirically supported treatment approaches not developed specifically for treating active duty service members or veterans. For example, **cognitive processing therapy** is an empirically supported treatment for PTSD. The therapist uses virtual reality to present traumatic stimuli, always controlling what is presented so as to increase or decrease the degree of client reaction. Cues—such as event-related odors—are carefully chosen. The social work counselor can monitor the client's physiological and mood reactions during the virtual reality presentation (Rubin et al., 2013, p. xxvii).

Cognitive information processing approaches may represent a useful strategy to employ with veterans who wish to rejoin the workforce (Bullock, Braud, Andrews, & Phillips, 2009). This approach emphasizes decision making and career problem solving, and requires a hefty dose of self-knowledge and job know-how. The social worker (therapist) can first administer a psychological inventory to help identify some of the negative thinking veterans may experience, or to assess the Big Five personality factors of openness, conscientiousness, extraversion, agreeableness, and emotional stability. Then a social worker could help military clients engage in multistage decision making. Studies have suggested that the strength of the helping relationship has a much greater impact on treatment outcome than does the specific intervention approach selected (Duncan, Miller, Wampold, & Hubble, 2009, p. 206).

SOCIAL WORK IN ACTION

Kristin Morrell Provides Therapy at a VA Hospital

KRISTIN Morrell, LCSW, MSW, has never served as an armed services member; however, her experience in hospice and home health care management has prepared her well for her social work position at the VA hospital. Trauma, loss, pain, suffering, and suicide are as familiar to her as the faces of recovery, courage, care, and catharsis. Her skill set includes cognitive behavioral therapy, motivational interviewing, exposure therapy, and couples therapy. These skills help her counsel veterans plagued by anxiety, depression, addiction, grief, anger, and more.

Kristin is genuine, honest, and direct in her communication with clients. She capably joins with male and female veterans and their family members, and gains trust during the first session. Kristin's empathy stems from a strong, yet gentle compassionate and caring spirit, coupled with stories she heard from her brother, father, and grandfather, who all experienced military culture, service, and life.

Her caseload varies. On Monday she counseled 7-year-old Aaron, a child whose dad was deployed 2 months ago. Since Aaron's birth his dad has been home for only about 3 1/2 years total. Aaron used to do well in school, but now he's tearful, aggressive toward peers, and inattentive in class.

On Wednesday Kristin counseled Staff Sergeant Talliba Bentley, a 37-year-old, African American Army reservist who has been married 15 years to her husband Kyle, a male nurse, with whom she has two children. She returned from combat with burn wounds from an improvised explosive device that killed one of her comrades. Her mother had helped care for her children while she was deployed. Talliba feels grief stricken not having resolved the loss of her comrade in combat. She feels depressed and unsupported by her husband, and much conflict exists in their marriage.

To help her clients, Kristin considers the cultural aspects of the military, gender, and ethnicity as she identifies reintegration, caregiving, and social support issues. As a civilian Kristin cannot fully imagine what Aaron and Talliba are feeling, but she meets them where they are and uses a biopsychosocial-spiritual assessment to discern what interventions may work best to improve their quality of life.

1. As a civilian, how can Kristin gain cultural competence as a military social worker?

2. What different skills and knowledge does the social worker require to work with Aaron and Talliba?

Multidisciplinary Team Approach

In military social work, a team approach is often required. Medical personnel may need to be consulted in cases of TBI and long-term physical impairments. In addition, military chaplains often possess fine relationship skills and can assist social workers to provide an environment where the soldier can start to share and better understand his or her ambivalence, especially in regard to substance issues. Religion, spirituality, and meaning-of-life issues deserve attention by chaplains and social workers alike in their work with members of the armed services and their family members.

DIVERSITY AND MILITARY SOCIAL WORK

In multiple ways, military service influences a young man's or woman's transition into adulthood. Active duty service members manage voluminous workloads and often work 24/7 with little leisure time. They experience a constant sense of hypervigilance and "mission readiness" that pervades their mind-sets. In addition to these deployment stressors, military service members and veterans must also grapple with diversity issues related to age, class, race/ethnicity, gender, and sexual orientation.

AGE

Across all military services, nearly half the force is between 17 and 24 years old. The age distribution of men and women is similar. There are slightly more women at younger ages and more men at older ages, mainly because of gender differences in retention: Women leave the military at earlier ages than men, perhaps because of family reasons (Kelty, Kleykamp, & Segal, 2010). The higher numbers of older men mainly reflect higher service rates among men who were at risk of being drafted into the military in the 1960s and 1970s. Military experience, rare among today's young people, was much more common in earlier generations.

By federal law (10 U.S.C., 505), the minimum age for enlistment in the U.S. military is 17 (with parental consent) and 18 (without parental consent). The maximum age is 35. However, DoD policy allows the individual branches to specify the maximum age of enlistment for active duty based on their own unique requirements. The service branches have set the following maximum ages for a person without any prior military service who has not completed basic training (Powers, 2014):

- Army: 35 (The Army experimented with raising the age limit to 42 for a brief time but reverted to the lower age limit in 2011.)
- Air Force: 27
- Navy: 34
- Marines: 28
- Coast Guard: 27

Age limits for enlistment are different for people who have prior service: For the Marine Corps and the Marine Corps Reserve, the maximum age of enlistment is 32; for the Army and Air National Guard, generally 59; for the Coast Guard, 32 for those selected to attend a high-level Coast Guard school directly upon enlistment. There are a few specific exceptions to these rules.

CLASS

The military has two distinct subcultures and lifestyles: the world of the officer and the life of the enlisted. The only equality between officers and enlisted is in dying on the battlefield. The distinction between the two classes is stark:

Nowhere in the United States is the dichotomy so omnipresent as on a military base; nowhere do the classes live and work in such close proximity; nowhere is every social interaction so freighted with class significance. . . . The thousands of people on a military base live together, have the same employer, dedicate their lives to the same purpose—yet they cannot, must not, socialize outside their class. (Wertsch, 1991, p. 285; as quoted in L. K. Hall, 2011, p. 10)

During the past 50 years, the DoD has endeavored to equalize the available services; however, all military systems function with rigid hierarchical systems based on dominance and subordination. What is essential for social workers to know is that a client's rank conveys important information, such as "stressors, military history of the client/family, length of service, and possibly certain duties and experiences," that will affect assessment, intervention, and care (Beder, 2012). Practitioners must also recognize that enlisted members will respond differently to services than will officers. Even children of the enlisted and officers who attend the same school will often feel discomfort when associating with peers of the other rank. First-generation student veterans who attend college also face social class issues and may experience poverty (Wurster, Rinaldi, Woods, & Liu, 2013).

ETHNICITY/RACE

The architects of the volunteer force had expected that the end of conscription would not affect the racial composition of the armed services. However, African American participation in the military increased dramatically during the 1970s and only dipped after the advent of the war on terror. Thus, overrepresentation of African Americans has decreased since the U.S. began military operations in Afghanistan and Iraq (Kelty et al., 2010). By contrast, African American participation in the civilian labor force since the late 1970s has remained constant.

Latino participation in the military has increased greatly since the early 1990s. Latinos are actually slightly overrepresented in the military compared with the civilian labor force. Latinos are most likely to enlist in the Air Force, whereas the Army has the highest amount of African American service members and the Marine Corps the lowest.

Immigrants are permitted to serve in the military and do. They make up about 5% of the active duty force. Serving in the military makes immigrants eligible for expedited citizenship. The DREAM (Development, Relief, and Education for Alien Minors) Act introduced in Congress in 2009 contained provisions to allow undocumented immigrants who came to the United States before age 16 a path to citizenship in exchange for 2 years of military service (Kelty et al., 2010, p. 187).

Over time, service personnel develop a unique identity that has been called an ethnic one (Daley, 1990; cited in Rubin et al., 2013, p. 23). It may even supersede ethnic

The DREAM Act

Annually, an estimated 65,000 undocumented students graduate from high school but cannot go to college, join the military, work, or otherwise follow the dreams associated with living in the United States. Why? As first-generation immigrants, these students were brought to the United States at a young age by parents or family members, but they are not citizens of this country. Unfortunately, many don't know that they aren't citizens until they apply for a driver's license, decide to enroll in college, or discover they don't have Social Security numbers and other legal documents.

On May 11, 2011, the DREAM Act was introduced in both the House of Representatives and the Senate. Provisions of the act would provide undocumented high school graduates or GED recipients eligibility to adjust to conditional lawful permanent resident (LPR) status if they have resided in the United States for at least 5 years and were younger than 16 when they first entered the country. This LPR status would be granted on a conditional basis and be valid for 6 years, during which time the student would be allowed to work, go to school, or join the military. The conditional status would be removed and the young adult granted LPR status after 6 years, once the student either completes 2 years in a program for a bachelor's degree or higher degree or serves in the uniformed services for at least 2 years and, if discharged, receives an honorable discharge. DREAM Act students would not be eligible for federal education grants. Students would, however, be eligible for federal work study and student loans, and individual states would not be restricted from providing financial aid to the students.

Proponents of the act argue that its passage would stimulate the economy by providing a pathway to permanent legal status, increasing the nation's workforce, and helping the military in recruitment. Opponents of the act are opposed to any form of immigration "amnesty" for undocumented students.

1. Do you think the DREAM Act should become law? Please describe at least three points that support your position.

2. If you were a school social worker who was working with an undocumented high school student, how would you inform her or him about the provisions of the DREAM Act?

3. Other than working directly with students, what advocacy action could a school social worker take on behalf of the DREAM Act's passage?

4. Relate the DREAM Act to the nation's broader crisis over immigration and border control, and its intersection with class, gender, and diversity.

---

identity based on geographic heritage. In the military ethnic identity, standards of conduct apply whether in or out of uniform. This unique identity forms because of shared commonalities that individuals and families encounter when they enter military culture. Such commonalities include aspects of language, exclusivity, status within command, branch of service, and military experience with or without combat. A sense of "we-ness" develops. Also, members who have served together in special operation forces may be extremely bonded to one another, and this phenomenon is labeled a "tribal experience" (Rubin et al., 2013, p. 24).

GENDER

Historically, military service has been a masculine role; however, the percentage of women serving in the armed forces has risen significantly since the advent of the all-volunteer force. Legal reforms have lifted official ceilings on women's service, allowing them to choose the military as their adult occupation. Women are currently employed in more than 90% of military occupations, are at risk for combat exposure, and serve multiple, lengthy deployments, similar to men (Larson et al., 2012; Manning & Wight, 2000). Over the past 20 years, women's representation in the senior enlisted and officer ranks has also grown, and it now accounts for almost 12% of senior enlisted personnel and officers in all services (Larson et al., 2012). One exception to women's growing opportunities in the military is the heavily combat-focused Marine Corps, which is only about 3% female (Kelty et al., 2010). Another is the Navy, which restricts women from serving aboard submarines.

The wars in Iraq and Afghanistan have unveiled the emotional and physical risks of combat service. The hypermasculine culture of the military devalues feminine qualities, and this devaluation has led to violence and harassment against women. Women endure multiple subtle but undermining "tests" in the service that men do not usually experience, such as constant scrutiny, sabotage, and indirect threats.

Women service members, in particular, contend with **military sexual trauma (MST)**, which includes rape, sexual assault, and sexual harassment. (Men experience MST as well but not to the degree that women do.) Sexual assault and sexual harassment have plagued multiple aspects of U.S. military life for years. Data from one West Los Angeles VA health center reveal that 41% of the female veterans said they were sexually assaulted while serving in the military, and 29% of them reported that they were raped during their military service (Bell, Turchik, & Karpenko, 2014; Pryce et al., 2012, pp. 12–13). Also consider that less than 10% of those affected by MST incidents throughout the military are believed to report those incidents, because they fear repercussions.

Women in uniform experience special challenges. Many military women are at risk for unsuccessful transitions to adulthood (Kelty et al., 2010). The marriages of military women are much more likely to fail than those of their male counterparts. Women are more likely than males to experience stressors related to family caregiving. And women service members face unique challenges in managing menstruation during field training and deployments.

Females continue to voluntarily enlist in the armed services despite the challenges of serving in a masculine military culture. The opportunities for women to serve have increased, as have the opportunities for camaraderie and support systems designed specifically for women.

▲ Women serve in all branches of the armed forces.

SEXUAL ORIENTATION

Since the Revolutionary War, homosexuals have served in the U.S. military, despite discrimination. From 1950 until 1993, however, gays were officially prohibited from service. Then in 1993 President Clinton signed the "Don't Ask, Don't Tell, Don't Pursue" policy on sexual orientation in the military. As long as gay soldiers' sexuality was not known, they were allowed to enlist and serve; if it did become known while they were in the service, they were discharged.

Over the years, shifts in public opinion have been evident. In 2010 President Obama signed the repeal of the "Don't Ask, Don't Tell" policy, which theoretically allowed gay and lesbian military members to serve openly. While some have viewed this repeal as an economic justice victory, allowing people of color and poor working-class LGBTQ people to join the military and to get better jobs and education, others do not believe that being allowed to serve in the military is economic justice. As many Americans applaud the repeal of this discriminatory policy, citizens must realize that overall militarism and war profiteering may not serve the interests of LGBTQ people, or people of color or poor people (Farrow, 2011).

LGBTQ veterans have higher rates of mental health needs than the general population. Therefore, social workers should realize that concealment of sexual orientation and identity may contribute to higher rates of anxiety, depression, and PTSD (Cochran, Balsam, Flentje, Malte, & Simpson, 2013; Moradi, 2009).

INTERSECTIONS OF DIVERSITY

As previously noted, although most sexual harassment research has focused on women, men also are targets of

Source: MCCS Robert J. Fluegel/CreativeCommons.

▲ The repeal of Don't Ask, Don't Tell went into effect in February 2011.

sexual harassment, particularly in the military. Sexual harassment is defined as unwanted gender-related comments and behaviors. African American men have reported more overall sexual harassment than have white men. Also, these African American armed service members tended to be enlisted personnel rather than officers (Settles, Buchanan, & Colar, 2012).

Latina women in military uniforms are rarely featured in news stories, although many come from a family heritage of military service. To better understand the invisibility of Latina veterans, an essay titled "Speaking Up for My Hermanas in Arms" was included in Betsy Beard and Joyce Gilmour's *Our Voices* (2013).

The military is one place where men of color can rise in the ranks based on merit. Consider Colin Powell, who after graduating from college and ROTC garnered numerous military and civilian awards and became the youngest man and first African American to become the chairman of the Joint Chiefs of Staff and the first African American secretary of state (CNN Library, 2014).

ADVOCACY FOR VETERANS AND MEMBERS OF THE MILITARY

Pressing contemporary issues are significantly related to military life and veteran clients, requiring social work advocacy. Some of these most prominent concerns include homelessness, incarcerated veterans, issues of military women and women veterans, and issues related to LGBTQ people in the military.

ECONOMIC AND SOCIAL JUSTICE

The military and military service raise several issues related to justice. First, the duties of military social workers are vastly different from those of civilian social workers. As mentioned earlier, military social workers are responsible both to the social work *Code of Ethics* and to military law and ethics, and the military's needs usually trump those of clients (Hall, 2009, p. 337). Military social work embraces seven social work fields of practice: aging, education, criminal justice, family and children, health, mental health, and work. Military social workers sometimes specialize, but for the most part they serve as flexible generalist practitioners.

Second, the military takes up a large portion of the federal budget, leaving small portions for social services to the needy. About half the U.S. budget in 2009 was made up of military spending (see Exhibit 15.7), and about half the national debt is caused by military costs (Barney, 2012). The amount of the budget spent on the military is more than the United States spent on the Department of Health and Human Services, Social Security Administration, Department of Housing and Urban Development, and Department of Education combined. Social safety net spending and a real jobs program to help the millions of young people who can barely make ends meet would be more economically just for U.S. society as a whole (Farrow, 2011). Media stories readily display the dissatisfaction of social justice groups regarding how taxpayer dollars are spent. For example, many citizens believe taxes should be used to fund social programs, job initiatives, and actions to fight climate change, rather than on increased military spending (Meador, 2013).

Since its official birth in 1943, military social work has been viewed as a microcosm of the social work profession, has served as a model for occupational social work, and has encountered multiple ethical dilemmas. Military social work advocacy concerns encompass how to optimally counsel military personnel in combat situations, how to prevent and treat alcohol and drug abuse, how to lend family support in the midst of domestic violence, and how to intervene with acute and chronic health and mental health issues that involve medications and monitoring.

TIME TO THINK

What do you think about the amount of funding the United States allocates to the military?

A third issue relates to exploitation of and support for service members, whose lives while in the military and once they depart can be considerably harsher than those of their civilian peers. Prior to Vietnam, conscription mainly affected young men who could not afford college, obtain psychiatric diagnoses, or use other common methods for avoiding the draft. Also, those who were drafted were quickly deployed to war zones and combat, which put them directly in harm's way. Since Vietnam, when all-voluntary service was put in place, enlistees have received better training and career opportunities. However, multiple deployments are the norm, thereby causing untold stress for returning forces and families.

Upon their return to civilian life, many veterans experience challenges finding employment. Career concerns of unemployed U.S. war veterans range from perceiving that their civilian coworkers will have different interests and values to worrying that the job skills they learned in the military will not be transferable to the civilian economy. In addition, retirement from the military with benefits is possible only after 20 years of service (unless one is injured in the line of duty). This reality often places undue stressors on women in the military, who often would like to take time out to have and raise children.

EXHIBIT 15.7   Amount Spent by the U.S. Government on the Military

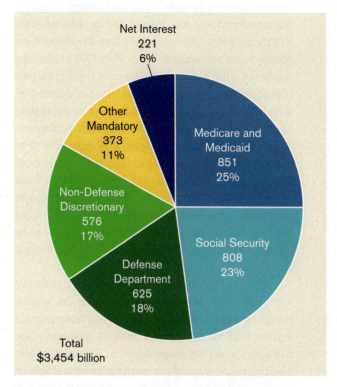

Total
$3,454 billion

Source: http://en.wikipedia.org/wiki/Military_budget_of_the_United_States.

SUPPORTIVE ENVIRONMENT

Military social work is inextricably linked with veterans social work. When military clients have been traumatized, injured, or in constant grief, social workers can and do advocate for supportive environments and help members of the armed forces and their families make adjustments and find housing. Social workers also help military families apply for benefits through the VA and other providers.

The military itself can be an extremely supportive environment, if you discount the hardships of deploying to a battle zone. Many veterans greatly miss the camaraderie and structured life they found in the military. Once they are discharged, they face many new challenges.

For example, veterans have experienced challenges and barriers to obtaining adequate housing. The National Coalition for Homeless Veterans has reported that nearly one third of all people experiencing homelessness in the United States are veterans, and about 1.5 million more veterans are at risk of homelessness "due to poverty, lack of support networks, and dismal living conditions in overcrowded or substandard housing." The coalition also reports that 56% of homeless veterans are black or Latino (Farrow, 2011).

Other studies show that 1 in 4 veterans become disabled as a result of physical violence or emotional trauma of war. There are currently 30,000 disabled veterans from the wars in Iraq and Afghanistan. Many records reveal how medical care, psychological care, and work rehabilitation provided by the U.S. military or government has been dismal in VA hospital environments.

HUMAN NEEDS AND RIGHTS

Military personnel are trained to go to war; they are placed in dangerous and austere environments that few civilians would understand; and their families are affected by extended separations, anxiety, and fear of loss. As a result, military members have special needs and rights, and require the support of civilians and the U.S. government.

Unfortunately, rape and sexual violence are common occurrences for women in the military. The American Civil Liberties Union is currently suing the Pentagon to get the real numbers on reported incidents. Women enrolled in the military are overwhelmingly drawn from the ranks of our country's poor and working classes. From 1973 to 2010, the number of active duty enlisted women in the military grew from 42,000 to 167,000 (Farrow, 2011). Military divorce rates differ by gender, race, and rank. Military men are less likely to be divorced than are their age-matched civilian counterparts, while women in uniform are significantly more likely to be divorced than are their civilian counterparts. Current research based on deployments in Iraq and Afghanistan shows that military marriages were stronger while one partner was deployed or on active duty (Kelty et al., 2010, p. 191). The needs of military families are immense, compounded by multiple deployments, physical and emotional suffering, and financial hardships.

Supportive family policies, a supportive community, and professional development opportunities to improve human capital via education, training, and leadership can improve financial opportunities (through promotions and postservice work) and personal growth. The Army provides marriage enrichment programs, often run by Army chaplains, and "exceptional family member" programs for families with special-needs members. Military housing policy is particularly favorable to married couples and families with children. Service members might have to live in barracks, while married soldiers can live in apartments or houses with their spouses, on or off military installations; regardless, one's housing needs are often met while serving in active duty.

POLITICAL ACCESS

Serving in a combat zone and engaging the enemy multiple times influences how you see the world. The military extracts a huge amount of allegiance from people who join that is literal and not just conceptual. Dual loyalties to one's "brothers/sisters" and one's family create great difficulties when veterans return home. Society must understand what the military experience has extracted from or given to someone who has served. Even soldiers who never shot at the enemy view their environment through a different lens upon returning home. Readjustment periods may be short-lived or can last a lifetime. Civilian social workers must at least understand the politics of military culture that relate to military occupations, rank, branches of service, the deployment cycle, the Uniform Code of Military Justice, the warrior ethos, and the perceived stigma associated with seeing a mental health professional (Jackson, 2013, p. 16).

Members of the military are able to affect U.S. policymaking. And military social workers are advocating for armed services members to have increased political access. For example military social workers from all branches have assisted with humanitarian relief efforts to help people suffering from natural disasters and have served survivors from hostage situations and mass-casualty efforts. Using media to evidence how military social work has made a difference in people's lives gets the attention of policymakers.

YOUR CAREER IN MILITARY SOCIAL WORK

A great need exists to increase the capacity of community, behavioral health providers, programs, and organizations to counsel and serve vets. In addition, the needs of active duty members, reservists, National Guard members, veterans, and those connected to the global war on terror will increasingly exceed the capacity of the VA and Veterans Centers. The need for military social work is so great that civilian social workers will increasingly be required to help veterans and their families. So if you are looking for a career with lots of growth, military social work may be for you.

Military social workers in and out of uniform may work contractually on a base or on staff in a VA hospital, Vet Center, or the Department of Homeland Security. They are involved with every possible social work role, from crisis intervention and assessment to administration and policy practice.

In addition, military social work has opportunities for clinical social workers, policy practitioners, educators, researchers, and direct practitioners at homeless shelters, domestic violence agencies, or substance abuse organizations that have clientele who are veterans. Social workers may also encounter veterans and military family members in private practice, medical clinics, schools, community agencies, and other typical settings for social work practice.

Social workers in any of these roles or settings must understand military jargon, culture, beliefs, and practices. This basic information gives them the tools they need when they do work with a military veteran or connected family. It is especially important for civilian clinicians to comprehend the realities of war and combat; if they don't connect with their veteran client in the first session, it is likely that the veteran will not return for subsequent sessions.

USC's Military Social Work Program

The University of Southern California (USC) offers a master's degree in social work with a military social work subconcentration. The program prepares students to engage in practice with service members, veterans, and their families. Additionally, students use practice skills to assist community-based agencies in identifying and serving military populations in their communities.

A unique feature of the USC program is its virtual client, Staff Sergeant Alamar Castilla—an avatar-based simulation program. Through interactive programming, students have the opportunity to see some of the probable or common behaviors of veterans exposed to combat stress and war fatigue. The animation introduces students to unfamiliar challenging life experiences and possible clinical approaches to assist veterans and their families as they transition into civilian life.

1. Why do you think the USC School of Social Work designed an avatar for teaching social work skills? Is this a learning tool you'd be interesting in using? Explain why or why not.

2. What aspects of military life could not be captured in a simulation program?

3. List some other social issues a social worker might confront that you think are well suited for a simulation program. What advocacy components could be introduced in the program?

The VA employs 11,000 social workers and has a clinical training program for social work students (U.S. Department of Veterans Affairs, 2014). The VA is affiliated with more than 180 graduate schools of social work and operates the biggest and most comprehensive clinical training program for social work students.

Social workers are required to have at least a master's degree to work with veterans in VA hospitals and to serve in the military. Increasingly, the DoD prefers that social workers also have 2 years of postgraduate experience and/or a license to practice independent clinical social work before serving in the armed forces. However, each branch has developed fieldwork for recent MSW-prepared social workers to help them get their clinical licensing while in the service (DoD, 2010; cited in Rubin et al., 2013, p. 18).

Given the increasing demand for social workers who have some understanding of the military, social work educators should integrate information about the military into courses on human behavior, practice and policy courses, and courses on topics such as child welfare, health, mental health, and gerontology (Pryce et al., 2012, p. xviii). Schools and departments of social work need to include at least one continuing education course on the topic. If you are interested in being both a social work educator and a military social worker, you could help develop or teach such a course.

SUMMARY

The military don't start wars. Politicians start wars.

—William Westmoreland

Current military organizations value social workers. The roots of military social work in the United States go back centuries before the field became officially recognized after World War II.

Military culture comprises behaviors, beliefs, norms, values, traditions, and perceptions that govern how members of the armed forces communicate, interact, and think. This culture also influences how military personnel and veterans view their life role and values.

War is stressful, dangerous, and requires adjustment. Fortunately, the field of military social work has grown, and both military and civilian social workers help war veterans and their families adjust. Active, discharged, and returning women and men in the armed services contend with biopsychosocial-spiritual issues because they have endured lengthy or multiple deployments and exposure to combat. To establish credibility with warrior clients, social work practitioners must know about military culture and understand and accept the nature of combat or war, and the stressors the soldiers and military family members experience.

Social work educators must help the social workers of tomorrow understand what service members, veterans, and their military families experience as at-risk populations. Veterans, warriors, and military families require deliberate attention from social work educators and civilian practitioners, too. Our U.S. government also needs to pay equal attention to a wide array of health and human services, issues, and policies to help meet the challenges and needs of returning veterans, from all branches of military service, and their loved ones.

TOP 10 KEY CONCEPTS

Department of Defense (DoD)
Department of Veterans Affairs (VA)
GI Bills
military sexual trauma (MST)
Operation Enduring Freedom

Operation Iraqi Freedom
reservists
secondary trauma
TRICARE
Uniform Code of Military Justice

DISCUSSION QUESTIONS

1. Posttraumatic stress disorder, major depressive disorder (and depressive symptoms), and traumatic brain injury are three invisible signature wounds that have emerged among current U.S. troops. What sorts of services should social workers and the VA medical system offer to soldiers for their physical, emotional, and moral injuries?

2. The VA hospital has been under fire in the media recently over cases of neglect. How has the U.S. government responded? What can VA social workers do to change the negative image that was portrayed as they help VA clients address their health, mental health, family, housing, and employment needs?

3. What portion of the federal budget should be allocated to the military versus social services? What is your rationale?

4. Imagine that you are counseling a young person who has expressed an interest in joining the military. Specify the demographic characteristics of this person (ethnicity, gender, class, and so forth). What are the social and economic pros and cons you would offer? Which aspects of the person's psychological makeup would you highlight?

5. Are military families and families of veterans entitled to the services now extended to them? Why or why not? From your reading of this chapter (and other knowledge you may have), which services would you say are still lacking? Which are perhaps too generous?

EXERCISES

1. You are asked to configure a 4-hour learning module for your social work program to teach students how to help clients who are veterans or armed services members, or their families. Sketch out your ideas for such a learning module. You may wish to view James Gandolfini's documentary film *Alive Day Memories: Home From Iraq,* which inspired Dr. Bender at Yeshiva to develop a course on social work practice with the military and to oversee a four-course certificate program related to the military and a field placement that serves the military. You may find more information about military curricula at Catholic University of

America in Washington, D.C.; Boston College; and SUNY Empire State College.

2. Read and reflect on the following excerpt from *War Is a Force That Gives Us Meaning* by Chris Hedges (2002), a *New York Times* correspondent and Harvard Divinity School graduate. Then discuss your reflections on the culture and attraction of war.

War forms its own culture. The rush of battle is a potent and often lethal addiction, for war is a drug, one I ingested for many years. It is peddled by mythmakers—historians, war correspondents, filmmakers, novelists, and the state—all of whom endow it with qualities it often does possess: excitement, exoticism, power, chances to rise above our small stations in life, and a bizarre and fantastic universe that has a grotesque and dark beauty. It dominates culture, distorts memory, corrupts language, and infects everything around it, even humor, which becomes preoccupied with the grim perversities of smut and death. Fundamental questions about the meaning, or meaninglessness, of our place on the planet are laid bare when we watch those around us sink to the lowest depths. War exposes the capacity for evil that lurks not far below the surface within all of us. And this is why for many, war is so hard to discuss once it is over.

The enduring attraction of war is this: Even with its destruction and carnage it can give us what we long for in life. It can give us purpose, meaning, a reason for living. Only when we are in the midst of conflict does the shallowness and vapidness of much of our lives become apparent. Trivia dominates our conversations and increasingly our airwaves. And war is an enticing elixir. It gives us resolve, a cause. It allows us to be noble. And those who have the least meaning in their lives, the impoverished refugees in Gaza, the disenfranchised North African immigrants in France, even the legions of young who live in the splendid indolence and safety of the industrialized world, are all susceptible to war's appeal. (p. 3)

3. Read and reflect on this excerpt from Allvord and Nowlin's (2008) *When Baseball Went to War*. Then discuss how people are forever changed by serving in the military and going to war.

Arguably one of the first victims in a war is a person's humanity, the memory of the person he was before the nightmare of war, before the sacrifice began and the long and tired feeling of war and regret set in as young boys became men much too early and much too fast. This was true in World War II and is still true today. . . .

In the Korean War, in Vietnam, in Desert Storm, and even today in Iraq, soldiers would burn off a little energy when they could and play baseball to regain a sense of the person they once were and hoped to become again. . . .

Veterans of America's current conflicts such as Desert Storm and Iraq also serve and play baseball with passion in their spare time. Navy pilot Lt. Commander Terry Allvord saw the importance of baseball as an essential element to morale, discipline, and hope. The U.S. Military All-Stars are servicemen and women from all branches who give up their leave time to play baseball, paying the cost out of their own pockets. World War II, where the players were flown from event to event by the government, the U.S. Military All Stars choose not to accept government money; they want the government to spend all funds for those serving in the War on Terror.

In 1990, then–Aviation Candidate Allvord had the honor of escorting President George H.W. Bush in Pensacola, Florida, and the conversation quickly turned to baseball. It was a subject for which both naval aviators held a deep passion. Bush mentioned how in his day, "Military baseball helped them pass the time, feel a sense of home, and gave them hope." Then the president asked how the current Navy team was doing.

"We don't have a (baseball) team, Mr. President," Allvord answered. The president was disappointed. "Someone should start a team," answered the former Yale baseball captain. Allvord agreed, and the U.S. Military All-Stars were born. In nearly two decades, those original teams grew to more than 35 single-service teams worldwide. Allvord selected players from those teams and the best players from worldwide tryouts to create the first and only combined armed forces team, U.S. Military All-Stars. Players from the U.S. Military All-Stars were among those who pulled Saddam Hussein from the depths of a spider hole in Iraq. Allvord notes, "There is something unique, something special, when an evil dictator is pulled out of his hole by a liberator, but the fact it was also one of our players makes it even better." These men are more than willing to give up their cherished free time to represent their country on and off the field. Former Dodgers farm hand and U.S. Military All-Star second baseman Ray Judy USN has a simple answer about playing baseball in the armed forces: "We love baseball, but we love our country more." (Allvord & Anton, 2008, pp. 239–244)

ONLINE RESOURCES

- Courage to Care for Me (www.couragetocareforme.org): An electronic health campaign for military and civilian professionals serving the military community, as well as for military men, women, and families; consists of electronic fact sheets on timely health topics relevant to military life that provide actionable information

- DoD Dictionary of Military Terms (www.dtic.mil/doctrine/dod_dictionary)
- Give an Hour Foundation (www.giveanhour.org): Provides free mental health counseling from private practitioners to U.S. military personnel and their families affected by the Iraq and Afghanistan conflicts
- Joining Forces (www.whitehouse.gov/joiningforces): A comprehensive initiative led by First Lady Michelle Obama and Second Lady Jill Biden to heighten awareness of the sacrifices made by the military; joined in July 2012 by the National Association of Social Workers
- Military OneSource (www.militaryonesource.com): Sponsored by the Department of Defense, the principal source of assistance for military members and military family members (active duty, National Guard, or other reserve components); also provides multiple websites for different service components and branches, as well as a full menu of topic-specific sites
- Motivational Interviewing (www.motivationalinterview.org): Provides information about motivational interviewing trainings, Internet links to related information, and information about the network of motivational interviewing trainers
- *NASW Standards for Social Work Practice With Service Members, Veterans, and Their Families* (www.socialworkers.org/practice/military/documents/MilitaryStandards2012.pdf)
- National Coalition for Homeless Veterans (www.nchv.org)
- National Women Veterans of America (www.wvanational.org): Unites women veterans, provides advocacy, and offers education services
- Operation R.O.S.E. (www.operationrose.com): Faith-based ministry resource provided by military wives for other military spouses to support and encourage the military lifestyle
- "PTSD Checklist–Military Version" (www.pdhealth.mil/guidelines/appendix4.asp)
- The Soldiers Project (www.thesoldiersproject.org): Provides free mental health counseling by private practitioners to U.S. military personnel and their families affected by the Iraq/Afghanistan conflicts
- Traumatic brain injury information (www.pdhealth.mil/TBI.asp)
- Uniform Code of Military Justice (www.au.af.mil/au/awc/awcgate/ucmj.htm): Guides armed services members in all they do
- Vet Center Program (www.vetcenter.va.gov): Provides readjustment counseling for veterans and their families to help transition from military to civilian life
- Veterans Affairs social workers (www.socialwork.va.gov/socialworkers.asp)

STUDENT STUDY SITE

Sharpen your skills with SAGE edge at **edge.sagepub.com/cox**

SAGE edge for Students provides a personalized approach to help you accomplish your coursework goals in an easy-to-use learning environment.

Chapter 16: ENVIRONMENTALISM

Learning Objectives

After reading this chapter, you should be able to

1. Define the terms *person-in-environment perspective* and *ecological social welfare and practice.*
2. Describe how environmental sustainability is linked to social work practice.
3. List various factors associated with misuse of the environment.
4. Apply the dynamic advocacy model to issues related to the environment.
5. Identify and describe the role of social workers in addressing environmental issues.

Pam and Her Special Needs Students Volunteer in a Cleanup

As a young child, Pam learned to fish and boat on the Chesapeake Bay, a waterway close to her home. As she grew older, Pam began volunteering with a national organization dedicated to Chesapeake Bay regulatory and restoration efforts. Over time, she participated in activities such as oyster restoration, chemical analysis of streams, and public meetings of local governing bodies.

When thinking about her career as a social worker, Pam thought she wanted to work with special needs children in a school setting. During her required yearlong field placement, Pam connected her interest in the Chesapeake Bay with her social work practice by organizing high school students with learning challenges in a waterway cleanup effort.

The outcome was phenomenal. Students learned to work as a team in the context of tasks where cooperation and dependability were essential. The learning environment was interdisciplinary; students connected their knowledge of biology with the life cycle of fish, water populations, and clean water. By talking with people working in the fishing industry, students learned the economic significance of the Chesapeake Bay. Pam realized how volunteering with a community activity enhanced the students' self-esteem while challenging community members' preconceived notions of students with special needs.

The person-in-environment perspective is integral to social work practice worldwide. It highlights the importance of understanding a person and his or her behavior in relationship to the environmental context in which that person lives and acts. An alternative to the commonly used disease and moral models, the person-in-environment model is client centered, dynamic, and interactive.

Social workers recognize that in daily interactions, people influence their environments and are in turn influenced by them. However, only recently has the social work profession considered the implications of the unhealthful and depleted ecology we all share. The social work profession, including the National Association of Social Workers (NASW) and the Council on Social Work Education (CSWE), has not always extended that ecological outlook to the human relationship with the natural world (Besthorn & Saleebey, 2003, p. 12).

This neglect of the natural world by the social work profession and its national organizations is no longer acceptable. Social workers know the environmental context is a prime determinant for quality of life. Consequently, the environmental issues of the natural world must become part of social workers' concerns. They are becoming **environmentalists.** As with efforts toward social justice, environmental social work highlights the inequalities and inequities experienced by the poorest and most marginalized populations. This chapter examines environmental social work practice through a social justice lens. Throughout this chapter, we suggest that social workers must understand that the logical consequence of exploitation of natural resources is the exploitation of people. By highlighting how populations have suffered as a result of environmental damage, we introduce creative and effective social work practice and policy that respond to the changes and stress.

TIME TO THINK

Think about a natural environment, such as an ocean, lake, mountain range, or desert, that left a lasting impression on you. What are the possible threats to that landscape?

Can you see yourself involved with an organization committed to protecting the natural environment you had in mind? Consider why or why not. If the answer is yes, think about the activities you would be willing to undertake to protect that environment.

ENVIRONMENTALISM AND SOCIAL WORK

The contemporary world presents social workers with challenges. From difficulties associated with the violation of human rights to the need for social justice and citizen participation, there is mounting pressure for the social work profession to expand its framework of practice. Interventions and theoretical perspectives are needed that address natural, human-influenced, and global environmental changes such as pollution and climate change. Social workers are positioned to act collaboratively with groups committed to ecology to recognize the connection between nature's life forces and people.

SOCIAL WORK LEADERSHIP IN ENVIRONMENTALISM

The social work profession has played an early and important role in raising awareness of **environmental justice**. The overriding goal is environmental sustainability that supports all of us and recognizes the interdependent aspects of the human and nonhuman worlds.

Mary Richmond

Mary Richmond is perhaps best known for her leadership in Charity Organization Societies in several cities in the late 1800s and early 1900s. These were the first organizations to develop a structured profession devoted to social work, through the work of "friendly visitors" with poor families. Within Charity Organization Societies, Richmond organized communities, developed casework practice, and focused on the person in the environment.

Richmond defined the sources of power available to clients and their social workers: the household, the person of the client, the neighborhood and wider social network, civil agencies, and private and public agencies (Hansan, n.d.). By doing this, Richmond connected components of the environment to the daily lives of people.

Within her book *Social Diagnosis* (1917), Richmond described the strengths of people and families. The shift from blaming people for deficits to recognizing the strengths and potential of individuals also highlighted the community as a potential resource. Indeed, Richmond's ideas were groundbreaking for her time and provided a cornerstone for much of social work education.

Jane Addams

Inspired by London's East End settlement houses, Jane Addams cofounded Hull House in Chicago with her friend Ellen Starr. Together, they focused on the living and working conditions of immigrants, which were negatively impacted

Angus, the School Social Worker, and the Regional Trash Dump

Angus lives in a rural community that has a significant waste dump. Trash from urban areas is transported to the dump. The arrangement is profitable to the community and advantageous to cities, but community members experience high rates of cancer and asthma.

Angus is concerned about the health of his two young children and mentioned the waste dump to a school social worker during a recent session about his son's asthma and subsequent absences from school. Angus explored the causes of asthma in childhood and then asked a community official about the type of trash being dumped in the landfill. When Angus realized that some of the disposed trash had chemicals and toxins associated with asthma, he asked his councilperson to allocate time for him to speak at the next council meeting. Angus also contacted the president of the Board of Education to list asthma and the waste dump on the agenda of the board's upcoming meeting.

1. What other consequences of the trash dump could impact Angus's hometown and its residents? How could the social worker and Angus help forestall these consequences?

2. Discuss the conflict between the community's need for income from the dump and the dump's effects on the health of citizens. What is social work's role in this discussion?

---

by the unregulated factories. Hull House challenged the housing, sanitation, and public health of crowded tenements and by doing so raised the public consciousness regarding these issues.

By waging a campaign to improve garbage collection in tenement neighborhoods, Addams and the members of the settlement movement gained political recognition. More specifically, in response to this campaign, Chicago hired its first garbage inspector, which helped link the government with environmental issues.

National Association of Social Workers

For several decades, awareness of the importance of environmental issues had little impact on social work practice. In part, this was because the profession's definition of environment included social elements but not physical and natural environments. In 1999 the **Delegate Assembly** of the NASW stated that "environmental exploitation violates the principle of social justice and is a direct violation of the NASW *Code of Ethics*." As a result, social work came to explore, if not fully embrace, natural environmental issues as part of the profession's mandate.

Currently, social workers purport to use an ecological and systems approach to help people with their problems. However, changes in social work curricula to include the natural environment are essential in establishing the social work profession in environmental research, policy, and practice.

Council on Social Work Education

The CSWE is the national accrediting body of social work education programs. In 2010, the Council declared that **sustainability,** or using resources in such a way as to maintain them for the future, was the social justice issue of the new century. The CSWE dedicated an annual program meeting to "Promoting Sustainability in Social Work."

The CSWE now recognizes that social workers have the skills needed for environmental practice. Community organizing, networking, advocacy, and program evaluation are but a few of the skills that can be used to further environmental justice and promote the inclusion of the natural environment in work with clients. There is growing support within social work for the idea that humans have constructed a social environment within the larger context of the natural environment. Elevating environmentalism in this way quickly gained the attention of national and international schools of social work.

ECOLOGICAL SOCIAL WELFARE AND PRACTICE

Over time, social workers have come to realize that practice involving the natural environment needs to be holistic. Said another way, social workers must recognize that all aspects of society are intricately related to one another. **Ecological social welfare,** sometimes called the new ecology, is defined as a social change process that promotes people's welfare and environmental justice through economic activities, such as examining the impact of deforestation on the control of river ways and subsequent flooding and landslides. The goal is "to meet the needs and aspirations of the present generation without compromising the ability of future generations to meet their needs" (Shaw, 2008, p. 22). From an ecological social welfare perspective, social workers become all too aware of the extent to which the poorest and most marginalized populations are hit by environmental fallout (Gray & Coates, 2012, p. 239).

The overarching principles that guide ecological social welfare practice are described in Exhibit 16.1. These principles encourage social work practice that is self-critical, values diversity and diverse solutions to problems, and encourages social workers to confront problems at a fundamental

level (Miller, Hayward, & Shaw, 2012). Most of all, these principles promote collaboration with community members to enhance the capacities of marginalized communities. They endorse a commitment to broad social change through participation in the political arena and community organizations (Miller, Lee, & Berle, 2012).

Sustainability

Implied in the principles of environmental social work is the idea of sustainability. The sustainability movement acknowledges the finite nature of resources and prioritizes the needs of the poor. It necessitates a global perspective and a positive commitment to a process of social change (Peeters, 2012). The practice implications for social workers are summarized in Exhibit 16.2.

Considering the political character of the sustainability movement, it is commonly understood within social work as the interaction of the social, ecological, economic, and process dimensions (Baker, 2006; Peeters, 2012). This means that social workers have to create situations that help overcome personal and societal difficulties while simultaneously working on the conditions needed for a sustainable future.

Ecological Justice

Extending rights to people in support of sustainability and ecological social work recognizes that our world does not

---

EXHIBIT 16.1   **New Ecology in Practice**

- Each individual has intrinsic value apart from the meaning or usefulness of the individual to others in his or her community.

- The diversity of culture and social organization offers the potential for unique solutions to emerge to share human challenges.

- Structural alliances between communities and the services that provide for them must act to increase the diversity of resources that are directly available to individuals and families to help them help themselves.

- A service delivery system that is managed by community members, not bureaucracies, is the most likely to contribute to social integration.

- Human systems work best when they are small, allowing resources to be divested to the communities being served.

- Public policy is needed that expands the capacity of communities and their members to function on their own by providing resources they need to sustain well-being.

- What is good for individuals and their communities is the benchmark of social and economic development.

- Social workers who support the above principles have an ethical obligation to move toward these goals by changing the methods of their practice, social welfare policy, and organizations.

Source: Adapted from Unger (2002).

EXHIBIT 16.2   Sustainable Development and Social Work

SUSTAINABLE DEVELOPMENT	SOCIAL WORK
Includes satisfaction of human needs but has a broader focus.	Enhancement of human well-being implies the satisfaction of needs.
Accepts ecological limits—the earth's finite resources.	Concern and respect for the earth's finite resources is not yet a core concern in social work discourse and depends on how notions of human well-being are understood across locations.
Common but differentiated responsibilities—in the first place between nations—result from general principles of fairness.	In the ethics of empowerment, social work holds people accountable for their actions, but fairness implies attention to the different possibilities and limits of people, both individuals and groups.
Concerned with global justice—although there are divergent conceptions of exactly what this entails.	Social work believes the state has a role in providing for its citizens.
Intragenerational equity and solidarity.	Social work is aligned with the goal of global justice.
Intergenerational equity and solidarity: Responsibility for future generations is an innovative principle.	Social work extols social solidarity, diversity, and empowerment, especially with disadvantaged and marginalized populations. This principle is compatible with social work's concern with people's futures.
Gender equality and respect for diversity.	Active participation of citizens is seen as crucial to sustainable development. Social work promotes gender equality and respect for diversity.

Source: Adapted from Peeters (2012).

operate separately from the rest of nature (Miller, Hayward, & Shaw, 2012). From the perspective of **ecological justice,** the earth is a holistic life source, which means all life deserves justice. Ecological justice upholds a sense of fairness for all life.

For social workers, ecological justice is global; there is an understanding that what occurs in one nation has a direct or indirect impact in many other geographic regions. For example, if a country neglects to implement policies on carbon emissions or ocean pollution, the impact is multinational. Conversely, population control in one nation helps address global inequalities worldwide.

Moving toward ecological justice in social work practice and policy means social workers will attempt to strike a balance between the needs of people and the natural world. Thus, the risks and needs of nature are not secondary to the needs of people but viewed in tandem.

Ecological Ethics

In many ways, where social work stands on ecological issues and environmental social work practice is an indication of the profession's respect for the natural world. Specifically, **ecological ethics** suggests that social workers must value

nature for the sake of nature, not just for the sake of the uses to which human beings might put the elements of nature. If nature is highly valued, then there might be times when people have to reconsider their needs and wants in light of natural resources. For example, ethical issues emerge when pesticides are used to increase the yield of food production but might increase health hazards to those who work close to the soil, such as immigrant workers.

Ecological ethics in the context of community development, social planning, and social welfare policy assumes that social workers will consider resource allocation and management in light of the needs of present and future generations. Ideally, such a multidimensional assessment is both pragmatic and democratic.

TIME TO THINK

Can you think of other instances when conflicting needs have been resolved in favor of the environment? How did the resolution affect needy people? Was it a fair resolution? Why or why not?

ENVIRONMENTAL ISSUES

Extreme natural events are part of the human experience and reflect the close interaction of people with the natural world. In the following discussion of some of the environmental issues and concerns that affect all of us, you will note that in some areas we are making gains and in others focused attention is needed. Therefore, social work practice and research needs to better highlight the connections among people, various environmental components, and social welfare issues.

OVERPOPULATION

The global population is growing like never before. It is estimated that 1 billion people are added to the world's population every 12 years. Currently, the world population totals more than 7 billion people. The rate at which a nation's population is growing has immense consequences related to resource allocation, overcrowding, social conflict, housing, and health conditions. For example, Exhibit 16.3 suggests that race and origin are factors to consider when projecting the nation's changing demographics and subsequent social welfare needs.

A concept closely associated with overpopulation is **doubling time,** which is how long it takes for a population to double. The calculation of doubling time is based on the extent to which birthrate exceeds the death rate. Doubling time has a compounding effect; so what may seem to be a relatively slow rate of population growth can produce dramatic results over time. The countries that tend to experience the fastest doubling times are those that are developing their economic base through industrialization and can least afford the cost associated with a growing population.

Surprisingly, overpopulation is not due to families having more children. Family size has not grown worldwide. What has changed is that more people are living to the age of fertility; that is, the mortality rate of babies and young children has decreased. These changes are related to improved nutrition, advances in health care, enhanced sanitation, and more effective responses to natural disasters.

Overpopulation is associated with a variety of social problems, and some of the most challenging are listed

EXHIBIT 16.3   Population by Race and Hispanic Origin: 2012 and 2060

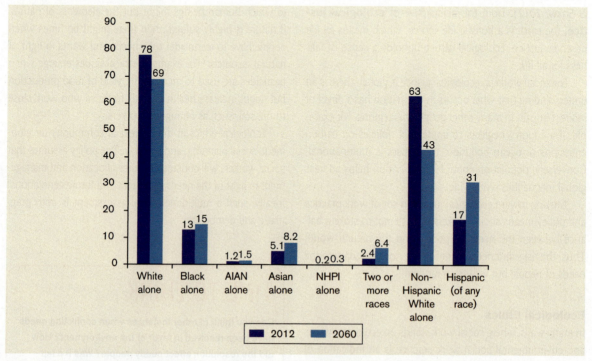

AIAN = American Indian and Alaska Native; NHPI = Native Hawaiian and Other Pacific Islander

Source: U.S. Census Bureau (2012).

SOCIAL WORK IN ACTION

Linda's Social Worker Encourages Her Environmentalism

LINDA and Bernie live with their three teenage sons in a small community on the outskirts of a large city. They are active in the community and enjoy the hiking and fishing it offers. The couple has noticed that people are dumping trash in a stream that runs through their town and into a lake. One weekend Linda and Bernie took their boys and attempted to clean up the debris, but it proved to be too much for them. The family also noticed that trash receptacles were not readily available by the stream, nor was there signage prohibiting trash disposal.

Linda, who was seeing a social worker at a community mental health center for work-related stress, mentioned during a counseling session her weekend cleanup effort and general concern for the community's environment. The social worker offered to provide Linda with contact information for a local environmental group and also for the councilperson responsible for community relationships.

Further, together Linda and the social worker explored the value of the community's environmental beauty and its calming effect. Linda related that she counted on her hikes with Bernie as a way to relax, reflect, and gain perspective on life circumstances.

1. Describe how the social worker used the new ecology perspective when working with Linda.

2. Define at least three ways the social worker could expand Linda's individual counseling to include action and advocacy on behalf of the community environment.

here. It is important to keep in mind that the problems may appear national or regional, but they are global and impact our planet in a significant way.

- *Global water and sanitation:* Global access to clean water, adequate sanitation, and proper hygiene are essential for improved health conditions and socioeconomic development. It is estimated that 780 million people worldwide do not have a safe water supply and appropriate sanitation (Centers for Disease Control and Prevention, 2014a).

- *Global hunger:* Hunger, or food insecurity, refers to conditions where people do not have physical or economic access to sufficient, safe, and nutritious food. Although global hunger has decreased 34% in the past decade, more than 840 million people worldwide still do not have enough to eat, with nearly 3 million children dying from hunger-related causes.

- *Energy:* Growing global consumption of energy resources extracted from the earth, including fossil fuels, threatens to result in lower-quality, less-accessible, and more-expensive energy. The likelihood of blackouts, heating crises, rising fuel prices, and dependency on foreign

Source: ©iStockphoto.com/Tarzan9280

▲ Industrializing nations experience the highest rates of population doubling time.

markets increases as it becomes harder to extract fossil fuels. Incentives to conserve energy and use alternative energy sources at the individual, residential, commercial, and industrial levels will help curb the use of fossil fuels.

- *Overcrowding:* Increasing urbanization continues throughout much of the world, and urban living is becoming a dominant lifestyle for much of the world's population. When more people are living within a dwelling or a specified area, space for movement is restricted and hygiene, privacy, and a quiet environment for sleeping become less available.

• *Migration*: About 3% of the people in the world have lived outside of their country of birth for a year or more. Migration across national borders is called the "third wave" of globalization, after the movement of goods (trade) and money (finances). The majority of people moving from their original country do so as a result of poverty and subsequent poor living conditions. Migration is associated with the search for economic opportunities and improved living conditions.

TIME TO THINK

Actor Matt Damon is involved with the website Water .org, which is devoted to providing clean, safe water and sanitation to various parts of the world. The projects are designed primarily to improve the lives of women and children. How would increasing the availability of water and sanitation improve the lives of women and children in particular?

Do you think celebrities can really influence environmental issues? Do you know of other organizations supported by "celebrity power"?

POLLUTION

A sign of our global connectedness is seen in **pollution,** the deposit of harmful materials into the air, water, and soil. Pollution is harmful to people and other living organisms,

Source: ©iStockphoto.com/yenwen.

⌃ Los Angeles is known for its smog.

and is a major challenge to a healthy and productive earth. Pollutants know no national boundaries or limitations.

Numerous environmental problems are related to pollutants, including these:

• *Air:* Since the industrial revolution, the United States has experienced problems with air pollution. Such pollution comprises industrial fumes, vehicle emissions, carbon grit, and other airborne material that contaminates the air and depletes the ozone, a region above the earth that absorbs the sun's radiation. Some of the diseases caused by air pollution are inflammation of the lungs, infections, chronic obstructive pulmonary disease, lung cancer, and heart disease.

• *Water:* Water covers 70% of the earth's surface and is a critical source of life. Some of the causes of water pollution include the release of sewage and wastewater, marine dumping, industrial waste, radioactive waste, oil pollution, underground sewage leakages, and global warming. All types of water pollution are harmful to general health. Some particular diseases related to water pollution are birth defects, cancers, immune suppression, reproductive failure, infant mortality, cholera, and typhoid fever.

• *Land:* Land pollution reflects the deterioration of soil, often a result of human activities or the misuse of land resources. There are various causes of land pollution: solid waste, pesticides and fertilizers, chemicals, deforestation, and ashes from nonbiodegradable products or chimneys and inclinators. The harmful effects of land pollution include repository problems, skin diseases, and various types of cancer.

CLIMATE CHANGE

Climate change refers to any significant change in the measures of climate lasting for an extended period of time, usually decades or centuries or more. Examples of climate change are changes in temperature, precipitation, and wind pattern.

According to the National Aeronautics and Space Administration (NASA), climate change is a product of certain long-lived gases that remain semipermanently in the atmosphere. The gases blanket the earth and disrupt the transfer of heat, a process referred to as the greenhouse effect. Gases that contribute to the greenhouse effect are

CURRENT TRENDS

Fracking

FOR well over 60 years, fracking—or hydraulic fracturing—has played a significant role in the obtainment of oil and natural gas. Fracking releases 2 to 3 times less carbon into the atmosphere than coal mining does, and it releases far less particulate matter as well. However, green energy advocates support technology that releases little to no carbon dioxide.

The health-related consequences from fracking are currently being examined by health experts, given that more large-scale drilling is under way. Exposure to toxic chemicals released during drilling has the potential to cause tremendous harm. Many of the health risks from such toxins do not manifest immediately and require studies looking into long-term health effects (see www.dangersoffracking.com).

What are your thoughts on fracking? Do you support the technique? Why or why not?

---

water vapor, carbon dioxide, methane, nitrous oxide, and chlorofluorocarbons. Further, the burning of fossil fuels such as coal and oil increases carbon dioxide and adds to the greenhouse effect.

The outcomes of climate change are varied but are likely to involve warmer temperatures, more evaporation and precipitation, the melting of glaciers and other ice, increasing sea levels, and impacts on plant communities. Climate change poses serious threats to human communities as well, in the form of water quality and availability, potential increase in forest fires, economic hardships of residents from crop failure, and potential extreme weather conditions.

ENVIRONMENTAL DISASTERS

Environmental disasters are events occurring in the natural world that cause serious disruptions to human activity. Consider the homes, personal property, and livelihoods lost in New Jersey after Hurricane Sandy in 2012 and along the Elkton River of West Virginia after the 2013 toxic spill. These are examples of the connection between environmental concerns and events that have simultaneously ravaged nature and people's lives. Note, however, that they are not all "natural" disasters. The toxic spill in West Virginia was the result of human activity that seriously affected the natural world and the lives of people living near the river.

Although social workers are trained to interpret and respond to crisis situations, their input in disaster relief at

Source: ©iStockphoto.com/Abenaa

⋏ Strip mining has harmful effects on the environment.

the local, state, national, and international levels has usually been negligible. In part, this reflects the profession's minimal research on the outcomes of disaster relief interventions and the absence of a well-trained cadre of social workers committed to interdisciplinary service provision in the aftermath of these events. Social workers could play an important role in helping people recover from environmental disasters, but the profession needs to do the following first:

- Educate social workers on trauma responses and the protracted recovery phase of disasters
- Understand the unique cultural features associated with disasters

- Understand the consequences of disasters for vulnerable populations
- Develop rigorous research on disaster responses
- Develop leadership in the area of disaster relief
- Design strategies that expedite the use of funds and services for victims of disasters (Rosenfeld, Caye, Lahad, & Gurwitch, 2010)

At the very least, social workers can start thinking about the types of environmental hazards that are most likely in the communities where they work and the human impact of these disasters. For example, the National Oceanic and Atmospheric Administration publishes the weekly *Harmful Algal Bloom Bulletin* to forecast for *Microcystis aeruginosa* blooms in western Lake Erie. These blooms produce toxins that may pose a significant risk to human and animal health, and may form scum that is unsightly and odorous to beach visitors, impacting the coastal economy. Forecasts depicting current and future locations of blooms will alert social workers, health care personnel, and scientists to possible threats to the Great Lakes beaches, and assist in mental health and health efforts.

Flooding

Floods are one of the most common environmental hazards, but not all floods are alike. Some floods develop slowly, giving people a chance to save some personal property and evacuate the area (Ready Campaign, 2014). Others develop in a matter of moments, catching people by surprise and leaving few opportunities to gather belongings and depart to a safe region.

Source: ©iStockphoto.com/gdagys

▲ Flooding and other natural disasters can have devastating effects on a community.

Overland floods, the most common type of flooding, typically occur when waterways such as rivers and streams overflow their banks and push water into surrounding areas. Flooding is usually a result of rainwater or a possible levee breach. It can also occur when rainfall or snowmelt exceeds the capacity of underground aquifers.

Those people that live downstream from a dam need to be aware of weather and water level conditions. Even the smallest of streams can cause significant damage if it receives more rainwater and rainwater runoff than it can hold.

Drought

A drought is a period of unusually persistent dry weather that lasts long enough to damage crops and threaten the well-being of all living things. The severity of the drought directly corresponds to moisture deficiency, duration, and location and size of the geographic region affected (National Aeronautics and Space Administration, 2014). Perhaps you will be surprised to learn that nearly all countries can experience a drought.

Historical records of precipitation in the United States show an increase in aridity since the 1950s (Anders, 2014). This trend and the evidence of long-term climate change suggest that droughts will become more common. The anticipated droughts will present in one of four ways:

- Meteorological—involves a departure of precipitation from normal
- Agricultural—occurs when the moisture in the soil does not sustain a particular crop region
- Hydrological—relates to surface or subsurface water supplies that are below normal
- Socioeconomic—happens when physical and water shortages begin to affect people

Unfortunately, little can be done to prevent droughts since they result from shifts in storm tracks. What we can do is better understand the relationship between droughts and changes in greenhouse gases, aerosols, and land use.

Hurricanes

Hurricanes—huge storms that can last as long as a week—gather heat and energy from warm ocean waters. When hurricanes meet land, heavy rain, strong winds, and large waves follow. The center or "eye" of the hurricane is the calmest part of the storm, but it is important to keep in mind that the hurricane's damaging rains and winds both precede and follow passage of the eye over a region.

Storm surges are frequently the most devastating element of a hurricane. As a hurricane's winds spiral around the storm, they push water into the storm's center. This mound of water becomes dangerous when the storm reaches land because it causes flooding along the coast.

Thanks to the tracking of hurricane conditions, residents in harm's way often have time to evacuate their homes before any lives are in danger. However, the damage to homes is often considerable, resulting in mental health conditions such as stress and depression. Social workers trained as first responders to disasters are needed to better prepare people and communities before and after storm devastation.

Volcanoes

Volcanoes are one of the earth's most dramatic agents of change. A volcano is a mountain that opens downward to a pool of molten rock below the surface of the earth. When pressure builds, eruptions occur. Gases and rock shoot up through the opening and spill over to fill the air with lava fragments. An erupting volcano can trigger tsunamis, flash floods, earthquakes, and rock falls (U.S. Geological Survey, 2014).

Volcanic eruptions are not common in the United States. The most recent were the sudden, violent eruption of Mount St. Helens in Oregon in 1980 and the slower, continuing eruption of Kilauea in Hawaii, which forced mass evacuations in the early 1990s. In regions of the world that have active volcanoes, the local residents are constantly alert to the possibility of an eruption.

Famine

Defined as the scarcity of food, famine is responsible for hunger, malnutrition, and starvation. Famine is associated with the overdrafting of groundwater, flooding, and other natural events that destroy crops, wars, internal strife, and inefficient distribution of food. Famine is especially common in sub-Saharan Africa and portions of Asia, where it causes extensive deaths.

The Green Revolution of the 1970s and 1980s was widely viewed as an answer to famine (Lobb, 2003). Hybrid strains of crops increased the worldwide production of grain

by 250%. But the increase in agriculture significantly drew down groundwater and resulted in the overuse of pesticides and other agricultural chemicals.

> ## TIME TO THINK
>
> Volunteers account for about 70% of all first responders in an environmental disaster. First responders are those who live in or near a community and are trained and willing to respond immediately to emergency situations. Do you have an interest in serving as a volunteer first responder? Would you be willing to attend training sessions, perform physical work, and be on call at any time of day?

DIVERSITY AND ENVIRONMENTALISM

Environmental issues intersect with factors associated with older people, socioeconomic class, gender, and sexual orientation in ways that draw attention to the interconnectedness between the person in the environment and the natural world. As social work more closely links practice and policy with the natural world, the call for ecological justice will gain increased attention from practitioners and scholars alike.

AGE

Understanding of the relationship between a worldwide aging demographic and changes in the environment is in the initial stages. There is evidence to suggest that flooding, famines, hurricanes, and drought cause a disproportionate amount of hardship and death for older people. Older adults made up 65% of the victims of the 2011 Japanese tsunami and about half the victims of the 2012 New Jersey hurricane. The reasons for this vary, including the inability of older people to move out of harm's away, reluctance to evacuate, and geographic and social isolation.

Unfortunately, countries typically do not have appropriate policies or services to address the needs of older people in environmental disasters. Of course, older people are a diverse group with different social, mental, physical, financial, and social variables; however, there is little doubt that these personal factors converge to support or challenge older people who are threatened by environmental issues. Some of the vulnerabilities associated with older people and environmental hazards are as follows:

- Physiological changes that coincide with aging and can alter one's degree of susceptibility
- Chronic diseases and the use of medications to treat those conditions
- Activities and lifestyles that can alter the types of environmental issues one is exposed to over time and place
- Factors such as socioeconomic and nutritional status that affect susceptibility to environmental conditions

In response, social workers are beginning to contribute to the interdisciplinary body of scholarship that integrates social justice with political ecology and the fair distribution of natural resources. To ensure a nurturing environment, older adults must be active in the care of the natural world through collaborations and lifestyle choices. Simultaneously, social workers must commit to practice on the national and international level to protect and enhance the natural environment's ability to sustain the well-being of older people.

CLASS

Around the world, poor people suffer the greatest losses from natural disasters, in both developing societies and industrialized nations. Poor people, who tend to be relegated to living in the riskiest areas, also have the most limited access to public and private recovery assets.

Preparedness behavior includes a variety of actions taken by families, households, and communities to get ready for a disaster. Devising a disaster plan, gathering emergency supplies, and educating residents about a potential disaster are all considered preparedness activities that can be undertaken by communities. However, preparedness activities for a natural disaster appear to correspond with socioeconomic indicators. Research has found that preparedness and disaster responses among individuals increase steadily with income levels (Turner, Nigg, & Paz, 1986).

Social workers know, based on their practice experience, that poor people tend to live in crisis before disaster occurs. It makes sense that when a natural disaster does occur, people living in poverty are impacted more severely than are other

members of society (Fothergill & Peek, 2004). The goal of social work is to decrease the vulnerability of people living in poverty, including their vulnerability to environmental issues. Clearly, a global examination of poverty and its implications for disaster planning is needed.

GENDER

Those most socially and economically insecure in any society or community are those who are least able to access or control the resources needed during and in the aftermath of an environmental disaster. Women and other socially marginalized populations are least likely to have the social power, economic resources, and physical capabilities to anticipate, survive, and recover from the effects of massive or extreme environmental events. Thus, economic insecurity is a key factor increasing the impact of disaster on women in their various roles in families, communities, and the workplace.

Knowledge of gender-specific impacts of environmental disasters is limited by lack of gender analysis in most disaster research. However, the most striking effect of disasters on women is the loss of economic resources and deterioration of economic status. Women on the margins who are living with "daily disasters" of poverty are especially vulnerable.

Social workers recognize that women's subordination and lack of power in decision making is a root cause of vulnerability in general and in particular with regard to environmental disasters. What is necessary is social work scholarship that integrates gender relationships as a factor in disaster vulnerability and response. Further, when social workers engage in community organization or design collaborative partnerships around disaster mitigation, women must be included as equal partners.

SEXUAL ORIENTATION

The human impacts of environmental disasters vary across different social groups. However, one group largely absent from scholarly and policy agenda is the LGBTQ (lesbian, gay, bisexual, transgender, and questioning) community. Research and discussion are needed to determine whether these minorities have particular experiences with the environment that need to be addressed.

What has developed of late is something known as "queer ecology," which integrates LGBTQ theories with those of ecology (Anderson et al., 2012). An integral task of queer ecology is to highlight the intersections of sexuality and environmental studies to illustrate that humans and the natural environment are capable of a much wider range of behaviors than they are often given credit (Mortimer-Sandilands & Erickson, 2010). The outcome is a perspective that relates patterns of domination and control over human diversity to patterns that impact the earth's resources.

INTERSECTIONS OF DIVERSITY

There is growing recognition that the diversity in life includes both environmental and cultural diversity. People have interacted with the natural environment for thousands of generations. In fact, in some cultures environmental and diversity factors intersect, as reflected in traditional symbols, behaviors, values, institutions, and religious practices. Consequently, a natural event, such as deforestation or erosion, may result in the loss of land-based cultures, particularly when coupled with economic or political stressors. Although the link between the world's diverse ecosystems and cultures is recognized, it needs to be better understood. Seeking answers to the questions listed in Exhibit 16.4 would go a long way toward achieving that understanding.

EXHIBIT 16.4   Ten Key Questions to Be Addressed to Support Environmental and Cultural Diversity Policy

PERSUASION AND POLICIES

1. How can governments and societies be persuaded that maintaining and improving both cultural and environmental diversity can be in their interest?

2. What are the best examples of enabling effective national and international policies that allow development of new approaches by grassroots communities and their sharing those approaches with others?

3. What are the best ways to deal with a change in tradition, such as when cultures and cultural traditions evolve and adapt?

BARRIERS TO RIGHTS

4. What are the barriers to governments' adopting and strengthening human rights declarations and land rights policies for all their own people?

REVITALIZATION PROJECTS

5. What are the most effective recovery or revitalization projects that can protect the cultures and values of both indigenous people and postindustrialized societies?

6. What are the best internal and external incentives for sustaining cultural and biological diversity? Can the benefits of the existing capitals of cultural and biological diversity be maximized in terms of income streams?

PARTICIPATION AND POWER

7. How can indigenous people and minority groups best be empowered while maintaining their own cultural values? How should conservation efforts respond to the fact that the cultural values of nature vary from place to place and also over time?

8. How can the promotion of increased participation by cultural minorities and a wider range of partners (e.g., responsible industry, faith groups, social action groups, and youth) be achieved in different political decision-making instances and processes?

CHANGING ASPIRATIONS

9. How can new aspirations be created for livelihoods and ways of life in all societies so as to change the consumption patterns that threaten nature and cultures worldwide?

YOUNG PEOPLE AND NATURE DISCONNECTIONS

10. How can younger generations be attracted back into contact with their local environment so as to prevent any further extinction of experience and the growing disconnection with nature?

Source: Adapted from Pretty et al. (2009).

ADVOCACY AND ENVIRONMENTALISM

It might be surprising to you, given the wealth, international power, and natural resources of the United States, that pollution, climate change, and carbon emissions are not more widely discussed. Similarly, perhaps it is puzzling that social work practice, given the profession's goal to enhance the quality of life, has been slow in supporting environmentalism in policies and programs.

The four interrelated and interlocking components of the dynamic advocacy model—economic and social justice, supportive environment, human needs and rights, and political access—provide a means for social workers to begin to evaluate environmental issues and facilitate a shift toward a more sustainable society. Ideally, using the model to outline in a broad way how social work could respond to environmental concerns will encourage you to think about knowledge systems, ideologies, lifestyles, and social care in the context of the environmental opportunities and challenges confronting us.

ECONOMIC AND SOCIAL JUSTICE

Our exploration of environmental hazards and social justice is based on the premise that all members of society need and deserve a healthy world in which to live, work, and engage with others. It follows that all people need and deserve input on creating a healthy world. In the United States, a formal definition of environmental justice has been crafted by the **Environmental Protection Agency** (EPA, 2014)—the federal entity responsible for protecting human health and the environment—and it reflects this view:

> Environmental Justice is the fair treatment and meaningful involvement of all people regardless of race, color, national origin, or income with respect to the development, implementation, and enforcement of environmental laws, regulations, and policies. EPA has this goal for all communities and persons across this Nation. It will be achieved when everyone enjoys the same degree of protection from environmental and health hazards and equal access to the decision-making process to have a healthy environment in which to live, learn, and work.

In short, environmental justice is the assurance that benefits of a healthy environment will be distributed to all members of society in an equitable fashion. Essentially, the quality of life for everyone in the general population must be approximately equal.

This view is supported by the Principles of Environmental Justice, compiled by the delegates to the first National People of Color Environmental Leadership Summit, held in 1991 in Washington, D.C. The summit derived from a class action suit under civil rights law regarding a 1979 dispute in Houston, Texas, to keep a sanitary landfill out of a largely African American community (Bullard, n.d.). The community won the case, providing impetus for a study that revealed that eight states in the South habitually located hazardous waste landfills in predominantly African American communities.

The 17 Principles of Environmental Justice that were drafted and adopted during the summit (see Exhibit 16.5) have served as a defining guide for the growing grassroots movement for environmental justice. The document provides a strong foundation and progressive perspective for environmentalism in social work. These principles encapsulated the intentions of summit participants to broaden the environmental movement to issues of public health, worker safety, and community empowerment; build a multiracial grassroots movement around environmental concerns; and call on all levels of government to address environmental needs in the context of justice. These principles are a good foundation for the social work profession as it locates itself in global environmental politics and expands awareness of the link between human society and the natural environment (Miller, Hayward, & Shaw, 2012).

SUPPORTIVE ENVIRONMENT

Social work maintains a strong emphasis on the person-in-environment perspective, which considers individuals as active participants in a larger society. Yet the perspective maintains a narrow definition of "environment" that includes the social but disregards the natural environment. Excluding the natural environment has perhaps contributed to the profession's slow involvement in worldwide issues regarding the natural environment, such as those described in this chapter.

While social workers reflect an awareness of the importance of environmental issues within the natural world, their practice and policies are not necessarily affected by those issues. But perhaps the notion of environmental ethics is what will drive the social work profession to address environmental concerns. The most practical arenas for addressing

EXHIBIT 16.5　　Seventeen Principles of Environmental Justice

PREAMBLE

WE, THE PEOPLE OF COLOR, gathered together at this multinational People of Color Environmental Leadership Summit, to begin to build a national and international movement of all peoples of color to fight the destruction and taking of our lands and communities, do hereby re-establish our spiritual interdependence to the sacredness of our Mother Earth; to respect and celebrate each of our cultures, languages and beliefs about the natural world and our roles in healing ourselves; to ensure environmental justice; to promote economic alternatives which would contribute to the development of environmentally safe livelihoods; and, to secure our political, economic and cultural liberation that has been denied for over 500 years of colonization and oppression, resulting in the poisoning of our communities and land and the genocide of our peoples, do affirm and adopt these Principles of Environmental Justice:

1. **Environmental Justice** affirms the sacredness of Mother Earth, ecological unity and the interdependence of all species, and the right to be free from ecological destruction.

2. **Environmental Justice** demands that public policy be based on mutual respect and justice for all peoples, free from any form of discrimination or bias.

3. **Environmental Justice** mandates the right to ethical, balanced and responsible uses of land and renewable resources in the interest of a sustainable planet for humans and other living things.

4. **Environmental Justice** calls for universal protection from nuclear testing, extraction, production and disposal of toxic/hazardous wastes and poisons and nuclear testing that threaten the fundamental right to clean air, land, water, and food.

5. **Environmental Justice** affirms the fundamental right to political, economic, cultural and environmental self-determination of all peoples.

6. **Environmental Justice** demands the cessation of the production of all toxins, hazardous wastes, and radioactive materials, and that all past and current producers be held strictly accountable to the people for detoxification and the containment at the point of production.

7. **Environmental Justice** demands the right to participate as equal partners at every level of decision-making, including needs assessment, planning, implementation, enforcement and evaluation.

8. **Environmental Justice** affirms the right of all workers to a safe and healthy work environment without being forced to choose between an unsafe livelihood and unemployment. It also affirms the right of those who work at home to be free from environmental hazards.

9. **Environmental Justice** protects the right of victims of environmental injustice to receive full compensation and reparations for damages as well as quality health care.

10. **Environmental Justice** considers governmental acts of environmental injustice a violation of international law, the Universal Declaration on Human Rights, and the United Nations Convention on Genocide.

11. **Environmental Justice** must recognize a special legal and natural relationship of Native Peoples to the U.S. government through treaties, agreements, compacts, and covenants affirming sovereignty and self-determination.

12. **Environmental Justice** affirms the need for urban and rural ecological policies to clean up and rebuild our cities and rural areas in balance with nature, honoring the cultural integrity of all our communities, and providing fair access for all to the full range of resources.

13. **Environmental Justice** calls for the strict enforcement of principles of informed consent, and a halt to the testing of experimental reproductive and medical procedures and vaccinations on people of color.

14. **Environmental Justice** opposes the destructive operations of multi-national corporations.

15. **Environmental Justice** opposes military occupation, repression and exploitation of lands, peoples and cultures, and other life forms.

16. **Environmental Justice** calls for the education of present and future generations which emphasizes social and environmental issues, based on our experience and an appreciation of our diverse cultural perspectives.

17. **Environmental Justice** requires that we, as individuals, make personal and consumer choices to consume as little of Mother Earth's resources and to produce as little waste as possible; and make the conscious decision to challenge and reprioritize our lifestyles to ensure the health of the natural world for present and future generations.

The Proceedings to the First National People of Color Environmental Leadership Summit are available from the United Church of Christ Commission for Racial Justice, 475 Riverside Dr., Suite 1950, New York, NY 10115.

Source: http://www.ejnet.org/ej/principles.html

environmental ethics at this point are education of social work students, social work practice with marginalized groups, and international advocacy in developing countries and in the national and international design of social welfare policies.

Social workers who are interested in the natural environment have roles to play as educators, researchers, community organizers, and policy analysts. In all these roles social workers would infuse the practice of social work with a holistic understanding of the mutually supportive relationship between people and their world.

HUMAN NEEDS AND RIGHTS

Concerns involving environmental issues interface with social workers' typical concerns about promoting people's mental, physical, financial, and social well-being. In all cases human rights are involved. The inequity is twofold: People who are poor or discriminated against on some other basis are the ones who have to deal with most of the results of pollution, and that pollution is typically the result of affluence in which they cannot participate (Coates & Gray, 2012; Rogge, 1994, p. 53). In addition, oppressed people are seldom consulted about, much less included in, decision making about how to manage pollution. When environmental initiatives are implemented, they seldom benefit oppressed people.

The dynamic advocacy model links human rights to the environment, viewing the well-being of people as the result of social justice. As a call to action, the model suggests that human rights are risked when the environmental degradation is ignored. Indeed, when the environment is ignored, human rights are also.

Environmental concerns present an excellent way for social workers to advance human rights laws. Victims of environmental neglect need to be protected by the laws and mechanisms established to address human rights abuses.

POLITICAL ACCESS

Social workers have a history of advocating for environmental justice. For example, they have collaborated with established environmental organizations such as the Sierra Club and Greenpeace to promote investigation, exposure, and resolution of environmental concerns.

Beginning in the 1950s and throughout most of the 1960s, environmental advocates have influenced Congress to react to the increasing concern about the impact of human activity on the environment. The organized action resulted in key legislation under the direction of the EPA. Over the years, laws have addressed atomic energy, chemical safety, clean air and water, emergency planning, and energy independence.

A current issue facing the United States, as well as other nations, is **fracking**, the process of drilling and inserting fluid into the earth to fracture shale rock and release natural gas. The decision to engage in fracking highlights many issues relevant to social work, such as the use of chemicals in a way that impacts well water and aquifers, the release of harmful compounds into the atmosphere, and possible health hazards. To date, the social work profession has not taken a strong position on the fracking debate, but practice from an environmental perspective would encourage the profession to do so.

YOUR CAREER IN ENVIRONMENTALISM

If you are interested in a career in social work, your courses will introduce you to the person-in-environment perspective and the role of policy in practice. The question is, how can you transfer this fund of knowledge to career paths in environmentalism? Take a moment to consider how developing a skill base in social work corresponds with human needs in the context of the environment. What might come to mind is how social workers serve as first responders when people have suffered directly and indirectly as a result of environmental destruction. Examples of such devastation are the significant loss of homes and livelihoods on the coast of New Jersey in the wake of Hurricane Sandy in 2012 and on the Gulf Coast after Hurricane Katrina in 2005. The 2010 BP oil spill in the Gulf of Mexico also showed all too clearly the impact of an environmental disaster on waterways, people, communities, and various forms of wildlife. In each of these cases, social workers were on the scene providing services to help ensure the physical, social, political, economic, and spiritual aspects of recovery.

Another career path that intersects social work and environmentalism involves advocacy on behalf of particular groups, such as the Sierra Club or the World Wide Fund for Nature. In this capacity social workers help organize communities, development and political campaigns, public education forums, and media releases related to environmental concerns. In this way social workers are proactive in prevention of misuse of the environment.

SUMMARY

What we are doing to the forests of the world is but a mirror reflection of what we are doing to ourselves and to one another.

–Mahatma Gandhi

While environmental issues are complex and the solutions challenging, social work has a role to play in this arena. Social workers can help inhibit environmental degradation that affects not only people worldwide but also the earth. Social work's mandate to serve the needs of people, especially those who are marginalized, is clearly the focus of these efforts. However, it is time to expand social work's framework to include practice and policy initiatives that protect people from natural and human-influenced environmental changes.

Confronting environmental issues necessitates that social work look within the profession to evaluate its mission. Further, the profession must look beyond its borders to recognize the relationship people have with the world of nature. In both cases, social workers need to work cooperatively with people in other disciplines to respond to the symptoms and causes that threaten the planet and all of life.

TOP 10 KEY CONCEPTS

climate change
doubling time
ecological ethics
ecological justice
ecological social welfare

environmental justice
Environmental Protection Agency
environmentalists
fracking
sustainability

DISCUSSION QUESTIONS

1. Consider what efforts your campus has made to enhance the physical environment. How do these efforts add quality to your life? What first brought your attention to these efforts?
2. Is there an organization on your campus involved in environmental issues? If so, what is the organization's mission and activities? If there isn't such an organization, why not?
3. What role does, or should, social media play in environmentalism?
4. When you think of the social work profession, does ecological practice and policy seem to add or distract from the notions of what social workers do?
5. What kinds of challenges and opportunities do environmental issues and disasters present for social workers?

EXERCISES

1. Review Nader.org, the website of Ralph Nader, a longtime advocate for environmental concerns. From your review, list at least five ways Nader has integrated issues such as poverty with environmental concerns.
2. Watch *An Inconvenient Truth,* the 2006 Academy Award–winning documentary narrated by former Vice President Al Gore. List six "takeaway points" from the film.
3. President Obama created the new position of assistant to the president for climate and energy. First, search for information on who holds this position. Then write what you think would be an appropriate job description for the position. What skills and knowledge should this person have, and what duties and responsibilities should come with the title?
4. Some people conclude that the environmental movement in the United States began with Rachel Carson's book *Silent Spring.* Read the book and discuss how Carson's warnings regarding exposure to the hazards of pesticides such as DDT have become evident in your lifetime.
5. Select a familiar community. It can be your hometown or college or university community. Track or map where your community's trash goes, sewage drains, water and electricity come from, and public transportation travels. What does this exercise tell you about your interaction with the community and resources?
6. Review social work's developing role in environmental issues by reading the position statements of the International Federation of Social Workers, the National

Association of Social Workers, and the Council on Social Work Education. What themes emerge from these statements? What do you think needs to be added to bring them up to date for today's environmental concerns?

7. The Brundtland Commission, formally the World Commission on Environment and Development, was established by the United Nations in 1983. The commission links peace, security, development, and the environment to oppression and degradation of the earth. Read an overview of the Brundtland Commission at www .un-documents.net/our-common-future.pdf. Select an opinion you endorse and another opinion you question, and explain your choices. In addition, answer this question: What possible direction could the report offer the profession of social work?

ONLINE RESOURCES

- EnviroLink Network (envirolink.org): This nonprofit organization provides access to thousands of online environmental resources
- Federal Emergency Management Agency (www .fema.gov): Site for the federal government's disaster response agency; provides comprehensive disaster assistance and prevention information
- Natural Resources Defense Council (nrdc.org): A national association of environmental, civil rights, mental health, and women's advocacy coalitions

- Sustainable Table (sustainabletable.org): A foundation that addresses a wide range of issues associated with water pollution and conservation
- WebEcoist (webecoist.momtastic.com/2008/09/24/25-environmental-agencies-and-organizations): Provides a comprehensive list and description of 25 organizations dedicated to environmental causes

STUDENT STUDY SITE

Sharpen your skills with SAGE edge at **edge.sagepub.com/cox**

SAGE edge for Students provides a personalized approach to help you accomplish your coursework goals in an easy-to-use learning environment.

Chapter 17: GLOBAL PRACTICE AND INTERNATIONAL SOCIAL WORK

Learning Objectives

After reading this chapter, you should be able to

1. Distinguish global practice from international social work.
2. Explain social work's professional commitment to global human needs and rights, and differentiate charity from empowerment.
3. Articulate key social work principles for global and international practice.
4. Identify and explain important considerations for culturally competent social work practice.
5. Describe major global issues in relationship to social work practice.
6. Identify and describe important considerations, including safety and self-care, for social workers entering global and international social work practice.

Teresa Applies Her Multicultural Background to Social Work

Teresa is a BSW-level social worker employed at her city's Latin American Coalition Organization (LACO). Teresa grew up in Venezuela and moved to the United States with her mother as a teenager, and she is fluent in Spanish and English. Following her senior-year field placement in an international refugee and resettlement program with Catholic Social Services, Teresa became convinced of her desire to work in global social work, specifically with local Latino population groups.

Teresa is enthusiastic about working for LACO. The mission of the organization, which was founded in 2008, is "providing assistance and support to local Latinos in need and promoting an understanding and respect for Latino and Hispanic cultures." LACO assists Latino individuals and families who are struggling with adapting to life in the United States. They face language barriers, unemployment, troubled family relationships, meager networks of social support, and a lack of access to basic needs (e.g., food, housing, and clothing), medical services, and transportation. LACO promotes cultural recognition and pride by backing local celebrations, cultural events, support groups, and business development. Although many Latinos in Teresa's area come from Mexico, Peru, and Argentina, Latinos have migrated to her city from nearly every country throughout Central and South America. Latinos predominantly live in an economically challenged section of town in small, distinct neighborhoods based on nation of origin. Conveniently located near Latino residences and on a major city bus route, LACO is highly accessible to the people being served and offers valuable meeting and recreational space.

TIME TO THINK

Do social workers have to come from or travel to another country to engage in global or international social work practice? Whether social workers practice inside their own country or abroad, how can they learn about the values, challenges, hardships, and strengths of the population groups they serve?

For many people, the globe has become smaller and more manageable. As a result of advanced communication technology (e.g., computers, phones, social media) and modes of rapid transportation (e.g., planes and bullet trains), it is commonplace for people to communicate, travel, and engage in social interaction and commerce across national boundaries. Those with the resources and ability to travel develop relationships internationally. Some move from one country to another to settle.

The United States is a relatively young country, less than 250 years old, with an increasingly complex racial and ethnic composition. With the exception of Native American Indians, the United States is a country founded by people who have migrated from other countries. People around the world, including an appreciable number of recent immigrants from Asia and Latin America, continue to come to the United States in pursuit of opportunities, freedom, and prosperity. High rates of racial and ethnic intermarriage have contributed to emerging American identities and a growing number of persons of mixed descent in the United States (Perez & Hirschman, 2009).

For decades, social workers have recognized the opportunities and challenges associated with this global interdependence. Notable organizations dedicated to promoting human rights and justice and aligned with the profession of social work include the International Federation of Social Workers, the International Association of Schools of Social Work, and the International Council on Social Welfare. Exhibit 17.1 describes the essential activities of each of these organizations.

EXHIBIT 17.1   International Social Work Organizations

INTERNATIONAL SOCIAL WORK ORGANIZATION	DESCRIPTION AND FUNCTIONS OF ORGANIZATION
International Federation of Social Workers (IFSW) ifsw.org	The IFSW is a federation of social work organizations producing a voice for the profession of social work around the world. A nongovernmental entity, the IFSW is organized into five regions around the world, with its global Secretariat located in Basel, Switzerland. The IFSW has more than 100 members and promotes worldwide social justice, human rights, and social development through the use of effective social work practices and international cooperation.
International Association of Schools of Social Work (IASSW) www.iassw-aiets.org	The IASSW is dedicated to supporting social work education and educators. It promotes international exchange of information, expertise, and research, and is dedicated to promoting global standards for social work education and training.
International Council on Social Welfare (ICSW) www.icsw.org	The ICSW gathers and distributes information (e.g., via reports, newsletters, and electronic means) about issues related to economic development and human rights around the globe. It supports research and consultation to assess problems, develop policies, and advocate for change. The ICSW facilitates meetings, forums, workshops, and conferences examining a variety of global topics.

CENTRAL CONCEPTS IN GLOBAL AND INTERNATIONAL SOCIAL WORK

At first glance, the terms *global social work practice* and *international social work* may seem synonymous. Both allude to the practice of social work involving, in some fashion, more than one country. But a closer examination highlights important distinctions:

- **Global practice:** Social work activities that are based on a special appreciation and understanding that **globalization** has made it possible for people around the world to experience multiple cultures and become involved in and affected by various social problems and causes. For example, through social media, social workers in the United States collaborate with social workers in Nigeria on a research project to design culturally appropriate strategies to decrease mother-to-child transfer of HIV/AIDS in their respective countries.

- **International social work**: Social work activities that involve people who cross national boundaries and focus on the universal characteristics of human beings and human needs in various environments. For example, child-care workers from Mexico travel to Texas to train and assist social workers in addressing the needs of unaccompanied immigrant children.

These definitions are by no means universally embraced within social work. In fact, there is ongoing discussion about the precise definition of each term. However, these are the ways we will use these terms in this chapter.

DIFFERENCES IN FOCUS OF GLOBAL AND INTERNATIONAL SOCIAL WORK

In global practice, social workers act to improve the circumstances and conditions of global citizens (Hong & Song, 2010). Social workers dedicated to global practice are committed to caring for and creating change via policy development and advocacy with population groups adversely affected by globalization. It should be noted that social workers in global practice are seen as thinking globally and acting locally (Lyons, 2006).

Thinking that international social work means only practice in another country is too simplistic. International social work is multifaceted and includes a variety of professional functions and activities, including working with social workers from other countries and participating in international advocacy and policy development (Healy, 2008). In international practice, social workers also participate directly in international development work (Healy, 2008, p. 15). Other activities include advocating for rights and justice for international populations and participating in social action and policy development to address global problems.

To summarize, global practice highlights social work's broad commitment to improving circumstances and conditions impacting people around the world (Hong & Song, 2010). International social work practice often refers to work within international development organizations, advocating for rights and justice, exchange of information, and social action and policy development.

LEVEL OF NATIONAL DEVELOPMENT

It is not unusual for much of global practice and international social work to involve countries and population groups struggling with economic and social development. The causes of delayed development are generally limited resources and oppressive political factors. Countries facing poverty, civil unrest, economic exploitation of labor and natural resources, war, environmental disaster, and political turmoil are especially noteworthy.

Decades ago, the term **third world country** was used to describe poor, nonindustrialized, and economically developing countries. Today, this term is viewed negatively, as it suggests a third-rate, backward, or nondesirable country. Contemporary thinking differentiates countries as either industrialized or developing:

- **Industrialized countries** have a developed economy, exhibit advanced technology, and are modernized.
- **Developing countries** have a less-developed economy, lack sophisticated technology, and possess a lower standard of living than do industrialized countries.

TIME TO THINK

Many people living in developing countries hope to migrate to industrialized countries. For example, people from Mexico and countries in Central America go to elaborate and often dangerous lengths to seek residency in the United States. What attracts people to industrialized countries? In the case of the United States, is it freedom and democracy? Or is the dominant factor economic opportunity and increasing one's standard of living (e.g., access to modern education, health care, and technological advancements)?

Does either of these goals justify Americans' allowing immigrants to move here? Where do you stand with regard to reform of immigration laws and allowing people from developing countries greater access to enter, live, work, and gain citizenship in the United States? Where do you stand in relation to the views of your family members, friends, and classmates?

SOCIAL WORK PRINCIPLES FOR GLOBAL AND INTERNATIONAL PRACTICE

As can be seen in the Bureau of Labor Statistics (2014) data presented in Exhibit 17.2, many social workers practice with children and families in the areas of health care, mental health, schools, and substance abuse. It is reasonable to suppose that international and global forms of social work practice are subsumed in these social work classifications and thus not discernable. Hence, data describing employment and employment projections for social workers can be misleading and often do not specifically recognize the amount of time and effort dedicated in everyday social work activities to international and global practice.

It is safe to say that many, if not most, social workers in the United States engage in some form of international or global practice. That being the case, all social workers should be aware of knowledge, principles, and best practices for working with people who have been affected by globalization or who live in other countries.

Transnational Identities

In Chapter 6, family members' maintaining lifestyles where they live across countries and cultures was defined as *transnational migration* (Furman & Negi, 2007, p. 108). The contemporary social worker frequently encounters people claiming to belong to two or more societies at one time. These individuals maintain family relationships, develop friendships, work, and/or keep social roots in more than one country. To understand the essence and identity of a transnational migrant, the social worker must conceptualize a person with allegiance to and a sense of home in more than one country.

Cultural Competence

International and global practice requires an ongoing commitment to acquiring knowledge about the values, traditions,

EXHIBIT 17.2   Employment Projections for Social Workers, 2012–2022

OCCUPATIONAL TITLE	EMPLOYMENT, 2012	PROJECTED EMPLOYMENT, 2022	CHANGE, 2012–2022	
			PERCENT	NUMERIC
Social workers	607,300	721,500	19	114,100
Child, family, and school social workers	285,700	328,800	15	43,100
Health care social workers	146,200	185,500	27	39,200
Mental health and substance abuse social workers	114,200	140,200	23	26,000
Social workers, all other	61,200	67,000	9	5,800

Source: Bureau of Labor Statistics (2014).

SOCIAL WORK IN ACTION

Jamal Seeks Bilingual Helping Professionals

JAMAL is a social worker practicing in a major city in the southeastern United States. Jamal's agency has employed a multicultural staff, including several support staff members fluent in English and Spanish, but the agency is very careful not to ask staff members to inappropriately engage in interpreting and translation activities. Yet the agency struggles with recruiting and retaining bilingual helping professionals. These professionals are in very high demand and costly to employ.

Jamal was tasked with examining the possibility of securing contracted services with an out-of-state company specializing in interpretation and translation services for social welfare agencies. Although a number of interpreting and translating companies have emerged in the United States,

Jamal began his search by looking at the ARCH Language Network. He will recommend it as a possible solution for his agency.

1. Which languages are most in use among the residents of your area? Have you noticed any organizations that intentionally hire helping professionals and staff for their multilingualism?

2. What other sorts of jobs in your area—including medical providers, court officials, and educators—need bilingual or multilingual staff to perform duties and responsibilities with people who have limited English proficiency?

customs, ways of thinking, and behaviors of client groups from a multitude of countries. **Cultural competence** is not simply a sensitivity to and appreciation for diversity. To be effective practitioners, social workers are also intentional in examining their own values, acquiring a cross-cultural understanding of clients, and developing culturally appropriate and relevant skills and approaches. The National Association of Social Workers (NASW) has identified and published standards for cultural competence in the areas of self-awareness, cross-cultural knowledge, cross-cultural skills, service delivery, empowerment and advocacy, a diverse workforce, professional education, language diversity, and cross-cultural leadership (NASW, 2001a).

Cultural knowledge can be attained in a number of ways, including reading, engaging in continuing education opportunities, attending events highlighting other cultures, and seeking out interaction with knowledgeable persons or groups. Clients and client groups also share valuable information.

Multilingualism

Multilingualism refers to the ability to speak or converse (e.g., sign) in more than one language. Social workers recognize that effective communication and use of language are

crucial factors for culturally appropriate practice. Commitment to linguistic competence is important for both professionals and social welfare agencies. In addition to being able to speak or sign effectively with clients, social workers promote and endorse programs and services through culturally appropriate and language-specific written information (e.g., posters, signs, electronic messaging, printed materials).

It is important to note that being able to converse in more than one language is different from **language interpretation**. To serve as an interpreter, the individual must typically undergo advanced training to be able to convert a thought or expression in one language to a comparable meaning in another language.

Comparative Social Policy

Beyond learning about values, traditions, and culture through direct interaction with people across the globe, social workers possess a rich history of expanding thought and ways of doing through the analysis of policies and service delivery in other countries (Long, 2009, p. 6). This practice is referred to as **comparative social policy**, or sometimes international social welfare.

If you decide to major in social work, a common assignment is to analyze a social policy (e.g., health care, public

Pope Francis on Global Capitalism

Pope Francis, the first Jesuit leader of the Roman Catholic Church, has challenged global capitalism. In his papal speech titled "Joy of the Gospel," Pope Francis acknowledged the productivity and material progress that results from global capitalism but pointed out that it often operates to the detriment of people who are poor and powerless (Cassidy, 2013). He labeled that situation as immoral. Pope Francis advances the view that economic growth in a global free market frequently does not result in social justice or inclusiveness, especially for people who are vulnerable, exploitable, and socially and economically oppressed.

Source: Agência Brasil/CreativeCommons.

▲ Pope Francis greets followers.

Although Pope Francis's critique of contemporary capitalism is likely unpopular with many of the rich and powerful, his position closely aligns with social work's view of social development. It also aligns with social work's commitment to advocating for rights and opportunities for all human beings.

1. Do you view Pope Francis as a relevant worldwide religious leader?

2. What are the pros and cons of social workers' aligning global advocacy efforts with religious leaders and institutions?

assistance, family leave, disability) from another country in comparison with policy implementation in the United States. Students are challenged to describe and explain how values and culture influence the practicality of such a policy's being approved and successfully implemented in the United States.

Principles of Ethics

The NASW (2008) *Code of Ethics* is a foundational and definitive source of information for ethical social work practice in the United States. However, in the context of global and international practice, recognition of and respect for codes of ethics in other countries is necessary. To address this need, the International Association of Schools of Social Work and the International Federation of Social Workers have approved a "Statement of Ethical Principles" that emphasizes professionalism, social justice, human rights and dignity, professional conduct, and evaluation of national codes of ethics.

Charity and Empowerment

Across country boundaries, a shared interest and commitment of social workers is to assist and help people in need. Historically, international efforts in social work have focused on **charity**, providing aid to those in need in the form of goods and services. Over past decades, social workers have been involved in worldwide relief organizations such as the United Nations, the World Health Organization, Catholic Relief Services, the International Committee of the Red Cross, Lutheran World Relief, and Save the Children, to name but a few. **International charity** is essential for addressing the immediate and oftentimes critical, life-threatening needs of people.

However, in global and international practice, it is important to see how charity might represent or mirror social injustices and inequities (Wehbi, 2011). Charity alone does little to challenge power differentials among people and forms of oppression. The recipients of charity are in no better position in the long run and often require more charity to fill their needs indefinitely.

Instead, people in need are better off receiving the gift of empowerment—that is, the encouragement, knowledge, and resources needed to influence decisions and decision-making processes. They should be educated to "see past the constructions of victimization" (Wehbi, 2011, p. 26). From a social work perspective, global and international social work are not simply a matter of providing money, goods, and services to those in need but also involve working with clients to advocate for and advance their rights and social–economic justice.

Social Development

Social workers in international practice are dedicated to **social development**, which refers to activities that combat exploitation and oppression by equitably distributing social and economic gains and by stimulating personal and social fulfillment for all members of society. It is not simply enhancing a country's assets and economic well-being as a means to increase growth in productivity for the benefit of a relative few; rather, social development is a means for changing social relations, unleashing creativity, and encouraging every member of the society to "grow to their full potential" (Dominelli, 1997, p. 75). In practice involving social development, social workers advocate for policies and practices that afford people meaningful employment, needed resources, opportunities for advancement, and an active voice in decision making.

CURRENT ISSUES FACING GLOBAL AND INTERNATIONAL SOCIAL WORKERS

In a complex and rapidly changing world, social workers are confronted with multiple issues, phenomena, and opportunities that cross borders and affect various population groups. The following topics illustrate the ways social work practice transcends national borders.

HIV/AIDS

At one time considered to be a death sentence, HIV/AIDS in the United States is now commonly viewed as a chronic illness. **HIV** is an abbreviation for human immunodeficiency

virus, which adversely affects the body's ability to combat disease and leads to AIDS. **AIDS** is an abbreviation for acquired immune deficiency syndrome, which occurs after the immune system becomes so compromised that it is unable to defend itself against bacteria or other viruses and often permits the development of certain forms of cancer (AIDS Healthcare Foundation, 2014).

Although no cure for HIV/AIDS exists, **antiretroviral medications** can stop the replication of HIV. When used properly, these medications have been very effective in suppression of HIV and AIDS, allowing people to live indefinitely. NBA basketball star and legend Ervin "Magic" Johnson was one of the first celebrities to openly discuss HIV infection, advancements in treatment, and long-term life expectancy. He was first diagnosed in 1991 and has, ever since, advocated for social justice in the treatment of HIV/AIDS.

HIV/AIDS is an infectious, not contagious disease that is typically transmitted through blood transfer, through sexual contact (via semen or vaginal fluid), or from mother to child (either at birth or via breast milk; Rowan, 2013, p. 281). Sexual practices (e.g., anal intercourse) and certain forms of drug use involving blood transfer (e.g., needle sharing) place people at high risk of infection. In many cultures, people resist discussion of HIV/AIDS and its prevention because topics such as anal sex, men having sex with men, and intravenous drug use are too controversial and threatening.

The global estimate of adults and children living with HIV in 2012 ranged from 32 million to 38 million, with an estimated 3 million to 3.7 million of those being children—defined as anyone 14 years of age or younger (UN Programme on HIV/AIDS, 2013). Estimates for the 2012 worldwide number of children who have been orphaned as a result of AIDS range from 16.1 million to 21.6 million (UN Programme on HIV/AIDS, 2013). In sub-Saharan Africa alone, an estimated 13.4 million to 16.9 million children have been orphaned as a result of AIDS (UN Programme on HIV/AIDS, 2013). The numbers are staggering and are testimony to the spread of the disease and its fatal nature when not diagnosed early and effectively treated with modern medicines.

CHILD WELFARE

The worldwide statistics for children infected with and orphaned by HIV/AIDS are stunning and disturbing; however, the global threats to children's welfare take many forms: diseases, loss of parents, hunger, housing, human trafficking

Diana Rowan and Her International Fight Against AIDS

Dr. Diana Rowan is an excellent example of a social worker, educator, and researcher who works internationally. She has developed extensive expertise and experience with the AIDS epidemic and global practice, particularly in Malawi (Rowan, 2009). In a service-learning course for her American students, she has even offered spring break trips to Malawi. Rowan and her international colleagues are innovators, using technology such as video recordings to help students in the United States and sub-Saharan Africa share their views, experiences, perspectives, and beliefs associated with HIV/AIDS (Rowan, Kabwira, Mmatli, Rankopo, & Long, 2012).

Rowan (2013) has also published a thorough review and case-based guide to social work practice with HIV/AIDS. In relationship to global and international practice, relevant topics highlighted in her book include cultural competence, work with Latinos and African Americans, medical care and treatment in developing countries, sexual practices and drug use in various countries, and U.S. AIDS policy.

1. How might Dr. Rowan's work serve as an inspiration for your involvement in international and global social work practice?

2. Would you ever consider working with people who have HIV/AIDS? Why or why not?

and exploitation (e.g., as laborers, prostitutes, or soldiers), neglect, abuse, and unsafe living conditions. Children constitute one of the most poverty-stricken groups in most locales and countries.

Developmentally, children are very vulnerable, especially at young ages. Regardless of nationality, children depend on human attachments and caretakers to meet their most basic needs, including nutrition, medicine, and shelter. Early childhood is also an especially crucial time for forming attachments to caretakers; without them, children may not learn to trust others, which puts them at risk of becoming antisocial.

Young children have no choice as to parents, caretakers, country of birth, and environmental conditions into which they are born. The availability and accessibility of child protective services, adoption, foster care, nutritional programs, child care, and medical services vary considerably from country to country, even among the wealthiest countries.

Investment in the welfare of children not only impacts individual lives but also contributes to each country's well-being and future. Provision of services and programs to protect children and enhance their abilities benefits all societal members. From a **human capital** perspective,

children represent a society's future assets, as long as the society invests in them; if it does not, those children may be future liabilities (Heiner, 2013, p. 118). Investment in children as human capital involves commitment and resources. It focuses on making children, a population group unable to advocate for themselves, a societal priority.

TIME TO THINK

In your view, is the United States a "child-centered" society? Consider the availability and affordability of health care, child care, and nutritional services and programs for all children. When compared with other, poorer countries, how can Americans argue an inability to fund child access to food, shelter, and health care?

In the United States we often make states and counties responsible for ensuring the welfare of children. In your opinion, is that approach successful or problematic?

In the United States there are also urban and rural distinctions in providing for children's welfare. Do you think those distinctions are relevant across nations?

POVERTY

Worldwide, the United States is revered as a country of great opportunity. People hope to migrate to the United States in pursuit of fame and fortune. Yet the American Dream of acquiring a high standard of living and wealth falls short of becoming a reality for most people in the United States. Especially since the housing crisis and Great Recession of 2008–2009, many Americans have struggled with maintaining and acquiring food, shelter, and employment sufficient to sustain and advance social–economic well-being. Many lower-wage earners work several jobs simply to "get by" and pay bills. Estimates suggest that about 1 in 6 Americans, many of them children, are consistently hungry (Kendall, 2013, p. 25).

The global scene with regard to poverty is even more discouraging. Worldwide, the measure for absolute poverty, how much a person needs to survive at the most basic level, is $1.25 per day. More than 1.4 billion people subsist at this level (Kendall, 2013, p. 29). Absolute poverty often results in severe malnutrition, preventable and treatable diseases, and poor overall health, resulting in human suffering and death.

As you can see, poverty is about much more than low income. The United Nations has developed the **Multidimensional Poverty Index** to measure deprivation. It takes into account health (e.g., nutrition and infant mortality), education (e.g., amount of schooling), and living standards (e.g., water, toilets, electricity, and flooring in residence). Based on this index, countries in sub-Saharan Africa, South Asia, and poorer areas of Latin America especially struggle with multidimensional poverty (Kendall, 2013, p. 29).

Impoverished nations, particularly nonindustrialized societies, have low national and personal incomes and limited resources. However, even in poverty-stricken nations, large differences in wealth exist between rich and very poor individuals and families.

It should be noted that both wealthy and poor countries exhibit **class systems**, where people are classified and stratified (divided and ranked into identifiable social groups) on the basis of social and economic inequalities (e.g., ownership, wealth, and control of resources). Disparities between the "haves" and "have-nots" within a country are typically rationalized by **ideologies** (sets of beliefs) and cultural values that justify privilege for people in power. Those disparities are usually larger, however, in poverty-stricken societies.

▲ The United Nations is one of several worldwide relief organizations involved with international charity and social work.

REFUGEES

At the beginning of 2012, the worldwide number of refugees was estimated at 10.4 million (UN High Commissioner for Refugees, 2013). **Refugees** are immigrants who are given special consideration because they have been forced to leave their country due to human rights violations (e.g., suffering or persecution as a result of race, religion, political belief, etc.). An **asylum seeker** is a person seeking or claiming the status of refugee but not yet formally evaluated and judged to be a refugee. National asylum systems have been developed to decide if asylum seekers qualify for international protection and the status of refugee. This distinction is often ignored, however, and all people fleeing violence are commonly called refugees.

War and generalized violence can lead to mass movements of asylum seekers across national borders in search of refugee status. The massive influx of people in a short period typically produces processing challenges, as authorities require asylum seekers to document their refugee status. If asylum seekers are not judged to be refugees, they can be sent back to their country of origin.

Asylum seekers, or refugees as they are commonly called, have dire needs for food, clothing, shelter, and health care. Transportation is a primary consideration for refugees when they leave one country to travel to another. With such a level of need, provision of goods and services for refugees can be a challenge for even wealthy countries. Usually countries rely on international and local **nongovernmental organizations** to address refugees' immediate needs and make arrangements for resettlement.

The United States and Canada accept an appreciable amount of the world's refugees. However, most refugees

CURRENT TRENDS

Civil War and Refugees

IN several parts of the world, especially the Middle East, political strife and social upheaval have led to violence between factions within a country. That violence has destroyed many homes across the region and is killing thousands of people. Many of the noncombatants are fleeing to safer places, where they usually face deprivation and other forms of danger.

One of the most severely affected regions is Syria, where 2.3 million people have left their homes and sought refuge in other countries (Vick, 2014, p. 24). About 900,000 are in make-shift camps in neighboring Lebanon. The Zaatari refugee camp was originally built for 30,000 people and now has 85,000 residents occupying a 2-square-mile area. The staple food is bread supplied by the World Food Programme; 92% of the people there have no private water storage (pp. 26–27). Residents

are overwhelmed by the cramped and insecure nature of their communal kitchens, water tanks, and storage facilities.

The Zaatari refugees have been not only displaced but also traumatized by the harsh civil war. Their situation is physically and emotionally distressing. In the first year of Zaatari's occupation, residents expressed their state of mind by throwing rocks at aid workers. Witnesses described the refugees as "angrier than many had ever seen" (Vick, 2014, p. 26).

1. What is the global responsibility to assist people fleeing war, especially civil war?

2. How might social workers from around the world bring attention to the plight of refugees and build commitment to addressing their needs?

---

from the world's poorest countries end up in neighboring countries, which are often struggling to take care of their own citizens (Mupedziswa, 1997, p. 112). Adding a large number of asylum seekers and refugees exacerbates the problem.

Social workers in the United States practice with people with a variety of immigration statuses. Some clients have been granted a legal right to be in the United States, and others have not. The nomenclature and issues associated with immigration status can be confusing and complex. For example, referring to a person as an **alien** is demeaning when compared with *undocumented* or *unauthorized person*. Similarly, the term *legal permanent resident* is more descriptive and more respectful than **green card holder**. These and other terms used in relation to immigration status are presented in Exhibit 17.3.

People with a different national origin often struggle with adapting to their new country and its values, language, traditions, expectations, and ways. Social workers partner with international organizations, human service agencies, and faith-based organizations to help immigrants, asylum seekers, and refugees address their needs, acclimate to new ways of thinking and behavioral expectations, and, from a

policy perspective, identify ways to protect and advance their rights in a new country.

SAFETY AND SELF-CARE

From a strengths-oriented perspective, global and international practice represent an opportunity for professional development. When introduced to and serving new population groups in practice, one's professional sense of self and comfort level are pushed. A key ingredient is humility, knowing your capabilities and limitations—what you know, don't know, and need to learn from others.

Whether social workers are practicing inside their own country or in a foreign land, safety and self-care are two very important considerations. As a general rule, to be effective professionals, social workers need to have first successfully addressed their own needs and safety concerns. **Self-care** refers to behaviors and actions that contribute to maintaining one's own sense of wellness and health. But in international social work, in developing countries in particular, safety can be the foremost concern. The "cardinal rule" is to avoid dangerous places and situations (Long, 2009, p. 17).

EXHIBIT 17.3   Immigration-Related Terminology Used in the United States

TERM	MEANING
National origin	A person's or his or her ancestors' country of birth
Alien	A person not a legal citizen of the United States
Undocumented or unauthorized person	A person not a legal citizen of the United States and without legal right and documentation to be in the United States; also sometimes referred to as an illegal immigrant or deportable alien
Documented person	A person not a legal citizen of the United States but with a legal right to be in the United States; also sometimes referred to as a documented alien
Legal permanent resident	A person legally admitted to the United States and with the privilege to be a permanent resident; also sometimes referred to as a green card holder or permanent resident alien
Nonimmigrant	A foreign-born person temporarily in the United States (e.g., a tourist, journalist, seasonal worker)
Temporary protected status	A temporary status granted to eligible nationals from designated countries as determined by the U.S. Secretary of Homeland Security. These people already reside in the United States, and a determination has been made that they are unable to return to their home countries as a result of safety or country circumstances.

Social workers giving serious consideration to employment in any of the world's trouble spots should contemplate the following advice:

- Seek appropriate oversight and supervision for your practice, especially in unstructured and fluid, undefined workplaces (Long, 2009, p. 17).
- Identify your own motivations and vulnerabilities (e.g., emotional, health, family) for working with international population groups. Self-analysis, professionally facilitated by a helping professional, may be useful and necessary (pp. 17–18).
- Identify your strengths and limitations concerning the kinds of expertise (e.g., language and knowledge of culture) that a social worker needs to develop to be effective (p. 17).
- Understand how foreign social workers may be viewed by the public as well as by professionals in the new location. Foreign social workers may be seen as being helpful or a hindrance.
- Establish adequate support systems (e.g., colleagues, family, friends, employer, in-country contacts) to support your involvement and be available for assistance in the event of difficulties.

DIVERSITY AND GLOBAL AND INTERNATIONAL PRACTICE

Social work practice with population groups and issues transcending country borders is an excellent way to examine the broader impact of variables such as age, class, ethnicity, race, gender, and sexual orientation. For example, countries vary tremendously concerning the meaning, bearing, and weight of sexual orientation. In recent years, views in the United States concerning gay and lesbian relationships, rights, and marriage have changed significantly, with many states passing legislation legalizing gay and lesbian marriage. In other countries, homosexuality is forbidden and against the law.

Values and views concerning specific forms of human diversity are often formed and supported in relationship to prevailing religious traditions. For social workers, the relationship between oppressive forms of behavior and dominant religious traditions presents a particular challenge. For example, in many Middle Eastern, Islamic countries, advocating for gay and lesbian rights would be seen by many people as offensive and an affront to both societal and religious beliefs. And yet social workers' ethical code impels them toward this sort of advocacy on behalf of their clients.

AGE

Many people think of oppression and discrimination on the basis of age solely in terms of the very young and very old in a particular country. However, age discrimination and oppression is a relative notion, contingent on country and culture.

Consider the employment situation in Mexico. Although the first article of Mexico's 1917 constitution prohibits discrimination motivated by age, employment discrimination on the basis of age flourishes in Mexico and impacts highly qualified candidates 35 years of age and older (Hawley & Solache, 2014). Job discrimination against people at this age may seem outrageous to Americans, but consider the conditions in Mexico. Mexico has a relatively young age structure, with a median age of 24, compared with the median age of 35 in the United States. Companies in Mexico hire younger, oftentimes less-qualified candidates to reduce expenses and save money. Younger workers also have fewer family responsibilities and accordingly are able to work longer, extended hours.

CLASS

Technology may be the new determinant of global class structures (Lamb, 2005). Instead of categorizing people on the basis of income, wealth, family status, social connections, and education, a worldwide class system has been developing on the basis of being technologically connected, semiconnected, or disconnected. The historical worldwide infatuation with American cars as a sign of power and success may well be giving way to infatuation with the newest, fastest, trendiest, and sleekest smartphone, tablet, smartwatch, and automobile technology package as symbols of class membership.

Client access to technology is a huge issue in social work practice. In advanced nations, in particular, the Internet has become an essential resource for obtaining information about housing and employment, and many forms of everyday information. Applying for or monitoring benefits from public assistance programs also often involves computer knowledge and access.

ETHNICITY

The United States has its own problems with discrimination based on ethnicity, but discrimination in some other parts of the world has far more impact on oppressed ethnic groups. For example, in the United States, many people have become actively engaged in humanitarian and resettlement efforts with Bhutanese refugees. Bhutan is a country bordered by Nepal, India, and China. In the 1980s, people from Southern Bhutan, who are ethnic Nepali (speaking Nepali and practicing Hinduism), were deemed as a political threat and systematically denationalized (stripped of their citizenship status and labeled antinationals). Some of the ethnic Nepali were imprisoned and faced discrimination and persecution, such as fines and harassment for no other reason than their ethnicity. Thousands of the ethnic Nepali moved during the 1990s to refugee camps in Nepal. The Bhutan government has been cited for committing racial discrimination and disregarding the human rights of ethnic Nepali (Carrick, 2008, p. 28).

These displaced Nepali have subsequently sought refuge in countries such as the United States. Bhutanese refugees are unique people, as they typically have a Nepali heritage (language and religion), have lived in a refugee camp (e.g., Nepal), and have faced oppression and discrimination in citizenship, property rights, housing, education, and employment. Given this history and these circumstances, it would be understandable for Bhutanese refugees living in the United States to be skeptical of government officials and alert to infringements on human rights.

RACE

As a result of high rates of racial and ethnic intermarriage in the United States, there are a growing number of persons of mixed descent (Perez & Hirschman, 2009). Thus, racial classification is becoming more complex. It is similarly complex in parts of the world that were colonized by a different racial group.

In everyday social work practice, racial and ethnic classifications are not assumed on the basis of skin color or legal definition and/or previous classification for statistical purposes, as in population surveys. In contemporary practice, race is especially important in regard to self-perception, self-identification, and any inherent meaning for a client. For many people from multiracial populations, a salient and practical question becomes, "What do I consider as my primary racial identification?"

The answer to that question may be fluid and depend on social circumstances. Gregory Williams is the former president of the University of Cincinnati and is known for his

1996 award-winning book *Life on the Color Line: The True Story of a White Boy Who Discovered He Was Black.* As the title implies, Williams grew up thinking of himself and being treated as white. But he found out when he was 10 that his father's family was black. Williams often speaks to audiences about his life as a black man who looks white.

GENDER

In many cultures throughout the world, men continue to oppress women. As with most forms of oppression, the plight of women is rooted in cultural values and traditions involving power. Globally, women continue to be dominated and exploited sexually, interpersonally, economically, and socially by men.

Helping women in an international or global context can be difficult, because discrimination against women is deeply ingrained in cultures, family relationships, and even their own identities. As has been pointed out,

> it is unrealistic and simplistic to expect women to rebuke male supremacy or that a society or culture, if prompted, will readily break with traditions and adopt different, more progressive postures and ways of doing. Instead, the challenge for the professional engaged in international social work is to assess the social environment and identify cultural and societal factors contributing to and supporting social relationships and realities that are detrimental to women yet amenable to social reform and change. (Long & Tice, 2009, p. 236)

SEXUAL ORIENTATION

In 2013, the United Nations called on all governments across the globe to protect the rights of lesbian, gay, bisexual, and transgender (LGBT) individuals. In his message, Secretary-General Ban Ki-moon couched his declaration of the fight to end homophobia in terms of a battle to gain human rights for all people:

> For far too long, their suffering was met with silence in the halls of power. As Secretary-General, I am committed to raising my voice. Along with many committed partners, we are working to elevate this struggle and draw greater attention to the

▲ It is important for social workers to consider the unique perspective of each person and the intersections of diversity they face.

Source: iStockphoto.com/pressdigital

specific challenges facing the LGBT members of our family. . . . Ending homophobia is a matter of personal security, dignity and even survival for countless individuals. (United Nations, 2013)

Statements such as this affirming LGBT rights constitute powerful endorsements and rallying points for social workers engaged in global practice. Social workers view newsworthy comments by powerful leaders as opportunities to partner with client groups and prompt international and local action to improve the conditions of global citizens.

INTERSECTIONS OF DIVERSITY

A key for learning about international population groups and global problems is to attempt to see behaviors, people, and phenomenon through the eyes of others (e.g., clients, important stakeholder groups). With people experiencing multiple forms of diversity, it is especially challenging to view the uniqueness, dignity, and worth of each person and his or her individual perspective.

Consider the experience of a social worker practicing with economically challenged Peruvian women at a communal kitchen in El Yurinaqui, Peru (Ramos, Botton, & Wright, 2009). One client demonstrated great reluctance to talk with the social worker, because as a Peruvian woman she had no time for herself; all her time was devoted to taking care of her father and children. In this situation, the social worker assured the client "of her self-worth and offered her unconditional assistance" (p. 222). This offer of help was very meaningful to a Peruvian woman living and working in a poor, rural setting.

ADVOCACY AND INTERNATIONAL SOCIAL WORK

As a profession, social work has a long-standing commitment to promoting human rights, challenging social injustice, and helping people address important social issues across the globe. Commitment is important, but converting dedication into action requires elaboration. Effective advocacy by social workers for global change often involves the following:

- *Interest*: Social workers are both rational and emotional human beings. In a cause pertaining to global human rights and/or social justice, some form of connection (personal or professional) to the issue can be helpful and motivating to the social worker. As a person with a developing understanding of social work, are you passionate about helping people and about advocacy concerning global issues such as poverty, child welfare, health care, hunger, human rights, refugees, social justice, environmental protection, and human exploitation?

- *Conducive employment*: Social workers are predominantly employed in human and social service agencies. Finding time for cause advocacy as a member of an organization dedicated to individual and family intervention can be a challenge for social workers committed to global change. When compared with salary, benefits, staffing, and workspace, how important to your choice of employment is your ability to advocate for rights and social justice on paid versus personal time?

- *Collaboration*: Advocacy is a collaborative process that relies on an ongoing assessment of "who is and is not represented at the planning table—people, groups, organizations, and constituencies" (Long, et al., 2006, p. 151). Social workers participate in partnerships and networking opportunities to build collaborations and coalitions to create change. "Flying solo" to advocate for rights and social justice is rarely advisable or impactful. Modern technology and forms of communication allow social workers to collaborate with and learn from people around the world to advocate for global issues. Do you enjoy working with other people to examine difficult questions and complex problems?

- *Strategic involvement in causes*: Prioritizing the use of one's professional self and the energies of clients is a noteworthy consideration when advocating for all kinds of causes. With international and global practice, it is important for social workers and clients to ascertain which cause(s) hold the greatest promise for making short- and long-term gains. In addition, thought needs to be given to what kinds of involvement (e.g., research, relationship building with decision makers, use of social media) are needed to advocate at a particular time in relationship to each specific cause. Are you good at making decisions to prioritize your time?

ECONOMIC AND SOCIAL JUSTICE

Taking a global perspective of issues of economic and social justice often means looking at the societal structures and forces that impinge on the situation (Finn & Jacobson, 2008, pp. 424–425). As an example, consider the activities of Amnesty International, a global movement aimed at protecting people wherever justice and rights are denied. It seeks a world where people live free from violence and is particularly concerned with ending the worldwide cycle of violence against women, which shatters the lives of millions of women and girls worldwide.

Amnesty International has not just committed to helping individual women. It has developed and is a supporter of the **International Violence Against Women Act**, a U.S. legislative initiative placing the end of global violence against women and girls as a top priority. The legislation would require U.S. agencies engaged in foreign assistance to take steps to prevent and intervene in violence against women and girls in at least five countries where gender-based violence is severe (Amnesty International, 2013–2014). Additionally, an Office of Global Women's Issues would be created in the State Department for coordinating programs and funding to combat worldwide violence against women and girls.

In the United States and across the globe, violence against women and girls takes many forms (e.g., physical abuse, rape, genital cutting, and human trafficking). As one of the most powerful countries in the world, the United States has a duty and obligation to be a leader in addressing human rights violations and promoting policies, programs, and practices to end violence against women and girls.

SUPPORTIVE ENVIRONMENT

People establish residency in another country for many reasons. **Migration** can take place as a result of both human desire and need, contingent on one's economic status

Avon's Global Believe Fund

Advocacy concerning social causes involves the general public, nonprofit organizations, clients, helping professionals, and often vital support from corporate partners. Avon, a beauty and cosmetic company founded in 1886, has a history of empowering women around the globe and improving their lives.

In 2004, Avon launched the Speak Out Against Domestic Violence program and has since donated more than $50 million to fund initiatives for intervening with violence against women in nearly 50 countries. Through Avon's Global Believe Fund, women's domestic violence shelters and organizations around the world have received additional grants to establish and improve programs for women. Since 2008, Avon has been a partner of the UN Development Fund for Women, which seeks to identify and implement ways to put an end to violence against women.

Source: AP Photo/PR NEWSWIRE

▲ The Avon Foundation's Speak Out Against Domestic Violence campaign advocates for victims of abuse and seeks for ways to prevent future violence.

1. Is it appropriate for social workers to partner with companies such as Avon to advance social development and improve the rights of women?

2. What are some considerations or concerns for social workers engaged in practice with large corporations?

and capability to move. Some countries and geographical locations possess highly desirable natural resources, social conditions, climates, and economic opportunities. Other countries, typically developing countries, struggle with difficult living and sanitary conditions (e.g., inadequate drinking water, pollution, and inefficient sewage systems), poor economies, and oppressive or ineffective governments. For people living in challenging environments, seeking residency in a more hospitable place is a way to improve their quality of life and life expectancy. Social work practice involves both helping people advocate for improvements to their native environment and assisting people with adapting to new places.

Migration not only occurs across country boundaries but also within countries, as exemplified in the United States. Contemplate the variation in the natural, social, and economic conditions that exist from state to state and between rural and urban areas within the United States. People often leave impoverished areas with support from family members and friends who have already relocated to places with higher standards of living.

For example, consider the motivations for rural-to-urban migration by poor families in Appalachia, a cultural region encompassing portions of Pennsylvania, Ohio, West Virginia, Tennessee, Virginia, North Carolina, South Carolina, Georgia, Alabama, and Missouri. The environment in Appalachia is characterized by "poor schools, healthcare, and other institutions and forms of inferior infrastructure, such as roads, public transportation, trash removal, water and sewer service, high-speed Internet service, and cell phone towers" (Sarnoff, 2009, p. 168). People from Appalachia may choose to move to urban areas for employment, higher-quality housing, convenient access to services, access to advanced medicine, and ability to use technology.

HUMAN NEEDS AND RIGHTS

Advocating for human needs and rights as a function of global and international practice is complex and draws significantly on social workers' ability to put their knowledge, skills, and professional values into action. Human needs and rights are relative to time, place, and the values of people involved. Cultural values defining the appropriateness of behaviors and actions vary tremendously by country. What is deemed sexist, oppressive, or abusive in one country may be seen by people in another, sometimes neighboring nations as acceptable or noble.

One example is the exploitation and abuse of children as prostitutes in Bangkok, Thailand. Girls, many in their early teens or younger, migrate from rural areas of Thailand to work as prostitutes in the city. The children are given a very small portion of the money paid for their services. From that money, these children send much-needed funds back to desperate family members in their native villages. Many times, parents and family members condone this behavior as an acceptable, dutiful, and admirable means of economic support. Meanwhile, men from countries around the world travel to Bangkok to sexually exploit these children, behavior deemed despicable by most human rights organizations. The men's behavior is probably also frowned on by their home countries, which is why they travel to Thailand. The effort to protect the rights of young Thai girls is an international cause attempting to stop exploitation of children that is open, flagrant, and disturbing.

More generally, the international community has taken steps to define the minimal standards for the treatment of human beings. In 1948, following the atrocities of World War II, the United Nations adopted a **Universal Declaration of Human Rights** applicable to the people of all nations. The declaration consists of a preamble and 30 articles delineating and describing various rights, freedoms, fair treatments, and entitlements for all humans (available at www.un.org/en/documents/udhr). Additionally, international organizations such as the International Council on Social Welfare perform an important role in promoting worldwide consideration of human rights. They do so by organizing international meetings and arranging for the exchange of information among professionals to facilitate dialog and raise global standards for human rights.

POLITICAL ACCESS

National laws defining a country's notions of acceptable and illegal behaviors are issued by politicians and political leaders. Those leaders can be elected, appointed, anointed (e.g., by virtue of their family or religious status), or simply installed through military might. In democratic countries, the notion of a fair and free election is valued; people have a right to vote for politicians and leaders, and votes are legitimately counted. But ensuring fair elections in countries whose politics are characterized by the use of force or plagued by corruption is a challenge. Former President Jimmy Carter was known for many years for volunteering to observe and monitor election practices in some of the most corrupt countries to ensure fair, democratic elections.

Even with fair and free elections, it is often difficult for a country's ordinary people, who do not have powerful connections and money, to mount a successful campaign. In the United States, for example, as with many countries, access to people able to contribute (individually or through special interest groups and political action campaigns) is a determining factor. The price of being elected to the U.S. presidency or a U.S. Senate or House seat is in the millions.

It is also unusual in the United States for a person from a disadvantaged group to be elected to national office. With the exception of President Barack Obama, all the presidents in the United States have been white men.

YOUR CAREER IN INTERNATIONAL SOCIAL WORK

Although there are indications that international social work practice is gaining momentum and prominence, as suggested earlier in this chapter, documenting the incidence and occupational outlook for international practice is difficult. In the United States, the occupational classification of international social worker is not prevalent, and data are not routinely available. Social workers in international practice often remain undifferentiated from other social workers and subsumed under employment classifications specifying population groups and problem areas.

Laws regulating the practice of social work are determined by the country or state in which one is employed and practices. Developing countries may not regulate the title or role of social worker at all, or may have very limited educational and training requirements. More sophisticated systems for regulating social work practice are generally in place in developed countries, where professionalism and advanced degrees are more common.

TIME TO THINK

In some developing countries, almost anyone can be called a social worker. A social work degree could be obtained through a 2- or 3-year college program. Or people could attain the title of social worker through their work experience in and with nonprofit organizations. How might a highly educated and trained BSW or MSW social worker from the United States be viewed by such colleagues? What would be the likely possibilities and barriers for collaboration between U.S. and non-U.S. social workers?

INTERNATIONAL JOB OPPORTUNITIES

International and global social work practice highlight the commitment, talents, and abilities of social workers for understanding cultural diversity and working with people from diverse backgrounds. Savvy global companies and international agencies tend to seek employees with refined interpersonal and communication skills, often labeled "soft skills," and thus may seek social workers. Social work is considered a people-oriented, respectful, and caring profession. Social workers possess valuable knowledge and skills for international commerce, and these skills are applicable to many occupations in the travel industry, diplomatic units, international government service (e.g., embassy work), higher education (e.g., advising, admissions, and exchange programs), and religious organizations.

With social work's heavy commitment to human rights and social justice, employment with companies and organizations emphasizing international human rights (e.g., Avon's Global Believe Fund) is a special consideration. Many international businesses seek ways to improve the human condition and spread corporate goodwill globally. These companies may hire social workers for jobs in public relations, product management, and human relations. A good rule of thumb when considering employment within and outside of traditional social work is to identify agencies, companies, and organizations with missions, goals, products, and services that are aligned with values such as human rights and social justice.

TIME TO THINK

People experience windows of opportunity in their lifetime for education and employment. Getting married, going through a divorce, losing a loved one, having children, becoming economically independent, and caring for parents are but a few factors that influence one's plans for education and career. Occupational decisions involving relocating for an international or global position require extra planning. When would be the appropriate time in your life for international or global employment?

VOLUNTEERING, EXPERIENTIAL LEARNING, AND FIELD EDUCATION

Many social workers in global and international practice have experienced a developmental journey that began with volunteering, experiential learning, or the thoughtful selection of field education placements. Here are some tips about professional development for a job dedicated to international social work (McLaughlin, 2007):

- Get some international experience through volunteering, humanitarian work, classes, and field experience involving or taking place in other countries (p. 26).
- Learn a new language (but also be open to in-country colleagues' helping with translation) (p. 26).
- Acquire cultural knowledge and experience (p. 26).
- Partner with others who are experienced with a different culture to learn new and different approaches (p. 26).
- Find ways for "getting your foot in the door" with international organizations that are prospective employers (p. 27).
- Be persistent in your efforts to seek knowledge and experience (p. 27).
- Realize that paid international social work positions may not be available or are very competitive and low paying, especially in nongovernmental organizations (p. 26).

Contemporary social work students typically are presented with a multitude of university-based experiential learning opportunities to facilitate international and global employment after graduation. Field education placements with agencies sponsoring programs that involve international and global practice foster the acquisition of a new language and familiarity with values, customs, symbols, thoughts, and traditions of local population groups. Many social work programs offer field placements for U.S. students in other countries. There are also numerous forms of immersion experiences in other countries (e.g., service learning and study tours) aimed at stimulating interest in and understanding of a culture (Cox, 2009, p. 126).

SUMMARY

If you're totally illiterate and living on one dollar a day, the benefits of globalization never come to you.

—President Jimmy Carter

In recent years, social work conferences and workshops in the United States have been abuzz with presentations and discussions about global and international practice. Every day, social workers are being confronted with many dire realities (e.g., poverty, exploitation, and oppression) and new opportunities (e.g., information sharing, learning about a variety of cultures, and expanded partnerships) associated with practice in a globally connected world. These are sometimes new and unique problems, issues, and population groups for American social workers. To keep abreast of and engaged in the dynamic world around them, social work students, practitioners, and educators will need to embrace both formal and informal continuing education.

TOP 10 KEY CONCEPTS

asylum seeker
comparative social policy
cultural competence
developing countries
global practice

industrialized countries
international social work
migration
refugees
social development

DISCUSSION QUESTIONS

1. Immigration law and policy regulating entry into the United States is a hotly debated national topic. Should the United States be more or less restrictive in allowing people to legally enter and reside here? Consider the ramifications of your position with regard to the provision of human services.
2. Does U.S. social work education, in both BSW and MSW programs, impart the cultural competence and understanding of values, beliefs, and customs needed to practice in another country or with a population group originating from another country? If not, what needs to be done differently?
3. How would a social work student or social worker interested in international or global practice select an issue

(e.g., poverty, child welfare, HIV/AIDS) for involvement in advocacy?
4. How can technology be effectively used to enhance social work practice with international population groups and to advocate for change with regard to global human needs and rights?
5. When social work students obtain international volunteer and field education experience in developing countries, do the benefits of their service to others outweigh the oversight and use of resources required to support their presence?

EXERCISES

1. Identify and reach out to classmates, friends, and acquaintances who have migrated to the United States. Discuss the differences in your cultural values, norms, ways, customs, and beliefs. You might consider going to a cultural event, restaurant, or area of town with that person as a means of stimulating discussion. Report on your experience.

2. Organize a group of students to plan an educational trip and course in another country during spring break, summer, or a January term. Which faculty members have the background and expertise to potentially lead such an experience? How could this trip align with education about human needs and rights? Is there an office of international study at your university that has established a similar educational offering or could assist with your ideas?

3. Organize a movie night and watch *Nepal's Stolen Children* (2011), produced by actress Demi Moore. After the showing, discuss how people and professionals can become involved in promoting global rights for women and children.

4. Invite a social worker from a community-based agency or organization involved in international or global practice to a student- or class-organized lunch. Ask the social worker to explain her or his work with a population group exhibiting specific needs in your area and to describe how students can get involved. Identify any student clubs or organizations that could be useful partners.

5. Organizations such as the International Association of Schools of Social Work provide small research grants for students and faculty members to examine issues related to international and global social work practice and causes. Your university might also provide this type of funding. Search the Internet to see what kinds of research initiatives are currently being funded for global and international study. Are there any appropriate opportunities for students and faculty members at your university to apply for such monies?

6. A career in international and global social work involves prep work. What countries, population groups, and causes are of interest to you? What will you need in the way of language acquisition and cultural education and awareness? Identify volunteer experiences, travel opportunities, internships, study-abroad trips, field placement opportunities, associations, and relationships with stakeholders that could prepare and position you for international and global practice.

ONLINE RESOURCES

- International Federation of Social Workers (ifsw.org/policies/statement-of-ethical-principles): Presents the "Statement of Ethical Principles"
- National Association of Social Workers: International (socialworkers.org/practice/intl/default.asp): Describes content on international affairs and human rights
- National Association of Social Workers: Social Workers Across Nations (www.socialworkers.org/nasw/swan/default.asp): Provides information about this mechanism to help social workers volunteer their skills internationally

- United Nations (unstats.un.org/UNSD/Demographic/sconcerns/migration/default.htm): Provides international migration data and statistics
- U.S. Citizenship and Immigration Services (www.uscis.gov/tools/glossary): Provides a glossary of important terms
- U.S. Homeland Security (www.dhs.gov/publication/refugees-and-asylees-2012): Provides information about refugees and asylees

STUDENT STUDY SITE

Sharpen your skills with SAGE edge at **edge.sagepub.com/cox**

SAGE edge for Students provides a personalized approach to help you accomplish your coursework goals in an easy-to-use learning environment.

EPILOGUE: SOCIAL WORK AND SELF-CARE

Social workers across multiple fields of practice will have to manage challenging situations and cases as they engage with individuals, families, communities, and populations with histories of trauma. Traumas that clients experience can include disabilities, divorce, death, terminal illnesses, neglect, fatal accidents, rape, disasters, and war (Dombo & Gray, 2013). People who have experienced traumas such as these are among the most oppressed and vulnerable of clients.

Stressors and traumatic life events are rather subjective and are experienced by people differently. Some people experience detachment from stimuli in their surroundings (dissociation), physical (or somatic) problems, and problems with the way they react to emotion (affect regulation). Others have no discernible problems at all due to traumatic experiences.

Social work counselors, as well as the family members of traumatized clients, may experience traumatic "secondary stress" by virtue of being indirectly exposed to people's stories of trauma and negative life events (American Psychiatric Association, 2013). **Secondary stress** takes several forms:

- **Vicarious trauma** occurs when a social worker takes in the emotions, experiences, and reactions of trauma while assisting in the healing or coping process (Trippany, Kress, & Wilcoxon, 2004).
- **Compassion fatigue** is the emotional strain or residue—in the form of losing optimism, hope, or humor—that results from being exposed to and working with people suffering from consequences of traumatic events. Vicarious trauma or secondary trauma is a form of compassion fatigue (Figley, 1995).
- **Burnout** is emotional exhaustion that causes an increasing depersonalization of clients and a decreased sense of personal accomplishment (Maslach & Jackson, 1981).
- **Moral injury** is secondary stress related to war trauma (Foy, Kelly, Leshner, Schultz, & Litz, 2011; Huss, Sarid, & Cwikel, 2010). It especially affects military social workers who actively listen to war stories.

Moral injury is a concept that was introduced by a psychiatrist named Jonathan Shay (2010), who counseled combat veterans for more than 20 years. It refers to a person's moral conscience being affected by something they did that causes them emotional shame. Combat veterans participate in war and they kill, which is an act that betrays their sense of right and wrong and invisibly wounds them. The concept of moral injury is now used in mental health literature in relation to military veterans who have observed or perpetrated a moral transgression in combat (Brock, 2013). Moral injury is a normal human response to an abnormal event, such as war, and it highlights the cultural, psychological, and spiritual aspects of trauma.

Understanding how to handle secondary stress and all four of the manifestations listed here is extremely important to social workers who want to continue being effective counselors to their clients. One source of support comes from colleagues, especially supervisors. Social work professionals are obligated to help fellow social workers who may feel overwhelmed by the abuse, neglect, illness, and death experiences they see or hear about. Social workers' supervisors should be on the lookout for situations in which stressed colleagues need mental health interventions to function optimally and healthily (National Association of Social Workers, 2008). Supervision is a great way to give support to social work counselors who may feel overwhelmed and traumatized.

Self-care, or taking action to alleviate one's own stress, is also essential for social workers (Bell, Kulkarni, & Dalton, 2003; Brady, Guy, Poelstra, & Brokaw, 1999; Dombo & Gray, 2013; Trippany et al., 2004). A variety of practices for self-care are available to social workers:

- Spirituality involves activities that renew, lift up, comfort, heal, and inspire. Spirituality is more than practicing a religion or having a faith perspective. Increasingly, social workers view spirituality as an ethical obligation (Collins, 2005; Dombo & Gray, 2013). Spiritual practice may take the form of spiritual readings, attending religious services, praying, meditating, singing in a choir, getting professional spiritual support, spiritual cleansing, and other personal spiritual practices such as chanting, drumming, exercising, and so on (Koenig, McCullough, & Larson, 2001; Pargament, 2007). Christianity, Buddhism, and other religions offer distinctive ideas for self-care as well. These activities can help social work practitioners clear their minds, stay in the present moment, breathe consciously, and truly "be" with clients. Exhibit E-1, featuring content from Dombo and Gray (2013), enumerates interventions related to the spiritual dimension of self-care across micro, mezzo, and macro levels of social work practice.

• **Rest taking** includes stopping what you are doing and doing very little—such as putting your feet up, taking a nap, or relaxing in a comfortable chair. This is a simple but effective restorative for stress (Chandler, 2008). Achieving work–life balance means you need to build downtime into your schedule, drop activities that sap your time or energy, rethink your errands, get moving, and relax.

• **Creative arts** are illustrated by drawing, sculpting, or creating some other representation of one's imagination. Creative activities can effectively counteract stress for clients who have experienced war, as well as the stress of social workers who counsel them. Art therapy literature reveals how art activities can reduce overexcitation of the senses, engage creative problem solving, and enable unconscious experiences to become conscious to the client in a non-threatening manner (Hass-Cohen & Carr, 2008; Huss et al., 2010; Kaye & Bleep, 1997; Liebman, 1996).

• **Mindfulness** is paying attention in the present moment, on purpose and without judgment. Multiple researchers have begun to investigate how mindfulness training may be used by helping professionals as a self-care strategy (Gockel, Burton, James, & Bryer, 2013; Lloyd, King, & Chenoweth, 2002; Shapiro, Brown, & Biegel, 2007). Meditations that incorporate imagery, play, and loving kindness or concentration on a word may be used to help social work practitioners find strength, joy, and peace to ground their daily work (Gockel et al., 2013). Similarly, social work professionals can flourish by using *Imago Dei*, a Judeo-Christian concept that encourages the notion that people have worth and value no matter their utility and function, just because of God's intent and action (Pooler, 2011).

• **Professional flourishing** occurs when one experiences job satisfaction, a feeling of effectiveness at work, and a balance between work and play. As social workers accumulate years of practice experience and achieve maturity, they realize how important self-care is. They recognize the importance to their professional well-being of quality supervision and diverse workplaces, environments, and organizational cultures. Ironically, being a healthy social worker is most likely linked to having an identity that goes beyond one in professional social work. Balanced social work professionals do not possess hidden agendas or unrealistic expectations for clients. They care about the client's well-being, rather than being driven to achieve a positive outcome with a client so they can feel better about themselves (Pooler, 2011).

• **Lifelong learning** facilitates growth. Social workers can alleviate stress by keeping abreast of cutting-edge policies and interventions that facilitate effectiveness.

EXHIBIT E.1   Self-Care Model

INTERVENTION LEVEL	INTERVENTION FOCUS	SPIRITUAL DIMENSION
Macro	Environmental factors; policies, procedures, and programs that contribute to vicarious trauma	Sacred space for spiritual practices; time allotted for use of space
Mezzo	Team meetings; mentoring relationships; supervision time to address self-care	Meditation practice for trauma work
Micro	Education on vicarious trauma and self-care techniques	Meditation practice for trauma work

Source: Dombo and Gray (2013, p. 94).

Perhaps even more important than lifelong learning is a lifelong commitment to balancing one's life. Social workers must learn how to literally leave work at the office, despite the inevitable calls they will receive to complete late discharges from hospitals or lengthy processes to remove children from family homes.

• **Social support** and mutual aid serve as protective factors. Healthy relationships are key to self-care and the reduction of stress. People need to be with others who allow them to be true to themselves and feel safe. That type of relationship may be found within one's family, with close friends, or in faith communities (Pooler, 2011).

Scant research literature exists on the self-care practices of social work students (Moore, Bledsoe, Perry, & Robinson, 2011). Yet knowing how to employ self-care is vital for students who are preparing to be full-fledged social work practitioners. While in school, they often simultaneously assume roles of student, parent, head of household, paid employee, caregiver for aging parents, and so on, and thus they have as great a need to know how to manage stress and enhance their well-being as practicing social workers do. Physical, spiritual, and social self-care activities are vitally important to help students and social work professionals achieve career longevity.

As a student, be aware that students are the lifeblood of the social work profession. Learn to protect yourself from stress, burnout, and compassion fatigue by practicing self-care and knowing yourself and your limits. Helping people cope with surprising life events and challenges can be amazingly satisfying work—especially when you are modeling how to construct a healthy life replete with physical, spiritual, and emotional health and well-being.

TOP 10 KEY CONCEPTS

burnout	professional flourishing
compassion fatigue	rest taking
creative arts	secondary stress
mindfulness	self-care
moral injury	vicarious trauma

APPENDIX: CODE OF ETHICS OF THE NATIONAL ASSOCIATION OF SOCIAL WORKERS

SUMMARY OF MAJOR PRINCIPLES

I. SOCIAL WORKERS' VALUES, COMMITMENT, AND CONDUCT

A. *Service.* Social workers' primary goal, above self-interest, is to help people and to address social problems.

B. *Social justice.* Social workers should challenge social injustice and pursue social change, particularly for vulnerable and oppressed people, and promote participation in decision making.

C. *Dignity and worth of the person.* Social workers should respect the inherent dignity and worth of all persons.

D. *Importance of human relationships.* Social workers should value relationships as a vehicle of change.

E. *Integrity.* Social workers should act in a trustworthy manner consistent with the profession's mission and values.

F. *Competence.* Social workers practice within and strive to increase their areas of knowledge and competence.

II. SOCIAL WORKERS' ETHICAL RESPONSIBILITIES TO CLIENTS

A. *Commitment to clients.* Social workers' primary responsibility is to clients, although this may be superseded by legal obligations or obligations to the larger society under some circumstances.

B. *Self-determination.* Social workers respect and promote the rights of clients to self-determination and assist them in attaining their goals, unless these could lead to serious harm to self or others.

C. *Informed consent.* Social workers should offer services to clients only with the informed consent of those clients, including making accessible information on client rights and on the potential outcomes of services.

D. *Competence.* Social workers should provide services only in those areas in which they are competent.

E. *Cultural competence.* Social workers should understand culture, have knowledge of their clients' cultures, recognize the strengths within cultures, and be aware of diversity and oppression.

F. *Conflicts of interest.* Social workers should avoid conflicts of interest, take action to inform clients of potential conflicts, maintain appropriate boundaries, and protect clients from negative consequences of dual relationships.

G. *Privacy and confidentiality.* Social workers should respect their clients' right to privacy, protecting client confidentiality and informing clients of the parameters of confidentiality.

H. *Access to records.* Social workers should provide clients with reasonable access to their own records.

I. *Sexual relationships.* Social workers should not engage in sexual contact with current clients. Social workers should usually not engage in sexual contact with people in the clients' personal lives. In most cases, social workers should not have sexual contact with former clients or take on clients with whom they have had a sexual relationship.

J. *Physical contact.* Social workers should engage in physical contact with clients only when such contact is not potentially harmful and when it is within clear, culturally appropriate boundaries.

K. *Sexual harassment.* Social workers should not sexually harass clients.

L. *Derogatory language.* Social workers should not use derogatory verbal or written language with or about clients.

M. *Payment for services.* Social workers should set fees that are fair and reasonable, and that give consideration to clients' ability to pay. They should not make bartering arrangements with clients.

N. *Clients who lack decision-making capacity.* Social workers should strive to protect the interests and rights of clients who are unable to make informed consent decisions.

O. *Interruption of services.* Social workers should try to maintain continuity of services.

P. *Termination of services.* Social workers should terminate services to clients when such services are no longer necessary or beneficial. They should attempt to avoid abandoning clients who are still in need of services. They may terminate services to clients for failure to pay only after attempts to address the issue with the clients and when such termination does not pose a danger.

III. SOCIAL WORKERS' ETHICAL RESPONSIBILITIES TO COLLEAGUES

A. *Respect.* Social workers should respect colleagues and their qualifications and views, avoiding unwarranted professional or personal criticism of colleagues. They should cooperate with colleagues when beneficial to clients.

B. *Confidentiality.* Social workers should respect the confidentiality of shared client information.

C. *Interdisciplinary collaboration.* Social workers on interdisciplinary teams should draw on the perspectives, values and experience of the social work profession. Ethical concerns of social workers on teams should be resolved.

Source: National Association of Social Workers (2008).

GLOSSARY

absolute needs   Involve products and services (e.g., food, clean water, medical care, shelter, and clothing) needed to support human survival (Long, 2004, p. 5)

absolute poverty   Used to designate survival at the most basic level. Measures have been established to determine which people live above and below the poverty level.

accountable care organization   Connotes a group of doctors, hospitals, and other health care providers who voluntarily collaborate to make sure Medicare patients get well-coordinated and high-quality care

active aging   A model for viewing aging as a positive experience of continued growth and participation in family, community, and societal activities, regardless of physical and cognitive decline

activists   Workers who try to shift power and resources, and encourage large-scale change

activities of daily living (ADLs)   Basic and complex dimensions of daily life, such as taking medicine, bathing, and preparing meals, as well as more instrumental activities such as managing money, preparing meals, shopping, and housekeeping; used to assess if older adults require interventions or services

acute illness   A sudden illness, often requiring hospitalization to remedy

acute inflammation   The inflammation that occurs in the immediate or short-term aftermath of an injury or disease. The five hallmarks of acute inflammation can be remembered by the acronym PRISH, which refers to the signs of inflammation, pain, redness, immobility, swelling, and heat.

adaptive behavior   The effectiveness or degree to which a person can be personally independent and socially responsible for a similar person who is of the same age or cultural group

addiction   Physiological and psychological dependence on a substance or behavior resulting in compulsive and habitual use; a synonym for *substance dependence* or *drug dependence*

addictive disorders   Behavioral addictions. In the DSM-5, gambling addiction is the only diagnosable addictive disorder.

adoption   The permanent rendering of legal and parental rights by a child's birth parents to other adults who will serve as parents

adult protective services   Those services provided to ensure the safety and well-being of elders and adults with disabilities who are in danger of being neglected or mistreated or who cannot take care of themselves or protect themselves from harm and may have no one to help them

advocacy   (1) Considered integral to all aspects of generalist social work practice. Defined by activities that influence resource allocation and decision making, advocacy occurs within social systems, institutions, and the political and economic arena. (2) Involves the act of defending or representing others through supporting or recommending action to secure or retain social justice. (3) Involves the act of representing and defending the rights of individuals, groups, or communities through direct intervention. Types of advocacy include legal advocacy, legislative advocacy, self-advocacy, and system advocacy.

advocacy practice and policy model (APPM)   Represents a change process that occurs in a sequential fashion and is directed at both the problems and strengths of individuals, families, communities, or organizations

advocate   (verb) One of many duties enacted by a social worker in relationship to her or his professional self; a salient and central act for both beginning- and advanced-level social workers for use in everyday practice to advance or champion the causes of consumers of services (noun) Someone who fights for the rights of others or fights to obtain needed resources or services

affirmative action   Refers to equal opportunity employment measures that federal contractors and subcontractors are legally required to adopt

Affordable Care Act (ACA)   Also called the Patient Protection and Affordable Care Act and less formally referred to as ObamaCare. Signed into law in 2010, this act passed reforms in the U.S. health care and health insurance system that were designed to expand health coverage, lower health coverage costs, and protect people from insurance practices such as denial of eligibility for health care coverage due to preexisting conditions.

affordable housing   A topic of considerable debate among researchers and scholars. Federally, housing is deemed to be affordable when a household has to pay no more than 30% of its income on mortgages and rents, including taxes and utilities.

ageism   Negative attitudes, beliefs, and conceptions of the nature and characteristics of older persons that are based on age and distort their actual characteristics and abilities

aggravated assault   Attacking another person physically

aging   Changes that occur to an organism during its life span, from development to maturation to *senescence*

aging in place   The ability to live in one's own home and community safely, independently, and comfortably, regardless of age, income, or ability level

AIDS   An abbreviation for acquired immune deficiency syndrome, which occurs after the immune system becomes so compromised that it is unable to defend itself against bacteria, other viruses, and so forth, often permitting the development of certain forms of cancer (AIDS Healthcare Foundation, 2014)

alcoholism   Physical and/or psychological dependence on alcohol; affected by many factors, such as family history, social environment, stress, and comorbid mental health conditions

alien   A person who is in the United States but not a legal citizen of the United States

alienation   The cognitive separation of people from one another and from control of their work

Alzheimer's disease   A progressive degenerative disorder that attacks the brain's nerve cells or neurons and causes premature senility

Americans with Disabilities Act (ADA)   Legislation passed in 1990 that prohibits discrimination against people living with disabilities. Under this act discrimination against a disabled person is illegal in employment, transportation, public accommodations, communications, and government activities.

analytical   Ability to use theoretical and research knowledge to inform community practice and change efforts

anorexia nervosa   An eating disorder that causes a person to obsess about the food she or he eats and about being overweight

antiretroviral medications   Used to stop the replication of HIV

anxiety disorders   An exaggeration of people's normal and adaptive reactions to stressful or fearful events

appreciation   Increase in value (e.g., home value)

apprenticing   Learning a trade such as shoemaking or blacksmithing from an expert

Area Agencies on Aging   A nationwide network of state and local agencies and programs that help people plan and care for their needs across the life span

arson   Malicious burning of property

Asperger's syndrome   An autistic (developmental) disorder most notable for the often great discrepancy between people's social and intellectual abilities, as well as issues with repetitive patterns

assessment   Involves an examination or investigation done in collaboration with a person, group, community, or organization to determine unique strengths, opportunities, and particular issues to include in the change process

assisted living   Apartment-style residences where older adults get individualized services (e.g., bathing, dressing, prepared meals, medication administration) to maximize their independence

assistive technology   A broad term comprising assistive, adaptive, and rehabilitative devices for people with disabilities; also includes the process of selecting, locating, and using such technological devices

asylum seeker   A person seeking or claiming the status of refugee but not yet formally evaluated and judged to be a refugee

at-risk communities   Geographical locations that exhibit documentable conditions of risk or danger to people

attention-deficit hyperactivity disorder (ADHD)   A problem of not being able to focus, being overactive, not being able to control behavior, or a combination of these. ADHD begins in childhood and endures across the life span.

autism   A general term for a group of complex neurodevelopmental disorders of brain development, characterized by trouble in communicating, social interaction, and repetitive behaviors; can be associated with intellectual disability, motor coordination issues, and sleep or gastrointestinal disturbances. Some high-functioning people with autism excel in visual skills, math, music, and art.

Bachelor of Social Work (BSW)   The entry-level position for the social work profession. The undergraduate degree involves graduation from a college or university with a social work program accredited by the Council on Social Work Education.

basic human rights   Can be thought of in a number of realms—personal, civil, and political. Generally, humans should be able to live in a fashion free of persecution, discrimination, and oppression, with access to important societal resources, which often include work, education, health care, and equality before the law.

battered child syndrome   Includes the set of injuries, symptoms, and signs of mistreatment observed on a repeatedly or severely abused child

behavioral health   How people act, feel, and think when faced with life events; how they see themselves, their lives, and the other people in their lives; how they evaluate their problems and challenges and explore choices

binge drinking   Drinking so much within about 2 hours that blood alcohol concentration levels reach 0.08%. For women this usually occurs after four drinks and for men after five.

biological age   Also physiological age; a measure of how well or poorly one's body is functioning in relation to one's actual calendar age. It describes a person's development based on biomarkers, such as a cellular or molecular event, looking at the person as he or she is and not just when he or she was born.

biopsychosocial environment   Refers to an interdisciplinary model that assumes that health and wellness are influenced by a complex interaction of biological, psychological, and sociocultural factors. The model is based on the systems perspective and rejects the biomedical model.

biopsychosocial-spiritual   A model for looking at the whole person and considering their biological, psychological, sociocultural, and spiritual dimensions together. Each aspect can be affected differently by a person's illness and history, and can interact with and affect other aspects of the person.

bipolar disorder   Used to be called manic-depressive disorder; associate with high and low mood swings

blended family   Family unit that includes two married persons, children from previous marriages or relationships, and any children resulting from the new marriage

block grants   Large sums of money provided by the federal government to the states, to be used for social services but without specific directions for how to spend the money

blood alcohol concentration (BAC)   Measure of the amount of alcohol in a person's body and thus degree of impairment; may be measured by blood or breath analysis. A BAC of 0.08% is a widespread indicator of being too impaired to drive.

broker   A professional role in which the social worker uses the processes of referral and follow-up to ensure that a family or person obtains needed resources; also links groups and individuals to needed community services

bulimia   An eating disorder, common in young women of nearly normal weight, characterized by episodic binge eating followed by depression, guilt, or self-condemnation

bullying   A systematic way of harming others, involving repeated physical, verbal, or psychological attacks, harassment, and intimidation directed against a victim who cannot properly defend himself or herself (Laursen, 2011, p. 4)

burglary   Breaking into a house or building to steal

burnout   A psychological term referring to long-term exhaustion and diminished interest in work. A clinical psychologist named Herbert Freudenberger first identified the construct of "burnout" in the 1970s. Later, social psychologists Christina Maslach and Susan Jackson (1981) developed a widely used instrument to assess burnout called the Maslach Burnout Inventory.

capitated   Insurance companies' placing strict limitations on the number of nights or amount of service allowable in inpatient treatment, depending on diagnosis

care work   Another word for caregiving that implies that such effort is really work done by people who care

case advocacy   Strategies used to attain and secure needed benefits or services on an individual-case basis (e.g., for individuals and families)

case manager   A person responsible for assessing client needs, arranging and coordinating services and goods that require delivery, and following up with clients to make sure resources have been obtained as planned

case plan   Like case management, a process to seek, advocate for, and monitor service resources and supports from various agencies to help clients meet their goals

categorical disabilities   Involve significant sensory impairment or mental illness and developmental delays, which may require long-term care and special education

cause advocacy   Creating social (structural) change by seeking benefits and services to address the needs of a segment of the population (Hoefer, 2012, p. 3)

cause to function   From a focus on politics to a focus on the efficient day-to-day administration of a social welfare bureaucracy

centenarians   People who are 100 or more years old

cerebral palsy   Involves a loss or impairment of motor function caused by brain damage and affects body movement, muscle control/coordination/tone, reflex, balance, and posture

charity   Aid in the form of money or goods and services

Charity Organization Society   Focused on the individual factors related to poverty, such as alcoholism, poor work habits, and inadequate money management

child   Typically defined as a human being under the age of 18

child maltreatment   A broad term used to encompass the abuse and victimization of children

child neglect   "Deficits in meeting a child's basic needs constitute child neglect" (Miller-Perrin & Perrin, 2009, p. 152)

child physical abuse   "The intentional use of physical force against a child that results in or has the potential to result in physical injury" (Miller-Perrin & Perrin, 2009, p. 58)

child protective services   A key component in publicly funded child welfare agencies, these services and social workers respond to reports of child maltreatment (Waldfogel, 1998)

child psychological maltreatment   "Intentional caregiver behavior (i.e., act of commission) that conveys to a child that he/she is worthless, flawed, unloved, unwanted, endangered, or valued only in meeting another's needs" (Leeb, Paulozzi, Melanson, Simon, & Arias, 2008, p. 11)

child sexual abuse   "Any completed or attempted (not-completed) sexual act, sexual contact with, or exploitation of (e.g., noncontact sexual interaction) of a child by a caregiver" (Leeb, Paulozzi, Melanson, Simon, & Arias, 2008, p. 11)

child trafficking   Recruiting, transporting, harboring, and exploiting children for labor, war, or sex

child welfare   A general term referring to practices, policies, and services to promote child well-being and safety (Pecora, Whittaker, Maluccio, Barth, & DePanfilis, 2009, p. vii)

child welfare agencies   Promote the safety, well-being, and best interests of children

childhood   In the United States, the period from birth to age 18

childhood mental disorder (CMD)   A general term that includes all mental disorders that begin and can be diagnosed in childhood

children's advocacy centers (CACs)   Designed with a multidisciplinary and integrative team approach to investigate, intervene, and

advocate for the protection of children (Wolfteich & Loggins, 2007, p. 334)

Children's Health Insurance Program   Federal program, a part of Medicaid, that provides health coverage to needy children

chronic disease   A long-lasting condition that can be controlled but not cured

chronic illness   The personal experience of living with chronic disease, which is a persistent, long-lasting health condition

chronic inflammation   Persists for weeks, months, or years and has an indefinite termination

chronological age   The number of years a person has lived; used as a standard to measure intelligence, behaviors, and so forth

class   A person's economic position in society

class systems   Where people are classified and stratified (divided and ranked into identifiable social groups) on the basis of social and economic inequalities (e.g., ownership, wealth, and control of resources)

client self-determination   Dictates that consumers of services make decisions and choices based on their will and value orientations

client system   The client and those in his or her environment who might influence or help find a solution. Social workers help nuclear families, extended families, neighbors, teachers, employers, religious leaders, and others who compose a client system.

climate change   Refers to any significant change in the measures of climate lasting for an extended period of time, usually decades or centuries or more. Examples are changes in temperature, precipitation, and wind pattern.

clinic   A place, often connected to a medical school or hospital, that treats nonresident patients, sometimes at a lower cost or for free

clinical social workers   A synonym for psychiatric social worker or social caseworker; typically emphasize a person-in-environment perspective

codependency   A relationship between two or more people who rely on each other to meet and provide reciprocal needs, especially unhealthy emotional ones. People pleasers are an example.

cognitive information processing   A theory that comprises multiple theoretical perspectives and attempts to explain human learning as the development of networked memory structures

cognitive processing therapy A 12-session approach, developed by Resick and Schnicke, to treat PTSD in people who have been sexually assaulted; combines cognitive therapy and exposure therapy

cohort A group of people of the same generation sharing a statistical trait such as age, ethnicity, or socioeconomic status

communal living Where people eat and sleep in common, shared areas

community A social organization based on shared geography or similar interests

community assets Encompasses many aspects of a community, including physical resources (e.g., buildings, housing, parks), businesses, schools, transportation, community participation, associations, leadership, civic groups, interorganizational networks, organizations, shared values, and the ability to exert power over decision makers

community capacity model Emphasizes the building and development of various assets, opportunities, and strengths in a community

community development Improvement of social and economic conditions in at-risk communities

Community Living Initiative An initiative led by the Department of Health and Human Services to implement solutions that address barriers to community living for individuals with disabilities and older Americans

community needs assessment Uses research methods to describe and specify the magnitude of community problems and the availability of local resources for addressing them

community organizing A term used to capture the process by which social workers bring interested people together through neighborhood associations, block parties, organizational affiliations, and religious entities to address social issues and seek solutions (e.g., policy changes, new laws, programs, and services) to community problems

community practice The process of stimulating and assisting the local community to evaluate, plan, and coordinate its efforts to provide for the community's health, welfare, and recreation needs; various labels of practice include social planning, community planning, locality development, community action, social action, macro practice, community organization, and community development

community reigns supreme perspective Setting aside self-interest and individual sacrifice to promote policies and practices for the benefit of a common good (McNutt, 1997)

comparative social policy Also sometimes called international social welfare, refers to examining "the appropriateness and applicability of policies and service delivery as defined and implemented in other countries" (Long, 2009, p. 6)

compassion fatigue Emotional strain or residue of being exposed to and working with people suffering from consequences of traumatic events. It differs from *burnout* but can coexist with it. Compassion fatigue can happen from exposure related to one case, or it can appear due to a "cumulative" level of trauma.

connectivity Easy access via transportation for large groups of people to other communities and industry

conscription Forced military service

conservative A political leaning that tends to favor personal responsibility over any form of government support or federally sponsored relief

continuing care retirement communities Combine parts of assisted-living, independent-living, and skilled nursing home care to offer a tiered approach to helping people who are aging and changing

continuous quality improvement A management philosophy that promotes the need for objective data to analyze and improve processes and asserts that most things can be improved; an approach to quality management that emphasizes "process" and systems and organizations rather than the individual

Continuum of Care Program Refers to a community-based approach where clients progress through a series of programs to become "housing ready," typically requiring sobriety and a commitment to mental health services (Groton, 2013, p. 51)

conversion therapies Sometimes called reparative or reorientation therapies, aimed at changing sexual orientation

co-occurring disabilities Implies that a person can have an intellectual disability or developmental disability in addition to a physical disability such as blindness, diabetes, an amputation, or the like

co-occurring disorders When individuals suffer from two or more disorders simultaneously. Substance abuse conditions often affect a person at the same time as other mental health disorders.

coronary heart disease The leading cause of death in the United States for males and females; caused by hardening of the arteries in the heart from plaque buildup

corporate criminals People who commit crimes on behalf of a corporation and with its support

correctional system Interventions, services, and programs (including probation, parole, and imprisonment) a person enters into as a result of involvement in the criminal justice system and courts

cost of advocacy All the real, intangible, and unintended ways that undertaking advocacy can deplete resources and work against the cause; includes determining the value of each person's time to engage in research, analyze and draft policies, attend meetings, develop media strategies, lobby, organize communities, campaign, and use technology (e.g., phone calls, text messages, websites, e-mails, blogs, wikis, and social networking sites)

Council on Social Work Education (CSWE) The professional body that accredits social work programs, establishes competencies, and oversees the growth in social work education

counselor This role focuses on improving social functioning, affirming strengths, and helping people deal with feelings and cope with stress, crises, or changing life circumstances

creative arts An umbrella term that describes multiple types of art, such as fine art, unique techniques, skills, media, film, music, museums, drawing, sculpting, and many more

crime Acts or behaviors that are prohibited by criminal law and punishable by negative sanctions (e.g., probation, fine, jail term)

criminal justice system Refers to a large network of organizations (e.g., courts, police departments, prisons, jails, probation agencies) dedicated to the enforcement of laws and the administration of justice

criminalization   Process by which acts and people become defined as criminal

criminals   People who have been found guilty and as a result are classified as having committed a crime (e.g., against person or property)

criminology   The scientific study of criminal behavior

critical thinking   The ability to reflect on and integrate information to form a position, opinion, or conclusion that you can support when questioned

cultural competence   The skill of communicating and working competently and effectively with people of contrasting cultures. Social workers need to become aware of culture and its pervasive influence, learn about their own cultures, recognize their own ethnocentricity, learn about other cultures, acquire cultural knowledge about their clients, and adapt social work skills and intervention approaches accordingly.

cultural neuroscience   The study of how cultural values, practice, and beliefs shape and are shaped by the mind, brain, and genes across multiple timescales

culture   The customs, habits, values, beliefs, skills, technology, arts, science, and religious and political behavior of a group of people in a specific time period

cyclical unemployment   The outcome of businesses laying off or not hiring workers because of a reduction in demand for goods and services

deinstitutionalization   The process of releasing from residential care facilities people who are dependent for their physical or mental care, assuming that they no longer require such care and can manage with community-based services

Delegate Assembly   National Association of Social Workers' body of social workers who are selected for specific terms to revise policies that get published in a book called *Social Work Speaks*

dementia   A syndrome rather than a single disease process, of which Alzheimer's disease and vascular dementia are the two most common manifestations, wherein people lose

functioning of their body, memory, and cognition

Department of Defense (DoD)   Otherwise known as the Pentagon; the capstone headquarters of the U.S. armed forces, headed by the secretary of defense, a civilian political appointee who serves at the pleasure of the president. The military branches subordinate to the DoD are the Army, Navy, Air Force, Marine Corps, and Coast Guard.

Department of Health and Human Services   Federal department that oversees the bulk of federal programs for services to the poor

Department of Veterans Affairs (VA)   A U.S. Cabinet department that provides patient care, veterans benefits, and other services to veterans of the U.S. armed services and their families. The VA provides disability compensation for those who were injured or contracted a disease while serving; education and training; medical, surgical, and rehabilitative care; readjustment counseling; bereavement counseling; surviving spouse benefits; care and benefits to homeless veterans; medical research; life insurance; vocational rehabilitation; headstones/burial markers; and home loan assistance.

depressive disorders   Also referred to as depression or unipolar depression, these are mental illnesses characterized by persistent and profound sad feelings, despair, and loss of interest in formerly pleasurable things. Appetite and sleep problems often accompany these disorders.

desensitization   Decreased sensitivity to fear about certain acts, which increases one's risk of engaging in violent behavior toward others

deserving poor   Associated with the Elizabethan Poor Laws; included orphan children, elderly individuals, and people with debilitating physical conditions, who could not provide for themselves

detoxification   Short-term medically supervised treatment program for alcohol or drug addiction designed to purge the body of intoxicating or addictive substances

developing countries   Have a less-developed economy, lack sophisticated technology, and possess a lower standard of living than do industrialized countries

developmental disability   One of a diverse group of chronic, severe conditions that evolve from physical and/or mental impairments

***Diagnostic and Statistical Manual of Mental Disorders* (DSM)**   The American Psychiatric Association's classification and diagnostic tool. The most current edition (DSM-5), published in 2013, contains descriptions, symptoms, and other diagnostic criteria for mental disorders.

direct practice   Social work activity that involves primarily one-on-one interactions with clients, many times individuals and families

disability   Implies a temporary or permanent reduction in function

distributive justice   Concerned with pursuing fair and equitable availability and access to goods and services, especially scarce and highly needed resources (Rawls, 1971)

division of labor   Organization of work by task and responsibility

domestic violence   Acts of violence (including assault, injury, and rape) by one family member against others in the family

doubling time   How long it takes for a population to double. Based on the extent to which birthrate exceeds the death rate, double time has a compound effect.

doubling up   Temporarily living with relatives or friends

Down syndrome   A genetic disorder caused when abnormal cell division results in extra genetic material from chromosome 21. People with this disorder have mild to moderate intellectual disability, short stature, and a flat facial profile.

dynamic advocacy model   Conceptualization of advocacy that depicts the ever-changing relationships among four interlocking values; social and economic justice, a supportive environment, human needs and rights, and political access

Earned-Income Tax Credit (EITC)   Tax-based relief for families living in poverty despite having earned income (wages from work)

eating disorders   A range of psychological disorders characterized by abnormal or disturbed eating habits (such as anorexia nervosa)

ecological ethics   Suggests that social work must consider its ethical position regarding the value placed on nature for the sake of nature

ecological justice   Extending fairness to all life on Earth

ecological map   A diagram that displays all the systems that compose a person's environment

ecological perspective   Builds on biological science and focuses on people and their social as well as physical environments

ecological social welfare   A process of planned, inclusive social change designed to promote people's welfare in conjunction with a comprehensive program of economic activities within the tenets of environmental justice; sometimes called the new ecology

economic and social justice   Can be conceptualized as "promoting and establishing equal liberties, rights, duties, and opportunities in the social institutions (economy, polity, family religion, education, etc.) of a society for all [people]" (Long, Tice, & Morrison, 2006, p. 208)

Educational Policy and Accreditation Standards (EPAS)   Guidelines established by the Council on Social Work Education to outline the requirements for accreditations of social work schools and programs. EPAS are reviewed every 8 years and set thresholds for competence that facilitate an integrated curriculum design.

elder abuse   Maltreatment of an older person

electronic medical records (EMRs)   Electronically maintained files of lab results, physicians' visit notes, diagnostic test results, insurance information, demographic information, health histories, and other medication information within the physician's office

Elizabethan Poor Laws   Passed in 1601 in Great Britain, these laws provided services to the poor and reflected social and economic forces associated with (1) the breakdown of England's feudal system, (2) the reduction of the labor force, and (3) the move toward industrialization

emancipated adult   Juvenile who has been granted the status of adulthood, usually by court order

emergency rooms (ERs)   The sections of health care facilities intended to give quick treatment for sufferers of trauma or sudden illness

emotional or psychological abuse   Speaking to or treating persons in ways that cause them emotional pain or distress

Employee Assistance Programs (EAPs)   An employer-paid benefit, EAPs are designed to provide services that address professional and personal issues that negatively impact job performance, work attendance, and collegial relationships

empowerment   Refers to clients' ability to exert influence over decision-making processes and their desired outcomes, both in service interventions and in regard to the development of policies, programs, and legislation

empowerment theory   An element in the change process that generalist social workers use to increase the change possibilities by helping people and groups access resource to gain control over their lives

engagement   Sets the tone for the change process and establishes a rapport with clients; involves verbal and nonverbal communication, such as body movement, facial expressions, and eye contact, which are used to put the client at ease and create a comfortable environment

environment of work   All factors that support employees' participation in the work placement itself, including relationship with coworkers and supervisors, organizational culture, and bridges for personal development and enhancement

environmental disasters   Events occurring in the natural world that cause serious disruptions to human activity

environmental justice   Involves the fair treatment and meaningful involvement of all people, regardless of race, color, national origin, or income, with respect to environmental laws, regulations, and policies

Environmental Protection Agency   The federal entity responsible for protecting human health and the environment

environmentalists   People who seek to protect the natural environment for the benefit of all, especially the disadvantaged

epilepsy   A condition that causes a person to have recurrent seizures, either petit mal or grand mal

ethnocentrism   Occurs when people believe their ethnic group and way of life are superior to others

evaluation   Involves monitoring the plan and ensuring that designated activities are accomplishing intended goals in an effective manner

eviction   Occurs when tenants or homeowners are removed from their housing, commonly for missing rent or mortgage payments

evidence-based practice   The use of research findings to inform and evaluate practice, and the sharing of practice experiences to inform and enrich research activities

extended family   In addition to parents and children, other relatives live in the same household or in close proximity to the family.

faith-based organizations   Programs such as churches, temples, synagogues, and others that receive funding to provide some level of social services or resources to clients

family   A social unit where people form relationships and make a commitment to live together as a defined family group and provide for the group's social, emotional, and economic needs, including care of children

family-based services   Programs and services addressing a wide range of family types to intervene with and prevent child abuse and neglect (Pecora, Whittaker, Maluccio, Barth, & DePanfilis, 2009, p. 167)

family foster care   Children are placed in licensed private homes of nonrelatives. Foster homes are supervised by child welfare professionals (Miller-Perrin & Perrin, 2009, p. 167).

family preservation   Supportive and in-home services designed to target families at risk of removal of a child (Miller-Perrin & Perrin, 2009, p. 85)

family service agencies   Provide programs and services to support and strengthen families during challenges and transitions

federally assisted housing   Includes social services to help low-income residents transition and move to nonsubsidized housing (Cohen, Mulroy, Tull, White, & Crowley, 2004, pp. 521–522)

felonies   Serious crimes (e.g., murder, rape, aggravated assault) that are punishable by extended imprisonment and sometimes death

feminization of poverty   Tendency for those living in poverty to be women, because of their workplace disadvantages and greater responsibility for children

fetal alcohol syndrome   A pattern of physical and mental defects that develop in some unborn babies when their mom drinks alcohol (or uses drugs) during pregnancy

fictive kin   Social ties based on neither blood relationships nor marriage

field education   Known as the signature pedagogy in social work education, and an essential component of both BSW and MSW education. Its goal is to connect theory from the classroom with practice in real-world settings.

financial abuse   Unauthorized use of a person's funds or property; includes exploitation

fiscal responsibility   Managing government spending to avoid budgetary crises, particularly (in the current U.S. political climate) by cutting spending on social programs and reducing government financial assistance

five-factor model (Big Five)   A trait approach used to categorize people on the basis of personality. The five traits are neuroticism, extraversion, openness to experience, agreeableness, and conscientiousness

foreclosure   Occurs when a residential mortgage borrower ceases making loan payments or otherwise violates the terms of the mortgage, and the lender (e.g., bank, credit union, savings and loan) takes legal action to terminate the loan and repossess or sell the property

forensic social work   Applies a social work outlook to legal issues and systems and litigation

foster care homes   Approved homes and foster care parents for the placement of children and sometimes older adults

four Ds   Death, dementia, depression, and disability—four conditions of aging that make the process seem negative

fracking   The process of drilling and inserting fluid into the earth to fracture shale rock and release natural gas

Fragile X syndrome   The most common known genetic (single-gene) cause of autism; the most common form of inherited intellectual disability in boys

frictional unemployment   A form of unemployment that is considered unavoidable and part of the normal labor market cycle; reflects the amount of time it takes an employer to find another worker

friendly visitor   Volunteer for the Charity Organization Society who visited the homes of families in need to provide relief and moral instruction

functional disabilities   Connotes a mental or physical impairment that limits how much a person can care for herself or himself. Often some personal care tasks can be done without help.

gender gap   Refers to a disproportionate difference, as in attitudes and voting preferences, between the sexes

gender inequality   Although sex discrimination laws have been passed, gender-based discrimination persists worldwide in the workplace and the political arena.

gender pay gap   Difference in earnings between men and women

gender stereotypes   Overgeneralizations about behaviors and characteristics (e.g., employment and education) based on gender

generalist practitioners   See *generalist social work practice.*

generalist social work practice   Uses generic practice processes to work with client systems of all sizes; recognizes change across multiple systems levels and consider behaviors in the social environment

genetic counseling   The process of helping people understand and adapt to the familial, medical, and psychological implications of genetic contributions to disease

gentrification   The purchase of low-value dwellings in economically challenged sections of a community or neighborhood for renovation, resale, and profit taking, which displaces poor people, often racial minorities

geographical communities   Formal social organizations that possess a defined physical territory (locality) and unique subculture

geriatrics   Also geriatric medicine; a specialty that focuses on health care for older adults

gerontology   The comprehensive study of aging and problems of older adults

GI Bills   Provide financial support for education and housing to veterans who have an honorable discharge. The Post-9/11 GI Bill is available to people with at least 90 days of aggregate service on or after September 11, 2001, or individuals discharged with a service-connected disability after 30 days.

global practice   Social work activities at a local level that are based on the understanding that globalization has made it possible for people to experience multiple cultures

globalization   International economic and social interdependence prompted by capital exchange, transnational production systems, and the trade of goods and services (Poole & Negi, 2008)

green card holder   A person legally admitted to the United States who has not gained citizenship but has the privilege to be a permanent resident

group homes   Commonly refers to group residential environments for people with mental or physical disabilities

group work   A method used by professional social workers to help individuals in a group setting experience positive adjustment and coping and greater participation in community activity by using the supportive mechanisms that occur in group life

guardian ad litem   A court-appointed individual who represents the voices and protects the best interests of children in court

Habitat for Humanity International (HFHI)   Faith-based nonprofit organization dedicated to building and rehabilitating homes across the United States to provide affordable housing for very poor families

halfway houses   Designed to facilitate transition from a restrictive inpatient or incarcerated residence to independent, community-based housing

harm reduction model   A model for substance abuse treatment that focuses on the reduction of harm rather than the cessation of the substance use itself. This method aims to reduce the harms of substance abuse when the individual is unwilling or unable to stop.

hate crimes   Involve intimidation and the intent to hurt people based on race, ethnicity, national origin, religion, sexual orientation, disability, and so on; include the use of verbal threats, acts of violence, fear, physical attack, and explosives

health   A state of complete physical, mental, and social well-being, and not merely the absence of disease or infirmity

health disparities Differences in health, disease rates and severity, and access to health care that are based on membership in less-privileged population groups

Health Insurance Portability and Accountability Act (HIPAA) An act created in 1996 to ensure individuals and their families continuity of health insurance despite job changes and possible unemployment

health maintenance organization (HMO) A specific type of health insurance system with different types of plans, where you choose your primary care physician from a list of covered physicians and that person is responsible for managing your health care needs

Healthy Meals for Healthy Americans Federal program that provides food, nutrition counseling, and access to health care to eligible women, infants, and children

heart disease An umbrella term that applies to a range of diseases that affect the heart

HIV An abbreviation for human immunodeficiency virus, which adversely affects the body's ability to combat disease and causes AIDS

home equity Paid-off portion of the house value

homelessness A condition of individuals or families who lack a fixed, regular, and adequate nighttime residence

homeownership Used to refer to outright owning a home and pursuing ownership of a home through mortgage payments

homicide Illegally causing the death of another person

hospice Not a place but a concept implying comfort care for a patient diagnosed as having 6 months or less to live

Housing and Urban Development housing project Designed as decent and safe housing units for low-income families; supported by the Department of Housing and Urban Development

Housing First programs Emphasize the rapid provision of permanent housing for the homeless, with the availability of supportive services

human capital People who can contribute to an organization's, community's, or society's long-term success

human needs and values Basic shelter, food, and the resources (e.g., emotional, economic, or tangible social support) and personal moral ethics that a person reveals as necessary to survive and function well in society

human relationship school of management Pertains to research in organizational development and the behavior of people in workplace groups

ideologies Sets of beliefs

illness A disease or period of sickness affecting the body or mind

implementation Performance of the steps in a plan. Actions included in the plan reflect the client's situation and view of reality in the context of his or her strengths and specified problems.

incarceration Being placed in prison

income Most commonly, a person's or household's wages for work provided; in some contexts, may include all money brought into a household in a year, whether as wages, the proceeds of investments, or cash benefits through government support programs

income support Income-related benefit for people who are on a low income

indenturing Contracting with a farm or business to work for a specific period

independent-living centers Community agencies, usually staffed by people with disabilities, who use peer counseling and advocacy to help others live on their own

individual reigns supreme perspective Social justice is cast in terms and ways that equate individual gain and interest with the common good (McNutt, 1997)

individualism The belief that success or failure depends on the individual

Individualized Education Program Federal legislation addressing how states and educational systems provide intervention to and address the educational needs of children with identified disabilities

Individuals with Disabilities Education Improvement Act Federal legislation addressing how states and educational systems provide intervention to and address the educational needs of children with identified disabilities

indoor relief In colonial America, services and housing provided in institutions called almshouses,

in exchange for the work of the nondeserving poor

industrialized countries Have a developed economy, exhibit advanced technology, and are modernized

inequality The persistently unequal distribution of wealth, income, and power

inflammation The body's attempt to protect itself from damaged cells, irritants, or pathogens so that a healing process can occur; part of our immune system, which is naturally present in our bodies at birth

inpatient treatment Refers to intervention taking place in an overnight residential treatment center or hospital

institutional or primary view of social welfare Humans are inherently good but are confronted with challenging needs (e.g., employment, health care, housing) and circumstances (e.g., unemployment, illness, divorce, loss of a loved one)

institutionalization The act or process of establishing something as a custom or common practice, or the act or process of placing someone in a mental, penal, or other type of institution

integrated care Involves coordinated care often led by a primary care provider to enhance close collaboration and communication among all members of a patient's health care team

integrative medicine Healing-oriented medicine that considers the body, mind, and spirit of people

intellectual disability A disability, originating before age 18, characterized by significant limitations in both intellectual functioning and adaptive behavior, which covers multiple social and daily skills

intensive treatment Within child and family services, specific types of counseling and social–psychological therapy developed as alternatives to residential care for children at risk

interactional abilities The use of relationship-building, interpersonal, and relational skills

international charity Providing foreign aid to those in need in the form of goods and services

international social work Social work activities that take place across national boundaries and focus on the universal characteristics of human beings and human needs in various environments

International Violence Against Women Act Proposed legislation that would require U.S. agencies engaged in foreign assistance to take steps to prevent and intervene in violence against women and girls in at least five countries where gender-based violence is severe

intersectionality Synonymous with "intersections of diversity"; a way of appreciating difference from multiple perspectives often related to age, class, gender, sexual orientation, race/ethnicity, ability, and religious or spiritual beliefs

irreconcilable differences Disagreements and differences are identified that cannot be resolved, and neither spouse is blamed for the breakdown of the relationship

judges and magistrates Attorneys elected or appointed to lead and rule over court and its processes

just practice An approach to social work practice that attempts to overcome social and economic inequalities while promoting equality, tolerance, and human rights

juvenile corrections Refers to intervention, services, and programs for minors as a result of their involvement in the criminal justice system and courts

juveniles Human beings under the age of 18

kinship Involves common ancestry, marriage, or adoption

landlord Person or entity renting a housing unit to a renter or tenant

language interpretation Typically requires advanced training to be able to convert a thought or expression in one language to a comparable meaning in another language

larceny Stealing of property

laws Legislative acts passed at local, state, and federal levels by corresponding political entities (e.g., city councils, state legislators, the U.S. Congress) to define and regulate acceptable and unacceptable behavior and action

learning disabilities or differences Affect the brain's ability to receive, process, store, respond to, and communicate information. A specific learning disability refers to a disorder in one or more basic psychological processes involved

in understanding or using language, spoken or written, which may affect a person's listening, thinking, speaking, reading, writing, spelling, or math skills.

level of practice The size (micro, mezzo/meso, macro) of the client system with which social workers intervene, including individual, family, group, organization, and community

liberal A political leaning that tends to support a large role of government in social welfare policy

liberal arts foundation The academic foundation of generalist social work practice; refers to a general fund of knowledge and academic skills. Courses within the liberal arts foundation may vary from university to university but typically include sociology, psychology, biology, economics, political science, and statistics.

licensed clinical social workers An advanced licensure classification available in many states that allows MSW- or doctoral-level social workers with appropriate education and supervised experience to practice independently and enter private practice. Typically, candidates are required to pass a designated test, and they often help people with mental health issues and daily living problems enhance their functioning. Sometimes they call themselves psychotherapists.

life expectancy How long, on average, a person is expected to live at a given age

life knowledge A social worker's personal, direct experience with the conditions in which needy clients live

life span A person's lifetime, the number of years a person actually lives

life stage A phase of life, such as being single, independent, and working, or being a parent of infants; assumedly linked to particular constraints or opportunities and significant to certain choices or activities. Also, the term suggests that different psychological tasks have to be done as a person matures and transitions between life stages, which could be times of crisis.

lifelong learning Pursued throughout life; flexible, diverse, and available at different times and places; crosses sectors and promotes learning beyond traditional schooling and across adult life

living wage Earnings sufficient to provide adequate and healthy living

longevity Living an active life longer than the average person

long-term care Often a synonym for nursing home care. Some states differentiate among intermediate or skilled levels of care (e.g., can't exit in case of fire, has a feeding tube or skin breakdown). Long-term care is also an intervention (health care, medical care, personal care, social support) developed to help chronically ill older adults or disabled people meet their daily needs. It may be delivered in the home, specialized rehabilitation centers, respite care facilities, adult day care centers, or nursing homes.

maladaptive Used in psychology to refer to patterns of behavior and thinking that cause and maintain emotional problems

managed care A health care system with administrative control over primary health care services in a medical group practice. The goal is to reduce costs and eliminate redundant facilities and services.

Master of Social Work (MSW) A social worker at the master's level of the profession

McKinney-Vento Homeless Assistance Act A federal law that ensures immediate enrollment and educational stability for homeless children and youth; provides federal funding to states for the purpose of supporting district programs that serve homeless students

means testing The calculations used by social welfare agencies and programs to determine a person's eligibility for benefits and services

mediator Intervenes and resolves disputes in a fair and equitable fashion. Finds common ground, compromises while reconciling differences, and assumes a neutral role.

Medicaid Federal program instituted through the Social Security Act of 1965 to provide matching funds to states to cover the costs of medical care for low-income people

medical home A concept first introduced in 1967 by the American Academy of Pediatrics. The modern medical home expands on its original foundation, becoming a home base for any child's medical and nonmedical care. Today's medical home is a cultivated partnership between the patient, family, and primary provider in cooperation with specialists and support from the community

(Health Resources and Services Administration, n.d.).

medicalization   Also called "pathologization," conveys who has the most power in mental health care decision making—professionals, patients, or corporations

Medicare   The U.S. government's national health insurance program for people age 65 and older who have worked for at least 10 years in Medicare-covered employment and are citizens or permanent residents of the United States. Medicare Part A covers inpatient hospital stays, and Medicare Part B covers physician and outpatient services.

Medicare Part D   A prescription drug benefit created through the U.S. Medicare Prescription Drug, Improvement, and Modernization Act of 2003. Part D coverage excludes drugs not approved by the Food and Drug Administration, those prescribed for off-label use, those not available in the United States, and those paid for by Medicare Part A or Part B benefits.

mental disorders   A medical condition characterized by impaired psychosocial, emotional, or cognitive functioning; vary in duration and severity, and can affect persons of any age, socioeconomic status, race, and ethnicity

mental health   Connotes psychological well-being and satisfactory adjustment to society and the ordinary demands of life

mental health literacy   Jorm et al. (1997) introduced this term and defined it as "knowledge and beliefs about mental disorders which aid their recognition, management or prevention"

mental health parity   A person who has been diagnosed with a mental disorder receives the same level of professional care as a person diagnosed with a physical disorder, and mental health professionals are reimbursed for their services as physicians and other medical personnel are

mental illness   A medical condition that disrupts a person's thinking, feeling, mood, ability to relate to others, and daily functioning

mental retardation   See *intellectual disability*

middle-old   Persons 75 to 84 years old

migration   Movement from one country to another to settle

military sexual trauma (MST)   A term the U.S. Department of Veterans Affairs (2014) uses to refer to sexual assault or repeated, threatening sexual harassment that occurred while the person was in the military. It includes any sexual activity where someone is involved against his or her will.

mindfulness   To pay attention in a certain way—on purpose, in the present moment, and nonjudgmentally

minimum wage   Lowest hourly-rate wage that employers may legally pay their workers

misdemeanor crimes   Relatively minor crimes (e.g., traffic violations, public drunkenness, shoplifting) that are punishable by a fine and a small amount of time (e.g., less than 1 year) in jail

moral injury   "Perpetrating, failing to prevent, bearing witness to, or learning about acts that transgress deeply held moral beliefs and expectations" (Litz et al., 2009, as quoted in Maguen & Litz, 2012, p. 1)

mortgage   A long-term housing loan (e.g., for 10, 15, or 30 years) provided through an approved financial institution (e.g., bank, savings and loan, home lender, or credit union)

motivational interviewing   A client-centered, directive method to enhance intrinsic motivation to change by exploring and resolving ambivalence

Multidimensional Poverty Index   Used to identify and measure deprivation based on health (e.g., nutrition and infant mortality), education (e.g., amount of schooling), and living standards (e.g., water, toilets, electricity, and flooring in residence)

multilingualism   The ability to speak or converse (e.g., sign) in more than one language

mutual aid   Refers to the cooperative (as opposed to competitive) factors operating in a society involving the voluntary exchange of resources and services for mutual benefit

National Alliance on Mental Illness (NAMI)   A national advocacy and self-help group composed of persons with mental illness and their family members; develops new treatment approaches and advocates issues to legislators and the general public

National Association of Social Workers (NASW)   An organization that formed in 1955 to represent and be the voice of the social work profession in the United States and its territories

National Institute of Mental Health (NIMH)   The largest scientific organization in the world that is devoted to research focused on the understanding and treatment of mental health disorders and biomedical and health-related research

National Organization of Forensic Social Work   A nationally recognized professional organization dedicated to the advancement of education in forensic social work

national origin   A person's or his or her ancestors' country of birth

naturally occurring retirement communities   Buildings or neighborhoods that were not originally built to serve older adults but over time have attracted a large proportion of residents who are older adults who intend to age in place

navigator   Assists clients in maneuvering through complex bureaucracies, such as the health care system, to gain needed services

neglect   Caregivers' failure to fulfill a caretaking obligation; includes abandonment

neurocognitive   Of or relating to cognitive functions associated with particular areas of the brain

neurocognitive disorders   Before the DSM-5, major neurocognitive disorder (NCD) was known as dementia; the main feature of all NCDs is an acquired decline in one or more cognitive domains. NCDs can affect attention, language, learning, memory, perception, and social cognition. They interfere markedly with a person's independence in major NCD; however, not so in minor NCD.

neurocognitive impairment   Refers to a condition starting in childhood wherein people show marked limitations in their ability to function and learn

neurodevelopmental disorders   A group of conditions that begin in children's developmental period, typically before they begin grade school, and feature developmental deficits that impair personal, social, academic, or job functioning

nicotine addiction   An addiction to nicotine, which can be found in all tobacco products. The dependency and use of tobacco/nicotine products is linked to serious health problems such as bronchitis, emphysema, heart disease, and various forms of cancer.

nondeserving poor   Able-bodied people who are judged as lazy and unwilling to work for a living

nongovernmental organizations   Not-for-profit, nongovernmental entities that often are involved in alleviating international crises and addressing dire human needs

norms   A standard or pattern, especially of social behavior, that is expected or typical of a group

nuclear family   One or more parents living with their dependent children, apart from other relatives

nursing homes   Homes for elderly people in which most residents require daily nursing care; include skilled nursing facilities and special care facilities such as those for patients with Alzheimer's disease

occupational health hazards   Conditions in the workplace that negatively impact the physical and emotional state of workers

Older Americans Act of 1965   Supports a range of home- and community-based services such as Meals on Wheels and other nutrition programs, in-home services, legal services, transportation, elder abuse prevention, and caregiver support. These programs help older adults stay as independent as possible in their homes and communities, with the goal of avoiding nursing home care and hospitalization and consequently saving state and federal dollars.

oldest-old   A general term that refers to the population over age 85, which is the fastest-growing age group in the United States and some other nations

Operation Enduring Freedom   When the United States invaded Afghanistan in 2001

Operation Iraqi Freedom   When the United States invaded Iraq in 2003

oppositional defiant disorder   A pattern of angry/irritable behavior or vindictiveness that, according to the DSM-5, lasts 6 months or more and is exhibited during an interaction with at least one person who is not a brother or sister. People must display four symptoms from one of the following categories: angry/irritable mood, argumentative/defiant behavior, or vindictiveness. Unlike children with *conduct disorder*, children with oppositional defiant disorder are not aggressive toward people or animals (even though this directly contradicts

the "signs and symptoms"), do not destroy property, and do not show a pattern of theft or deceit. A diagnosis of this disorder cannot be given if the child presents with conduct disorder.

orthopedic problems   Involve the need to correct or prevent deformities, disorders, or injuries of the skeleton and associated structures (such as tendons and ligaments). Such problems include arthritis; fractures; joint replacement; pain management; rheumatology; sports medicine; back, spine, or hand surgery; hip and shoulder injuries; and more.

outdoor relief   In colonial America, provided assistance to the deserving poor in their own homes and communities

outpatient treatment   Sometimes called partial treatment, occurs when clients partake of intervention services at a treatment center without staying overnight

pain   When people have inflammation that hurts. They feel stiff, uncomfortable, or distressed and in agony depending on its severity.

palliative care   An approach that improves quality of life for patients and their families who face issues connected to a life-threatening illness, through prevention and relief of suffering by early identification and excellent assessment and treatment of pain and other physical, psychosocial, and spiritual problems

panic disorders   Sudden and repeated attacks of fear that last for several minutes or longer; may run in families and involve the brain

parole   The early release of an inmate from prison, supervised by a parole officer. Much like probation, parole specifies conditions (e.g., regular reporting, counseling, drug testing, substance treatment) for offenders.

peer support   Takes many forms—phone calls, text messaging, online groups, home visits, group meetings, walking together, grocery shopping, and so on. Peer support links people living with a chronic condition or common illness so they can share their experiences and knowledge, beyond what even health workers may know.

perpetrators   People who inflict violence on others

person with a disability (PWD)   A term used to describe a person whose mental or physical condition or impairment limits his or her ability

to complete daily responsibilities; the condition can be partial or total. In the United States, the Social Security Administration deems someone disabled if he or she can't do any type of appropriate work because of a chronic disability (e.g., lasting 1 year or more).

personal responsibility   References a belief that people should be responsible for their own welfare and life circumstances, diminishing the role or need for governmental intervention

personality   The combination of characteristics or qualities that form a person's distinctive character

personality disorders   A group of mental disturbances defined by the DSM-5 as an enduring pattern of inner experience and behavior that deviates markedly from the expectations of the person's culture and typically causes conflicts in a person's social or occupational environments

person-first language   Respectfully puts the person before the disability; the practice of using care in language when talking about people with disabilities

person-in-environment perspective   A principle integral to social work practice worldwide, this perspective highlights the importance of understanding an individual and individual behavior in relationship to the environmental context in which that person lives and acts. Sometimes referred to as an ecological perspective to highlight how people are affected both positively and negatively by their surroundings.

phobias   Extreme or irrational fears or aversions to particular objects or situations

physical abuse   Nonaccidental use of force that results in physical pain, injury, or impairment; includes hitting, shoving, and inappropriate use of drugs, restraints, and confinement

planning   An activity that results in formation of short- and long-term goals and corresponding strategies, sometimes including family members, friends, and the neighborhood in the planning process and plan

plea bargaining   A negotiation, often conducted by an attorney, with the prosecution for a reduced charge or sentence

police officers   Sworn and authorized officers recognized by local, state, county, or federal authorities to enforce and uphold laws

pollution   The deposit of harmful materials into the air, water, and soil

posttraumatic stress disorder (PTSD)   A psychological reaction that can occur when a person either sees, hears about, or experiences a traumatic event outside of the range of common human experience, such as sexual assault, military combat, or a natural disaster. It is not known why some people develop PTSD from trauma and others do not.

poverty   Lacking basic needs or resources such as money and all that it buys—food, clothing, housing, transportation, and medical care

poverty guidelines   Issued each year in the *Federal Register* by the Department of Health and Human Services as a simplification of the poverty thresholds for administrative use—for instance, determining financial eligibility for certain federal programs

poverty line (poverty threshold, poverty index)   The official measure of poverty, adjusted each year to account for inflation

power   The ability of a person to gain control despite the resistance of others

Prader-Willi syndrome   A syndrome that features floppiness and feeding problems in early infancy, followed later by excessive eating that, if unchecked, leads to severe obesity. All children with this syndrome show developmental delays and mild-to-moderate mental retardation with multiple learning disabilities.

preferred provider organization (PPO)   An organization that provides health care to people at a lower cost if they use the doctors, hospitals, and so forth that belong to the organization

prison   A broad term that encompasses being held in local and county jails as well as state and federal prisons

private child welfare agencies   Usually focus on specific problems and subpopulations, rely on pay for service, see fewer clients, and are less bureaucratic in nature

private practice   In social work, the autonomous provision of professional services by a licensed/qualified social worker who assumes responsibility for the nature and quality of the services provided to the client in exchange for direct payment or third-party reimbursement

privatization   Transferring governmental duties, functions, and roles to business or private organizations

pro bono   Without payment or at a reduced rate

probation   Constitutes a sentence given to an offender by a judge, typically in lieu of prison, carrying specific requirements and conditions (e.g., regular reporting, counseling, drug testing, substance treatment) monitored by a probation officer

profession   Refers to a group of people who use a common system of skills, techniques, knowledge, values, and beliefs to meet a particular social need. The group enhances its public credibility by expanding and disseminating its knowledge; refining its skills and values; making sure members adhere to ethical standards, regulations, and licensing criteria; and publicizing how the group reaches these goals.

professional flourishing   To be in a period of the highest productivity, excellence, or influence possible

professional identity   How a person, who might also have a social work degree, integrates his or her own understandings and experiences with a composite collage of shifting understandings and life views, because she or he has been trained to act in accordance with a code of ethics and use particular knowledge and skills learned in social work courses and training

profiling   When information about crimes and stereotypes about who commits crimes are used to identify and question suspects

property crimes   Refers to crimes involving the taking of money or property (e.g., shoplifting, theft, car theft, vandalism)

prosecutor   An attorney representing a government entity (e.g., city, county, state, federal), arguing that the accused is guilty

psychoactive   Affecting the brain

psychological age   A subjective description of one's experience using nonphysical features

psychopharmacology   The study and use of medications in treating mental disorders and their effects on mood, sensation, thought processing and formation, personality, and behavior

psychotropic medications   Drugs prescribed by psychiatrists and other physicians to manage behavioral,

psychological, and emotional health; includes antidepressant medication, antianxiety drugs, antipsychotic medication, and antimanic medication

public accommodations   Public facilities, such as food, lodging, entertainment, health care, sales or rental services, and other professional services and recreation facilities, that allow use by people with disabilities

public assistance   Social services that are means tested

public child welfare agencies   Typically serve large numbers of people, offer a variety of programs, and are less costly to clients

public housing   Dwelling unit funded by the government for the benefit of low-income persons

qualitative research   Highlights data that are descriptive in nature and not quantified into numbers

quantitative research   Involves collecting data (e.g., through surveys and checklists) about social behaviors, phenomena, programs, and various social units that are converted into numbers and often involve larger sample sizes and statistical analysis

quintiles   Fifths of the population, used to rank groups according to wealth and income

rape   Sexual penetration through the use of force

rational-recovery model   An alternative treatment model to 12-step programs for substance abuse; teaches addicts Addictive Voice Recognition Training to recognize and dispute irrational thoughts that encourage substance abuse

reasonable accommodation   Adjustments or modifications provided by an employer to enable people with disabilities to enjoy equal employment opportunities

recidivism   The tendency for former inmates to return to prison

recovery   The lifelong period in the process of overcoming a substance use disorder that involves treatment and pursuit of well-being

redistributive justice   References the unequal distribution of goods, services, and property and wealth, and attempts to redistribute and equalize their spread in a social unit (e.g., society)

refugees   Immigrants who are given special consideration because they have been forced to leave their country due to human rights violations

(e.g., suffering or persecution as a result of race, religion, political belief, etc.)

rehabilitation   Bringing a person back to a normal, healthy condition after an illness, injury, drug problem, or the like; includes vocational rehabilitation, neurological or traumatic brain injury healing, addiction or substance abuse recovery, or occupational and physical therapy

relational justice   Also called processual justice and refers to "decision making processes that lead to decisions about distribution and to the relationships between dominant and subordinate groups" (Longres & Scanlon, 2001, p. 448)

relative needs   Focus on human dignity and well-being, emphasizing what people need (e.g., soap, hygiene products, indoor plumbing, electronic means of communication, and transportation) to address everyday expectations in a given culture or society (Long, 2004, p. 5)

relative poverty   Compares a person's wages with what is the norm or average to determine if that person is experiencing poverty

religion   Organized spiritual practice that tends to focus on the link between a higher power and human existence

researcher   Conducts research projects and program evaluations to gain evidence that informs practice and policy

reservists   Members of the military who are civilians during peacetime but may be obligated to report for duty during conflicts

residential care   Group homes and other forms of out-of-home residential care facilities intended to provide a stable, structured, and enriching living environment for child development

residential instability   Moving frequently and often once a year

residual or secondary view of social welfare   People, especially the poor and downtrodden, should be responsible for their own position and lot in life and not expect government intervention

resilience   An interaction between risk and protective factors within a person's background that can interrupt and reverse a potentially damaging process

respite care   Temporary assistance to relieve family members from the emotional, physical, and social demands of care work for an older person who lives at home. This assistance is typically provided by friends, volunteers, relatives, or community agencies, including adult day-care programs.

rest taking   Simply stopping what you are doing and doing very little—such as putting your feet up, taking a nap, or relaxing in a comfortable chair

restorative justice perspective   Highlights the notion that many crimes are first and foremost an offense against human relations and offenders should be held accountable to the people they have violated (Finn & Jacobson, 2008, p. 341)

robbery   Stealing from another person

safety net   The concept that people experiencing dramatic and survival-oriented falls in life should be provided with only enough to spare them from perishing

Sandwich Generation   Caregivers who find themselves squeezed in between caring for their children and their elder parents or other older adult family members

schizophrenia   A psychotic disorder (or group of disorders) marked by severely impaired thinking, emotions, and behaviors. People with schizophrenia are typically unable to filter sensory stimuli and may have enhanced perceptions of sounds, colors, and other features of their environment. Most people with schizophrenia, if left untreated, will gradually withdraw from interacting with other people and lose their ability to take care of personal needs and grooming.

school social workers   A specialized form of social work practice for work with students and school systems

secondary stress   Stress resulting from exposure to other people's stories of trauma and negative life events

secondary trauma   Commonly used to refer to "the stress resulting from helping or wanting to help a traumatized or suffering person." Dr. Laurie Pearlman, an expert in the trauma field, prefers the term *vicarious trauma* to describe the "cumulative transformative effect of working with survivors of traumatic life events."

Section 8 housing   Rental housing provided to low-income individuals and families through the Housing and Urban Development Act of 1965

Section 8 vouchers   Certificates from the U.S. Department of Housing and Urban Development that low-income people can use to rent nonprofit and for-profit housing

segregated communities   People living in communities separated on the basis of factors such as race and ethnicity

self-awareness   The capacity to notice the self. Our ability to notice ourselves *in the present moment* can potentially help us break bad habits if we are motivated to change.

self-care   Behaviors and actions that contribute to maintaining one's own sense of wellness and health

self-determination   Involves the rights of people, groups, communities, and organizations to decide their course of action; supports the idea of freedom of choice

self-interest   Actions to promote one's own interest and/or benefit

senescence   The gradual decline of all organ systems, especially after age 30; all the changes associated with the normal process of aging

settlement laws   A feature of the Elizabethan Poor Laws that was implemented throughout the 13 colonies as a standard requirement for receiving welfare assistance and as a method for localities to monitor the cost of such assistance

settlement movement   Began in 19th century England in response to rising unemployment and poverty. Jane Addams brought the movement to the United States by establishing Hull House, which took a holistic approach to neighborhood improvement and social change through community leadership.

sexual abuse   Intimate contact without the person's consent, or forcing the person to watch sex acts

shaken baby syndrome   Serious brain injury to infants and toddlers as a result of being physically shaken

shelters   Short-term havens for people to inhabit during a life transition

slow medicine   Shares with hospice care the goal of comfort rather than cure; a plan for caring, and for living well, in the time an older adult has left (McCullough, 2008)

slum landlord   A negative term applied to landlords who specialize in the purchase and renting out of inferior, low-cost units in need of repair, often to desperate tenants

social action   Efforts aimed at creating social change and advancing the interests and causes of vulnerable and oppressed groups of people (clients and constituents)

social age   An estimate of a person's capabilities in social situations, relative to normal standards. In clinical situations with young children, social age often is assigned by interviewing parents and other adults to produce scores.

social constructs   The ideas and perceptions gathered from life knowledge that are used to define people, circumstances, and actions

social control   Processes in society and government designed and implemented to regulate conformity and compliance in people's behavior; a motive embedded in social welfare policy for addressing the needs of poor and vulnerable people

social development   Activities that combat exploitation and oppression by equitably distributing social and economic gains and by stimulating personal and social fulfillment for all members of a society

social inequality   Occurs when societal resources are distributed unevenly and the distribution is based on typically defined categories of people

social insurance   Programs to prevent poverty, such as Social Security and workers compensation

social justice   Exists when a society as a whole shares in civil liberties, has a voice in political affairs, and has equal access to resources and opportunities

social responsibility   The notion that society should address people's needs but only if they are considered to be worthy

Social Security   A federal program designed to provide benefits to adults who become disabled or retire; composed of four trust funds   (1) Old Age Survivors Insurance, (2) Disability Insurance, (3) Hospital Insurance Trust Fund—Medicare Part A, and (4) Supplementary Medical Insurance—Medicare Part B. Social Security is also known as Old-Age, Survivors, and Disability Insurance, and it supports retirement for workers who contribute to the federal social insurance program.

social stigma   See *stigma*

social support   Typically defined as the existence of people on whom we can rely, people who let us know they care about, value, and love us

social welfare   The array of programs, services, and institutions designed to maintain the stability and well-being of society

social welfare policy   The legal mandates that specify the profession's clients, what services will be made available to designated populations, how services will be delivered, the duration of services, and how intervention outcomes will be evaluated and measured

social work   The recognized profession that nationally and globally provides social services in governmental and private organizations; persons with social work degrees endeavor to help people to prevent problems or find solutions and strengths in biopsychosocial-spiritual functioning, to achieve life-enhancing goals, and to create a civil and just society.

social workers   Graduates of accredited departments, programs, or schools of social work (with either a bachelor's or master's degree) who use their knowledge and skills to provide social services for clients, as defined by the National Association of Social Workers

socioeconomic status   A person's or group's position within a hierarchical structure that depends on variables such as education, occupation, income, wealth, and place of residence. Researchers often use it as a way to predict behavior.

spirituality   Has multiple definitions that go beyond practicing a religion or having a faith perspective. Broadly defined, spirituality comprises activities that renew, lift up, comfort, heal, and inspire both ourselves and those with whom we interact. Spirituality is also the motivational and emotional source of a person's search for a personal relationship with a higher being that can lead to increased well-being, inner peace, and life satisfaction.

standard of living   The level of wealth, material goods, housing, services, and education available to people in a certain geographic region or country

status   A person's prestige, social recognition, honor, or popularity in society

stigma   When someone views you negatively because you have a personal trait that is thought to be or actually is a disadvantage (a negative stereotype). Stigma can lead to discrimination.

strengths perspective   Supports the role of clients in defining or assessing their conditions and describing what they would like to change based on their needs

structural unemployment   A form of unemployment caused largely by conditions in the economy that mismatch available jobs with potential workers

subsidized housing   A general term referencing government-supported housing, where low-income populations receive financial assistance to provide or help them afford housing

substance abuse   A maladaptive pattern of using certain drugs, alcohol, medications, and toxins despite their adverse consequences; thought to be less of a problem than *substance dependence* in that *tolerance* and *withdrawal symptoms* have not yet occurred. This term is a synonym for drug abuse.

Substance Abuse and Mental Health Services Administration (SAMHSA)   Program within the federal government that promotes prevention of and treatment for substance use disorders

substance dependence   Continued use or craving associated with greater tolerance to alcohol, certain drugs, medications, and toxins. If *tolerance* or *withdrawal* symptoms have not yet occurred, then the condition is known as *substance abuse*.

substance use   Consumption of harmful, potentially addictive substances

substance use disorder   A classification associated with the consumption of a harmful addictive substance; includes both *substance abuse* and *dependence*

substandard housing   Housing that falls below local health and/or building codes

successful aging   Refers to a combination of three actions and outcomes; (1) avoiding disease and disability, (2) continuing effective physical and psychological functioning in later years, and (3) continuing to actively engage in a social life (Crowther, Parker, Achenbaum, Larimore, & Koenig, 2002; Rowe & Kahn, 1997, 1999).

supercentenarian   A person who is significantly older than 100 years of age; typically one who has reached the age of 110

Supplemental Nutrition Assistance Program (SNAP) Federal nutritional assistance program for low-income people

Supplemental Security Income (SSI) Federal program providing cash assistance to any person who is 65 years or older or is blind or has a disability, and whose income falls below the poverty line

sustainability Prioritizing the needs of the poor and accepting the finite nature of resources; using resources in such a way as to maintain them for the future

systems theory Used by social workers to conceptualize problems within human systems and to introduce a change process. It allows for a multidimensional analysis of function, cause, and interrelations when considering avenues of change.

telehealth Encompasses the use of digital technologies to deliver health services and education, medical care, and public health services by connecting multiple users who are in different locations. This term includes telemedicine, which entails diagnosing through video conferencing, remote patient monitoring, and more.

Temporary Assistance for Needy Families (TANF) A program designed to help needy families achieve self-sufficiency. States receive block grants to meet specific needs of their residents.

terminal illness Legal and medical definitions indicate that this is when an active, progressive illness has no cure.

third world country An outdated term used to describe poor, nonindustrialized, and economically developing countries. Today, this term is viewed negatively, as it suggests a third-rate, backward, or nondesirable country.

systems–ecological approach Contends that human development is impacted by various environmental systems. Consequently, behavior at home may be very different from behavior in the workplace.

traditional families Families in which children are reared by two married, heterosexual parents

transnational migration Leads to family members maintaining lifestyles across separate countries and cultures (Furman & Negi, 2007, p. 108)

traumatic brain injury A nondegenerative, nongenetic insult to the brain from an external mechanical force that may lead to permanent or temporary impairment of cognitive, physical, and psychosocial functions, with an associated diminished or altered state of consciousness

TRICARE Military insurance program

trickle-down economics An economic theory that the prosperity of the rich will "trickle down" to middle-class and poorer Americans through the creation of new industries and jobs

Trisomy 21 See *Down syndrome*.

12-step approach A 12-step substance abuse recovery program designed to assist people in admitting they have a problem and taking steps toward lifelong sobriety

UN Convention on the Rights of the Child (UNCRC) A treaty defining the rights of children and forbidding the capital punishment of children across the globe

underemployment Related to workers who are employed but unsatisfied or frustrated in their ability to do a job commensurate with their skills and availability because they are overqualified, do not work enough hours to support costs of living, or have not been credentialed

Uniform Code of Military Justice The foundation of military law in the United States

Uniform Crime Report An annual publication of the Federal Bureau of Investigation and the primary source for reporting crime statistics in the United States

Universal Declaration of Human Rights Policy statement by the countries of the United Nations about the minimal standards for the treatment of human beings, adopted in the aftermath of World War II

urgent care centers Provide accessible primary care, urgent care for illnesses or injuries that are non-life-threatening, family medicine to patients of all ages, and comprehensive occupational medicine to businesses and organizations of all sizes and scopes

vascular dementia Dementia caused by stroke

vicarious trauma Secondary stress that occurs when a social worker takes in the emotions, experiences, and reactions of trauma while assisting in the healing or coping process (Trippany, Kress, & Wilcoxon, 2004)

victim assistance programs Programs designed to support and assist survivors and witnesses of acts of victimization in understanding what has happened and seeking appropriate crisis help and services

victimless crimes Illegal acts that (arguably) do not have a readily identifiable victim. Examples include prostitution, illegal gambling, and the selling of drugs.

victims People who have experienced a traumatic or violent act committed by a perpetrator. Because the term *victim* carries negative and helpless connotations, many professionals prefer the term *survivor*.

violent crimes Crimes against people that involve the use of force or threatened force

wage laborers Workers who sell their work hours in return for pay

wealth A person's or family's accumulation of valuable resources and possessions

welfare General, usually stigmatizing term for programs and services to assist the poor

welfare capitalism Business philosophy holding the view that capitalists should take some responsibility for policies and programs benefiting workers

welfare secretaries Staffers for welfare programs established by businesses

white flight In the early years of desegregation, Caucasian families moved from the city to the suburbs to escape desegregated schools and enrolled their children in better-resourced public or private schools.

white-collar crime Acts (e.g., fraud, theft, falsification of records) that occur in the course of employment or normal work activities

work ethic The moral belief in the necessity and benefit of work; attached to the character of individuals and the perceptions others have of individuals

workers' compensation Social insurance program that provides most employees who are injured on the job the right to medical care for any injury and, in many cases, monetary payments to compensate for resulting temporary or permanent disabilities; also provides benefits to the families of workers who are killed on the job

young-old Used to denote a person who is between 55 and 75 years of age

zero tolerance Policy of requiring total abstinence from substances and behaviors that may lead or have led to a substance use disorder

REFERENCES

Accius, J. C. (2010, March). *The Village: A growing option for aging in place* (AARP Public Policy Institute Fact Sheet 177). Retrieved from http://assets.aarp.org/rgcenter/ppi/liv-com/fs177-village.pdf

Acevedo, E. (2005). The Latina paradox: Cultural barriers to the equitable receipt of welfare services under modern welfare reform. *Berkeley Journal of Gender, Law & Justice, 20*, 199–215.

Acker, G. M. (2011). Burnout among mental health care providers. *Journal of Social Work, 12*(5), 475–490.

Adams, J., & Joshi, K. Y. (2010). Religious oppression. In M. Adams, W. J. Blumenfeld, C. Castaneda, H. W. Hackman, M. L. Peters, & X. Zuniga (Eds.), *Readings for diversity and social justice* (pp. 226–234). New York: Routledge.

AIDS Healthcare Foundation. (2014). *HIV/AIDS info.* Retrieved from http://www.aidshealth.org/#/healthcare/hiv-aids-info/

Albrecht, G. L. (2006). The sociology of health and illness. In C. Calhoun, C. Rojek, & B. Turner (Eds.), *The SAGE handbook of sociology* (pp. 267–283). Thousand Oaks, CA: Sage. Retrieved on July 10, 2014, from http://www.sagepub.com/oswmedia3e/study/chapters/handbooks/handbook14.1.pdf

Alcoholics Anonymous. (2001). *The story of how many thousands of men and women have recovered from alcoholism* (4th ed.). New York: Alcoholics Anonymous World Services.

Aldwin, C. (2007). *Stress, coping, and development* (2nd ed.). New York: Guilford Press.

Allvord, T., & Anton, T. (2008). Afterword: Baseball and war. In T. Anton & B. Nowlin (Eds.), *When baseball went to war* (pp. 239–244). Chicago, IL: Triumph Books.

American Association of Suicidology. (2012). *Elderly suicide fact sheet* (based on 2010 data). Retrieved from http://www.suicidology.org/Portals/14/docs/Resources/FactSheets/Elderly2012.pdf

American Cancer Society. (2014, January 16). *Americans with Disabilities Act: Information for people facing cancer.* Retrieved from http://www.cancer.org/treatment/findingandpayingfortreatment/understandingfinancialandlegalmatters/americans-with-disabilities-act

American Civil Liberties Union. (n.d.). *Affirmative action.* Retrieved from https://www.aclu.org/racial-justice/affirmative-action

American Medical Association. (2014). *Health information technology.* Retrieved from http://ww.ama-assn.org/ama/pub/physician-resources/health-information-technology/health-it-basics/emrs-ehrs.page?

American Psychiatric Association. (2013). *Diagnostic and statistical manual of mental disorders* (5th ed.). Washington, DC: Author.

Amnesty International. (2013–2014). The International Violence Against Women Act (I-VAWA). *Issue Brief,* (3). Retrieved from http://www.amnestyusa.org/pdfs/IVAWAIBCongressJUNE2013.pdf

Anders, A. M. (2014, July 24). Earth science: Rain on the parade. *Nature, 511*, 413–414. Retrieved from http://www.nature.com/nature/journal/v511/n7510/full/511413a.html

Anderson, C. A., & Bushman, B. J. (2001). Effects of violent games on aggressive behavior, aggressive cognition, aggressive affect, physiological arousal, and prosocial behavior: A meta-analysis of the scientific literature. *Psychological Science, 12*, 353–359.

Anderson, D., & Wiscott, R. (2003). Comparing social work and non-social work students' attitudes about aging: Implications to promote work with elders. *Journal of Gerontological Social Work, 42*, 21–36.

Anderson, J. E., Azzarello, R., Brown, G., Hogan, K., Ingram, G. B., Morris, M. J., & Stephens, J. (2012). Queer ecology: A roundtable discussion. *European Journal of Ecopsychology, 3*, 82–103.

Aneshensel, C. S. (2009). Toward explaining mental health disparities. *Journal of Health and Social Behavior, 50*(4), 377–394. Retrieved from http://www.jstor.org/stable/20617650

Anton, T., & Nowlin, B. (Eds.). (2008). *When baseball went to war.* Chicago, IL: Triumph Books.

The Arc. (2014). *What is people first language?* Retrieved from http://www.thearc.org/page.aspx?pid=2523

Asch, A., & Mudrick, N. R. (1995). Disability. In R. L. Edwards & J. G. Hopps (Eds.), *The encyclopedia of social work* (19th ed., p. 758). Washington, DC: NASW Press.

Askeland, G. A., & Payne, M. (2006). Social work education's cultural hegemony. *International Social Work, 49*(6), 731–743.

Atchley, R. C. (2009). *Spirituality and aging.* Baltimore, MD: Johns Hopkins University Press.

Auerbach, C., & Mason, S. E. (2010). The value of the presence of social work in emergency departments. *Social Work in Health Care, 49*(4), 314–326. doi:10.1080/00981380903426772

Axinn, J., & Levin, H. (1992). *Social welfare: A history of the American response to need.* New York: Longman.

Axinn, J., & Stern, M. (1988). *Dependency and poverty: Old problems in a new world.* Lexington, MA: Lexington Books.

Axinn, J., & Stern, M. (2005). *A history of the American response to need.* New York: Longman.

Baker, S. (2006). *Sustainable development.* London: Routledge.

Barker, R. L. (2014). *The social work dictionary* (6th ed.). Washington, DC: NASW Press.

Barney, F. (2012, January–February). How to save the global economy: Cut defense spending. *Foreign Policy, 191*, 1–4.

Barry, C. L., & Huskamp, H. A. (2011). Moving beyond parity: Mental health and addiction care under the ACA. *New England Journal of Medicine, 365*, 973–975.

Beall, A. E. (2004). Body language speaks: Reading and responding more effectively to hidden communication. *Communication World, 21*(2), 18.

Beard, B., & Gilmour, J. (2013). *Our voices: Military writers.* Bridgeville, PA: Red Engine Press.

Beard, J. H., Propst, R. N., & Malamud, T. J. (1982, January). The Fountain House model of psychiatric rehabilitation. *Psychosocial Rehabilitation Journal, 5*(1), 47–53.

Beattie, M. (2009). *The new codependency: Help and guidance for today's* generation. New York: Simon & Schuster.

Beattie, M. (2011). *Codependent no more workbook.* Center City, MN: Hazelden.

Beder, J. (2012). *Advances in social work practice with the military.* New York: Routledge.

Beder, J., Postiglione, P., & Strolin-Goltzman, J. (2012). Social work in the Veterans Administration hospital system: Impact of the work. *Social Work in Health Care, 51*(8), 661–679. doi:10.1080/00981389.2012.699023

Beinecke, R., & Huxley, P. (2009). Mental health social work and nursing in the USA and the UK: Divergent paths coming together? *International Journal of Social Work, 55*(3), 214–225.

Bell, H., Kulkarni, S., & Dalton, L. (2003). Organizational prevention of vicarious trauma. *Families in Society, 84*(4), 463–470.

Bell, M. E., Turchik, J. A., & Karpenko, J. A. (2014). Impact of gender on reactions to military sexual assault and harassment. *Health & Social Work, 39*(1), 25–33.

Belluomini, E. (2013). Technology changing the face of social work. *The New Social Worker, 20*(2). Retrieved from http://www.socialworker.com/feature-articles/technology-articles/Technology_Changing_the_Face_of_Social_Work/

Benjamin, A. (1981). *The helping interview* (3rd ed.). Boston, MA: Houghton Mifflin.

Benshoff, L. (2014, July 18). U.S. star goalie Tim Howard puts name on Tourette syndrome "leadership academy." *Newsworks.* Retrieved from http://www.newsworks.org/index.php/local/healthscience/70518usstargoalietimhowardputsnameontourettesyndromelead

Beresford, P. (2000). Service users' knowledge and social theory: Conflict or collation? *British Journal of Social Work, 30,* 489–503.

Berg-Weger, M., Meuser, T. M., & Stowe, J. (2013). Addressing individual differences in mobility transition counseling with older adults. *Journal of Gerontological Social Work, 56*(3), 201–218.

Berkman, B., Dobrof, R., Damron-Rodriguez, J., & Harry, L. (1997). Social work. In S. M. Klein (Ed.), *A national agenda for geriatric education: White papers* (pp. 53–85). New York: Springer.

Bernard-Kuhn, L. (2014, January 13). Surgeon's 1st trial wrapping up. *Cincinnati Enquirer,* p. A6.

Besthorn, F. H., & Saleebey, D. (2003). Nature, genetics, and the biophilia connection: Exploring linkages with social work values and practice. *Advances in Social Work, 4*(1), 1–18.

Bickenbach, J. E., Chatterji, S., Badley, E. M., & Üstün, T. B. (1999). Models of disablement, universalism and the international classification of impairments, disabilities and handicaps. *Social Science and Medicine, 48*(9), 1173–1187.

Blau, J., & Abramovitz, M. (2004). *The dynamics of social welfare policy.* New York: Oxford University Press.

Blieszner, R. (2014). The worth of friendship: Can friends keep us happy and healthy? *Generations, 38*(1), 24–30.

Bloch, M., Ericson, M., & Giratikanon, T. (2013, December 18). Mapping uninsured Americans. *New York Times.* Retrieved from www.nytimes.com/newsgraphics/2013/12/18/uninsured-map/

Blume, S. B. (1992). Alcohol and other drug problems in women. In J. H. Lowinson, P. Ruiz, R. Milliman, & J. G. Langrod (Eds.), *Substance abuse: A comprehensive textbook* (2nd ed., pp. 794–807). Baltimore, MD: Williams & Wilkins.

Boeri, M. W., Sterk, C. E., & Elifson, K. W. (2008). Reconceptualizing early and late onset: A life course analysis of older heroin users. *The Gerontologist, 48*(5), 637–645.

Boomsma, D., Cacioppo, J., Muthén, B., Asparouhov, T., & Clark, S. (2007). Longitudinal genetic analysis for loneliness in Dutch twins. *Twin Research and Human Genetics, 10,* 267–273.

Boushey, H., O'Leary, A., & Glynn, S. J. (2013, February 5). Our working nation in 2013: An updated national agenda for work and family politics. *Center for American Progress.* Retrieved from http://www.americanprogress.org/issues/labor/report/2013/02/05/51720/our-working-nation-in-2013/

Bowen, E. A. (2012, June). Clean needles and bad blood: Needle exchange as a morality policy. *Journal of Sociology & Social Welfare, 39*(2), 121–137.

Boylan, J., & Dalrymple, J. (2011). Advocacy, social justice and children's rights. *Practice: Social Work in Action, 23*(1), 19–30.

Bradshaw, C. P., & Johnson, R. M. (2011). The social context of bullying and peer victimization: An introduction to the special issue. *Journal of School Violence, 10,* 107–114.

Bradshaw, C. P., Sawyer, A. L., & O'Brennan, L. M. (2007). Bullying and peer victimization at school: Perceptual differences between students and school staff. *School Psychology Review, 6,* 361–382.

Brady, J. L., Guy, J. D., Poelstra, P. L., & Brokaw, B. F. (1999). Vicarious traumatization, spirituality, and the treatment of sexual abuse survivors: A national survey of women psychotherapists. *Professional Psychology: Research and Practice, 30*(4), 386–393.

Bragg, E., & Hansen, J. E. (2011). A revelation of numbers: Will America's eldercare workforce be ready to care for an aging America? *Generations, 34*(4), 11–19.

Bresnahan, M., Begg, M. D., Brown, A., Schaefer, C., & Sohler, N. (2007). Race and risk of schizophrenia in a U.S. birth cohort: Another example of health disparity. *International Journal of Epidemiology, 36,* 751–758.

Brock, R. N. (2013). *Soul repair: Recovering from moral injury after war.* Boston, MA: Beacon Press.

Brydon, K. (2010). Social work advocacy in Singapore: Some reflections on the constraints and opportunities. *Asian Social Work and Policy Review, 4,* 119–133.

Bullard, R. D. (n.d.). *Environmental justice in the 21st century.* Retrieved from http://www.ejrc.cau.edu/ejinthe21century.htm

Bullock, E. E., Braud, J., Andrews, L., & Phillips, J. (2009). Career concerns of unemployed U.S. war veterans: Suggestions from a cognitive information processing approach. *Journal of Employment Counseling, 46,* 171–180.

Bullock, H. E. (1995). Class acts: Middle-class responses to their poor. In B. Lott & D. Maluso (Eds.), *The social psychology of interpersonal discrimination* (pp. 118–159). New York: Guilford Press.

Bureau of Labor Statistics. (2012, July 25). *Number of jobs held, labor market activity, and earnings growth among the youngest baby boomers: Results from a longitudinal survey* [Press release]. Retrieved from http://www.bls.gov/news.release/pdf/nlsoy.pdf

Bureau of Labor Statistics. (2014). Social workers. In *Occupational Outlook Handbook* (2014–2015 ed.).

Washington, DC: U.S. Department of Labor. Retrieved from http://www .bls.gov/ooh/community-and-social-service/social-workers.htm

Burock, J., & Naqvi, L. (2014). Practical management of Alzheimer's dementia. *Rhode Island Medical Journal, 97*(6), 36–40.

California WIC. (2012, April). *Program at a glance.* Retrieved from http://www .cdph.ca.gov/programs/wicworks/ Documents/WICProgramAaGlance.pdf

Callanan, V., & Davis, M. (2012). Gender differences in suicide methods. *Social Psychiatry & Psychiatric Epidemiology, 47*(6), 857–869.

Caplan, R. B. (1969). *Psychiatry and the community in nineteenth-century America.* New York: Basic Books.

Carl, J. D. (2012). *Think social problems: 2010 census update.* Boston, MA: Pearson.

Carolla, B. (2014). *What has your state done to improve health care?* Retrieved from http://www.nami.org/Content/ NavigationMenu/Top_Story/What_Has_ Your_State_Done_to_Improve_Mental_ Health_Care_.htm

Carr, D., & Sharp, S. (2014). Do afterlife beliefs affect psychological adjustment to late-life spousal loss? *The Gerontologist, 69*(1), 103–112. doi:10.1093/geronb/gbt063

Carrick, B. (2008). The rights of the Nepali minority in Bhutan. *Asian-Pacific Journal on Human Rights and the Law, 1,* 13–28.

Carter, I. (1977). Social work in industry: A history and a viewpoint. *Social Thought, 3*(1), 7–17.

Cassidy, J. (2013, December 4). Pope Francis's challenge to global capitalism. *New Yorker.* Retrieved from http:// www.newyorker.com/online/blogs/ johncassidy/2013/12/pope-francis-is-no-marxist-hes-a-marian.html

Catholic Relief Services. (2014). *Slavery and human trafficking.* Retrieved from http://crs.org/slavery-human-trafficking /?gclid=Cly37ZK62b8CFQyGaQod MgYAIQ

Cavalieri, T. A. (2005). Management of pain in older adults. *Journal of the American Osteopathic Association, 105*(3), 12S–17S.

Center for Teaching and Learning, Cedarville University (with Furj, J.). (2014). Timeline of social welfare history. *Social Welfare Policy.* Retrieved from http://ctl.cedarville.edu/swk/socialpol/ content/timeline.pdf

Center on Budget and Policy Priorities. (2008). CBPP calculations from U.S.

Census Bureau Data. Washington, D.C.: Center on Budget and Policy Priorities.

Centers for Disease Control and Prevention. (2008, October 16). *Racial and ethnic differences in self-related health status among adults with and without disabilities.* Retrieved from http://www.cdc.gov/Features/ dsDisabilityAndHealthStatus/

Centers for Disease Control and Prevention. (2011a, February 11). *Effects of blood alcohol concentration (BAC).* Retrieved from http://www.cdc.gov/ Motorvehiclesafety/Impaired_Driving/ bac.html

Centers for Disease Control and Prevention. (2011b). *47.5 million U.S. adults report a disability; arthritis remains most common cause.* Retrieved from http://www.cdc.gov/features/ dsadultdisabilitycauses/

Centers for Disease Control and Prevention. (2012a). *About arthritis disabilities and limitations.* Retrieved from http:// www.cdc.gov/arthritis/data_statistics/ disabilities-limitations.htm

Centers for Disease Control and Prevention. (2012b). *Health risks among sexual minority youth.* Retrieved from http:// www.cdc.gov/healthyyouth/disparities/ smy.htm

Centers for Disease Control and Prevention. (2012c, October). *Teen drinking and driving: A dangerous mix.* Retrieved from http://www.cdc.gov/vitalsigns/ teendrinkinganddriving/

Centers for Disease Control and Prevention. (2013, May 16). *Health disparities.* Retrieved from http://www.cdc.gov/ healthyyouth/disparities/index.htm

Centers for Disease Control and Prevention. (2014a). *Global water, sanitation, and hygiene (WASH).* Retrieved from http:// www.cdc.gov/healthywater/global/

Centers for Disease Control and Prevention. (2014b). *Heart disease facts.* Retrieved from http://www.cdc.gov/heartdisease/ facts.htm

Centers for Disease Control and Prevention. (2014c). *Types of disabilities.* Retrieved from http://www.cdc.gov/ncbddd/ disabilityandhealth/types.html

Centers for Disease Control and Prevention, National Center for Chronic Disease Prevention and Health Promotion. (2011, May 11). *Healthy aging: Helping people to live long and productive lives and enjoy a good quality of life.* Retrieved from http://www.cdc.gov/ chronicdisease/resources/publications/ aag/aging.htm

Centers for Medicare and Medicaid Services. (2014). *Medicaid.gov* [Website]. Retrieved from http://www.medicaid.gov

Cesta, T. (2012). Acute care social work in today's environment. *Hospital Case Management, 20*(6), 88–89.

Chamber, C. (1986). Women in the creation of the profession of social work. *Social Service Review, 60,* 141–180.

Chandler, D. (2008). Pastoral burnout and the impact of pastoral spiritual renewal, rest taking, and support system practices. *Pastoral Psychology, 58,* 273–287.

Chen, S. (2010). Boy, 12, faces grown up murder charges. *CNN Justice.* Retrieved from http://www .cnn.com/2010/CRIME/02/10/ pennsylvania.young.murder.defendant/

Cherlin, A. J. (2010). Demographic trends in the United States: A review of research in the 2000s. *Journal of Marriage and Family, 72,* 403–419.

Chinman, M., Lucksted, A., Gresen, R., Davis, M., Losonczy, M., Sussner, B., & Martone, L. (2008). Early experiences of employing consumer providers in the VA. *Psychiatric Services, 59,* 1315–1321.

Choi, N., Nathan, M. C., Bruce, M. L., Hegel, M. T., Wilson, N. L., & Kunik, M. E. (2014). Six month postintervention depression and disability outcomes of in-home telehealth problem-solving therapy for depressed, low-income homebound older adults. *Depression & Anxiety, 31*(8), 653–661.

Chou, C., & Chronister, J. (2011). Social tie characteristics and psychiatric rehabilitation outcomes among older adults with serious mental illness. *Rehabilitation Counseling Bulletin, 55*(2), 92–102.

Cire, B. (2014, June 30). *NIH-commissioned Census Bureau report highlights effect of aging boomers.* Bethesda, MD: National Institute on Aging. Retrieved from http://www .nia.nih.gov/newsroom/2014/06/nih-commissioned-census-bureau-report-highlights-effect-aging-boomers

Clark, E. J. (2012, March). Social Work Month matters. *NASW News, 57*(3). Retrieved from http://www.naswdc .org/pubs/news/2012/03/social-work-month-matters.asp

Classes and Careers. (2014). *Outlook for counseling careers.* Retrieved from http://www.classesandcareers .com/online-degrees_social-sciences/ courses_counseling

CNN Library. (2014, March 31). Colin Powell fast facts. *CNN U.S.*

Retrieved from http://www.cnn.com/2013/08/20/us/colin-powell-fast-facts/

Coates, J., & Gray, M. (2012). The environment and social work: An overview and introduction. *International Journal of Social Welfare, 21,* 230–238.

Cochran, B. N., Balsam, K., Flentje, A., Malte, C. A., & Simpson, T. (2013). Mental health characteristics of sexual minority veterans. *Journal of Homosexuality, 60*(2–3), 419–435. doi:10.1080/00918369.2013.744932

Cohen, C. S., Mulroy, E., Tull, T., White, C., & Crowley, S. (2004). Housing plus services: Supporting vulnerable families in permanent housing. *Child Welfare, 63*(5), 509–528.

Cohen, D., de la Vega, R., & Watson, G. (2001). *Advocacy for social justice: A global action and reflection guide.* Bloomfield, CT: Kumarian Press.

Collins, P. H. (2010). Toward a new vision: Race, class, gender. In M. Adams, W. J. Blumenfeld, C. Castaneda, H. W. Hackman, M. L. Peters, & X. Zuniga (Eds.), *Readings for diversity and social justice* (pp. 604–609). New York: Routledge.

Constable, R. (2009). The role of the school social worker. In C. R. Massat, R. Constable, S. McDonald, & J. P. Flynn (Eds.), *School social work: Practice, policy, and research* (7th ed., pp. 3–29). Chicago, IL: Lyceum Books.

Constable, R., & Alvarez, M. (2006). Moving into specialization in school social work. *School Social Work Journal, 30*(3), 116–131.

Cook, C. C., Crull, S. R., Fletcher, C. N., Hinnant-Bernard, T., & Peterson, J. (2002). Meeting family housing needs: Experiences of rural women in the midst of welfare reform. *Journal of Family and Economic Issues, 23*(3), 285–316.

Cook, J. A., Copeland, M. E., Hamilton, M. M., Jonikas, J. A., Razzano, L. A., Floyd, C. B., Hudson, W. B., . . . Grey, D. D. (2009). Initial outcomes of a mental illness self-management program based on wellness recovery action planning. *Psychiatric Services, 60*(2), 285–316.

Cook, S. J. (2010). "Oh dear! How the factory girls do rig up!": Lowell's self-fashioning workingwomen. *New England Quarterly, 83*(2), 219–249.

Copen, C. A., Daniels, K., Vespa, J., & Mosher, W. D. (2012, March 22). First marriages in the United States: Data from the 2006–2010 National Survey of Family Growth (National Health Statistics Report No. 49). Hyattsville, MD: National Center for Health Statistics. Retrieved from http://www.cdc.gov/nchs/data/nhsr/nhsr049.pdf

Corcoran, J., & Walsh, J. M. (2012). *Mental health in social work: A casebook on diagnosis and strengths-based assessment* (2nd ed.). Boston, MA: Pearson.

Cornell University. (2013). *Disability statistics: Online resources for U.S. disability statistics.* Retrieved from http://www.disabilitystatistics.org/

Cornwell, E. Y., & Waite, L. J. (2009). Social disconnectedness, perceived isolation, and health among older adults. *Journal of Health and Social Behavior, 50*(1), 31–48.

Costa, P. T., Jr., & McCrae, R. R. (1980). Still stable after all these years: Personality as a key to some issues of adulthood and old age. In P. B. Baltes & O. G. Brim Jr. (Eds.), *Life-span development and behavior* (Vol. 3, pp. 65–102). New York: Academic Press.

Council on Social Work Education (CSWE). (2008). *Educational policy and accreditation standards.* Alexandria, VA: Author. Retrieved from http://www.cswe.org/Accreditation/2008EPASDescription.aspx

Council on Social Work Education (CSWE). (2014). *Accreditation.* Retrieved from http://www.cswe.org/Accreditation.aspx

Cox, L. E. (2009). Costa Rica: A cultural study tour. In C. Tice & D. Long (Eds.), *International social work policy and practice: Practical insights and perspectives* (pp. 125–160). Hoboken, NJ: John Wiley.

Cravey, T., & Mitra, A. (2011). Demographics of the Sandwich Generation by race and ethnicity in the United States. *Journal of Behavioral and Experimental Economics, 40*(3), 306–311. doi:10.1016/j.socec.2010.12.003

Crowther, M. R., Parker, M. W., Achenbaum, W. A., Larimore, W. L., & Koenig, H. G. (2002). Rowe and Kahn's model of successful aging revisited: Positive spirituality—the forgotten factor. *The Gerontologist, 42*(5), 613–620.

Damron-Rodriguez, J. A. (2006). Moving ahead: Developing geriatric social work competencies. In B. Berkman (Ed.), *Handbook of social work in health and aging* (pp. 1051–1068). New York: Oxford University Press.

Daniels, A. S. "Peer support Services- What does the Research Reveal about Peer Support Services?" Pillars of Peer Support -2 Summit. October, 2010. Atlanta, GA Carter Center. http://www.dbsalliance.org/pdfs/training/PillarsIIresearchPresentation10_10final-Daniels.pdf

Davidson, Chinman, et.al. *Clinical Psychology: Science and Practice V6 N2, SUMMER 1999.*

Davis, K. (2008). The mental health field of practice. In K. M. Sowers & C. N. Dulmus (Eds.), *Comprehensive handbook of social work and social welfare* (pp. 253–266). New York: John Wiley.

Debate: Are doctors fleeing the ObamaCare exchange? (2014, March 4). *Fox News Insider.* Retrieved from http://foxnewsinsider.com/2014/03/04/bill-o%E2%80%99reilly-ezekiel-emanuel-debate-whether-doctors-are-fleeing-obamacare-exchange

Defense and Veterans Brain Injury Center. (2014). *DoD worldwide numbers for TBI.* Retrieved from http://dvbic.dcoe.mil/dod-worldwide-numbers-tbi

DeFina, R., & Hannon, L. (2009). Diversity, racial threat, and metropolitan housing segregation. *Social Forces, 88*(1), 373–394.

Deitch, R. (2003). *Hemp—American history revisited.* New York: Algora.

DeKosky, S. T., Ikonomovic, M. D., & Gandy, S. (2010). Traumatic brain injury—Football, warfare, and long-term effects. *New England Journal of Medicine, 363,* 1293–1296.

DePoy, E., & Gilson, S. F. (2007). *The human experience: Description, explanation, and judgment.* Lanham, MD: Rowman & Littlefield.

Desilver, D. (2014, February 18). Minimum wage hasn't been enough to lift most out of poverty for decades. *Fact Tank.* Retrieved from http://www.pewresearch.org/fact-tank/2014/02/18/minimum-wage-hasnt-been-enough-to-lift-most-out-of-poverty-for-decades/

DeWeaver, K. L. (1983). Deinstitutionalization of the developmentally disabled. *Social Work, 28*(6), 435–439.

Diamond, P. (2013). Cyclical unemployment, structural unemployment. *IMF Economic Review, 61*(3), 410–455.

Diana, L. (1960). What is probation? *Journal of Criminal Law, Criminology, and Police Science, 51,* 189–208.

Dittman, M. (2003). Fighting ageism. *Monitor on Psychology, 34*(5), 50. Retrieved from http://www.apa.org/monitor/May03/fighting.html

Doherty, L. (2013, October). The village movement senior care. *New Hampshire Magazine*. Retrieved from http://www.nhmagazine.com/October-2013/The-Village-Movement-Senior-Care/

Dohrenwend, B. S., Dohrenwend, B. P., Dodson, M., & Shrout, P. E. (1984). Symptoms, hassles, social supports, and life events: Problems of confounded measures. *Journal of Abnormal Psychology, 93*, 222–230.

Dolgoff, R., Feldstein, D., & Skolnik, L. (1993). *Understanding social welfare* (3rd ed.). New York: Longman.

Dombo, E., & Gray, C. (2013). Engaging spirituality in addressing vicarious trauma in clinical social workers: A self-care model. *Social Work & Christianity, 40*(1), 89–104.

Dominelli, L. (1997). International social development. In M. Hokenstad & J. Midgley (Eds.), *Issues in international social work: Challenges for a new century* (pp. 74–91). Washington, DC: NASW Press.

DuBois, B., & Miley, K. (2014). *Generalist social work practice: An empowerment approach* (8th ed.). Upper Saddle River, NJ: Pearson Education.

Duncan, B. L., Miller, S. D., Wampold, B. E., & Hubble, M. A. (2009). *The heart and soul of change: Delivering what works in therapy* (2nd ed.). Washington, DC: American Psychological Association.

Durose, M. R., Cooper, A. D., & Snyder, H. N. (2014, April). *Recidivism of prisoners released in 30 states in 2005: Patterns from 2005 to 2010.* Washington, DC: Bureau of Justice Statistics. Retrieved from http://www.bjs.gov/content/pub/pdf/rprts05p0510.pdf

Emanuel, E. J. (2014a). *Reinventing American health care.* New York: PublicAffairs.

Emanuel, E. J. (2014b, January 18). Sex and the single senior. *New York Times.* Retrieved from http://www.nytimes.com/2014/01/19/opinion/sunday/emanuel-sex-and-the-single-senior.html

Environmental Protection Agency (EPA). (2014). *What is environmental justice?* Retrieved from http://www.epa.gov/environmentaljustice/

Evans, D. R., Hearn, M. T., Uhlemann, M. R., & Ivey, A. E. (2004). *Essential interviewing: A programmed approach to effective communication* (6th ed.). Belmont, CA: Thomson Brooks/Cole.

Ezell, M. (2001). *Advocacy in the human services.* Belmont, CA: Brooks/Cole Cengage Learning.

Faherty, C. (2008). *Understanding death and illness and what they teach about life: An interactive guide for individuals with autism or Asperger's and their loved ones.* Arlington, TX: Future Horizons.

Farmer, R. (2009). *Neuroscience and social work practice: The missing link.* Thousand Oaks, CA: Sage.

Farrow, K. (2011). A military job is not economic justice. *Huffington Post.* Retrieved from http://www.huffingtonpost.com/kenyon-farrow/post_1732_b_824046.html?view=print&comm_ref=false

Fauci, A. S., Braunwald, E., Kasper, D. L., Hauser, S. L., Longo, D. L., Jameson, J. L., & Loscalzo, J. (Eds.). (2008). *Harrison's principles of internal medicine* (17th ed.). New York: McGraw-Hill.

Federal Bureau of Investigation (FBI). (2011). Table 1A. In *Crime in the United States, 2011.* Washington, DC: U.S. Department of Justice. Retrieved from http://www.fbi.gov/about-us/cjis/ucr/crime-in-the-u.s/2011/crime-in-the-u.s.-2011/tables/table-1

Federal Bureau of Investigation (FBI). (2012, June 11). *Crime rates are down according to 2011 preliminary report.* Retrieved from http://www.fbi.gov/news//stories/2012/june/crimes_061112/crimes_061112

Figley, C. R. (1995). *Compassion fatigue: Secondary traumatic stress.* New York: Brunner/Mazel.

FindLaw. (2014). *Medical marijuana laws by state.* Retrieved from http://healthcare.findlaw.com/patient-rights/medical-marijuana-laws-by-state.html

Finkelhor, D. (2008). *Childhood victimization: Violence, crime, and abuse in the lives of young people.* New York: Oxford University Press.

Finn, J. L., & Jacobson, M. (2008). *Just practice: A social justice approach to social work practice.* Peosta, IA: Eddie Bowers.

Fisher, R., & Harding, S. (2008). Political economy and public life: The context for community organizing. In J. Rothman, J. L. Erlich, & J. E. Tropman (Eds.), *Strategies of community intervention* (pp. 5–26). Peosta, IA: Eddie Bowers.

Flynn, M. (2010). Guest editorial: Unique challenges of war in Iraq and Afghanistan. *Journal of Social Work Education, 46*(2), 169–173.

Fothergill, A., & Peek, L. A. (2004). Poverty and disasters in the United States: A review of recent sociological findings. *Natural Hazards, 32*, 89–110.

Fountain House. (2014a). *History.* Retrieved from http://www.fountainhouse.org/content/history-timeline

Fountain House. (2014b). *Housing.* Retrieved from http://www.fountainhouse.org/content/housing

Fowler, T. (2014, August 6). World Cup star Tim Howard helps teens who have Tourette syndrome—just like him. *People.* Retrieved from http://www.people.com/article/tim-howard-world-cup-tourettes-syndrome

Foy, D. W., Kelly, G., Leshner, A., Schultz, K., & Litz, B. (2011). An exploration of the viability and usefulness of the construct of moral injury in war veterans. *Traumatology, 17*(1), 1–8.

Frances, A. (2013). *Essentials of psychiatric diagnosis: Responding to the challenge of DSM-5.* New York: Guilford Press.

Frankenhaeuser, M. (1980). Psychobiological aspects of life stress. In S. Levine & H. Ursin (Eds.), *Coping and health* (pp. 203–223). New York: Plenum.

Franklin, D. (2012, March 1). How hospital gardens help patients heal. *Scientific American, 306*(3). Retrieved from http://www.scientificamerican.com/article/nature-that-nurtures/

Friedman, H. S., & Martin, L. R. (2012). *The Longevity Project: Surprising discoveries for health and long life from the landmark eight-decade study.* New York: Plume.

Friedman, R. A. (2013, April 29). A rising tide of substance abuse. *New York Times.* Retrieved from http://newoldage.blogs.nytimes.com/2013/04/29/a-rising-tide-of-mental-distress/?_php=true&_type=blogs&_r=0

Frith, U. (2014). Autism and dyslexia: A glance over 25 years of research. *Perspectives on Psychological Science, 86*(6), 670–672.

Furman, R., & Negi, N. J. (2007). Social work practice with transnational populations. *International Social Work, 50*, 107–112.

Fusenig, E. (2012). *The role of emergency room social worker: An exploratory study.* Unpublished Master of Social Work clinical research paper, St. Catherine University, St. Paul, MN. Retrieved from http://sophia.stkate.edu/msw_papers/26

Galper, J. H. (1975). *The politics of social services.* Englewood Cliffs, NJ: Prentice Hall.

Gambrill, E. (1997). Social work education: Current concerns and possible future. In M. Reisch & E. Gambrill (Eds.),

Social work in the 21st century (pp. 317–327). Thousand Oaks, CA: Pine Forge Press.

Gargiulo, R. M. (2006). *Special education in contemporary society* (2nd ed.). Belmont, CA: Wadsworth.

Garrett, P. M. (2009). The "whalebone" in the (social work) "corset"? Notes on Antonio Gramsci and social work education. *Social Work Education, 28*(5), 461–475.

Geewax, M. (2012, May 8). Long-term care insurance: Who needs it? *Family matters: The money squeeze.* Retrieved from http://www.npr.org/2012/05/08/151970188/long-term-care-insurance-who-needs-it

Gellis, Z. D., Sherman, S., & Lawrance, F. (2003). First year graduate social work students' knowledge of and attitude toward older adults. *Educational Gerontology, 29*, 1–16.

Gibleman, M. (1995). *What social workers do.* Washington, DC: NASW Press.

Giffords, E. D., & Garber, K. R. (2014). *New perspectives on poverty: Policies, programs, and practice.* Chicago, IL: Lyceum Books.

Ginsberg, L. (2001). *Careers in social work.* New York: Allyn & Bacon.

Gliedman, J., & Roth, W. (1980). *The unexpected minority: Handicapped children in America.* New York: Harcourt, Brace, Jovanovich.

Glisson, C. A. (1994). Should social work take greater leadership in research on total systems of service? Yes. In W. Hudson & P. Nurius (Eds.), *Controversial issues in social work research* (pp. 155–159). Boston, MA: Allyn & Bacon.

Gockel, A., Burton, D., James, S., & Bryer, E. (2013). Introducing mindfulness as a self-care and clinical training strategy for beginning social work students. *Mindfulness, 4,* 343–353. doi:10.1007/s12671-012-0134-1

Goffman, E. (1963). *Stigma: Notes on the management of spoiled identity.* New York: Prentice Hall.

Googins, B., & Godfrey, J. (1987). *Occupational social work.* Englewood Cliffs, NJ: Prentice Hall.

Gordon, E. (2014, August 27). Hello, may I help you plan your final months? *Shots: Health News from NPR.* Retrieved from http://www.npr.org/blogs/health/2014/08/27/339861118/hello-may-i-help-you-plan-your-final-months

Gorin, S. (2001). Medicare and prescription drugs: Prospects for reform. *Health & Social Work, 26*(2), 115–118.

Grandin, T. (2011). *The way I see it* (2nd ed.). Arlington, TX: Future Horizons.

Gray, M., & Coates, J. (2012). Environmental ethics for social work: Social work's responsibility to the non-human world. *International Journal of Social Work, 21,* 239–247.

Gray, M., Coates, J., & Hetherington, T. (2012). *Social work in a sustainable world.* Chicago, IL: Lyceum Books.

Green, M. A., & Rowell, J. C. (2014). *Understanding health insurance: A guide to billing and reimbursement* (12th ed.). Stamford, CT: Cengage Learning.

Green, R. G., Kiernan-Stern, M., & Baskind, F. (2005). White social workers' attitudes about people of color. *Journal of Ethnic & Cultural Diversity in Social Work, 14*(1–2), 47–68.

Greene, R. R. (2002). *Resiliency: An integrated approach to practice, policy, and research.* Washington, DC: NASW Press.

Greene, R., & Galambos, C. (2002). *Social work's pursuit of a common professional framework: Have we reached a milestone? Advancing gerontological social work education.* New York: Haworth Press.

Greenfield, E. A., Morton, C., Birkenmaier, J., & Rowan, N. L. (2013). Optimizing geriatric social work education: Program and individual characteristics that promote competencies. *Journal of Gerontological Social Work, 56*(4), 356–377. doi:10.1080/01634372.2013.771807

Griffiths, M. D. (2012). Internet sex addiction: A review of empirical research. *Addiction Research and Theory, 20*(2), 111–124. doi:10.3109/16066359.2011.588351

Grob, G. N. (1991). *From asylum to community: Mental health policy and modern America.* Princeton, NJ: Princeton University Press.

Groskind, F. (1994). Ideological influences on public support for assistance to poor families. *Social Work, 39,* 81–89.

Groton, D. (2013). Are housing first programs effective? A research note. *Journal of Sociology and Social Welfare, 40*(1), 51–63.

Groton, D., Teasley, M. L., & Canfield, J. P. (2013). Working with homeless school-aged children: Barriers to school social work practice. *School Social Work Journal, 37*(2), 37–51.

Hacking, I. (1999). *The social construction of what?* Boston, MA: Harvard University Press.

Hall, J. (2009). Utilizing social support to conserve the fighting strength: Important considerations for military social workers. *Smith College Studies in Social Works, 79*(3–4), 335–343. doi:10.1080/00377310903115465

Hall, L. K. (2008). *Counseling military families: What mental health professionals need to know.* New York: Routledge.

Hall, L. K. (2011). The importance of understanding military culture. *Social Work in Health Care, 50*(1), 4–18.

Hall, P. (2011). A biopsychosocial view of sex addiction. *Sexual and Relationship Therapy, 26*(3), 217–228.

Hallahan D. P., Kauffman, J. M., & Pullen, P. C. (2012). *Exceptional learners: An introduction to special education* (12th ed.). Boston, MA: Pearson.

Hall-Flavin, D. (2011, October 13). Does caffeine make depression worse? *Mayo Clinic.* Retrieved from http://www.mayoclinic.org/diseases-conditions/depression/expert-answers/caffeine-and-depression/faq-20057870

Hansan, J. E. (n.d.). Charity Organization Societies: 1877–1893. *Social Welfare History Project.* Retrieved from http://www.socialwelfarehistory.com/organizations/charity-organization-societies-1877-1893/

Harms, W. (2014, February 16). AAAS 2014: Loneliness is a major health risk for older adults. *UChicago News.* Retrieved from http://news.uchicago.edu/article/2014/02/16/aaas-2014-loneliness-major-health-risk-older-adults

Harrington, M. (1962). *The other America: Poverty in the United States.* New York: Penguin Books.

Hartwell, R. M. (1971). *The industrial revolution and economic growth.* London: Methuen.

Hass-Cohen, N., & Carr, R. (2008). *Art therapy and clinical neuroscience.* London: Jessica Kingsley.

Hawley, C., & Solache, S. (2014, March 5). Age discrimination flourishes in Mexico. *ABCNews.* Retrieved from http://abcnews.go.com/Business/story?id=3641173

Hayflick, L. (1994). *How and why we age.* New York: Ballantine.

Haynes, K., & Mickelson, J. (2006). *Affecting change: Social workers in the political arena* (6th ed.). Boston, MA: Pearson Allyn & Bacon.

Health Resources and Services Administration. (n.d.). *What is a medical home? Why is it important?*

Retrieved from http://www.hrsa.gov/healthit/toolbox/Childrenstoolbox/BuildingMedicalHome/whyimportant.html

Healy, L. M. (2008). *International social work: Professional action in an interdependent world.* New York: Oxford University Press.

Hedges, C. (2002). *War is a force that gives us meaning.* New York: Anchor Press.

Hegewisch, A., Williams, C., Hartmann, H., & Hudiburg, S. K. (2014, March). *The gender wage gap: 2013; Differences by race and ethnicity, no growth in real wages for women.* Washington, DC: Institute for Women's Policy Research. Retrieved from http://www.iwpr.org/publications/pubs/the-gender-wage-gap-2013-differences-by-race-and-ethnicity-no-growth-in-real-wages-for-women

Heiner, R. (2013). *Social problems: An introduction to critical constructionism.* New York: Oxford University Press.

Hellmich, N. (2012a, July 10). Sitting less could extend your life. *USA Today.* Retrieved from http://usatoday30.usatoday.com/news/health/story/2012-07-09/sitting-less-could-extend-life/56117870/1

Hellmich, N. (2012b, August 13). Take a stand against "sitting disease" *USA Today.* Retrieved from http://usatoday30.usatoday.com/news/health/story/2012-07-19/sitting-disease-questions-answers/57016756/1

Hepworth, D. H., Rooney, R. H., Rooney, G. D., Strom-Gottfried, K., & Larsen, J. (2010). *Direct social work practice: Theory and skills* (8th ed.). Belmont, CA: Brooks/Cole, Cengage Learning.

Herek, G. M., Cogan, J. C., & Gillis, J. R. (2002). Victim experiences in hate crimes based on sexual orientation. *Journal of Social Issues, 58,* 319–339.

Hermans, H., & Evenhuis, H. (2013). Factors associated with depression and anxiety in older adults with intellectual disabilities: Results of the healthy ageing and intellectual disabilities study. *International Journal of Geriatric Psychiatry, 28*(7), 691–699.

Hershner, S. D., & Chervin, R. D. (2014). Causes and consequences of sleepiness among college students. *Natural Science Sleep, 6,* 73–84.

Hoefer, R. (2012). *Advocacy practice for social justice* (2nd ed.). Chicago, IL: Lyceum Books.

Hoeger, L. W., & Hoeger, W. W. K. (1995). *Lifetime: Physical fitness and wellness.* Englewood, CO: Norton.

Hollis, F. (1964). *Casework: A psychosocial therapy.* New York: Random House.

Hong, P. Y., & Song, I. H. (2010). Globalization of social work practice: Global and local response to globalization. *International Social Work, 53,* 656–670.

Hooyman, N. R. (2006). *Achieving curricular and organizational change: Impact of the CSWE geriatric enrichment in social work education project.* Alexandria, VA: Council on Social Work Education.

Hooyman, N. R., & Kiyak, H. A. (2010). *Social gerontology* (10th ed.). Boston, MA: Pearson/Allyn & Bacon.

Hooyman, N., & Lubben, J. (2009). The need for gerontological social workers. In N. Hooyman (Ed.), *Transforming social work education: The first decade of the Hartford Geriatric Social Work Initiative* (pp. 3–20). Alexandria, VA: Council on Social Work Education.

Hoyer, W. J., & Roodin, P. A. (2009). *Adult development and aging* (6th ed.). New York: McGraw-Hill.

Hsia, H., Bridges, G. S., & McHale, R. (2004). *Disproportionate minority confinement: 2002 update.* Washington, DC: U.S. Department of Justice, Office of Justice Programs, Office of Justice and Delinquency Prevention.

Human Rights Campaign. (2014). *Resources: Maps of state laws and policies.* Retrieved from http://www.hrc.org/resources/entry/maps-of-state-laws-policies

Huss, E., Sarid, O., & Cwikel, J. (2010). Using art as a self-regulating tool in a war situation: A model for social workers. *Health & Social Work, 35*(3), 201–209.

Huttman, E. (1985). *Social services for the elderly.* New York: Free Press.

Ife, J. (2001). *Human rights and social work: Rights-based practice.* New York: Cambridge University Press.

Institute for Research on Poverty. (2014). *What are poverty thresholds and poverty guidelines?* Retrieved from http://www.irp.wisc.edu/faqs/faq1.htm#thresholds

Internal Revenue Service. (2014, June 27). *EITC home page.* Retrieved from http://www.irs.gov/individuals/article/0,,id=96406,00.html

International Essential Tremor Foundation. (n.d.). *Utensils: Liftware.* Retrieved from http://essentialtremor.org/treatments/assistive-devices/

International Federation of Social Workers. (2004). *Ethics in social work, statement of principles.* Geneva, Switzerland: Author.

Isett, K. R., Ellis, A. R., Topping, S., & Morrissey, J. P. (2009). Managed care and provider satisfaction in mental health settings. *Community Mental Health Journal, 45,* 209–221. doi:10.1007/s10597-008-9171-6

Ivey, A. E., Ivey, M. B., & Zalaquett, C. P. (2010). *Intentional interviewing and counseling* (7th ed.). Belmont, CA: Brooks/Cole.

Jackson, K. (2013). Working with veterans and military families. *Social Work Today, 13*(2), 12–16.

Jackson, M. (Director). (2010). *Temple Grandin* [Motion picture]. Los Angeles, CA: HBO Films.

Jacobson, J. (2006). Compassion fatigue, compassion satisfaction, and burnout: Reactions among employee assistance professionals providing workplace crisis intervention and disaster services. *Journal of Behavioral Health, 21*(3–4), 133–152.

Jani, J., Pierce, D., Ortiz, L., & Sowbel, L. (2011). Access to intersectionality, content to competence: Deconstructing social work education diversity standards. *Journal of Baccalaureate Social Work, 47*(2), 283–301.

Jannson, B. S. (1999). Becoming an effective policy advocate: From policy practice to social justice. Pacific Grove, CA: Brooks/Cole.

Jenner, M. S. (2011). International drug trafficking: A global problem with a domestic solution. *Indiana Journal of Global Legal Studies, 18*(2), 901–927.

Jette, A. M. (2006). Toward a common language for function, disability, and health. *Physical Therapy, 86,* 726–734. Retrieved from http://ptjournal.apta.org/content/86/5/726.full.pdf+html

John A. Hartford Foundation. (2009). *2009 annual report.* New York: Author.

Johnson, B. D., & Betsinger, S. (2009). Punishing the "model minority": Asian-American criminal sentencing outcomes in federal district courts. *Criminology, 47,* 1045–1090.

Johnson & Johnson. (n.d.). *Prevention and wellness.* Retrieved from http://www.jnj.com/sites/default/files/pdf/prevention-and-wellness.pdf

Joiner, T. (2005). *Why people die by suicide.* Cambridge, MA: Harvard University Press.

Jonas, W. B., O'Connor, F. G., Deuster, P., Peck, J., Shake, C., & Frost, S. S.

(2010). Why Total Force Fitness? *Military Medicine, 175*(8), 6–13.

Jones, J. (2012, April 27). Expected retirement age in U.S. up to 67. *Gallup.* Retrieved from http://www.gallup.com/poll/154178/Expected-Retirement-Age.aspx

Joo, J. H., Wittink, M., & Dahlberg, B. (2011). Shared conceptualizations and divergent experiences of counseling among African American and white older adults. *Qualitative Health Research, 21*(8), 1065–1074.

Jorm, A. F., Korten, A. E., Jacomb, P. A., Christensen, H., Rodgers, B., & Pollitt, P. (1997). "Mental health literacy": A survey of the public's ability to recognise mental disorders and their beliefs about the effectiveness of treatment. *Medical Journal of Australia, 166*(4), 182–186.

Joseph, A. L., Slovak, K., & Broussard, C. A. (2010). School social workers and a renewed call to advocacy. *School Social Work Journal, 35*(1), 1–20.

Joslyn, S. A., & West, M. M. (2000). Racial differences in breast carcinoma survival. *Cancer, 88*(1), 114–123.

Judd, R. G., & Sheffield, S. (2010). Hospital social work: Contemporary roles and professional activities. *Social Work in Health Care, 49*(9), 856–871.

Kahn, S. (1994). *How people get power.* Washington, DC: National Association of Social Workers.

Kaye, S., & Bleep, M. (1997). *Arts and healthcare.* London: Jessica Kingsley.

Keller, C. E., & Hallahan, D. P. (1990). The coverage of persons with disabilities in American newspapers. *Journal of Special Education, 24*(3), 271–273.

Kelley-Moore, J. A., & Ferraro, K. F. (2004). The black/white disability gap: Persistent inequality in later life? *Journal of Gerontology, 59B*(1), S34–S43.

Kelty, R., Kleykamp, M., & Segal, D. R. (2010). The military and the transition to adulthood. *The Future of Children, 20*(1), 181–207.

Kempe, C. H., Silverman, F. N., Steele, B. F., Droegemueller, W., & Silver, H. K. (1962). The battered child syndrome. *Journal of the American Medical Association, 17*, 17–24.

Kendall, D. (2013). *Social problems in a diverse society.* Boston, MA: Pearson.

Kilty, K. M., & Meenaghan, T. M. (1995). Social work and the convergence of politics and science. *Social Work, 40*(4), 445–453.

Kitterlin, M., & Moreo, P. J. (2012). Pre-employment drug-testing in the full-service restaurant industry and its relationship to employee work performance factors. *Journal of Human Resources in Hospitality & Tourism, 11*, 36–51.

Klein, B. S. (Director). (2006). *Shameless: The art of disability.* Quebec: National Film Board of Canada. Retrieved from http://onf-nfb.gc.ca/en/our-collection/?idfilm=51620

Kleinhans, R., van der Land, M., & Doff, W. (2010). Dealing with living in poor neighborhoods. *Journal of Housing and the Built Environment, 25*, 381–389.

Knox, J., & Price, D. H. (1995, September). The changing American military family: Opportunities for social work. *Social Service Review*, 479–497.

Knudson, T. M., & Terrell, H. K. (2012). Codependency, perceived interparental conflict, and substance abuse in the family of origin. *American Journal of Family Therapy, 40*(3), 245–257.

Koenig, H., McCullough, M., & Larson, D. (2001). *Handbook of religion and health.* Oxford, UK: Oxford University Press.

Koenig, T. L., Lee, J. H., Fields, N. L., & Macmillan, K. R. (2011). The role of the gerontological social worker in assisted living. *Journal of Gerontological Social Work, 54*(5), 494–510. doi:10.1080/01634372.2011.576424

Konovsky, M. A., & Cropanzano, R. (1991). Perceived fairness of employee drug testing as a predictor of employee attitudes and job performance. *Journal of Applied Psychology, 76*(5), 698–707. doi:10.1037/0021-9010.76.5.698

Kretzmann, J. P., & McKnight, J. (1993). *Building communities from the inside out: A path toward finding and mobilizing a community's assets.* Evanston, IL: Center for Urban Affairs and Policy Research, Northwestern University.

Krumer-Nevo, M. (2005). Listening to "life knowledge": A new research direction in poverty studies. *International Journal of Social Welfare, 14*, 99–106.

Krumer-Nevo, M., & Barak, A. (2007). Service users and personal social services in Israel: Are we ready to hear what clients want to tell us? *Journal of Social Services, 34*(1), 27–42.

Krumer-Nevo, M., Weiss-Gal, I., & Monnickendam, M. (2009). Poverty aware social work practice: A conceptual framework for social work

education. *Journal of Social Work Education, 45*(2), 225–243.

Kruse, M. W. (2005, November 28). Generation archetypes. *Kruse Kronicle.* Retrieved from http://www.krusekronicle.com/kruse_kronicle/2005/11/generation_arch.html#.VCtc3vldWSo

Kulshreshtha, A., Goyal, A., Dabhadkar, K., Veledar, E., & Vaccarino, V. (2014). Urban-rural differences in coronary heart disease mortality in the United States: 1999–2009. *Public Health Reports, 129*(1), 19–29.

Lamanna, M. A., & Riedmann, A. (2012). *Marriages and families: Making choices in a diverse society* (11th ed.). Belmont, CA: Wadsworth/Cengage.

Lamb, P. (2005, November 1). Perspective: Technology and the new class divide. *CNET.* Retrieved from http://news.cnet.com/2100-1028_3-5924758.html

Larson, M. J., Wooten, N. R., Adams, R. S., & Merrick, E. L. (2012). Military combat deployments and substance use: Review and future directions. *Journal of Social Work Practice in the Addictions, 12*, 6–27. doi:10.1080/1533256X.2012.647586

Laser, J. A., & Stephens, P. M. (2011). Working with military families through deployment and beyond. *Clinical Social Work Journal, 39*(1), 28–38. doi:10.1007/s10615-010-0310-5

Laursen, E. K. (2011). Bullying and violence in schools and communities. *Counseling and Human Development, 44*(2), 1–16.

Lazarus, R. S. (1966). *Psychological stress and the coping process.* New York: McGraw-Hill.

Leeb, R. T., Paulozzi, L., Melanson, C., Simon, T., & Arias, I. (2008). *Child maltreatment surveillance: Uniform definitions for public health and recommended data elements.* Atlanta, GA: Centers for Disease Control and Prevention, National Center for Injury Prevention and Control.

Lemley, B. (n.d.). What is integrative medicine? *DrWeil.com.* Retrieved from http://www.drweil.com/drw/u/ART02054/Andrew-Weil-Integrative-Medicine.html

Lemongello, S. (2014, May 25). During a World War II flight, Ewing Roddy nearly went down with the bomb. *Press of Atlantic City.* Retrieved from http://www.pressofatlanticcity.com/news/breaking/during-a-world-war-ii-flight-ewing-roddy-nearly-went/article_98f4588a-e475-11e3-9dea-001a4bcf887a.html

Lester, D., Haines, J., & Williams, C. L. (2012). Firearm suicides among males in Australia: An analysis of Tasmanian coroner's incest files. *International Journal of Men's Health, 11*(2), 170–176.

Levin, R. F. (1994). *Heartmates: A guide for the spouse and family of the heart patient* (Rev. ed.). New York: Simon & Schuster.

Levy, B. R. (2003). Mind matters: Cognitive and physical effects of aging self-stereotypes. *Journals of Gerontology Series B: Psychological Sciences, 58B,* P203–P211.

Levy, B. R., Slade, M. D., Kunkel, S. R., & Kasl, S. V. (2002). Longevity increased by positive self-perceptions of aging. *Journal of Personality and Social Psychology, 83*(2), 261–270.

Lieberman, A. (2011). *The social workout book: Strength-building exercises.* Thousand Oaks, CA: Sage.

Liebman, M. (1996). *Arts approaches to conflict.* London: Jessica Kingsley.

Lindsell-Roberts, S. (2011). *New rules for today's workplace: Strategies for success in the virtual world.* New York: Houghton Mifflin Harcourt.

Lister, R. (2004). *Poverty.* London: Polity Press.

Lloyd, C., King, R., & Chenoweth, L. (2002). Social work, stress and burnout: A review. *Journal of Mental Health, 11,* 255–265. doi:10.1080/09638230020023642

Lobb, R. L. (2003). Green Revolution. In *Encyclopedia of Food and Culture.* Retrieved from http://www.encyclopedia.com/topic/Green_Revolution.aspx

Loecher, B., & Harrar, S. (2001). Link between gambling and depression. *Prevention, 53*(10), 164.

Logsdon-Breakstone, S. L. (2012, April 23). Disability History 101—The rise of the institution. *Disability Right Now.* Retrieved from www.disabilityrightnow.wordpress.com/2012/04/23/dis-hist-101

Long, D. D. (2000). Welfare reform: A social work perspective for assessing success. *Journal of Sociology and Social Welfare, 28*(4), 59–74.

Long, D. D. (2004). Introduction to social welfare. In A. Sallee (Ed.), *Social work and social welfare: An introduction.* Peosta, IA: Eddie Bowers.

Long, D. D. (2009). International social work education and practice. In C. Tice & D. Long (Eds.), *International social work policy and practice: Practical insights and perspectives* (pp. 1–22). Hoboken, NJ: John Wiley.

Long, D. D., & Holle, M. C. (2007). *Macro systems in the social environment* (2nd ed.). Belmont, CA: Cengage Learning.

Long, D. D., Long, J. H., & Kulkarni, S. J. (2007). Interpersonal violence and animals: Mandated cross-sector reporting. *Journal of Sociology and Social Welfare, 34*(3), 147–164.

Long, D. D., & Tice, C. J. (2009). Lessons learned from international practice and policy. In C. Tice & D. Long (Eds.), *International social work policy and practice: Practical insights and perspectives* (pp. 231–249). Hoboken, NJ: John Wiley.

Long, D. D., Tice, C. J., & Morrison, J. D. (2006). *Macro social work practice: A strengths perspective.* Belmont, CA: Brooks/Cole Cengage Learning.

Longres, J. F., & Scanlon, E. (2001). Social justice and the research curriculum. *Journal of Social Work Education, 37,* 447–463.

Lowry, F. (2014, February 11). Mental health services still lack racial-ethnic diversity. *Medscape Medical News.* Retrieved from http://www.medscape.com/viewarticle/820466

Lucksted, A., McNulty, K., Brayboy, L., & Forbes, C. (2009). Initial evaluation of the peer-to-peer program. *Psychiatric Services, 60,* 250–253.

Lurigio, A. J. (2011). Examining prevailing beliefs about people with serious mental illness in the criminal justice system. *Federal Probation, 75,* 11–18.

Lyons, K. (2006). Globalization and social work: International and local implications. *British Journal of Social Work, 36,* 365–380.

Mackelprang, R. W., & Salsgiver, R. O. (2009). *Disability: A diversity model approach in human service practice* (2nd ed.). Chicago, IL: Lyceum Books.

Maguen, S., & Litz, B. (2012). Moral injury in veterans of war. *PTSD Research Quarterly, 23*(1). Retrieved from http://www.ptsd.va.gov/professional/newsletters/research-quarterly/v23n1.pdf

Makin-Byrd, K., Gifford, E., McCutcheon, S., & Glynn, S. (2011). Family and couples treatment for newly returning veterans. *Professional Psychology: Research and Practice, 42*(1), 47–55. doi:10.1037/a0022292

Malick, A. (2014, June 12). Study: Pot increases heart attack risks. *ABC News.* Retrieved from http://abcnews.go.com/Health/story?id=117399

Manetta, A., & Cox, L. E. (2013). Suicidal behavior and HIV/AIDS: A partial test of Joiner's theory of why people die by suicide. *Social Work in Mental Health, 12*(1), 20–35. doi:10.1080/15332985.2013.832717

Manfredi, C. (2009). Golden years. *American Fitness, 27*(2), 55.

Manning, L., & Wight, V. R. (2000). *Women in the military: Where they stand* (3rd ed.). Washington, DC: Women's Research & Education Institute.

Markel, H. (2009). Case shined first light on abuse of children. *New York Times.* Retrieved from http://www.nytimes.com/2009/12/15/health/15abus.html?_r=1&

Mars, S. G., & Ling, P. M. (2008, October). Meanings and motives: Experts debating tobacco addiction. *American Journal of Public Health, 98*(10), 1793–1802. doi:10.2105AJPH.2007.114124

Martin, T. C., Lewis, T., Josiah-Martin, J. A., & Sinnott, T. (2010). Client family-member participation is associated with improved residential treatment program completion at an international drug and alcohol treatment center. *Journal of Groups in Addiction & Recovery, 5,* 34–44. doi:10.1080/15560350903543931

Mary, N. (2008). *Social work in a sustainable world.* Chicago, IL: Lyceum Books.

Masala, C., & Petretto, D. R. (2008). From disablement to enablement: Conceptual models of disability in the 20th century. *Disability and Rehabilitation, 30*(17), 1233–1244.

Maschi, T., & Killian, M. L. (2011). The evolution of forensic social work in the United States: Implications for 21st century practice. *Journal of Forensic Social Work, 1,* 8–36.

Masiriri, T. (2008). The effects of managed care on social work mental health practice. *SPNA Review, 4*(1), 83–98.

Maslach, C., & Jackson, S. (1981). The measurement of experienced burnout. *Journal of Occupational Behaviour, 2,* 99–113.

Mason, S. E., & Sanders, G. R. (2004). Social work student attitudes on working with older clients. *Journal of Gerontological Social Work, 42,* 61–75.

Massat, C. P., Essex, E. L., Hare, I., & Rome, S. H. (2009). The developing social, political, and economic context for school social work. In C. R. Massat, R. Constable, S. McDonald, & J. P. Flynn (Eds.), *School social work: Practice, policy, and research* (7th ed., pp. 114–139). Chicago, IL: Lyceum Books.

May, B., & LaMont, E. (2014). Rethinking learning disabilities in the college classroom: A multicultural perspective. *Social Work Education, 33*(7), 959–975.

Mayo Clinic. (2014). *Traumatic brain injury.* Retrieved from http://www.mayoclinic.org/diseases-conditions/traumatic-brain-injury/basics/definition/con-20029302

Mayo Clinic Staff. (2014, February 12). *Compulsive gambling: Definition.* Retrieved from http://www.mayoclinic.org/diseases-conditions/compulsive-gambling/basics/definition/con-20023242

McConnell, K. J. (2013, October). The effect of parity on expenditures for individuals with severe mental illness. *Health Services Research, 48*(5), 1634–1652. doi:10.1111/1475-6773.12058

McCullough, D. (2008, Spring). Slow medicine. *Dartmouth Medicine.* Retrieved from http://dartmed.dartmouth.edu/spring08/html/grand_rounds.php

McGowan, B. G. (1978). The case advocacy function in child welfare practice. *Child Welfare, 57*(5), 275–284.

McInnis-Dittrich, K. (2014). *Social work with older adults* (4th ed.). New York: Pearson.

McKay, J. R., & Hiller-Sturmhoefel, S. (2011). Treating alcoholism as a chronic disease: Approaches to long-term clinical care. *Alcohol Research & Health, 33*(4), 356–370.

McLaughlin, A. (2007). How to snag a job in international social work. *New Social Worker, 14*(2), 26–27.

McLaughlin, S. (2014, May 12). More beds open to help Butler County heroin addicts. *Cincinnati Enquirer,* pp. A11–A12.

McLeod, S. A. (2014). Abnormal psychology. *Simply Psychology.* Retrieved from http://www.simplypsychology.org/abnormal-psychology.html

McNutt, J. (1997). New communitarian thought and the future of social policy. *Journal of Sociology and Social Welfare, 24*(4), 45–56.

McNutt, J. (2011). Is social work advocacy worth the cost? Issues and barriers to an economic analysis of social work political practice. *Research on Social Work Practice, 21*(4), 397–403.

Meador, A. (2013). Social justice groups demand Congress slash military budget, spend money on people, peace, planet. *Truthout.* Retrieved from http://truth-out.org/news/item/20598-social-justice-groups-demand-congress-slash-military-budget-spend-money-on-people-peace-planet

Mealer, W. F., Singh, D. N., & Murray, S. O. (1981). The social worker's role in genetic counseling. *Journal of the National Medical Association, 73*(12), 1159–1162.

Meenaghan, T. M., Kilty, K. M., Long, D. D., & McNutt, J. G. (2013). *Policy, politics, and ethics: A critical approach.* Chicago, IL: Lyceum Books.

Mendenhall, A. N., & Frauenholtz, S. (2013, October). Mental health literacy: Social work's role in improving public mental health. *Social Work, 58*(4), 365–368.

Metz, P. (1997). Staff development for working with lesbian and gay elders. In J. K. Quam (Ed.), *Social services for senior gay men and lesbians* (pp. 35–45). New York: Haworth Press.

Meyer, M. H. (Ed.). (2000). *Care work: Gender, labor, and the welfare state.* New York: Routledge.

Miller, S. E., Hayward, R. A., & Shaw, T. V. (2012). Environmental shifts for social work: A principles approach. *International Journal of Social Welfare, 21,* 270–277.

Miller, S. E., Lee, J. S., & Berle, D. (2012). Community engagement from the ground up: An interdisciplinary service-learning after-school garden program. *Journal of Agriculture, Food Systems, and Community Development, 2*(3), 121–135.

Miller, W. R., & Rollnick, S. (2013). *Motivational interviewing: Helping people change* (3rd ed.). New York: Guilford Press.

Miller-Perrin, C. L., & Perrin, R. D. (2009). *Child maltreatment: An introduction.* Thousand Oaks, CA: Sage.

Miller-Perrin, C. L., & Perrin, R. D. (2013). *Child maltreatment: An introduction* (3rd ed.). Thousand Oaks, CA: Sage.

Minorities expected to be majority in 2050. (2008, August 13). *CNN.com.* Retrieved from http://www.cnn.com/2008/US/08/13/census.minorities/index.html?iref=hpmostpop

Mirick, R. (2014). Engagement in child protective services: The role of substance abuse, intimate partner violence, and race. *Child & Adolescent Social Work Journal, 31*(3), 267–279. doi:10.100/s 10560-013-0320-6

Moniz, C., & Gorin, S. (2014). *Health care policy and practice: A biopsychosocial perspective* (4th ed.). New York: Routledge.

Moody, H. R., & Sasser, J. R. (2012). *Aging concepts and controversies* (8th ed.). Thousand Oaks, CA: Sage.

Moore, S., Bledsoe, L., Perry, A., & Robinson, M. (2011). Social work students and self-care: A model assignment for teaching. *Journal of Social Work Education, 47*(3), 545–553. doi:10.5175/JSWE.2011.201000004

Moradi, B. (2009). Sexual orientation disclosure, concealment, harassment, and military cohesion: Perceptions of LGBT military veterans. *Military Psychology, 21*(4), 513–533. doi:10.1080/08995600903206453

Mortimer-Sandilands, C., & Erickson, B. (2010). *Queer ecologies: Sex, nature, politics, desire.* Bloomington: Indiana University Press.

Mu-Jung, A., & Lin, P. (1995). Mental health overview. In R. L. Edwards & J. G. Hopps (Eds.), *The encyclopedia of social work* (19th ed., Vol. 2, pp. 1705–1711). Washington, DC: NASW Press.

Mullen, M. (2011). On Total Force Fitness in war and peace. *Military Medicine, 175*(8), 1–2.

Munson, C. (2011). Forensic social work practice standards: Definition and specification. *Journal of Forensic Social Work, 1,* 37–60.

Mupedziswa, R. (1997). Social work refugees: The growing international crisis. In M. Hokenstad & J. Midgley (Eds.), *Issues in international social work: Challenges for a new century* (pp. 110–124). Washington, DC: NASW Press.

Murdach, A. D. (2011). Is social work a human rights profession? *Social Work, 56*(3), 281–283.

Museum of Modern Art (MoMA). (2009). *Meet me: Making art accessible to people with dementia.* New York: Author. Retrieved from http://www.moma.org/momaorg/shared/pdfs/docs/meetme/MeetMe_FULL.pdf

Namkee, G. C., & DiNitto, D. M. (2013). Mental health and substance use: Challenges for serving older adults. *Indian Journal of Medical Research, 138*(4), 439–442.

National Aeronautics and Space Administration. (2014, February 7). *California drought.* Retrieved from http://science.nasa.gov/science-news/science-at-nasa/2014/07feb_drought/

National Alliance for Partnerships in Equity. (n.d.). *Paycheck Fairness Act and Lilly Ledbetter Fair Pay Act.*

Retrieved from http://www.napequity
.org/public-policy/current-laws-and-
bills/paycheck-fairness-act/

National Alliance on Mental Illness. (2012).
*Cultural competence in mental health
care.* Retrieved from http://www.nami
.org/Content/NavigationMenu/Find_
Support/Multicultural_Support/Cultural_
Competence/Cultural_Competence.htm

National Alliance on Mental Illness. (2013,
October 28). *State legislation report
2013: Trends, themes, and practices
in state mental health legislation.*
Arlington, VA: Author. Retrieved
from http://www.nami.org/Content/
NavigationMenu/State_Advocacy/
Tools_for_Leaders/2013StateLegisla
tionReportFinal.pdf

National Association of Social Workers
(NASW). (1973). *NASW standards for
social service manpower.* Washington,
DC: Author.

National Association of Social Workers
(NASW). (1982). *Standards for the
classification of social work practice.*
Washington, DC: Author.

National Association of Social Workers
(NASW). (2000, January 21).
*"Reparative" and "conversion" therapies
for lesbians and gay men.* Retrieved
from http://www.naswdc.org/diversity/
lgb/reparative.asp

National Association of Social Workers
(NASW). (2001a). *NASW standards
for cultural competence in social work
practice.* Washington, DC: Author.

National Association of Social Workers
(NASW). (2001b, October 31). *Update
on mental health parity.* Retrieved from
http://www.socialworkers.org/archives/
advocacy/updates/2001/103101.htm

National Association of Social Workers
(NASW). (2008). *Code of ethics of the
National Association of Social Workers*
(Rev. ed.). Washington, DC: Author.
Retrieved from http://www
.socialworkers.org/pubs/code/code.asp

National Association of Social Workers
(NASW). (2009). *Turning priorities into
action: How the social work profession
will help.* Washington, DC: Author.
Retrieved from http://www
.socialworkers.org/advocacy/
resources/ObamaBook.pdf

National Association of Social Workers
(NASW). (2012). *NASW standards for
social service manpower* [Electronic
version]. Retrieved from http://www
.naswdc.org

National Association of Social Workers
(NASW). (2013). *A social work
perspective on drug policy reform:
Public health approach.* Washington,
DC: Author.

National Association of Social Workers
(NASW). (2014). *NASW professional
social work credentials and advanced
practice specialty credentials.* Retrieved
from http://www.naswdc
.org/credentials/default.asp

National Association of Social Workers
(NASW). (n.d.). *Mental health.*
Retrieved from http://www.naswdc.org/
pressroom/features/issue/mental.asp

National Association of Social Workers
(NASW). (in press). *NASW standards
for social work practice in health
care settings.* Washington, DC:
Author. Draft retrieved from http://
www.socialworkers.org/practice/
naswstandards/Health%20care%20
standardsfinal%20draft.pdf

National Association of the Deaf. (2011).
*Community and culture—frequently
asked questions.* Retrieved on
December 18, 2013, from http://
www.nad.org/issues/american-sign-
language/community-and-culture-faq

National Coalition for the Homeless.
(2009). *How many people experience
homelessness?* Washington, DC:
Author. Retrieved from http://www
.nationalhomeless.org/factsheets/
How_Many.html

National Institute of Mental Health. (2013).
*Serious mental illness (SMI) among
adults.* Retrieved from http://www.nimh
.nih.gov/statistics/SMI_AASR.shtml

National Institute on Aging. (2011, May).
AgePage: Elder abuse. Washington,
DC: National Institutes of Health U.S.
Department of Health & Human Services.

National Institute on Drug Abuse. (2011a,
March). *Commonly abused drugs chart.*
Retrieved from http://www.drugabuse
.gov/drugs-abuse/commonly-abused-
drugs/commonly-abused-drugs-chart

National Institute on Drug Abuse. (2011b,
October). *Commonly abused
prescription drugs chart.* Retrieved from
http://www.drugabuse.gov/drugs-abuse/
commonly-abused-drugs/commonly-
abused-prescription-drugs-chart

National Institute on Drug Abuse. (2014,
July). *Prescription drugs and cold
medicine: What is prescription
drug abuse?* Retrieved from http://
www.drugabuse.gov/drugs-abuse/
prescription-drugs

National Multifamily Housing Council.
(2013). *Quick facts: Resident
demographics.* Retrieved from
https://www.nmhc.org/Content.
aspx?id=4708#Rent_v_Own

National Research Council and Institute of
Medicine. (2009). *Preventing mental,
emotional, and behavioral disorders
among young people: Progress and
possibilities.* Washington, DC: National
Academic Press.

National Society of Genetic Counselors.
(n.d.). *About NSGC: The leading voice
for genetic counselors.* Retrieved from
http://nsgc.org/p/cm/ld/fid=6

National Women's Law Center. (2013,
January 29). *Lilly Ledbetter Fair Pay Act.*
Retrieved from http://www.nwlc.org/
resource/lilly-ledbetter-fair-pay-act-0

Nelson, J. A., & Gingerich, B. S. (2010). Rural
health: Access to care and services.
*Home Health Care Management &
Practice, 22*(5), 339–343.

Nelson Mandela Foundation. (2014).
Biography. *The Life and Times of
Nelson Mandela.* Retrieved from
http://www.nelsonmandela.org/content/
page/biography

Neumark, D., & Wascher, W. (2006).
*Minimum wages and employment:
A review of evidence from the new
minimum wage research.* Cambridge,
MA: National Bureau of Economic
Research.

Nielsen, K. (2012). *A disability history of the
United States.* Boston, MA: Beacon
Press.

Northeastern University Institute on Urban
Health Research. (2010, June 8). *Study
correlates sexual orientation and health
disparities.* Retrieved from http://www
.northeastern.edu/news/stories/
2010/06/ConronHealthDisparities.html

Novak, J. (2014, May 8). *The six living
generations in America.* Retrieved from
http://www.marketingteacher.com/
the-six-living-generations-in-america/

Obama, B. (2014, January 28). *2014 state
of the union.* Retrieved from http://
www.whitehouse.gov/sotu

O'Brennan, L. M., Bradshaw, C. P., &
Sawyer, A. L. (2009). Examining
developmental differences in the social-
emotional problems among frequent
bullies, victims, and bully/victims.
Psychology in the Schools, 46(2),
100–115.

O'Connor v. Donaldson, 422 U.S. 563
(1975).

Odier, N. (2010). The U.S. health-care
system: A proposal for reform. *Journal
of Medical Marketing, 10*(4), 279–304.

Olson, L. K. (2014, June 30). VA failures
go beyond hospitals. *Philly.com.*
Retrieved from http://www.philly.com/
philly/opinion/inquirer/20140630_VA_
failures_go_beyond_hospitals.html

O'Melia, M. (2002). From person to context: The evolution of an empowering practice. In M. W. O'Melia & K. K. Miley (Eds.), *Pathways to power: Readings in contextual social work practice* (pp. 1–14). Boston, MA: Pearson Allyn & Bacon.

Organization for Economic Cooperation and Development. (2013, November 21). *Health at a Glance 2013: OECD indicators.* Paris: OECD Publishing.

Orshansky, M. (1964). Measuring poverty. *In The social welfare forum: Official proceedings* (p. 214). New York: Columbia University Press.

Ozawa, M. N., & Yeo, Y. H. (2011). Net worth accumulation by different quintiles of older adults approaching retirement age and 10 years later. *Journal of Sociology & Social Welfare, 38*(3), 9–30.

Pace, P. R. (2012). Social workers key players in criminal justice system. *NASW News, 57*(10). Retrieved from http://www.socialworkblog.org/nasw-news-article/2012/11/social-workers-key-players-in-criminal-justice-system/

Palmore, E. (2001). The ageism survey: First findings. *The Gerontologist, 41*(5), 572–575.

Pargament, K. (2007). *Spiritually integrated psychotherapy.* New York: Guilford Press.

Park, J., Hirz, C. E., Manotas, K., & Hooyman, N. (2013). Nonpharmacological pain management by ethnically diverse older adults with chronic pain: Barriers and facilitators. *Journal of Gerontological Social Work, 56*(6), 487–508. doi: 10.1080/01634372.2013.808725

Park, J., & Hughes, A. K. (2012). Nonpharmacological approaches to the management of chronic pain in community-dwelling older adults: A review of empirical evidence. *Journal of the American Geriatrics Society, 60,* 555–568. doi:10.1111/j.1532 5415.2011.038646.x

Parker, K., & Wang, W. (2013, March 13). *Modern parenthood: Roles of moms and dads converge as they balance work and family.* Washington, DC: Pew Research Center. Retrieved from http://www.pewsocialtrends.org/2013/03/14/modern-parenthood-roles-of-moms-and-dads-converge-as-they-balance-work-and-family/

Payne, M. (2012). *Citizenship social work with older people.* Chicago, IL: Lyceum Books.

Payton, A., & Thoits, P. (2011). Medicalization, direct-to-consumer advertising, and mental illness stigma.

Society and Mental Health, 1(1), 55–70.

Pearce, D. (1978). The feminization of poverty: Women, work, and welfare. *Urban and Social Change Review, 11,* 28–36.

Pecora, P. J., Whittaker, J. K., Maluccio, A. N., Barth, R. P., & DePanfilis, D. (2009). *The child welfare challenge: Policy, practice, and research.* New Brunswick, NJ: Aldine Transaction.

Pedram, P., Wadden, D., Amini, P., Gulliver, W., Randell, E., Cahill, F., & Sun, G. (2013). Food addiction: Its prevalence and significant association with obesity in the general population. *PLOS ONE, 8*(9), 1–6. doi:10.1371/journal.pone.0074832

Peeters, J. (2012). The place of social work in sustainable development: Towards ecosocial practice. *International Journal of Social Welfare, 21,* 297–298.

Perez, A. D., & Hirschman, C. (2009). The changing racial and ethnic composition of the US population: Emerging American identities. *Population and Development Review, 35*(1), 1–51.

Perkes, C. (2013, January 23). Doctors often don't advise the obese. *Orange County Register.* Retrieved from http://www.ocregister.com/articles/weight-408996-patients-doctors.html

Perlman, H. H. (1957). *Social casework: A problem-solving process.* Chicago, IL: University of Chicago Press.

Perlman, R., & Gurin, A. (1972). *Community organization and social planning.* New York: Wiley.

Peternelj-Taylor, C. (2008). Criminalization of the mentally ill. *Journal of Forensic Nursing, 4,* 185–187. doi:10.1111/j.1939-3938.2008.00031.x

Peters, C. M. (2011). Social work and juvenile probation: Historical tensions and contemporary convergences. *Social Work, 56,* 355–365.

Pew Research. (2013, December 11.) *On Pay Gap, Millennial Women Near Parity — For Now Despite Gains, Many See Roadblocks Ahead.http://www.pewsocialtrends.org/2013/12/11/on-pay-gap-millennial-women-near-parity-for-now/*

Pew Research Center. (2013, December 4). 5 *Facts about the minimum wage.* Desilver, D. http://www.pewresearch.org/fact-tank/2013/12/04/5-facts-about-the-minimum-wage/Number 2 Fact

Pew Research Center. (2008, December 18). *Bush and public opinion: Reviewing the Bush years and the

public's final verdict.* Washington, DC: Author. Retrieved from http://www.people-press.org/2008/12/18/bush-and-public-opinion/

Pilcher, J. (2014, May 30). What will happen to sober living homes? *Cincinnati Enquirer,* pp. A1, A4–A5.

Piven, F. F., & Cloward, R. A. (1982). *The new class war: Reagan's attack on the welfare state and its consequences.* New York: Pantheon.

Pizer, J. C., Sears, B., Mallory, C., & Hunter, N. D. (2012). *Evidence of persistent and pervasive workplace discrimination against LGBT people: The need for federal legislation prohibiting discrimination and providing equal employment benefits.* Retrieved from http://digitalcommons.lmu.edu/llr/vol45/iss3/3/

Pollitz, K., & Sorian, R. (2000, October). Ensuring health security: Is the individual market ready for prime time? *Health Affairs.* Retrieved from http://content.healthaffairs.org/content/early/2002/10/23/hlthaff.w2.372.full.pdf+html

Poole, D. L., & Negi, N. (2008). Transnational community enterprises for social welfare in global civil society. *International Journal of Social Welfare, 17,* 243–246.

Pooler, D. (2011). Professional flourishing: Re-visioning self-care using Imago Dei. *Social Work & Christianity, 38*(4), 440–452.

Powers, G. T., Meenaghan, T. M., & Toomey, B. G. (1985). *Practice focused research: Integrating human service practice and research.* Englewood Cliffs, NJ: Prentice Hall.

Powers, R. (2014, May 30). U.S. military enlistment standards: Age limits. *About Careers.* Retrieved from http://usmilitary.about.com/od/joiningthemilitary/a/enlage.htm

President's New Freedom Commission on Mental Health. (2003). *Achieving the promise: Transforming mental health care in America.* Rockville, MD: Author. Retrieved from http://www.nami.org/template.cfm?section=New_Freedom_Commission

Pretty, J., Adams, B., Berkes, F., Ferreira de Athayde, S., Dudley, N., Hunn, E., Maffi, L., . . . Pilgrim, S. (2009). The intersections of biology diversity and cultural diversity: Towards integration. *Conservation and Society, 7*(2), 100–112.

Prisons Bureau. (2013, March 18). Annual determination of average cost of incarceration. *Federal Register*. Retrieved from https://www .federalregister.gov/articles/2013/ 03/18/2013-06139/annual-determination-of-average-cost-of-incarceration

Prochaska, J. O., & DiClemente, C. C. (1982). Transtheoretical therapy: Toward a more integrative model of change. *Psychotherapy: Theory, Research and Practice, 19*(3), 276–288.

Pryce, J. G., Pryce, D. H., & Shackelford, K. K. (2012). *The costs of courage: Combat stress, warriors, and family survival*. Chicago, IL: Lyceum Books.

Qualls, S. H. (2014). Yes, health and social relationships are inextricably linked. *Generations, 38*(1), 6–7.

Quanbeck, A. R., Gustafson, D. H., Marsch, L. A., McTavish, F., Brown, R. T., Mares, M. L., Johnson, R., . . . McDowell, H. (2014). Integrating addiction treatment into primary care using mobile health technology: Protocol for an implementation research study. *Implementation Science, 9*(1), 1–22. doi:10.1186/1748-5908-9-65

Quillian, L. (2012). Segregation and poverty concentration: The role of three segregations. *American Sociological Review, 77*(3), 354–379.

Ramos, B. M., Botton, M. L., & Wright, G. A. (2009). Peru: A focus on individual practice. In C. Tice & D. Long (Eds.), *International social work policy and practice: Practical insights and perspectives* (pp. 209–229). Hoboken, NJ: John Wiley.

Rappaport, J. (1981). In praise of paradox: A social policy of empowerment over prevention. *American Journal of Community Psychology, 9*, 1–25.

Rawls, J. (1971). *A theory of justice*. Cambridge, MA: Harvard University Press.

Ready Campaign. (2014, April 17). *Floods*. Retrieved from http://www.ready.gov/ floods

Reamer, F. (2005). Ethical and legal standards in social work: Consistency and conflict. *Families in Society: The Journal of Contemporary Social Services, 86*(2), 163–169.

Reardon, C. (2012). The changing face of older adult substance abuse. *Social Work Today, 12*(1), 8.

Reardon, G., Nelson, W. W., Patel., A. A., Philpot, T., & Neidecker, M. (2012). Prevalence of atrial fibrillation in U.S. nursing homes: Results from the National Nursing Home Survey, 1984–2004. *Journal of the American Medical Directors Association, 13*(6), 529–534. doi:10.1016/j.jamda .2012.03.007

Reed, C. C., Beall, S. C., & Baumhover, L. A. (1992). Gerontological education for students in nursing and social work: Knowledge, attitudes, and perceived barriers. *Educational Gerontology, 18*, 625–636.

Reese, D. J., & Brown, D. R. (1997). Psychosocial and spiritual care in hospices: Differences between nursing, social work, and clergy. *Hospice Journal, 12*, 29–41.

Reisch, M. (1998). The sociopolitical context and social work methods. *Social Service Review, 72*, 161–181.

Reisch, M. (2000). The future of social work in the United States: Implications for field education. *Journal of Social Work Education, 36*(2), 201–214.

Reisch, M. (2002). Defining social justice in a socially unjust world. *Families in Society: The Journal of Contemporary Human Services, 83*(4), 343–354.

Reisch, M. (2012). The challenges of health care reform for hospital social work in the United States. *Social Work in Health Care, 51*(10), 873–893.

Remafedi, G., French, S., Story, M., Reshnick, M. D., & Blum, R. (1998). The relationship between suicide risk and sexual orientation: Results of a population-based study. *American Journal of Public Health, 88*(1), 57–60.

Rennison, C., Dragiewicz, M., & DeKeseredy, W. (2013). Context matters: Violence against women and reporting to police in rural, suburban and urban areas. *American Journal of Criminal Justice, 38*, 141–159.

Reynolds, B. C. (1951). *Social work and social living*. New York: Citadel Press.

Rice, V. (2012). Theories of stress and its relationship to health. In V. H. Rice (Ed.), *Handbook of stress, coping, and health: Implications for nursing research, theory, and practice* (pp. 22–42). Thousand Oaks, CA: Sage.

Richmond, M. (1917). *Social diagnosis*. New York: Russell Sage Foundation.

Richmond, M. (1922). *What is social case work?* New York: Russell Sage Foundation.

Rickwood, D. (2012). Entering the e-spectrum: An examination of new interventions for youth mental health. *Youth Studies Australia, 31*(4), 18–27.

Riebschleger, J. (2007). Social worker's suggestions for effective rural practice. *Families in Society, 88*(2), 203–213. doi:10.1606/1044-3894.3618

Rizvi, Z. M. (2012). Pro-poor affordable housing: The issue we know, the answers we need. *Housing Finance International, 26*(4), 14–15.

Rizzo, V. M., & Rowe, J. (2006). Studies of the cost-effectiveness of social work services in aging: A review of the literature. *Research on Social Work Practice, 16*(1), 67–73. doi:10.1177/1049731505276080

Robbins, L. A., & Rieder, C. H. (2002). The John A. Hartford Foundation geriatric social work initiative. *Journal of Gerontological Social Work, 39*(3), 71–90.

Robinson, H. H. (1898). The Lowell Mill Girls go on strike, 1836. In *Loom and spindler, or life among the early Mill Girls* (pp. 83–86). New York: T. Y. Crowell. Retrieved from http:// historymatters.gmu.edu/d/5714/

Rogge, M. E. (1994). Environmental justice: Social welfare and toxic waste. In M. D. Hoff & J. G. McNutt (Eds.), *The global environmental crisis: Implications for social welfare and social work* (pp. 53–74). Brookfield, VT: Ashgate.

Roman, P. M. (2014). Seventy-five years of policy on alcohol problems: An American perspective. *Journal of Studies on Alcohol and Drug*, (Suppl. 17), 116–124.

Rome, S. H. (2010). Social work and civic engagement: The political participation of professional social workers. *Journal of Sociology and Social Welfare, 37*(3), 107–129.

Rosenberg, C. M. (2011). *The life and times of Francis Cabot Lowell, 1775–1817*. Layham, MD: Lexington Books.

Rosenberg, J. (n.d.). Vietnam War. *About Education*. Retrieved from http:// history1900s.about.com/od/ vietnamwar/a/vietnamwar.htm

Rosenfeld, L. B., Caye, J. S., Lahad, M., & Gurwitch, R. H. (2010). *When their world falls apart: Helping families and children manage the effects of disasters* (2nd ed.). Washington, DC: NASW Press.

Rosenhan, D. L., & Seligman, M. E. P. (1989). *Abnormal psychology* (2nd ed.). New York: W. W. Norton.

Rothman, D. J. (1971). *The discovery of asylum: Social order and disorder in the new republic*. Boston, MA: Little, Brown.

Rothman, J. (2007). Multi modes of intervention at the macro level. *Journal of Community Practice, 15*(4), 11–40.

Rowan, D. (2009). Malawi and AIDS: Examining diversity and populations at risk. In C. Tice & D. Long (Eds.), *International social work policy and practice: Practical insights and perspectives* (pp. 185–207). Hoboken, NJ: John Wiley.

Rowan, D. (2013). *Social work with HIV and AIDS: A case-based guide.* Chicago, IL: Lyceum Books.

Rowan, D., Kabwira, D., Mmatli, T., Rankopo, M., & Long, D. (2012). Using video as pedagogy for globally connected learning about the HIV/AIDS pandemic. *Journal of Social Work Education, 48,* 691–706.

Rowe, J. W., & Kahn, R. L. (1997). Successful aging. *The Gerontologist, 37*(4), 433–440. doi:10.1093/geront/37.4.433

Rowe, J. W., & Kahn, R. L. (1999). *Successful aging.* New York: Pantheon.

Roy, A. (2012, April 30). How George W. Bush would have replaced Obamacare. *Forbes.* Retrieved from http://www.forbes.com/sites/theapothecary/2012/04/30/how-george-w-bush-would-have-replaced-obamacare/

Rubin, A. (2012, October). Civilian social work with veterans returning from Iraq and Afghanistan: A call to action. *Social Work, 57*(4), 293–296.

Rubin, A., Weiss, E. L., & Coll, J. E. (Eds.). (2013). *Handbook of military social work.* Hoboken, NJ: John Wiley.

Rusch, M. L., Schall, M. C., Lee, J. D., Dawson, J. D., & Rizzo, M. (2014). Augmented reality cues to assist older drivers with gap estimation of left-turns. *Accident Analysis & Prevention, 71,* 210–221.

Ryan, C., & Futterman, D. (1998). *Lesbian and gay youth, care and counseling: A comprehensive guide to health and mental health care.* New York: Columbia University Press.

Saleebey, D. (2009). *The strengths perspective in social work practice* (5th ed.). Boston, MA: Allyn & Bacon.

Salzer, M. S., Schwenk, E., & Brusilovskiy, E. (2010). Certified peer specialist roles and activities: Results from a national survey. *Psychiatric Services, 61,* 520–523.

Sandler, E. P. (2009, October 28). Promoting hope, preventing suicide. *Psychology Today.* Retrieved from http://www.psychologytoday.com/blog/promoting-hope-preventing-suicide/200910/behavioral-health-versus-mental-health

Sarnoff, S. K. (2009). An Appalachian example: Issues of social and economic justice. In C. Tice & D. Long (Eds.), *International social work policy and practice: Practical insights and perspectives* (pp. 161–184). Hoboken, NJ: John Wiley.

Scheyett, A. (2005). The mark of madness: Stigma, serious mental illnesses, and social work. *Social Work in Mental Health, 3,* 79–97.

Schild, S., & Black, R. B. (1984). *Social work and genetics: A guide for practice.* New York: Haworth Press.

Schroeder, S. A. (2010). Confronting a neglected epidemic: Tobacco cessation for persons with mental illness and substance abuse problems. *Annual Review of Public Health, 31*(1), 297–314.

Schulte, M. T., & Hser, Y. (2014). Substance use and associated health conditions throughout the lifespan. *Public Health Reviews, 35*(2), 1–27.

Schwalbe, C., Hatcher, S., & Maschi, T. (2009). The effects of treatment needs and prior social services utilization on juvenile court decision making. *Social Work Research, 33,* 31–40.

Scotch, R. (1988). Disability as the basis for a social movement: Politics and the advocacy of definition. *Journal of Social Issues, 44*(1), 173–188.

Searle, J. (1995). *The construction of social reality.* New York: Free Press.

Seccombe, K. (2011). *So you think I drive a Cadillac: Welfare recipients' perspectives on the system and its reform.* Boston, MA: Pearson/Allyn & Bacon.

Segal, E. A., & Brzuzy, S. (1998). *Social welfare policy, programs, and practices.* Itasca, IL: F. E. Peacock.

Segal, S. P. (1995). Deinstitutionalization. In R. L. Edwards & J. G. Hopps (Eds.), *The encyclopedia of social work* (19th ed., Vol. 1, pp. 704–712). Washington, DC: NASW Press.

Selye, H. (1980). *Selye's guide to stress research.* New York: Van Nostrand Reinhold.

SenGupta, G. (2009). *From slavery to poverty: The racial origins of welfare in New York, 1840–1918.* New York: New York University Press.

Settles, I. H., Buchanan, N. T., & Colar, B. (2012). The impact of race and rank on the sexual harassment of black and white men in the U.S. military. *Pscychology of Men & Masculinity, 13*(3), 256–263.

Shapiro, S. L., Brown, K. W., & Biegel, G. M. (2007). Teaching self-care to caregivers: Effects of mindfulness-based stress reduction on the mental health of therapists in training. *Training and Education in Professional Psychology, 1,* 105–115. doi:10.1037/1931-3918.1.2.105

Shaw, T. V. (2008). An ecological contribution to social welfare theory. *International Consortium for Social Development, 30*(3), 13–26.

Shay, J. (2010). *Odysseus in America: Combat trauma and the trials of homecoming.* New York: Scribner.

Sidell, N., & Smiley, D. (2008). *Professional communication skills in social work.* New York: Pearson/Allyn & Bacon.

Simmons, C. A., & Rycraft, J. R. (2010). Ethical challenges of military social workers serving in a combat zone. *Social Work, 55*(1), 9–18.

Sinacola, R. S., & Peters-Strickland, T. S. (2012). *Basic psychopharmacology for counselors and psychotherapists* (2nd ed.). New York: Pearson.

Singer, J. B. (2009). The role and regulations for technology in social work practice and e-therapy: Social Work 2.0. In A. R. Roberts (Ed.), *Social workers' desk reference* (pp. 186–193). New York: Oxford University Press.

Singh, V. (2013). Exploring the concept of work across generations. *Journal of Intergenerational Relationships, 11*(3), 272–285. doi:10:1080/15350770.2013.810498

Skobba, K., Bruin, M. J., & Yust, B. L. (2013). Beyond renting and owning: The housing accommodations of low-income families. *Journal of Poverty, 17*(2), 234–252.

Skocpol, T. (1995). *Social policy in the United States: Future possibilities in historical perspective.* Princeton, NJ: Princeton University Press.

Smith, A. (2002). Effects of caffeine on human behavior. *Food and Chemical Toxicology, 40,* 1243–1255.

Smith, C. A. (2013). The rise of Habitat for Humanity subdivisions. *Focus on Geography, 56*(3), 95–104.

Smith-Osborne, A., & Felderhoff, B. (2014). Veterans' informal caregivers in the "Sandwich Generation": A systematic review towards a resilience model. *Journal of Gerontological Social Work, 57*(6–7), 556–584. doi:10.1080/01634372.2014.880101

Smyth, N. J. (1995). Substance abuse: Direct practice. In R. L. Edwards & J. G. Hopps (Eds.), *The encyclopedia of social work* (19th ed., pp. 2328–2337). Washington, DC: NASW Press.

Social Security Administration. (2014). *Contribution and benefit base.* Retrieved from http://www.ssa.gov/oact/cola/cbb.html

Social Security Timeline. (n.d.). *Annenberg Classroom.* Retrieved from http://www.annenbergclassroom.org/Files/Documents/Timelines/SocialSecurity.pdf

Soydan, H. (2008, July). Applying randomized controlled trials and systematic reviews in social work research. *Research on Social Work Practice, 18*(4), 311–318. doi:10.1177/1049731507307788

Special Olympics. (2014). *Special Olympics mission.* Retrieved from http://www.specialolympics.org/mission.aspx

Spitzer, W. J., & Davidson, K. W. (2013). Future trends in health and health care: Implications for social work practice in an aging society. *Social Work in Health Care, 52,* 959–986.

Spitzer, W., & Nash, K. (1996). Educational preparation for contemporary health care social work practice. *Social Work in Health Care, 24*(1–2), 9–34.

Stalker, K. (2003). Managing risk and uncertainty in social work. *Journal of Social Work, 3*(2), 211–233. doi:10.1177/14680173030032006

Stiglitz, J. E. (2012). *The price of inequality.* New York: W. W. Norton.

Stine, G. J. (2014). *AIDS update 2014.* New York: McGraw-Hill.

Stix, G. (2012). The mind recovery act. *Scientific American, 306*(4), 12.

Stoesz, D., & Karger, H. J. (2009). Reinventing social work accreditation. *Research on Social Work Practice, 19*(1), 104–111. doi:10.1177/1049731507313976

Stotzer, R. L., & Alvarez, A. R. (2009). Porter R. Lee and advocacy in the social work profession. *Journal of Community Practice, 17*(3), 323–326.

Straits-Troster, K. A., Brancu, M., Goodale, B., Pacelli, S., Wilmer, C., Simmons, E. M., & Kudler, H. (2011). Developing community capacity to treat post-deployment mental health problems: A public health initiative. *Psychological Trauma: Theory, Research, Practice, and Policy, 3*(3), 289–291. doi:10.1037/a0024645

Straussner, S. L. A., & Isralowitz, R. (2008). Alcohol and drug problems: Overview. In T. Mizrahi & L. E. Davis (Eds.), *Encyclopedia of social work* (20th ed., Vol. 1, pp. 126–127). Washington, DC: NASW Press and Oxford University Press.

Substance Abuse and Mental Health Services Administration. (2011a). *Results from the 2010 National Survey on Drug Use and Health: Summary of national findings.* Rockville, MD: Author.

Substance Abuse and Mental Health Services Administration. (2011b, December 22). *SAMHSA announces a working definition of "recovery" from mental disorders and substance use disorders* [Press release]. Retrieved from http://www.samhsa.gov/newsroom/advisories/1112223420.aspx

Sullivan, J. E., & Zayas, L. E. (2013). Passport biopsies: Hospital deportations and implications for social work. *Social Work, 58*(3), 281–284.

Sutherland, E. H. (1939). *Principles of criminology.* Philadelphia, PA: Lippincott.

Swank, E. W. (2012). Predictors of political activism among social work students. *Journal of Social Work Education, 48*(2), 245–266.

Sweeten, G., Piquero, A., & Steinberg, L. (2013). Age and the explanation of crime, revisited. *Journal of Youth and Adolescence, 42,* 921–938.

Syme, M. L. (2014). The evolving concept of older adult sexual behavior and its benefits. *Generations, 38*(1), 35–41.

Taylor, D. (2012). *Concordia's Social Work Club participates in area Special Olympics.* Retrieved from http://www.ccal.edu/?q=node/683

Taylor-Brown, S., & Johnson, A. M. (1998, February). *Social work's role in genetic services.* Washington, DC: National Association of Social Workers. Retrieved from http://www.naswdc.org/practice/health/genetics.asp

Theriot, M. T. (2013). From the guest editor. *Journal of Baccalaureate Social Work, 18,* 3–4.

Theriot, M. T., & Lodato, G. A. (2012, Fall). Attitudes about mental illness and professional danger among new social work students. *Journal of Social Work Education, 48*(3), 403–423.

Thomas, A. C., Allen, F. L., Phillips, J., & Karantzas, G. (2011). Gaming machine addiction: The role of avoidance, accessibility and social support. *Psychology of Addictive Behaviors, 25*(4), 738–744. doi:10.1037/a0024865

Thomas, L. E., & Eisenhandler, S. A. (1999). *Religion, belief, and spirituality in late life.* New York: Springer.

Tice, C. J., & Perkins, K. (1996). *Mental health issues and aging: Building on the strengths of older persons.* Pacific Grove, CA: Brooks/Cole.

Tice, C. J., & Perkins, K. (2002). *The faces of social policy: A strengths perspective.* Pacific Grove, CA: Brooks/Cole.

Tidball, K. G., & Krasny, M. E. (2014). *Greening in the red zone.* New York: Springer.

Torrey, E. F. (1995). Editorial: jails and prisons—America's new mental hospitals. *American Journal of Public Health, 85*(12), 1612.

Trattner, W. I. (1999). *From poor law to welfare state: A history of social welfare in America* (6th ed.). New York: Free Press.

Trimpey, J. (1994). AVRT: The rational recovery technique. *Behavioral Health Management, 14*(1), 30.

Trippany, R. L., Kress, V. E. W., & Wilcoxon, S. A. (2004). Preventing vicarious trauma: What counselors should know when working with trauma survivors. *Journal of Counseling and Development, 82,* 31–37.

Turner, R. H., Nigg, J. M., & Paz, D. H. (1986). *Waiting for disaster: Earthquake watch in California.* Berkeley: University of California Press.

The 25 best Master of Social Work degree programs. (2012). *The Best Schools.* Retrieved from http://www.thebestschools.org/blog/2012/04/16/25-master-social-work-degree-programs/

UN Enable. (n.d.-a). *The United Nations and indigenous people with disabilities.* Retrieved from http://www.un.org/disabilities/default.asp?id=1605

UN Enable. (n.d.-b). *Women and girls with disabilities.* Retrieved from http://www.un.org/disabilities/default.asp?navid=13&pid=1514

UN High Commissioner for Refugees. (2013). *UNHCR global appeal 2013 update: Populations of concern to UNHCR.* Retrieved from http://www.unhcr.org/50a9f81b27.html

UN Programme on HIV/AIDS. (2013). *Global report: UNAIDS report on the global AIDS epidemic 2013.* Geneva, Switzerland: Author. Retrieved from http://www.unaids.org/en/media/unaids/contentassets/documents/epidemiology/2013/gr2013/UNAIDS_Global_Report_2013_en.pdf

UNC Center for Aging and Health. (2005). Who mistreats older adults? *Elder Mistreatment Learning Module.* Chapel Hill: University of North Carolina. Retrieved from http://www.med.unc.edu/aging/eldermistreatment/overview5.htm

Unger, M. (2002). More social ecological social work practice. *Social Service Review, 76*(3), 480–497.

UNICEF. (2010). *Advocacy toolkit*. New York: Author. Retrieved from http://www.unicef.org/evaluation/files/Advocacy_Toolkit.pdf

United Nations. (2013, May 16). *Secretary-General's message to the International Forum on the International Day against Homophobia and Transphobia* [Delivered by Navanethem Pillay, High Commissioner for Human Rights]. Retrieved from http://www.un.org/sg/statements/?nid=6822

U.S. Census Bureau. (2010). *Income, poverty, and health insurance coverage in the United States: 2010*. Retrieved from http://www.npc.umich.edu/poverty

U.S. Census Bureau. (2011). *Statistical abstract of the United States: 2012*. Washington, DC: Author.

U.S. Department of Agriculture, Food and Nutrition Service. (2013, November 18). *Women, Infants and Children (WIC)*. Retrieved from http://www.fns.usda.gov/wic/aboutwic/mission.htm

U.S. Department of Health and Human Services. (2014). Health disparities. *HealthyPeople.gov*. Retrieved from http://www.healthypeople.gov/2020/about/disparitiesAbout.aspx

U.S. Department of Health and Human Services, Administration for Children and Families, Children's Bureau. (2011). *Child maltreatment 2010*. Washington, DC: Author. Retrieved from http://www.acf.hhs.gov/programs/cb/research-data-technology/statistics-research/child-maltreatment

U.S. Department of Health and Human Services, National Institutes of Health, Office of Behavioral and Social Sciences Research. (2007, August). *The contributions of behavioral and social sciences research to improving the health of the nation: A prospectus for the future*. Washington, DC: Author. Retrieved from http://obssr.od.nih.gov/pdf/OBSSR_Prospectus.pdf

U.S. Department of Homeland Security. (2013, April 5). *White House drug policy director, Secretary Napolitano highlight progress in disrupting drug trafficking along southwest border* [Press release]. Retrieved from http://www.dhs.gov/news/2013/04/05/white-house-drug-policy-director-secretary-napolitano-highlight-progress-disrupting

U.S. Department of Health and Human Services. (1999). *Stress . . . at work. Publication* 99–101.

U.S. Department of Housing and Urban Development (HUD). (2013, November 21). *HUD reports continued decline in U.S. homelessness since 2010* [Press release]. Retrieved from http://portal.hud.gov/hudportal/HUD?src=/press/press_releases_media_advisories/2013/HUDNo.13-173

U.S. Department of Housing and Urban Development (HUD). (n.d.-a). *Affordable housing*. Retrieved from http://portal.hud.gov/hudportal/HUD?src=/program_offices/comm_planning/affordablehousing/

U.S. Department of Housing and Urban Development (HUD). (n.d.-b). *HUD history*. Retrieved from http://portal.hud.gov/hudportal/HUD?src=/about/hud_history

U.S. Department of Labor, Office of Disability Employment Policy. (2014). *Older workers*. Retrieved from http://www.dol.gov/odep/topics/OlderWorkers.htm

U.S. Department of Labor, Office of Unemployment Insurance. (2014, April). *Unemployment compensation: Federal–state partnership*. Washington, DC: Author. Retrieved from http://workforcesecurity.doleta.gov/unemploy/pdf/partnership.pdf

U.S. Department of Labor, U.S. Bureau of Labor Statistics. (2011). Distribution of full-time wage and salary employment, by sex and major occupation group, 2010 annual averages. Highlights of women's earnings in 2010, Report 1031, Chart 4. Retrieved from http://www.bls.gov/cps/cpswom2010.pdf

U.S. Department of State. (2012). *Bureau of Democracy, Human Rights, and Labor*. Retrieved from http://www.state.gov/j/drl/

U.S. Department of Veterans Affairs. (2014). *VA social work*. Retrieved from http://www.socialwork.va.gov/

U.S. Equal Employment Opportunity Commission. (2014). *Disability discrimination*. Retrieved from http://www.eeoc.gov/laws/types/disability.cfm

U.S. Geological Survey. (2014). *Volcano Hazards Program*. Retrieved from http://volcanoes.usgs.gov/

Vick, K. (2014, February 3). No home in sight. *TIME*, 24–33.

Vital Decisions. (2014). *What we do*. Retrieved from http://www.vitaldecisions.net/what-we-do.asp

von Herbay, A. (2014). Letter to the editor: Otto Von Bismarck is not the origin of old age at 65. *The Gerontologist, 54*(1), 5.

Waldfogel, J. (1998). Rethinking the paradigm for child protection. *Future of Children: Protecting Children from Abuse and Neglect, 8*(1), 104–119.

Wang, D., & Chonody, J. (2013). Social workers' attitudes toward older adults: A review of the literature. *Journal of Social Work Education 49*, 150–172. doi:10.1080/10437797 2013755104

Wang, K. H., Fiellin, D. A., & Becker, W. C. (2014). Source of prescription drugs used nonmedically in rural and urban populations. *American Journal of Drug & Alcohol Abuse, 40*(4), 292–303.

Ward, D. (1971). *Cities and immigrants: A geography of change in nineteenth century America*. New York: Oxford University Press.

Waterstone, M. E. (2014). Disability constitutional law. *Emory Law Journal, 63*(3), 527–580.

Weber, M. (1964). *The theory of social and economic organization* (T. Parsons, Ed.). New York: Free Press. (Original work published in 1922)

Wehbi, S. (2011). Key theoretical concepts for teaching international social work. *Revista de Asistenţă Socială, 10*, 23–29.

Weiss, R. S. (1973). *Marital separation*. New York: Basic Books.

Weitzer, R., & Tuch, S. A. (2004). Race and perceptions of police misconduct. *Social Problems, 51*, 305–325.

Wertsch, M. W. (1991). *Military brats: Legacies of childhood inside the fortress*. New York: Harmony Books.

Whitaker, T. (2008). *Who wants to be a social worker? Career influences and timing. NASW Membership workforce study*. Washington, DC: National Association of Social Workers.

Whitaker, T., & Arrington, P. (2008). *Social workers at work: NASW membership workforce study*. Washington, DC: National Association of Social Workers.

White House. (2014, March). *The impact of raising the minimum wage on women: And the importance of ensuring a robust tipped minimum wage*. Washington, DC: Author. Retrieved from http://www.whitehouse.gov/sites/default/files/docs/20140325minimumwageand womenreportfinal.pdf

White House. (n.d.). *A new patient's bill of rights*. Retrieved from http://www.whitehouse.gov/files/documents/healthcare-fact-sheets/patients-bill-rights.pdf

Wilensky, H. L., & Lebeaux, C. N. (1958). *Industrial society and social welfare*. New York: Russell Sage Foundation.

Wiles, J. L., Leibing, A., Guberman, N., Reeve, J., & Allen, R. E. S. (2014). The meaning of "aging in place" to older people. *The Gerontologist, 52*(3), 357–366.

Wilmoth, J. D., Adams-Price, C., Turner, J. J., Blaney, A. D., & Downey, L. (2014). Examining social connections as a link between religious participation and well-being among older adults. *Journal of Religion, Spirituality & Aging, 26*(2–3), 259–278.

Wilson, W. J. (1996). *When work disappears: The world of the new urban poor.* New York: Vintage Books.

Witkin, S. (1998). Human rights and social work. *Social Work, 43*(3), 197–201.

Wolfteich, P., & Loggins, M. S. (2007). Evaluation of the children's advocacy center model: Efficiency, legal and revictimization outcomes. *Child and Adolescent Social Work Journal, 24*(4), 333–352.

World Health Organization. (2003). *WHO definition of health.* Retrieved from http://www.who.int/about/definition/en/print.html

World Health Organization. (2013). *Disability and health.* Retrieved from http://www.who.int/mediacentre/factsheets/fs352/en/

World Health Organization. (2014). *Stress at the workplace.* Retrieved from http://www.who.int/occupational_health/topics/stressatwp/en/

Wu, L., & Blazer, D. G. (2011). Illicit and nonmedical drug use among older adults: A review. *Journal of Aging and Health, 23*(3), 481–504. doi:10.1177/08982643.10386224

Wurster, K. G., Rinaldi, A. P., Woods, T. S., & Liu, W. (2013). First-generation student veterans: Implications of poverty for psychotherapy. *Journal of Clinical Psychology, 69*(2), 127–137. doi:10.1002/jclp.21952

Wyatt v. Stickney, 325 F. Supp. 781 (M.D. Ala. 1971).

Yakowicz, W. (2014, June 20). Proof is in the pot: Legal weed gives Colorado business a boost. *Inc.* Retrieved from http://www.inc.com/will-yakowicz/legal-marijuana-gives-colorado-businesses-a-lift.html

Yarvis, J. S. (2011). A civilian social worker's guide to the treatment of war-induced PTSD. *Social Work in Health Care, 50*(1), 51–72.

Yee, S. (2011, August). *Health and health care disparities among people with disabilities.* Berkeley, CA: Disability Rights Education and Defense Fund. Retrieved from http://dredf.org/healthcare/Health-and-Health-Care-Disparities-Among-People-with-Disabilities.pdf

Young, B. B. (2010). Using the tidal model of mental health recovery to plan primary health care for women in residential substance abuse recovery. *Issues in Mental Health Nursing, 31,* 569–575. doi:10.3109/01612840.2010.487969

Zamora, E., Nodar, D., & Ogletree, K. (2013). Long term care insurance: A life raft for baby boomers. *St. Thomas Law Review, 26*(1), 70–102.

Zastrow, C. (2014). *Introduction to social work and social welfare: Empowering people* (11th ed.). Belmont, CA: Brooks/Cole, Cengage Learning.

Zinn, H. (1980). *A people's history of the United States.* New York: Harper Row.

Zoroya, G. (2014, March 3). Study: High suicide rates for soldiers in, out of war. *USA Today.* Retrieved from http://www.usatoday.com/story/news/nation/2014/03/03/suicide-army-rate-soldiers-institute-health/5983545/

INDEX

SAGE researchmethods

The essential online tool for researchers from the world's leading methods publisher

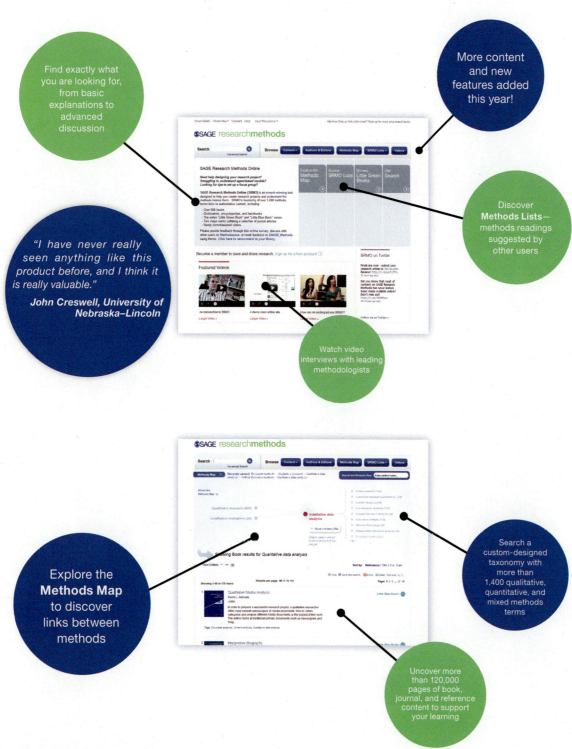

Find exactly what you are looking for, from basic explanations to advanced discussion

More content and new features added this year!

"I have never really seen anything like this product before, and I think it is really valuable."

John Creswell, University of Nebraska–Lincoln

Discover **Methods Lists**— methods readings suggested by other users

Watch video interviews with leading methodologists

Explore the **Methods Map** to discover links between methods

Search a custom-designed taxonomy with more than 1,400 qualitative, quantitative, and mixed methods terms

Uncover more than 120,000 pages of book, journal, and reference content to support your learning

Find out more at
www.sageresearchmethods.com